S TEPHEN JONES is the winner of two World Fantasy Awards and two Horror Writers of America Bram Stoker Awards, as well as being a nine-time recipient of the British Fantasy Award and a Hugo Award nominee. A full-time columnist, television producer/director and genre film publicist and consultant (all three *Hellraiser* movies, *Night Life*, *Nightbreed*, *Split Second* etc.), he is the co-editor of *Horror: 100 Best Books*, *The Best Horror from Fantasy Tales*, *Gaslight & Ghosts*, *Now We Are Sick*, *The Giant Book of Best New Horror* and the *Best New Horror*, *Dark Voices* and *Fantasy Tales* series. He has also compiled *The Mammoth Book of Terror*, *The Mammoth Book of Vampires*, *Clive Barker's Shadows in Eden*, *James Herbert: By Horror Haunted*, *Clive Barker's The Nightbreed Chronicles*, *The Hellraiser Chronicles*, *The Illustrated Vampire Movie Guide* and *The Illustrated Dinosaur Movie Guide*.

The Mammoth Book of
ZOMBIES

Edited by
STEPHEN JONES

Carroll and Graf Publishers, Inc.
New York

Carroll & Graf Publishers, Inc.
260 Fifth Avenue
New York
New York 10001
USA

This collection first published in Great Britain 1993
First Carroll & Graf edition 1993

Collection copyright © by Stephen Jones 1993
Illustrations copyright © by Martin McKenna

ISBN 0–7867–0023–8

Typeset by Hewer Text Composition Services, Edinburgh

Printed and bound by HarperCollins, Glasgow.

10 9 8 7 6 5 4 3 2 1

CONTENTS

ACKNOWLEDGEMENTS

Special thanks to Sue and Lou Irmo for their generosity, and to Jo Fletcher for helping me meet the deadlines.

"Sex, Death and Starshine" copyright © 1984 by Clive Barker. Originally published in *Books of Blood Volume 1*. Reprinted by permission of Little, Brown and Company (UK) Limited.

"Rising Generation" copyright © 1975 by Ramsey Campbell. Originally published in *World of Horror* No.4, January, 1975.

"The Song of the Slaves" copyright © 1940 by *Weird Tales*. Originally published in *Weird Tales*, March 1940. Reprinted by permission of the author's executor.

"The Ghouls" copyright © 1975 by Ronald Chetwynd-Hayes. Originally published in *The Night Ghouls*. Reprinted by permission of the author.

"The Facts in the Case of M. Valdemar" by Edgar Allan Poe. Originally published in *American Whig Review* (1845).

"Sticks" copyright © 1974 by Stuart David Schiff. Originally published in *Whispers*, March 1974. Reprinted by permission of the author.

"Quietly Now" copyright © 1981 by Charles L. Grant. Originally published in *The Arbor House Necropolis*. Reprinted by permission of the author.

"The Grey House" copyright © 1966 by Basil Copper. Originally published in *Not After Nightfall*. Reprinted by permission of the author.

"A Warning to the Curious" by M. R. James. Originally published in *A Warning to the Curious* (1925).

"The Crucian Pit" copyright © 1993 by Nicholas Royle.

"The Disapproval of Jeremy Cleave" copyright © 1989 by the Terminus Publishing Company, Inc. Originally published in *Weird Tales* No.295, Winter 1989/90. Reprinted by permission of the author and the author's agent.

For Dave Carson
who, after all these years,
still just likes to draw monsters.

Introduction

The Dead That Walk

ZOMBIES . . . OR *Zombis* . . . *the Walking Dead* . . . soulless automatons risen from the grave to do the bidding of their masters. They have their factual basis in the voodoo ceremonies of Haiti and other Caribbean islands, and accounts of the real-life phenomenon range from William Seabrook's 1929 study *The Magic Island* to Wade Davis' modern bestseller *The Serpent and the Rainbow*.

However, despite blending many of horror fiction's major thematic archetypes – witchcraft, a mindless monster, the living dead – the zombie has rarely made a successful transition to the novel form (in the same way as, say, the vampire has). Although there are, of course, a number of exceptions (Breer, the appalling Razor-Eater in Clive Barker's *The Damnation Game* and Hugh, the reanimated lover of Gordon Honeycombe's *Neither the Sea Nor the Sand* come to mind), the true home of the zombie has always been the movies.

Ever since Bela Lugosi's sinister "Murder" Legendre ordered the revived corpses of his plantation workers to shamble across the screen in *White Zombie* (1932), it has been the cinema which has most influenced our perception of the walking dead. From Bob Hope's comedic capers in *The Ghost Breakers* (1940) and producer Val Lewton's atmospheric reworking of *Jane Eyre*, *I Walked With a Zombie* (1943), through to George Romero's epic dystopian trilogy

(*Night of the Living Dead* [1969], *Dawn of the Dead* [1978] and *Day of the Dead* [1985]) and the numerous European rip-offs, the zombie has reached a level of identification in the horror pantheon equal to that of its generic companions: the vampire, the Frankenstein monster, the werewolf, and the mummy. Yet, despite these and other memorable titles, the walking (dancing?) dead probably reached a commercial pinnacle in 1983 with Michael Jackson's *Thriller* video.

An area in which the zombie still continues to thrive is the short story, with several all-new anthologies devoted to the theme in recent years. *The Mammoth Book of Zombies* brings together twenty-six stories ranging from traditional Haitian rituals to futuristic science as a means of reviving the dead. Within these pages you'll discover such classic tales of the macabre as Edgar Allan Poe's "The Facts in the Case of M. Valdemar", M. R. James' "A Warning to the Curious" and J. Sheridan Le Fanu's "Schalken the Painter", plus memorable stories from the pulp magazines by Manly Wade Wellman ("The Song of the Slaves"), H. P. Lovecraft and Robert Bloch (with their respective novellas "Herbert West – Reanimator" and "The Dead Don't Die!", both the basis for movie adaptations).

Also collected together for the first time are stories from such established masters as Clive Barker, Ramsey Campbell, Brian Lumley, Karl Edward Wagner, Dennis Etchison, Lisa Tuttle, Les Daniels, Charles L. Grant, R. Chetwynd-Hayes, Basil Copper, Kim Newman and Joe R. Lansdale, plus original fiction by Graham Masterton, Christopher Fowler, Peter Tremayne, Nicholas Royle, Michael Marshall Smith, David Sutton, and new novellas by David Riley and Hugh B. Cave.

As with my other *Mammoth* volumes, *The Mammoth Book of Terror* and *The Mammoth Book of Vampires,* the main criteria for choosing these stories is because they are particular favourites of mine. However, they also present the discerning reader with a unique gamut of zombies, ranging from the traditional to the *outré*.

So listen to the sound of ragged nails scraping against hard wood, while cold fingers claw up through the damp earth and mist-shrouded graveyards once more give up their long-silent tenants. As Bela Lugosi gleefully explained to one hapless victim back in 1932, *"For you, my friend, they are the Angels of Death . . ."*

Stephen Jones,
London, England

Clive Barker

Sex, Death and Starshine

Never one to rest on his laurels, Clive Barker has been busy with numerous projects which utilize his polymorphic talents. On the film side these include a continuation of the Hellraiser *saga, inspired by his original novella and directing debut, following the success of* Hellraiser III: Hell on Earth *(1992); a sequel to the critically-acclaimed* Candyman *(1992), based on his original story, "The Forbidden"; and an animated feature adaptation of his recent fantasy novel,* The Thief of Always.

In 1993 his paintings and drawings were exhibited at New York's Bess Cutler Gallery, and graphic versions of his stories and concepts continue to proliferate. He describes his latest novel, Everville, *as "a look at the dark heart of America".*

"Sex, Death and Starshine" was originally published in Barker's ground-breaking Books of Blood *series, and comes out of the author's early career in the theatre. "Zombies are the ideal late-twentieth century monsters," according to Barker. "A zombie is the one thing you can't deal with. It survives anything. Frankenstein and Dracula could be sent down in many ways. Zombies, though, fall outside all this. You can't argue with them. They just keep coming at you.*

"Zombies are about dealing with death. They represent a specific face of death. And the fact that we can even talk like this about a horror movie creation puts down the theory that the genre can't be taken seriously."

I'm not sure that the story which follows takes the genre very seriously, but prepare to meet some of the sexiest and most urbane walking dead you're ever likely to find in modern horror fiction . . .

DIANE RAN HER scented fingers through the two days' growth of ginger stubble on Terry's chin.

"I love it," she said, "even the grey bits."

She loved everything about him, or at least that's what she claimed.

When he kissed her: I love it.

When he undressed her: I love it.

When he slid his briefs off: I love it, I love it, I love it.

She'd go down on him with such unalloyed enthusiasm, all he could do was watch the top of her ash-blonde head bobbing at his groin, and hope to God nobody chanced to walk into the dressing-room. She was a married woman, after all, even if she was an actress. He had a wife himself, somewhere. This tête-à-tête would make some juicy copy for one of the local rags, and here he was trying to garner a reputation as a serious-minded director; no gimmicks, no gossip; just art.

Then, even thoughts of ambition would be dissolved on her tongue, as she played havoc with his nerve-endings. She wasn't much of an actress, but by God she was quite a performer. Faultless technique; immaculate timing: she knew either by instinct or by rehearsal just when to pick up the rhythm and bring the whole scene to a satisfying conclusion.

When she'd finished milking the moment dry, he almost wanted to applaud.

The whole cast of Calloway's production of *Twelfth Night* knew about the affair, of course. There'd be the occasional snide comment passed if actress and director were both late for rehearsals, or if she arrived looking full, and he flushed. He tried to persuade her to control the cat-with-the-cream look that crept over her face, but she just wasn't that good a deceiver. Which was rich, considering her profession.

But then La Duvall, as Edward insisted on calling her, didn't need to be a great player, she was famous. So what if she spoke Shakespeare like it was Hiawatha, dum de dum de dum de dum? So what if her grasp of psychology was dubious, her logic faulty, her projection inadequate? So what if she had as much sense of poetry as she did propriety? She was a star, and that meant business.

There was no taking that away from her: her name was money.

The Elysium Theatre publicity announced her claim to fame in three inch Roman Bold, black on yellow:

"Diane Duvall: star of *The Love Child*."

The Love Child. Possibly the worst soap opera to cavort across the screens of the nation in the history of that genre, two solid hours a week of under-written characters and mind-numbing dialogue, as a result of which it consistently drew high ratings, and its performers became, almost overnight, brilliant stars in television's rhinestone heaven. Glittering there, the brightest of the bright, was Diane Duvall.

Maybe she wasn't born to play the classics, but Jesus was she good box-office. And in this day and age, with theatres deserted, all that mattered was the number of punters on seats.

Calloway had resigned himself to the fact that this would not be the definitive *Twelfth Night*, but if the production were successful, and with Diane in the role of Viola it had every chance, it might open a few doors to him in the West End. Besides, working with the ever-adoring, ever-demanding Miss D. Duvall had its compensations.

Calloway pulled up his serge trousers, and looked down at her. She was giving him that winsome smile of hers, the one she used in the letter scene. Expression Five in the Duvall repertoire, somewhere between Virginal and Motherly.

He acknowledged the smile with one from his own stock, a small, loving look that passed for genuine at a yard's distance. Then he consulted his watch.

"God, we're late, sweetie."

She licked her lips. Did she really like the taste that much?

"I'd better fix my hair," she said, standing up and glancing in the long mirror beside the shower.

"Yes."

"Are you OK?"

"Couldn't be better," he replied. He kissed her lightly on the nose and left her to her teasing.

On his way to the stage he ducked into the Men's Dressing Room to adjust his clothing, and dowse his burning cheeks with cold water. Sex always induced a giveaway mottling on his face and upper chest. Bending to splash water on himself Calloway studied his features critically in the mirror over the sink. After thirty-six years of holding the signs of age at bay, he was beginning to look the part. He was no more the juvenile lead. There was an indisputable puffiness beneath his eyes, which was nothing to do with sleeplessness and there were lines too, on his forehead, and round his mouth. He didn't look the *wunderkind* any longer; the secrets of his debauchery were written all over his face. The excess of sex, booze and ambition, the frustration of aspiring and just missing the main chance so many times. What would he look like now, he thought bitterly, if he'd been content to be some unenterprising nobody working in a minor rep, guaranteed a house of ten aficionados every night, and devoted to Brecht? Face as smooth as a baby's bottom probably, most of the people in the socially-committed theatre had that look. Vacant and content, poor cows.

"Well, you pays your money and you takes your choice," he told himself. He took one last look at the haggard cherub in the mirror, reflecting that, crow's feet or not, women still couldn't resist him, and went out to face the trials and tribulations of Act III.

On stage there was a heated debate in progress. The carpenter, his name was Jake, had built two hedges for Olivia's garden. They still had to be covered with leaves, but they looked quite impressive, running the depth of the stage to the cyclorama, where the rest of the garden would be painted. None of this symbolic stuff. A garden was a garden: green grass, blue sky. That's the way the audience liked it North of Birmingham, and Terry had some sympathy for their plain tastes.

"Terry, love."

Eddie Cunningham had him by the hand and elbow, escorting him into the fray.

"What's the problem?"

"Terry, love, you cannot be serious about these fucking (it came trippingly off the tongue: fuck-ing) hedges. Tell Uncle Eddie you're not serious before I throw a fit." Eddie pointed towards the offending hedges. "I mean look at them." As he spoke a thin plume of spittle fizzed in the air.

"What's the problem?" Terry asked again.

"Problem? Blocking, love, blocking. *Think* about it. We've rehearsed this whole scene with me bobbing up and down like a March hare. Up right, down left – but it doesn't work if I haven't got access round the back. And look! These fuck-ing things are flush with the backdrop."

"Well they have to be, for the illusion, Eddie."

"I can't get round though, Terry. You must see my point."

He appealed to the few others on stage: the carpenters, two technicians, three actors.

"I mean – there's just not enough time."

"Eddie, we'll re-block."

"Oh."

That took the wind out of his sails.

"No?"

"Um."

"I mean it seems easiest, doesn't it?"

"Yes . . . I just liked . . ."

"I know."

"Well. Needs must. What about the croquet?"

"We'll cut that too."

"All that business with the croquet mallets? The bawdy stuff?"

"It'll all have to go. I'm sorry, I haven't thought this through. I wasn't thinking straight."

Eddie flounced.

"That's all you ever do, love, think straight . . ."

Titters. Terry let it pass. Eddie had a genuine point of criticism; he had failed to consider the problems of the hedge-design.

"I'm sorry about the business; but there's no way we can accommodate it."

"You won't be cutting anybody else's business, I'm sure," said Eddie. He threw a glance over Calloway's shoulder at Diane, then headed for the dressing-room. Exit enraged actor, stage left. Calloway made no attempt to stop him. It would have worsened the situation considerably to spoil his departure. He just breathed out a quiet "oh Jesus", and dragged a wide hand down over his face. That was the fatal flaw of this profession: actors.

"Will somebody fetch him back?" he said.

Silence.

"Where's Ryan?"

The Stage Manager showed his bespectacled face over the offending hedge.

"Sorry?"

"Ryan, love – will you please take a cup of coffee to Eddie and coax him back into the bosom of the family?"

Ryan pulled a face that said: you offended him, you fetch him. But Calloway had passed this particular buck before: he was a past master at it. He just stared at Ryan, defying him to contradict his request, until the other man dropped his eyes and nodded his acquiescence.

"Sure," he said glumly.

"Good man."

Ryan cast him an accusatory look, and disappeared in pursuit of Ed Cunningham.

"No show without Belch," said Calloway, trying to warm up the atmosphere a little. Someone grunted: and the small half-circle of onlookers began to disperse. Show over.

"OK, OK," said Calloway, picking up the pieces, "let's get to work. We'll run through from the top of the scene. Diane, are you ready?"

"Yes."

"OK. Shall we run it?"

He turned away from Olivia's garden and the waiting actors just to gather his thoughts. Only the stage working lights were on, the auditorium was in darkness. It yawned at him insolently, row upon row of empty seats, defying him to entertain them. Ah, the loneliness of the long-distance director. There were days in this business when the thought of life as an accountant seemed a consummation devoutly to be wished, to paraphrase the Prince of Denmark.

In the Gods of the Elysium, somebody moved. Calloway looked up from his doubts and stared through the swarthy air. Had Eddie taken residence on the very back row? No, surely not. For one thing, he hadn't had time to get all the way up there.

"Eddie?" Calloway ventured, capping his hand over his eyes. "Is that you?"

He could just make the figure out. No, not a figure, figures. Two people, edging their way along the back row, making for the exit. Whoever it was, it certainly wasn't Eddie.

"That isn't Eddie, is it?" said Calloway, turning back into the fake garden.

"No," someone replied.

It was Eddie speaking. He was back on stage, leaning on one of the hedges, cigarette clamped between his lips.

"Eddie . . ."

"It's all right," said the actor good-humouredly, "don't grovel; I can't bear to see a pretty man grovel."

"We'll see if we can slot the mallet-business in somewhere," said Calloway, eager to be conciliatory.

Eddie shook his head, and flicked ash off his cigarette.

"No need."

"Really – "

"It didn't work too well anyhow."

The Grand Circle door creaked a little as it closed behind the visitors. Calloway didn't bother to look round. They'd gone, whoever they were.

*   *   *

"There was somebody in the house this afternoon."

Hammersmith looked up from the sheets of figures he was poring over.

"Oh?" his eyebrows were eruptions of wire-thick hair that seemed ambitious beyond their calling. They were raised high above Hammersmith's tiny eyes in patently fake surprise. He plucked at his bottom lip with nicotine stained fingers.

"Any idea who it was?"

He plucked on, still staring up at the younger man; undisguised contempt on his face.

"Is it a problem?"

"I just want to know who was in looking at the rehearsal that's all. I think I've got a perfect right to ask."

"Perfect right," said Hammersmith, nodding slightly and making his lips into a pale bow.

"There was talk of somebody coming up from the National," said Calloway. "My agents were arranging something. I just don't want somebody coming in without me knowing about it. Especially if they're important."

Hammersmith was already studying the figures again. His voice was tired.

"Terry: if there's someone in from the South Bank to look your opus over, I promise you, you'll be the first to be informed. All right?"

The inflexion was so bloody rude. So run-along-little-boy. Calloway itched to hit him.

"I don't want people watching rehearsals unless I authorize it, Hammersmith. Hear me? And I want to know who was in today."

The Manager sighed heavily.

"Believe me, Terry," he said, "I don't know myself. I suggest you ask Tallulah – she was front of house this afternoon. If somebody came in, presumably she saw them."

He sighed again.

"All right . . . Terry?"

Calloway left it at that. He had his suspicions about Hammersmith. The man couldn't give a shit about theatre, he never failed to make that absolutely plain; he affected an exhausted tone whenever anything but money was mentioned, as though matters of aesthetics were beneath his notice. And he had a word, loudly administered, for actors and directors alike: butterflies. One day wonders. In Hammersmith's world only money was forever, and the Elysium Theatre stood on prime land, land a wise man could turn a tidy profit on if he played his cards right.

Calloway was certain he'd sell off the place tomorrow if he could manoeuvre it. A satellite town like Redditch, growing as Birmingham grew, didn't need theatres, it needed offices, hypermarkets, warehouses: it needed, to quote the councillors, growth through investment in new industry. It also needed prime sites to build that industry upon. No mere art could survive such pragmatism.

Tallulah was not in the box, nor in the foyer, nor in the Green Room.

Irritated both by Hammersmith's incivility and Tallulah's disappearance, Calloway went back into the auditorium to pick up his jacket and go to get drunk. The rehearsal was over and the actors long gone. The bare hedges looked somewhat small from the back row of the stalls. Maybe they needed an extra few inches. He made a note on the back of a show bill he found in his pocket: Hedges, bigger?

A footfall made him look up, and a figure had appeared on stage. A smooth entrance, up-stage centre, where the hedges converged. Calloway didn't recognize the man.

"Mr Calloway? Mr Terence Calloway?"

"Yes?"

The visitor walked down stage to where, in an earlier age, the footlights would have been, and stood looking out into the auditorium.

"My apologies for interrupting your train of thought."

"No problem."

"I wanted a word."

"With me?"

"If you would."

Calloway wandered down to the front of the stalls, appraising the stranger.

He was dressed in shades of grey from head to foot. A grey worsted suit, grey shoes, a grey cravat. Piss-elegant, was Calloway's first, uncharitable summation. But the man cut an impressive figure nevertheless. His face beneath the shadow of his brim was difficult to discern.

"Allow me to introduce myself."

The voice was persuasive, cultured. Ideal for advertisement voice-overs: soap commercials, maybe. After Hammersmith's bad manners, the voice came as a breath of good breeding.

"My name is Lichfield. Not that I expect that means much to a man of your tender years."

Tender years: well, well. Maybe there was still something of the *wunderkind* in his face.

"Are you a critic?" Calloway inquired.

The laugh that emanated from beneath the immaculately-swept brim was ripely ironical.

"In the name of Jesus, no," Lichfield replied.

"I'm sorry, then, you have me at a loss."

"No need for an apology."

"Were you in the house this afternoon?"

Lichfield ignored the question. "I realize you're a busy man, Mr Calloway, and I don't want to waste your time. The theatre is my business, as it is yours. I think we must consider ourselves allies, though we have never met."

Ah, the great brotherhood. It made Calloway want to spit, the familiar claims of sentiment. When he thought of the number of so-called allies that had cheerfully stabbed him in the back; and in return the playwrights whose work he'd smilingly slanged, the actors he'd crushed with a casual quip. Brotherhood be damned, it was dog eat dog, same as any over-subscribed profession.

"I have," Lichfield was saying, "an abiding interest in the Elysium." There was a curious emphasis on the word abiding. It sounded positively funereal from Lichfield's lips. Abide with me.

"Oh?"

"Yes, I've spent many happy hours in this theatre, down the years, and frankly it pains me to carry this burden of news."

"What news?"

"Mr Calloway, I have to inform you that your *Twelfth Night* will be the last production the Elysium will see."

The statement didn't come as much of a surprise, but it still hurt, and the internal wince must have registered on Calloway's face.

"Ah . . . so you didn't know. I thought not. They always keep the artists in ignorance don't they? It's a satisfaction the Apollonians will never relinquish. The accountant's revenge."

"Hammersmith," said Calloway.

"Hammersmith."

"Bastard."

"His clan are never to be trusted, but then I hardly need to tell you that."

"Are you sure about the closure?"

"Certainly. He'd do it tomorrow if he could."

"But why? I've done Stoppard here, Tennessee Williams – always played to good houses. It doesn't make sense."

"It makes admirable financial sense, I'm afraid, and if you think in figures, as Hammersmith does, there's no riposte to simple arithmetic. The Elysium's getting old. We're *all* getting old. We creak. We feel our age in our joints: our instinct is to lie down and be gone away."

Gone away: the voice became melodramatically thin, a whisper of longing.

"How do you know about this?"

"I was, for many years, a trustee of the theatre, and since my retirement I've made it my business to – what's the phrase? – keep my ear to the ground. It's difficult, in this day and age, to evoke the triumph this stage has seen . . ."

His voice trailed away, in a reverie. It seemed true, not an effect.

Then, business-like once more: "This theatre is about to die, Mr Calloway. You will be present at the last rites, through no fault of your own. I felt you ought to be . . . warned."

"Thank you. I appreciate that. Tell me, were you ever an actor yourself?"

"What makes you think that?"

"The voice."

"Too rhetorical by half, I know. My curse, I'm afraid. I can scarcely ask for a cup of coffee without sounding like Lear in the storm."

He laughed, heartily, at his own expense. Calloway began to warm to the fellow. Maybe he was a little archaic-looking, perhaps even slightly absurd, but there was a full-bloodedness about his manner that caught Calloway's imagination. Lichfield wasn't apologetic about his love of theatre, like so many in the profession, people who trod the boards as a second-best, their souls sold to the movies.

"I have, I will confess, dabbled in the craft a little," Lichfield confided, "but I just don't have the stamina for it, I'm afraid. Now my wife – "

Wife? Calloway was surprised Lichfield had a heterosexual bone in his body.

"– My wife Constantia has played here on a number of occasions, and I may say very successfully. Before the war of course."

"It's a pity to close the place."

"Indeed. But there are no last act miracles to be performed, I'm afraid. The Elysium will be rubble in six weeks' time, and there's an end to it. I just wanted you to know that interests other than the crassly commercial are watching over this closing production. Think of us as guardian angels. We wish you well, Terence, we all wish you well."

It was a genuine sentiment, simply stated. Calloway was touched by this man's concern, and a little chastened by it. It put his own stepping-stone ambitions in an unflattering perspective. Lichfield went on: "We care to see this theatre end its days in suitable style, then die a good death."

"Damn shame."

"Too late for regrets by a long chalk. We should never have given up Dionysus for Apollo."

"What?"

"Sold ourselves to the accountants, to legitimacy, to the likes of Mr Hammersmith, whose soul, if he has one, must be the size of my fingernail, and grey as a louse's back. We should have had the courage of our depictions, I think. Served poetry and lived under the stars."

Calloway didn't quite follow the allusions, but he got the general drift, and respected the viewpoint.

Off stage left, Diane's voice cut the solemn atmosphere like a plastic knife.

"Terry? Are you there?"

The spell was broken: Calloway hadn't been aware how hypnotic Lichfield's presence was until that other voice came between them. Listening to him was like being rocked in familiar arms. Lichfield stepped to the edge of the stage, lowering his voice to a conspiratorial rasp.

"One last thing, Terence – "

"Yes?"

"Your Viola. She lacks, if you'll forgive my pointing it out, the special qualities required for the role."

Calloway hung fire.

"I know," Lichfield continued, "personal loyalties prevent honesty in these matters."

"No," Calloway replied, "you're right. But she's popular."

"So was bear-baiting, Terence."

A luminous smile spread beneath the brim, hanging in the shadow like the grin of the Cheshire Cat.

"I'm only joking," said Lichfield, his rasp a chuckle now. "Bears can be charming."

"Terry, there you are."

Diane appeared, over-dressed as usual, from behind the tabs. There was surely an embarrassing confrontation in the air. But Lichfield was walking away down the false perspective of the hedges towards the backdrop.

"Here I am," said Terry.

"Who are you talking to?"

But Lichfield had exited, as smoothly and as quietly as he had entered. Diane hadn't even seen him go.

"Oh, just an angel," said Calloway.

The first Dress Rehearsal wasn't, all things considered, as bad as Calloway had anticipated: it was immeasurably worse. Cues were lost, props mislaid, entrances missed; the comic business seemed ill-contrived and laborious; the performances either hopelessly over-wrought or trifling. This was a *Twelfth Night* that seemed to last a year. Halfway through the third act Calloway glanced at his watch, and realized an uncut performance of *Macbeth* (with interval) would now be over.

He sat in the stalls with his head buried in his hands, contempla-ting the work that he still had to do if he was to bring this production up to scratch. Not for the first time on this show he felt helpless in the face of the casting problems. Cues could be tightened, props rehearsed with, entrances practised until they were engraved on the memory. But a bad actor is a bad actor is a bad actor. He could labour till doomsday neatening and sharpening, but he could not make a silk purse of the sow's ear that was Diane Duvall.

With all the skill of an acrobat she contrived to skirt every significance, to ignore every opportunity to move the audience, to avoid every nuance the playwright would insist on putting in her way. It was a performance heroic in its ineptitude, reducing the delicate characterization Calloway had been at pains to create to a single-note whine. This Viola was soap-opera pap, less human than the hedges, and about as green.

The critics would slaughter her.

Worse than that, Lichfield would be disappointed. To his con-siderable surprise the impact of Lichfield's appearance hadn't dwindled; Calloway couldn't forget his actorly projection, his posing, his rhetoric. It had moved him more deeply than he was prepared to admit, and the thought of this *Twelfth Night*, with this Viola, becoming the swan-song of Lichfield's beloved Elysium perturbed and embarrassed him. It seemed somehow ungrateful.

He'd been warned often enough about a director's burdens, long before he became seriously embroiled in the profession. His dear departed guru at the Actors' Centre, Wellbeloved (he of the glass eye), had told Calloway from the beginning:

"A director is the loneliest creature on God's earth. He knows what's good and bad in a show, or he should if he's worth his salt, and he has to carry that information around with him and keep smiling."

It hadn't seemed so difficult at the time.

"This job isn't about succeeding," Wellbeloved used to say, "it's about learning not to fall on your sodding face."

Good advice as it turned out. He could still see Wellbeloved handing out that wisdom on a plate, his bald head shiny, his living eye glittering with cynical delight. No man on earth, Calloway had thought, loved theatre with more passion than Wellbeloved, and surely no man could have been more scathing about its pretensions.

It was almost one in the morning by the time they'd finished the wretched run-through, gone through the notes, and separated, glum and mutually resentful, into the night. Calloway wanted none of their company tonight: no late drinking in one or others' digs, no mutual ego-massage. He had a cloud of gloom all to himself, and neither wine, women nor song would disperse it. He could barely bring himself to look Diane in the face. His notes to her, broadcast in front of the rest of the cast, had been acidic. Not that it would do much good.

In the foyer, he met Tallulah, still spry though it was long after an old lady's bedtime.

"Are you locking up tonight?" he asked her, more for something to say than because he was actually curious.

"I always lock up," she said. She was well over seventy: too old for her job in the box office, and too tenacious to be easily removed. But then that was all academic now, wasn't it? He wondered what her response would be when she heard the news of the closure. It would probably break her brittle heart. Hadn't Hammersmith once told him Tallulah had been at the theatre since she was a girl of fifteen?

"Well, goodnight Tallulah."

She gave him a tiny nod, as always. Then she reached out and took Calloway's arm.

"Yes?"

"Mr Lichfield . . ." she began.

"What about Mr Lichfield?"

"He didn't like the rehearsal."

"He was in tonight?"

"Oh yes," she replied, as though Calloway was an imbecile for thinking otherwise, "of course he was in."

"I didn't see him."

"Well . . . no matter. He wasn't very pleased."

Calloway tried to sound indifferent.

"It can't be helped."

"Your show is very close to his heart."

"I realize that," said Calloway, avoiding Tallulah's accusing looks. He had quite enough to keep him awake tonight, without her disappointed tones ringing in his ears.

He loosed his arm, and made for the door. Tallulah made no attempt to stop him. She just said: "You should have seen Constantia."

Constantia? Where had he heard that name? Of course, Lichfield's wife.

"She was a wonderful Viola."

He was too tired for this mooning over dead actresses; she was dead wasn't she? He had said she was dead, hadn't he?

"Wonderful," said Tallulah again.

"Goodnight, Tallulah. I'll see you tomorrow."

The old crone didn't answer. If she was offended by his brusque manner, then so be it. He left her to her complaints and faced the street.

It was late November, and chilly. No balm in the night-air, just the smell of tar from a freshly laid road, and grit in the wind. Calloway pulled his jacket collar up around the back of his neck, and hurried off to the questionable refuge of Murphy's Bed and Breakfast.

In the foyer Tallulah turned her back on the cold and dark of the outside world, and shuffled back into the temple of dreams. It smelt so weary now: stale with use and age, like her own body. It was time to let natural processes take their toll; there was no point in letting things run beyond their allotted span. That was as true of buildings as of people. But the Elysium had to die as it had lived, in glory.

Respectfully, she drew back the red curtains that covered the portraits in the corridor that led from foyer to stalls. Barrymore, Irving: great names and great actors. Stained and faded pictures perhaps, but the memories were as sharp and as refreshing as spring water. And in pride of place, the last of the line to be unveiled, a portrait of Constantia Lichfield. A face of transcendent beauty; a bone structure to make an anatomist weep.

She had been far too young for Lichfield of course, and that had been part of the tragedy of it. Lichfield the Svengali, a man twice her age, had been capable of giving his brilliant beauty everything she desired; fame, money, companionship. Everything but the gift she most required: life itself.

She'd died before she was yet twenty, a cancer in the breast. Taken so suddenly it was still difficult to believe she'd gone.

Tears brimmed in Tallulah's eyes as she remembered that lost and wasted genius. So many parts Constantia would have illuminated had she been spared. Cleopatra, Hedda, Rosalind, Electra . . .

But it wasn't to be. She'd gone, extinguished like a candle in a hurricane, and for those who were left behind life was a slow and joyless march through a cold land. There were mornings now, stirring to another dawn, when she would turn over and pray to die in her sleep.

The tears were quite blinding her now, she was awash. And oh dear, there was somebody behind her, probably Mr Calloway back for something, and here was she, sobbing fit to burst, behaving like the silly old woman she knew he thought her to be. A young man like him, what did he understand about the pain of the years, the deep ache of irretrievable loss? That wouldn't come to him for a while yet. Sooner than he thought, but a while nevertheless.

"Tallie," somebody said.

She knew who it was. Richard Walden Lichfield. She turned round and he was standing no more than six feet from her, as fine a figure of a man as ever she remembered him to be. He must be twenty years older than she was, but age didn't seem to bow him. She felt ashamed of her tears.

"Tallie," he said kindly, "I know it's a little late, but I felt you'd surely want to say hello."

"Hello?"

The tears were clearing, and now she saw Lichfield's companion, standing a respectful foot or two behind him, partially obscured. The figure stepped out of Lichfield's shadow and there was a luminous, fine-boned beauty Tallulah recognized as easily as her own reflection. Time broke in pieces, and reason deserted the world. Longed-for faces were suddenly back to fill the empty nights, and offer fresh hope to a life grown weary. Why should she argue with the evidence of her eyes?

It was Constantia, the radiant Constantia, who was looping her arm through Lichfield's and nodding gravely at Tallulah in greeting.

Dear, dead Constantia.

The rehearsal was called for nine-thirty the following morning. Diane Duvall made an entrance her customary half hour late. She looked as though she hadn't slept all night.

"Sorry I'm late," she said, her open vowels oozing down the aisle towards the stage.

Calloway was in no mood for foot-kissing.

"We've got an opening tomorrow," he snapped, "and everybody's been kept waiting by you."

"Oh really?" she fluttered, trying to be devastating. It was too early in the morning, and the effect fell on stony ground.

"OK, we're going from the top," Calloway announced, "and everybody please have your copies and a pen. I've got a list of cuts here and I want them rehearsed in by lunchtime. Ryan, have you got the prompt copy?"

There was a hurried exchange with the ASM and an apologetic negative from Ryan.

"Well get it. And I don't want any complaints from anyone, it's too late in the day. Last night's run was a wake, not a performance. The cues took forever; the business was ragged. I'm going to cut, and it's not going to be very palatable."

It wasn't. The complaints came, warning or no, the arguments, the compromises, the sour faces and muttered insults. Calloway would have rather been hanging by his toes from a trapeze than manoeuvering fourteen highly-strung people through a play two-thirds of them scarcely understood, and the other third couldn't give a monkey's about. It was nerve-wracking.

It was made worse because all the time he had the prickly sense of being watched, though the auditorium was empty from Gods to front stalls. Maybe Lichfield had a spyhole somewhere, he thought, then condemned the idea as the first signs of budding paranoia.

At last, lunch.

Calloway knew where he'd find Diane, and he was prepared for the scene he had to play with her. Accusations, tears, reassurance, tears again, reconciliation. Standard format.

He knocked on the Star's door.

"Who is it?"

Was she crying already, or talking through a glass of something comforting?

"It's me."

"Oh."

"Can I come in?"

"Yes."

She had a bottle of vodka, good vodka, and a glass. No tears as yet.

"I'm useless, aren't I?" she said, almost as soon as he'd closed the door. Her eyes begged for contradiction.

"Don't be silly," he hedged.

"I could never get the hang of Shakespeare," she pouted, as though it were the Bard's fault. "All those bloody words." The squall was on the horizon, he could see it mustering.

"It's all right," he lied, putting his arm around her. "You just need a little time."

Her face clouded.

"We open tomorrow," she said flatly. The point was difficult to refute.

"They'll tear me apart, won't they?"

He wanted to say no, but his tongue had a fit of honesty.

"Yes. Unless – "

"I'll never work again, will I? Harry talked me into this, that damn half-witted Jew: good for my reputation, he said. Bound to give me a bit more clout, he said. What does he know? Takes his ten bloody per cent and leaves me holding the baby. I'm the one who looks the damn fool aren't I?"

At the thought of looking a fool, the storm broke. No light shower this: it was a cloudburst or nothing. He did what he could, but it was difficult. She was sobbing so loudly his pearls of wisdom were drowned out. So he kissed her a little, as any decent director was bound to do, and (miracle upon miracle) that seemed to do the trick. He applied the technique with a little more gusto, his hands straying to her breasts, ferreting under her blouse for her nipples and teasing them between thumb and forefinger.

It worked wonders. There were hints of sun between the clouds now; she sniffed and unbuckled his belt, letting his heat dry out the last of the rain. His fingers were finding the lacy edge of her panties, and she was sighing as he investigated her, gently but not too gently, insistent but never too insistent. Somewhere along the line she knocked over the vodka bottle but neither of them cared to stop and right it, so it sloshed on to the floor off the edge of the table, counterpointing her instructions, his gasps.

Then the bloody door opened, and a draught blew up between them, cooling the point at issue.

Calloway almost turned round, then realized he was unbuckled, and stared instead into the mirror behind Diane to see the intruder's face. It was Lichfield. He was looking straight at Calloway, his face impassive.

"I'm sorry, I should have knocked."

His voice was as smooth as whipped cream, betraying nary a tremor of embarrassment. Calloway wedged himself away, buckled up his belt and turned to Lichfield, silently cursing his burning cheeks.

"Yes . . . it would have been polite," he said.

"Again, my apologies. I wanted a word with — " his eyes, so
deep-set they were unfathomable, were on Diane "— your star,"
he said.

Calloway could practically feel Diane's ego expand at the word.
The approach confounded him: had Lichfield undergone a volte-
face? Was he coming here, the repentant admirer, to kneel at the
feet of greatness?

"I would appreciate a word with the lady in private, if that were
possible," the mellow voice went on.

"Well, we were just — "

"Of course," Diane interrupted. "Just allow me a moment,
would you?"

She was immediately on top of the situation, tears forgotten.

"I'll be just outside," said Lichfield, already taking his leave.

Before he had closed the door behind him Diane was in front of
the mirror, tissue-wrapped finger skirting her eye to divert a rivulet
of mascara.

"Well," she was cooing, "how lovely to have a well-wisher. Do
you know who he is?"

"His name's Lichfield," Calloway told her. "He used to be a
trustee of the theatre."

"Maybe he wants to offer me something."

"I doubt it."

"Oh don't be such a drag, Terence," she snarled. "You just can't
bear to have anyone else get any attention, can you?"

"My mistake."

She peered at her eyes.

"How do I look?" she asked.

"Fine."

"I'm sorry about before."

"Before?"

"You know."

"Oh . . . yes."

"I'll see you in the pub, eh?"

He was summarily dismissed apparently, his function as lover or
confidant no longer required.

In the chilly corridor outside the dressing room Lichfield was
waiting patiently. Though the lights were better here than on the
ill-lit stage, and he was closer now than he'd been the night before,
Calloway could still not quite make out the face under the wide brim.
There was something — what was the idea buzzing in his head? —
something artificial about Lichfield's features. The flesh of his face
didn't move as interlocking system of muscle and tendon, it was too

stiff, too pink, almost like scar-tissue.

"She's not quite ready," Calloway told him.

"She's a lovely woman," Lichfield purred.

"Yes."

"I don't blame you . . ."

"Um."

"She's no actress though."

"You're not going to interfere are you, Lichfield? I won't let you."

"Perish the thought."

The voyeuristic pleasure Lichfield had plainly taken in his embarrassment made Calloway less respectful than he'd been.

"I won't have you upsetting her – "

"My interests are your interests, Terence. All I want to do is see this production prosper, believe me. Am I likely, under those circumstances, to alarm your Leading Lady? I'll be as meek as a lamb, Terence."

"Whatever you are," came the testy reply, "you're no lamb."

The smile appeared again on Lichfield's face, the tissue round his mouth barely stretching to accommodate his expression.

Calloway retired to the pub with that predatory sickle of teeth fixed in his mind, anxious for no reason he could focus upon.

In the mirrored cell of her dressing-room Diane Duvall was just about ready to play her scene.

"You may come in now, Mr Lichfield," she announced.

He was in the doorway before the last syllable of his name had died on her lips.

"Miss Duvall," he bowed slightly in deference to her. She smiled; so courteous. "Will you please forgive my blundering in earlier on?"

She looked coy; it always melted men.

"Mr Calloway – " she began.

"A very insistent young man, I think."

"Yes."

"Not above pressing his attentions on his Leading Lady, perhaps?"

She frowned a little, a dancing pucker where the plucked arches of her brows converged.

"I'm afraid so."

"Most unprofessional of him," Lichfield said. "But forgive me – an understandable ardour."

She moved upstage of him, towards the lights of her mirror, and turned, knowing they would back-light her hair more flatteringly.

"Well, Mr Lichfield, what can I do for you?"

"This is frankly a delicate matter," said Lichfield. "The bitter fact is – how shall I put this? – your talents are not ideally suited to this production. Your style lacks delicacy."

There was a silence for two beats. She sniffed, thought about the inference of the remark, and then moved out of centre-stage towards the door. She didn't like the way this scene had begun. She was expecting an admirer, and instead she had a critic on her hands.

"Get out!" she said, her voice like slate.

"Miss Duvall – "

"You heard me."

"You're not comfortable as Viola, are you?" Lichfield continued, as though the star had said nothing.

"None of your bloody business," she spat back.

"But it is. I saw the rehearsals. You were bland, unpersuasive. The comedy is flat, the reunion scene – it should break our hearts – is leaden."

"I don't need your opinion, thank you."

"You have no style – "

"Piss off."

"No presence and no style. I'm sure on the television you are radiance itself, but the stage requires a special truth, a soulfulness you, frankly, lack."

The scene was hotting up. She wanted to hit him, but she couldn't find the proper motivation. She couldn't take this faded poseur seriously. He was more musical comedy than melodrama, with his neat grey gloves, and his neat grey cravat. Stupid, waspish queen, what did he know about acting?

"Get out before I call the Stage Manager," she said, but he stepped between her and the door.

A rape scene? Was that what they were playing? Had he got the hots for her? God forbid.

"My wife," he was saying, "has played Viola – "

"Good for her."

"– and she feels she could breathe a little more life into the role than you."

"We open tomorrow," she found herself replying, as though defending her presence. Why the hell was she trying to reason with him; barging in here and making these terrible remarks. Maybe because she was just a little afraid. His breath, close to her now, smelt of expensive chocolate.

"She knows the role by heart."

"The part's mine. And I'm doing it. I'm doing it even if I'm the worst Viola in theatrical history, all right?"

She was trying to keep her composure, but it was difficult. Something about him made her nervous. It wasn't violence she feared from him: but she feared something.

"I'm afraid I have already promised the part to my wife."

"What?" she goggled at his arrogance.

"And Constantia will play the role."

She laughed at the name. Maybe this was high comedy after all. Something from Sheridan or Wilde, arch, catty stuff. But he spoke with such absolute certainty. *Constantia will play the role*; as if it was all cut and dried.

"I'm not discussing this any longer, Buster, so if your wife wants to play Viola she'll have to do it in the fucking street. All right?"

"She opens tomorrow."

"Are you deaf, or stupid, or both?"

Control, an inner voice told her, you're overplaying, losing your grip on the scene. Whatever scene this is.

He stepped towards her, and the mirror lights caught the face beneath the brim full on. She hadn't looked carefully enough when he first made his appearance: now she saw the deeply-etched lines, the gougings around his eyes and his mouth. It wasn't flesh, she was sure of it. He was wearing latex appliances, and they were badly glued in place. Her hand all but twitched with the desire to snatch at it and uncover his real face.

Of course. That was it. The scene she was playing: the Unmasking.

"Let's see what you look like," she said, and her hand was at his cheek before he could stop her, his smile spreading wider as she attacked. This is what he wants, she thought, but it was too late for regrets or apologies. Her fingertips had found the line of the mask at the edge of his eye-socket, and curled round to take a better hold. She yanked.

The thin veil of latex came away, and his true physiognomy was exposed for the world to see. Diane tried to back away, but his hand was in her hair. All she could do was look up into that all-but fleshless face. A few withered strands of muscle curled here and there, and a hint of a beard hung from a leathery flap at his throat, but all living tissue had long since decayed. Most of his face was simply bone: stained and worn.

"I was not," said the skull, "embalmed. Unlike Constantia."

The explanation escaped Diane. She made no sound of protest, which the scene would surely have justified. All she could summon was a whimper as his hand-hold tightened, and he hauled her head back.

"We must make a choice, sooner or later," said Lichfield, his breath smelling less like chocolate than profound putrescence, "between serving ourselves and serving our art."

She didn't quite understand.

"The dead must choose more carefully than the living. We cannot waste our breath, if you'll excuse the phrase, on less than the purest delights. You don't want art, I think. Do you?"

She shook her head, hoping to God that was the expected response.

"You want the life of the body, not the life of the imagination. And you may have it."

"Thank . . . you."

"If you want it enough, you may have it."

Suddenly his hand, which had been pulling on her hair so painfully, was cupped behind her head, and bringing her lips up to meet his. She would have screamed then, as his rotting mouth fastened itself on to hers, but his greeting was so insistent it quite took her breath away.

Ryan found Diane on the floor of her dressing-room a few minutes before two. It was difficult to work out what had happened. There was no sign of a wound of any kind on her head or body, nor was she quite dead. She seemed to be in a coma of some kind. She had perhaps slipped, and struck her head as she fell. Whatever the cause, she was out for the count.

They were hours away from a Final Dress Rehearsal and Viola was in an ambulance, being taken into Intensive Care.

"The sooner they knock this place down, the better," said Hammersmith. He'd been drinking during office hours, something Calloway had never seen him do before. The whisky bottle stood on his desk beside a half-full glass. There were glass-marks ringing his accounts, and his hand had a bad dose of the shakes.

"What's the news from the hospital?"

"She's a beautiful woman," he said, staring at the glass. Calloway could have sworn he was on the verge of tears.

"Hammersmith? How is she?"

"She's in a coma. But her condition is stable."

"That's something, I suppose."

Hammersmith stared up at Calloway, his erupting brows knitted in anger.

"You runt," he said, "you were screwing her, weren't you? Fancy yourself like that, don't you? Well, let me tell you something, Diane Duvall is worth a dozen of you. A dozen!"

"Is that why you let this last production go on, Hammersmith? Because you'd seen her, and you wanted to get your hot little hands on her?"

"You wouldn't understand. You've got your brain in your pants." He seemed genuinely offended by the interpretation Calloway had put on his admiration for Miss Duvall.

"All right, have it your way. We still have no Viola."

"That's why I'm cancelling," said Hammersmith, slowing down to savour the moment.

It had to come. Without Diane Duvall, there would be no *Twelfth Night*; and maybe it was better that way.

A knock on the door.

"Who the fuck's that?" said Hammersmith softly. "Come."

It was Lichfield. Calloway was almost glad to see that strange, scarred face. Though he had a lot of questions to ask of Lichfield, about the state he'd left Diane in, about their conversation together, it wasn't an interview he was willing to conduct in front of Hammersmith. Besides, any half-formed accusations he might have had were countered by the man's presence here. If Lichfield had attempted violence on Diane, for whatever reason, was it likely that he would come back so soon, so smilingly?

"Who are you?" Hammersmith demanded.

"Richard Walden Lichfield."

"I'm none the wiser."

"I used to be a trustee of the Elysium."

"Oh."

"I make it my business – "

"What do you want?" Hammersmith broke in, irritated by Lichfield's poise.

"I hear the production is in jeopardy," Lichfield replied, unruffled.

"No jeopardy," said Hammersmith, allowing himself a twitch at the corner of his mouth. "No jeopardy at all, because there's no show. It's been cancelled."

"Oh?" Lichfield looked at Calloway.

"Is this with your consent?" he asked.

"He has no say in the matter; I have sole right of cancellation if circumstances dictate it; it's in his contract. The theatre is closed as of today: it will not reopen."

"Yes it will," said Lichfield.

"What?" Hammersmith stood up behind his desk, and Calloway realized he'd never seen the man standing before. He was very short.

"We will play *Twelfth Night* as advertised," Lichfield purred. "My wife has kindly agreed to understudy the part of Viola in place of Miss Duvall."

Hammersmith laughed, a coarse, butcher's laugh. It died on his lips however, as the office was suffused with lavender, and Constantia Lichfield made her entrance, shimmering in silk and fur. She looked as perfect as the day she died: even Hammersmith held his breath and his silence at the sight of her.

"Our new Viola," Lichfield announced.

After a moment Hammersmith found his voice. "This woman can't step in at half a day's notice."

"Why not?" said Calloway, not taking his eyes off the woman. Lichfield was a lucky man; Constantia was an extraordinary beauty. He scarcely dared draw breath in her presence for fear she'd vanish.

Then she spoke. The lines were from Act V, Scene I:

"If nothing lets to make us happy both
But this my masculine usurp'd attire,
Do not embrace me till each circumstance
Of place, time, fortune, do cohere and jump
That I am Viola."

The voice was light and musical, but it seemed to resound in her body, filling each phrase with an undercurrent of suppressed passion.

And that face. It was wonderfully alive, the features playing the story of her speech with delicate economy.

She was enchanting.

"I'm sorry," said Hammersmith, "but there are rules and regulations about this sort of thing. Is she Equity?"

"No," said Lichfield.

"Well you see, it's impossible. The union strictly precludes this kind of thing. They'd flay us alive."

"What's it to you, Hammersmith?" said Calloway. "What the fuck do you care? You'll never need set foot in a theatre again once this place is demolished."

"My wife has watched the rehearsals. She is word perfect."

"It could be magic," said Calloway, his enthusiasm firing up with every moment he looked at Constantia.

"You're risking the Union, Calloway," Hammersmith chided.

"I'll take that risk."

"As you say, it's nothing to me. But if a little bird was to tell them, you'd have egg on your face."

"Hammersmith: give her a chance. Give all of us a chance. If Equity blacks me, that's my look-out." Hammersmith sat down again.

"Nobody'll come, you know that, don't you? Diane Duvall was a star; they would have sat through your turgid production to see her, Calloway. But an unknown . . .? Well, it's your funeral. Go ahead and do it, I wash my hands of the whole thing. It's on your head, Calloway, remember that. I hope they flay you for it."

"Thank you," said Lichfield. "Most kind."

Hammersmith began to rearrange his desk, to give more prominence to the bottle and the glass. The interview was over: he wasn't interested in these butterflies any longer.

"Go away," he said. "Just go away."

"I have one or two requests to make," Lichfield told Calloway as they left the office. "Alterations to the production which would enhance my wife's performance."

"What are they?"

"For Constantia's comfort, I would ask that the lighting levels be taken down substantially. She's simply not accustomed to performing under such hot, bright lights."

"Very well."

"I'd also request that we install a row of footlights."

"Footlights?"

"An odd requirement, I realize, but she feels much happier with footlights."

"They tend to dazzle the actors," said Calloway. "It becomes difficult to see the audience."

"Nevertheless . . . I have to stipulate their installation."

"OK."

"Thirdly – I would ask that all scenes involving kissing, embracing or otherwise touching Constantia be re-directed to remove every instance of physical contact whatsoever."

"Everything?"

"Everything."

"For God's sake why?"

"My wife needs no business to dramatize the working of the heart, Terence."

That curious intonation on the word "heart". Working of the *heart*.

Calloway caught Constantia's eye for the merest of moments. It was like being blessed.

"Shall we introduce our new Viola to the company?" Lichfield suggested.

"Why not?"

The trio went into the theatre.

The re-arranging of the blocking and the business to exclude any physical contact was simple. And though the rest of the cast were initially wary of their new colleague, her unaffected manner and her natural grace soon had them at her feet. Besides, her presence meant that the show would go on.

At six, Calloway called a break, announcing that they'd begin the Dress at eight, and telling them to go out and enjoy themselves for an hour or so. The company went their ways, buzzing with a new-found enthusiasm for the production. What had looked like a shambles half a day earlier now seemed to be shaping up quite well. There were a thousand things to be sniped at, of course: technical shortcomings, costumes that fitted badly, directorial foibles. All par for the course. In fact, the actors were happier than they'd been in a good while. Even Ed Cunningham was not above passing a compliment or two.

Lichfield found Tallulah in the Green Room, tidying.

"Tonight . . ."

"Yes, sir."

"You must not be afraid."

"I'm not afraid," Tallulah replied. "What a thought. As if – "

"There may be some pain, which I regret. For you, indeed for all of us."

"I understand."

"Of course you do. You love the theatre as I love it: you know the paradox of this profession. To play life . . . ah, Tallulah, to play life . . . what a curious thing it is. Sometimes I wonder, you know, how long I can keep up the illusion."

"It's a wonderful performance," she said.

"Do you think so? Do you really think so?" He was encouraged by her favourable review. It was so galling, to have to pretend all the time; to fake the flesh, the breath, the look of life. Grateful for Tallulah's opinion, he reached for her.

"Would you like to die, Tallulah?"

"Does it hurt?"

"Scarcely at all."

"It would make me very happy."

"And so it should."

His mouth covered her mouth, and she was dead in less than a minute, conceding happily to his inquiring tongue. He laid her out on the threadbare couch and locked the door of the Green Room with her own key. She'd cool easily in the chill of the room, and be up and about again by the time the audience arrived.

At six-fifteen Diane Duvall got out of a taxi at the front of the Elysium. It was well dark, a windy November night, but she felt fine; nothing could depress tonight. Not the dark, not the cold.

Unseen, she made her way past the posters that bore her face and name, and through the empty auditorium to her dressing-room. There, smoking his way through a pack of cigarettes, she found the object of her affection.

"Terry."

She posed in the doorway for a moment, letting the fact of her reappearance sink in. He went quite white at the sight of her, so she pouted a little. It wasn't easy to pout. There was a stiffness in the muscles of her face but she carried off the effect to her satisfaction.

Calloway was lost for words. Diane looked ill, no two ways about it, and if she'd left the hospital to take up her part in the Dress Rehearsal he was going to have to convince her otherwise. She was wearing no make-up, and her ash-blonde hair needed a wash.

"What are you doing here?" he asked, as she closed the door behind her.

"Unfinished business," she said.

"Listen . . . I've got something to tell you . . ."

God, this was going to be messy. "We've found a replacement, in the show." She looked at him blankly. He hurried on, tripping over his own words, "We thought you were out of commission, I mean, not permanently, but, you know, for the opening at least . . ."

"Don't worry," she said.

His jaw dropped a little.

"Don't worry?"

"What's it to me?"

"You said you came back to finish – "

He stopped. She was unbuttoning the top of her dress. She's not serious, he thought, she can't be serious. Sex? Now?

"I've done a lot of thinking in the last few hours," she said as she shimmied the crumpled dress over her hips, let it fall, and stepped out of it. She was wearing a white bra, which she tried, unsuccessfully, to unhook. "I've decided I don't care about the theatre. Help me, will you?"

She turned round and presented her back to him. Automatically he unhooked the bra, not really analysing whether he wanted this or not. It seemed to be a *fait accompli*. She'd come back to finish what they'd been interrupted doing, simple as that. And despite the bizarre noises she was making in the back of her throat, and the glassy look in her eyes, she was still an attractive woman. She turned again, and Calloway stared at the fullness of her breasts, paler than he'd remembered them, but lovely. His trousers were becoming uncomfortably tight, and her performance was only worsening his situation, the way she was grinding her hips like the rawest of Soho strippers, running her hands between her legs.

"Don't worry about me," she said. "I've made up my mind. All I really want . . ."

She put her hands, so recently at her groin, on his face. They were icy cold.

"All I really want is you. I can't have sex *and* the stage . . . There comes a time in everyone's life when decisions have to be made."

She licked her lips. There was no film of moisture left on her mouth when her tongue had passed over it.

"The accident made me think, made me analyse what it is I really care about. And frankly – " She was unbuckling his belt. "– I don't give a shit – "

Now the zip.

"– about this, or any other fucking play."

His trousers fell down.

"– I'll show you what I care about."

She reached into his briefs, and clasped him. Her cold hand somehow made the touch sexier. He laughed, closing his eyes as she pulled his briefs down to the middle of his thigh and knelt at his feet.

She was as expert as ever, her throat open like a drain. Her mouth was somewhat drier than usual, her tongue scouring him, but the sensations drove him wild. It was so good, he scarcely noticed the ease with which she devoured him, taking him deeper than she'd ever managed previously, using every trick she knew to goad him higher and higher. Slow and deep, then picking up speed until he almost came, then slowing again until the need passed. He was completely at her mercy.

He opened his eyes to watch her at work. She was skewering herself upon him, face in rapture.

"God," he gasped, 'that is *so* good. Oh yes, oh yes."

Her face didn't even flicker in response to his words, she just continued to work at him soundlessly. She wasn't making her usual noises, the small grunts of satisfaction, the heavy breathing through the nose. She just ate his flesh in absolute silence.

He held his breath a moment, while an idea was born in his belly. The bobbing head bobbed on, eyes closed, lips clamped around his member, utterly engrossed. Half a minute passed; a minute; a minute and a half. And now his belly was full of terrors.

She wasn't breathing. She was giving this matchless blow-job because she wasn't stopping, even for a moment, to inhale or exhale.

Calloway felt his body go rigid, while his erection wilted in her throat. She didn't falter in her labour; the relentless pumping continued at his groin even as his mind formed the unthinkable thought:

She's dead.

She has me in her mouth, in her cold mouth, and she's dead. That's why she'd come back, got up off her mortuary slab and come back. She was eager to finish what she'd started, no longer caring about the play, or her usurper. It was this act she valued, this act alone. She'd chosen to perform it for eternity.

Calloway could do nothing with the realization but stare down like a damn fool while this corpse gave him head.

Then it seemed she sensed his horror. She opened her eyes and looked up at him. How could he ever have mistaken that dead stare for life? Gently, she withdrew his shrunken manhood from between her lips.

"What is it?" she asked, her fluting voice still affecting life.

"You . . . you're not . . . breathing."

Her face fell. She let him go.

"Oh darling," she said, letting all pretence to life disappear, "I'm not so good at playing the part, am I?"

Her voice was a ghost's voice: thin, forlorn. Her skin, which he had thought so flatteringly pale was, on second view, a waxen white.

"You are dead?" he said.

"I'm afraid so. Two hours ago: in my sleep. But I had to come, Terry; so much unfinished business. I made my choice. You should be flattered. You are flattered, aren't you?"

She stood up and reached into her handbag, which she'd left beside the mirror. Calloway looked at the door, trying to make his limbs work, but they were inert. Besides, he had his trousers round his ankles. Two steps and he'd fall flat on his face.

She turned back on him, with something silver and sharp in her hand. Try as he might, he couldn't get a focus on it. But whatever it was, she meant it for him.

* * *

Since the building of the new Crematorium in 1934, one humiliation had come after another for the cemetery. The tombs had been raided for lead coffin-linings, the stones overturned and smashed; it was fouled by dogs and graffiti. Very few mourners now came to tend the graves. The generations had dwindled, and the small number of people who might still have had a loved one buried there were too infirm to risk the throttled walkways, or too tender to bear looking at such vandalism.

It had not always been so. There were illustrious and influential families interred behind the marble façades of the Victorian mausoleums. Founder fathers, local industrialists and dignitaries, any and all who had done the town proud by their efforts. The body of the actress Constantia Lichfield had been buried here ('Until the Day Break and the Shadows Flee Away'), though her grave was almost unique in the attention some secret admirer still paid to it.

Nobody was watching that night, it was too bitter for lovers. Nobody saw Charlotte Hancock open the door of her sepulchre, with the beating wings of pigeons applauding her vigour as she shambled out to meet the moon. Her husband Gerard was with her, he less fresh than she, having been dead thirteen years longer. Joseph Jardine, en famille, was not far behind the Hancocks, as was Marriott Fletcher, and Anne Snell, and the Peacock Brothers; the list went on and on. In one corner, Alfred Crawshaw (Captain in the 17th Lancers), was helping his lovely wife Emma from the rot of their bed. Everywhere faces pressed at the cracks of the tomblids – was that not Kezia Reynolds with her child, who'd lived just a day, in her arms? and Martin van de Linde (the Memory of the Just is Blessed) whose wife had never been found; Rosa and Selina Goldfinch: upstanding women both; and Thomas Jerrey, and –

Too many names to mention. Too many states of decay to describe. Sufficient to say they rose: their burial finery flyborn, their faces stripped of all but the foundation of beauty. Still they came, swinging open the back gate of the cemetery and threading their way across the wasteland towards the Elysium. In the distance, the sound of traffic. Above, a jet roared in to land. One of the Peacock brothers, staring up at the winking giant as it passed over, missed his footing and fell on his face, shattering his jaw. They picked him up fondly, and escorted him on his way. There was no harm done; and what would a Resurrection be without a few laughs?

So the show went on.

"If music be the food of love, play on,
  Give me excess of it; that, surfeiting,

The appetite may sicken and so die – ”

Calloway could not be found at Curtain; but Ryan had instructions from Hammersmith (through the ubiquitous Mr Lichfield) to take the show up with or without the Director.

“He’ll be upstairs, in the Gods,” said Lichfield. “In fact, I think I can see him from here.”

“Is he smiling?” asked Eddie.

“Grinning from ear to ear.”

“Then he’s pissed.”

The actors laughed. There was a good deal of laughter that night. The show was running smoothly, and though they couldn’t see the audience over the glare of the newly-installed footlights they could feel the waves of love and delight pouring out of the auditorium. The actors were coming off stage elated.

“They’re all sitting in the Gods,” said Eddie, “but your friends, Mr Lichfield, do an old ham good. They’re quiet of course, but such big smiles on their faces.”

Act I, Scene II; and the first entrance of Constantia Lichfield as Viola was met with spontaneous applause. Such applause. Like the hollow roll of snare drums, like the brittle beating of a thousand sticks on a thousand stretched skins. Lavish, wanton applause.

And, my God, she rose to the occasion. She began the play as she meant to go on, giving her whole heart to the role, not needing physicality to communicate the depth of her feelings, but speaking the poetry with such intelligence and passion the merest flutter of her hand was worth more than a hundred grander gestures. After that first scene her every entrance was met with the same applause from the audience, followed by almost reverential silence.

Backstage, a kind of buoyant confidence had set in. The whole company sniffed the success; a success which had been snatched miraculously from the jaws of disaster.

There again! Applause! Applause!

In his office, Hammersmith dimly registered the brittle din of adulation through a haze of booze.

He was in the act of pouring his eighth drink when the door opened. He glanced up for a moment and registered that the visitor was that upstart Calloway. Come to gloat I daresay, Hammersmith thought, come to tell me how wrong I was.

“What do you want?”

The punk didn’t answer. From the corner of his eye Hammersmith had an impression of a broad, bright smile on Calloway’s face. Self-satisfied half-wit, coming in here when a man was in mourning.

"I suppose you've heard?"

The other grunted.

"She died," said Hammersmith, beginning to cry. "She died a few hours ago, without regaining consciousness. I haven't told the actors. Didn't seem worth it."

Calloway said nothing in reply to this news. Didn't the bastard care? Couldn't he see that this was the end of the world? The woman was dead. She'd died in the bowels of the Elysium. There'd be official enquiries made, the insurance would be examined, a post-mortem, an inquest: it would reveal too much.

He drank deeply from his glass, not bothering to look at Calloway again.

"Your career'll take a dive after this, son. It won't just be me: oh dear no."

Still Calloway kept his silence.

"Don't you care?" Hammersmith demanded.

There was silence for a moment, then Calloway responded. "I don't give a shit."

"Jumped up little stage-manager, that's all you are. That's all *any* of you fucking directors are! One good review and you're God's gift to art. Well let me set you straight about that – "

He looked at Calloway, his eyes, swimming in alcohol, having difficulty focussing. But he got there eventually.

Calloway, the dirty bugger, was naked from the waist down. He was wearing his shoes and his socks, but no trousers or briefs. His self-exposure would have been comical, but for the expression on his face. The man had gone mad: his eyes were rolling around uncontrollably, saliva and snot ran from mouth and nose, his tongue hung out like the tongue of a panting dog.

Hammersmith put his glass down on his blotting pad, and looked at the worst part. There was blood on Calloway's shirt, a trail of it which led up his neck to his left ear, from which protruded the end of Diane Duvall's nail-file. It had been driven deep into Calloway's brain. The man was surely dead.

But he stood, spoke, walked.

From the theatre, there rose another round of applause, muted by distance. It wasn't a real sound somehow; it came from another world, a place where emotions ruled. It was a world Hammersmith had always felt excluded from. He'd never been much of an actor, though God knows he'd tried, and the two plays he'd penned were, he knew, execrable. Book-keeping was his forte, and he'd used it to stay as close to the stage as he could, hating his own lack of art as much as he resented that skill in others.

The applause died, and as if taking a cue from an unseen prompter, Calloway came at him. The mask he wore was neither comic nor tragic, it was blood and laughter together. Cowering, Hammersmith was cornered behind his desk. Calloway leapt on to it (he looked so ridiculous, shirt-tails and balls flip-flapping) and seized Hammersmith by the tie.

"Philistine," said Calloway, never now to know Hammersmith's heart, and broke the man's neck — snap! — while below the applause began again.

"Do not embrace me till each circumstance
Of place, time, fortune, do cohere and jump
That I am Viola."

From Constantia's mouth the lines were a revelation. It was almost as though this *Twelfth Night* were a new play, and the part of Viola had been written for Constantia Lichfield alone. The actors who shared the stage with her felt their egos shrivelling in the face of such a gift.

The last act continued to its bitter-sweet conclusion, the audience as enthralled as ever to judge by their breathless attention.

The Duke spoke: "Give me thy hand;
And let me see thee in thy woman's weeds."

In the rehearsal the invitation in the line had been ignored: no-one was to touch this Viola, much less take her hand. But in the heat of the performance such taboos were forgotten. Possessed by the passion of the moment the actor reached for Constantia. She, forgetting the taboo in her turn, reached to answer his touch.

In the wings Lichfield breathed "no" under his breath, but his order wasn't heard. The Duke grasped Viola's hand in his, life and death holding court together under this painted sky.

It was a chilly hand, a hand without blood in its veins, or a blush in its skin.

But here it was as good as alive.

They were equals, the living and the dead, and nobody could find just cause to part them.

In the wings, Lichfield sighed, and allowed himself a smile. He'd feared that touch, feared it would break the spell. But Dionysus was with them tonight. All would be well; he felt it in his bones.

The act drew to a close, and Malvolio, still trumpeting his threats, even in defeat, was carted off. One by one the company exited, leaving the clown to wrap up the play.

"A great while ago the world began,

With hey, ho, the wind and the rain,
But that's all one, our play is done
And we'll strive to please you every day."
The scene darkened to blackout, and the curtain descended. From
the gods rapturous applause erupted, that same rattling, hollow
applause. The company, their faces shining with the success of the
Dress Rehearsal, formed behind the curtain for the bow. The curtain
rose: the applause mounted.

In the wings, Calloway joined Lichfield. He was dressed now: and
he'd washed the blood off his neck.

"Well, we have a brilliant success," said the skull. "It does seem
a pity that this company should be dissolved so soon."

"It does," said the corpse.

The actors were shouting into the wings now, calling for Calloway
to join them. They were applauding him, encouraging him to show
his face.

He put a hand on Lichfield's shoulder.

"We'll go together, sir," he said.

"No, no, I couldn't."

"You must. It's your triumph as much as mine." Lichfield nodded,
and they went out together to take their bows beside the company.

In the wings Tallulah was at work. She felt restored after her sleep
in the Green Room. So much unpleasantness had gone, taken with
her life. She no longer suffered the aches in her hip, or the creeping
neuralgia in her scalp. There was no longer the necessity to draw
breath through pipes encrusted with seventy years' muck, or to rub
the backs of her hands to get the circulation going; not even the need
to blink. She laid the fires with a new strength, pressing the detritus
of past productions into use: old backdrops, props, costuming. When
she had enough combustibles heaped, she struck a match and set the
flame to them. The Elysium began to burn.

Over the applause, somebody was shouting:

"Marvellous, sweethearts, marvellous."

It was Diane's voice, they all recognized it even though they
couldn't quite see her. She was staggering down the centre aisle
towards the stage, making quite a fool of herself.

"Silly bitch," said Eddie.

"Whoops," said Calloway.

She was at the edge of the stage now, haranguing him.

"Got all you wanted now, have you? This your new lady-love is
it? Is it?"

She was trying to clamber up, her hands gripping the hot metal hoods of the footlights. Her skin began to singe: the fat was well and truly in the fire.

"For God's sake, somebody stop her," said Eddie. But she didn't seem to feel the searing of her hands; she just laughed in his face. The smell of burning flesh wafted up from the footlights. The company broke rank, triumph forgotten.

Somebody yelled: "Kill the lights!"

A beat, and then the stage lights were extinguished. Diane fell back, her hands smoking. One of the cast fainted, another ran into the wings to be sick. Somewhere behind them, they could hear the faint crackle of flames, but they had other calls on their attention.

With the footlights gone, they could see the auditorium more clearly. The stalls were empty, but the Balcony and the gods were full to bursting with eager admirers. Every row was packed, and every available inch of aisle space thronged with audience. Somebody up there started clapping again, alone for a few moments before the wave of applause began afresh. But now few of the company took pride in it.

Even from the stage, even with exhausted and light-dazzled eyes, it was obvious that no man, woman or child in that adoring crowd was alive. They waved fine silk handkerchiefs at the players in rotted fists, some of them beat a tattoo on the seats in front of them, most just clapped, bone on bone.

Calloway smiled, bowed deeply, and received their admiration with gratitude. In all his fifteen years of work in the theatre he had never found an audience so appreciative.

Bathing in the love of their admirers, Constantia and Richard Lichfield joined hands and walked down-stage to take another bow, while the living actors retreated in horror.

They began to yell and pray, they let out howls, they ran about like discovered adulterers in a farce. But, like the farce, there was no way out of the situation. There were bright flames tickling the roof-joists, and billows of canvas cascaded down to right and left as the flies caught fire. In front, the dead: behind, death. Smoke was beginning to thicken the air, it was impossible to see where one was going. Somebody was wearing a toga of burning canvas, and reciting screams. Someone else was wielding a fire extinguisher against the inferno. All useless: all tired business, badly managed. As the roof began to give, lethal falls of timber and girder silenced most.

In the Gods, the audience had more or less departed. They were ambling back to their graves long before the fire department appeared, their cerements and their faces lit by the glow of the fire

as they glanced over their shoulders to watch the Elysium perish.
It had been a fine show, and they were happy to go home, content
for another while to gossip in the dark.

The fire burned through the night, despite the never less than gallant
efforts of the fire department to put it out. By four in the morning the
fight was given up as lost, and the conflagration allowed its head. It
had done with the Elysium by dawn.

In the ruins the remains of several persons were discovered,
most of the bodies in states that defied easy identification. Dental
records were consulted, and one corpse was found to be that of
Giles Hammersmith (Administrator), another that of Ryan Xavier
(Stage Manager) and, most shockingly, a third that of Diane Duvall.
"Star of *The Love Child* burned to death", read the tabloids. She was
forgotten in a week.

There were no survivors. Several bodies were simply never
found.

They stood at the side of the motorway, and watched the cars
careering through the night.

Lichfield was there of course, and Constantia, radiant as ever.
Calloway had chosen to go with them, so had Eddie, and Tallulah.
Three or four others had also joined the troupe.

It was the first night of their freedom, and here they were on the
open road, travelling players. The smoke alone had killed Eddie,
but there were a few more serious injuries amongst their number,
sustained in the fire. Burned bodies, broken limbs. But the audience
they would play for in the future would forgive them their petty
mutilations.

"There are lives lived for love," said Lichfield to his new company,
"and lives lived for art. We happy band have chosen the latter
persuasion."

"There was a ripple of applause amongst the actors.

"To you, who have never died, may I say: welcome to the
world!"

Laughter: further applause.

The lights of the cars racing north along the motorway threw the
company into silhouette. They looked, to all intents and purposes,
like living men and women. But then wasn't that the trick of their
craft? To imitate life so well the illusion was indistinguishable from
the real thing? And their new public, awaiting them in mortuaries,
churchyards and chapels of rest, would appreciate the skill more
than most. Who better to applaud the sham of passion and pain they

would perform than the dead, who had experienced such feelings, and thrown them off at last?

The dead. They needed entertainment no less than the living; and they were a sorely neglected market.

Not that this company would perform for money, they would play for the love of their art, Lichfield had made that clear from the outset. No more service would be done to Apollo.

"Now," he said, "which road shall we take, north or south?"

"North," said Eddie. "My mother's buried in Glasgow, she died before I ever played professionally. I'd like her to see me."

"North it is, then," said Lichfield. "Shall we go and find ourselves some transport?"

He led the way towards the motorway restaurant, its neon flickering fitfully, keeping the night at light's length. The colours were theatrically bright: scarlet, lime, cobalt, and a wash of white that splashed out of the windows on to the car park where they stood. The automatic doors hissed as a traveller emerged, bearing gifts of hamburgers and cake to the child in the back of his car.

"Surely some friendly driver will find a niche for us," said Lichfield.

"All of us?" said Calloway.

"A truck will do; beggars can't be too demanding," said Lichfield. "And we are beggars now: subject to the whim of our patrons."

"We can always steal a car," said Tallulah.

"No need for theft, except in extremity," Lichfield said. "Constantia and I will go ahead and find a chauffeur."

He took his wife's hand.

"Nobody refuses beauty," he said.

"What do we do if anyone asks us what we're doing here?" asked Eddie nervously. He wasn't used to this role; he needed reassurance.

Lichfield turned towards the company, his voice booming in the night:

"What do you do?" he said, "Play life, of course! And smile!"

Ramsey Campbell

Rising Generation

Ramsey Campbell's new Arkham House volume, Alone With the Horrors, *collects together thirty-nine stories written by the author between 1961 and 1991. His other recent books include* Uncanny Banquet, *an anthology of Great Tales of the Supernatural, the annual* Best New Horror *series (co-edited with Stephen Jones), the collection* Strange Things and Stranger Places, *and such novels as* Midnight Sun, The Count of Eleven *and* The Long Lost.

Described as "the most respected living British horror writer", Campbell has received the Horror Writers of America Bram Stoker Award, the World Fantasy Award three times and the British Fantasy Award seven times – more awards for horror fiction than any other writer. He also reviews films for BBC Radio Merseyside, is president of The British Fantasy Society, and is much in demand as a reader of his stories to audiences.

With "Rising Generation" the author is obviously having fun with the trappings of the zombie genre, but he still manages to give it a darkly atmospheric twist that is uniquely Campbell.

As THEY APPROACHED the cave beneath the castle some of the children began to play at zombies, hobbling stiffly, arms outstretched. Heather Fry frowned. If they knew the stories about the place, despite her efforts to make sure they didn't, she hoped they wouldn't frighten the others. She hadn't wanted to come at all; it had been Miss Sharp's idea, and she'd been teaching decades longer than Heather, so of course she had her way. The children were still plodding inexorably toward their victims. Then Joanne said "You're only being like those men in that film last night." Heather smiled with relief. "Keep together and wait for me," she said.

She glanced up at the castle, set atop the hill like a crown, snapped and bent and discovered by time. Overhead sailed a pale blue sky, only a wake of thin foamy clouds on the horizon betraying any movement. Against the sky, just below the castle, Heather saw three figures toiling upward. Odd, she thought, the school had been told the castle was forbidden to visitors because of the danger of falling stone, which was why they'd had to make do with the cave. Still, she was glad she hadn't had to coax her class all the way up there. The three were moving slowly and clumsily, no doubt exhausted by their climb, and even from where Heather stood their faces looked exceptionally pale.

She had to knock several times on the door of the guide's hut before he emerged. Looking in beyond him, Heather wondered what had taken his time. Not tidying the hut, certainly, because the desk looked blitzed, scattered and overflowing with forms and even an upset ink-bottle, fortunately stoppered. She looked at the guide and her opinion sank further. Clearly he didn't believe in shaving or cutting his nails, and he was pale enough to have been born in a cave, she thought. He didn't even bother to turn to her; he stared at the children lined up at the cave entrance, though by his lack of expression he might as well have been blind. "I'd rather you didn't say anything about the legend," she said.

His stare swivelled to her and held for so long she felt it making a fool of her. "You know what I mean," she said, determined to show him she did too. "The stories about the castle. About how the baron was supposed to keep zombies in the cave to work for him, until someone killed him and walled them up. I know it's only a story but not for the children, please."

When he'd finished staring at her he walked toward the cave, his hands dangling on his long arms and almost brushing his knees. At least he won't interrupt, she thought. I wonder how much he's paid and for what? There was even a propped-up boot poking out from beneath the desk.

As she reached the near end of the line of children he was trudging into the cave. Daylight slipped from his back and he merged with the enormous darkness, then the walls closed about him as his torch awakened them. Heather switched on her own torch. "Stay with your partner," she called, paragraphing with her fingers. "Stay in the light. And don't lag."

The children, fourteen pairs of them, were hurrying after the guide's light. The cave was wide at the entrance but swiftly narrowed as it curved, and when Heather glanced back a minute later, lips of darkness had closed behind them. As the guide's torch wavered the corrugations of the walls rippled like the soft gulping flesh of a throat. The children were glancing about uneasily like young wild animals, worried by the dark sly shifting they glimpsed at the edge of their vision. Heather steadied her beam about them, and the thousands of tons of stone above their heads closed down.

Not that it was easy to steady the beam. In the cave he'd picked up speed considerably, and she and the children had to hurry so as not to be left behind. Maybe he feels at home, she thought angrily. "Will you slow down, please," she called and heard Debbie at the front of the line say "Miss Fry says you've got to slow down."

The guide's light caught a wide flat slab of roof that looked as if it were sagging. Scattered earth crunched softly beneath Heather's feet. About now, she was sure, they would be heading up and out the other side of the hill. Joanne, who hadn't let Debbie convince her as a zombie, and Debbie squeezed back to Heather along the contracting passage. "I don't like that man," Joanne said. "He's dirty."

"What do you mean?" Heather said, sounding too worried. But Joanne said, "He's got earth in his ears."

"Will you hold our hands if we're frightened?" Debbie said.

"Now I can't hold everyone's hand, can I?" Earth slid from beneath Heather's feet. Odd, she thought: must come from the guide's ears and beneath his nails, and began to giggle, shaking her head when they asked why. He was still forcing them to hurry, but she was beginning to be glad that at least they wouldn't have to depend on him much longer. "If you think of questions don't ask them yet," she called. "Wait until we're outside."

"I wish we didn't have to come underground," Joanne said.

Then you should have said before, Heather thought. "You'll be able to look for things in the field later," she said. And at least you haven't had Miss Sharp herding you as well as her own class. If they hadn't come on ahead they would have had to suffer her running their picnic.

"But why do we have to come down when it's nice? Sharon didn't have to."

"It'll still be nice this afternoon. Sharon can't go into places that are closed in, just as you don't like high places. So you see, you're lucky today."

"I don't feel lucky," Joanne said.

The ridges of the walls were still swaying gently, like the leaves of a submarine plant, and now one reached out and tugged at Heather's sleeve. She flinched away, then saw that it was a splintered plank, several of which were propped against the wall, looking as if they'd once been fastened together. Ahead the cave forked, and the children were following the shrinking rim of light into the left-hand passage, which was so low that they had to stoop. "Go on, you're all right," she told Debbie, who was hesitating. Stupid man, she raged.

It was tighter than she'd thought. She had to hold one arm straight out in front of her so that the light urged the children on, leaving herself surrounded by darkness that coldly pressed her shoulders down when she tried to see ahead. If this passage had been fenced off, as she suspected, she was sorry it had been re-opened. The children's ridged shadows rippled like caterpillars. Suddenly Debbie halted. "There's someone else in here," she said.

"Well?" Joanne said. "It's not your cave."

Now all the children had gone quiet, and Heather could hear it too: the footsteps of several people tramping forward from deeper within the cave. Each step was followed by a scattering sound like brief dry rain. "Men working in the caves," she called, waiting for someone to ask what the dry sound was so that she could say they were carrying earth. Don't ask why, she thought. Something to do with the castle, perhaps with the men she'd seen on the hill. But the footsteps had stopped.

When she straightened up at last the darkness clenched on her head: she had to steady herself against the wall. Her vertigo gradually steadied, and she peered ahead. The children had caught up with the guide, who was silhouetted against a gaping tunnel of bright pale stone. As she started toward him he pulled something from his pocket and hurled it beyond her.

Debbie made to retrieve it. "It's all right," Heather said, and ushered the pair of them with her light toward the other children. Then, cursing his rudeness, she turned the beam on what she assumed he'd thrown her to catch. She peered closer, but it was exactly what it seemed: a packed lump of earth. Right, she thought, if I can lose you your job, you're out of work now.

She advanced on him. He was standing in the mouth of a side tunnel, staring back at her and pointing his torch deeper into the main passage. The children were hurrying past him into the hard tube of light. She was nearly upon him when he plodded out of the side tunnel, and she saw that the children were heading for a jagged opening at the limit of the beam, surrounded by exploded stone sprinkled with earth. She'd opened her mouth to call them back when his hand gripped her face and crushed her lips, forcing her back into the side tunnel.

His cold hand smelled thickly of earth. His arm was so long that her nails flailed inches short of his face. "Where's Miss Fry?" Debbie called, and he pointed ahead with his torch. Then he pushed Heather further into the cave, though she hacked at his shins. All at once she remembered that the boot beneath the desk had been propped on its toe: there might have been a leg beyond it.

Then the children screamed; one chorus of panic, then silence. Heather's teeth closed in the flesh of his hand, but he continued to shove her back into the cave. She saw her torch gazing up at the roof of the main passage, retreating. His own torch drooped in his hand, and its light drew the walls to leap and struggle, imitating her.

Now he was forcing her toward the cave floor. She caught sight of a mound of earth into which he began to press her head, as if for baptism. She fought upward, teeth grinding in his flesh, and saw figures groping past her upturned torch. They were the children.

She let herself go limp at once, and managed to twist out of the way as he fell. But he kept hold of her until she succeeded in bringing her foot forward and grinding his face beneath her heel like a great pale insect. He still made no vocal sound. Then she fled staggering to her torch, grabbed it and ran. The stone wrinkles of the low roof seemed more hindering, as if now she were battling a current. Before she was free of the roof she heard him crawling in the darkness at her heels, like a worm.

When the children appeared at the end of her swaying tunnel of light she gave a wordless cry of relief. She could feel nothing but relief that they were covered with dirt: they'd been playing. They still were just short of the border of daylight, and they'd even persuaded Joanne to be a zombie. "Quickly," Heather gasped. "Run to Miss Sharp's class." But they continued playing, turning stiffly toward her, arms groping. Then, as she saw the earth trickling from their mouths and noses, she knew they weren't playing at all.

Manly Wade Wellman

The Song of the Slaves

Since his death in 1986, Manly Wade Wellman (b. 1903) has continued to entertain a whole new generation of horror fans with reprints of his classic pulp magazine stories in various anthologies around the world.

One of the most prolific contributors to the pulps during the 1930s and 40s, Wellman's horror, fantasy and science fiction stories graced the pages of Weird Tales, Strange Stories, Unknown *and* The Magazine of Fantasy & Science Fiction, *to name only a few. He wrote more than seventy-five books in all genres, more than two hundred short stories, and numerous comic books and articles. Twice a winner of the World Fantasy Award, Wellman's best short stories can be found in the collections* Who Fears the Devil?, Worse Things Waiting, Lonely Vigils *and* The Valley so Low.

Although the author was born in Africa and retained many sentimental feelings about the country, this was rarely reflected in his work. One of the notable exceptions is "The Song of the Slaves," a chilling tale of revenge from beyond the grave . . .

GENDER PAUSED AT the top of the bald rise, mopped his streaming red forehead beneath the wide hat-brim, and gazed backward at his forty-nine captives. Naked and black, they shuffled upward from the narrow, ancient slave trail through the jungle. Forty-nine men, seized by Gender's own hand and collared to a single long chain, destined for his own plantation across the sea . . . Gender grinned in his lean, drooping mustache, a mirthless grin of greedy triumph.

For years he had dreamed and planned for this adventure, as other men dream and plan for European tours, holy pilgrimages, or returns to beloved birthplaces. He had told himself that it was intensely practical and profitable. Slaves passed through so many hands – the raider, the caravaner, the seashore factor, the slaver captain, the dealer in New Orleans or Havana or at home in Charleston. Each greedy hand clutched a rich profit, and all profits must come eventually from the price paid by the planter. But he, Gender, had come to Africa himself, in his own ship; with a dozen staunch ruffians from Benguela he had penetrated the Bihé-Bailundu country, had sacked a village and taken these forty-nine upstanding natives between dark and dawn. A single neck-shackle on his long chain remained empty, and he might fill even that before he came to his ship. By the Lord, he was making money this way, fairly coining it – and money was worth the making, to a Charleston planter in 1853.

So he reasoned, and so he actually believed, but the real joy to him was hidden in the darkest nook of his heart. He had conceived the raider-plan because of a nature that fed on savagery and mastery. A man less fierce and cruel might have been satisfied with hunting lions or elephants, but Gender must hunt men. As a matter of fact, the money made or saved by the journey would be little, if it was anything. The satisfaction would be tremendous. He would broaden his thick chest each day as he gazed out over his lands and saw there his slaves hoeing seashore cotton or pruning indigo; his forty-nine slaves, caught and shipped and trained by his own big, hard hands, more indicative of assured conquest than all the horned or fanged heads that ever passed through the shops of all the taxidermists.

Something hummed in his ears, like a rhythmic swarm of bees. Men were murmuring a song under their breath. It was the long string of pinch-faced slaves. Gender stared at them, and mouthed one of the curses he always kept at tongue's end.

"Silva!" he called.

The lanky Portuguese who strode free at the head of the file turned aside and stood before Gender. "*Patrao*?" he inquired respectfully, smiling teeth gleaming in his walnut face.

"What are those men singing?" demanded Gender. "I didn't think they had anything to sing about."

"A slave song, *patrao*." Silva's tapering hand, with the silver bracelet at its wrist, made a graceful gesture of dismissal. "It is nothing. One of the things that natives make up and sing as they go."

Gender struck his boot with his coiled whip of hippopotamus hide. The afternoon sun, sliding down toward the shaggy jungle-tops, kindled harsh pale lights in his narrow blue eyes. "How does the song go?" he persisted.

The two fell into step beside the caravan as, urged by a dozen red-capped drivers, it shambled along the trail. "It is only a slave song, *patrao*," said Silva once again. "It means something like this: 'Though you carry me away in chains, I am free when I die. Back will I come to bewitch and kill you.'"

Gender's heavy body seemed to swell, and his eyes grew narrower and paler. "So they sing that, hmm?" He swore again. "Listen to that!"

The unhappy procession had taken up a brief, staccato refrain:

"*Hailowa – Genda! Haipana – Genda!*"

"Genda, that's my name," snarled the planter. "They're singing about me, aren't they?"

Silva made another fluid gesture, but Gender flourished his whip under the nose of the Portuguese. "Don't you try to shrug me off. I'm not a child, to be talked around like this. What are they singing about me?"

"Nothing of consequence, *patrao*," Silva made haste to reassure him. "It might be to say: 'I will bewitch Gender, I will kill Gender.'"

"They threaten me, do they?" Gender's broad face took on a deeper flush. He ran at the line of chained black men. With all the strength of his arm he slashed and swung with the whip. The song broke up into wretched howls of pain.

"I'll give you a music lesson!" he raged, and flogged his way up and down the procession until he swayed and dripped sweat with the exertion.

But as he turned away, it struck up again:

"*Hailowa – Genda! Haipana – Genda!*"

Whirling back, he resumed the rain of blows. Silva, rushing up to second him, also whipped the slaves and execrated them in their own tongue. But when both were tired, the flayed captives began to sing once more, softly but stubbornly, the same chant.

"Let them whine," panted Gender at last. "A song never killed anybody."

Silva grinned nervously. "Of course not, *patrao*. That is only an idiotic native belief."

"You mean, they think that a song will kill?"

"That, and more. They say that if they sing together, think together of one hate, all their thoughts and hates will become a solid strength – will strike and punish for them."

"Nonsense!" exploded Gender.

But when they made camp that night, Gender slept only in troubled snatches, and his dreams were of a song that grew deeper, heavier, until it became visible as a dark, dense cloud that overwhelmed him.

The ship that Gender had engaged for the expedition lay in a swampy estuary, far from any coastal town, and the dawn by which he loaded his goods aboard was strangely fiery and forbidding. Dunlapp, the old slaver-captain that commanded for him, met him in the cabin.

"All ready, sir?" he asked Gender. "We can sail with the tide. Plenty of room in the hold for that handful you brought. I'll tell the men to strike off those irons."

"On the contrary," said Gender, "tell the men to put manacles on the hands of each slave."

Dunlapp gazed in astonishment at his employer. "But that's bad for blacks, Mr Gender. They get sick in chains, won't eat their food. Sometimes they die."

"I pay you well, Captain," Gender rumbled, "but not to advise me. Listen to those heathen."

Dunlapp listened. A moan of music wafted in to them.

"They've sung that cursed song about me all the way to the coast," Gender told him. "They know I hate it – I've whipped them day after day – but they keep it up. No chains come off until they hush their noise."

Dunlapp bowed acquiescence and walked out to give orders. Later, as they put out to sea, he rejoined Gender on the after deck.

"They do seem stubborn about their singing," he observed.

"I've heard it said," Gender replied, "that they sing together because they think many voices and hearts give power to hate, or to other feelings." He scowled. "Pagan fantasy!"

Dunlapp stared overside, at white gulls just above the wavetips. "There may be a tithe of truth in that belief, Mr Gender; sometimes there is in the faith of wild people. Hark ye, I've seen a good fifteen hundred Mohammedans praying at once, in the Barbary countries. When they bowed down, the touch of all those heads to the ground banged like the fall of a heavy rock. And when they straightened, the motion of their garments made a swish like the gust of a gale. I couldn't help but think that their prayer had force."

"More heathen foolishness," snapped Gender, and his lips drew tight.

"Well, in Christian lands we have examples, sir," Dunlapp pursued. "For instance, a mob will grow angry and burn or hang someone. Would a single man do that? Would any single man of the mob do it? No, but together their hate and resolution becomes – "

"Not the same thing at all," ruled Gender harshly. "Suppose we change the subject."

On the following afternoon, a white sail crept above the horizon behind them. At the masthead gleamed a little blotch of color. Captain Dunlapp squinted through a telescope, and barked a sailorly oath.

"A British ship-of-war," he announced, "and coming after us."

"Well?" said Gender.

"Don't you understand, sir? England is sworn to stamp out the slave trade. If they catch us with this cargo, it'll be the end of us." A little later, he groaned apprehensively. "They're overtaking us. There's their signal, for us to lay to and wait for them. Shall we do it, sir?"

Gender shook his head violently. "Not we! Show them our heels, Captain."

"They'll catch us. They are sailing three feet to our two."

"Not before dark," said Gender. "When dark comes, we'll contrive to lessen our embarrassment."

And so the slaver fled, with the Britisher in pursuit. Within an hour, the sun was at the horizon, and Gender smiled grimly in his mustache.

"It'll be dark within minutes," he said to Dunlapp. "As soon as you feel they can't make out our actions by glass, get those slaves on deck."

In the dusk the forty-nine naked prisoners stood in a line along the bulwark. For all their chained necks and wrists, they neither stood nor gazed in a servile manner. One of them began to sing and the others joined, in the song of the slave trail:

"Hailowa – Genda! Haipana – Genda!"

"Sing on," Gender snapped briefly, and moved to the end of the line that was near the bow. Here dangled the one empty collar, and he seized it in his hand. Bending over the bulwark, he clamped it shut upon something – the ring of a heavy spare anchor, that swung there upon a swivel-hook. Again he turned, and eyed the line of dark singers.

"Have a bath to cool your spirits," he jeered, and spun the handle of the swivel-hook.

The anchor fell. The nearest slave jerked over with it, and the next and the next. Others saw, screamed, and tried to brace themselves against doom; but their comrades that had already gone overside were too much weight for them. Quickly, one after another, the captives whipped from the deck and splashed into the sea. Gender leaned over and watched the last of them as he sank.

"Gad, sir!" exclaimed Dunlapp hoarsely.

Gender faced him almost threateningly.

"What else to do, hmm? You yourself said that we could hope for no mercy from the British."

The night passed by, and by the first grey light the British ship was revealed almost upon them. A megaphoned voice hailed them; then a shot hurtled across their bows. At Gender's smug nod, Dunlapp ordered his men to lay to. A boat put out from the pursuer, and shortly a British officer and four marines swung themselves aboard.

Bowing in mock reverence, Gender bade the party search. They did so, and remounted the deck crestfallen.

"Now, sir," Gender addressed the officer, "don't you think that you owe me an apology?"

The Englishman turned pale. He was a lean, sharp-featured man with strong, white teeth. "I can't pay what I owe you," he said with deadly softness. "I find no slaves, but I smell them. They were aboard this vessel within the past twelve hours."

"And where are they now?" teased Gender.

"We both know where they are," was the reply. "If I could prove in a court of law what I know in my heart, you would sail back to England with me. Most of the way you would hang from my yards by your thumbs."

"You wear out your welcome, sir," Gender told him.

"I am going. But I have provided myself with your name and that of your home city. From here I go to Madeira, where I will cross a packet bound west for Savannah. That packet will bear with it a letter to a friend of mine in Charleston, and your neighbors shall hear what happened on this ship of yours."

"You will stun slave-owners with a story of slaves?" inquired Gender, with what he considered silky good-humor.

"It is one thing to put men to work in cotton fields, another to tear them from their homes, crowd them chained aboard a stinking ship, and drown them to escape merited punishment." The officer spat on the deck. "Good day, butcher. I say, all Charleston shall hear of you."

Gender's plantation occupied a great, bluff-rimmed island at the mouth of a river, looking out toward the Atlantic. Ordinarily that island would be called beautiful, even by those most exacting followers of Chateaubriand and Rousseau; but, on his first night at home again, Gender hated the fields, the house, the environs of fresh and salt water.

His home, on a seaward jut, resounded to his grumbled curses as he called for supper and ate heavily but without relish. Once he vowed, in a voice that quivered with rage, never to go to Charleston again.

At that, he would do well to stay away for a time. The British officer had been as good at his promise, and all the town had heard of Gender's journey to Africa and what he had done there. With a perverse squeamishness beyond Gender's understanding, the hearers were filled with disgust instead of admiration. Captain Hogue had refused to drink with him at the Jefferson House. His oldest friend, Mr Lloyd Davis of Davis Township, had crossed the street to avoid meeting him. Even the Reverend Doctor Lockin had turned coldly away as he passed, and it was said that a sermon was forthcoming at Doctor Lockin's church attacking despoilers and abductors of defenseless people.

What was the matter with everybody? savagely demanded Gender of himself; these men who snubbed and avoided him were slave-holders. Some of them, it was quite possible, even held slaves fresh from raided villages under the Equator. Unfair! . . . Yet he could not but feel the animosity of many hearts, chafing and weighing upon his spirit.

"Brutus," he addressed the slave that cleared the table, "do you believe that hate can take form?"

"Hate, Marsa?" The sooty face was solemnly respectful.

"Yes. Hate, of many people together." Gender knew he should not confide too much in a slave, and chose his words carefully. "Suppose a lot of people hated the same thing, maybe they sang a song about it – "

"Oh, yes, Marsa," Brutus nodded. "I heah 'bout dat, from ole gran-pappy when I was little. He bin in Affiky, he says many times dey sing somebody to deff."

"Sing somebody to death?" repeated Gender. "How?"

"Dey sing dat dey kill him. Afta while, maybe plenty days, he die – ".

"Shut up, you black rascal" Gender sprang from his chair and clutched at a bottle. "You've heard about this somewhere, and you dare to taunt me!"

Brutus darted from the room, mortally frightened. Gender almost pursued, but thought better and tramped into his parlor. The big, brown-paneled room seemed to give back a heavier echo of his feet.

The windows were filled with the early darkness, and a hanging lamp threw rays into the corners.

On the center table lay some mail, a folded newspaper and a letter. Gender poured whisky from a decanter, stirred in spring water, and dropped into a chair. First he opened the letter.

"Stirling Manor," said the return address at the top of the page. Gender's heart twitched. Evelyn Stirling, he had hopes of her . . . but this was written in a masculine hand, strong and hasty.

> Sir:
>   Circumstances that have come to my knowledge compel me, as a matter of duty, to command that you discontinue your attention to my daughter.

Gender's eyes took on the pale tint of rage. One more result of the Britisher's letter, he made no doubt.

> I have desired her to hold no further communication with you, and I have been sufficiently explicit to convince her how unworthy you are of her esteem and attention. It is hardly necessary for me to give you the reasons which have induced me to form this judgement, and I add only that nothing you can say or do will alter it.
>
>   Your obedient servant,
>   JUDGE FORRESTER STIRLING.

Gender hastily swigged a portion of his drink, and crushed the paper in his hand. So that was the judge's interfering way – it sounded as though he had copied it from a complete letter-writer for heavy fathers. He, Gender, began to form a reply in his mind:

> Sir:
>   Your unfeeling and arbitrary letter admits of but one response. As a gentleman grossly misused, I demand satisfaction on the field of honor. Arrangements I place in the hands of . . .

By what friend should he forward that challenge? It seemed that he was mighty short of friends just now. He sipped more whisky and water, and tore the wrappings of the newspaper.

It was a Massachusetts publication, and toward the bottom of the first page was a heavy cross of ink, to call attention to one item.

A poem, evidently, in four-line stanzas. Its title signified nothing –
The Witnesses. Author, Henry W. Longfellow; Gender identified him
vaguely as a scrawler of Abolitionist doggerel. Why was this poem
recommended to a southern planter?

> *In Ocean's wide domains,*
> *Half buried in the sands,*
> *Lie skeletons in chains,*
> *With shackled feet and hands.*

Once again the reader swore, but the oath quavered on his lips.
His eye moved to a stanza farther down the column:

> *These are the bones of Slaves;*
> *They gleam from the abyss;*
> *They cry, from yawning waves . . .*

But it seemed to Gender that he heard, rather than read, what that
cry was.

He sprang to his feet, paper and glass falling from his hands.
His thin lips drew apart, his ears strained. The sound was faint,
but unmistakable – many voices singing.

The Negroes in his cabins? But no Negro on his plantation would
know that song. The chanting refrain began:

"*Hailowa – Genda! Haipana – Genda!*"

The planter's lean mustaches bristled tigerishly. This would surely
be the refined extremity of his persecution, this chanting of a weird
song under his window-sill. It was louder now. *I will bewitch, I will
kill* – but who would know that fierce mockery of him?

The crew of his ship, of course; they had heard it on the writhing
lips of the captives, at the very moment of their destruction. And
when the ship docked in Charleston, with no profit to show, Gender
had been none too kindly in paying them off.

Those unsavory mariners must have been piqued. They had
followed him, then, were setting up this vicious serenade.

Gender stepped quickly around the table and toward the window.
He flung up the sash with a violence that almost shattered the glass,
and leaned savagely out.

On that instant the song stopped, and Gender could see only
the seaward slope of his land, down to the lip of the bluff that
overhung the water. Beyond that stretched an expanse of waves,
patchily agleam under a great buckskin-colored moon, that even
now stirred the murmurous tide at the foot of the bluff. Here were

no trees, no brush even, to hide pranksters. The singers, now silent, must be in a boat under the shelter of the bluff.

Gender strode from the room, fairly tore open a door, and made heavy haste toward the sea. He paused, on the lip of the bluff. Nothing was to be seen, beneath him or farther out. The mockers, if they had been here, had already fled. He growled, glared, and tramped back to his house. He entered the parlor once more, drew down the sash, and sought his chair again. Choosing another glass, he began once more to mix whisky and water. But he stopped in the middle of his pouring.

There it was again, the song he knew; and closer.

He rose, took a step in the direction of the window, then thought better of it. He had warned his visitors by one sortie, and they had hidden. Why not let them come close, and suffer the violence he ached to pour out on some living thing?

He moved, not to the window, but to a mantelpiece opposite. From a box of dark, polished wood he lifted a pistol, then another. They were duelling weapons, handsomely made, with hair-triggers; and Gender was a dead shot. With orderly swiftness he poured in glazed powder from a flask, rammed down two leaden bullets, and laid percussion caps upon the touchholes. Returning, he placed the weapons on his center table, then stood on tiptoe to extinguish the hanging lamp. A single light remained in the room, a candle by the door, and this he carried to the window, placing it on a bracket there. Moving into the gloomy center of the parlor, he sat in his chair and took a pistol in either hand.

The song was louder now, lifted by many voices:

"Hailowa – Genda! Haipana – Genda!"

Undoubtedly the choristers had come to land by now, had gained the top of the bluff. They could be seen, Gender was sure, from the window. He felt perspiration on his jowl, and lifted a sleeve to blot it. Trying to scare him, hmm? Singing about witchcraft and killing? Well, he'd show them who was the killer.

The singing had drawn close, was just outside. Odd how the sailors, or whoever they were, had learned that chant so well! It recalled to his mind the slave trail, the jungle, the long procession of crooning prisoners. But here was no time for idle revery on vanished scenes. Silence had fallen again, and he could only divine the presence, just outside, of many creatures.

Scratch-scratch-scratch; it sounded like the stealthy creeping of a snake over rough lumber. That scratching resounded from the window where something stole into view in the candlelight. Gender fixed his eyes there, and his pistols lifted their muzzles.

The palm of a hand, as grey as a fish, laid itself on the glass. It was wet; Gender could see the trickle of water descending along the pane. Something clinked, almost musically. Another hand moved into position beside it, and between the two swung links of chain.

This was an elaborately devilish joke, thought Gender, in an ecstasy of rage. Even the chains, to lend reality . . . and as he stared he knew, in a split moment of terror that stirred his flesh on his bones, that it was no joke after all.

A face had moved into the range of the candlelight, pressing close to the pane between the two palms.

It was darker than those palms, of a dirty, slaty deadness of color. But it was not dead, not with those dull, intent eyes that moved slowly in their blistery sockets . . . not dead, though it was foully wet, and its thick lips hung slackly open, and seaweed lay plastered upon the cheeks, even though the flat nostrils showed crumbled and gnawed away, as if by fish. The eyes quested here and there across the floor and walls of the parlor. They came to rest, gazing full into the face of Gender.

He felt as though stale sea-water had trickled upon him, but his right hand abode steady as a gun-rest. He took aim and fired.

The glass crashed loudly, and fell in shattering flakes to the floor beneath the sill.

Gender was on his feet, moving forward, dropping the empty pistol on the table and whipping the loaded one into his right hand. Two leaping strides took him almost to the window, before he reeled backward.

The face had not fallen. It stared at him, a scant yard away. Between the dull, living eyes showed a round black hole, where the bullet had gone in. But the thing stood unflinchingly, somehow serenely. Its two wet hands moved slowly, methodically, to pluck away the jagged remains of the glass.

Gender rocked where he stood, unable for the moment to command his body to retreat. The shoulders beneath the face heightened. They were bare and wet and deadly dusky, and they clinked the collar-shackle beneath the lax chin. Two hands stole into the room, their fish-colored palms opening toward Gender.

He screamed, and at last he ran. As he turned his back, the singing began yet again, loud and horribly jaunty – not at all as the miserable slaves had sung it. He gained the seaward door, drew it open, and looked full into a gathering of black, wet figures, with chains festooned among them, awaiting him. Again he screamed, and tried to push the door shut.

He could not. A hand was braced against the edge of the panel –

many hands. The wood fringed itself with gleaming black fingers. Gender let go the knob, whirled to flee into the house. Something caught the back of his coat, something he dared not identify. In struggling loose, he spun through the doorway and into the moonlit open.

Figures surrounded him, black, naked, wet figures; dead as to sunken faces and flaccid muscles, but horribly alive as to eyes and trembling hands and slack mouths that formed the strange primitive words of the song; separate, yet strung together with a great chain and collar-shackles, like an awful fish on the gigantic line of some demon-angler. All this Gender saw in a rocking, moon-washed moment, while he choked and retched at a dreadful odor of death, thick as fog.

Still he tried to run, but they were moving around him in a weaving crescent, cutting off his retreat toward the plantation. Hands extended toward him, manacled and dripping. His only will was to escape the touch of those sodden fingers, and one way was open – the way to the sea.

He ran toward the brink of the bluff. From its top he would leap, dive and swim away. But they pursued, overtook, surrounded him. He remembered that he held a loaded pistol, and fired into their black midst. It had no effect. He might have known that it would have no effect.

Something was clutching for him. A great, inhuman talon? No, it was an open collar of metal, with a length of chain to it, a collar that had once clamped to an anchor, dragging down to ocean's depths a line of shackled men. It gaped at him, held forth by many dripping hands. He tried to dodge, but it darted around his throat, shut with a ringing snap. Was it cold . . . or scalding hot? He knew, with horror vividly etching the knowledge into his heart, that he was one at last with the great chained procession.

"*Hailowa – Genda! Haipana – Genda!*"

He found his voice. "No, no!" he pleaded. "No, in the name of – "

But he could not say the name of God. And the throng suddenly moved explosively, concertedly, to the edge of the bluff.

A single wailing cry from all those dead throats, and they dived into the waves below.

Gender did not feel the clutch and jerk of the chain that dragged him alone. He did not even feel the water as it closed over his head.

R. Chetwynd-Hayes

The Ghouls

"I see that more often than not I am now described as a veteran author,"
observes Ronald Chetwynd-Hayes, "which roughly means I am getting (or
have grown) old and have published a fair amount of material, little of which
can the average reader remember. Yet amazing to relate, I still continue to turn
stuff out and those in high places (such as editors) pause every now and again
to give me a nod."

The author of ten novels, two novelizations, some nineteen short story collec-
tions and editor of thirty-three anthologies, the self-effacing Chetwynd-Hayes
is as busy as ever, with recent appearances in Weird Tales, Dark Voices
4: The Pan Book of Horror, *and a whole clutch of reprint anthologies.*
His latest novels are Kepple *and* The Psychic Detective, *the latter*
featuring his series characters Fred and Francis and recently optioned by
Hammer Films.

When asked about the genesis of the following story, the author explains:
"I am of the opinion that anyone in politics can rise very quickly to the top
if they are not weighed down by talent or integrity, so I could quite easily
picture our current Prime Minister conceiving the soul-shattering idea of using
the dead as an unpaid labour force while drinking his late night cup of cocoa.
Naturally, government controlled zombies would not be in tip-top condition,
hence the need for a waste bin in which to deposit the bits and pieces that fall
off while receiving their ration of methy.

"Should the current tenant of 10 Downing Street require more advice regarding this astounding idea, he is cordially invited to contact me . . ."

THE DOORBELL RANG. A nasty long shrill ring that suggested an impatient caller or a faulty bell-button. Mr Goldsmith did not receive many visitors. He muttered angrily, removed the saucepan of baked beans from the gas ring, then trudged slowly from the tiny kitchen across the even smaller hall and opened the front door. The bell continued to ring.

A tall, lean man faced him. One rigid finger seemed glued to the bell-button. The gaunt face had an unwholesome greenish tinge. The black, strangely dull eyes stared into Mr Goldsmith's own and the mouth opened.

"Oosed o love hore . . ."

The shrill clatter of the doorbell mingled with the hoarse gibberish and Mr Goldsmith experienced a blend of fear and anger. He shouted at the unwelcome intruder.

"Stop ringing the bell."

"Oosed o love hore . . ." the stranger repeated.

"Stop ringing the bloody bell." Mr Goldsmith reached round the door frame and pulled the dirt-grimed hand away. It fell limply down to its owner's side, where it swung slowly back and forth, four fingers clenched, the fifth – the index finger – rigid, as though still seeking a bell-button to push. In the silence that followed, Mr Goldsmith cleared his throat.

"Now, what is it you want?"

"Oosed o love hore." The stranger said again unintelligibly, then pushed by Mr Goldsmith and entered the flat.

"Look here . . ." The little man ran after the intruder and tried to get in front of him, but the tall, lean figure advanced remorselessly towards the living-room, where it flopped down in Mr Goldsmith's favourite armchair and sat looking blankly at a cheap Gauguin print that hung over the fireplace.

"I don't know what your little game is," Mr Goldsmith was trying hard not to appear afraid, "but if you're not out of here in two minutes flat, I'll have the law around. Do you hear me?"

The stranger had forgotten to close his mouth. The lower jaw hung down like a lid with a broken hinge. His threadbare, black overcoat was held in place by a solitary, chipped button. A frayed, filthy red scarf was wound tightly round his scrawny neck. He presented a horrible, loathsome appearance. He also smelt.

The head came round slowly and Mr Goldsmith saw the eyes were now watery, almost as if they were about to spill over the puffy lids and go streaming down the green-tinted cheeks.

"Oosed o love hore."

The voice was a gurgle that began somewhere deep down in the constricted throat and the words seemed to bubble like stew seething in a saucepan.

"What? What are you talking about?"

The head twisted from side to side. The loose skin round the neck concertinaed and the hands beat a tattoo on the chair arms.

"O-o-sed t-o-o l-o-v-e h-o-r-e."

"Used to live here!" A blast of understanding lit Mr Goldsmith's brain and he felt quite pleased with his interpretative powers. "Well, you don't live here now, so you'll oblige me by getting out."

The stranger stirred. The legs, clad in a pair of decrepit corduroy trousers, moved back. The hands pressed down on the chair arms, and the tall form rose. He shuffled towards Mr Goldsmith and the stomach-heaving stench came with him. Mr Goldsmith was too petrified to move and could only stare at the approaching horror with fear-glazed eyes.

"Keep away," he whispered. "Touch me and . . . I'll shout . . ."

The face was only a few inches from his own. The hands came up and gripped the lapels of his jacket and with surprising strength, he was gently rocked back and forth. He heard the gurgling rumble; it gradually emerged into speech.

"Oi . . . um . . . dud . . . Oi . . . um . . . dud . . ."

Mr Goldsmith stared into the watery eyes and had there been a third person present he might have supposed they were exchanging some mutual confidence.

"You're . . . what?"

The bubbling words came again.

"Oi . . . um . . . dud."

"You're bloody mad," Mr Goldsmith whispered.

"Oi . . . um . . . dud."

Mr Goldsmith yelped like a startled puppy and pulling himself free, ran for the front door. He leapt down the stairs, his legs operating by reflex, for there was no room for thought in his fear-misted brain.

Shop fronts slid by; paving stones loomed up, their rectangular shapes painted yellow by lamplight; startled faces drifted into his blurred vision, then disappeared and all the while the bubbling, ill-formed words echoed along the dark corridors of his brain.

"Oi . . . um . . . dud."

"Just a moment, sir."

A powerful hand gripped his arm and he swung round as the impetus of his flight was checked. A burly policeman stared down at him, suspicion peeping out of the small, blue eyes.

"Now, what's all this, sir. You'll do yourself an injury, running like that."

Mr Goldsmith fought to regain his breath, eager to impart the vital knowledge. To share the burden.

"He's . . . he's dead."

The grip on his arm tightened.

"Now, calm yourself. Start from the beginning. Who's dead?"

"He . . ." Mr Goldsmith gasped . . . "he rang the bell, wouldn't take his finger off the button . . . used to live there . . . then he sat in my chair . . . then got up . . . and told me . . . he was dead . . ."

A heavy silence followed, broken only by the purr of a passing car. The driver cast an interested glance at the spectacle of a little man being held firmly by a large policeman. The arm of the law finally gave utterance.

"He told you he was dead?"

"Yes." Mr Goldsmith nodded, relieved to have shared his terrible information with an agent of authority. "He pronounced it *dud*."

"A northern corpse, no doubt," the policeman remarked with heavy irony.

"I don't think so," Mr Goldsmith shook his head. "No, I think his vocal cords are decomposing. He sort of bubbles his words. They . . . well, ooze out."

"Ooze out," the constable repeated drily.

"Yes." Mr Goldsmith remembered another important point.

"And he smells."

"Booze?" enquired the policeman.

"No, a sort of sweet, sour smell. Rather like bad milk and dead roses."

The second silence lasted a little longer than the first, then the constable sighed deeply:

"I guess we'd better go along to your place of residence and investigate."

"Must we?" Mr Goldsmith shuddered and the officer nodded.

"Yes, we must."

The front door was still open. The hall light dared Mr Goldsmith to enter and fear lurked in dark corners.

"Would you," Mr Goldsmith hesitated, for no coward likes to bare his face, "would you go in first?"

"Right." The constable nodded, squared his shoulders, and entered the flat. Mr Goldsmith found enough courage to advance as far as the doormat.

"In the living-room," he called out. "I left him in the living-room. The door on the left."

The police officer walked ponderously into the room indicated and after a few minutes came out again.

"No one there," he stated simply.

"The bedroom." Mr Goldsmith pointed to another door. "He must have gone in there."

The policeman dutifully inspected the bedroom, the kitchen, then the bathroom before returning to the hall.

"I think it's quite safe for you to come in," he remarked caustically. "There's no one here — living or dead."

Mr Goldsmith reoccupied his domain, much like an exiled king remounting his shaky throne.

"Now," the policeman produced a notebook and ball-point pen, "let's have a description."

"Pardon?"

"What did the fellow look like?" the officer asked with heavy patience.

"Oh. Tall, thin — very thin, his eyes were sort of runny, looked as if they might melt at any time, his hair was black and matted and he was dressed in an overcoat with one button . . ."

"Hold on," the officer admonished. "You're going too fast. Button . . ."

"It was chipped," Mr Goldsmith added importantly. "And he wore an awful pair of corduroy trousers. And he looked dead. Now I come to think of it, I can't remember him breathing. Yes, I'm certain, he didn't breathe."

The constable put his notebook away, and took up a stance on the hearthrug.

"Now, look, Mr . . ."

"Goldsmith. Edward. J. Goldsmith."

"Well, Mr Goldsmith . . ."

"The J is for Jeremiah but I never use it."

"As I was about to say, Mr Goldsmith," the constable wore the expression of a man who was labouring under great strain, "I've seen a fair number of stiffs — I should say, dead bodies — in my time, and not one of them has ever talked. In fact, I'd say you can almost bank on it. They can burp, jerk, sit up, flop, bare their teeth, glare, even clutch when rigor mortis sets in, but never talk."

"But he said he was." Mr Goldsmith was distressed that this nice, helpful policeman seemed unable to grasp the essential fact. "He said he was *dud*, and he looked and smelt dead."

"Ah, well now, that's another matter entirely." The constable looked like Sherlock Holmes, about to astound a dim-witted Watson. "This character you've described sounds to me like old Charlie. A proper old lay-about, sleeps rough and cadges what he can get from hotel kitchens and suchlike. A meths drinker no doubt and long ago lost whatever wits he ever had. I think he came up here for a hand-out. Probably stewed to the gills and lumbered by you when the door was open, intending to doss down in your living-room. I'll report this to the station sergeant and we'll get him picked up. No visible means of subsistence, you understand."

"Thank you." Mr Goldsmith tried to feel relieved. "But . . ."

"Don't you worry anymore." The constable moved towards the door. "He won't bother you again. If you are all that worried, I'd have a chain put on your front door, then you can see who's there before you let them in."

Mr Goldsmith said, "Yes", and it was with a somewhat lighter heart that he accompanied the policeman to the front-door and politely handed him his helmet.

"A talking dead man!" The constable shook his head and let out a series of explosive chuckles. "Strewth!"

Mr Goldsmith shut the door with a little bang and stood with his back leaning against its mauve panels. By a very small circle of friends he was considered to be wildly artistic.

"He was." He spoke aloud. "He was dead. I know it."

He reheated the baked beans, prepared toast under the grill and opened a tin of mushrooms, then dined in the kitchen.

The evening passed. The television glared and told him things he did not wish to know; the newspaper shocked him and the gas fire went out. There were no more fivepenny pieces so he had no option but to go to bed.

The bed was warm; it was safe, it was soft. If anything dreadful happened he could always hide under the sheets. His book was comforting. It told a story of a beautiful young girl who could have been a famous film star if only she would sleep with a nasty, fat producer, but instead she cut the aspiring mogul down to size, and married her childhood sweetheart who earned twenty pounds a week in the local bank. Mr Goldsmith derived much satisfaction from this happy state of affairs and, placing the book under his pillow, turned out the light and prepared to enter the land of dreams.

He almost got there.

His heart slowed down its heat. His brain flashed messages along the intricate network of nerves and contented itself all was well, although the stomach put in a formal complaint regarding the baked beans. It then began to shut off his five senses, before opening the strong-room where the fantasy treasures were stored. Then his ears detected a sound and his brain instantly ordered all senses on the alert.

Mr Goldsmith sat up and vainly fumbled for the light switch, while a series of futile denials tripped off his tongue.

"No . . . no . . . no . . ."

The wardrobe doors were opening. It was a nice, big wardrobe, fitted with two mirror doors and Mr Goldsmith watched the gleaming surfaces flash as they parted. A dark shape emerged from the bowels of the wardrobe; a tall, lean, slow-moving figure. Mr Goldsmith would have screamed, had such a vocal action been possible, but his throat was dry and constricted and he could only manage a few croaking sounds. The dark figure shuffled towards the bed, poised for a moment like a tree about to fall, then twisted round and sat down. Mr Goldsmith's afflicted throat permitted a whimpering sound as the long shape swung its legs up and lay down beside him. He could not see very well but he could smell and he could also hear. The strangled words bubbled up through the gloom.

"Oo . . . broot . . . cupper . . . Oi . . . hote . . . cuppers . . ."

They lay side by side for a little while, Mr Goldsmith's whimpers merging with the bubbling lament.

"Oo . . . broot cupper . . . Oi . . . um . . . dud . . . hote . . . cuppers . . . oll . . . cuppers . . . stunk . . ."

Mr Goldsmith dared to toy with the idea of movement. He longed to put distance between himself and whatever lay bubbling on the bed. His hand moved prior to pulling back the bedclothes. Instantly cold fingers gripped his wrist, then slid down to his palm to grasp his hand.

"Oi . . . um . . . dud . . ."

"Not again," Mr Goldsmith pleaded. "Not again."

Minutes passed. Mr Goldsmith tried to disengage his hand from the moist, cold grip, but it only tightened. Eventually, the form stirred and to Mr Goldsmith's horror, sat up and began to grope around with its free hand. The light shattered the gloom, chasing

the shadows into obscure corners and Mr Goldsmith found himself
looking at that which he did not wish to see.

The face had taken on a deeper tinge of green; the eyes were
possibly more watery and seemed on the point of dribbling down
the cheeks. The mouth was a gaping hole where the black tongue
writhed like a flattened worm. The bubbling sound cascaded up the
windpipe with the threatening roar of a worn out geyser.

"G-oot dr-oosed . . ."

The figure swung its legs off the bed and began to move towards
the fireplace, still retaining its icy grip on Mr Goldsmith's hand,
and forcing him to wriggle through the bedclothes and go stumbling
after it. Over the mantelpiece was an old brass-handled naval cutlass,
picked up for thirty shillings, back in the days when Mr Goldsmith
had first read *The Three Musketeers*. This, the creature laboriously
removed from its hooks and turning slowly, raised it high above
the terrified little man's head. The bubbling sound built up and
repeated the earlier order.

"G-oot dr-oosed . . ."

Mr Goldsmith got dressed.

They walked down the empty street, hand-in-hand, looking at times
like a father dragging his reluctant son to school. Mr Goldsmith
hungered for the merest glimpse of his friend the policeman, but
the creature seemed to know all the back streets and alleys, pulling
its victim through gaping holes in fences, taking advantage of every
shadow, every dark corner. This, Mr Goldsmith told himself in the
brief periods when he was capable of coherent thought, was the
instinct of an alley cat, the automatic reflexes of a fox. The creature
was making for its hole and taking its prey with it.

They were in the dock area. Black, soot-grimed buildings reached
up to a murky sky. Cobbled alleys ran under railway arches, skirted
grim-faced warehouses, and terminated in litter-ridden wastelands
cleared by Hitler's bombs, thirty years before. Mr Goldsmith
stumbled over uneven mounds crowned with sparse, rusty grass.
He even fell down a hole, only to be promptly dragged out as the
creatures advanced with the ponderous, irresistible momentum of a
Sherman tank.

The ground sloped towards a passage running between the
remnants of brick walls. Presently there was a ceiling to which
morsels of plaster still clung. Then the smell of burning wood —
and a strange new stench of corruption.

They were in what had once been the cellar of a large warehouse.
The main buildings had been gutted and their skeletons removed,

but the roots, too far down to be affected by flame or bomb, still remained. The walls wept rivulets of moisture, the ceiling sagged, the floor was an uneven carpet of cracked cement, but to all intents, the cellar existed. An ancient bath stood on two spaced rows of bricks. Holes had been pierced in its rusty flanks, and it now held a pile of burning wood. Flame tinted smoke made the place look like some forgotten inferno; it drifted up to the ceiling and coiled lazily round the black beams like torpid snakes looking for darkness. A number of hurricane lamps hung from beams and walls, so that once again Mr Goldsmith was forced to look at that which he would rather have not seen.

They were crouched in a large circle round the fire, dressed in an assortment of old clothes, with green tinted faces and watery eyes, gaping mouths and rigid fingers. Mr Goldsmith's companion quelled any lingering doubts he might have had with the simplicity of a sledgehammer cracking a walnut.

"Oll . . . dud . . . oll . . . dud . . ."

"What's all this then?"

Two men stood behind Mr Goldsmith and his companion. One was a tall, hulking fellow and the other a little runt of a man with the face of a crafty weasel. It was he who had spoken. He surveyed Mr Goldsmith with a look of profound astonishment, then glared at the creature.

"Where the hell did you find him?"

The bubbling voice tried to explain.

"Oooosed o love thore . . ."

"You bloody stupid git." The little man began to pummel the creature about the stomach and chest and it retreated, the bubbling voice rising to a scream, like a steam kettle under full pressure.

"Oosed o love thore . . . broot cupper . . ."

The little man ceased his punitive operations and turned an anxious face towards his companion.

"'Ere what's all this, then? Did 'e say copper? His Nibs won't like that. Don't get the law worked up, 'e said."

The big man spoke slowly, his sole concern to calm his friend.

"Don't carry on, Maurice. Old Charlie's about 'ad it, ain't 'e? 'E'll be dropping apart soon if they don't get 'im mended and varnished up. The old brainbox must be in an 'ell of a state."

But Maurice would not be comforted. He turned to Mr Goldsmith and gripped his coat front.

"Did you bring the law in? You call a copper?"

"I certainly summoned a police officer, when this," Mr Goldsmith hesitated, "when this . . . person, refused to leave my flat."

"Cor strike a light." Maurice raised his eyes ceilingward. "'E calls a copper a police officer! Respectable as Sunday dinner. Probably got a trouble and strife who'll scream to 'igh 'eavens when 'er little wandering boy don't come 'ome for his milk and bickies."

"You married?" the big man asked and Mr Goldsmith, inspired by the wish to pacify his captors, shook his head.

"Live alone, aye?" The big man chuckled. "Thought so. Recognize the type. Keep yer 'air on, Maurice, he'll be just another missing person. The DPs will handle it."

"Yeah, Harry." Maurice nodded and released Mr Goldsmith. "You're right. We'd better tie 'im up somewhere until His Nibs gets 'ere. He'll decide what to do with 'im."

Harry produced a length of rope and Mr Goldsmith meekly allowed himself to be tied up, while "Charlie", for such it appeared was the creature's name, kept nudging Maurice's arm.

"Um . . . woont . . . meethy . . ."

"You don't deserve any methy." Maurice pushed the terrible figure to one side. "Making a bugger-up like this."

"Meethy . . ." Charlie repeated, "um . . . woont . . . meethy . . ."

"Bit of a waste of the blue stuff," Maurice remarked drily. "'E's coming apart at the seams. Let me bash 'is 'ead in."

"Naw." Maurice shook his head. "'Is Nibs don't like us taking liberties with units. Besides the new repairing and varnishing machine can do wonders with 'em. "E'd better have 'is ration with the rest."

Mr Goldsmith, suitably bound, was dumped into a corner where he soon witnessed a scene that surpassed all the horror that had ridden on his shoulders since Charlie had rung his doorbell.

Harry came out of a cubby hole bearing a large saucepan with no handle. Maurice followed with a chipped mug. At once there was a grotesque stirring round the nightmare circle; legs moved, arms waved, mouths opened in the familiar bubbling speech and raucous cries. Placing the saucepan on a rickety table, Maurice began to call out in a high pitched voice.

"Methy . . . come on then . . . methy, methy, methy . . ."

There was a scrambling and scuffling, a united, bubbling, gurgling, raucous scream, and the entire pack came lumbering forward, pushing the feeble to one side, clawing in their determination to reach the enamel saucepan and the chipped mug. One scarecrow figure, clad in the remnants of an old army overcoat, fell or was pushed and landed with a resounding crash a few yards from Mr Goldsmith. When he tried to rise, his left leg crumbled under him and the horrified spectator saw the jagged end of a thigh bone jutting out from a tear in threadbare trousers. There was no expression of pain on the green-tinted face but whatever spark of intelligence that still flickered in the brain finally prompted the creature to crawl over the uneven ground until it reached the table. Maurice looked down and kicked the writhing figure over on to its back. It lay howling in protest, like an up-turned beetle, legs and arms flailing helplessly.

The chipped mug was dipped into the saucepan, a quarter filled with some blue liquid, then presented to the nearest gaping mouth. A green-tinted, wrinkled neck convulsed, then the mug was snatched away to be filled for the next consumer. Harry pulled the "fed one" to one side, then gave it a shove that sent the bundle of skin-wrapped bones lurching across the floor. Whatever the liquid was that came out of the saucepan, its effect on the receiver was little short of miraculous. All straightened up; some danced in a revolting, flopping, jumping movement. One creature did six knee-bends before its right knee made an ominous cracking sound. Another began clapping its hands and Maurice called out, "Cut that out," but his warning came too late. One hand fell off and landed on the floor with a nasty, soft thud. Mr Goldsmith's stomach was considering violent action when Harry sauntered over and pointed to the offending item.

"Pick that up," he ordered.

The creature, still trying to clap with one hand, gazed at the big man with blank, watery eyes.

"Glop . . . glop," it bubbled.

"Never mind the glop-glop business. Pick the bloody thing up. I'm not 'aving you leave yer bits and pieces about. I'm telling yer for the last time – pick it up."

He raised a clenched fist and the creature bent down and took hold of its late appendage.

"Now put it in the bin," Harry instructed, pointing to an empty oil drum by the far wall. "You lot might be bone idle, but yer not going to be dead lazy."

Harry then turned to Maurice, who was completing his culinary duties.

"This lot's dead useless, Maurice. They're falling to bits. If this goes on, all we'll 'ave is a load of wriggling torsos. You've put too much EH471 in that stuff."

"Balls." Maurice cuffed a too eager consumer, who promptly retreated with one ear suspended by a strand of skin. "We can do some running repairs, can't we? A bit of tape, a few slats of wood, a few brooms. You carry on like a nun in a brothel."

"Well, so long as you explain the breakages to 'Is Nibs, it's all right with me," Harry stated, kicking a wizened little horror that was trying to turn a somersault on one hand and half an arm. "What's 'e hope to do with this lot?"

"Search me," Maurice shrugged. "Probably carve 'em up. 'E could take a leg from one, an arm from another, swop a few spare parts, and get 'imself a few working models."

Mr Goldsmith had for some time been aware that some of the more antiquated models were displaying an unhealthy interest in his person. One, who appeared to have a faulty leg, shuffled over and examined the little man's lower members with a certain air of deliberation. A rigid forefinger poked his trouser leg, then the creature whose vocal cords seemed to be in better working order than Charlie's, croaked: "Good . . . good."

"Go away," Mr Goldsmith ordered, wriggling his legs frantically. "Shush, push off."

The creature pulled his trouser leg up and stared at the plump white flesh, like a cannibal viewing the week-end joint. He dribbled.

"Maurice – Harry." A sharp voice rang out. "What is the meaning of this? Get the units lined up at once."

It could have been the voice of a sergeant-major admonishing two slack NCOs; or a managing-director who has walked in on an office love-in. Maurice and Harry began to shout, pulling their charges into a rough file, pushing, swearing, punching, occasionally kicking the fragile units. His own particular tormentor was seized by the scruff of the neck and sent hurling towards the ragged line, that drooped, reeled, gurgled and bubbled in turn.

"Careful, man," the voice barked, "units cost money. Repairs take time."

"Sir." Maurice froze to a momentary attitude of attention, then went on with his marshalling activity with renewed, if somewhat subdued energy.

"Get into line, you dozy lot. Chests out, chins in, those who 'ave 'ands, down to yer flipping sides. Harry, a couple of brooms for that basket, three from the end. If 'e falls down, 'is bleeding 'ead will come off."

For the first time Mr Goldsmith had the opportunity to examine the newcomer. He saw a mild looking, middle-aged man, in a black jacket and pin-striped trousers. Glossy bowler hat, horn-rimmed spectacles and a brief case, completed the cartoonist conception of a civil servant. Maurice marched up to this personage and swung up a rather ragged salute.

"Units lined up and ready for your inspection, sir."

"Very well." His Nibs, for such Mr Goldsmith assumed him to be, handed his brief case to Harry, then began to walk slowly along the file, scrutinizing each unit in turn.

"Maurice, why has this man got a hand missing?"

"Clapping, sir. The bleeder . . . beg pardon, the unit got carried away after methy, sir. Sort of came off in his 'and, sir."

His Nibs frowned.

"This is rank carelessness, Maurice. I have stressed time and time again, special attention must be paid to component parts at all times. Spare hands are hard to come by and it may become necessary to scrap this unit altogether. Don't let me have to mention this matter again."

"Sir."

His Nibs passed a few more units without comment, then stopped at the man whose ear still dangled by a single thread. He made a tut-tutting sound.

"Look at this, Maurice. This unit is a disgrace. For heaven's sake get him patched up. What HQ would say if they saw this sort of thing, I dare not think."

"Sir." Maurice turned his head and barked at Harry over one shoulder. "Take this unit and put his lughole back on with a strip of tape."

When His Nibs reached the unit propped up on two brooms, he fairly exploded.

"This is outrageous. Really, Maurice, words fail me. How you could allow a unit to come on parade in this condition, is beyond my comprehension."

"Beg pardon, sir, it fell over, sir."

"Look at it," His Nibs went on, ignoring the interruption. "The neck's broken." He touched the head and it wobbled most alarmingly. "The eyeballs are a disgrace, half an arm is missing, one leg is as about as useful as a woollen vest at a nudist picnic, and one foot is back to front."

Maurice glared at the unfortunate unit who was doing his best to bubble-talk. His Nibs sighed deeply.

"There is little point in berating the unit now, Maurice. The damage is done. We'll have to salvage what we can and the rest had better go into the scrap-bin."

Having completed his inspection, His Nibs turned and almost by chance his gaze alighted on Mr Goldsmith.

"Maurice, what is this unit doing tied up?"

"Beg pardon, sir, but this ain't no unit, sir. It's a consumer that Charlie Unit brought in by error, sir."

His Nibs took off his spectacles, wiped them carefully on a black edged handkerchief, then replaced them.

"Let me get this clear, Maurice. Am I to understand that this is a live consumer? An actual, Mark one, flesh and blood citizen? In fact, not to mince words – a voter?"

"Yes, sir. A proper old Sunday-dinner-eater, go-to-Churcher, and take-a-bath-every-dayer, sir."

"And how, may I ask, did this unfortunate mistake occur?"

"Sent Charlie Unit out with a resurrection party, sir. Wandered off on his own; sort of remembered a place where 'e used to live, found this geezer – beg pardon, sir – this consumer, and brought 'im back 'ere, sir."

"Amazing!" His Nibs examined Mr Goldsmith with great care. "A bit of luck, really. I mean, he'll need no repairs and with care he'll be ready for a Mark IV MB in no time at all."

"That's what I thought, sir." Maurice smirked and looked at Mr Goldsmith with great satisfaction. "Might start a new line, sir. Bring 'em back alive."

"That's the next stage." His Nibs took his brief case from Harry. "In the meanwhile you had better untie him and I'll take him down to the office."

The office was situated through the cubby hole and down twelve steps. It was surprisingly comfortable. A thick carpet covered the floor, orange wallpaper hid the walls and His Nibs seated himself behind a large, mahogany desk.

"Take a seat, my dear fellow," he invited, "I expect you'd like a cup of tea after your ordeal."

Mr Goldsmith collapsed into a chair and nodded. The power of speech would return later, of that he felt certain. His Nibs picked up a telephone receiver.

"Tea for two," he ordered, "and not too strong. Yes, and some digestive biscuits. You'll find them filed under pending."

He replaced the receiver and beamed at Mr Goldsmith.

"Now, I expect you're wondering what this is all about. Probably got ideas that something nasty is taking place, eh?"

Mr Goldsmith could only nod.

"Then I am delighted to put your mind at rest. Nothing illegal is taking place here. This, my dear chap, is a government department."

Mr Goldsmith gurgled.

"Yes," His Nibs went on, "a properly constituted government department, sired by the Ministry of Health, and complete with staff, filing cabinets and teacups. When I tell you this project sprang from the brain of a certain occupier of a certain house, situated in a certain street, not far from the gasworks at Westminster, I am certain that whatever doubts you may have entertained will be instantly dispelled."

Mr Goldsmith made a sound that resembled an expiring bicycle tyre.

"I expect," His Nibs enquired, "you are asking yourself – why?"

Mr Goldsmith groaned.

"The answer to your intelligent question, can be summed up in two words. Industrial strife. Until recently there was a dire labour shortage, and the great man to whom I referred was bedevilled by wage claims, strikes and rude men in cloth caps who would never take no for an answer. Then one night over his bedtime cup of cocoa, the idea came to him. The idea! Nay, the mental earthquake."

The door opened and a blonde vision came in, carrying a tea tray. The vision had long blonde hair and wore a neat tailored suit with brass buttons. Mr Goldsmith said: "Cor."

"Ah, Myna and the cup that cheers," announced His Nibs with heavy joviality. "Put it down on the desk, my dear. Did you warm the pot?"

"Yes, sir." Myna smiled and put her tray down.

"Have the national intake figures come through yet?" His Nibs enquired.

"Yes, sir."

"And?"

"Three thousand, nine hundred and thirty four."

"Capital, capital." His Nibs rubbed his hands together in satisfaction, then aimed a slap at Myna's bottom which happened to be conveniently to hand. The after effect was alarming.

Myna jerked, stiffened her fingers, opened her mouth and bubbled three words.

"Oi . . . um . . . dud . . ."

"Excuse me," His Nibs apologized to Mr Goldsmith, "Merely a technical hitch."

Rising quickly, he hurried round to Myna's front and twisted two brass buttons. The fingers relaxed, the eyes lit up and the mouth closed.

"Anything else, sir?" she enquired.

"No thank you, my dear," His Nibs smiled genially, "not for the time being."

Myna went out and His Nibs returned to his desk.

"Latest stream-lined model," he confided, "fitted with the Mark

IV computer brain, but one has to be jolly careful. Slightest pat in
the wrong place and puff – the damn thing goes haywire. Now where
was I? Oh, yes. The great idea."

He leant forward and pointed a finger at Mr Goldsmith.

"Do you know how many living people there are in Britain
today?"

"Ah – ah . . ." Mr Goldsmith began.

"Precisely," His Nibs sat back, "Sixty-two million, take or lose
a million. Sixty-two million actual or potential voters. Sixty-two
million consumers, government destroyers and trade unionists. Now,
what about the others?"

"Others," echoed Mr Goldsmith.

"Ah, you've got the point. The dead. The wastage, the unused.
One person in two thousand dies every twenty-four hours. That
makes 30,000 bucket-kickers a day, 3,000,000 a year. One man,
and one man only, saw the potential. Sitting there in his terrace
house, drinking his cocoa and watching television, it came to him
in a flash. Why not use the dead?"

"Use the dead," Mr Goldsmith agreed.

"Taking up valuable building space." His Nibs was becoming
quite heated, "Rotting away at the state's expense, using up
marble and stonemason's time, and not paying a penny in taxes.
He knew what had to be done. How to get down to the 'bones' of
the matter."

For a while His Nibs appeared to be lost in thought. Mr Goldsmith
stared at a slogan that had been painted in black letters on the
opposite wall

WASTE NOT – WANT NOT

Presently the precise voice went on.

"First we imported a few voodoo experts from the West Indies.
After all, they had been turning out zombies for centuries. But we had
to improve on their technique of course. I mean to say, we couldn't
have them dancing round a fire, dressed up in loincloths and slitting
cockerels' throats. So our chaps finally came up with METHY. *Ministry
Everlasting Topside Hardened Youth.* No one knows what it means of
course, but that is all to the good. If some of Them from the other
side got hold of the formula, I shudder to think what might happen.
The basis is methylated spirit – we found that pickled fairly well –
then there's R245 and a small amount of E294 and most important,
25 per cent EH471 with 20 per cent HW741 to cancel it out. You do
follow me?"

Mr Goldsmith shook his head, then fearful of giving offence, nodded violently.

"You have keen perception," His Nibs smiled. "It makes a nice change to talk to a consumer of the lower-middle class who does not confuse the issue by asking embarrassing questions. The latest stage is the Mark IV Mechanical Brain. After the unit has been repaired, decoked, and sealed with our all-purpose invisible varnish the nasty old, meddling brain is removed and Dr You-Know-Who inserts his M. IV M. B., which does what it's told and no nonsense. No trade unions, no wage claims – no wages, in fact – no holidays, no food. Give 'em a couple of cups of METHY a day and they're good for years. Get the idea?"

Mr Goldsmith found his voice.

"Who employs them?"

"Who doesn't?" His Nibs chuckled, then lowered his voice to a confidential whisper.

"Keep this under your hat, but you may remember a certain very large house situated at the end of the Mall, which had rather a lot of problems over the housekeeping bills."

Mr Goldsmith turned pale.

"Not any more. All the lower servants were elevated from the churchyard, and some of the senior go out through one door and come back in through another, if you get my meaning. In fact there has been a suggestion. . . . Well, never mind, that is still but a thought running round in a cabinet.

"Now, what are we going to do about you?"

Mr Goldsmith stared hopefully at his questioner. He dared to put forward a suggestion.

"I could go home."

His Nibs smilingly shook his head.

"I fear not. You've seen too much and thanks to my flapping tongue, heard too much. No, I think we'd better give you the treatment. A nice little street accident should fill the bill. You wouldn't fancy walking under a moving bus, I suppose?"

Mr Goldsmith displayed all the symptoms of extreme reluctance.

"You're sure? Pity. Never mind, Harry can simulate these things rather well. A broken neck, compound fracture of both legs; nothing we can't fix later on, then a tip-top funeral at government expense and the certainty of life after death. How's that sound?'

Mr Goldsmith gulped and started a passionate love affair with the door.

"I can see you are moved," His Nibs chuckled. "You've gone quite pale with joy. I envy you, you know. It's not all of us who can serve

our country. Remember: 'They also serve who only lie and rotticate.'
Ha . . . ha . . . ha . . ."

His Nibs roared with uncontrollable merriment and lifted the
receiver of his desk telephone.

"Myna, be a good girl and get Harry on the intercom. What!
Teabreak! We'll have none of that nonsense here. Tell him to get
down here in two minutes flat, or I'll have him fitted with a M. IV
MB before he can put water to teabag."

He slammed the receiver down and glared at Mr Goldsmith.

"Teabreak! I promise you, in five years time there'll be no more
tea breaks or dinner breaks, or three weeks holiday with pay. We'll
teach 'em."

The door opened and Harry all but ran into the office.

He stamped his feet, stood rigidly to attention and swung up
a salute.

"Resurrection Operator Harry Briggs reporting, sir."

His Nibs calmed down, wiped his brow on the black-edged handkerchief and reverted to his normal, precise manner of speech.

"Right, Harry, stand easy. This consumer is to be converted into a
unit. I thought something in the line of a nice, tidy street accident. He
won't be a missing person then, see. What are your suggestions?"

"Permission to examine the consumer, sir?"

His Nibs waved a languid hand.

"Help yourself, Harry."

Harry came over to Mr Goldsmith and tilted his head forward so
that his neck was bared.

"A couple of nifty chops should break his neck, sir, and I
could rough his face up a bit – bash it against the wall. Then,
with your permission, sir, run a ten-ton truck over his stomach – won't do 'is guts much good but 'e won't be needing
'em."

"Methy," His Nibs explained to Mr Goldsmith, "works through
the nervous system. The stomach is surplus to requirements."

"Then I thought a couple of swipes with an iron bar about 'ere."
Harry pointed to Mr Goldsmith's trembling thighs. "And 'ere." He
indicated a spot above the ankles. "Won't do to touch the knee caps,
seeing as 'ow they're 'ard to replace."

"You'll have no trouble with repairs afterwards?" His Nibs
enquired.

"Gawd bless us, no, sir. A couple of rivets in the neck, a bit of
patching up here and there. We'll have to replace the eyes. They
gets a bit runny after a bit. Otherwise, 'e'll make a first class unit,
such as you can be proud of, sir."

"Very creditable." His Nibs beamed his approval. "You'd better fill in an LD142 and lay on transport to transfer the, eh . . . unit to the accident point. Let me see . . ." He consulted a desk diary. "Today's Wednesday – coroner's inquest on Friday – yes, we can fit the funeral in next Tuesday."

"Tuesday, sir," Harry nodded.

"Then your resurrection units can get cracking Tuesday night. No point in letting things rot, eh?"

His Nibs roared again and Harry permitted himself a respectful titter.

"Well, my dear chap," His Nibs said to Mr Goldsmith. "This time next week you should be doing something useful."

"Where were you thinking of fitting 'im in, sir?" Harry enquired.

"We'll start him off as a porter at Waterloo Station. The railway union have a wage claim in the pipeline and one more non-industrial action vote will do no harm. Right, Harry, take him away."

Fear may make cowards; it can also transform a coward into a man of action. The sight of Harry's large hand descending on to his neck triggered off a series of reflexes in Mr Goldsmith which culminated in him leaping from his chair and racing for the door. His behaviour up to that moment had been co-operative, so both His Nibs and Harry were taken by surprise and for three precious moments could only stare after him with speechless astonishment. Meanwhile, Mr Goldsmith was through the door and passing Myna, who presumably had not been programmed for such an emergency, for she sat behind her desk, typing away serenely, ignoring Harry's bellows of rage. But they spurred the little man to greater efforts and he mounted the stairs with the determination of an Olympic hurdler chasing a gold medal. He burst into the cellar, by-passing the recumbent units and was on his way to the exit before a startled Maurice had been galvanized into action.

He was like a rabbit chased by two blood-thirsty hounds, when he pounded up the ramp and came to the waste ground. A sickly moon played hide and seek from behind scudding clouds and a black cat screamed its fear and rage, as he went stumbling over mounds and potholes, discarded tins clattering before his blundering feet. They were about twenty feet behind, silent now, for the unmentionable was heading for the domain of the commonplace and their business must be done in shadows without sound or word.

Mr Goldsmith crossed a cobbled road, galloped under a railway arch and stumbled into a narrow alley. A convenient hole in a fence presented itself; he squeezed through just before running footsteps rounded the nearest corner. They came to a halt only a few paces from his hiding place. Maurice's voice was that of a weasel deprived of a supper.

"The little bleeder's got away."

"Won't get far," Harry comforted.

"Better get back," Maurice admitted reluctantly. "His Nibs will have to notify a DPC."

The footsteps shuffled, then retreated and Mr Goldsmith dared to breathe again. He emerged from his hole and began to trudge wearily down the alley. He wandered for a long time, completely lost, shying from shadows, running before a barking dog, adrift in a nightmare. He came out into a small square and there on the far side, its steeple reaching up towards the moon, was a church. The doors were tight shut, but the building evoked childhood memories, and he knelt on the steps, crying softly, like a child locked out by thoughtless parents.

Heavy footsteps made him start and he rose quickly, before casting a terrified glance along the moonlit pavement. A tall, burly figure was moving towards him with all the majesty of a frigate under full sail. His silver buttons gleamed like stars in a velvet sky. His badge shone like a beacon of hope. Mr Goldsmith gave a cry of joy and ran towards his protector. He gripped the great, coarse hands; he thrust his face against the blue tunic and sobbed with pure relief.

"Now, what's all this?" the officer enquired. "Not more dead men that talk?"

"Hundreds of them." Mr Goldsmith stammered in his effort to be believed. "They are emptying the churchyards. You've got to stop them."

"There, there. You leave it all to me, sir. Just come along to the station and we'll get it all down in a statement."

"Yes . . . yes." Mr Goldsmith perceived the sanity in such an arrangement. "Yes, I . . . I will make a statement. Then you'll lock me up, won't you? So they can't reach me?"

"Anything you say," the constable agreed. "We'll lock you up so well, no one will ever be able to reach you again. Come along now."

They moved away from the locked church with Mr Goldsmith pouring out a torrent of words. The policeman was a good listener and encouraged him with an occasional: "Beyond belief, sir . . . You don't say so, sir . . . It only goes to show . . . Truth is stranger than fiction."

Mr Goldsmith agreed that it was, but a disturbing factor had caused a cold shiver to mar his newly acquired sense of well-being.

"Why are we going down this alley?"

"A short cut, sir," the constable replied. "No sense in tiring ourselves with a long walk."

"Oh." Mr Goldsmith snatched at this piece of logic like a condemned man at the rope which is to hang him. "Is the station far?"

"A mere stone's throw, sir. A last, few steps, you might say."

They progressed the length of the passage, then turned a corner. The officer trod on an upturned dustbin lid and promptly swore. "Damned careless of someone. You might have broken your neck, sir."

"This is the way I came," Mr Goldsmith stated and the policeman's grip tightened.

"Is it now, sir? Sort of retracing your footsteps."

Hope was sliding down a steep ramp as Mr Goldsmith started to struggle. "You . . ." But the grip on his arm was a band of steel. He clawed at the blue tunic and twisted a silver button. The bubbling words came from a long way off.

"Oi . . . um . . . dud . . ."

The moon peeped coyly from behind a cloud and watched a burly, but dead policeman drag a struggling little man towards eternity.

Edgar Allan Poe

The Facts in the Case of M. Valdemar

Edgar Allan Poe (1809–49) has been described as "the father of modern horror" and his often unstable state of mind, due to depression and alcohol, is reflected in such classic stories of the macabre as "The Fall of the House of Usher", "The Murders in the Rue Morgue", "The Black Cat" and "The Pit and the Pendulum". His only novel, The Narrative of A. Gordon Pym *(1837), was left incomplete.*

"The Facts in the Case of M. Valdemar" was originally filmed by Roger Corman as part of his three-episode anthology movie Tales of Terror *(1962), starring Vincent Price and Basil Rathbone. It was updated to lesser effect in 1989 by director George Romero as half of* Two Evil Eyes *(aka* Due Occhi Diabolici*), featuring Adrienne Barbeau and Bingo O'Malley as the walking corpse. Neither version really does justice to the nightmare vision of Poe's original . . .*

OF COURSE I shall not pretend to consider it any matter for wonder, that the extraordinary case of M. Valdemar has excited discussion. It would have been a miracle had it not – especially under the circumstances. Through the desire of all parties concerned, to keep the affair from the public, at least for the present, or until we had further opportunities for investigation – through our endeavors to effect this – a garbled or exaggerated account made its way into society, and became the source of many unpleasant misrepresentations; and, very naturally, of a great deal of disbelief.

It is now rendered necessary that I give the *facts* – as far as I comprehend them myself. They are, succinctly, these:

My attention, for the last three years, had been repeatedly drawn to the subject of Mesmerism; and, about nine months ago, it occurred to me, quite suddenly, that in the series of experiments made hitherto, there had been a very remarkable and most unaccountable omission: – no person had as yet been mesmerized *in articulo mortis*. It remained to be seen, first, whether, in such condition, there existed in the patient any susceptibility to the magnetic influence; secondly, whether, if any existed, it was impaired or increased by the condition; thirdly, to what extent, or for how long a period, the encroachments of Death might be arrested by the process. There were other points to be ascertained, but these most excited my curiosity – the last in especial, from the immensely important character of its consequences.

In looking around me for some subject by whose means I might test these particulars, I was brought to think of my friend, M. Ernest Valdemar, the well-known compiler of the "Bibliotheca Forensica," and author (under the *nom de plume* of Issachar Marx) of the Polish versions of "Wallenstein" and "Gargantua." M. Valdemar, who has resided principally at Harlem, N.Y., since the year of 1839, is (or was) particularly noticeable for the extreme spareness of his person – his lower limbs much resembling those of John Randolph; and, also, for the whiteness of his whiskers, in violent contrast to the blackness of his hair – the latter, in consequence, being very generally mistaken for a wig. His temperament was markedly nervous, and rendered him a good subject for mesmeric experiment. On two or three occasions I had put him to sleep with little difficulty, but was disappointed in other results which his peculiar constitution had naturally led me to anticipate. His will was at no period positively, or thoroughly, under my control, and in regard to *clairvoyance*, I could accomplish with him nothing to be relied upon. I always attributed my failure at these points to the disordered state of his health. For some months previous to my becoming acquainted with him, his physicians had declared him in a confirmed phthisis. It was his custom, indeed, to speak calmly of his approaching dissolution, as of a matter neither to be avoided nor regretted.

When the ideas to which I have alluded first occurred to me, it was of course very natural that I should think of M. Valdemar. I knew the steady philosophy of the man too well to apprehend any scruples from *him*; and he had no relatives in America who would be likely to interfere. I spoke to him frankly upon the subject; and, to my surprise, his interest seemed vividly excited. I say to my surprise; for, although he had always yielded his person freely to my experiments, he had never before given me any tokens of sympathy with what I did. His disease was of that character which would admit of exact calculation in respect to the epoch of its termination in death; and it was finally arranged between us that he would send for me about twenty-four hours before the period announced by his physicians as that of his decease.

It is now rather more than seven months since I received, from M. Valdemar himself, the subjoined note:

My Dear P——

You may as well come now. D—— and F—— are agreed that I cannot hold out beyond to-morrow midnight; and I think they have hit the time very nearly.

Valdemar

I received this note within half an hour after it was written, and in fifteen minutes more I was in the dying man's chamber. I had not seen him for ten days, and was appalled by the fearful alteration which the brief interval had wrought in him. His face wore a leaden hue; the eyes were utterly lustreless; and the emaciation was so extreme, that the skin had been broken through by the cheek-bones. His expectoration was excessive. The pulse was barely perceptible. He retained, nevertheless, in a very remarkable manner, both his mental power and a certain degree of physical strength. He spoke with distinctness – took some palliative medicines without aid – and, when I entered the room, was occupied in penciling memoranda in a pocket-book. He was propped up in the bed by pillows. Doctors D—— and F—— were in attendance.

After pressing Valdemar's hand, I took these gentlemen aside, and obtained from them a minute account of the patient's condition. The left lung had been for eighteen months in a semi-osseous or carti-laginous state, and was, of course, entirely useless for all purposes of vitality. The right, in its upper portion, was also partially, if not thoroughly, ossified, while the lower region was merely a mass of purulent tubercles, running one into another. Several extensive perforations existed; and, at one point, permanent adhesion to the ribs had taken place. These appearances in the right lobe were of comparatively recent date. The ossification had proceeded with very unusual rapidity; no sign of it had been discovered a month before, and the adhesion had only been observed during the three previous days. Independently of the phthisis, the patient was suspected of aneurism of the aorta; but on this point the osseous symptoms rendered an exact diagnosis impossible. It was the opinion of both physicians that M. Valdemar would die about midnight on the morrow (Sunday). It was then seven o'clock on Saturday evening.

On quitting the invalid's bedside to hold conversation with myself, Doctor D—— and F—— had bidden him a final farewell. It had not been their intention to return; but, at my request, they agreed to look in upon the patient about ten the next night.

When they had gone, I spoke freely with M. Valdemar on the subject of his approaching dissolution, as well as, more particularly, of the experiment proposed. He still professed himself quite willing and even anxious to have it made, and urged me to commence it at once.

A male and a female nurse were in attendance; but I did not feel myself altogether at liberty to engage in a task of this character with no more reliable witnesses than these people, in case of sudden accident, might prove. I therefore postponed operations until about eight the next night, when the arrival of a medical student, with whom I had some acquaintance (Mr Theodore L——l), relieved me from further embarrassment. It had been my design, originally, to wait for the physicians; but I was induced to proceed, first by the urgent entreaties of M. Valdemar, and secondly, by my conviction that I had not a moment to lose, as he was evidently sinking fast.

Mr L——l was so kind as to accede to my desire that he would take notes of all that occurred; and it is from his memoranda that what I now have to relate is, for the most part, either condensed or copied *verbatim*.

It wanted about five minutes of eight when, taking the patient's hand, I begged him to state, as distinctly as he could, to Mr L——l, whether he (M. Valdemar) was entirely willing that I should make the experiment of mesmerizing him in his then condition.

He replied feebly, yet quite audibly: "Yes, I wish to be mesmerized" – adding immediately afterward: "I fear you have deferred it too long."

While he spoke thus, I commenced the passes which I had already found most effectual in subduing him. He was evidently influenced with the first lateral stroke of my hand across his forehead; but, although I exerted all my powers, no further perceptible effect was induced until some minutes after ten o'clock, when Doctors

D—— and F—— called, according to appointment. I explained to them, in a few words, what I designed, and as they opposed no objection, saying that the patient was already in the death agony, I proceeded without hesitation – exchanging, however, the lateral passes for downward ones, and directing my gaze entirely into the right eye of the sufferer. By this time his pulse was imperceptible and his breathing was stertorous, and at intervals of half a minute.

This condition was nearly unaltered for a quarter of an hour. At the expiration of this period, however, a natural although a very deep sigh escaped from the bosom of the dying man, and the stertorous breathing ceased – that is to say, its stertorousness was no longer apparent; the intervals were undiminished. The patient's extremities were of an icy coldness.

At five minutes before eleven, I perceived unequivocal signs of the mesmeric influence. The glassy roll of the eye was changed for that expression of uneasy *inward* examination which is never seen except in cases of sleep-waking, and which it is quite impossible to mistake. With a few rapid lateral passes I made the lids quiver, as in incipient sleep, and with a few more I closed them altogether. I was not satisfied, however, with this, but continued the manipulations vigorously, and with the fullest exertion of the will, until I had completely stiffened the limbs of the slumberer, after placing them in a seemingly easy position. The legs were at full length; the arms were nearly so, and reposed on the bed at a moderate distance from the loins. The head was very slightly elevated.

When I had accomplished this, it was fully midnight, and I requested the gentlemen present to examine M. Valdemar's condition. After a few experiments, they admitted him to be in an unusually perfect state of mesmeric trance. The curiosity of both the physicians was greatly excited. Dr D—— resolved at once to remain with the patient all night, while Dr F—— took leave with a promise to return at daybreak. Mr L——l and the nurses remained.

We left M. Valdemar entirely undisturbed until about three o'clock in the morning, when I approached and found him in precisely the same condition as when Dr F—— went away – that is to say, he lay in the same position; the pulse was imperceptible; the breathing was gentle (scarcely noticeable, unless through the application of a mirror to the lips); the eyes were closed naturally; and the limbs were as rigid and as cold as marble. Still, the general appearance was certainly not that of death.

As I approached M. Valdemar I made a kind of half effort to influence his right arm into pursuit of my own, as I passed the latter gently to and fro above his person. In such experiments with the patient, I had never perfectly succeeded before, and assuredly I had little thought of succeeding now; but to my astonishment, his arm very readily, although feebly, followed every direction I assigned it with mine. I determined to hazard a few words of conversation.

"M. Valdemar," I said, "are you asleep?" He made no answer, but I perceived a tremor about the lips, and was thus induced to repeat the question, again and again. At its third repetition, his whole frame was agitated by a very slight shivering; the eyelids unclosed themselves so far as to display a white line of a ball; the lips moved sluggishly, and from between them, in a barely audible whisper, issued the words:

"Yes; – asleep now. Do not wake me! – let me die so!"

I here felt the limbs, and found them as rigid as ever. The right arm, as before, obeyed the direction of my hand. I questioned the sleep-waker again:

"Do you still feel pain in the breast, M. Valdemar?"

The answer now was immediate, but even less audible than before:

"No pain – I am dying!"

I did not think it advisable to disturb him further just then, and nothing more was said or done until the arrival of Dr F——, who came a little before sunrise, and expressed unbounded astonishment at finding the patient still alive. After feeling the pulse and applying a mirror to the lips, he requested me to speak to the sleep-waker again. I did so, saying:

"M. Valdemar, do you still sleep?"

As before, some minutes elapsed ere a reply was made; and during the interval the dying man seemed to be collecting his energies to speak. At my fourth repetition of the question, he said very faintly, almost inaudibly:

"Yes; still asleep – dying."

It was now the opinion, or rather the wish, of the physicians, that M. Valdemar should be suffered to remain undisturbed in his present apparently tranquil condition, until death should supervene – and this, it was generally agreed, must now take place within a few minutes. I concluded, however, to speak to him once more, and merely repeated my previous question.

While I spoke, there came a marked change over the countenance of the sleep-waker. The eyes rolled themselves slowly open, the pupils disappearing upwardly; the skin generally assumed a cadaverous hue, resembling not so much parchment as white paper; and the circular hectic spots which, hitherto, had been strongly defined in the centre of each cheek, *went out* at once. I use this expression, because the suddenness of their departure put me in mind of nothing so much as the extinguishment of a candle by a puff of the breath. The upper lip, at the same time, writhed itself away from the teeth, which it had previously covered completely; while the lower jaw fell with an audible jerk, leaving the mouth widely extended, and disclosing in full view the swollen and blackened tongue. I presume that no member of the party then present had been unaccustomed to death-bed horrors; but so hideous beyond conception was the appearance of M. Valdemar at this moment, that there was a general shrinking back from the region of the bed. I now feel that I have reached a point of this narrative at which every reader will be startled into positive disbelief. It is my business, however, simply to proceed.

There was no longer the faintest sign of vitality in M. Valdemar; and concluding him to be dead, we were consigning him to the charge of the nurses, when a strong vibratory motion was observable in the tongue. This continued for perhaps a minute. At the expiration of this period, there issued from the distended and motionless jaws a voice – such as it would be madness in me to attempt describing. There are, indeed, two or three epithets which might be considered as applicable to it in part; I might say, for example, that the sound was harsh, and broken and hollow; but the hideous whole is indescribable, for the simple reason that no similar sounds have ever jarred upon the ear of humanity. There were two particulars, nevertheless, which I thought then, and still think, might fairly be stated as characteristic of the intonation – as well adapted to convey some idea of its unearthly peculiarity. In the first place, the voice seemed to reach our ears – at least mine – from a vast distance, or from some deep cavern within the earth. In the second place, it impressed me (I fear, indeed, that it will be impossible to make myself comprehended) as gelatinous or glutinous matters impress the sense of touch.

I have spoken both of "sound" and of "voice." I mean to say that the sound was one of distinct – of even wonderfully, thrillingly distinct – syllabification. M. Valdemar *spoke* – obviously in reply to the question I had propounded to him a few minutes before. I had asked him, it will be remembered, if he still slept.

He now said:

"Yes; – no; – I *have been* sleeping – and now – now – *I am dead*."

No person present even affected to deny, or attempted to repress, the unutterable, shuddering horror which these few words, thus uttered, were so well calculated to convey. Mr L——l (the student) swooned. The nurses immediately left the chamber, and could not be induced to return. My own impressions I would not pretend to render intelligible to the reader. For nearly an hour, we busied ourselves, silently – without utterance of a word – in endeavors to revive Mr L——l. When he came to himself, we addressed ourselves again to an investigation of M. Valdemar's condition.

It remained in all respects as I have last described it, with the exception that the mirror no longer afforded evidence of respiration. An attempt to draw blood from the arm failed. I should mention, too, that this limb was no further subject to my will. I endeavored in vain to make it follow the direction of my hand. The only real indication, indeed, of the mesmeric influence, was now found in the vibratory movement of the tongue, whenever I addressed M. Valdemar a question. He seemed to be making an effort to reply, but had no longer sufficient volition. To queries put to him by any other person than myself he seemed utterly insensible – although I endeavored to place each member of the company in mesmeric *rapport* with him. I believe that I have now related all that is necessary to an understanding of the sleep-waker's state at this epoch. Other nurses were procured; and at ten o'clock I left the house in company with the two physicians and Mr L——l.

In the afternoon we called again to see the patient. His condition remained precisely the same. We had now some discussion as to the propriety and feasibility of awakening him; but we had little difficulty in agreeing that no good purpose would be served by so doing. It was evident that, so far, death (or what is usually termed death) had been arrested by the mesmeric process. It seemed clear to us all that to awaken M. Valdemar would be merely to insure his instant, or at least his speedy, dissolution.

From this period until the close of last week – *an interval of nearly seven months* – we continued to make daily calls at M. Valdemar's house, accompanied, now and then, by medical and other friends. All this time the sleep-waker remained *exactly* as I have last described him. The nurses' attentions were continual.

It was on Friday last that we finally resolved to make the experiment of awakening, or attempting to awaken him; and it is the (perhaps) unfortunate result of this latter experiment which has given rise to so much discussion in private circles – to so much of what I cannot help thinking unwarranted popular feeling.

For the purpose of relieving M. Valdemar from the mesmeric trance, I made use of the customary passes. These for a time were unsuccessful. The first indication of revival was afforded by a partial descent of the iris. It was observed, as especially remarkable, that this lowering of the pupil was accompanied by the profuse outflowing of a yellowish ichor (from beneath the lids) of a pungent and highly offensive odor.

It was now suggested that I should attempt to influence the patient's arm as heretofore. I made the attempt and failed. Dr F—— then intimated a desire to have me put a question. I did so, as follows:

"M. Valdemar, can you explain to us what are your feelings or wishes now?"

There was an instant return of the hectic circles on the cheeks; the tongue quivered, or rather rolled violently in the mouth (although the jaws and lips remained rigid as before), and at length the same hideous voice which I have already described, broke forth:

"For God's sake! – quick! – quick! – put me to sleep – or, quick! – waken me! – quick! – *I say to you that I am dead!*"

I was thoroughly unnerved, and for an instant remained undecided what to do. At first I made an endeavor to recompose the patient; but, failing in this through total abeyance of the will, I retraced my steps and as earnestly struggled to awaken him. In this attempt I soon saw that I should be successful – or at least I soon fancied that my success would be complete – and I am sure that all in the room were prepared to see the patient awaken.

For what really occurred, however, it is quite impossible that any human being could have been prepared.

As I rapidly made the mesmeric passes, amid ejaculations of "dead! dead!" absolutely *bursting* from the tongue and not from the lips of the sufferer, his whole frame at once – within the space of a single minute, or less, shrunk – crumbled – absolutely *rotted* away beneath my hands. Upon the bed, before that whole company, there lay a nearly liquid mass of loathsome – of detestable putrescence.

Karl Edward Wagner

Sticks

In his introduction to Karl Edward Wagner's superb short story collection In a Lonely Place, *Peter Straub decribes "Sticks" as the author's "clearest expression of devotion and mastery of the pulp tradition, being simultaneously a hommage to Lee Brown Coye, the artist who created many of pulpdom's strongest images, and one of the cleverest modern additions to Lovecraft's Cthulhu myth."*

As Wagner reveals, "The story is really Lee Brown Coye's and is about Lee Brown Coye, as the Afterword explains. Coye had described the events upon which 'Sticks' is based to me, and when Stuart David Schiff decided to bring out a special Lee Brown Coye issue of Whispers, *I stole time from my final few months of medical school to write a story inspired by Coye's experiences. 'Sticks' is shot through with in-jokes and references which the serious fantasy/horror fan will recognize. I wrote the story as a favour and tribute to Lee, and I never expected it to be read by anyone beyond the thousand or so fans who read* Whispers. *To my surprise, 'Sticks' became one of my best known and best liked stories. It won the British Fantasy Award and was a runner-up in the World Fantasy Award for best short fiction. The story has been anthologized numerous times and translated into several languages. It was broadcast on National Public Radio on Hallowe'en 1982 and was to have been produced for the short-lived television series,* Darkroom. *Not bad for an in-joke."*

More recent projects from one of the most talented writer/editors in the field include the 21st volume in his annual The Year's Best Horror Stories *series, a new collection entitled* Exorcisms and Ecstasies, *and a medical chiller,* The Fourth Seal. *Penguin/ROC in the UK is reprinting his classic Kane series of heroic fantasy novels, but he disowns the recent graphic novel* Tell Me, Dark *after DC Comics decided to tamper with his deliberately enigmatic storyline. Here's a chance to read the pure stuff . . .*

THE LASHED TOGETHER framework of sticks jutted from a small cairn alongside the stream. Colin Leverett studied it in perplexment – half a dozen odd lengths of branch, wired together at cross angles for no fathomable purpose. It reminded him unpleasantly of some bizarre crucifix, and he wondered what might lie beneath the cairn.

It was the spring of 1942 – the kind of day to make the War seem distant and unreal, although the draft notice waited on his desk. In a few days Leverett would lock his rural studio, wonder if he would see it again – be able to use its pens and brushes and carving tools when he did return. It was goodbye to the woods and streams of upstate New York, too. No fly rods, no tramps through the countryside in Hitler's Europe. No point in putting off fishing that troutstream he had driven past once, exploring back roads of the Otselic Valley.

Mann Brook – so it was marked on the old Geological Survey map – ran southeast of DeRuyter. The unfrequented country road crossed over a stone bridge old before the first horseless carriage, but Leverett's Ford eased across and onto the shoulder. Taking fly rod and tackle, he included a pocket flask and tied an iron skillet to his belt. He'd work his way downstream a few miles. By afternoon he'd lunch on fresh trout, maybe some bullfrog legs.

It was a fine clear stream, though difficult to fish as dense bushes hung out from the bank, broken with stretches of open water hard to work without being seen. But the trout rose boldly to his fly, and Leverett was in fine spirits.

From the bridge the valley along Mann Brook began as fairly open pasture, but half a mile downstream the land had fallen into disuse and was thick with second growth evergreens and scrub-apple trees. Another mile, and the scrub merged with dense forest, which continued unbroken. The land here, he had learned, had been taken over by the state many years back.

As Leverett followed the stream he noted the remains of an old railroad embankment. No vestige of tracks or ties – only the embankment itself, overgrown with large trees. The artist rejoiced in the beautiful dry-wall culverts spanning the stream as it wound through the valley. To his mind it seemed eerie, this forgotten railroad running straight and true through virtual wilderness.

He could imagine an old wood-burner with its conical stack, steaming along through the valley dragging two or three wooden coaches. It must be a branch of the old Oswego Midland Rail Road, he decided, abandoned rather suddenly in the 1870s. Leverett, who had a memory for detail, knew of it from a story his grandfather told of riding the line in 1871 from Otselic to DeRuyter on his honeymoon. The engine had so labored up the steep grade over Crumb Hill that he got off to walk alongside. Probably that sharp grade was the reason for the line's abandonment.

When he came across a scrap of board nailed to several sticks set into a stone wall, his darkest thought was that it might read "No Trespassing." Curiously, though the board was weathered featureless, the nails seemed quite new. Leverett scarcely gave it much thought, until a short distance beyond he came upon another such contrivance. And another.

Now he scratched at the day's stubble on his long jaw. This didn't make sense. A prank? But on whom? A child's game? No, the arrangement was far too sophisticated. As an artist, Leverett appreciated the craftsmanship of the work – the calculated angles and lengths, the designed intricacy of the maddeningly inexplicable devices. There was something distinctly uncomfortable about their effect.

Leverett reminded himself that he had come here to fish and continued downstream. But as he worked around a thicket he again stopped in puzzlement.

Here was a small open space with more of the stick lattices and an arrangement of flat stones laid out on the ground. The stones – likely taken from one of the many dry-wall culverts – made a pattern maybe twenty by fifteen feet, that at first glance resembled a ground plan for a house. Intrigued, Leverett quickly saw that this was not so. If the ground plan for anything, it would have to be for a small maze.

The bizarre lattice structures were all around. Sticks from trees and bits of board nailed together in fantastic array. They defied description; no two seemed alike. Some were only one or two sticks lashed together in parallel or at angles. Others were worked into complicated lattices of dozens of sticks and boards. One could have been a child's tree house – it was built in three planes, but was so abstract and useless that it could be nothing more than an insane conglomeration of sticks and wire. Sometimes the contrivances were stuck in a pile of stones or a wall, maybe thrust into the railroad embankment or nailed to a tree.

It should have been ridiculous. It wasn't. Instead it seemed some-how sinister – these utterly inexplicable, meticulously constructed stick lattices spread through a wilderness where only a tree-grown embankment or a forgotten stone wall gave evidence that man had ever passed through. Leverett forgot about trout and frog legs, instead dug into his pockets for a notebook and stub of pencil. Busily he began to sketch the more intricate structures. Perhaps someone could explain them; perhaps there was something to their insane complexity that warranted closer study for his own work.

Leverett was roughly two miles from the bridge when he came upon the ruins of a house. It was an unlovely colonial farmhouse, box-shaped and gambrel-roofed, fast falling into the ground. Win-dows were dark and empty; the chimneys on either end looked ready to topple. Rafters showed through open spaces in the roof, and the weathered boards of the walls had in places rotted away to reveal hewn timber beams. The foundation was stone and disproportionately massive. From the size of the unmortared stone blocks, its builder had intended the foundation to stand forever.

The house was nearly swallowed up by undergrowth and rampant lilac bushes, but Leverett could distinguish what had been a lawn with imposing shade trees. Farther back were gnarled and sickly apple trees and an overgrown garden where a few lost flowers still bloomed – wan and serpentine from years in the wild. The stick lattices were everywhere – the lawn, the trees, even the house were covered with the uncanny structures. They reminded Leverett of a hundred misshapen spider webs – grouped so closely together as to almost ensnare the entire house and clearing. Wondering, he sketched page on page of them, as he cautiously approached the abandoned house.

He wasn't certain just what he expected to find inside. The aspect of the farmhouse was frankly menacing, standing as it did in gloomy desolation where the forest had devoured the works of man – where the only sign that man had been here in this century were these insanely wrought latticeworks of sticks and board. Some might have turned back at this point. Leverett, whose fascination for the macabre was evident in his art, instead was intrigued. He drew a rough sketch of the farmhouse and the grounds, overrun with the enigmatic devices, with thickets of hedges and distorted flowers. He regretted that it might be years before he could capture the eeriness of this place on scratchboard or canvas.

The door was off its hinges, and Leverett gingerly stepped within, hoping that the flooring remained sound enough to bear even his sparse frame. The afternoon sun pierced the empty windows, mottling the decaying floorboards with great blotches of light. Dust drifted in the sunlight. The house was empty – stripped of furnishings other than indistinct tangles of rubble mounded over with decay and the drifted leaves of many seasons.

Someone had been here, and recently. Someone who had literally covered the mildewed walls with diagrams of the mysterious lattice structures. The drawings were applied directly to the walls, crisscrossing the rotting wallpaper and crumbling plaster in bold black lines. Some of vertiginous complexity covered an entire wall like a mad mural. Others were small, only a few crossed lines, and reminded Leverett of cuneiform glyphics.

His pencil hurried over the pages of his notebook. Leverett noted with fascination that a number of the drawings were recognizable as schematics of lattices he had earlier sketched. Was this then the planning room for the madman or educated idiot who had built these structures? The gouges etched by the charcoal into the soft plaster appeared fresh – done days or months ago, perhaps.

A darkened doorway opened into the cellar. Were there drawings there as well? And what else? Leverett wondered if he should dare it. Except for streamers of light that crept through cracks in the flooring, the cellar was in darkness.

"Hello?" he called. "Anyone here?" It didn't seem silly just then. These stick lattices hardly seemed the work of a rational mind. Leverett wasn't enthusiastic with the prospect of encountering such a person in this dark cellar. It occurred to him that virtually anything might transpire here, and no one in the world of 1942 would ever know.

And that in itself was too great a fascination for one of Leverett's temperament. Carefully he started down the cellar stairs. They were stone and thus solid, but treacherous with moss and debris.

The cellar was enormous – even more so in the darkness. Leverett reached the foot of the steps and paused for his eyes to adjust to the damp gloom. An earlier impression recurred to him. The cellar was too big for the house. Had another dwelling stood here originally – perhaps destroyed and rebuilt by one of lesser fortune? He examined the stonework. Here were great blocks of gneiss that might support a castle. On closer look they reminded him of a fortress – for the dry-wall technique was startlingly Mycenaean.

Like the house above, the cellar appeared to be empty, although without light Leverett could not be certain what the shadows hid. There seemed to be darker areas of shadow along sections of the foundation wall, suggesting openings to chambers beyond. Leverett began to feel uneasy in spite of himself.

There was something here – a large table-like bulk in the center of the cellar. Where a few ghosts of sunlight drifted down to touch its edges, it seemed to be of stone. Cautiously he crossed the stone paving to where it loomed – waist-high, maybe eight feet long and less wide. A roughly shaped slab of gneiss, he judged, and supported by pillars of unmortared stone. In the darkness he could only get a vague conception of the object. He ran his hand along the slab. It seemed to have a groove along its edge.

His groping fingers encountered fabric, something cold and leathery and yielding. Mildewed harness, he guessed in distaste.

Something closed on his wrist, set icy nails into his flesh.

Leverett screamed and lunged away with frantic strength. He was held fast, but the object on the stone slab pulled upward.

A sickly beam of sunlight came down to touch one end of the slab. It was enough. As Leverett struggled backward and the thing that held him heaved up from the stone table, its face passed through the beam of light.

It was a lich's face – desiccated flesh tight over its skull. Filthy strands of hair were matted over its scalp, tattered lips were drawn away from broken yellowed teeth, and, sunken in their sockets, eyes that should be dead were bright with hideous life.

Leverett screamed again, desperate with fear. His free hand clawed the iron skillet tied to his belt. Ripping it loose, he smashed at the nightmarish face with all his strength.

For one frozen instant of horror the sunlight let him see the skillet crush through the mould-eaten forehead like an axe – cleaving the dry flesh and brittle bone. The grip on his wrist failed. The cadaverous face fell away, and the sight of its caved-in forehead and unblinking eyes from between which thick blood had begun to ooze would awaken Leverett from nightmare on countless nights.

But now Leverett tore free and fled. And when his aching legs faltered as he plunged headlong through the scrub-growth, he was spurred to desperate energy by the memory of the footsteps that had stumbled up the cellar stairs behind him.

When Colin Leverett returned from the War, his friends marked him a changed man. He had aged. There were streaks of gray in his hair; his springy step had slowed. The athletic leanness of his body had withered to an unhealthy gauntness. There were indelible lines to his face, and his eyes were haunted.

More disturbing was an alteration of temperament. A mordant cynicism had eroded his earlier air of whimsical asceticism. His fascination with the macabre had assumed a darker mood, a morbid obsession that his old acquaintances found disquieting. But it had been that kind of a war, especially for those who had fought through the Apennines.

Leverett might have told them otherwise, had he cared to discuss his nightmarish experience on Mann Brook. But Leverett kept his own counsel, and when he grimly recalled that creature he had struggled with in the abandoned cellar, he usually convinced himself it had only been a derelict – a crazy hermit whose appearance had been distorted by the poor light and his own imagination. Nor had his blow more than glanced off the man's forehead, he reasoned, since the other had recovered quickly enough to give chase. It was best not to dwell upon such matters, and this rational explanation helped restore sanity when he awoke from nightmares of that face.

Thus Colin Leverett returned to his studio, and once more plied his pens and brushes and carving knives. The pulp magazines, where fans had acclaimed his work before the War, welcomed him back with long lists of assignments. There were commissions from galleries and collectors, unfinished sculptures and wooden models. Leverett busied himself.

There were problems now. *Short Stories* returned a cover painting as "too grotesque." The publishers of a new anthology of horror stories sent back a pair of his interior drawings – "too gruesome, especially the rotted, bloated faces of those hanged men." A customer returned a silver figurine, complaining that the martyred saint was too thoroughly martyred. Even *Weird Tales*, after heralding his return to its ghoul-haunted pages, began returning illustrations they considered "too strong, even for our readers."

Leverett tried half-heartedly to tone things down, found the results vapid and uninspired. Eventually the assignments stopped trickling in. Leverett, becoming more the recluse as years went by, dismissed the pulp days from his mind. Working quietly in his isolated studio, he found a living doing occasional commissioned pieces and gallery work, from time to time selling a painting or sculpture to major museums. Critics had much praise for his bizarre abstract sculptures.

The War was twenty-five years history when Colin Leverett received a letter from a good friend of the pulp days – Prescott Brandon, now editor-publisher of Gothic House, a small press that specialized in books of the weird-fantasy genre. Despite a lapse in correspondence of many years, Brandon's letter began in his typically direct style:

The Eyrie/Salem, Mass./Aug. 2
To the Macabre Hermit of the Midlands:

    Colin, I'm putting together a deluxe 3-volume collection of H. Kenneth Allard's horror stories. I well recall that Kent's stories were personal favorites of yours. How about shambling forth from retirement and illustrating these for me? Will need 2-color jackets and a dozen line interiors each. Would hope that you can startle fandom with some especially ghastly drawings for these – something different from the hackneyed skulls and bats and werewolves carting off half-dressed ladies.

    Interested? I'll send you the materials and details, and you can have a free hand. Let us hear – Scotty

Leverett was delighted. He felt some nostalgia for the pulp days, and he had always admired Allard's genius in transforming visions of cosmic horror into convincing prose. He wrote Brandon an enthusiastic reply.

He spent hours rereading the stories for inclusion, making notes and preliminary sketches. No squeamish sub-editors to offend here; Scotty meant what he said. Leverett bent to his task with maniacal relish.

Something different, Scotty had asked. A free hand. Leverett studied his pencil sketches critically. The figures seemed headed in the right direction, but the drawings needed something more – something that would inject the mood of sinister evil that pervaded Allard's work. Grinning skulls and leathery bats? Trite. Allard demanded more.

The idea had inexorably taken hold of him. Perhaps because Allard's tales evoked that same sense of horror; perhaps because Allard's visions of crumbling Yankee farmhouses and their depraved secrets so reminded him of that spring afternoon at Mann Brook . . .

Although he had refused to look at it since the day he had staggered in, half-dead from terror and exhaustion, Leverett perfectly recalled where he had flung his notebook. He retrieved it from the back of a seldom used file, thumbed through the wrinkled pages thoughtfully. These hasty sketches reawakened the sense of foreboding evil, the charnel horror of that day. Studying the bizarre lattice patterns, it seemed impossible to Leverett that others would not share his feeling of horror that the stick structures evoked in him.

He began to sketch bits of stick lattice work into his pencil roughs. The sneering faces of Allard's degenerate creatures took on an added shadow of menace. Leverett nodded, pleased with the effect.

*   *   *

Some months afterward a letter from Brandon informed Leverett he
had received the last of the Allard drawings and was enormously
pleased with the work. Brandon added a postscript:

> For God's sake Colin — *What is it* with these insane sticks
> you've got poking up everywhere in the illos! The damn
> things get really creepy after awhile. How on earth did you
> get onto this?

Leverett supposed he owed Brandon some explanation. Dutifully
he wrote a lengthy letter, setting down the circumstances of his
experience at Mann Brook — omitting only the horror that had
seized his wrist in the cellar. Let Brandon think him eccentric, but
not madman and murderer.

Brandon's reply was immediate:

> Colin — Your account of the Mann Brook episode is fascinat-
> ing — and incredible! It reads like the start of one of Allard's
> stories! I have taken the liberty of forwarding your letter to
> Alexander Stefroi in Pelham. Dr Stefroi is an earnest scholar
> of this region's history — as you may already know. I'm certain
> your account will interest him, and he may have some light to
> shed on the uncanny affair.
>
> Expect 1st volume, *Voices from the Shadow*, to be ready from the
> binder next month. The proofs looked great. Best — Scotty

The following week brought a letter postmarked Pelham,
Massachusetts:

> A mutual friend, Prescott Brandon, forwarded your fasci-
> nating account of discovering curious sticks and stone artifacts
> on an abandoned farm in upstate New York. I found this
> most intriguing, and wonder if you recall further details?
> Can you relocate the exact site after 30 years? If possible,
> I'd like to examine the foundations this spring, as they call
> to mind similar megalithic sites of this region. Several of us
> are interested in locating what we believe are remains of
> megalithic construction dating back to the Bronze Age, and
> to determine their possible use in rituals of black magic in
> colonial days.
>
> Present archeological evidence indicates that ca. 1700–2000

BC there was an influx of Bronze Age peoples into the North-
east from Europe. We know that the Bronze Age saw the rise of
an extremely advanced culture, and that as sea-farers they were
to have no peers until the Vikings. Remains of a megalithic
culture originating in the Mediterranean can be seen in the
Lion Gate in Mycenae, in Stonehenge, and in dolmens, passage
graves and barrow mounds throughout Europe. Moreover,
this seems to have represented far more than a style of
architecture peculiar to the era. Rather, it appears to have
been a religious cult whose adherents worshipped a sort of
earth-mother, served her with fertility rituals and sacrifices,
and believed that immortality of the soul could be secured
through interment in megalithic tombs.

That this culture came to America cannot be doubted
from the hundreds of megalithic remnants found – and now
recognized – in our region. The most important site to date
is Mystery Hill in N.H., comprising a great many walls and
dolmens of megalithic construction – most notably the Y
Cavern barrow mound and the Sacrificial Table (see postcard).
Less spectacular megalithic sites include the group of cairns
and carved stones at Mineral Mt., subterranean chambers
with stone passageways such as at Petersham and Shutesbury,
and uncounted shaped megaliths and buried 'monk's cells'
throughout this region.

Of further interest, these sites seem to have retained their
mystic aura for the early colonials, and numerous megalithic
sites show evidence of having been used for sinister purposes
by colonial sorcerers and alchemists. This became particularly
true after the witchcraft persecutions drove many practitioners
into the western wilderness – explaining why upstate New York
and western Mass have seen the emergence of so many cultist
groups in later years.

Of particular interest here is Shadrach Ireland's 'Brethren
of the New Light,' who believed that the world was soon to be
destroyed by sinister 'Powers from Outside' and that they, the
elect, would then attain physical immortality. The elect who
died beforehand were to have their bodies preserved on tables
of stone until the 'Old Ones' came forth to return them to life.
We have definitely linked the megalithic sites at Shutesbury to
later unwholesome practices of the New Light cult. They were
absorbed in 1781 by Mother Ann Lee's Shakers, and Ireland's
putrescent corpse was hauled from the stone table in his cellar
and buried.

Thus I think it probable that your farmhouse may have figured in similar hidden practices. At Mystery Hill a farmhouse was built in 1826 that incorporated one dolmen in its foundations. The house burned down ca. 1848–55, and there were some unsavory local stories as to what took place there. My guess is that your farmhouse had been built over or incorporated a similar megalithic site – and that your 'sticks' indicate some unknown cult still survived there. I can recall certain vague references to lattice devices figuring in secret ceremonies, but can pinpoint nothing definite. Possibly they represent a development of occult symbols to be used in certain conjurations, but this is just a guess. I suggest you consult Waite's Ceremonial Magic or such to see if you can recognize similar magical symbols.

Hope this is of some use to you. Please let me hear back.

Sincerely, Alexander Stefroi

There was a postcard enclosed – a photograph of a 4½-ton granite slab, ringed by a deep groove with a spout, identified as the Sacrificial Table at Mystery Hill. On the back Stefroi had written:

You must have found something similar to this. They are not rare – we have one in Pelham removed from a site now beneath Quabbin Reservoir. They were used for sacrifice – animal and human – and the groove is to channel blood into a bowl, presumably.

Leverett dropped the card and shuddered. Stefroi's letter reawakened the old horror, and he wished now he had let the matter lie forgotten in his files. Of course, it couldn't be forgotten – even after thirty years.

He wrote Stefroi a careful letter, thanking him for his information and adding a few minor details to his account. This spring, he promised, wondering if he would keep that promise, he would try to relocate the farmhouse on Mann Brook.

Spring was late that year, and it was not until early June that Colin Leverett found time to return to Mann Brook. On the surface, very little had changed in three decades. The ancient stone bridge yet stood, nor had the country lane been paved. Leverett wondered whether anyone had driven past since his terror-sped flight.

He found the old railroad grade easily as he started downstream.

Thirty years, he told himself — but the chill inside him only tightened. The going was far more difficult than before. The day was unbearably hot and humid. Wading through the rank underbrush raised clouds of black flies that savagely bit him.

Evidently the stream had seen severe flooding in the past years, judging from piled logs and debris that blocked his path. Stretches were scooped out to barren rocks and gravel. Elsewhere gigantic barriers of uprooted trees and debris looked like ancient and mouldering fortifications. As he worked his way down the valley, he realized that his search would yield nothing. So intense had been the force of the long ago flood that even the course of the stream had changed. Many of the drywall culverts no longer spanned the brook, but sat lost and alone far back from its present banks. Others had been knocked flat and swept away, or were buried beneath tons of rotting logs.

At one point Leverett found remnants of an apple orchard groping through weeds and bushes. He thought that the house must be close by, but here the flooding had been particularly severe, and evidently even those ponderous stone foundations had been toppled over and buried beneath debris.

Leverett finally turned back to his car. His step was lighter.

A few weeks later he received a response from Stefroi to his reported failure:

Forgive my tardy reply to your letter of 13 June. I have recently been pursuing inquiries which may, I hope, lead to the discovery of a previously unreported megalithic site of major significance. Naturally I am disappointed that no traces remained of the Mann Brook site. While I tried not to get my hopes up, it did seem likely that the foundations would have survived. In searching through regional data, I note that there were particularly severe flashfloods in the Otselic area in July 1942 and again in May 1946. Very probably your old farmhouse with its enigmatic devices was utterly destroyed not very long after your discovery of the site. This is weird and wild country, and doubtless there is much we shall never know.

I write this with a profound sense of personal loss over the death two nights ago of Prescott Brandon. This was a severe blow to me — as I am sure it was to you and to all who knew him. I only hope the police will catch the vicious killers who did this senseless act — evidently thieves surprised while ransacking his office. Police believe

the killers were high on drugs from the mindless brutality of
their crime.

I had just received a copy of the third Allard volume,
Unhallowed Places. A superbly designed book, and this tragedy
becomes all the more insuperable with the realization that
Scotty will give the world no more such treasures.

                                    In Sorrow, Alexander Stefroi

Leverett stared at the letter in shock. He had not received news of
Brandon's death – had only a few days before opened a parcel from
the publisher containing a first copy of *Unhallowed Places*. A line in
Brandon's last letter recurred to him – a line that seemed amusing
to him at the time:

> Your sticks have bewildered a good many fans, Colin, and
> I've worn out a ribbon answering inquiries. One fellow in
> particular – a Major George Leonard – has pressed me for
> details, and I'm afraid that I told him too much. He has
> written several times for your address, but knowing how you
> value your privacy I told him simply to permit me to forward
> any correspondence. He wants to see your original sketches,
> I gather, but these overbearing occult-types give me a pain.
> Frankly, I wouldn't care to meet the man myself.

"Mr Colin Leverett?"

Leverett studied the tall lean man who stood smiling at the
doorway of his studio. The sports car he had driven up in was black
and looked expensive. The same held for the turtleneck and leather
slacks he wore, and the sleek briefcase he carried. The blackness
made his thin face deathly pale. Leverett guessed his age to be late
40 by the thinning of his hair. Dark glasses hid his eyes, black driving
gloves his hands.

"Scotty Brandon told me where to find you," the stranger said.

"Scotty?" Leverett's voice was wary.

"Yes, we lost a mutual friend, I regret to say. I'd been talking
with him just before . . . But I see by your expression that Scotty
never had time to write."

He fumbled awkwardly. "I'm Dana Allard."

"Allard?"

His visitor seemed embarrassed. "Yes – H. Kenneth Allard was
my uncle."

"I hadn't realized Allard left a family," mused Leverett, shaking the extended hand. He had never met the writer personally, but there was a strong resemblance to the few photographs he had seen. And Scotty had been paying royalty checks to an estate of some sort, he recalled.

"My father was Kent's half-brother. He later took his father's name, but there was no marriage, if you follow."

"Of course." Leverett was abashed. "Please find a place to sit down. And what brings you here?"

Dana Allard tapped his briefcase. "Something I'd been discussing with Scotty. Just recently I turned up a stack of my uncle's unpublished manuscripts." He unlatched the briefcase and handed Leverett a sheaf of yellowed paper. "Father collected Kent's personal effects from the state hospital as next-of-kin. He never thought much of my uncle, or his writing. He stuffed this away in our attic and forgot about it. Scotty was quite excited when I told him of my discovery."

Leverett was glancing through the manuscript – page on page of cramped handwriting, with revisions pieced throughout like an indecipherable puzzle. He had seen photographs of Allard manuscripts. There was no mistaking this.

Or the prose. Leverett read a few passages with rapt absorption. It was authentic – and brilliant.

"Uncle's mind seems to have taken an especially morbid turn as his illness drew on," Dana hazarded. "I admire his work very greatly but I find these last few pieces . . . Well, a bit *too* horrible. Especially his translation of his mythical *Book of Elders*."

It appealed to Leverett perfectly. He barely noticed his guest as he pored over the brittle pages. Allard was describing a megalithic structure his doomed narrator had encountered in the crypts beneath an ancient churchyard. There were references to "elder glyphics" that resembled his lattice devices.

"Look here," pointed Dana. "These incantations he records here from Alorri-Zrokros's forbidden tome: 'Yogth-Yugth-Sut-Hyrath-Yogng' – Hell, I can't pronounce them. And he has pages of them."

"This is incredible!" Leverett protested. He tried to mouth the alien syllables. It could be done. He even detected a rhythm.

"Well, I'm relieved that you approve. I'd feared these last few stories and fragments might prove a little too much for Kent's fans."

"Then you're going to have them published?"

Dana nodded. "Scotty was going to. I just hope those thieves weren't searching for this – a collector would pay a fortune. But

Scotty said he was going to keep this secret until he was ready for an announcement." His thin face was sad.

"So now I'm going to publish it myself – in a deluxe edition. And I want you to illustrate it."

"I'd feel honored!" vowed Leverett, unable to believe it.

"I really liked those drawings you did for the trilogy. I'd like to see more like those – as many as you feel like doing. I mean to spare no expense in publishing this. And those stick things . . ."

"Yes?"

"Scotty told me the story on those. Fascinating! And you have a whole notebook of them? May I see it?"

Leverett hurriedly dug the notebook from his file, returned to the manuscript.

Dana page through the book in awe. "These things are totally bizarre – and there are references to such things in the manuscript, to make it even more fantastic. Can you reproduce them all for the book?"

"All I can remember," Leverett assured him. "And I have a good memory. But won't that be overdoing it?"

"Not at all! They fit into the book. And they're utterly unique. No, put everything you've got into this book. I'm going to entitle it *Dwellers in the Earth*, after the longest piece. I've already arranged for its printing, so we begin as soon as you can have the art ready. And I know you'll give it your all."

He was floating in space. Objects drifted past him. Stars, he first thought. The objects drifted closer.

Sticks. Stick lattices of all configurations. And then he was drifting among them, and he saw that they were not sticks – not of wood. The lattice designs were of dead-pale substance, like streaks of frozen starlight. They reminded him of glyphics of some unearthly alphabet – complex, enigmatic symbols arranged to spell . . . what? And there *was* an arrangement – a three-dimensional pattern. A maze of utterly baffling intricacy . . .

Then somehow he was in a tunnel. A cramped, stone-lined tunnel through which he must crawl on his belly. The dank, moss-slimed stones pressed close about his wriggling form, evoking shrill whispers of claustrophobic dread.

And after an indefinite space of crawling through this and other stone-lined burrows, and sometimes through passages whose angles hurt his eyes, he would creep forth into a subterranean chamber. Great slabs of granite a dozen feet across formed the walls and ceiling of this buried chamber, and between the slabs other burrows pierced the earth. Altar-like, a gigantic slab of gneiss waited in the center of the chamber. A spring welled darkly between the stone pillars that supported the table. Its outer edge was encircled by a groove, sickeningly stained by the substance that clotted in the stone bowl beneath its collecting spout.

Others were emerging from the darkened burrows that ringed the chamber – slouched figures only dimly glimpsed and vaguely human. And a figure in a tattered cloak came toward him from the shadow – stretched out a claw-like hand to seize his wrist and draw him toward the sacrificial table. He followed unresistingly, knowing that something was expected of him.

They reached the altar and in the glow from the cuneiform lattices chiselled into the gneiss slab he could see the guide's face. A mouldering corpse-face, the rotted bone of its forehead smashed inward upon the foulness that oozed forth . . .

And Leverett would awaken to the echo of his screams . . .

He'd been working too hard, he told himself, stumbling about in the darkness, getting dressed because he was too shaken to return to sleep. The nightmares had been coming every night. No wonder he was exhausted.

But in his studio his work awaited him. Almost fifty drawings finished now, and he planned another score. No wonder the nightmares.

It was a grueling pace, but Dana Allard was ecstatic with the work he had done. And *Dwellers in the Earth* was waiting. Despite problems with typesetting, with getting the special paper Dana wanted – the book only waited on him.

Though his bones ached with fatigue, Leverett determinedly trudged through the greying night. Certain features of the nightmare would be interesting to portray.

The last of the drawings had gone off to Dana Allard in Petersham, and Leverett, fifteen pounds lighter and gut-weary, converted part of the bonus check into a case of good whiskey. Dana had the offset presses rolling as soon as the plates were shot from the drawings. Despite his precise planning, presses had broken down, one printer quit for reasons not stated, there had been a bad accident at the new printer – seemingly innumerable problems, and Dana had been furious at each delay. But the production pushed along quickly for all that. Leverett wrote that the book was cursed, but Dana responded that a week would see it ready.

Leverett amused himself in his studio constructing stick lattices

and trying to catch up on his sleep. He was expecting a copy of the
book when he received a letter from Stefroi:

> Have tried to reach you by phone last few days, but no
> answer at your house. I'm pushed for time just now, so must
> be brief. I have indeed uncovered an unsuspected megalithic
> site of enormous importance. It's located on the estate of
> a long-prominent Mass. family – and as I cannot receive
> authorization to visit it, I will not say where. Have investigated
> secretly (and quite illegally) for a short time one night and
> was nearly caught. Came across reference to the place in
> collection of 17th century letters and papers in a divinity
> school library. Writer denouncing the family as a brood of
> sorcerers and witches, references to alchemical activities and
> other less savory rumors – and describes underground stone
> chambers, megalithic artifacts etc. which are put to 'foul usage
> and diabolic praktise.' Just got a quick glimpse but his descrip-
> tion was not exaggerated. And Colin – in creeping through the
> woods to get to the site, I came across dozens of your mysterious
> 'sticks!' Brought a small one back and have it here to show you.
> Recently constructed and exactly like your drawings. With
> luck, I'll gain admittance and find out their significance –
> undoubtedly they have significance – though these cultists can
> be stubborn about sharing their secrets. Will explain my inter-
> est is scientific, no exposure to ridicule – and see what they say.
> Will get a closer look one way or another. And so – I'm off!
>   Sincerely, Alexander Stefroi

Leverett's bushy brows rose. Allard had intimated certain dark
rituals in which the stick lattices figured. But Allard had written over
thirty years ago, and Leverett assumed the writer had stumbled onto
something similar to the Mann Brook site. Stefroi was writing about
something current.

He rather hoped Stefroi would discover nothing more than an
inane hoax.

The nightmares haunted him still – familiar now, for all that the
scenes and phantasms were visited by him only in dream. Familiar.
The terror that they evoked was undiminished.

Now he was walking through forest – a section of hills that seemed
to be close by. A huge slab of granite had been dragged aside, and a
pit yawned where it had lain. He entered the pit without hesitation,
and the rounded steps that led downward were known to his tread.

A buried stone chamber, and leading from it stone-lined burrows. He knew which one to crawl into.

And again the underground room with its sacrificial altar and its dark spring beneath, and the gathering circle of poorly glimpsed figures. A knot of them clustered about the stone table, and as he stepped toward them he saw they pinned a frantically writhing man.

It was a stoutly built man, white hair disheveled, fresh gouged and filthy. Recognition seemed to burst over the contorted features, and he wondered if he should know the man. But now the lich with the caved in skull was whispering in his ear, and he tried not to think of the unclean things that peered from that cloven brow, and instead took the bronze knife from the skeletal hand, and raised the knife high, and because he could not scream and awaken, did with the knife as the tattered priest had whispered . . .

And when after an interval of unholy madness, he at last did awaken, the stickiness that covered him was not cold sweat, nor was it nightmare the half-devoured heart he clutched in one fist.

Leverett somehow found sanity enough to dispose of the shredded lump of flesh. He stood under the shower all morning, scrubbing his skin raw. He wished he could vomit.

There was a news item on the radio. The crushed body of noted archeologist, Dr Alexander Stefroi, had been discovered beneath a fallen granite slab near Whately. Police speculated the gigantic slab had shifted with the scientist's excavations at its base. Identification was made through personal effects.

When his hands stopped shaking enough to drive, Leverett fled to Petersham – reaching Dana Allard's old stone house about dark. Allard was slow to answer his frantic knock.

"Why, good evening, Colin! What a coincidence your coming here just now! The books are ready. The bindery just delivered them."

Leverett brushed past him. "We've got to destroy them!" he blurted. He'd thought a lot since morning.

"Destroy them?"

"There's something none of us figured on. Those stick lattices – there's a cult, some damnable cult. The lattices have some significance in their rituals. Stefroi hinted once they might be glyphics of some sort, I don't know. But the cult is still alive. They killed Scott . . . they killed Stefroi. They're onto me – I don't know what they intend. They'll kill you to stop you from releasing this book!"

Dana's frown was worried, but Leverett knew he hadn't impressed him the right way. "Colin, this sounds insane. You really have been overextending yourself, you know. Look, I'll show you the books. They're in the cellar."

Leverett let his host lead him downstairs. The cellar was quite large, flagstoned and dry. A mountain of brown-wrapped bundles awaited them.

"Put them down here where they wouldn't knock the floor out," Dana explained. "They start going out to distributors tomorrow. Here, I'll sign your copy."

Distractedly Leverett opened a copy of *Dwellers in the Earth*. He gazed at his lovingly rendered drawings of rotting creatures and buried stone chambers and stained altars – and everywhere the enigmatic lattice work structures. He shuddered.

"Here." Dana Allard handed Leverett the book he had signed. "And to answer your question, they *are* elder glyphics."

But Leverett was staring at the inscription in its unmistakable handwriting : "For Colin Leverett, Without whom this work could not have seen completion – H. Kenneth Allard."

Allard was speaking. Leverett saw places where the hastily applied flesh-toned makeup didn't quite conceal what lay beneath. "Glyphics symbolic of alien dimensions – inexplicable to the human mind, but essential fragments of an evocation so unthinkably vast that the 'pentagram' (if you will) is miles across. Once before we tried – but your iron weapon destroyed part of Althol's brain. He erred at the last instant – almost annihilating us all. Althol had been formulating the evocation since he fled the advance of iron four millennia past.

"Then you reappeared, Colin Leverett – you with your artist's knowledge and diagrams of Althol's symbols. And now a thousand new minds will read the evocation you have returned to us, unite with our minds as we stand in the Hidden Places. And the Great Old Ones will come forth from the earth, and we, the dead who have steadfastly served them, shall be masters of the living."

Leverett turned to run, but now they were creeping forth from the shadows of the cellar, as massive flagstones slid back to reveal the tunnels beyond. He began to scream as Althol came to lead him away, but he could not awaken, could only follow.

AFTERWORD

Some readers may note certain similarities between characters and events in this story and the careers of real-life figures, well known to fans of this genre. This was unavoidable, and no disrespect is intended. For much of this story *did* happen, though I suppose you've heard that one before.

In working with Lee Brown Coye on Wellman's *Worse Things Waiting*, I finally asked him why his drawings so frequently included sticks in their design. Lee's work is well known to me, but I had noticed that the "sticks" only began to appear in his work for Ziff-Davis in the early 60s. Lee finally sent me a folder of clippings and letters, far more eerie than this story – and factual.

In 1938 Coye *did* come across a stick-ridden farmhouse in the desolate Mann Brook region. He kept this to himself until fall of 1962, when John Vetter passed the account to August Derleth and to antiquarian-archeologist Andrew E. Rothovius. Derleth intended to write Coye's adventure as a Lovecraft novelette, but never did so. Rothovius discussed the site's possible megalithic significance with Coye in a series of letters and journal articles on which I have barely touched. In June 1963 Coye returned to the Mann Brook site and found it obliterated. It is a strange region, as HPL knew.

Coye's fascinating presentation of their letters appeared in five weekly instalments of his "Chips and Shavings" column in the *Mid York Weekly* from 22 August to 26 September 1963. Rothovius, whose research into the New England megaliths has been published in many journals, wrote an excellent and disquieting summary of his research in Arkham House's *The Dark Brotherhood*, to which the reader is referred.

Charles L. Grant

Quietly Now

It's getting hard to keep track of Charles L. Grant's multifarious careers as he continues to publish adventure fiction as "Geoffrey Marsh", humorous fantasy as "Lionel Fenn", and young adult fiction as "Steven Charles", among other pseudonyms. On the horror front, recent novels under his own name include In a Dark Dream, Stunts, Something Stirs *and* Raven.

*The author of more than one hundred short stories and editor of numerous anthologies (*In the Fog *is the latest), Grant is a three-time winner of the* World Fantasy Award, *and has also received two Nebula Awards and the British Fantasy Award for Life Achievement.*

As the title implies, the story which follows is another example of the author's unique style of "quiet" horror. However, it is no less disturbing for that.

THE HILLS OF northwestern New Jersey are low and ancient, densely forested and, for the most part, state protected. In those areas, however, which the state has kept clear there are children's camps and winter resorts, lakes natural and manmade, villages where only a radio tells them the year – and sufficient distances to exclude them all from New York City's commuting umbrella. Scarcely a wilderness by the Far West's standards, yet wilderness enough

to make the ordinary tourist somewhat cautious after dark. And
wilderness enough to spawn midnight stories of travelers wandering
into the woodland and seldom returning.

Stories resurrected during the time of the darkmoon.

There are nights, poets' nights, when the stars are perfect against
a backdrop of perfect black, and the air is cool and the streams are
running, and vision seems unlimited except for the moon. It could
be crescent, it could be full, waxing or waning, yet darkened by a
haze not born of a cloud. Silverlight becomes grey, shadows lose
definition, and old-timers head for the nearest tavern or hearth.

And travelers take walks, and the stories begin.

And like everyone else who lived there year-round, Keith Prior
read the inevitable news with a slow-shaking head and a continuing
wonderment that city people could be so eternally foolhardy, so
infernally stupid. The darkmoon was legend, a Halloween tale, but
it didn't change the fact that people sometimes died. He thought it
would have been sufficient for them to see one two-column photo of
a spring-thaw corpse huddled in a small cave, of a partially devoured
woman huddled beneath a tree, of a fleshless family unprotected in
their tents, sleeping bags slashed and clothes rent at the seams. But at
least once a year someone refused to heed common-sense warnings,
and once a year the stories returned.

Not, he thought, that he himself dwelled in a rustic log cabin
and chopped wood for heat and hunted his meals and fashioned
his wrappings from the pelts of the wild. That was a fancy he left
to the movies, and his New York friends who thought he lived like
a hermit.

The Greenwitch Arms Apartments complex was much more a
place to foster a recluse's nightmares.

It had been constructed a decade before on a deserted farm just
below a two-lane highway, sixty miles west of the Hudson River.
Seventy-two two-story buildings of varicolored brick shaded by oaks
still reaching for the eaves; a dozen units to a building – the upstairs
with a narrow slatted balcony, the downstairs with a concrete slab
that masked as a patio. Nearly two thousand people who thought
they lived in the country.

It was May now, and warm, and the sky was of a blue better suited
to a lover's eyes. He sat in his living room – a desk, two chairs, white
walls buried behind unfinished bookcases – waiting for inspiration
to lure him back to work.

Outside, on the twenty-yard patch of grass and shrubs between
his building and the next, was a large, red plastic wading pool
currently invaded by an army of young children. They splashed and

complained and laughed so loudly he was unable to concentrate on the research he was doing – reading for an article on the fantasy whims of poets and prophets, for a magazine he'd never heard of, but which paid fifteen cents a word.

He sighed, and wondered if perhaps he shouldn't try calling Jane to apologize, though he had no idea if one was really necessary. It would be nice if he had to, because that would imply he might have another chance. But he doubted it. The affair had slowed to stasis during winter, had not thawed with spring. They were friends, they had drinks, he even visited now and then, but instinct warned him momentum had died. Probably, he thought sourly, he'd been preempted by Carl Andrews.

Another sigh, mockingly melodramatic, and he rose to stand at the sliding screen door to watch the kids playing. He counted eight, all of them trying to wedge into the pool without touching the ground now muddy with spillage. Suddenly, two of them – a carrot-top and a white-blond – broke away in disgust and wandered listlessly toward him. They looked up and waved before he could back off. He slid the door aside, stepped out, and rested his forearms on the railing.

"Hi, Uncle Keith!" A chorus high-pitched and pleasant. The title was honorary but he didn't mind it a bit.

"Gentlemen," he said solemnly, and nodded toward the others. "Too crowded at the beach?"

They scowled. They wore identical pairs of blue jogging shorts with gold piping. Chest, legs, arms bare and tanned. They seemed ill at ease, as if they missed having pockets in which their hands could hide.

"Did you guys have a good time yesterday?" he said. "See any neat freaks in the city?"

"No," said Peter, the carrot-top and older. "There wasn't anything but a bunch of dead animals. Bones and a lot of pictures. Nuts. Who wants to see bones?" And with a grimace of disgust he headed home, the first-floor apartment one over from Keith's.

"Hey, don't worry about him," Keith said when Philip looked stricken at his brother's desertion. "It's hard being ten these days. He'll grow up, I promise."

Philip considered, then shrugged with a rueful smile. "He still doesn't like it that Danny went away."

Keith only nodded. Euphemisms for death irritated him without exception, and when they were used by children he felt annoyingly helpless. Especially in this case. Danny Ramera had been found in the woodland tract behind the schoolhouse across the highway. He'd been missing for five days, and the police medical team had judged death by exposure. No matter the temperature hadn't dropped below sixty-five for a week or more, and no matter the body had been discovered less than eighty yards from the school; the boy had been playing, had fallen, had struck his head on a rock, and Nature was blamed for doing the rest.

That was the word circulated through the township, and that was the word accepted by the local paper.

"Mrs German," Philip said suddenly, "thinks all those animals are damned or something because they're not human."

"What?" Keith blinked slowly and leaned farther over the railing.

The boy repeated himself, and Keith wondered what kind of teachers they were turning out these days. Jane, on the other hand –

"I think she's crazy," Philip declared.

"Well . . . she is rather strange."

"No, she's not," the boy said. "She's a vampire."

"So was my third mother-in-law, but I don't brag about it."

"No, I mean it," Philip said, moving closer, craning his neck and squinting against the sun. "She's a real vampire."

"No kidding."

"Really! She keeps the shades down in her room all the time. She *says* she doesn't want us looking outside, but I know it's because vampires can't take the sun. And you know something else?"

"No," he said. "What?"

"She never leaves the school!"

"That's because you don't see her," he said. "You leave before she does."

The boy shook his head vigorously. "No, I mean it! She doesn't have a car and she never leaves. Really. I'm not lying."

He smiled gentle tolerance for a boy who often seemed so much older than his years, and rubbed his chin thoughtfully against his forearm. "Listen, Phil, do you really think Mr Bonachek would allow one of his teachers to – "

"He's right, you know."

He scowled and rolled his eyes, a tongue-in-cheek indication that a Great Truth had been interrupted. Phil dashed away, avoiding his mother's outstretched arm to duck into his home. Moira Leary was short, slim for bearing two children a year apart, and wore oversized sunglasses that made her eyes too wide, too innocent for the dark lips glistening in the afternoon's heat. She was almost Jane's twin, though she seemed years older. He saluted her silently.

"German's a vampire, right?"

A hand lifted to shade her eyes. "If not that, something else again, believe me. She knows her stuff, don't get me wrong, but there are times when she acts like she's right out of the Dark Ages."

"I would commiserate," he said, "but you'd only tell me that bachelors – especially ones three times divorced – don't know anything about raising children so what do I know anyway, right?"

She laughed. "What're you working on now, Hemingway?"

Several decidedly lecherous responses came to mind, but he discarded them reluctantly. Though he'd never met her salesman husband in the two years he'd been here, and though he was positive she'd made a pass at him more than once, he didn't dare consider her more than a friend – though it hadn't stopped him from sneaking a sex-starved glance once in a while. He grinned, she grinned back knowingly, and he told her about the article. She laughed again, brightly, brushed the bangs from her forehead and waved him a farewell.

He waited until she was gone, then returned to his desk. A bored glance at his calendar made him realize with a start he'd promised Mike Bonachek he'd talk this Monday to the fourth graders about a book of his they were using, on astronomy and NASA. My God, he thought, me and my big mouth.

But it wasn't that bad, he admitted when it was over. The book had been read, and he'd been asked intelligent questions. The only argument he'd suffered centered on his refusal to believe in flying saucers; the classes – two jammed into a single room – had seen too much television, and they knew better.

Five minutes before the talk ended, however, the room abruptly stilled. He turned automatically to the door, and just managed not to gape.

Mrs German stood on the threshold. She was nearly six feet tall, slightly overweight, wearing a shapeless print dress whose colors had faded. Her hair was black and flat, her features sharp to the point of emaciation. Her shoes were brown, sturdy and laced, and he bet himself her dark stockings ended just above the knee with a darker band of elastic that left a red belt around her thighs.

He couldn't help it; he glanced at Philip who grinned an *I told you so*.

Jane Disanza smiled politely. "Yes, Mrs German?"

The older woman did not turn. She kept her heavily veined hands clasped at her waist and stared at the class. "I am visiting all the rooms at Mr Bonachek's request. I'm sorry for the interruption. It seems someone had been prying at the basement lock." Her gaze was stern, condemnation without trial. "It is not permitted."

The children said nothing; Jane said nothing; and Keith merely pursed his lips in a silent whistle and stared at the floor.

"Not permitted," she repeated, and nodded once before leaving. There was a rustling quelled by a sharp word from Jane. A bee droning against a pane. A fussing with books until the bell finally rang and he found himself surrounded. He grinned, shook a few hands, and stood with a groan once the last child was gone.

Jane had slumped into her desk chair, fluffed idly at the hair curling darkly to her shoulders. "Bitch," she said. "She's been here so long she thinks she owns the place. Hell, Keith, nobody wants to go into the stupid basement anyway, for God's sake."

He wanted to stand behind her then, massage her shoulders and bring back the days when they could laugh without strain. And the worst of it was, he understood all too well why their relationship had ended. Three times married, four years each time, and she had every right to be skeptical whenever he protested *but this time it's different, it isn't like the others*. She'd reasoned rightly he had said it (and had meant it) twice before, and at thirty-two (to his forty) a four-year contract was hardly a promise of security and heaven.

He shoved his hands into his pockets and leaned against the blackboard. "She sure looks old enough to have been here forever. As a matter of fact, your nephew thinks she's a vampire."

"That would be Philip. Peter's the one with the better command of street language." She shuffled paper for a moment, and stood. "How are you?"

"Hanging in," he said quietly.

She picked up a pencil and tapped it hard against her blotter. "Carl thinks we should get together, a double date or something."

He nodded. Death knell. Finishing touch. "Sure, why not?"

She reached for her purse in the desk's bottom drawer. "I'm supposed to feed you lunch."

"Fine," he said. "I never carp a free meal."

The cafeteria was midway along the central corridor – white wooden walls and green slippery tiles – and they tagged the end of a softly babbling line. Students giggled and gossiped, faculty feigning extreme patience. Keith played the stoic, smiling automatically while he wondered why he didn't feel more devastated than disappointed. But before he could consider further, a grizzled winter-bent man in greyed coveralls and carrying a stiff broom sidled up to him and tugged on his jacket.

"Mac, you gotta light?"

"You been drinking?" he said from the corner of his mouth.

Jane turned around briefly, pursed her lips and turned back.

"Not a drop, mac. Not since German found my whisky and curdled it with a look."

Keith barked a laugh and jabbed Stan Linkholm's scrawny arm with a loose fist. The man was three weeks away from retirement as the school's custodian, and was looking forward to spending the rest of his life watching dirt join him in his house. They had met at the Deer Head, the only bar on the highway within walking distance that didn't feature country music six nights out of seven. And it had been there Keith had heard the stories of the darkmoon, of the dogs tourists left behind in summer to run wild in the hills.

"Well, you gonna help my cancer or what?"

He pulled matches from his pocket and Linkholm nodded thanks, peered into the cafeteria with a sneer and grunted as he left – back bent, head down, a deceptively frail man tracking wisps of dust.

"You like him?" Jane asked innocently as the line finally drifted forward.

He shrugged. "He tells great jokes, he buys me a drink now and then, and he speaks his mind."

"Ah," she said, grinning, "he's mentioned his skirmishes with sweet Mrs German."

Skirmishes, Keith thought, was hardly the word for what sounded like all-out warfare. It was Stan's contention that he should be permitted into the basement once in a while, just to see if the foundations were still holding the place up; the math teacher, however, informed him that his utensils and the boiler were in a different section of the building, and nothing in the records kept below the steepled core should have the slightest interest for a man who shaved only once or twice a month.

It was an impasse Stan was determined to break before he retired.

Jane then spent the next twenty minutes avoiding Keith's questions about her life with Carl Andrews. And finally, when he felt self-pity beginning to well, he excused himself with a blown kiss to her cheek and walked outside to let the fresh air calm him. He stood in front, just below the once-belled steeple, and directly ahead the ground sloped gently toward the highway; beyond, a steeper incline, and behind a row of thick-boled elms the apartments began, rising and falling on the gentle swells of the old farm until the woodland reasserted itself, dark with noon shadows.

He lit a cigarette and turned around to look at the school. It was an oddity, he thought – originally one room, it had been added to here and there, modernized, bloated and extended around the central building, which seemed now beneath flanking willows like a dwarfed New England church. He didn't like it. Innocent and white and crawling with children, and he didn't like it. It was, he thought, as if contemporary builders had known something everyone else hadn't, and had tried to hide it by disguising it, badly.

He tossed the cigarette away without finishing it, angry with the way his mood had soured, blame in equal parts on himself and Jane. He walked slowly, a conscious effort to clear his mind, and by the time he reached home he was at least ready to smile.

And he did when he saw Peter waiting there for him.

The entrance to his apartment was recessed beneath a slate roof, the door on the right his downstairs neighbors', the one on the left belonging to him. Peter was standing on the concrete stoop, his red hair awry, faint shadows over his eyes.

"Hi, Uncle Keith." Desultory, uncomfortable.

Keith leaned against the door frame. "You cut out of school early, m'boy. Does your mother know you're home yet?"

Peter shook his head, staring with a scowl at the building across the way. "Mrs German wants to suspend me."

"What? For God's sake, you're only in fifth grade!"

There was almost a grin. "Well . . . I put a tack on her chair."

He couldn't help it – he laughed. Unoriginal and stupid and demeaning to the teacher, but he laughed and slipped an arm around the boy's shoulders, cool here in the shade, almost cold. "I don't believe it. Of all the people in the world . . . my God, don't tell your mother I think I approve."

"She's gonna kill me."

"You want me to talk to her?"

Peter pulled away instantly, brightening and smiling. "No kidding, you will?"

"Sure, why not. But you have to tell her first. Then I'll come over later to talk."

"But we're going to grandma's for dinner."

"You're always going to grandma's for dinner. She must be a hell of a cook. Nope. You first, then me, or no deal." He waited. "How high did she jump?"

"That's the dumb part. She didn't feel a thing. Elsie Franks snitched."

He was gone before Keith could make further comment. Great, he thought; I think I've just been conned. He shrugged and reached for the doorknob, stopped when he saw deep scratch marks around the lock. The door wasn't closed.

He glanced around, looked for Peter, then gently nudged the door with his shoe. It swung open slowly. Immediately to the right were the stairs, carpeted in dim gold and badly needing a vacuum. He listened and heard nothing, but took the steps cautiously, his gaze on the dim light that blocked the room above. His arms were stiff, the breath caught in his lungs spilling over to cold. He blinked rapidly, swallowed, told himself to go back down and call the cops from Moira's. For all he knew the robbers, the vandals, the murderers were still up there, hiding behind the recliner, in the bedroom, in the kitchen, behind the plastic shower curtain in the bath. For all he knew the whole place had been stripped and he was left with nothing but the clothes on his back.

He reached the top and paused.

The room was twenty-five feet from front to balcony, twelve feet wide in the living room area. It was dark, the drapes drawn and all the other doors closed. Darker than it should have been on a May afternoon. And colder. Much colder. He felt his breath pluming between lips growing chapped. He shivered, and clenched his left hand before reaching for the light switch. Clicked it and waited, but the lights wouldn't flare on.

Fuse, he thought; the circuit breaker's busted.

His vision adjusted, and he could see nothing wrong. All the books were on their shelves, his desk undisturbed, the manuscript by the typewriter still stacked in disarray.

But the cold persisted, and he hugged himself tightly.

Go away, he thought then; go away and leave me alone. But he wasn't at all sure whether he was talking to himself or the intruder.

He backed down one step, and the cold began to leave.

The lights winked on.

And when he looked across the room he saw the drapes hadn't been drawn at all, that there was sun out there spilling onto the carpet.

He sat suddenly and hard, his hands gripping his knees and his gaze fixed on the open door below. He knew there was an explanation for everything that had happened. He was tired. He was self-admittedly overworked. He was reacting to losing another woman from his life. It would be natural for his mind to overload, to punish him for the abuse and teach him a lesson. That was the logical path to pursue, and pursue it he did – sitting in the stairwell until just before sunset, then rising and going down, pulling the door closed, glancing at the lock and not seeing any scratches.

He walked away quickly. Away from the apartment, up the hill to the highway. His fingers were trembling and he hid them in his pockets, jumping to one side when the white-globed streetlamps reacted to their times and filled the complex with soft light. There were low hills below the sky, their ragged western edges shading from grey to brilliant rose. And as he walked along the verge gusts from passing buses and trucks kept his eyes in a squint. A few headlights were on, and dusk gave the air a black-spotted complexion.

At Frazier's – a mom-and-pop luncheonette and grocery – he ate a tasteless sandwich, drank four cups of coffee, and bought a carton of cigarettes he tucked swagger-stick under his arm. He felt better for the food and the quiet company the Fraziers gave him, and he'd just stepped outside when he remembered his promise to Peter.

"Great," he muttered, and stepped out in a hurry.

The scent of rain, a rising wind, tires on the blacktop already hissing wetly. He'd almost broken into a guilt-prodded run when an aborted siren's wail stopped and turned him. With his free hand screening the side of his face against the wind he looked toward the school. On the curved drive in front was a patrol car with blue lights swirling, and a rescue squad van whose rear doors were open, whose attendants were lifting a white-covered stretcher into the back. He checked the traffic quickly, then sprinted across and stood at the base of the grassy slope while Carl Andrews walked toward him.

"Carl," he said, as neutrally as he could while he eyed the van.

"How's it going, Keith?" He was tall, brawny and dark-haired. His left palm rested on his revolver's wooden stock, in his right hand a clipboard.

"Could be better, I suppose. You got trouble it seems."

"We can handle it."

"Yeah. Anybody I know? Jesus, not another kid, is it?"

Andrews didn't move.

"Dead?"

"Yeah. Dead." Andrews licked at his lips. "Very. It's Stan Linkholm."

"Ah . . . Christ." Keith looked back to the highway and shook his head slowly. "Heart attack, something like that?"

"Something like that."

Keith frowned slight irritation. "Carl, look, if you're going to tell me, then tell me. I mean, I knew him and I'd like to know. But if you're not going to tell me, then don't. I've got work to do."

Carl Andrews turned away.

He spent the next two days finishing the article, keeping his door locked and the phone off the hook. No one bothered him. No mail was delivered. He worked until his fingers cramped, ate and worked again. He slept badly. There were dreams, and there was a lingering memory of the cold he'd discovered after talking to Peter. The cold that had him lying under two layers of blankets.

On Thursday morning the weekly paper was shoved through the door's mail slot and he hurried down to grab it, sitting on the bottom step and snapping it open to the front page. A short piece about Stan, about a cardiac arrest, about his years with the school and a long quote from Bonachek. A grainy photograph. A story on page three about a New York couple who'd been missing since Monday from their campsite in the hills. An editorial demanding action, citing the tourism the county needed to survive.

It was spring, and it was business as usual, and he threw the paper into the corner and didn't believe it.

Stan's heart was as sound as his broomstick, and if Danny Ramera died of exposure he'd turn in his typewriter and dig ditches instead.

But it wasn't the stories that had finally convinced him, it was the memory of the cold, of the vanished scratches on the lock, of the way the children cowered when Mrs German walked by.

He knew it was stupid. He knew he was driving himself out of the Jane-induced depression by grasping at whatever straws the wind carried his way. Mrs German was odd, but no odder than the teachers he'd had himself as a child; and people who weren't used to the hills were always disappearing, always turning up, always changing their minds and heading for home without notification.

But the cold . . . it was the cold.

As soon as he dressed he drove to the hospital eight miles away, and was refused permission to check the medical records. The police stalled him, Andrews wouldn't meet with him, and when he talked to Philip after school he was given nothing more than bits of gossip about Jack the Ripper and Godzilla the Monster and everybody knew it was Mrs German anyway so why don't we just get some stakes and catch her in the basement.

He punched at his typewriter, so hard his knuckles burned. There was a murderer out there, dammit, and no one was helping!

Another hour to stoke courage, and he grabbed his windbreaker and hurried to stand beside one of the highway's guardian elms. He was a hundred yards from the school, watching as the lights in each room died, as the faculty left in pairs and alone to vanish into an evening beginning too soon.

Five cigarettes. A handful of patrol cars that passed him, slowed, recognized him and moved on. The wind again, and the clouds, and the stars died before rising.

He tried to grin. Silliness is what it was. He understood that, and he approved. His early panic, his dreams, a combination of nonsense that produced further nonsense. But it was working, at least – he realized with a start not at all guilty that he hadn't thought of Jane in more than three days. Nevertheless, he was here, playing a country-boy Humphrey Bogart against a prickling at his nape that would not scratch away.

And just before seven he straightened and inched behind the tree. Mrs German, tall even at this distance, stepped around the corner of the school, walking slowly and holding a deep-blue shawl closed at her throat. She seemed to be checking the windows, the front door, searching the grass for items dropped by the students. She disappeared. Reappeared with purse in hand and made her way briskly through the playground and into the trees.

Stupid, Keith thought as he raced across the road; stupid, he repeated as he cut between the swings and found the narrow path between two cages of birch.

Light faded, slipping swiftly through twilight to full dark as the foliage closed like lacing clouds overhead. His footfalls were muffled, but the slap and scrape of twigs against his trousers had him holding his breath, brought a hand to his forehead to wipe away the perspiration. Road sounds died. The day's warmth hung in patches of humid mist to the branches, to the hollowed ground, to the linings of his lungs. He gulped to breathe. He pulled at his shirt, his belt. His socks felt wet. He scolded himself impatiently when he glanced up through a leafy gap and saw the darkmoon hanging.

Ten minutes, and he wondered if he'd already passed the spot where Danny had been found. Where Stan had been found.

Another ten minutes and he stopped. Listened. Shadowswift whispers of wind through an elm, the scurrying of something small to his right, the lumbering of something large to his left.

He moved on, his sense of direction skewed, the silliness buried beneath a blanket of sour regret.

And when time finally blurred and his watch was unreadable, the trees thinned, the underbrush cleared, and he was staring at the backs of several clapboard houses. A street beyond. Fences around the yards. He felt his jaw lowering, and he snapped it shut with a curse. Mopped his face with a sleeve, and saw the kitchen light in the house directly ahead switch on to reveal Mrs German at the window. She was holding a tea kettle close to her eyes, shaking it slowly.

A tea kettle. A goddamned copper tea kettle.

"Jesus," he whispered. "God . . . damn!" And he walked away with a gesture condemning the tract to hell, berating himself for almost believing she might be living in a coffin. "Idiot!" It sounded right. "Idiot!"

And all because he'd listened to the children.

He shivered, then, and slowed. It was cold. December had become dislodged and slipped down around him, tightening his cheeks and knifing through his chest. His nose began to run, his ears began to ache, and it took him several moments to hear the walking in the woods.

It was off to his left, deep in the black, at one point sounding furtive, at another perfectly calm. And as far as he knew he was on the only trail. He smothered a cough – God, it was cold! – and hurried on, left hand out in a wavering semaphore to keep the branches from his face, right hand clasping the wind-breaker's collar tight to his neck.

It kept pace, then fell slowly behind.

He tried to stare through the dark, and succeeded only in making the boles twist, the brush climb, the leaves reach out to ensnare him. He faced forward, searching for the highway's lights. Nearer, then; he was positive the sounds were nearer. He tried to whistle; his mouth was too dry. He tried reciting all the lines of memorized verse, but the first line that came was from Bryant's "Thanatopsis."

The cold deepened. Dry, ancient, crackling as he passed through it, snapping as his shoes slapped against the ground.

Deathcold, and black, and digging through his scalp like the claws of an angry cat.

The shrubbery gave way behind him; whatever it was had broken from the trees.

And despite the fact he knew he wouldn't die, that he was like all men immortal, that he was only a writer who lived just over the low rise ahead and beyond the old school . . . he ran. He jumped as if working from a starting gun and he ran, heedless now of the twigs and the branches, leaping whenever he thought he saw a root, swerving whenever he thought he saw a boulder.

He ran until he reached the playground, falling against one of the canted iron legs (cold; it was cold) supporting the swings, grasping it and gasping, sliding down to his knees as his gaze fixed on a car's headlights speeding west to east.

The school was dark, its white turned to shadow. Lights from the complex were trapped by the sky, a glow not quite white, not quite grey, that shimmered like a storm cloud uncertain of its power. He stared at it, shivering, until he heard the steps behind him. Then he broke from the swings and loped across the grass, slid down the slope and stumbled like a drunk until he reached his doorway.

Keys jumped and jangled while he cursed them; the doorknob was curiously slick in his hand.

One step inside, and something poked him in the back.

"You ever do that again," he said to Carl Andrews, who was on the stoop and laughing, "I don't care if I give away ten years and a hundred pounds, I'll break your goddamned neck."

It was fifteen minutes before he stopped shaking, before he felt warm again. By that time drinks had been poured and Andrews was in the recliner, while Keith, pacing through a narration loudly defensive and belligerently shamefaced, told him where he'd gone, though he couldn't explain exactly why.

"I just did, that's all," he said, finally allowing his legs to fold him to the floor. "It seemed like a good idea at the time." But he didn't tell him about the dark, about the cold.

"I believe it," Carl said. "That old broad's been around for damn ever. Easy to see why you'd think she – "

"I did not say she killed anybody," he snapped. "I just . . . hell, I don't know. I just did, and that's all there is to it." Thinking: first thing in the morning he was going to borrow Moira's car and take the boys around to German's house, to show them where she lived before he broke both their necks.

Carl emptied his glass and placed it on the floor beside him. "Let's talk about Stan."

"Why? We saw each other a few times, had a few drinks, and I mostly listened to his war stories, that's all."

Andrews seemed disappointed. "He never talked about school?"

Keith shook his head, then caught himself. "Well, hardly a word. If he'd had a bad day he'd bitch, but nothing more than that." He looked up. "Good Lord, Carl, you're not suggesting . . ." He laughed nervously. "No, I see you're not. I guess they aren't nasty enough."

Andrews squirmed slightly. "You didn't see Stan. And you didn't see the kid."

"Bad?"

"Worse. Thought for a while we had wild dogs. They were done like that. Not all over. Just in . . . pieces."

Keith stared at his hands, pondering. "Rabies maybe. Animals don't eat even though they want to. You might – "

"We did. All over the damned place."

"The paper sure keeps quiet about it."

"The paper gets read by tourists."

A pause while Keith pulled at the side of his neck. "So, what do you think?"

"If I knew I'd be out there."

They talked a few minutes more, saying little, getting nowhere. Then Andrews thanked him for the drink and left, leaving Keith on the floor to decide finally that he had to see the school's basement. He wasn't sure why, but he knew if he didn't he wouldn't sleep for days.

The following morning he broached Bonachek, arming himself with an article premise he'd thought up on the way over. The principal refused politely.

"But those records," Keith protested gently. "I mean, they'd be invaluable."

"I understand," the man said, "but I'm afraid my hands are tied. It's school board property. You'll have to fill out a request, and they meet in two weeks."

Keith shrugged and left, stood in the corridor for a moment fuming over bureaucrats even in country schools, then checked for watchers before hurrying toward the back. Steps led down to the rear double doors. A sharp right, and another staircase leading to a thick-planked door bolted and padlocked. And though he knew he was no expert, he also knew by looking that neither bolt nor padlock was stiff from disuse.

Somebody, he thought, is lying through his teeth, and when he said as much to Jane when he stopped her before lunch, she turned to him, scowled, and told him to mind his own business.

"You're crazy," she said, and he had to trot up to keep up as she hastened outside. "There's nothing down there but dust."

"Then what's the harm?" he said softly, taking hold of her arm. "Come on, Jane. You know where Checkie keeps the keys. Show a little leg or something. I'll wait for your call after school." He kissed her cheek before she could refuse, almost ran home, and almost collided with Moira, who was standing by his door. Her blouse was unbuttoned midway down her chest, her sunglasses off, and her jeans snugly inviting. Moira, whose husband he hadn't seen in over two years. A shadow behind the window, a just-closed door. Whenever he went over for lunch or dinner the man was gone on a trip, and small wonder the boys had taken him for an uncle.

Moira. Jane. How much of a lecher are you, he wondered as he pushed in the door, though remained outside.

"The kids again, right?" he said.

She shook her head. "It's Jane. I'm worried about her."

"No kidding?"

A finger touched his hand, cool and demanding. Standing with her was like lying in shade, and it didn't take him long to make up his mind her husband was a fool, and fools deserve fooling.

"Have you seen her today?"

"Can you keep a secret?" And before she could answer he told her about the keys, Mrs German, and the scare he'd given himself. When he was done, she shook her head and looked pointedly up the staircase. "You're crazy," she told him. "No wonder the boys love you."

Not like. Love.

He swallowed. "I . . ." A hand to her shoulder. "I've got some work, Moira."

"That's all right," she said brightly. "I just wanted to invite you to dinner."

"Deal. And afterward I'll tell you all about my adventures."

She leaned into him suddenly, kissed him lightly on the chin. "It's Jane's loss," she whispered, and was gone.

He had no idea how long he'd stood there, gaping at the image she'd left in her wake, but the next thing he knew Peter and Philip were standing there, grinning. "He's a Greek god," Peter said solemnly to his brother.

"Nope, he's one of those dinosaur things we saw in the city. All stuffed and stuff."

Keith roused himself with a mock scowl. "Beat it, punks, or I won't give you dinner."

"We don't care," Peter said. "We're going to grandma's."

Keith almost contradicted him, but the telephone was ringing. He waved and ran up, snatched at the receiver on the fifth harsh summons. It was Carl, demanding to know where the hell Jane was. Keith explained what he knew – which wasn't much – and Carl complained she hadn't answered any of his messages, complained a moment longer before suddenly hanging up.

So what am I, Keith thought sourly, your girl friend's keeper?

But the call bothered him. It wasn't like Jane to ignore messages; nor, he remembered as he aimed a finger toward the dial, does she like personal calls at school.

He dropped into his chair and stared at the telephone, willing it to ring. Willing, squirming, rising once to fetch a beer and returning at a run.

Moira called at six, and he told her he'd be late.

Twice he called the school, and received no response.

At seven Carl called back, worried and angry and warning him not to go off on one of his half-assed explorations.

Seven-thirty, and he stood. Wavered. Then he took a look at the

sky and grabbed his raincoat from the closet, a flashlight from the
desk drawer, and whispered an apology to Moira before he ran
outside.

All he could think of was Mrs German, and the cold.

The air was a curious shade of dim grey-green, and the leaves were
turning belly up to the keening damp wind. Mutters of thunder. No
traffic at all.

By the time he reached the school he was gasping for breath,
and cursing the cigarettes he could feel in his pocket. The clouds
were shifting rapidly, the steeple that once housed the morning bell
seeming to topple when he approached the front steps. He glanced
to either side, took the six steps two at a time and yanked at the door.
It rattled but didn't give. He tried again, fighting panic, then swung
off the porch and walked quickly around the side. All the shades had
been drawn halfway, eyelids drowsing, but the sills were too high for
him to see if the windows were unlocked.

He pulled the flashlight from his coat pocket and tapped it
impatiently against a palm.

It darkened.

There was lightning.

He bunched his shoulders in frustration and turned a circle against
the wind. She must have changed her mind, he decided, and had
finally gone to Carl's. Or gone for a drive. Or gone through the
woods to Mrs German's for a cup of her damned tea. The wind
gusted, and he ducked, stopped when he saw the playground in a
flash of blue-white.

Slides. Swings. A sandbox. An iron horse.

He held his breath and began to walk slowly over the wet
trampled grass.

Swings.

At one end there was a bench with a plank floor, two seats facing
each other. Jane was sitting with her back to the school, her legs too
long, her feet touching the ground. He didn't call out, and he didn't
break into a run. He vaguely heard the rear doors slamming open
with the wind, vaguely heard the rain pattering on his shoulders.

Blue-white again, and he saw without blinking the red gleaming
in her hair.

He stopped directly behind her, reached out a hand and dropped
it as if he'd been burned. The blood had trailed down the back of
the seat and had gathered blackly on the ground. He swallowed. He
whispered her name. He took a step to one side, and spun down to
his knees.

Her face. It was gone.

The rain, then, and the lightning, and the darkmoon above the storm, and he rocked back to his heels and screamed at the thunder. Staggered to his feet and lurched toward the school. The door. He remembered the door, saw it now waiting through sheets of cold water. There was no time to think, no time for grand designs; he stumbled over the threshold and down the steps to the basement. Then he looked to his hands; the flashlight was gone. A slap to his sides and the feel of a matchbox crammed into his pocket.

A tearing shriek of lightning, and he saw his shadow slip through the open basement door.

He walked quickly, then, and down four more steps, pulled out a match and struck it on the railing, a quick sound that made him wince, the simultaneous hiss of burning sulphur that flared to lighten the dark and narrow his eyes. But there was nothing else. No breathing. No footfalls. No creaks of rotting planks or sighs of storm wind sneaking down behind him; only the light that wavered a curious blue-yellow above his pinched fingers.

He waited for a moment, then moved away from the stairs.

The basement was large, a disturbingly silent cave that extended beneath the entire central core of the school building above. On the left, along a rough-stone wall mottled by dampness, were rows of crates that seemed as if they would disintegrate at a touch; on the right, the same. Along the uneven stone flooring were aisles created by warped shelving atop crumbling brick, four tiers of them, with more cartons, mildewed books, papers wrapped with string or faded yarn – all of it nibbled at, eaten, littered with droppings like tiny black pebbles.

Beams hung low from the sagging stone ceiling, and there were no windows. There was only the silence and the mausoleum cold.

He hissed suddenly as the flame scorched his fingers, dropped the match and fumbled with a heel to crush it. He lit another quickly, and wished he hadn't lost the flashlight. But Jane . . . Jane . . . he felt the bile rising and swallowed hard and often.

When he felt dizziness slip by him, then, he stepped into the center aisle, shivering now with a cold that hadn't come with the storm. Shadows writhing, wind soughing, the weight of the building blackly descending. Toward the front he shuffled, cursing the children and all their foolish talk about vampires, cursing the stories about the travelers and the darkmoon.

At aisle's end he stopped, and waited.

For the first time since entering he knew he wasn't alone.

And for the first time since it started he knew who was with him.

Overhead and behind him a bare lightbulb flickered, painting his image darkly against the sweating blocks of stone. He would not move. He would not give his company the satisfaction of his fear. Instead, with movement so slow he wanted to scream, he slipped his hands into his pockets and bunched them to fists.

Remembered a time, too much time ago, when his father had brought him out at twilight onto a lake's shore and they'd waited for the bats to come out for their feeding. "Quietly now," the old man had told him. "Quietly now, you don't want him to hear."

Quietly now.

Don't let him hear you.

He turned to face the staircase, and the figure waiting by the railing. He glanced up at the ceiling. "Has . . . anyone guessed?"

"Danny," a voice said, made sexless by thunder and by the dead time in the basement. "Stan broke in. A few others over the years."

"Those people from New York?"

"One gets hungry, you know. I can't do anything about that."

"I don't believe it."

"You don't believe I get hungry, or you don't believe what I am."

"I don't believe in vampires, no matter what the children say."

A laugh slipped through the darkness. "To them everything monstrous is a vampire. Surely you can forgive them that."

I'm afraid, he thought; I'm afraid and I can't run. But he knew it wasn't the fear that held him; it was worse, much worse – he wanted to know. There was a good chance of his dying, but he wanted to know.

"Werewolf," he said then. "Or are you a ghoul?"

A pause, more a hesitation, and he closed his eyes briefly, grunting silently as he fought against the loosening of his bowels.

The voice, then, and the cold.

"I'm too old to remember exactly how it began. But it did. One moment I was normal, the next . . ." An invisible shrug. "And living out here has made it very easy. Here, and places like here, all over the country. You move on when you're suspected, before someone can kill you. A nibble here" – a giggle – "a nibble there. It all adds up, Keith. It all adds up."

"You bitch! You killed Jane."

The cold was on the outside, but there was a heated rage working through the marrow, through the blood. His head was spinning, his eyes fighting a squint.

"You didn't have to, you know, Moira. You could've let her live.

But then, you've known her for so long she must have suspected, must have wondered what wonder drugs you were taking."

A noise. Rumbling, snarling, cut off as if bitten. The figure shifted, and he shaded his eyes, glancing from side to side as he tried to make her out, tried to find something he could throw while escaping. She wouldn't follow; she couldn't. She knew he'd called Carl, he'd be here soon to hunt for his lover. All he had to do was keep talking, and make his way to the stairs. The door was still open, and he could hear the rain on the landing.

"How did you manage the children?" he said, moving an inch at a time back up the aisle.

"What children?" the voice said, and he stopped when she moved directly under the bulb.

Her face was moon pale, her lips dark and gleaming, her teeth when she smiled coated with saliva.

The cold. He could feel the cold now, could hear the yellowed papers rustling as they crumpled, could hear the orange crates creaking as they buckled.

The cold in his apartment.

He put a hand to his forehead, trying to think. It was important he keep on using his mind, to prevent its collapse in the face of her smiling.

Cold. A signal, perhaps, that portends her feeding, and the longer she's denied it, the colder she gets.

Moira touched a long finger to her chin. "The children," she said as though the thought amused her. "No, Keith, we're just one tiny family, kindred spirits if you will. It doesn't matter where we came from; we just came, that's all. Back there in the hills, and we decided to stick together. Strength in numbers, my love."

He heard the boys shifting quietly behind him.

Danny, Stan, Jane: *We're going to grandma's for dinner tonight.*

He bolted. Whatever he believed, whatever madness he was facing, it shrieked through his enforced calm and sent him charging toward the doorway. Moira yelled when he shoved her aside, clawed at his arm, and he was halfway to the door when the boys each snared a leg. He kicked frantically, punched wildly, slipped to the floor and was stunned when his skull cracked against the bottom step.

"No," he whispered. "No, please, Moira."

Philip sat on his stomach, Peter on his thighs. Moira loomed behind them, the light from the ceiling turning her face black and giving her hair an umbra of stark white.

"You don't know what it's like," she said then, reaching between the boys and coldly stroking his cheek. "To have to fake a husband.

A man who's never home. Leaving yourself open to every damned horny bastard who comes to your door, and you're not even hungry."

His mind faded from a whimpering to a daze; there was only the cold, and the sound of her voice.

"I've had enough," she said wearily. "I've had quite enough."

Maneuvered, he thought; all this time I've been maneuvered.

He swallowed. He sobbed once.

"Hey, don't worry," Peter told him. So old. So old.

Moira nodded. "You're not going to die, love. At least not for long."

He closed his eyes, opened them. Wide, and staring.

"Yes, dear, Jane is our meal. Little Jane is our meal. We brought you down here because I'm tired of all the deceptions. And besides, the boys need a father they can point to with pride."

Peter nodded quickly, his eyes bright and eager.

"Just a little pain," Moira whispered, dead wind over velvet. "Don't worry, just a little pain, a little dying. Then I'll say the words, the incantation, and you'll be just as good as new."

Philip leaned closer, his breath fetid and iced. "And then I can call you daddy. Boy, won't that be great?"

Basil Copper

The Grey House

Basil Copper has been called "one of the last of the great traditionalists of English fiction" by Colin Wilson and "Britain's leading purveyor of the macabre" by Peter Haining. The author has been busy recently with the publication of his horror novel The Black Death *in a handsome hardcover edition from Fedogan & Bremer, who have also issued his Sherlock Holmes pastiches,* The Exploits of Solar Pons, *with a limited commemorative pipe to coincide with Copper's special guest of honour appearance at the 1993 World Fantasy Convention.*

His major new novella, "Wish You Were Here", appeared in Richard Dalby's anthology Horror for Christmas, *and he has written the introductions for the Chivers Press reprints of the Crime Writers' Association "Black Dagger" novels. The Norwegian Broadcasting Corporation recently transmitted the BBC Radio play "Invitation to the Vaults", based on his story "The Recompensing of Albano Pizar"; his hard-boiled Mike Faraday thrillers continue to sell to Australia, and he recently had his work translated in Finland for the first time.*

As the author explains, the genesis for the story which follows "was in an ancient house in France my mother-in-law purchased when it was a dilapidated ruin. It had a terrace which looked down on a romantic and deserted park belonging to a large house nearby, with the river Armançon winding past a rustic summerhouse. The building, with massive beams and walls about two feet thick, dated from the fifteenth century and has now been restored to a comfortable house with every modern convenience."

Perhaps "The Grey House" can be read as a dark flip-side of the recent *bestseller* A Year in Provence . . .

I

To ANGELE, STANDING in the sunlight of a late summer afternoon, The Grey House, as they came to call it, had an air of chill desolation that was at variance with the brightness and warmth of the day. It was uninhabited and had evidently been so for many years. But Philip was delighted with the place; he clapped his hands like a child of five and then strolled around, his arms folded, lost in silent admiration. He needs must have it and wouldn't rest until he had rooted out the local agent and made an offer for the house.

Philip, her husband, was a writer; apart from a series of successful detective stories which brought him the larger part of his income, he was the author of a number of striking tales of mystery and the macabre. The Grey House would give him inspiration, he chuckled: Angele, stifling her doubts, didn't like to dampen her husband's enthusiasm and trailed round behind him and the estate agent with growing dislike.

They had spotted the place after a long day's drive in the older parts of Burgundy. Then in early afternoon, they had stopped for a late lunch in the small medieval city which nestled among the blue haze of the surrounding mountains. The view was enchanting and after lunch they spent a pleasant hour on the ramparts, tracing out the path of a small river which wound its way foaming between great boulders and woods of dark pines.

It was Philip who first sighted The Grey House. It was down a narrow lane and the path to it was long choked with nettles. It was the last house, separated from its neighbours by several hundreds of yards of rough cartway and trees, overgrown shrubbery and bushes. It was unquestionably a ruin. The place looked something like a barn or stable.

It was largely constructed of great blocks of grey stone, which decided them on its name, with one round-capped turret hanging at an insane angle over the big front door, large as a church. There was a round tower at one side, immensely old and covered in lichen. The roof, of red crab tiles, sagged ominously and would obviously need a lot of repairs.

The big old wooden door was locked but Philip led the way with

enthusiasm, cutting a swathe through breast-high nettles for his
wife. They followed the great frowning wall down the lane until
the property obviously came to an end. The rest of the lane was
an impenetrable mass of brambles. But Philip had seen enough.
Through the trees below the bluff he could see the rusted iron
railings of a balcony and there were even some outbuildings and
what looked like an old water mill.

"We could get this place for a song," he told his wife gleefully.
"It would want a lot of doing up of course, but the terrace would
be ideal for my writing and what a view!"

Against such enthusiasm Angele could find no valid argument so
half an hour later found them back in the city square, at the office
of M. Gasion, the principal of the main firm of estate agents in
the area.

M. Gasion, a short broad-shouldered man of cheerful aspect and
obviously addicted to the grape was shattered at the prospect of such
a sale. The property had been on his books for more than forty years,
over twenty years before he acquired the firm. Therefore, he was a
little hazy about the antecedents of the estate. Yes, it would need a
lot of doing up, he agreed; he did not think monsieur need worry
about the price.

It would not be heavy and as they would see, though it needed a
great deal of renovation, it had possibilities, distinct possibilities. He
positively purred with enthusiasm and Angele could not help smiling
to herself. A purchaser like Philip would hardly happen more than
once in a lifetime; no wonder M. Gasion was pleased.

It was absurdly cheap, she had to agree. The asking price was
£300, which included the main building and tower, the terrace,
out-buildings and mill house, together with a short strip of orchard
below the bluff on which the terrace was set. Nothing would do but
that Philip must conclude the deal then and there. This called for
a great deal of bustle and the notaire was sent for, while Angele,
Philip and the agent went on a tour of the building. There was
further delay while the key was hunted up but at last the small
procession set off.

The big door gave back with a creak after M. Gasion's repeated
applications and the first ray of sunshine for something like forty
years found difficulty in penetrating the interior. The unusual
activity round the old building had not passed notice among the
local people who lived higher up the lane and Angele had seen the
curious glances they cast towards her, though Philip, as usual, was
too absorbed in talk with the agent to notice anything.

Angele glanced over her shoulder as they went in the main door and was not surprised to see a small knot of gawping householders standing at the last bend in the lane in front of the house. Surprisingly, the house was wired for electricity but the main switchboard inside the door, fixed by great bolts directly into the ancient stone, was bare except for fragments of rusted wire and fittings covered with verdigris. The electricity had been cut off in the twenties, when the last tenants left, explained M. Gasion.

He carried a powerful electric lantern, despite the brightness of the afternoon. The house had formerly belonged to the de Menevals, the great landed proprietors who had now died out. They had owned a chateau which formerly stood in a vast park on the mountain opposite. The building had burned down in a great fire and explosion over a hundred years earlier and now only the stones remained. The last de Meneval, Gaston, had died a violent death, said M. Gasion with relish. He was apparently a great one for the ladies and had kept The Grey House for entertaining his girl friends.

"Une maison d'assignation," he explained to Philip with a smile, man to man. Philip returned the smile with a grin and the trio went into the house. Angele could not repress a shudder at the interior and wondered what deeds the old house had seen. She and Philip had visited the ruins of the old chateau earlier the same afternoon; it was one of the sights of the district. The park was now kept as a public pleasaunce, and the guide had told the stories of blood and violence with distinct enthusiasm.

But one did not need even that to picture dark scenes of lust centuries before, as they gazed at the ruined and distorted remains of the house, which even now bore traces of charring on ancient beams and on the undersides of blackened stones. She was disquieted to hear that The Grey House had belonged to the de Menevals too, and her own French ancestry – her mother had come from these very parts – with its heightened sensibilities, rang a little bell somewhere back in her brain.

When the door swung open even the agent was not prepared for the long undisturbed foetor which met them; it was so strong that it seemed almost to darken the sunlight and they were forced to open the main door and remain outside for a few minutes before they could enter.

"Faugh!" said M. Gasion, with unrestrained disgust, but even this did not seem to dampen Philip's ardour.

"Loads of atmosphere, eh?" he said, turning to Angele with a smile. After a minute they descended some broad stone steps. The smell was still strong but not so offensive and Angele had to admit that it was probably due to vegetable decay. To her surprise, the light of the agent's torch, supplemented by small windows high up, disclosed a vast stone hall. There was a fireplace to one side in which an ox could have been roasted and the remains of an old gallery which had collapsed with age and woodworm.

But the floor was covered with an indescribable medley of old rubbish. It was impossible to do more than look hurriedly around and be careful where one trod. Many of the massive roof beams would need replacing and Philip's face became more thoughtful as the tour continued. The house would evidently need a great deal more renovation than he had bargained for. However, he brightened as they went through into the other rooms. The stones of the house were sound and would merely need replastering and painting. There were two more large reception rooms, though nothing on the scale of the old hall, which was partly subterranean; another room was used as a kitchen.

On the top floor, under vast, sagging roof beams, through which the sky could be seen, was another huge room over the Great Hall below. This could be partitioned and would make a corridor with bathroom, and three large bedrooms, said Philip. Or he could make a study and leave one spare bedroom for guests. The open mass of the tower spread out from one end room of this large upper storey and Philip could find no place for that at the moment, in his ready-made scheme of things.

They had saved the best for last; off the kitchen, whose door was finally forced with screaming protest, they came upon the glory of The Grey House. It was nothing more or less than a large tiled terrace, but it gave the place a cachet that finally clinched the deal in Philip's mind, weighing the cost, as he was, against the utility and suitability of the house for his writing purposes.

The rusty iron railings which enclosed the terrace, had evidently been of great elegance, and would no doubt be so again; Philip was already confiding to M. Gasion that he would have them painted pale blue. He could have his writing table *comme ça* and they could eat dinner under electric light at night *sur le balcon*. Even the agent was momentarily impressed by his enthusiasm.

For the view was magnificent; that could not be gainsaid. Below the balcony, the terrain dropped sheer for forty feet or so over a stone outcrop, to the small strip of orchard which was part of the purchase. A thick belt of leafy trees blotted out the immediate view, but above them were wooded hills and valleys, with the stream trickling between until the eye was arrested by the mountain opposite surmounted by the ruins of the old chateau. Angele was surprised to see how the white of the stones stood out against the dark blue haze, even at that distance. Just below and to the left was the small stone building of the old water mill, through which the stream meandered beyond the orchard.

When they tore themselves away from the unearthly beauties of that sylvan view, dusk was already falling and the tinkle of the water in the mill house had assumed a melancholy that it had lacked in the sunlight of the earlier afternoon. A thin mist was already rising above the belt of dark trees which abutted the orchard. Angele pointed this out to Philip as perhaps being undesirable, unhealthy.

"Oh, no," said Philip with a short laugh. "Bound to get a mist with water at this time of the year, especially after the heat of the day. We're too high up for it to affect us in any case." But nevertheless, even as he spoke, the mist, white and clammy, almost like thick smoke, drifted up over the trees and already the farthest trees were wavering in its tendrils.

No more was said; the party went back indoors, led by M. Gasion's enormous torch and once outside, the door was firmly locked and secured by double padlocks. The trio were silent on the way back to the town and after a little reflection, M. Gasion spoke to Angele. Philip had gone to get something from the car and they were alone for a moment in the office.

"You do not like the house, madame?"

Angele was non-committal. She did not want to spoil Philip's evident delight in the property, but at the same time she had many reservations of her own about the dark, silent grey pile above the water mill, which sounded so eerily in the dusk. Instead, she stammered some words about the property being so derelict and the enormous expense she was afraid her husband would be put to.

The agent's face cleared as though it had been sponged. If that was all that was worrying madame, he was prepared to lower the price.

Quite frankly, he had been rather taken aback by the degree of decay; he would be quite happy to take the equivalent of £250 to effect a quick sale. Philip had just returned from the car at this moment and was delighted with the news; so Angele had unwittingly been the means of sealing the bargain.

The notaire also; a lean, vulpine man named Morceau had just arrived, cross at being disturbed at his favourite cafe. Introductions were made, M. Gasion produced a bottle and some glasses and over much agreeable smacking of lips and handing round of delectable little biscuits, the details of the sale were worked out.

An hour later Philip and Angele left the office, potential owners of The Grey House. They were to stay at a hotel in the city for a few days until the legal niceties had been gone into; that would take time, but there was nothing to stop monsieur from having the property surveyed or putting work in hand, for the remainder of the proceedings were a formality. So Philip signed a paper, handed over a cheque, wired his literary agent in London that he was staying on and would write, and worked himself into an agreeable enthusiasm over the possibilities of The Grey House.

It was decided between him and Angele that they would return to London for a couple of weeks, to wind up their immediate affairs and then return to Burgundy for the autumn. They would occupy themselves during that time by working on the house, assisted by local labour and then decide, with the assistance of a local architect, just what major repairs and alterations would be necessary. They would go back to London in November and keep in touch with the work through the architect. Then they intended to return to The Grey House in the spring to supervise the final stages and arrange for a house-warming.

By next summer Philip hoped they would be fully installed for a six-month season of prolific and profitable writing for him and a period of pleasure and entertaining for her. He was determined that they would make the old house a show place, a necessary pilgrimage for their London friends and all that night, long after the rest of the hotel was asleep he kept Angele awake with plans and possibilities. Angele had her reservations but kept her own counsel. She felt that she might be mistaken in her intuitions and after all, carpenters and builders could make a magnificent job of the old house. She would wait and see what transpired.

II

A month later The Grey House was already under siege. Philip had engaged a local builder and he, two assistants and Philip and Angele in their oldest clothes, were in a frenzy of demolition and renovation. Philip had decided that they would tackle the Great Hall first. It was mainly of stone and once they had got rid of the loathsome accumulation which littered the floor, they would rid the house of that putrescent smell. But first there was one setback.

Pierre, the builder they had engaged, was a stolid, good-looking man, broad as a barrel, in his early fifties; as was the custom he worked with his hands with his assistants, taking his share of the heavy work as well as directing operations. He was surprised, as were all the local people that The Grey House was to be re-opened and lived in after all this time, but he was quite glad of the job.

But the first afternoon, there was a short consultation among his two workmen and they drew the builder to one side. Philip, who had been down the lane, returned at that moment and Pierre asked to speak to him. He seemed embarrassed and eventually said that nothing could be done until the electric light was in operation; his point was that the loathsome conditions underfoot in the Great Hall made good lighting essential.

This was understandable enough but Angele thought she could discern odd expressions in the eyes of the two workmen. Despite herself, she was convinced that they had other reasons for their request. Fortunately, a modern water supply was already laid on to the house, and Philip had merely to request the local electricity company to restore the current. Like many English people he was naive about local conditions and Angele had laughingly assured him that it would take a month or more before anything would be done about it.

Philip told the assembled workmen that the current would be turned on that afternoon. There was a general air of disbelief but Philip said he had an appointment with the electricity people at two o'clock and sat down upon an upturned box in front of the house to wait. Pierre and his workmen chatted among themselves. Philip was the only person present to believe the statement.

When half-past three came with not a stroke of work done it became obvious even to Philip that the electricity would not be connected. He jumped up angrily and drove off in his car. He was unable to achieve any satisfaction and found the company office locked; no doubt the official in charge was in one of the local cafes.

Incensed at this lack of efficiency Philip phoned M. Gasion, who presently came down to the house himself. He assured Philip that he had sorted out the misunderstandings and that the workmen would be at The Grey House without fail the following day. Mollified, Philip announced that they could still get some work done while daylight lasted. It was not half past four, so, lighting a couple of lanterns the party of five – M. Gasion having returned to his office – set off through the gloomy reception rooms to the terrace. Here, restored by the bright sunlight and the atmosphere of open countryside, the workmen unloaded their tools and set about clearing the area, amid jokes and laughter.

The whole terrace seemed to be covered with lichen and here and there fungoid growths; two of the workmen started scraping this off to reveal the intricately patterned tiles beneath, while Pierre, Philip and Angele busied themselves with clearing the area of brushwood, fallen branches and other debris which had accumulated over the years. This they threw off the balcony into the orchard below; it made loud crashing noises in the brittle branches of dead trees and for some reason gave Angele considerable uneasiness.

She looked sharply down to the water mill and the dark trees at the orchard end, but nothing moved and she attributed her feelings to nerves and the thin tinkle of falling water. In an hour, good progress had been made and when repeated applications with buckets of water had been carried out to the considerable area of tiling cleared by the workmen, it was seen that the whole terrace was one of considerable elegance and beauty.

Philip had recovered his good humour when he saw what an excellent start it was and how pleasantly and efficiently the workmen had carried out their task.

It was evident that with this team the house would be in good hands and Philip was obviously in a great hurry to complete the preliminaries and get to grips with the major problems. He spoke with Pierre of the work to be done to the main roof and the sagging turret; this would have to be a priority and needed to be started well before the winter. Pierre told him that work on this would commence within a fortnight, once working arrangements had been achieved inside.

It was in this atmosphere of mutual satisfaction that the day's work ended. Dusk was falling and the lanterns had been carried on to the terrace to complete the clearing of the tiles. Another of the workmen was already chipping rust from the great sweep of the balcony. It made an ugly sound in the dusk and was re-echoed from the dark woods below. As they finished and carried the tools back into the house for the night, there was a faint rustling in the underbrush at the back of the house down by the water mill. Angele was the only one to hear it; she strained her eyes down to the orchard below and thought she could see the faintest shadow slip into the dark shade of the old trees at the end of the orchard.

Probably a cat. There were lots of them haunting the lanes down near The Grey House. Big, grey brutes they were, and sometimes she heard them howling sadly in the dusk when she and Philip went out. The big door of the house shrieked, as though annoyed at the intrusion into the long silence of forty years, when they left. Outside, on the small terrace in front of The Grey House, where Philip intended to lay tiles and build a small garage later, the employer and the employed congratulated one another and there was much shaking of hands.

Then Philip insisted on buying everyone a drink at the first cafe they came across. All parted with mutual expressions of goodwill and it was quite dark when Philip and Angele had got back to their hotel. He was resolved to make a good start the next day and had asked the electricity people to come in at nine o'clock. The workmen would arrive at twelve and with luck and sufficient illumination they could make a good start on clearing the Great Hall.

The following morning the electricity employees surprisingly arrived almost at the specified hour; The Grey House was opened again and around midday a jubilant Philip was allowed to pull the master switch and the Great Hall was flooded with light. Much of the house would need re-wiring and Philip had many special schemes for heating and outdoor floodlighting, but that would come later.

For the moment, naked bulbs and trailing lengths of flex were draped all over the house in order to give the workmen good light to work by. Philip hoped also to have two great picture windows opened up in the stonework of the Great Hall to let light into the building during daytime.

This, and a number of other anomalies puzzled him and he resolved to look up the history of the de Menevals in the great historical library in the City Museum, when time would afford. That opportunity did not arise until the next year; in the meantime Philip and his wife, with their team of workmen, followed by the interest of M. Gasion, M. Morceau and later, the architect, went at the work of restoration with enthusiasm.

But strangely, the progress of the first day wasn't repeated. One of the workmen went sick the second afternoon and, assuredly, the stench from the floor of the Great Hall was such as to turn a strong stomach; Philip got round that with buckets of hot water and disinfectant and after a while they cleared some of the miasma which seemed to hang around the old foundations.

Lorry load after lorry load of malodorous rubbish left for the city tip and even the sick workman, who returned to duty the next day, had to admit there had been a great improvement. But there was something which made Angele vaguely uneasy, though Philip seemed as blind to the atmosphere of the place as ever. He was puzzled at the inordinate number of lights and flex positions the workmen were obliged to insist on, especially when working among the noisome rafters and complained that the cost of electricity and bulbs would soon gross the total cost of the house if things went on that way.

Yet Angele understood perfectly the feelings of the workmen and marvelled again at the insensitivity of her husband to the atmosphere; especially as his name as an author had been largely made through the description of just such situations. About a week after the renovation of the house had begun the workmen were still clearing the upper storey and Pierre expected an early start to the roof repairs; Philip had been delighted with some unusual finds among the debris of centuries. A curiously marked ring, evidently belonging to a man of rank; a sword hilt, a tankard with a strange inscription in the Latin tongue and some porcelain jars and containers for which none of them could assign any known use.

Philip took them back to his hotel for cleaning and said he would use them for decorating the house when restoration was complete. One afternoon one of the workmen came to Philip with a bizarre object he had found in one of the upper rooms. It was a long instrument with a spike of very old metal on one end of it; the other end was a sort of whip or switch. The thongs were made of wire, stained with the rust of centuries.

A learned Abbé from the City University, with whom Philip had become great friends, was visiting The Grey House on the afternoon in question. Monsignor Joffroy turned quite pale, Angele noticed.

"May I see?" he asked, taking the whip from Philip with unseemly haste. He drew him on to one side. The good Abbé looked worried.

"I do not wish to alarm you, my friend, but this is an unclean thing," he said, almost fiercely.

"See," He pointed out an inscribed tablet on the shaft of the instrument. "These are the arms of the de Menevals. We have a locked room of the Musée d'Antiquités at the University, devoted to such relics of the sadistic de Menevals. If you would permit me, I will see it is deposited for safe keeping. It is not fit that such mementoes should be allowed in the outside world."

He crossed himself and Angele could not repress a shudder. Though inclined to be amused, Philip could not but be impressed by the earnestness and deadly seriousness of Monsignor Joffroy's manner and he readily assented to his friend's request.

"I should like to hear something of the history of the de Menevals from you, some time," he said. "It would make good material for some of my books."

The Abbé laid his hand on Philip's arm and looked steadily into his eyes.

"Believe me, my friend, such things are not for books – or rather for books of your sort. Your essays in the macabre, admirable and successful as they are, are children's nursery tales compared with the things that went on in the chateau above – now no more, praise be to God."

A few minutes later the Monsignor excused himself, made his

farewells to Angele and returned to the university; he left behind him a somewhat thoughtful Philip and a thoroughly disturbed Angele. Sensibly, Philip said nothing to Pierre and the workmen and to M. Gasion, whom he met for an occasional glass of cassis at the latter's home, he was guarded; he made no comment on the curious whip, but discussed some of the other finds which the workmen had made. He did learn one thing about the de Menevals from the inscription on the tankard, but of this he said nothing, even to Angele.

She herself had one more unusual experience on the afternoon of the same day as Monsignor Joffroy's visit. She was alone on the terrace at dusk; she was no longer afraid of the low tinkling of water, to which she had become accustomed and even the mist did not affect her with uneasiness. She was trimming branches of an old tree which overhung the balcony.

This was now almost complete, wanting only a few final touches and, with an electric light above the glazed double doors, was taking on an unaccustomed elegance. She had gone down to Philip to ask him about something and when she came back the last glow of the fading sun was sinking behind the mountain. She was overcome by the melancholy of the scene and had remained seated while her gaze played over the terrain spread out so enticingly before her. It was while she was so occupied that she felt rather than saw a faint, dark shadow steal out from one orchard tree and disappear behind another.

Why she did the next thing she was not quite sure; but on some obscure impulse she suddenly stooped, picked up a large bundle of chopped branches from the tree, stepped noiselessly to the edge of the balcony and hurled the mass of wood and foliage through the air into the orchard below. The bundle fell where she had aimed, quite by chance, and with a sharp, almost frightening crash into the tree beneath which the shape had melted.

More branches fell to the ground and from the midst of the splintered wood something dark and long launched itself like a streak through the orchard; the creature poised and jumped up on to the edge of an outbuilding of the water mill. As far as she could judge, Angele saw a huge, grey cat. It had enormous yellow eyes that flickered with anger in the dusk. It looked back over its shoulder at her reproachfully and then disappeared into the bushes.

A moment later she heard a stealthy swish as it vanished and was evidently making its way through the dark trees at the back of the orchard. More startled than alarmed she left the terrace rather hurriedly for the welcome shelter of the house, which now blazed with lights from every room.

The next day Monsignor Joffroy was dining with them on the terrace of their hotel and Angele mentioned the cat. It was the first time she had spoken of it. Philip seemed only mildly interested but the effect on the Abbé was electric. His hand twitched and his glass of cognac soaked the table cloth. There was a flurry of apologies and in the midst of mopping up, Angele felt the Abbé's eyes fixed on her.

"There is no such animal, Madame," he said with terrible emphasis.

"Oh, come now, Monsignor," Philip laughed good-naturedly. "There's nothing so remarkable about that. There are dozens of cats around the lanes leading to The Grey House. I've seen 'em myself."

The Abbé continued to look at the girl. "Nevertheless, I must insist, there is no such animal. A trick of the light . . ."

Angele did not press the point and a moment or two later the conversation passed on to other topics. But she felt the Abbé's eyes on her from time to time during the evening, and she read concern in their friend's eyes.

The house was making excellent progress. As the autumn colours deepened and the melancholy around The Grey House gradually gave way to orderliness and a more modern atmosphere, Angele's unease subsided. The couple had arranged to leave for England in November as planned and would return in April, when the main architectural changes would be made and Philip would be on hand to supervise and give advice. They were due to depart on the following Tuesday, and in the meantime wandered about the house, idly watching the workmen and planning even more grandiose effects for the spring.

The architect they had finally engaged, Roget Frey, was thoroughly in accord with Philip's ideas and he had been enthusiastic about the designs the gifted young man had produced. Philip knew he could trust him to realize the effect he wanted. The house was to be a blend of ancient and modern, with every comfort, yet the medieval atmosphere was to be retained, particularly in the Great Hall and in the rooms above it.

The roof was more than half finished and two great picture windows had been punched into the ancient stonework high up in the eastern wall of the Great Hall, more than thirty feet above the fireplace.

Philip had ideas about these windows and he didn't want to reveal his special plans to Angele or the workmen until their return; Roget had worked out a fine design for his *pièce de resistance* and he was convinced his house would be a showplace for his friends if the final result was only half as spectacular as his designs.

The work to be done in the winter would be long and arduous and Philip was glad they would be in the comfort of their London flat; there was no heating in The Grey House as yet and the wind and rain on that exposed ledge would find them totally unprepared. Pierre had promised that all would be up to schedule by spring, and in the warmer weather he and Angele could work out the elegant details, the central heating and style of radiators, the furnishings the curtains and the hundred and one other things that would make The Grey House a masterful blend of old and new.

In the meantime Pierre and his men were to finish the roof; prepare and glaze new windows; install the central heating plant; build a garage and terrace in front of the house; scrape and plaster the interior walls and line the Great Hall with oak panelling. Philip could imagine the stupendous effect the whole thing would have when it was finished; he strolled around the house in a delighted daze, noting the fine new staircases, the cedar handrails in the modern parts of the house and the start already made in creating a streamlined kitchen for Angele.

The whole of the upper storey had yet to be converted into several rooms; there was much to be done. But he was glad he had given his confidence to Pierre and Roget. They would see that the work had a quality seldom seen nowadays. The men had already made a start on the interior of the Great Hall and their scaffolding and lights lined the walls at a dizzy height from the flagged floor; another gang was at work on the roof outside and the place resembled a great, humming factory.

A striking contrast to the mist-haunted ambience of their first sight of the place. Philip was pacing about on the terrace, smoking a pipe, and picturing himself writing a new series of novels of the macabre in this evocative atmosphere. He had two novels coming out shortly, but he would have to get down to some hard work in England in the coming winter. Then he would return to The Grey House and by late summer would be well back in his stride.

His publisher was pleased with the consistency of his output and he had no doubt that the quiet surroundings here would contribute a great deal to his writing. If only Angele liked the place a little better . . . Still, she had seemed more pleased with the house lately and he felt that when she saw the new kitchen and all the latest gadgets he proposed to install for her, she would be as delighted with The Grey House as he.

His musings were suddenly interrupted by a startled cry.

It came from the direction of the Great Hall and in a few moments more he heard the sharp noise of running footsteps on the stone floor. It was Pierre.

"Monsieur!" There was a hard excitement in the voice, but no alarm. He quickened his own steps towards the builder. The couple met at the entrance of the Great Hall and an instant later Philip was sharing Pierre's excitement.

The workmen had been scraping down the wall of the Great Hall over the fireplace, preparatory to re-plastering; Philip had long pondered a centrepiece which would provide a striking point for the eye in this chamber and now he had the answer. Beneath the layers of old plaster on the surface of the ancient wall, a painting had begun to reveal itself.

When Philip arrived, two workmen were engrossed in clearing away an area which appeared to depict a man's blue waistcoat with gold gilt buttons. Philip joined them on the scaffolding and studied the painting, as it began to appear, with mounting excitement. Pierre seized a paint brush and a can of water and started clearing another area; the four men worked on.

The rest of the house was silent, Angele and Monsignor Joffroy having gone for a walk and the men on the roof having a temporary break from their labours.

After an hour, a painting of unique and demoniac nature had emerged; viewing it from the floor of the Great Hall by the brilliant electric light which the workman held to illuminate it, Philip was jubilantly aware of having found his centrepiece – remarkably appropriate in view of his profession as a novelist of the macabre – and yet at the same time he could not help having serious doubts as to the effect it might have on his visitors.

The radiant colours were unblurred by their long sojourn under the whitewash of an earlier age and the painting really stood out remarkably. It depicted a singularly sinister old man, in a grey tricorn hat and blue coat with gold buttons. His knee breeches were caught in with gold cords and his black shoes had silver gilt buckles. He was pushing his way through some sort of dark, wet undergrowth with concentrated ferocity. In his arms and hanging head downwards as he dragged her into the darkling bushes was a young girl.

She was stark naked, her pink body, depicted with pitiless detail by the unknown painter of obvious genius, streaked with gouts of blood where the brambles had gashed her. Her eyes were closed, either in death or a faint, it was impossible to tell, and her long gold hair dragged through the wet grass. It was difficult to convey the hideous effect this painting of diabolical brilliance had upon the viewer.

In the old man's left hand, held towards the observer, was the curious spiked whip which Philip had seen in this very house not so many weeks before. The workmen were still busy washing away the covering whitewash from the bottom righthand corner of the picture and their backs obscured the details from Philip's view. He strode about the floor of the hall, trying to get a better perspective.

At the very bottom of the painting was an enamelled coat of arms with a Latin inscription underneath, which he would have translated later. He was no scholar and would ask Monsignor Joffroy what he made of it. As the workmen again began their interminable hammering upon the roof above his head, the footsteps of the Abbé himself were heard upon the entrance stair.

His face was pale in the light of the electric lamps and he seemed to stagger and made a warding off gesture with his hand, as he caught sight of the painting, which the workmen had now finished uncovering.

"For the love of God, Monsieur," he cried harshly. "Not this horror . . ."

Amazed, Philip ran to meet him but a startled shriek from the stairhead above interrupted the projected dialogue. Monsignor Joffroy, remarkably agile for his late middle-age, was even before Philip on the stair. The two men were just in time to save Angele as she fell fainting to the stone floor.

"Let us get her out of this hall," the priest whispered, his head close to Philip's, as they began to lift her. He waved off the alarmed workmen who were swarming down the scaffolding. "Nothing, nothing at all. Just a fainting fit – Madame was merely startled by the painting."

Half an hour later, Philip re-entered the hall. Angele, pale and distraught, had returned to the hotel, driven by Roget Frey, who had called to see the work in progress. Finally calm, she had refused to say what was the cause of her alarm and had attributed it to the shock of seeing the painting in such vivid detail.

Viewed from the top of the stairs, it did strike one with terrific effect, Philip had to admit, pausing at the spot where Angele had stood. But even his stolid materialism had begun to crack with what he had learned in the past few minutes. Monsignor Joffroy, before leaving to comfort Angele, had advised him to have the painting effaced, or bricked over.

"No good can come of it," he insisted, but he would not, or could not, explain anything further. He had, however, confirmed what

Philip had already guessed. The arms beneath the strange picture were those of the de Menevals. The motto beneath the escutcheon was the old and terrible one by which the de Menevals had lived; "Do as thou wilt."

But the thing which disturbed Philip most of all was the painting's final detail, which the workmen had uncovered last of all. Upon this point Monsignor Joffroy had persisted in a stubborn silence.

Philip looked at the picture again and certain words of the Abbé's came to his mind. Following behind the dreadful couple and gazing with sardonic expression at the viewer was a terrible cat, three times larger than any ever seen in this mortal life. A great, grey cat, with blazing yellow eyes.

III

In London, Angele and Philip resumed the interrupted round of their life. The events of the previous autumn seemed blurred and far away and their strangeness something of the imagining, rather than reality. Their friends constantly chaffed them about their old grey house and their preferring to live in such a remote place, rather than to enjoy London life and all the privileges of a successful novelist there.

Philip, however, never tired of telling his friends what a fascinating gem he had unearthed and in truth he had a most interesting way of relating his stories so that his listeners were more than half convinced; even the most hidebound and deskbound of their acquaintances. A good dozen or more couples accepted invitations to visit them the following summer, seduced by the lilt of Philip's voice, for his narration of the tale of The Grey House was almost as fascinating as his printed work.

Angele was, perhaps, pleased at his success and now that she was back in her own familiar atmosphere, the events at The Grey House seemed trivial and commonplace. She supposed it was something that could have happened to anybody. And environment could do many things. The Grey House had an undeniable ambiance that spoke of matters best forgotten, but electric light and modern fittings would dispel them.

She should have been the novelist; Philip often teased her and said she was the one with all the imagination. It was true in a way, too; as she thought this she looked over at him in a corner of the lounge, pipe in mouth and a pint tankard in one hand. He looked young and supple at forty-five, not a grey hair in his glossy black head; she was proud of him and the success they had made of life and their marriage.

It was silly to worry so about The Grey House and a ridiculous atmosphere; it was all the same in old houses. Come to that, she had exactly the same sensation in the Paris Conciergerie, with all its terrible associations with the Comité de Salut Public and Marie Antoinette. She dismissed the thoughts from her mind and listened with an interest that was not feigned when Philip read her the latest progress reports from Roget Frey or M. Gasion.

Sometimes, too, the Abbé would write them little notes in his scholarly handwriting, but he never referred to The Grey House, save in the most general way, or the painting. Particularly not the painting. Angele herself had seen it again since her stupid fainting fit on the staircase; she had to admit that in the daylight and with her husband and friends around her, it no longer frightened.

It was a diabolical subject and he was a disgusting old man – the painter had caught a most sinister expression on his face, which left the viewer feeling uneasy – but that was all. Even the cat wasn't the same as the one she had fancied in the orchard; the one in the picture was at least the size of a bloodhound, but the eyes and face were different.

They even laughed at it, she and Philip and Roget; Philip had said it might have had nine lives but even a cat as big as that could hardly have lived for two hundred years into the late twentieth century. No, that no longer worried her. But what did worry her then, if the cause of the worry – the sight of a cat in an orchard; the atmosphere of an old house; the discovery of a painting – had no fear for her?

She was hard put to it to define a reason and eventually forgot all about it as her normal London life went on. Philip's two books were published, one in December, one in early spring and achieved an even greater success than before. They had money in abundance and life seemed to hold great promise.

The progress reports on the house were satisfactory and as late spring advanced, Philip began to tear his thoughts away from his life in England and his mind flew to The Grey House, waiting for him to give it the final touches. A flurry of invitations went out from him and Angele and then the couple found themselves with only two weeks to go before they were off again.

The regular letters told Philip that the roof had been completed; all the domestic arrangements were in the final stages; the panelling of the Great Hall and its picture windows had gone smoothly; the electric lighting was functioning satisfactorily. Roget Frey said that the surprise he and Philip had planned was also going to schedule;

he had the work carried out in sections and the structure would be erected whenever Philip chose. The garage and the front terrace too, were nearly complete; the remainder of the work, including the reconstruction of the upper storey would await Philip's supervision in the spring.

The author was more than pleased; indeed, judging by the excellent photographs Roget had sent him, the house seemed even more impressive than he had envisaged when he started out on his elaborate scheme of renovation. The terrace overlooking the water mill also looked superb and he hoped to erect a glass marquee on one side so that they could eat in the open in summer even when it rained.

Much against the Abbé's advice, he had decided to keep the painting as the centrepiece of the Great Hall; from his researches he had considered that it represented the old Vicompte Hector de Meneval, one of the most debauched and sadistic of the line. It was no doubt how the old boy liked to see himself, in an obscene and allegorical situation, representing the black arts.

So he had instructed Frey to have the painting framed in oak and preserved under glass. In deference to Angele, the Abbé and other friends of more tender nerves, he had decided to have a plain sliding panel in the modern Swedish style erected over the work. In that way he could have his cake and eat it, he reflected. And at the press of a button the old rogue would be revealed, to shock his friends on a cold winter's night.

The two weeks drew to an end at last; Philip attended a dinner given in his honour by his publisher, extended the last of his invitations, drank through his last farewell party and in the first week in May – rather later than he had intended – he and Angele with the car set off on the cross-Channel ferry. They stopped at Fontainebleau for the night and next day made an uneventful journey south.

They had decided to camp out in the house temporarily, as the greater part was habitable; from what Roget had said, the bathroom was partly in order, the working parts of the kitchen completely so. They could extemporize and superintend the final arrangements themselves. But even so, both liked comfort and rather than arrive late in the afternoon with inadequate provision for food, they had booked in at their old hotel for two nights before deciding to launch themselves completely on to the facilities of The Grey House.

Their telegrams had preceded them and their old friends M. Gasion, Roget and the Abbé presented themselves punctually for dinner. It was a time of laughter and jokes shared, which

Philip always remembered and when the builder Pierre put in an appearance just as they had given him up, the evening seemed complete. Afterwards, they sat out on the balcony, smoking, drinking their cognac and looking over the lights of the quiet city.

All was well at the house, the couple learned; things had gone even better than expected and Pierre and Roget Frey were obviously bubbling with enthusiasm. If they could decently have done so, they would have dragged Philip and Angele into the car that night and over to the house, late as it was.

Roget Frey and Philip chaffed the Abbé over what they called the "boxing in" of the painting, but though he good-humouredly smiled at their sallies, it was obvious that his eyes had a serious and thoughtful look. The party broke up late and Philip never had a chance to speak to any of his friends alone. The pair rose late the next morning.

It was after midday before Frey, the builder Pierre and M. Gasion arrived at the hotel to escort their friends in triumph to their new home. There had certainly been an extraordinary change in The Grey House. In front of the house was a terrace of pink tiles, the great entrance door sparkled with pale yellow paint and boxes of flowers garlanded the facade, with more flowers hanging in baskets on hooks suspended from the walls.

On the roof, new red tiles caught the sunshine and the straightened turret must have looked as it did in the eighteenth century. On one side, a new garage was nearing completion, needing but a final coat of paint while white balustrades edging the terrace gave the last touch in a notable and inspired piece of restoration.

The ancient and the modern blended in perfect harmony and even Angele could not resist a gasp of pleasure. With congratulations on all sides, architect, builder and agent passed inside the great door to show the couple the wonders of the interior. It was a happy afternoon and Philip was well pleased, not only with his choice of restorers but in his own ability to choose good men.

When the mutual congratulations were over, the party stayed on for a convivial dinner and while the majority remained in the dining room, chatting over coffee and cognac, served by a local domestic, Philip and Roget Frey retired to the Great Hall to discuss the next stages of the work. Even the Abbé, when he put in an appearance around nine o'clock in the evening, had to admit that the house now had great charm and style; if he had any reservations he, at any rate, was wise enough to keep them to himself.

He glanced up at the space over the fireplace when he entered the Great Hall and appeared relieved to see nothing but a smooth wooden panel where the painting was formerly visible. During the next few days Philip and Angele settled down into a more or less stable routine. They had two small portable beds installed in one of the half-completed rooms on the first floor and ate in the kitchen or on the terrace.

This was in order to avoid inconvenience and extra trouble for the workmen, who were now proceeding with the later stages of the work under Pierre and Roget's direction. Philip was already writing and the steady clack of his typewriter could be heard from the terrace several hours each day. Roget was in and out several times a day, the work went well; all in all, it was a busy time for the young couple. Some evenings they would drive into the city for a meal or a drink with their friends and several afternoons a week, Angele would go shopping, either alone or with Philip.

She was busy ordering furniture, domestic utensils, hangings and the many hundreds of individual items which the house would need. Surprisingly, the renovation of The Grey House was not costing as much as they had budgeted for, despite the extensive nature of the work; this was mainly due to Roget's goodness in the matter of fees and to the builder's reasonable rates and friendly attitude.

This meant that Angele had more to spend on furnishings and she wanted to make sure that her side of the decorating measured up to the high standards set by her husband. Angele was not troubled by any more disturbing thoughts and she had grown used to the tinkling of the water mill. The mist was now rising thickly from the area of trees at the bottom of the orchard, due to the extremely hot weather, but she paid no more attention to that either.

About the third week in July, the first of their friends from London arrived to inspect the progress of the house. Doreen and Charles Hendry were a jolly couple and they were delighted with The Grey House as they first saw it from their sports car one afternoon. But for some reason their enthusiasm evaporated after their first raptures. One of the guest rooms was now ready for occupation, though still unpainted. It overlooked, from a higher point, the orchard and the grove of trees at the foot of the terrace and it was this room which Doreen and Charles occupied their first night at The Grey House.

The next morning, at breakfast on the terrace, Angele could not help noticing that Doreen looked drawn and tired. Even Philip sensed this, for he asked, "Sleep well?"

Charles looked embarrassed. He glanced round the breakfast table and said with a short laugh, "Well, as a matter of fact we didn't sleep a wink. There was such a howling of cats all night, that we were awake most of the time. Never heard anything like it. One great brute was in the orchard. I got up to sling some water at it. It had burning yellow eyes – gave me quite a turn."

"Sorry about that," said Philip. "Yes, there are a lot of cats round here, now that you come to mention it, but I can't say they've bothered us to that extent. Have you heard them, dear?" he said, turning to Angele.

His wife had turned quite white. She stammered some casual remark and quickly excused herself. There was nothing else of moment during the Hendrys' short stay. And short it was. They had originally intended to remain for two weeks but after a few days Charles pleaded urgent business which necessitated his return to England. As their sports car headed up the lane and Angele and Philip waved them off, Angele could have sworn there was relief in Doreen's eyes as they drove away from The Grey House.

Imagined or not, there was no doubt that Charles' business was a pretext, for Philip ran into him in one of the main squares of the city a couple of afternoons later, to their mutual embarrassment. On the Friday of the same week Philip made a startling discovery which did something to disturb the peace of his mind, while the effect on Angele was deeply felt. Philip returned from a walk with Roget and asked Pierre, "I say, did you know there was an old graveyard at the end of the lane?"

Pierre shrugged and answered that he believed that was so; but it was a good way from the house, well screened by trees. He could not see that it was of any importance. In face of this indifference Philip had to agree that the affair seemed of little moment. But the way of its discovery had been a shock to him, though he was loath to admit it.

He and Roget had been out surveying the extent of the property; Philip had wanted to have a closer look at the orchard and the water mill building and there was also the question of repair of walls and fences. When they had gone some way towards their boundary, forcing their way through breast-high nettles in places, Philip was surprised to see a large area of rusted iron railings and the white gleam of marble through the trees.

Roget was almost as surprised as he. The two men, impelled by some curiosity, the source of which was obscure, were soon confronted by an elaborate ironwork gate with a rusted metal scroll, whose hieroglyphs seemed familiar; the stone pillars on either side were covered with lichens and moss and the stone ball on one column had long fallen into the grass.

The gate was ajar and after some hesitation, the two men pushed it open and went on into the cemetery. Its extent was quite small but there was a frightful mouldering stench emanating from the ancient tombs with which they were surrounded, and the long, echoing screech the gate made as it went back on its age-old hinges, set the young men's teeth on edge.

There seemed to be about thirty tombs in the cemetery and it was evident that a hundred years or more had passed since the latest occupant was laid to rest. As they gazed round, Roget said with a nervous catch in his breath, "This must be the old de Meneval graveyard. They were brought here from the chateau above. They had to be laid in this place, far from the town, because of the public outcry. I seem to remember in the old histories that the townspeople said they were an accursed strain and there was a great ecclesiastical debate over their being interred in the municipal cemetery. So the Bishop of the province had this private *cimetière* set aside for the use of the family."

Philip could not hold back a shiver at these words, reinforced by the melancholy scene around him. He saw now that the dark grove of trees below the orchard had screened the graveyard from view, as no doubt it was meant to do. There was no doubt, however, as to the reasons for the dark mist which rose over the orchard and surrounds at night. The place was unhealthy and Philip would have to seek the advice of the health authorities.

The pair had been traversing the small avenues which bisected the old graveyard and now found themselves in front of an imposing monument which stood in the most secluded part; overgrown hedges of laurel surrounded it and the lower part of the tomb was effaced by the encroachment of brambles and tangled grasses. Philip noticed with interest that the mausoleum was in the form of a great marble portico, in the style of a Greek temple, which evidently covered a vault of considerable proportions below.

On the face of the portico was repeated the escutcheon which appeared below the painting in the Great Hall of The Grey House; he saw the name of Hector de Meneval and others of his house, the dates of birth and death obliterated with time. But as he looked closer, he saw that he had been mistaken; the dates of birth were clearly given, but the remainder of the legend was left blank after each name – there was not even the customary dash. This was decidedly curious.

Roget had left his side for a moment and was puzzling out a massive Latin inscription which extended along the side of the mausoleum. Roughly translated it ran, "Mighty are they, great joy is theirs; they shall taste of Life Everlasting." Somehow, this inscription left a vaguely unpleasant impression on Philip's mind and he could not help remembering, for the first time, the sly and cunning expression of the old man in the painting.

He was about to retrace his steps towards the gate when there was a sharp exclamation from Roget. He joined his friend and saw, following the line of Roget's somewhat unsteady finger, that one side of the tomb had collapsed, after long years of erosion by wind and rain. The earth had fallen in, carrying with it fragments of marble and through the gaping hole in the side of the mausoleum could be seen part of the interior of the vault.

There were dark steps and even what looked like part of a catafalque some distance below. A faint miasma exuded from this charnel place and seemed to poison the air around the tomb. A little farther off, Philip noted another curious feature. The grass around the hole in the marble seemed crushed and torn, as though something heavy had been dragged along; the trail continued for some distance into the dark and sombre bushes which bordered the cemetery gate.

Neither man liked the idea of following that trail and after a few moments, by mutual, unspoken consent they hurried away to the healthy sanity of the upper lanes which led to the house. The gate shrieked mockingly behind them. Philip did not mention their visit to the old cemetery in any detail and after her first shock of alarm, Angele gave the matter no more thought. And the following week there was a minor celebration, culminating in the unveiling of Philip's surprise.

The principal of Philip's publishing firm was to be in Burgundy for a few days and had promised to spend a day with them and inspect their new quarters. Philip had laid on a party in his honour and the climax was to be the architectural coup he had planned for the Great Hall. This chamber had been barred to all members of the household and friends for three days beforehand and the noise of hammering and sawing echoed throughout the house all day long; Roget and Philip were in conference behind the locked doors and workmen carrying heavy baulks of timber and elaborately carved beams in and out, smilingly disclaimed all knowledge of the nature of the affair.

The party was a big success and the unlocking of the Great Hall set the seal on a momentous occasion; tables laden with wine and food were set down the middle, an epic fire blazed in the hearth, for the stone hall was a cold place even in summer, despite the wooden panelling; and lights blazed from half a hundred metal wall fittings. But what enchanted the guests was the architectural feature on which Philip and Roget had worked for such a long time.

Completely surrounding the upper part of the hall, like a minstrel gallery, ran an airy balcony which continued over the fireplace round to a point above the huge door. Each side of the entrance, beautifully carved oak balustrades ran up to the balcony, encasing polished oak staircases. The whole length of the balconies themselves, except where the two great picture windows pierced the wall, were a blaze of colour; thousands of books, the cream of Philip's collection, lined the walls in finely fitted mahogany bookcases. The whole thing was a triumph and the guests could not resist audible murmurs of admiration.

A few minutes later, ascending the first staircase, hand in hand with Philip, Angele had to admit that the idea was the crown of the Great Hall. Thirty feet above the flagged pavement she looked down on the shimmering dazzle of faces and the babble of the guests' conversation rose like the noise of the sea above the clink of glasses. On the balconies themselves visitors could browse among the books set out row on row, spreading from wall to wall; the views from the picture windows were magnificent and with the stout railing at her back, Angele could see across mile after mile of hazy blue mountain.

The balcony ran across and dipped a little below the great central panel of the fireplace and this was the only unfortunate feature of the affair from her point of view; for whenever the panel was unrolled it must bring the viewer on the balcony in close proximity to the disturbing painting, even though it were still a good half dozen feet above.

It was this which caused the only disrupting element of the party for Angele. She and Philip were admiring the setting from this point when Roget or another friend in the hall below decided to demonstrate the ingenious panel for an intrigued guest. The button was pressed, the panel slid silently back and there, not two yards away, Angele saw with a shock the same hideous scene. The sight was so unexpected that she gave a gasp and reeled back against the railing.

Philip was beside her in an instant, his face wrinkled with worry.

"What is it?" he asked, looking round him swiftly, in a manner she had never seen before.

"Nothing," she said. "I just feel faint, that's all. It must be the height."

As Philip led her below, a girl who had never had a qualm on even the loftiest mountain top, she looked again at the picture but she did not see repeated the optical illusion which had so unnerved her. That it must be an optical illusion, she did not doubt. But she could have sworn that the baleful eye of the old Vicomte had closed, for just the faintest fraction, in an obscene wink. The effect must be one of the texture of the paint, combined with the light on the glass above it. But she could not recapture the sensation, though she tried again as they went downstairs; and a few minutes later the panel closed again over it, to the wondering murmur of the assembled guests.

IV

It was now again turning towards late summer. Philip was beginning to get into his stride with writing, Roget came seldom to the house, the remaining one or two workmen were pottering amiably on the sunny days, putting the finishing touches to the decor. Angele had been too busy to spare any thoughts for morbid imaginings, and she was well satisfied with the effect of the furniture and hangings she was arranging with such competent art.

But the Abbé came more often to the house than ever. Angele was glad of his company and his benign eye, in which there shone such wisdom and benevolence, gave her a solid feeling of comfort and safety. Monsignor Joffroy spoke little of the matters which so deeply troubled him, but with humorous and interesting discourse kept the little dinner parties gay with laughter, as the night moths fluttered round the lamps as they took their evening ease on the balcony, whose magnificent views never ceased to delight them.

The couple had on two or three occasions been the guests of the Abbé at his quarters in the old university, and had duly marvelled at the extent and antiquity of the great library which was its proudest boast. It was on one of these occasions that Philip asked the old man if he could consult one of the rare and unexpurgated histories of the de Meneval family.

Monsignor Joffroy was reluctant to do this, but assented at last and eventually left Philip alone in his study with a great brass-bound book which had four locks. Translating the crabbed Latin was a long and tiresome task but Philip eventually unravelled a sickening story which explained much that was dark and horrifying about the de Menevals. He replaced the book on the shelf and sat pondering; for the first time he had some doubts about the wisdom of his purchase of The Grey House.

He ever afterwards refused to speak of what he had seen in the locked book, but he did hint to Roget Frey something of

the unspeakable practices of the old de Menevals which had led
the people of the city a hundred years before to lay siege to the
chateau and burn it about the ears of the atrocious occupants.
The events which led the citizenry to this extreme measure had
concerned the abduction of young girls from the neighbourhood,
which the de Menevals were in the habit of procuring for their
unspeakable rites.

Philip could not go on – the details were too blasphemous and
appalling to contemplate, even in the Latin, but it did explain
the curious content of the painting in the Great Hall. Philip was
now convinced that the study depicted a literal subject and not an
allegorical one and this caused him great disquiet. When he left the
Abbé's library, the old man refused to discuss the subject with him.
But Monsignor Joffroy looked him in the eye with great intensity and
said with emphasis, "Take care of your wife, Monsieur!"

For some days afterwards Philip was seen to wander about The
Grey House with an odd and abstracted air, but he gradually
recovered his spirits as the warm and sunny days went by. He
had been to see the sanitary authorities regarding the old graveyard
and had been promised that the thing would be looked into. But, as
is the way in rural France, no action was immediately forthcoming,
the weeks went by and Philip eventually forgot about it.

It was in early September, on a day of golden and benevolent
splendour, that Angele had an odd experience. She had been
standing on the balcony drinking in the beauty of the wild scene,
against the backcloth of the far mountains. There was a hush, broken
only by the faint tinkle of water. Philip had gone into town to see
about some business with Roget and the only other thing which
disturbed the silence was the occasional chink of china as Gisele,
the hired girl, washed up the crockery from lunch.

She was thinking about nothing in particular, except possibly what
they would be having for dinner. As she lowered her gaze from the
distant mountain peaks and the white stones of the chateau on the
heights above, her eye was arrested by the early leaves of autumn
which fell like faint flakes of snow on to the golden foliage of the
old orchard. She then heard a faint rustling sound and presently
noticed the figure of a man.

He was standing in the far corner of the orchard, near the water
mill, and she could not see him at all clearly. He wore a blue coat,
like most French workmen wear, and he seemed to be shading his
eyes against the sun. She was not at all alarmed and as she cast
her eyes on him, he gave her a long, piercing glance back over his
shoulder, but owing to the intervening foliage she was not able to see

his features with any detail. The gesture reminded her of something, though she could not for the moment place it, and when she looked again the man had gone.

She mentioned the matter to Philip when he arrived home and he only said with studied casualness, "Oh, I expect the sanitary people have got around to doing that work I asked them about."

This view was reinforced the following day when Pierre and Philip had occasion to go down the far lane on a matter connected with the outfall of the drainage. Philip pointed out to Pierre a long swathe which had been forced through the nettles.

The trail, which was in a different place to the route taken by Philip and Roget on the occasion of their visit, appeared to run from the old graveyard to a point by an ancient, broken-down fence, and then through the orchard below the house. Pierre said nothing but gave Philip a very curious look. The two men made no further reference to the matter.

It was when they were turning to go back that Philip asked Pierre whether they might not visit the orchard. He had never been there since his original inspection of the water mill, but his curiosity had been aroused by the tracks and he wanted to see if the municipal authorities had taken action. Pierre seemed strangely reluctant and mentioned the lateness of the hour; the setting sun was already casting long shadows and a faint swathe of mist could be seen faintly outlining the furthest trees.

Both men were by now rather disturbed by the atmosphere and Philip started when the long drawn-out yowl of a cat sounded from far away. They stood listening for a moment at the entrance of the orchard but the noise was not repeated. Then Philip went boldly crunching his way through a tangle of brush into the old place, more for his own peace of mind than to impress the builder with his English phlegm.

There was nothing out of the way in the orchard. The trail gave out in the centre. There were only a few rusted agricultural implements, half-hidden in the grass. But Philip was surprised to see that a long iron ladder, wreathed in a tangle of branches and mossy lichen, was stapled to the wall below The Grey House. It led up to a point just below the balcony. This was something he felt he ought to look into.

A few minutes later the two men were back in the sunlit uplands of the inhabited lanes leading to the town and were able to forget the strange, brooding atmosphere of the orchard area. Pierre shook his head when Philip mentioned the matter of the ladder. He imagined it would have been placed there in case of fire. For some reason this gave Philip an enormous peace of mind. He expanded in the glow of the sun and insisted that Pierre accompany him to a cafe for an aperitif.

When he arrived back at the house, he found Angele setting the table on the terrace, with Gisele prattling commonplaces as she bustled to and from the kitchen. On pretext of admiring the view, he looked eagerly for the ladder. Yes, there it was, in a rather different position from what he had imagined below. It must be the foreshortening. He did not know why, but he was disturbed to find that anyone coming from below could gain the balcony by this means, old and rusty as the ladder was. Though this in itself was illogical, for the ladder was surely designed to ensure that people from the house could gain the orchard in case of fire.

This again puzzled him, for the ladder ended about three feet from the balcony, in a tangle of brambles and bushes. He saw something else too, which disturbed him more than he cared to admit. The edges of the ladder were covered with lichen and moss. On all the rungs which he could see, the green of years had been torn away, as though by ascending feet.

Philip slept badly that night, but as day succeeded day and the calm of the Indian summer brought with it nothing but blue skies and contentment, he warmed again to The Grey House.

Angele was in good spirits and the couple made their usual visits. Though the work on the house was finished, their local friends were as before; Pierre, Roget, M. Gasion and the Abbé.

Philip was writing better than ever in the more peaceful atmosphere. A book of demoniac tales which he had finished shortly after arrival in Burgundy in May was having a sensational sale in England and the Continental and American rights were being negotiated. He had reason to feel satisfied. And though the Abbé had attempted to dissuade them from the idea, he had started on his most ambitious novel of the macabre to date, a history based loosely on that of the de Menevals. He had quite recovered his spirits and the odd events which earlier had set his mind on strange and sombre paths, now provided much the same material for his book.

His enthusiasm blazed up as day after day found him hunched over his typewriter and Angele could hear the machine clacking on into the long hours of the night. He preferred to work on the balcony even when the nights began to turn cold in early October. Angele remonstrated with him about this, but he laughed at her and her old wives' remedies for colds, and told her not to worry. He had a good sweater on and his pipe for company.

The days of October continued scorching hot, though the nights were cool and Philip was pleased with his progress on the book; he had five chapters finished and another three shaped out in the rough. He began to talk of finishing before the end of November so that he could get an early draft to the publishers before the new year.

Angele was pleased for his sake but troubled at his appearance. Philip had begun to get pale with overwork and his eyes had deep hollows under them which she had never seen before. She had hoped that they would be away to England before the winter set in, but to her alarm Philip had begun to talk of staying at The Grey House the whole winter round. It was all very well for him, with all his work to occupy him, but it would be a dull existence for her once the long, dark, wet days of the Burgundy winter set in.

They had left the matter open, without quarrelling over it, and Angele had Philip's promise that if the book was finished within the next month, as well it might be, then they would go back to London and he would deliver the manuscript to the publishers himself. He would not show her the material, for fear of spoiling the effect.

"It's the best thing I've ever done," he said, biting hard on his pipe in his enthusiasm. "I've never known a book come along so well. It's almost as though it's writing itself."

Angele shot him a sharp look, but said nothing.

"It's a curious thing," he went on, after a bit, his brows wrinkled over the mass of typed sheets before him. "There's some of this stuff I don't even remember writing. There's a bit here which gets the medieval atmosphere exactly . . . no, perhaps you'd better not read it now. Wait until the end. It spoils it to take it out of context."

Angele continued to watch her husband's progress on the novel with mounting alarm; she had never seen him like this, but consoled herself with the thought that it would do no good to interfere and at the rate he was going they would soon be away to England for the winter.

A few days later, Philip announced in triumph that the last chapter was in progress and that he would revise and re-shape the book in England. Angele greeted the news with unconcealed relief. Philip looked at her in surprise. His face was white and his eyes looked wild with his long hours of composition. Then he put down his pipe and took her in his arms.

"I know it hasn't been much fun for you, darling," he said. "But it will only be a few days more now and then we're off home. I can promise you that the book will be the biggest thing I've ever done. I'm sure you will agree with me that it has all been worthwhile."

Husband and wife, both pleased at the turn of events, occupied themselves with planning their departure and in the evenings Philip pressed on at fever heat with the final pages of the book. They were to leave on the following Wednesday and some of their effects were already packed. The car was to go in for servicing the following day and Angele felt strangely content with her life, with her relationship with Philip and even with The Grey House. She supposed that by next year she would be quite used to its strange atmosphere.

On the Saturday evening Philip finished his work early. He had been at the book hard all afternoon but the climax he was shaping had finally eluded him. He had got up from the table on the terrace with an exclamation of disgust and carried the typewriter and the thick bundle of manuscript through into the dining room. She remembered him putting a fresh sheet of paper into the machine and then they went up to bed.

It was in the middle of the night when she awoke. At first she half drifted back into sleep but then came wide awake, her mind puzzled by a series of sharp, scratching noises. Then she turned, her mind at ease, as she realized Philip must be working again. He had evidently gone back to the novel he had discarded. But then a great fear came into her mind as her arm came into contact with her husband's body at her side and she heard his steady breathing. The scratching noise, loud in the still night, went on from the dining room, arousing a thousand fears in her confused brain.

By a great effort of will-power, for she was a brave woman, she steeled herself to get out of bed without waking her husband. Not bothering to put on a dressing gown, she tip-toed out of the room and down the short flight of stairs; she did not heed the chill of the night air on her skin or notice the coldness of the flagstones on her bare feet.

When she had closed the door of the bedroom behind her, she switched on the light. The blaze of yellow radiance on familiar things steadied her and left her with a core of hard anger; she went down the remaining stairs with a firm step. The scratching which had aroused her attention went on. As she advanced, she threw switch after switch and as light sprang up beneath her hand so her courage rose. When she was about ten yards away from the dining room a board suddenly creaked under her feet. The scratching immediately stopped and she heard an odd scrabbling noise on the floor.

As she pushed open the door with a furiously thudding heart and threw the switch, the sudden glare of light showed her that the room was empty. All was in its place, the whole house now silent, except for the faint tapping of the night wind against the balcony outside. As she thought of this, she set the great lights of the terrace aflame in the gloom but nothing moved in all the expanse of tile and wrought iron.

She forced herself to look at the table. Several sheets of new paper were laid on top of the typewriter ready for copying. The last sheet was in French, in painfully formed handwriting, covering half the page. She read, "And the flesh of virgins is desirable above all others and whosoever acquires this tenderest of all meat shall find the Everlasting Life. And the fairest of all the married women shall be taken to bride by the Whore-Master and the tomb shall flame forth brighter than the wedding-bower . . ." The words ended there, in mid-sentence, the ink still wet.

Angele, shaking and sick, as she backed away from the table, still had time to notice something on the cloth by the machine. It was a small piece of green lichen.

V

On the Tuesday, Philip and Angele had invited their friends to a farewell dinner and Philip was to read them portions of his novel. The remainder of the previous week-end was occupied in packing and on Monday afternoon Philip rushed in to Angele, jubilant. The book was finished and he waved the thick mass of manuscript over his head in triumph. Angele had not mentioned to him the events of Saturday evening; something dark hung over the house and she knew in her heart that whatever she could say would make no difference. She was only glad that she would soon be gone without the winter to face; in the meantime she shared Philip's joy in his completed work – on the surface at any event.

The pair spent the mid-afternoon talking over future plans and after an early tea, Philip left for Roget's house; he had arranged to have a drink with his friend and discuss some business. He had plans for the orchard and he proposed to have a big stone wall built to block off the old graveyard – a scheme with which Angele fervently agreed. Gisele was to stay with Angele and Philip intended to return about nine o'clock so that they could get in an early night.

They had to prepare for the party the following day and there would be much to do. It had been a hot day again and Gisele and her mistress sat chatting on the balcony; the steepening sun dyed the opposite mountains a deep carmine and as the rays dipped below the hills it left the valley in deep shadow. It began to be cold, the tinkle of water from the old mill house sounded oddly loud in the silence and thick swathes of mist billowed silently across the orchard.

The cats in the lane below the house seemed to be noisy tonight and Angele abruptly got up and went to fetch a woolly sweater.

After a while, she and Gisele moved into the kitchen to continue their conversation but they kept the terrace lights on. Philip had left his thick bundle of manuscript to read; she had promised to give him her opinion on it when he returned, though she felt sure it would take her more than the three hours she had allowed herself.

From time to time, as the two girls were talking, Angele turned to look at the great pile of paper which stood on the typing table in the corner of the terrace where Philip usually worked. Presently she excused herself; Gisele had some cleaning to do and went to get out her vacuum cleaner. Angele took a cup of coffee on to the terrace and sat down at the table. She did not know why she did this, but she felt that Philip's novel had to be read on the terrace, where most of it had been written. The title page was headed; IN THE VALE OF CROTH.

She read on, fascinated. It was the most extraordinary thing Philip had ever written. She did not know how she could have found the ideas in it revolting; perhaps she had started at the wrong page. Taken out of context such a book could give the wrong impression. An hour must have passed, an hour in which the silence was broken only by the measured rustle of turning pages or the faint noises of Gisele's cleaning operations. Her cup of coffee grew cold, untasted.

Presently she looked up, startled. Her eyes were shining and had an intense expression. Strangely, too, the terrace had suddenly grown oppressively hot. She knew she had to be properly prepared for the final part of the book. She had too many clothes on for this heat – she had to be prepared. When she emerged from her bedroom ten minutes later she had a strange, sly look on her face but her cheeks were burning and her eyes bright with longing. She was naked except for a flimsy nightgown which revealed every detail of her figure.

Her hair was freshly combed and she crept almost furtively past the room where Gisele was dusting. Once on the terrace she flung herself on the book and began to devour the pages with her eyes. Eight o'clock fled past and there were only a few dozen pages left. There was a lustful expression on her face and her whole body had begun to tremble. She paid no attention to the thin mist which had begun to envelop the balcony. She strained her eyes to learn the unmentionable secret revealed in the last page of the novel.

Her eyes glazed as she read what no woman was meant to read; something aeons old called through the pages to her. She thought of the whip with the spike and her flesh quivered with delicious terror. As she reached the last sentence of the book there was a rustling on the balcony, which did not distract her.

Her eyes took in the last words on the pages before her, "Nude thou shalt be, naked thou shalt be, unashamed thou shalt be. Prepare thou then to do thy Master's will. Prepare thou, BRIDE OF CROTH."

Angele was already on her feet; her eyes were closed, her tongue lolled out of her mouth, a bead of moisture rolled from under one eyelid.

"Take me, Master," she breathed. Something slit the thin silk of her nightgown, exposing her breasts to the chill air. An unutterable stench was in her nostrils, but she smiled happily as ancient arms lifted her from the balcony.

VI

Philip returned happily from Roget's house a little after nine, but his casual homecoming soon changed into bewilderment, then terror. The maid, Gisele, sunk into an unnaturally deep sleep on a divan in the dining room, when aroused, expressed only astonishment; the last thing she remembered, she had been dusting the room. Philip went through the house calling his wife's name.

He found the floor of their bedroom littered with every last stitch of his wife's clothing. But it was on the balcony that stark fear leapt out at him for the first time. It was not the overturned coffee cup, the jumble of typed paper littered across the terrace or even the green, lichenous mould. But something had forced its way through the mass of brambles from the old ladder below the balcony; it was this, and the strands of his wife's blonde hair caught on the thorns which sent him almost out of his mind.

Seizing a powerful electric searchlight from the garage, he set off down the steep, nettle-grown lane, calling his wife's name. His voice echoed back eerily and once again he caught the loathsome stench of putrescence which seemed to emanate from the mist which swirled about these lower parts. His heart leaped in his throat as the beam of his lamp picked out something white in the gloom. It was then, he thinks, that he gave up hope of seeing Angele again; in the darkest moment of his life idiot fear babbled out at him as the probing beam caught Angele's pathetic, torn, blood-stained scrap of nightgown fast on a patch of nettles as the unnameable thing had carried her through the night.

Philip's knees gave under him and he trembled violently; for the path through the nettles led directly to the old graveyard and he knew that, much as he loved his wife, he dare not go there alone at night to face such forces. It was a nightmare journey as he stumbled back up the lane; falling, hacking his shins on outcrops of rock, cutting his face with brambles. He looked an appalling sight as he staggered into a cafe on the edge of the town and made his pathetic telephone plea to Roget Frey.

The young architect not only came in his car at once, but collected Monsignor Joffroy from the university on his way over. The couple were with the demented Philip in a quarter of an hour. His appearance shocked them both but a few words only, told the old Abbé all he had suspected and feared from the first.

He had come fully prepared. Round his neck he had an ornate silver crucifix; he carried a prayer book in one hand and, curiously, a crowbar. Roget Frey had also armed himself with a revolver and in the back of his car were two enormous electric lamps, like car headlights.

"Courage, *mon pauvre ami*," said Monsignor Joffroy, helping Philip into a seat beside him. "What must be done, must be done. I fear it is too late to save your dear wife, but we must do all we can to destroy this evil being in order to save her soul." Horrified, half dazed, understanding only a quarter of what he was told, Philip clutched the Monsignor's arm as Roget's sports car leapt like a demented thing down the narrow lane at suicidal speed.

At the bottom Frey drove straight at the wall of brambles and stinging nettles as far as he could. The headlights shone a brilliant radiance right down towards the cemetery gates. Frey left the lights on and the engine running.

"To remind us of normality," he said with great emphasis.

"This will do," said Monsignor Joffroy, making a great sign of the cross in the air before him. "The rest is in God's hands."

Roget handed a long crowbar to Philip, the prelate carried one searchlight and the other crowbar, and Roget had his revolver in one hand and the second searchlight in his left. The three men walked abreast through the wet grass, making no attempt at concealment. Philip put down his own flashlight at the cemetery entrance, which lit up a considerable part of the graveyard; he had recovered his courage now and led the way towards the de Meneval tomb.

Their feet echoed hollowly over the gravel and Philip dropped to one knee as a thing with great flaming eyes drove at them from the top of a gravestone. Frey's revolver roared twice, with deafening impact, and a broken-backed, yowling creature that had been the great cat went whimpering to die in the bushes. Monsignor Joffroy had jumped up instantly and without swerving set off at a run towards the de Meneval tomb. The others followed, trembling from the sudden shock of the revolver shots.

Philip could never forget that charnel house scene. Like a tableau out of Goya, it ever haunted his life. The nude body of Angele, quite dead, slashed with gouts of blood, but with an expression of diabolical happiness on her face, was clutched fast in the arms of a thing which lay on its side at the entrance of the tomb, as though exhausted. It was dressed in a frayed and faded blue coat and the abomination had apparently broken one of its old and brittle legs as it dropped from the balcony. This had accounted for its slow progress to the malodorous lair beneath the old de Meneval mausoleum.

But the worst horror was to come. In one withered and grey, parchment-like paw was clutched a whip-and-spike instrument dabbled with fresh young blood. The face, half eaten away and with the broken bones protruding from the split, rotted skin, was turned towards them. Something moved and the eyes, which were still alive, gazed balefully at the three men. Old de Meneval was malevolent to the last.

Monsignor Joffroy hesitated not an instant. Pronouncing the name of the Father, the Son and the Holy Ghost in a voice like thunder, he held aloft the cross. Then, handing it to Philip, he brought down the great crowbar again and again on the brittle ancient blasphemy that had once been a man. Teeth and hair flew in all directions, old bones cracked and split and dust and putrefaction rose in the still air. At length, all was quiet.

Panting, the Monsignor led the two men away. "This is all we can do for tonight," he said. "Much remains to be done in the morning, but this abomination will never walk again."

He sprinkled holy water from a bottle over the remains of Angele and covered it with a blanket from the car. To Philip's anguished protests over his wife, he remained adamant.

"We must not move her," he insisted. "She is no longer your wife, my poor friend. She belongs to them. For her own sake and for her immortal soul we must do what has to be done."

Little remains to be told, though the city will remember for many a long year the horrors which were found in the old de Meneval tomb. Monsignor Joffroy obtained a special dispensation from the Bishop that same night and the very next morning, at first light, a battalion of the Infanterie Coloniale were called in to work under the Abbé's directions.

These soldiers, hardened and toughened on the forge of war as they were, saw sights which made them act like frightened children when the vault below was opened. Monsignor Joffroy, calm and strong, prevented a panic and bore himself like a true man of the church that day. Indeed, many said that the sights he saw and the things he had to do hastened the good man's own end.

The body of Angele was taken to a hastily prepared pyre behind a canvas shelter in the old cemetery and burned while priests conducted a service. In the vault of the de Menevals a stupefying sight awaited the intruders, priest and soldier alike. Some say that there were more than thirty bodies, de Menevals and the naked corpses of fresh young girls, as undecayed as the day they were abducted from the neighbourhood upwards of two hundred years before.

The searchers also found vast passages and chambers under the earth, equipped as for the living, where the undead dead still held obscene and blasphemous rites. Be that as it may, and no one can now say for certain that all this is true, the Bishop himself with Monsignor Joffroy as his chaplain held a service of exorcism and afterwards the troops went in with flame guns and destroyed every last one of those horrors as they lay.

The underground chambers were blown up by Army engineers and the whole of the area cauterized and purified. Later, by order of the Bishop the field was concreted over and from that day to this the people of the city have remained unmolested, neither does mist appear in the orchard by the mill house.

The Grey House still stands, now fast falling to ruin and deserted. M. Gasion, greyer now, has retired and gone to live in a villa in Normandy; Monsignor Joffroy is dead; and Roget Frey is a successful architect, practising in Paris.

VII

Philip is still a successful novelist. He lives in London, with a very young wife, who is not serious at all, and is content with what she calls the simple things of life. He seldom goes abroad, very occasionally to France, and never to Burgundy. His stories now, while very popular in the English-speaking world, are not what they were.

They are mainly comedies and light pieces, with an occasional political drama. Though he is still a year or so short of fifty, his hair is quite white and his face that of an old man. It is only when one looks closely into his eyes that one can see the fires of the pit.

Two small footnotes. Afterwards, in The Grey House, Roget Frey found a great pile of grey ash in a circular stone jar on the terrace.

In the Great Hall, the painting of the old man and the girl had disappeared; the whole wall had been gouged out from the balcony and the solid stone pitted as though with a pickaxe.

He did not make any inquiries and he had no theories so the mysteries remain. But one does not feel it is very hard to guess.

M. R. James

A Warning to the Curious

Montague Rhodes James (1862–1936) remains one of the most influential writers of horror fiction, thanks to his landmark collections Ghost Stories of an Antiquary, More Ghost Stories of an Antiquary, A Thin Ghost and Others, A Warning to the Curious *and* The Collected Ghost Stories. *He also wrote a fantasy novel for children,* The Five Jars, *which was published in 1922.*

He is best remembered for such classic tales of the supernatural as "Oh, Whistle and I'll Come to You, My Lad", "Casting the Runes", "The Mezzotint", "Canon Alberic's ScrapBook" and the following story, which effectively combines many of the recurring themes explored by James throughout his fiction.

"A Warning to the Curious" was filmed in the early 1970s by BBC-TV as part of their "A Ghost Story for Christmas" series, with Peter Vaughan playing the luckless treasure-hunter pursued by a dead guardian of an ancient crown . . .

THE PLACE ON the east coast which the reader is asked to consider is Seaburgh. It is not very different now from what I remember it to have been when I was a child. Marshes intersected by dykes to the south, recalling the early chapters of *Great Expectations*; flat fields to the north, merging into heath; heath, fir woods, and, above all, gorse, inland. A long sea-front and a street: behind that a spacious church of flint, with a broad, solid western tower and a peal of six bells. How well I remember their sound on a hot Sunday in August, as our party went slowly up the white, dusty slope of road towards them, for the church stands at the top of a short, steep incline. They rang with a flat clacking sort of sound on those hot days, but when the air was softer they were mellower too. The railway ran down to its little terminus farther along the same road. There was a gay white windmill just before you came to the station, and another down near the shingle at the south end of the town, and yet others on higher ground to the north. There were cottages of bright red brick with slate roofs . . . but why do I encumber you with these commonplace details? The fact is that they come crowding to the point of the pencil when it begins to write of Seaburgh. I should like to be sure that I had allowed the right ones to get on to the paper. But I forgot. I have not quite done with the word-painting business yet.

Walk away from the sea and the town, pass the station, and turn up the road on the right. It is a sandy road, parallel with the railway, and if you follow it, it climbs to somewhat higher ground. On your left (you are now going northward) is heath, on your right (the side towards the sea) is a belt of old firs, wind-beaten, thick at the top, with the slope that old seaside trees have; seen on the sky-line from the train they would tell you in an instant, if you did not know it, that you were approaching a windy coast. Well, at the top of my little hill, a line of these firs strikes out and runs towards the sea, for there is a ridge that goes that way; and the ridge ends in a rather well-defined mound commanding the level fields of rough grass, and a little knot of fir trees crowns it. And here you may sit on a hot spring day, very well content to look at blue sea, white windmills, red cottages, bright green grass, church tower, and distant martello tower on the south.

As I have said, I began to know Seaburgh as a child; but a gap of a good many years separates my early knowledge from that which is more recent. Still it keeps its place in my affections, and any tales of it that I pick up have an interest for me. One such tale is this: it came to me in a place very remote from Seaburgh, and quite accidentally, from a man whom I had been able to oblige – enough in his opinion to justify his making me his confidant to this extent.

I know all that country more or less (he said). I used to go to Seaburgh pretty regularly for golf in the spring. I generally put up at the "Bear," with a friend – Henry Long it was, you knew him perhaps – ("Slightly," I said) and we used to take a sitting-room and be very happy there. Since he died I haven't cared to go there. And I don't know that I should anyhow after the particular thing that happened on our last visit.

It was in April, 19 –, we were there, and by some chance we were almost the only people in the hotel. So the ordinary public rooms were practically empty, and we were the more surprised when, after dinner, our sitting-room door opened, and a young man put his head in. We were aware of this young man. He was rather a rabbity anæmic subject – light hair and light eyes – but not unpleasing. So when he said: "I beg your pardon, is this a private room?" we did not growl and say: "Yes, it is," but Long said, or I did – no matter which: "Please come in." "Oh, may I?" he said, and seemed relieved. Of course it was obvious that he wanted company; and as he was a reasonable kind of person – not the sort to bestow his whole family history on you – we urged him to make himself at home. "I dare say you find the other rooms rather bleak," I said. Yes, he did: but it was really too good of us, and so on. That being got over, he made some pretence of reading a book. Long was playing Patience, I was writing. It became plain to me after a few minutes that this visitor of ours was in rather a state of fidgets or nerves, which communicated itself to me, and so I put away my writing and turned to at engaging him in talk.

After some remarks, which I forget, he became rather confidential. "You'll think it very odd of me" (this was the sort of way he began), "but the fact is I've had something of a shock." Well, I recommended a drink of some cheering kind, and we had it. The waiter coming in made an interruption (and I thought our young man seemed very jumpy when the door opened), but after a while he got back to his woes again. There was nobody he knew in the place, and he did happen to know who we both were (it turned out there was some common acquaintance in town), and really he did want a word of advice, if we didn't mind. Of course we both said: "By all means," or "Not at all," and Long put away his cards. And we settled down to hear what his difficulty was.

"It began," he said, "more than a week ago, when I bicycled over to Froston, only about five or six miles, to see the church; I'm very much interested in architecture, and it's got one of those pretty porches with niches and shields. I took a photograph of it, and then an old man who was tidying up in the churchyard came and asked if I'd care to look into the church. I said yes, and he produced a key and let me in. There wasn't much inside, but I told him it was a nice little church, and he kept it very clean, 'but,' I said, 'the porch is the best part of it.' We were just outside the porch then, and he said, 'Ah, yes, that is a nice porch; and do you know, sir, what's the meanin' of that coat of arms there?'

"It was the one with the three crowns, and though I'm not much of a herald, I was able to say yes, I thought it was the old arms of the kingdom of East Anglia.

"'That's right, sir,' he said, 'and do you know the meanin' of them three crowns that's on it?'

"I said I'd no doubt it was known, but I couldn't recollect to have heard it myself.

"'Well, then,' he said, 'for all you're a scholard, I can tell you something you don't know. Them's the three 'oly crowns what was buried in the ground near by the coast to keep the Germans from landing – ah, I can see you don't believe that. But I tell you, if it hadn't have been for one of them 'oly crowns bein' there still, them Germans would a landed here time and again, they would. Landed with their ships, and killed man, woman and child in their beds. Now then, that's the truth what I'm telling you, that is; and if you don't believe me, you ast the rector. There he comes: you ast him, I says.'

"I looked round, and there was the rector, a nice-looking old man, coming up the path; and before I could begin assuring my old man, who was getting quite excited, that I didn't disbelieve him, the rector struck in, and said: 'What's all this about, John? Good day to you, sir. Have you been looking at our little church?'

"So then there was a little talk which allowed the old man to calm down, and then the rector asked him again what was the matter.

"'Oh,' he said, 'it warn't nothink, only I was telling this gentleman he'd ought to ast you about them 'oly crowns.'

"'Ah, yes, to be sure,' said the rector, 'that's a very curious matter, isn't it? But I don't know whether the gentleman is interested in our old stories, eh?'

"'Oh, he'll be interested fast enough,' says the old man, 'he'll put his confidence in what you tells him, sir; why, you known William Ager yourself, father and son too.'

"Then I put in a word to say how much I should like to hear all about it, and before many minutes I was walking up the village street with the rector, who had one or two words to say to parishioners, and then to the rectory, where he took me into his study. He had made out, on the way, that I really was capable of taking an intelligent interest in a piece of folk-lore, and not quite the ordinary tripper. So he was very willing to talk, and it is rather surprising to me that the particular legend he told me has not made its way into print before. His account of it was this: 'There has always been a belief in these parts in the three holy crowns. The old people say they were buried in different places near the coast to keep off the Danes or the French or the Germans. And they say that one of the three was dug up a long time ago, and another has disappeared by the encroaching of the sea, and one's still left doing its work, keeping off invaders. Well, now, if you have read the ordinary guides and histories of this county, you will remember perhaps that in 1687 a crown, which was said to be the crown of Redwald, King of the East Angles, was dug up at Rendlesham, and alas! alas! melted down before it was even properly described or drawn. Well, Rendlesham isn't on the coast, but it isn't so very far inland, and it's on a very important line of access. And I believe that is the crown which the people mean when they say that one has been dug up. Then on the south you don't want me to tell you where there was a Saxon royal palace which is now under the sea, eh? Well, there was the second crown, I take it. And up beyond these two, they say, lies the third.'

"'Do they say where it is?' of course I asked.

"He said, 'Yes, indeed, they do, but they don't tell,' and his manner did not encourage me to put the obvious question. Instead of that I waited a moment, and said: 'What did the old man mean when he said you knew William Ager, as if that had something to do with the crowns?'

"'To be sure,' he said, 'now that's another curious story. These Agers – it's a very old name in these parts, but I can't find that they were ever people of quality or big owners – these Agers say, or said, that their branch of the family were the guardians of the last crown. A certain old Nathaniel Ager was the first one I knew – I was born and brought up quite near here – and he, I believe, camped out at the place during the whole of the war of 1870. William, his son, did the same, I know, during the South African War. And young William, *his* son, who has only died fairly recently, took lodgings at the cottage nearest the spot, and I've no doubt hastened his end, for he was a consumptive, by exposure and night watching. And he was the last of that branch. It was a dreadful grief to him to think that he was the last, but he could do nothing, the only relations at all near to him were in the colonies. I wrote letters for him to them imploring them to come over on business very important to the family, but there has been no answer. So the last of the holy crowns, if it's there, has no guardian now.'

"That was what the rector told me, and you can fancy how interesting I found it. The only thing I could think of when I left

him was how to hit upon the spot where the crown was supposed
to be. I wish I'd left it alone.

"But there was a sort of fate in it, for as I bicycled back past the
churchyard wall my eye caught a fairly new gravestone, and on it
was the name of William Ager. Of course I got off and read it. It
said 'of this parish, died at Seaburgh, 19 –, aged 28.' There it was,
you see. A little judicious questioning in the right place, and I should
at least find the cottage nearest the spot. Only I didn't quite know
what was the right place to begin my questioning at. Again there
was fate: it took me to the curiosity-shop down that way – you know
– and I turned over some old books, and, if you please, one was a
prayerbook of 1740 odd, in a rather handsome binding – I'll just go
and get it, it's in my room."

He left us in a state of some surprise, but we had hardly time to
exchange any remarks when he was back, panting, and handed us
the book opened at the fly-leaf, on which was, in a straggly hand:

> *Nathaniel Ager is my name and England is my nation,*
> *Seaburgh is my dwelling-place and Christ is my Salvation,*
> *When I am dead and in my Grave, and all my bones are rotton,*
> *I hope the Lord will think on me when I am quite forgotton.*

This poem was dated 1754, and there were many more entries
of Agers, Nathaniel, Frederick, William, and so on, ending with
William, 19 –.

"You see," he said, "anybody would call it the greatest bit of luck.
I did, but I don't now. Of course I asked the shopman about William
Ager, and of course he happened to remember that he lodged in a
cottage in the North Field and died there. This was just chalking
the road for me. I knew which the cottage must be: there is only one
sizeable one about there. The next thing was to scrape some sort of
acquaintance with the people, and I took a walk that way at once. A
dog did the business for me: he made at me so fiercely that they had to
run out and beat him off, and then naturally begged my pardon, and
we got into talk. I had only to bring up Ager's name, and pretend I
knew, or thought I knew something of him, and then the woman said
how sad it was him dying so young, and she was sure it came of him
spending the night out of doors in the cold weather. Then I had to
say: "Did he go out on the sea at night?" and she said: "Oh, no, it
was on the hillock yonder with the trees on it." And there I was.

"I know something about digging in these barrows: I've opened
many of them in the down country. But that was with owner's leave,
and in broad daylight and with men to help. I had to prospect very

carefully here before I put a spade in: I couldn't trench across the mound, and with those old firs growing there I knew there would be awkward tree roots. Still the soil was very light and sandy and easy, and there was a rabbit hole or so that might be developed into a sort of tunnel. The going out and coming back at odd hours to the hotel was going to be the awkward part. When I made up my mind about the way to excavate I told the people that I was called away for a night, and I spent it out there. I made my tunnel: I won't bore you with the details of how I supported it and filled it in when I'd done, but the main thing is that I got the crown."

Naturally we both broke out into exclamations of surprise and interest. I for one had long known about the finding of the crown at Rendlesham and had often lamented its fate. No one has ever seen an Anglo-Saxon crown – at least no one had. But our man gazed at us with a rueful eye. "Yes," he said, "and the worst of it is I don't know how to put it back."

"Put it back?" we cried out. "Why, my dear sir, you've made one of the most exciting finds ever heard of in this country. Of course it ought to go to the Jewel House at the Tower. What's your difficulty? If you're thinking about the owner of the land, and treasure-trove, and all that, we can certainly help you through. Nobody's going to make a fuss about technicalities in a case of this kind."

Probably more was said, but all he did was to put his face in his hands, and mutter: "I don't know how to put it back."

At last Long said: "You'll forgive me, I hope, if I seem impertinent, but are you *quite* sure you've got it?" I was wanting to ask much the same question myself, for of course the story did seem a lunatic's dream when one thought over it. But I hadn't quite dared to say what might hurt the poor young man's feelings. However, he took it quite calmly – really, with the calm of despair, you might say. He sat up and said: "Oh, yes, there's no doubt of that: I have it here, in my room, locked up in my bag. You can come and look at it if you like: I won't offer to bring it here."

We were not likely to let the chance slip. We went with him; his room was only a few doors off. The boots was just collecting shoes in the passage: or so we thought: afterwards we were not sure. Our visitor – his name was Paxton – was in a worse state of shivers than before, and went hurriedly into the room, and beckoned us after him, turned on the light, and shut the door carefully. Then he unlocked his kit-bag, and produced a bundle of clean pocket-handkerchiefs in which something was wrapped, laid it on the bed, and undid it. I can now say I *have* seen an actual Anglo-Saxon crown. It was of silver – as the Rendlesham one is always said to have been – it was set with some gems, mostly antique intaglios and cameos, and was of rather plain, almost rough workmanship. In fact, it was like those you see on the coins and in the manuscripts. I found no reason to think it was later than the ninth century. I was intensely interested, of course, and I wanted to turn it over in my hands, but Paxton prevented me. "Don't *you* touch it," he said, "I'll do that." And with a sigh that was, I declare to you, dreadful to hear, he took it up and turned it about so that we could see every part of it. "Seen enough?" he said at last, and we nodded. He wrapped it up and locked it in his bag, and stood looking at us dumbly. "Come back to our room," Long said, "and tell us what the trouble is." He thanked us, and said: "Will you go first and see if — if the coast is clear?" That wasn't very intelligible, for our proceedings hadn't been, after all, very suspicious, and the hotel, as I said, was practically empty. However, we were beginning to have inklings of — we didn't know what, and anyhow nerves are infectious. So we did go, first peering out as we opened the door, and fancying (I found we both had the fancy) that a shadow, or more than a shadow — but it made no sound — passed from before us to one side as we came out into the passage. "It's all right," we whispered to Paxton — whispering seemed the proper tone — and we went, with him between us, back to our sitting-room. I was preparing, when we got there, to be ecstatic about the unique interest of what we had seen, but when I looked at Paxton I saw that would be terribly out of place, and I left it to him to begin.

"What *is* to be done?" was his opening. Long thought it right (as he explained to me afterwards) to be obtuse, and said: "Why not find out who the owner of the land is, and inform — " "Oh, no, no!" Paxton broke in impatiently, "I beg your pardon: you've been very kind, but don't you see it's *got* to go back, and I daren't be there at night, and daytime's impossible. Perhaps, though, you don't see: well, then, the truth is that I've never been alone since I touched it." I was beginning some fairly stupid comment, but Long caught my eye, and I stopped. Long said: "I think I do see, perhaps: but wouldn't it be — a relief — to tell us a little more clearly what the situation is?"

Then it all came out: Paxton looked over his shoulder and beckoned to us to come nearer to him, and began speaking in a low voice: we listened most intently, of course, and compared notes afterwards, and I wrote down our version, so I am confident I have what he told us almost word for word. He said: "It began when I was first prospecting, and put me off again and again. There was always somebody — a man — standing by one of the firs. This was in daylight, you know. He was never in front of me. I always saw him with the tail of my eye on the left or the right, and he was never there when I looked straight for him. I would lie down for quite a long time and take careful observations, and make sure there was no one, and then when I got up and began prospecting again, there he was. And he began to give me hints, besides; for wherever I put that prayer-book – short of locking it up, which I did at last – when I came back to my room it was always out on my table open at the fly-leaf where the names are, and one of my razors across it to keep it open. I'm sure he just can't open my bag, or something more would have happened. You see, he's light and weak, but all the same I daren't face him. Well, then, when I was making the tunnel, of course it was worse, and if I hadn't been so keen I should have dropped the whole thing and run. It was like someone scraping at my back all the time: I thought for a long time it was only soil dropping on me, but as I got nearer the – the crown, it was unmistakable. And when I actually laid it bare and got my fingers into the ring of it and pulled it out, there came a sort of cry behind me – oh, I can't tell you how desolate it was! And horribly threatening too. It spoilt all my pleasure in my find – cut it off that moment. And if I hadn't been the wretched fool I am, I should have put the thing back and left it. But I didn't. The rest of the time was just awful. I had hours to get through before I could decently come back to the hotel. First I spent time filling up my tunnel and covering my tracks, and all the while he was there trying to thwart me. Sometimes, you know, you see him, and sometimes you don't, just as he pleases, I think: he's there, but he has some power over your eyes. Well, I wasn't off the spot very long before sunrise, and then I had to get to the junction for Seaburgh, and take a train back. And though it was daylight fairly soon, I don't know if that made it much better. There were always hedges, or gorsebushes, or park fences along the road – some sort of cover, I mean – and I was never easy for a second. And then when I began to meet people going to work, they always looked behind me very strangely: it might have been that they were surprised at seeing anyone so early; but I didn't think it was only that, and I don't now: they didn't look exactly at *me*. And the porter at the train was like that too. And the guard held open the door after I'd got into the carriage – just as he would if there was somebody else coming, you know. Oh, you may be very sure it isn't my fancy," he said with a dull sort of laugh. Then he went on: "And even if I do get it put back, he won't forgive me: I can tell that. And I was so happy a fortnight ago." He dropped into a chair, and I believe he began to cry.

We didn't know what to say, but we felt we must come to the rescue somehow, and so – it really seemed the only thing – we said

if he was so set on putting the crown back in its place, we would
help him. And I must say that after what we had heard it did seem
the right thing. If these horrid consequences had come on this poor
man, might there not really be something in the original idea of the
crown having some curious power bound up with it, to guard the
coast? At least, that was my feeling, and I think it was Long's too.
Our offer was very welcome to Paxton, anyhow. When could we do
it? It was nearing half-past ten. Could we contrive to make a late
walk plausible to the hotel people that very night? We looked out
of the window: there was a brilliant full moon – the Paschal moon.
Long undertook to tackle the boots and propitiate him. He was to
say that we should not be much over the hour, and if we did find it
so pleasant that we stopped out a bit longer we would see that he
didn't lose by sitting up. Well, we were pretty regular customers of
the hotel, and did not give much trouble, and were considered by the
servants to be not under the mark in the way of tips; and so the boots
was propitiated, and let us out on to the sea-front, and remained, as
we heard later, looking after us. Paxton had a large coat over his
arm, under which was the wrapped-up crown.

So we were off on this strange errand before we had time to think
how very much out of the way it was. I have told this part quite
shortly on purpose, for it really does represent the haste with which
we settled our plan and took action. "The shortest way is up the hill
and through the churchyard," Paxton said, as we stood a moment
before the hotel looking up and down the front. There was nobody
about – nobody at all. Seaburgh out of the season is an early, quiet
place. "We can't go along the dyke by the cottage, because of the
dog," Paxton also said, when I pointed to what I thought a shorter
way along the front and across two fields. The reason he gave was
good enough. We went up the road to the church, and turned in at
the churchyard gate. I confess to having thought that there might
be some lying there who might be conscious of our business: but if it
was so, they were also conscious that one who was on their side, so
to say, had us under surveillance, and we saw no sign of them. But
under observation we felt we were, as I have never felt it at another
time. Specially was it so when we passed out of the churchyard into
a narrow path with close high hedges, through which we hurried as
Christian did through that Valley; and so got out into open fields.
Then along hedges, though I would sooner have been in the open,
where I could see if anyone was visible behind me; over a gate or
two, and then a swerve to the left, taking us up on to the ridge which
ended in that mound.

As we neared it, Henry Long felt, and I felt too, that there were what I can only call dim presences waiting for us, as well as a far more actual one attending us. Of Paxton's agitation all this time I can give you no adequate picture: he breathed like a hunted beast, and we could not either of us look at his face. How he would manage when we got to the very place we had not troubled to think: he had seemed so sure that that would not be difficult. Nor was it. I never saw anything like the dash with which he flung himself at a particular spot in the side of the mound, and tore at it, so that in a very few minutes the greater part of his body was out of sight. We stood holding the coat and that bundle of handkerchiefs, and looking, very fearfully, I must admit, about us. There was nothing to be seen: a line of dark firs behind us made one skyline, more trees and the church tower half a mile off on the right, cottages and a windmill on the horizon on the left, calm sea dead in front, faint barking of a dog at a cottage on a gleaming dyke between us and it: full moon making that path we know across the sea: the eternal whisper of the Scotch firs just above us, and of the sea in front. Yet, in all this quiet, an acute, an acrid consciousness of a restrained hostility very near us, like a dog on a leash that might be let go at any moment.

Paxton pulled himself out of the hole, and stretched a hand back to us. "Give it to me," he whispered, "unwrapped." We pulled off the handkerchiefs, and he took the crown. The moonlight just fell on it as he snatched it. We had not ourselves touched that bit of metal, and I have thought since that it was just as well. In another moment Paxton was out of the hole again and busy shovelling back the soil with hands that were already bleeding. He would have none of our help, though. It was much the longest part of the job to get the place to look undisturbed: yet – I don't know how – he made a wonderful success of it. At last he was satisfied, and we turned back.

We were a couple of hundred yards from the hill when Long suddenly said to him: "I say, you've left your coat there. That won't do. See?" And I certainly did see it – the long dark overcoat lying where the tunnel had been. Paxton had not stopped, however: he only shook his head, and held up the coat on his arm. And when we joined him, he said, without any excitement, but as if nothing mattered any more: "That wasn't my coat." And, indeed, when we looked back again, that dark thing was not to be seen.

Well, we got out on to the road, and came rapidly back that way. It was well before twelve when we got in, trying to put a good face on it, and saying – Long and I – what a lovely night it was for a walk. The boots was on the look-out for us, and we made remarks like that for his edification as we entered the hotel. He gave another look up and down the sea-front before he locked the front door, and said:

"You didn't meet many people about, I s'pose, sir?" "No, indeed, not a soul," I said; at which I remember Paxton looked oddly at me. "Only I thought I see someone turn up the station road after you gentlemen," said the boots. "Still, you was three together, and I don't suppose he meant mischief." I didn't know what to say; Long merely said "Good night," and we went off upstairs, promising to turn out all lights, and to go to bed in a few minutes.

Back in our room, we did our very best to make Paxton take a cheerful view. "There's the crown safe back," we said; "very likely you'd have done better not to touch it" (and he heavily assented to that), "but no real harm has been done, and we shall never give this away to anyone who would be so mad as to go near it. Besides, don't you feel better yourself? I don't mind confessing," I said, "that on the way there I was very much inclined to take your view about – well, about being followed; but going back, it wasn't at all the same thing, was it?" No, it wouldn't do: "*You've* nothing to trouble yourselves about," he said, "but I'm not forgiven. I've got to pay for that miserable sacrilege still. I know what you are going to say. The Church might help. Yes, but it's the body that has to suffer. It's true I'm not feeling that he's waiting outside for me just now. But – " Then he stopped. Then he turned to thanking us, and we put him off as soon as we could. And naturally we pressed him to use our sitting-room next day, and said we should be glad to go out with him. Or did he play golf, perhaps? Yes, he did, but he didn't think he should care about that to-morrow. Well, we recommended him to get up late and sit in our room in the morning while we were playing, and we would have a walk later in the day. He was very submissive and *piano* about it all: ready to do just what we thought best, but clearly quite certain in his own mind that what was coming could not be averted or palliated. You'll wonder why we didn't insist on accompanying him to his home and seeing him safe into the care of brothers or someone. The fact was he had nobody. He had had a flat in town, but lately he had made up his mind to settle for a time in Sweden, and he had dismantled his flat and shipped off his belongings, and was whiling away a fortnight or three weeks before he made a start. Anyhow, we didn't see what we could do better than sleep on it – or not sleep very much, as was my case – and see what we felt like to-morrow morning.

We felt very different, Long and I, on as beautiful an April morning as you could desire; and Paxton also looked very different when we saw him at breakfast. "The first approach to a decent night I seem ever to have had," was what he said. But he was going to do as we had settled: stay in probably all the morning, and come out with us later. We went to the links; we met some other men and played with them in the morning, and had lunch there rather early, so as not to be late back. All the same, the snares of death overtook him.

Whether it could have been prevented, I don't know. I think he would have been got at somehow, do what we might. Anyhow, this is what happened.

We went straight up to our room. Paxton was there, reading quite peaceably. "Ready to come out shortly?" said Long, "say in half an hour's time?" "Certainly," he said: and I said we would change first, and perhaps have baths, and call for him in half an hour. I had my bath first, and went and lay down on my bed, and slept for about ten minutes. We came out of our rooms at the same time, and went together to the sitting-room. Paxton wasn't there – only his book. Nor was he in his room, nor in the downstair rooms. We shouted for him. A servant came out and said: "Why, I thought you gentlemen was gone out already, and so did the other gentleman. He heard you a-calling from the path there, and run out in a hurry, and I looked out of the coffee-room window, but I didn't see you. 'Owever, he run off down the beach that way."

Without a word we ran that way too – it was the opposite direction to that of last night's expedition. It wasn't quite four o'clock, and the day was fair, though not so fair as it had been, so there was really no reason, you'd say, for anxiety: with people about, surely a man couldn't come to much harm.

But something in our look as we ran out must have struck the servant, for she came out on the steps, and pointed, and said, "Yes, that's the way he went." We ran on as far as the top of the shingle bank, and there pulled up. There was a choice of ways: past the houses on the sea-front, or along the sand at the bottom of the beach, which, the tide being now out, was fairly broad. Or of course we might keep along the shingle between these two tracks and have some view of both of them; only that was heavy going. We chose the sand, for that was the loneliest, and someone *might* come to harm there without being seen from the public path.

Long said he saw Paxton some distance ahead, running and waving his stick, as if he wanted to signal to people who were on ahead of him. I couldn't be sure: one of these sea-mists was coming up very quickly from the south. There was someone, that's all I could say. And there were tracks on the sand as of someone running who wore shoes; and there were other tracks made before those – for the shoes sometimes trod in them and interfered with them – of someone not in shoes. Oh, of course, it's only my word you've got to take for all this: Long's dead, we'd no time or means to make sketches or take casts, and the next tide washed everything away. All we could do was to notice these marks as we hurried on. But there they were over and over again, and we had no doubt whatever that what we saw was the track of a bare foot, and one that showed more bones than flesh.

The notion of Paxton running after – after anything like this, and supposing it to be the friends he was looking for, was very dreadful to us. You can guess what we fancied: how the thing he was following might stop suddenly and turn round on him, and what sort of face it would show, half-seen at first in the mist – which all the while was getting thicker and thicker. And as I ran on wondering how the poor wretch could have been lured into mistaking that other thing for us, I remembered his saying, "He has some power over your eyes." And then I wondered what the end would be, for I had no hope now that the end could be averted, and – well, there is no need to tell all the dismal and horrid thoughts that flitted through my head as we ran on into the mist. It was uncanny, too, that the sun should still be bright in the sky and we could see nothing. We could only tell that we were now past the houses and had reached that gap there is between them and the old martello tower. When you are past the tower, you know, there is nothing but shingle for a long way – not a house, not a human creature, just that spit of land, or rather shingle, with the river on your right and the sea on your left.

But just before that, just by the martello tower, you remember there is the old battery, close to the sea. I believe there are only a few blocks of concrete left now: the rest has all been washed away, but at this time there was a lot more, though the place was a ruin. Well, when we got there, we clambered to the top as quick as we could to take breath and look over the shingle in front if by chance the mist would let us see anything. But a moment's rest we must have. We had run a mile at least. Nothing whatever was visible ahead of us, and we were just turning by common consent to get down and run hopelessly on, when we heard what I can only call a laugh: and if you can understand what I mean by a breathless, a lungless laugh, you have it: but I don't suppose you can. It came from below, and swerved away into the mist. That was enough. We bent over the wall. Paxton was there at the bottom.

You don't need to be told that he was dead. His tracks showed that he had run along the side of the battery, had turned sharp round the corner of it, and, small doubt of it, must have dashed straight into the open arms of someone who was waiting there. His mouth was full of sand and stones, and his teeth and jaws were broken to bits. I only glanced once at his face.

At the same moment, just as we were scrambling down from the battery to get to the body, we heard a shout, and saw a man running down the bank of the martello tower. He was the caretaker stationed there, and his keen old eyes had managed to descry through the mist that something was wrong. He had seen Paxton fall, and had seen us a moment after, running up – fortunate this, for otherwise we could hardly have escaped suspicion of being concerned in the dreadful business. Had he, we asked, caught sight of anybody attacking our friend? He could not be sure.

We sent him off for help, and stayed by the dead man till they came with the stretcher. It was then that we traced out how he had come, on the narrow fringe of sand under the battery wall. The rest was shingle, and it was hopelessly impossible to tell whither the other had gone.

What were we to say at the inquest? It was a duty, we felt, not to give up, there and then, the secret of the crown, to be published in every paper. I don't know how much you would have told; but what we did agree upon was this: to say that we had only made acquaintance with Paxton the day before, and that he had told us he was under some apprehension of danger at the hands of a man called William Ager. Also that we had seen some other tracks besides Paxton's when we followed him along the beach. But of course by that time everything was gone from the sands.

No one had any knowledge, fortunately, of any William Ager living in the district. The evidence of the man at the martello tower freed us from all suspicion. All that could be done was to return a verdict of wilful murder by some person or persons unknown.

Paxton was so totally without connections that all the inquiries that were subsequently made ended in a No Thoroughfare. And I have never been at Seaburgh, or even near it, since.

Nicholas Royle

The Crucian Pit

Nicholas Royle has been described by Interzone *as the "leading light of the British horror scene", while* Fear *called him "Britain's most successful young writer of short horror fiction."*

He has had more than sixty short stories published in a wide variety of publications, including various volumes of Best New Horror, The Year's Best Horror Stories *and* The Year's Best Fantasy and Horror, *as well as such recent books and magazines as* Blood and Roses, Peeping Tom, Dark Voices 4 and 5, *and* Narrow Houses. *Royle's first novel,* Counterparts, *appeared in 1993 from Barrington Books as a limited edition paperback.*

He won the 1991 British Fantasy Award for his original anthology of psychological horror stories, Darklands, *and followed up with a second volume in 1992. Both books are being published in mass-market editions by New English Library.*

About "The Crucian Pit", the author asks: "Should you or shouldn't you go back to special places? It's probably a bad idea, especially if you hope to feel what you felt before. But I'm drawn very strongly to certain places which seem to contain latent power in relation to me and my past. The crucian pit exists, but is full of tiny rudd now, nice fish but not as exciting as crucian."

Get ready for a trip back into a past where the horror has never gone away . . .

IT ISN'T *always* a bad idea to go back. Sometimes you have to.

Nicci and I drove up north on Friday morning in my red Citroen. She'd managed to get someone to cover for her at the bookshop and I'd simply told my art director I needed the day off. As a freelance designer that meant losing a day's pay but I'd been waiting a long time to make this trip, even since before I met Nicci, and I wasn't going to waste half the weekend by driving up on a Saturday. It was bad enough on the Friday morning thanks to two stretches of roadworks between the M25 and Newport Pagnell. By 11.30, however, we were clear and belting up the M1 with the windows down and Chris Rea cranked up to full volume. It was a beautiful day, bright sunshine, no wind – not even the sprawl of the Midlands could spoil it. We invented stories about other drivers. The mid-30s blonde in the BMW was on her way to meet a younger lover in Macclesfield; the rep in the Sierra was working his last day for a pharmaceuticals company and would start a new job as picture researcher for a girlie magazine on Monday. Drivers who'd been pulled over by speed cops we either felt sorry for or laughed at – depending on what car they drove. We were both doing pretty well financially and I'd bought the Citroen almost new as an ex-demonstration model, but we still both felt more of an affinity with the young rocker in his souped-up Singer Vogue than the tosser on the phone in his Porsche.

Nicci's bookshop job was filling in time between college and something more interesting, she said. Acting or music, she was vague about it but she was happy enough. I'd come on since my first job – stuffing envelopes – and prospects were looking good, but I couldn't fully relax at anything until I'd gone back up north and laid certain ghosts to rest. That's why I was getting more and more excited – and nervous – the closer we got. This weekend was important. I wasn't expecting to enjoy every moment but there would be pleasures to be had in touring round the old haunts. We wouldn't be seeing my folks – even though Nicci still hadn't met them – as they had left the area years ago for Scotland and well-earned retirement.

As I began recognizing landmarks I pointed them out to Nicci and she made up little episodes from my childhood to fit around them. "Yes, that's the water tower you walked to from home once in the middle of the night completely naked. You walked all the way because you thought you could hear it singing. The next day you visited your family doctor, Dr Naik, and he diagnosed tinnitus. Since that day you've been suspicious of water towers." I glanced sideways at her and said, "You're mad, Nicci, completely mad." She threw her head back and laughed, then she said, "This is shit," and ejected the Chris Rea.

"So choose something else," I said, checking my rearview mirror. She went through the tapes on the shelf, picking them up, reading the labels and chucking them over her shoulder into the back as she muttered to herself about how they were all shit and why didn't I have any decent music. It was good fun and I was enjoying it as much as her. She did in fact like most of the tapes but she'd obviously decided only one thing would do. "Ah," she cried in triumph. "This is more like it." And she slid a tape into the machine.

It was Gary Glitter. I looked at her again and laughed. She was right, of course. If I was going back I should have the right soundtrack to go back with. So it was to the accompaniment of 'Rock and Roll Part I' that we left the motorway and sailed up the long, straight A road that led back to my childhood. All the place names were practically dripping with nostalgia.

"You loved your childhood, didn't you?" Nicci said. I nodded. But I remembered it with sadness as well as pleasure. Even sitting there in the car with Nicci was tinged with sadness. I was hoping, of course, that the weekend would do something about that.

I wasn't planning to go and look for the Crucian Pit until later, perhaps that evening while it was still light. First I just wanted to drive around the city and outskirts looking for anything that would take me back to what it was like then. This kind of stuff, of course, doesn't mean a great deal to someone who wasn't there, but Nicci had insisted she wanted to come.

We drove past the railway depot where I used to go clambering about in old rolling stock and sneaking into the sheds to look at the locomotives. Other kids took down numbers but I just liked being around the place, the smells of diesel and grease, the black-faced engineers working down the inspection pits, the crunch of the chippings between the tracks. Anyone who's ever looked twice at a train will know what I mean. There's romance in railway sheds. We parked for a minute or two and Nicci sat on the bonnet of the car swinging her legs while I went and peered over the fence which I had scaled as a child. I recognized the corner of a shed, the pattern of the tracks going into the sidings. For all I knew they could have been the same old diesels standing idle beside the main line.

We drove on and stopped outside my old school and watched boys playing cricket in front of the pavilion. "A bit posh, isn't it?" Nicci said with a heavy frown. "You weren't by any chance an over-privileged little git, were you?"

I smiled at her and she raised her eyebrows a fraction just like

Kathy would have done. Just occasionally she reminded me of Kathy. Who knows, maybe you do spend your whole life looking for one person, someone you were shown a photograph of before you were born, and that's why all your partners look the same. Nicci was funnier than Kathy though and as far as I was concerned they were unalike, apart from the odd expression – the eyebrows, stuff like that.

"I haven't upset you, have I?" she said, worried.

"No, of course not. Sorry, I was miles away. It's seeing the old school. I loved it."

I tried not to mention Kathy. There's nothing worse than going on about your old girlfriend to your current partner. She pretends not to care but she does. Who wouldn't?

I felt Nicci's hand on the back of my neck and turned to smile at her. I *had* to stop thinking about Kathy. She was in the past. They say your first love leaves an indelible impression and they could be right. But this trip was meant to be about forgetting Kathy.

Nicci and I drove away from the school but I was still thinking about her. Ten years ago I didn't drive and if Kathy and I went anywhere out of town we had to use bikes or go by train. We had a few picnics in outlying parks, an unforgettable day in the dunes at Formby, a couple of visits to the Crucian Pit.

I first came into contact with Kathy when we were both about fifteen. Out of the girls who caught my bus to school and sat on the top deck she was the one I fancied the most. I probably fancied them all – even those you could never own up to fancying because they were too fat or had greasy hair – but she was the only one who made my heart beat faster and my mouth go dry. It was largely for her benefit that I ostentatiously folded back the huge pages of the *New Musical Express* each week, thinking it would make me look cool. I made sure the knot of my tie never reached my neck and almost certainly I would have had my blazer collar turned up. For all the trouble I took to look good I didn't have the bottle to speak to her and ask her out, so I wrote a note and left it on her seat one morning. It said something like, "Would you like to go to a gig? I can get tickets."

When she got on, her just-washed fair hair shone in the spring sunlight and she looked as gorgeous as ever. She might have only been fifteen; she was a woman to me, deeply mysterious and alluring, her maroon and blue uniform concealing a body I had wild fantasies about every night. She picked the note up off the seat before she sat down and read it. Instead of looking round immediately she looked out of the window. When she did look round, her eyes giving nothing away, she saw me watching her and that's when our eyes met for the first time. Her friends got on at the next stop and I spent the rest of the journey in an agony of waiting. When they got up in a group to go Kathy avoided looking at me and one of her friends passed me a folded note. The friend even gave me a tiny smile.

It was a very encouraging rejection. Not because she indicated she might ever change her mind but because of the nice tone in which it was written. She hadn't used the opportunity to take the piss, as some girls would have done. She'd been nice about it. Thank you very much, but no thank you. "I think I ought to point out," she wrote "that I am already going out with someone, and have been for the last two months." I pictured him instantly – taller and darker than me with clear skin and a deeper voice. He would live in one of the posh southern suburbs and would be able to afford to take her out anywhere whenever she wanted. He was a total bastard, obviously: didn't have to revise for exams, never suffered from respiratory diseases, probably even smoked joints and tried on Nazi uniforms at home in front of his mirror.

It almost didn't matter that she'd said no because now I had a scrap of paper with her handwriting on. I carried it with me for months, taking it out in school assembly to examine every curve of her signature and feel the underside of the paper where the ballpoint had pressed through, the ballpoint that she'd held in her hand. A kid in my class called Andrew Rosemarine told me there was nothing nobler than unrequited love. I tried hard to believe in this for a few weeks.

I still got the same bus to school and so did Kathy but I made less of an effort. I even started getting *Angling Times* instead of the *NME*. Maybe it was exactly that lack of effort which swung it in the end because when we happened both to be at the same party one Saturday night late in the summer it was Kathy who came out into the garden to look for me and we sort of took it from there. I never asked her about the other boyfriend in case I found out she'd just made him up to have an excuse to turn me down.

Nicci and I stopped for some fish and chips at Jon's Fish Bar. "I know," she said. "You used to nick 50p out of your mum's purse and use 10p of it to get the bus, then you'd spend 40p on a bag of chips which you'd eat walking home. Then you wouldn't want your tea but you wouldn't be able to explain why and you always ended up feeling guilty so it wasn't really worth it."

"Yes," I said, "but you left out the bit about discovering a murdered woman on the way home and not being able to report it because then it would come out about nicking the money to get chips." We were crossing the road and already I could smell the chips. "No. Whenever we went out in the evening and were coming back along this road I'd drop heavy hints about getting some fish and chips, and if my dad was in a good mood we'd stop. He'd park exactly where I've parked in that side street and I'd cross the road to get them just like we're doing now."

It wasn't the same man in Jon's but the chips tasted the same.

We drove further south and soon we were sitting in the car outside the house where I'd been brought up. "It's so upsetting," I said, looking at the huge hole dug in the front garden presumably for foundations to be laid so they could build an extension. I desperately wanted to knock on the door and ask if I could have a look round. But at the same time I knew it wasn't a good idea. Sometimes it *is* just best to keep things as you remember them.

"Shall we go?" Nicci said, picking up on my mood.

I turned in my seat to look at her and reached out for her hands. I held them tightly. "I mustn't lose you," I said, and thought: like I lost Kathy.

Ten minutes later we were driving south out of town towards the airport. The Crucian Pit was right next to the airport, very close to the main runway. Or it had been in the old days. I didn't know if it would still be there, but I hoped so. It was important I found it.

"When I've had a look at the Crucian Pit we'll find somewhere to stay," I said as I calmly negotiated the double roundabout which I remembered so clearly. Ten years ago and more I'd made this trip on my push-bike, tackle box strapped on the little luggage rack, rod bag slung over my back. By this stage I'd be knackered and longing for the peace of the poolside, the sun beating down on the lily pads, the surprisingly tough little crucian carp throwing themselves at my bread punch.

Getting there had always been a struggle but with paradise at the end of it all.

"Do you want to wait in the car, Nicci?" I asked her. "I won't be long." She looked at me and smiled and nodded.

"Don't be nervous," she said. "I'm sure it'll still be there. I'll wait here for you."

I wanted to tell her I loved her but for some reason felt shy or too much in awe of her. She could tell I wanted to go up there by myself and she didn't mind. Even if she did mind she wasn't going to show it because she knew how important this was to me. Maybe in that moment she seemed too good to be true. I nearly said it but instead left it to my eyes to tell her what I felt.

I walked away from the car, which I'd had to park fifty yards down
a narrow track off the main road which itself was too dangerous to
park on at that point because of the tunnel – about a hundred yards
from the track the main road went into the tunnel under the end of
the main runway. I looked back at the car and could see the back
of Nicci's head. For some reason I whispered, "I love you."

I crossed the main road and started to climb up the embankment
that led to the thick copse that in the old days had concealed the
Crucian Pit.

I heard a plane take off but didn't look up. My breathing became
quicker and shallower as I climbed and it wasn't just the effort
involved. Ten years ago, for a number of reasons, the Crucian Pit
had been one of the most important places in my life, probably *the*
most important.

I reached the top of the slope and stopped to catch my breath. I
looked back down at the road. Cars sped past and were swallowed
by the tunnel. I could see the entrance to the little track down which
I'd parked the Citroen but the car was out of sight.

One change I had noticed on my way up the embankment was
that a mesh fence had been erected along the ridge at head height,
replacing an old wooden fence which in my day had been broken in
various places. This was a bad sign. I parted the foliage of a young
tree to get a look through the fence. My heart sank. The flat land
beyond had been cleared. What before had been a virtual forest of
entangled vines and brambles and shrubs was now as clear as the
runways beyond. I tried to look to the left to see if any vegetation
remained but the fence prevented me. I backed away and began
picking my way along the top of the slope between trees and
overgrown hawthorn hedge. I was oblivious to the sharp little thorns
that caught my hands. Already I'd gone beyond the point at which
in the past I had climbed through a hole in the wooden fence and
started to make my way past a mysterious group of outbuildings to
the pit. I was fast losing hope and beginning to curse the authorities
for filling in the pit when I noticed a tall hedge on the other side of
the fence that met the wire at right angles. I pushed aside branches
and tangles of creeper to get a look beyond the fence. There was a
small paddock. I didn't remember this, but then I had never needed
to come this far along the ridge. On the far side of the paddock was
another high hedge. I needed to discover what lay beyond that.

I looked at my watch. I'd been gone ten minutes. I didn't want
to leave Nicci waiting too long, but she had seemed to understand
what was going on. From beyond the trees I heard the roar of a jet
as it accelerated for take-off. I heard it come screaming down the

runway and knew exactly when its wheels had left the tarmac. The plane appeared above the trees and I watched it climb with my heart in my mouth.

The fence was high but I was agile and very light. I was over in seconds. The paddock was as quiet as the grave. No planes were taking off or landing. The road seemed to have become distant as well. A light breeze touched my face and whispered through the tops of the trees. A hornet buzzed somewhere behind me and I heard the distinct chirrup of a grasshopper.

I hoped Nicci was all right. The car now seemed a long way away as I approached the hedge on the far side of the paddock. It was thick but I worked my way through it and over a low wire fence. I found a rough path and followed it through a stand of trees until I began to recognize landmarks – a fallen log, a sleek bed of nettles – and I knew I was back on familiar ground.

I smelt the Crucian Pit before it came into view. I felt enormous relief that it was still there. I walked another fifty yards until I could see it before me, not smaller than I remembered it – as I had feared it might be, if I were to find it at all – but slightly bigger if anything. I shivered at the sight of it, feeling a mixture of pleasure and unease. Over on the runway a jet began its take-off run but I looked down at the surface of the pit. There were lily pads still covering the surface at the eastern end. Lose a crucian in them and you wouldn't ever get it out.

I'd fished the pit maybe twenty times in all, in a variety of swims, and it was easily the best stillwater I'd ever visited. If it was stocked with any fish other than crucian carp I'd never caught any. And in all my visits I never saw another angler. I never knew if I was permitted to fish there, though I doubted it because of the difficulty in finding the place, and because there was never anyone else about. The man who had told me about it and given me vague directions – flame-haired Jim, our window cleaner – claimed to have fished there for a couple of seasons and never seen a soul. He stopped going because the cycle ride got too much for him. I was younger and fitter and perhaps fonder of crucians than Jim, who later developed an obsession with specimen mirror and leather carp.

The first day I fished there is as clear in my mind as the last. I broke through the last line of bushes and was profoundly shocked by this sudden expanse of water hidden away in between semi-urban farmland and the airport. Nothing Jim had told me had prepared me for the reality. It was an angler's paradise, nothing less, with its deep green unpolluted water and hosts of lily pads. The bank undulated as it made its way slowly around the water so that there were small promontories and inlets, ideal for getting your bait out among the feeding crucians and steering the exhausted fish into shallow water to land it. There were bulrushes, reeds and weeping willows, and at the far end nearest the airport fences an explosion of yellow gorse.

I completed a circuit of the pit before choosing a swim. Often a previous angler's debris will tell you where there has at least been activity, but there was no sign of anybody having been here at all. Jim, obviously, was not one to give anglers a bad name by leaving old nylon line and maggot dumps lying around. I still didn't know for sure that there were fish to be caught, though I had Jim's word and a growing sense of my own that the pit was teeming with life. I chose a swim where the ground was not too muddy for my basket and I tackled up with nervous fingers. Twice I dropped a size 20 hook in the grass at my feet and had to get down on hands and knees to find it rather than allow it to defile the perfection of the place. I wanted to leave it exactly as I had found it.

I used my favourite float – an orange-tipped quill – with two lead shot pinched on to the line half way up from the hook. I elected to fish without any cocking shot directly under the float, so that if a crucian took the bait on the way down I'd know because the float would continue to lie flat on the surface instead of cocking. This method of presentation had already proved irresistible to crucians and rudd in one of my local ponds that summer. I cast out no more than twenty feet and waited for the float to cock, which it didn't. I imagined the shot caught up with the float and the bread fifty yards away having flown off the hook. But just in case, I struck lightly upwards and to the left and immediately bent into a fighting crucian. The quick, edgy runs and strong tugs would have betrayed the species even without prior knowledge. I landed it in half a minute without a net and admired its beautiful golden flanks.

That was the first of at least twenty five crucians caught in three hours. I got lightly sunburned. I fished until about eight when the colours in the sky were turning heavier and the landing jets flashed vivid messages across the water. Prior to packing up I pulled my keepnet out of the water and using the pocket camera I always kept in the basket took a perfect little picture before returning my finest catch to the water.

Not all my memories of the Crucian Pit were recorded in this way however. I looked at my watch and thought about Nicci waiting in the car. Would she be getting pissed off? I decided not. She had seemed happy to let me do this on my own. I started to walk around the pit. Much of the vegetation that had graced the shallows was there again ten years later, though the willows and other trees that had stood by the edge of the water were no longer around. I walked past the bulrushes and round the far end by the gorse bushes until I reached the trees on the north side of the pit.

After I'd gone on endlessly about the Crucian Pit to Kathy she had said she wanted to come, so on a scorching afternoon in August I left my tackle at home and took Kathy instead. She fell in love with it at first sight and I swore her to secrecy.

"It can be our secret place," I said. "Whatever happens to us in the future, we can come back here and as good as be with each other." She gave me a sad look. We both knew the summer was drawing to a close and not only were we at the transition between school and university – which had threatened to split us up – but Kathy's father had accepted a twelve-month lecturing post at Phillips Academy, Massachusetts. As far as everyone except Kathy and I were concerned, she was going too, along with the rest of the family. I naturally hoped she would stay. Kathy herself was still undecided. "I know what I want," she said. "But I know what I should do."

I took her hand and we wandered round to the trees on the north side. There were enough trees to shield us from the runway – though airport ground staff rarely happened to come out this far – and from the farmland on the other side. But in any case, the only people I ever saw while I was at the Crucian Pit were the faces at the windows of planes taking off and landing. Them and Kathy, on the three occasions she came there with me.

We lay down in the long grass using a soft mound as a pillow and I held Kathy by her shoulders and kissed her slowly. She moved like a lizard beneath me and we hugged each other so fiercely a bright pain flared up at the front of my skull. We were both still virgins, but not for very much longer. I whispered my love to her. She responded, "I need you, I need you." We had so far had precious few opportunities to go beyond the limit of our meagre experience, taking advantage of evenings when her parents and sister went out, but never quite to the full.

Kathy was wearing a white T shirt with Peugeot written across the chest and a pair of baggy shorts. As our kissing became more and more urgent I slipped my hand inside her T shirt and touched her breast, squeezing it and then slipping two fingers inside her bra. With the sun beating down on my back and in the knowledge that we were completely alone I was becoming almost unbearably excited. But still I was nervous and shy. I couldn't bring myself to be adventurous. After a couple of minutes Kathy sat up and peeled her T shirt over her head and unclipped her bra, pulling it off and dropping it on the grass.

I was shocked by so much bare flesh. We had previously made our limited explorations of each other's bodies in semi-darkness, due partly to shyness and partly to guilt. If we did it in the dark it wasn't so bad. It was that sort of logic.

Shocked but turned on in a way I never had been before I reached out and touched her.

It wasn't awkward and fumbled, nor was it over in seconds and all something of a disappointment. Rocked in the sun's honeyed embrace we pushed out slowly into the furthest reaches of sensation and soared to such heights of emotion as neither of us had imagined to exist. Afterwards we clung to each other and wept. Over on the runway the thrust of jet engines propelled hundreds of helpless passengers time after time into the skies. Gnats danced crazily above our heads as the slowly sinking sun dried the moisture on our bodies. We whispered promises to each other, believing in them with utter conviction. Tiny playful crucians splashed their tails and fins clear of the surface of the pit. If I'd had my fishing basket we would have used my penknife to carve some message into the bark of one of the trees, and we would have taken photographs of each other – one each only. But we sensed it would prove to be an unforgettable afternoon even without photographs. There was a solemnity about us as we got dressed and sat with our arms around each other to watch the sun go down. Then we walked once round the Crucian Pit and regretfully made our way through the bushes and undergrowth to climb back down the embankment and return to a world which would now be transformed.

I was still standing beneath the trees studying the exact spot where we had lain ten years earlier when I heard the faintest of noises behind me and then felt hot breath on my neck. I turned to face Nicci standing right behind me. I was too surprised to speak.

"This was where you made love," she said, laying a light hand to my shoulder and raising her eyebrow a fraction in that way that was not entirely hers.

Head bent again over the soft mound of earth I could only nod silently amid a storm of questions. How did she know that? How had she found me? How had she approached so quietly?

I don't know how many minutes passed but it seemed like there had been an ellipsis in time – almost as if I had blacked out – before I turned round again to find myself alone. "Nicci," I called, my voice tearing through the idyllic scene like a vandal destroying a painting. "Nicci. Where've you gone?" There wasn't a single sign that she'd been there at all, except for a slight chill on the back of my neck. I spun round looking in every direction but couldn't see her. She couldn't have vanished so quickly. Had I imagined her?

Then like a punch in the chest it hit me and I ran, tearing my way through the gorse and trees at the airport end of the pit to get to the thick hedge which led to the paddock. Branches whipped this way and that as I forced my way through. A jet took off from the runway barely a hundred yards away with a great whoosh and its engines screaming. I shuddered with fear.

Imagining her so clearly that I even felt her breath on my neck could only have been a premonition. She was in danger.

I jumped over the low wire fence into the paddock and suddenly everything seemed to slow down. I felt completely exhausted. The long grass drained the energy from my legs and I wanted to lie down. The jet that had just taken off banked steeply so that it seemed to be nosediving towards the paddock. I just wanted to sleep but my legs kept moving. I struggled to reach the fence and somehow found the strength to climb it.

I landed in a crouch and scampered in a crab-like fashion down the embankment, then ran across the main road which was empty, although I had hardly given it a glance. The little track was slippery with gravel underfoot and I was fortunate to stay upright as I sprinted breathlessly to the Citroen. From a distance it looked empty and I prayed it was an optical illusion. When I reached the car and saw that it was no trick I became hysterical – chanting out loud in the thick warm air of the lengthening evening – praying that Nicci had just gone for a walk. I flung open the driver's door and looked at the floor in front of the passenger's seat. Her bag was gone. I looked in the back. The cassettes were still strewn over the back seat where she had tossed them.

My heart beating furiously I looked in the rearview mirror for any lingering shadows but all I saw was my own distraught face, mouth twisted in panic.

Some time later I found myself walking dejectedly back across the road and mounting the embankment. The Crucian Pit was now as still as the paddock had been earlier. No fish jumped and the clouds of gnats had dispersed. I became aware that I was crying. For some perverse reassurance I patted the inside pocket of my jacket. It was still there, the photograph I'd carried for ten years. Over on the runway a jet fired up its engines for maximum thrust then allowed them to die down, presumably in receipt of some instruction from the tower. I sat on the soft mound where Kathy and I had opened ourselves up to each other and contemplated the leathery surface of the pit. The sun had fallen beneath the horizon but the sky was still aglow. As I looked round in case Nicci was about to slip out from behind a tree like some sprite I slipped the photograph from my inside pocket and ran my fingers over its surface. I knew each crease that had appeared in the ten years since I had taken it. I knew every minute detail of the image but I always carried it nevertheless. It was like an act of faith, the patient work of an unquestioning servant. And now the waiting was almost over. It was time to put the past behind me time to lay all the ghosts to rest. I'd heard their cries in my head every day for ten years.

I continued to fish the Crucian Pit after Kathy and I had christened it. The small carp were still lining up to take my bread punch but as the summer stretched into early September my visits were fruited with the fungus of melancholy. Kathy had bowed to pressure to go with her family to Massachusetts for a year off before she took her place at Southampton. There were tears every time we saw each other after that decision was made. We went for long walks on the Edge and sat on the huge, flat, overhanging rocks for hours dangling our feet into nothingness. I would notice movement out of the corner of my eye and know that Kathy's shoulders were shaking as she sobbed. My own face would crumple like an expiring balloon, but not before I had put my arm around her shoulders and drawn her to me. She would know but not see that I was crying too. We walked by the river south of the Edge, meandering in our conversation too: looking back over the summer and forward to our own personal ambitions. We would keep in touch, we both promised – indeed, Kathy said she would write every day – and, after all, a year was not a long time.

But we both knew that back then it was a very long time.

In an unguarded moment one evening as we sat watching the old men play bowls on the green behind my parents' house Kathy said, "You'll find someone else." I broke down and cried until long after the men had packed up their bowls in their little brown leather cases and shouted their good-byes to each other across the darkening grass. Of course, I didn't want to find anyone else, but the suggestion that I might raised the spectre I had not dared to confront: the near certainty that some handsome freshman would sweep Kathy off her feet and she might never come back. I imagined her returning here grey-haired and pudding-shaped to share her early memories with the good grey man that college kid had grown into.

I was crying for more than a lost love though. I was going away too and would have some growing up to do. The summer we'd enjoyed together was the last one in this part of my life. I'd never recapture these scorching afternoons playing the eager, flighty carp as I had. The Crucian Pit was already a memory before the summer was over.

I looked at the photograph in my hand and felt a brief chill invade my chest.

I still don't really know what made me take it; some deep instinct, a need to seize the last guttering of the candle before an indifferent draught snuffed it out. Some compulsion made me delve into the basket for the camera.

It was going to be my last visit to the Crucian Pit in any case. Two weeks into September the carp were neither as hungry nor as lively as they had been. I was trying to concentrate on the fishing but my mind was on other things. Planes took off throughout the afternoon and, whereas normally they hardly impinged on my consciousness, today the constant noise was giving me a headache. I was ready to pack up and go when it happened.

I was watching a plane which had just taken off, at first because its engines sounded different and then because it banked steeply and lost altitude suddenly. The pilot seemed to try to bring the nose around so that he could land again. I heard a bang and saw flames licking out of one of the jet engines at its rear. I stood up though my legs had gone weak and I felt sick. In that moment I was more terrified than I had ever been and I was transfixed. Hundreds of people were about to die and I would be a witness to it and yet could do nothing. I don't know if I imagined it later or if I really could see faces at the porthole windows lining the fuselage. It was only the realization that the crashing plane was heading towards the Crucian Pit that enabled me to move. But before running for my life I thrust my hand into my basket and took out the little camera. I pointed it and took one picture. Then I ran.

I was at the bottom of the embankment when it hit, so thankfully I didn't see the impact. What I did see was an enormous fireball which burst gloriously into flower above the trees and, of course, I felt it. I was thrown to the ground and hit my head, knocking myself out. When I came to there were people around me shouting things, brushing my hair out of my eyes, asking if I could see straight. Apparently I just kept screaming, "Was that the one? Was that the one she was on?" They didn't know what I was talking about. I found out later it was the one she was on. It was no coincidence I was at the Crucian Pit the day she was to fly to Massachusetts. Where else could I go? What else could I do? It was one of those things you don't really have any choice in. It was the obvious place to be. I wouldn't know which plane she would fly out on but I would

be right there, as close to her as I could be until the last moment.
The idea was it would be better, more appropriate and less painful
than saying good-bye in the airport itself.

The plane plummeted into the Crucian Pit and everyone on board,
passengers and crew, died on impact, they said. The fire had spread
to the cabin before the crash. Because of the fire and the nature of
the crash and resulting explosion no actual bodies were recovered.
For once the papers were sparing with the detail. The decision was
made not to drain the pit and construct some elaborate memorial,
but to leave it all pretty much as it was. The accident investigators
never arrived at an explanation for the crash, though they did rule
out the possibility of a bomb. Pictures of the disaster site appeared
in the press but there were no pictures of the plane in the air.

While I'd been sitting on the grassy mound fingering the photograph the sky had slowly got darker. There was still a glimmer
however and I pored over the photograph as I had countless times
before. I never showed the picture to another living soul; not only
was there my private grief but I felt it would be an invasion of
some sort into the lives – the lives as they were lived in their very
last moments – of all 326 passengers and crew. Time and time again
I thought about taking it to a newspaper. As an image it seemed to
me to hold great power but I could never work out whether it was
potentially a power for good – for healing – or for bad. Would it
simply cause fresh hurt to the bereaved? I played safe and kept it
to myself. But the pressure told and I knew the day would come
when I would have to let go of the past.

The day came. I sat there by the pit as the darkness thickened
in the trees like a web. The surface of the water, now black like a
pool of engine oil, waited. I took a last look at the photograph –
the cigar-like fuselage, the punctuation marks of tiny windows, the
terror smeared on faces glimpsed for the last time, the lick of flame
– and skimmed it gently on to the water's surface. I watched it drift
towards the centre of the pit until the water seeped over the image
itself – as if tasting it – and swallowed the photograph.

There. I had let go.

In the same way that some mornings I just cannot get out of bed,
I found I couldn't leave the waterside. Not so soon after unloading
my secret cargo. I sat very still, resting my head in my hands, until
I felt part of the landscape. It was by now quite dark. The runway
lights were largely obscured by the trees and gorse bushes. I wasn't
surprised when I heard the first splash. I supposed this had been at
the back of my mind all along and was the real reason why it had
taken me ten years to come back.

They say when you take a photograph of someone you steal a small part of their soul.

Now I was giving back what I'd taken.

There was no great frenzy of activity, nothing to match the accident itself, just the sounds of water parting and subsiding, little splashes and trails of drips. I didn't look up but stared at the ground between my feet feeling as if my body and my skull had been completely scoured. I didn't know what I really felt deep down. There was the terror of responsibility but there was also – and I was ashamed and sickened by this – a dull thrill, a terrifying excitement.

I felt something wet brush the back of my neck and rest on my shoulder. I moved my head a fraction and saw a small hand smeared with mud and dripping water on to the front of my jacket. All feeling left me and I rose to my feet. Without focusing on any of the figures in the trees and bushes around me I walked as if in a dream round the edge of the pit towards the thick hedge that led to the paddock. Several times the hand was removed from and replaced on my shoulder.

Passage through the hedge was easy. I scaled the fence with the automatic ease of one who has drunk so much they will attempt – and achieve – any physical act. This was how I was feeling now: dissociated from the world and just passing through it. I clearly recognized the sounds of accompaniment behind me as I descended the embankment. I knew she was there but I couldn't bring myself to turn round and look at her. Crossing the main road I had the impression I was in a corridor which led back to the car. I was beyond fear. I heard water dripping off her body; her shoes made a damp, sucking noise with each small step.

When I reached the car I just opened my door and got in. She did the same. Still I hadn't looked at her. I was sufficiently conscious of what was happening to keep my eyes averted. To that extent, then, I was terrified, but I managed to function. The car started and I backed out of the little track on to the main road. I changed into first gear and started to move forward. Looking up I saw the darkness swarming down the embankment and into the road and I felt a tug of panic. "What about them?" I heard myself say. "I've got to do something."

Kathy spoke for the first time. In a voice dredged up through sediment, slurred and distorted by water and mud in her lungs, she said, "Just drive."

I drove.

Brian Lumley

The Disapproval of Jeremy Cleave

Brian Lumley's career has come a long way in the past twenty-five years. His first short story, "The Cyprus Shell", was published in The Arkham Collector *in 1968, while the author was still serving in the Army in Germany and Cyprus. These days he is a bestselling writer on both sides of the Atlantic with most of his titles going into multiple reprints and translations.*

His five-volume "Necroscope" series – comprising Necroscope, Wamphyri!, The Source, Deadspeak *and* Deadspawn – *has proved phenomenally successful and resulted in a line of collector's model kits, a series of bestselling comic books, and a follow-up trilogy (*Blood Brothers, The Last Aerie *and* Bloodwars!*).*

Some of his short fiction has been collected in The Last Rite, Fruiting Bodies and Other Fungi *(including the British Fantasy Award-winning title story), and* The Return of the Deep Ones and Other Mythos Novels, *while recent anthology appearances include* Best New Horror, The Year's Best Horror Stories XX, Dark Voices 5: The Pan Book of Horror, The Mammoth Book of Vampires *and* Final Shadows.

"The Disapproval of Jeremy Cleave" is a blackly comic chiller which shows that not all zombies have to come back from the grave complete . . .

"MY HUSBAND'S EYE," she said quite suddenly, peering over my shoulder in something of morbid fascination. "Watching us!" She was very calm about it, which ought to say quite a lot about her character. A very cool lady, Angela Cleave. But in view of the circumstances, a rather odd statement; for the fact was that I was making love to her at the time, and somewhat more alarming, her husband had been dead for six and a half weeks!

"*What*!?" I gasped, flopping over onto my back, my eyes following the direction of her pointing finger. She seemed to be aiming it at the dresser. But there was nothing to be seen, not anywhere in that huge, entirely extravagant bedroom. Or perhaps I anticipated too much, for while it's true that she had specified an "eye," for some reason *I* was looking for a complete person. This is perhaps readily understandable – the shock, and what all. But no such one was there. Thank God!

Then there came a rolling sound, like a marble down a gentle slope, and again I looked where she was pointing. Atop the dresser, a shape wobbled into view from the back to the front, being brought up short by the fancy gilt beading around the dresser's top. And she was right, it was an eye – a glass eye – its deep green pupil staring at us somehow morosely.

"Arthur," she said, in the same breathless, colourless voice, "this really makes me feel very peculiar." And truth to tell it made me feel that way, too. Certainly it ruined my night.

But I got up, went to the dresser and brought the eye down. It was damp, or rather sticky, and several pieces of fluff had attached themselves to it. Also, I fancied it smelled rather, but in a bedroom perfumed as Angela Cleave's that was hard to say. And not something one *would* say, anyway.

"My dear, it's an eye," I said, "only a glass eye!" And I took it to the vanity basin and rinsed it thoroughly in cold water. "Jeremy's, of course. The . . . vibrations must have started it rolling."

She sat up in bed, covering herself modestly with the silk sheet (as if we weren't sufficiently acquainted) and brushed back a lock of damp, golden hair from her beautiful brow. And: "Arthur," she said, "Jeremy's eye was buried with him. He desired to be put to rest looking as perfectly natural as possible – *not* with a patch over that hideous hole in his face!"

"Then it's a spare," I reasoned, going back to the bed and handing it to her. She took it – an entirely unconscious act – and immediately snatched back her hand, so that the thing fell to the floor and rolled under the bed. And:

"*Ugh!*" she said. "But I didn't *want* it, Arthur! And anyway, I never knew he had a spare."

"Well, he obviously did," I sighed, trying to get back into bed with her. But she held the covers close and wouldn't have me.

"This has quite put me off," she said. "I'm afraid I shall have a headache." And suddenly, for all that she was a cool one, it dawned on me how badly this silly episode had jolted her. I sat on the bed and patted her hand, and said: "Why don't you tell me about it, my dear?"

"It?" she looked at me curiously, frowning.

"Well, it has to be something more than just a silly old glass eye, now doesn't it? I mean, I've never seen you so shaken." And so she told me.

"It's just something he said to me," she explained, "one night when I was late home after the opera. In fact, I believe I'd spent a little time with you that night? Anyway, in that perfectly *vulgar* way of his he said: 'Angela, you must be more discreet. Discretion, my girl! I mean, I know we don't have it off as often as you'd possibly like – but you can't accuse me of holding too tight a rein, now can you? I mean – har! har! – I don't keep too close an eye on you – eh? Eh? Not *both* of 'em anyway, har! har!'

"So I asked him what on earth he meant? And he answered, 'Well, those damned *boyfriends*, my dear! Only right you should have an escort, me being incapacitated and all, but I've a position to maintain and scandal's something I won't hear of. So you just watch your step!'"

"Is that all?" I said, when it appeared she'd finished. "But I've always understood that Jeremy was perfectly reasonable about . . . well, your *affairs* in general." I shrugged. "It strikes me he was simply trying to protect his good name – and yours!"

"Sometimes, Arthur," she pouted then, "you sound just like him! I'd hate to think you were going to turn out just like *him!*"

"Not at all!" I answered at once. "Why, I'm not at all like him! I do . . . everything he didn't do, don't I? And I'm, well, entire? I just can't understand why a fairly civil warning should upset you so – especially now that he's dead. And I certainly can't see the connection between that and . . . and this," and I kicked the eye back under the bed, for at that moment it had chosen to trundle out again.

"A civil warning?" she looked at me, slowly nodded her agreement. "Well, I suppose it was, really." But then, with a degree more animation: "But he wasn't very civil the next time!"

"He caught you out again?"

"No," she lifted her chin and tossed back her hair, peevishly, I thought, "in fact it was *you* who caught me out!"

"Me?" I was astonished.

"Yes," she was pouting again, "because it was that night after the ball, when you drove me home and we stopped off at your place for a drink and . . . and slept late."

"Ah!" I said. "I suspected there might be trouble that time. But you never *told* me!"

"Because I didn't want to put you off; us being so good together, and you being his closest friend and all. Anyway, when I got in he was waiting up for me, stamping round the place on that pot leg of his, blinking his one good eye furiously at me. I mean he really was raging! 'Half past three in the morning?' he snorted. 'What? *What*? By God, but if the neighbours saw you coming in, I'll . . . I'll – '"

"Yes," I prompted her. "'I'll –?'"

"And then he threatened me," she said.

"Angela, darling, I'd already guessed that!" I told her. "But *how* did he threaten you – and what has it to do with this damned eye?"

"Arthur, you know how I dislike language," her tone was disapproving. But on the other hand she could see that I was getting a bit ruffled and impatient. "Well, he reminded me how much older he was than I, and how he probably only had a few years left, and that when he was gone everything would be mine. *But*, he also pointed out how it wouldn't be very difficult to change his will – which he would if there should be any sort of scandal. Well of course there wasn't a scandal and he didn't change his will. He didn't get the chance, for it was . . . all so very sudden!" And likewise, she was suddenly sniffling into the hankie she keeps under the pillow. "Poor Jeremy," she sobbed, "over the cliff like that." And just as quickly she dried up and put the hankie away again. It helps to have a little cry now and then.

"But there you go!" I said, triumphantly. "You've said it yourself: he *didn't* change the will! So . . . not much of a threat in that!"

"But that's not all," she said, looking at me straight in the eye now. "I mean, you know how Jeremy had spent all of that time with those *awful* people up those *awful* rivers? Well, and he told me he'd learned something of their jojo."

"Their juju," I felt obliged to correct her.

"Oh, jojo, juju!" She tossed her hair. "He said that they set spells when they're about to die, and that if their last wishes aren't carried out to the letter, then that they send, well, *parts* of themselves back to punish the ones they held to trust!"

"Parts of them –?" I began to repeat her, then tilted my head on one side and frowned at her very seriously. "Angela, I – "

But off she went, sobbing again, face down in the pillows. And this time doing it properly. Well, obviously the night was ruined. Getting dressed, I told her: "But of course that silly glass eye *isn't* one of Jeremy's parts; it's artificial, so I'm sure it wouldn't count – *if* we believed in such rubbish in the first place. Which we don't. But I do understand how you must have felt, my darling, when you saw it wobbling about up there on the dresser."

She looked up and brushed away her tears. "Will I see you tomorrow night?" And she was anxious, poor thing.

"Of course you will," I told her, "tomorrow and every night! But I've a busy day in the morning, and so it's best if I go home now. As for you: you're to take a sleeping draft and get a good night's sleep. And meanwhile – " I got down on my knees and fished about under the bed for the eye, "– did Jeremy have the box that this came in?"

"In that drawer over there," she pointed. "What on earth do you want with that?"

"I'm simply putting it away," I told her, "so that it won't bother us again." But as I placed the eye in its velvet-lined box I glanced at the name of the suppliers – Brackett and Sanders, Jewellers, Brighton – and committed their telephone number to memory . . .

The next day in the City, I gave Brackett and Sanders a ring and asked a question or two, and finished by saying: "Are you absolutely sure? No mistake? Just the one? I see. Well . . . thank you very much. And I'm sorry to have troubled you . . ." But that night I didn't tell Angela about it. I mean, so what? So he'd used two different jewellers. Well, nothing strange about that; he got about a fair bit in his time, old Jeremy Cleave.

I took her flowers and chocolates, as usual, and she was looking quite her old self again. We dined by candlelight, with a background of soft music and the moon coming up over the garden, and eventually it was time for bed.

Taking the open, somewhat depleted box of chocolates with us, we climbed the stairs and commenced a ritual which was ever fresh and exciting despite its growing familiarity. The romantic preliminaries, sweet prelude to boy and girl togetherness. These were broken only once when she said:

"Arthur, darling, just before I took my draft last night I tried to open the windows a little. It had got very hot and sticky in here. But that one – " and she pointed to one of a pair of large, pivot windows,

"– wouldn't open. It's jammed or something. Do be a dear and do something with it, will you?"

I tried but couldn't; the thing was immovable. And fearing that it might very well become hot and sticky again, I then tried the other window, which grudgingly pivoted. "We shall have them seen to," I promised.

Then I went to her where she lay; and in the next moment, as I held her in my arms and bent my head to kiss the very tip of a brown, delicious . . .

Bump!

It was perfectly audible – a dull thud from within the wardrobe – and both of us had heard it. Angela looked at me, her darling eyes startled, and mine no less; we both jerked bolt upright in the bed. And:

"What . . .?" she said, her mouth staying open a very little, breathing lightly and quickly.

"A garment, falling from its hanger," I told her.

"Nevertheless, go and see," she said, very breathlessly. "I'll not be at ease if I think there's something trapped in there."

Trapped in there? In a wardrobe in her bedroom? What could possibly be trapped in there? She kept no cats. But I got out of bed and went to see anyway.

The thing fell out into view as soon as I opened the door. Part of a manikin? A limb from some window-dresser's storeroom? An anatomical specimen from some poor unfortunate's murdered, dismembered torso? At first glance it might have been any of these things. And indeed, with the latter in mind, I jumped a foot – before I saw that it was none of those things. By which time Angela was out of bed, into her dressing-gown and haring for the door – which wouldn't open. For she had seen it, too, and unlike me she'd known exactly what it was.

"His leg!" she cried, battering furiously at the door and fighting with its ornate, gold-plated handle. "His bloody *awful* leg!"

And of course it was: Jeremy Cleave's pot left leg, leather straps and hinged knee-joint and all. It had been standing in there on its foot, and a shoe carton had gradually tilted against it, and finally the force of gravity had won. But at such an inopportune moment. "Darling," I said, turning to her with the thing under my arm, "but it's only Jeremy's pot leg!"

"Oh, of *course* it is!" she sobbed, finally wrenching the door open and rushing out onto the landing. "But what's it doing there? It should be buried with him in the cemetery in Denholme!" And then she rushed downstairs.

Well, I scratched my head a little, then sat down on the bed with the limb in my hands. I worked its joint to and fro for a while, and peered down into its hollow interior. Pot, of one sort or another, but tough, quite heavy, and utterly inanimate. A bit smelly, though, but not unnaturally. I mean, it probably smelled of Jeremy's thigh. And there was a smear of mud in the arch of the foot and on the heel, too . . .

By the time I'd given it a thorough bath in the vanity basin Angela was back, swaying in the doorway, a glass of bubbly in her trembling little hands. And she looked like she'd consumed a fair old bit of the rest of the bottle, too. But at least she'd recovered something of her former control. "His leg," she said, not entering the room while I dried the thing with a fluffy towel.

"Certainly," I said, "Jeremy's *spare* pot leg." And seeing her mouth about to form words: "Now don't say it, Angela. Of *course* he had a spare, and this is it. I mean, can you imagine if he'd somehow broken one? What then? Do you have spare reading glasses? Do I have spare car keys? Naturally Jeremy had spare . . . things. It's just that he was sensitive enough not to let you see them, that's all."

"Jeremy, sensitive!" she laughed, albeit hysterically. "But very well – you must be right. And anyway, I've never been in that wardrobe in a donkey's years. Now do put it away – no. not there, but in the cupboard under the stairs – and come to bed and love me."

And so I did. Champagne has that effect on her.

But afterwards – sitting up in bed in the darkness, while she lay huddled close, asleep, breathing across my chest – I thought about him, the "Old Boy," Jeremy.

Adventurer, explorer, wanderer in distant lands. That was him. Jeremy Johnson Cleave, who might have been a Sir, a Lord, a Minister, but chose to be himself. Cantankerous old (old-*fashioned*) bugger! And yet in many ways quite modern, too. Naïve about certain things – the way he'd always trusted me, for instance, to push his chair along the airy heights of the cliff tops when he didn't much feel like hobbling – but in others shrewd as a fox, and nobody's fool. Never for very long, anyway.

He'd lost his eye to an N'haqui dart somewhere up the Orinoco or some such, and his leg to a croc in the Amazon. But he'd always made it back home, and healed himself up, and then let his wanderlust take him off again. As for juju: well, a man is liable to see and hear and touch upon some funny things in the far-flung places of the world, and almost certainly he's like to go a bit native, too . . .

*   *   *

The next day (today, in fact, or yesterday, since it's now past midnight) was Friday, and I had business which took me past Denholme. Now don't ask me why, but I bought a mixed posy from the florist's in the village and stopped off at the old graveyard, and made my way to Jeremy's simple grave. Perhaps the flowers were for his memory; there again they could have been an alibi, a reason for my being there. As if I needed one. I mean I had been his friend, after all! Everyone said so. But it's also a fact that murderers do, occasionally, visit their victims.

The marble headstone gave his name and dates, and a little of the Cleave history, then said:

> Distant lands ever called him;
> he ever ventured,
> and ever returned.
> Rest in Peace.

Or pieces? I couldn't resist a wry chuckle as I placed my flowers on his hollow plot.

But . . . hollow?

"Subsidence, sir," said a voice directly behind me as a hand fell on my arm. Lord, how I jumped!

"What?" I turned my head to see a gaunt, ragged man leaning on his shovel: the local gravedigger.

"Subsidence," he said again, his voice full of dialect and undisguised disgust, gravelly as the path he stood on. "Oh, they likes to blame me for it – saying as 'ow I don't pack 'em down tight enough, an' all – but the fact is it's the subsidence. One in every 'alf-dozen or so sinks a little, just like Old J. J.'s 'ere. This was 'is family seat, y'know: Denholme. Last of the line, 'e were – *and* a rum un'! But I suppose you knows all that."

"Er, yes," I said. "Quite." And, looking at the concave plot: "Er, a little more soil, d'you think? Before they start blaming it on you again?"

He winked and said, "I'll see to 'er right this minute, sir, so I will! Good day to you." And I left him scratching his head and frowning at the grave, and finally trundling his barrow away, doubtless to fetch a little soil.

And all of this was the second thing I wasn't going to report to Angela, but as it happens I don't suppose it would have made much difference anyway . . .

So tonight at fall of dark I arrived here at their (hers, now) country home, and from the moment I let myself in I knew that things weren't right. So would anyone have known, the way her shriek came knifing down the stairs:

"Arthur! *Arthur!*" her voice was piercing, penetrating, very nearly unhinged. "Is that you? Oh, for *God's sake* say it's you!"

"But of course it's me, darling, who else would it be?" I shouted up to her. "Now what on earth's the matter?"

"The matter? The matter?" She came flying down the stairs in a towelling robe, rushed straight into my arms. "I'll tell you what's the matter . . ." But out of breath, she couldn't. Her hair was wet and a mess, and her face wasn't done yet, and . . . well, she looked rather floppy all over.

So that after a moment or so, rather brusquely, I said: "So tell me!"

"It's *him!*" she gasped then, a shudder in her voice. "Oh, it's him!" And bursting into tears she collapsed against me, so that I had to drop my chocolates and flowers in order to hold her up.

"Him?" I repeated her, rather stupidly, for by then I believe I'd begun to suspect that it might indeed be "him" after all – or at least something of his doing.

"Him!" she cried aloud, beating on my chest. "Him, you fool – *Jeremy!*"

Well, "let reason prevail" has always been my family motto, and I think it's to my merit that I didn't break down and start gibbering right there and then, along with Angela . . . Or on the other hand, perhaps I'm simply stupid. Anyway I didn't, but picked up my flowers and chocolates – yes, and Angela, too – and carried them all upstairs. I put her down on the bed but she jumped up at once, and commenced striding to and fro, to and fro, wringing her hands.

"Now what *is* it?," I said, determined to be reasonable.

"*Not* in that tone of voice!" she snarled at me, coming to a halt in front of me with her hands clenched into tight little knots and her face all twisted up. "Not in that 'oh, Angela's being a silly again' voice! I said it's him, and I *mean* it's him!"

But now I was angry, too. "You mean he's here?" I scowled at her.

"I mean he's *near*, certainly!" she answered, wide-, wild-eyed. "His bloody bits, anyway!" But then, a moment later, she was sobbing again, those deep racking sobs I just can't put up with; and so once more I carried her to the bed.

"Darling," I said, "just tell me all about it and I'll sort it out from there. And that's a promise."

"Is it, Arthur? Is it? Oh, I do hope so!"

So I gave her a kiss and tried one last time, urging: "Now come on, do tell me about it."

"I . . . I was in the bath," she started, "making myself nice for you, hoping that for once we could have a lovely quiet evening and night together. So there I am soaping myself down, and all of a sudden I feel that someone is watching me. And he was, he was! Sitting there on the end of the bath! Jeremy!"

"Jeremy," I said, flatly, concentrating my frown on her. "Jeremy . . . the man?"

"No, you fool – *the bloody eye*!" And she ripped the wrapper from the chocolates (her favourite liqueurs, as it happens) and distractedly began stuffing her mouth full of them. Which was when the thought first struck me: *maybe she's cracked up*!

But: "Very well," I said, standing up, striding over to the chest of drawers and yanking open the one with the velvet-lined box, "in that case – "

The box lay there, open and quite empty, gaping at me. And at that very moment there came a well-remembered rolling sound, and damned if the hideous thing didn't come bowling out of the bathroom and onto the pile of the carpet, coming to a halt there with its malefic gaze directed right at me!

And: **Bump**! – **bump**! from the wardrobe, and **BUMP**! again: a final kick so hard that it slammed the door back on its hinges. And there was Jeremy's pot leg, jerking about on the carpet like a claw freshly wrenched from a live crab! I mean not just lying there but . . . active! Lashing about on its knee-hinge like a wild thing!

Disbelieving, jaw hanging slack, I backed away from it – backed right into the bed and sat down there, with all the wind flown right out of me. Angela had seen everything and her eyes were threatening to pop out of her head; she dribbled chocolate and juice from one corner of her twitching mouth, but still her hand automatically picked up another liqueur. Except it wasn't a liqueur.

I waved a fluttery hand, croaked something unintelligible, tried to warn her. But my tongue was stuck to the roof of my mouth and the words wouldn't come. "*Gurk*!" was the only thing I managed to get out. And that too late, for already she'd popped the thing into her mouth. Jeremy's eye – but not his glass eye!

Oh, and what a horror and a madness and an asylum then as she bit into it! Her throat full of chocolate, face turning blue, eyes bulging as she clawed at the bedclothes going "Ak – ak – *ak*!" And me trying to massage her throat, and the damned pot leg kicking its way across the floor towards me, and that bloody nightmare glass eye wobbling there for all the world as if its owner were laughing!

Then . . . Angela clawed at me one last time and tore my shirt right down the front as she toppled off the bed. Her eyes were standing out like organ stops and her face was purple, and her dragging nails opened up the shallow skin of my chest in five long red bleeding lines, but I scarcely noticed. For Jeremy's leg was still crashing about on the floor and his eye was still laughing.

I started laughing, too, as I kicked the leg into the wardrobe and locked it, and chased the eye across the floor and under Angela's dressing-table. I laughed and I laughed – laughed until I cried – and perhaps wouldn't have sobered yet, except . . .

What was that?

That bumping, out there on the landing!

And it – he – Jeremy, is still out there, bumping about even now. He's jammed the windows again so that I can't get out, but I've barricaded the door so that *he* can't get in; and now we're both stuck. I've a slight advantage, though, for I can see, while he's quite blind! I mean, I *know* he's blind, for his glass eye is in here with me and his real eye is in Angela! And his leg will come right through the panelling of the wardrobe eventually I suppose but when it does I'll jump on it and pound the thing to pieces.

And he's out there blind as a bat, hopping around on the landing, going *gurgle*, *gurgle*, *gurgle* and stinking like all Hell! Well sod you Jeremy Johnson Cleave for I'm not coming out. I'm just going to stay here always. I won't come out for you or for the maid when she comes in the morning or for the cook or the police or anybody.

I'll just stay here with my pillows and my blankets and my thumb where it's nice and safe and warm. Here under the bed.

Do you hear me, Jeremy?

Do you hear me?

I'm – not – coming – out!

H. P. Lovecraft

Herbert West — Reanimator

Howard Phillips Lovecraft (1890–1937) is probably the most important and influential author of supernatural fiction in the twentieth-century. Almost every major writer working in the horror field today has been inspired in some way by his work. What makes this fact even more impressive is that Lovecraft was never prolific, and his short stories, poems and essays mostly appeared in the amateur press or such pulp magazines as Weird Tales *during his lifetime.*

Two years after Lovecraft's untimely death, his young protégés August Derleth and Donald Wandrei established Arkham House to publish a posthumous collection, The Outsider and Others, *and eventually bring all Lovecraft's work back into print.*

"Herbert West – Reanimator" is, admittedly, one of the author's earliest professional sales and, as such, lacks much of the power he brought to his later work. In 1921, Lovecraft was approached by fellow amateur journalist George Julian Houtain to write a series of six connected horror stories to appear in Houtain's new professional magazine, Home Brew. *These were originally published under the title "Grewsome Tales" beginning with the January 1922 issue. Lovecraft complained about "the burthen of hack labour" and "the arid waste of ochreous commercialism" but still accepted $5.00 per episode (which worked out to a quarter of a cent a word, or $30.00 in total – a measly sum even in 1922). To add insult to injury, although Houtain paid promptly for*

the first two instalments, he kept Lovecraft waiting months for the rest of the money.

It's impossible that Lovecraft could have foreseen (much less approved) that the story would eventually form the basis for Stuart Gordon's outrageous 1985 cult movie hit Re-Animator *and its equally splattery sequel* Bride of Re-Animator *(1989), both featuring Jeffrey Combs as the death-defying medical student Herbert West.*

I FROM THE DARK

OF HERBERT WEST, who was my friend in college and in other life, I can speak only with extreme terror. This terror is not due altogether to the sinister manner of his recent disappearance, but was engendered by the whole nature of his life-work, and first gained its acute form more than seventeen years ago, when we were in the third year of our course at the Miskatonic University medical school in Arkham. While he was with me, the wonder and diabolism of his experiments fascinated me utterly, and I was his closest companion. Now that he is gone and the spell is broken, the actual fear is greater. Memories and possibilities are ever more hideous than realities.

The first horrible incident of our acquaintance was the greatest shock I ever experienced, and it is only with reluctance that I repeat it. As I have said, it happened when we were in medical school, where West had already made himself notorious through his wild theories on the nature of death and the possibility of overcoming it artificially. His views, which were widely ridiculed by the faculty and by his fellow-students, hinged on the essentially mechanistic nature of life; and concerned means for operating the organic machinery of mankind by calculated chemical action after the failure of natural processes. In his experiments with various animating solutions he had killed and treated immense numbers of rabbits, guinea-pigs, cats, dogs, and monkeys, till he had become the prime nuisance of the college. Several times he had actually obtained signs of life in animals supposedly dead; in many cases violent signs; but he soon saw that the perfection of his process, if indeed possible, would necessarily involve a lifetime of research. It likewise became clear that, since the same solution never worked alike on different organic species, he would require human subjects for further and more specialized progress. It was here that he first came into conflict with the college authorities, and was debarred from future experiments by no less a dignitary than the dean of the medical school himself – the learned and benevolent Dr Allan Halsey, whose work in behalf of the stricken is recalled by every old resident of Arkham.

I had always been exceptionally tolerant of West's pursuits, and we frequently discussed his theories, whose ramifications and corollaries were almost infinite. Holding with Haeckel that all life is a chemical and physical process, and that the so-called "soul" is a myth, my friend believed that artificial reanimation of the dead can depend only on the condition of the tissues; and that unless actual decomposition has set in, a corpse fully equipped with organs may with suitable measures be set going again in the peculiar fashion known as life. That the psychic or intellectual life might be impaired by the slight deterioration of sensitive brain-cells which even a short period of death would be apt to cause, West fully realized. It had at first been his hope to find a reagent which would restore vitality before the actual advent of death, and only repeated failures on animals had shown him that the natural and artificial life-motions were incompatible. He then sought extreme freshness in his specimens, injecting his solutions into the blood immediately after the extinction of life. It was this circumstance which made the professors so carelessly skeptical, for they felt that true death had not occurred in any case. They did not stop to view the matter closely and reasoningly.

It was not long after the faculty had interdicted his work that West confided to me his resolution to get fresh bodies in some manner, and continue in secret the experiments he could no longer perform openly. To hear him discussing ways and means was rather ghastly, for at the college we had never procured anatomical specimens our-selves. Whenever the morgue proved inadequate, two local negroes attended to this matter, and they were seldom questioned. West was then a small, slender, spectacled youth with delicate features, yellow hair, pale blue eyes, and a soft voice, and it was uncanny to hear him dwelling on the relative merits of Christ Church Cemetery and the potter's field, because practically every body in Christ Church was embalmed; a thing of course ruinous to West's researches.

I was by this time his active and enthralled assistant, and helped him make all his decisions, not only concerning the source of bodies but concerning a suitable place for our loathsome work. It was I who thought of the deserted Chapman farmhouse beyond Meadow Hill, where we fitted up on the ground floor an operating room and a laboratory, each with dark curtains to conceal our midnight doings. The place was far from any road, and in sight of no other house, yet precautions were none the less necessary; since rumours of strange lights, started by chance nocturnal roamers, would soon

bring disaster on our enterprise. It was agreed to call the whole
thing a chemical laboratory if discovery should occur. Gradually
we equipped our sinister haunt of science with materials either
purchased in Boston or quietly borrowed from the college – materials
carefully made unrecognizable save to expert eyes – and provided
spades and picks for the many burials we should have to make in
the cellar. At the college we used an incinerator, but the apparatus
was too costly for our unauthorized laboratory. Bodies were always
a nuisance – even the small guinea-pig bodies from the slight
clandestine experiments in West's room at the boarding-house.

We followed the local death-notices like ghouls, for our specimens
demanded particular qualities. What we wanted were corpses
interred soon after death and without artificial preservation; pre-
ferably free from malforming disease, and certainly with all organs
present. Accident victims were our best hope. Not for many weeks
did we hear of anything suitable; though we talked with morgue and
hospital authorities, ostensibly in the college's interest, as often as
we could without exciting suspicion. We found that the college had
first choice in every case, so that it might be necessary to remain in
Arkham during the summer, when only the limited summer-school
classes were held. In the end, though, luck favoured us; for one day
we heard of an almost ideal case in the potter's field; a brawny young
workman drowned only the morning before in Summer's Pond, and
buried at the town's expense without delay or embalming. That
afternoon we found the new grave, and determined to begin work
soon after midnight.

It was a repulsive task that we undertook in the black small hours,
even though we lacked at that time the special horror of graveyards
which later experiences brought to us. We carried spades and oil
dark lanterns, for although electric torches were then manufactured,
they were not as satisfactory as the tungsten contrivances of today.
The process of unearthing was slow and sordid – it might have been
gruesomely poetical if we had been artists instead of scientists – and
we were glad when our spades struck wood. When the pine box was
fully uncovered West scrambled down and removed the lid, dragging
out and propping up the contents. I reached down and hauled the
contents out of the grave, and then both toiled hard to restore the
spot to its former appearance. The affair made us rather nervous,
especially the stiff form and vacant face of our first trophy, but we
managed to remove all traces of our visit. When we had patted down
the last shovelful of earth we put the specimen in a canvas sack and
set out for the old Chapman place beyond Meadow Hill.

On an improvised dissecting-table in the old farmhouse, by the

light of a powerful acetylene lamp, the specimen was not very
spectral looking. It had been a sturdy and apparently unimaginative
youth of wholesome plebeian type – large-framed, grey-eyed, and
brown-haired – a sound animal without psychological subtleties, and
probably having vital processes of the simplest and healthiest sort.
Now, with the eyes closed, it looked more asleep than dead; though
the expert test of my friend soon left no doubt on the score. We had
at last what West had always longed for – a real dead man of the
ideal kind, ready for the solution as prepared according to the most
careful calculations and theories for human use. The tension on our
part became very great. We knew that there was scarcely a chance
for anything like complete success, and could not avoid hideous
fears at possible grotesque results of partial animation. Especially
were we apprehensive concerning the mind and impulses of the
creature, since in the space following death some of the more delicate
cerebral cells might well have suffered deterioration. I, myself, still
held some curious notions about the traditional "soul" of man, and
felt an awe at the secrets that might be told by one returning from
the dead. I wondered what sights this placid youth might have seen
in inaccessible spheres, and what he could relate if fully restored to
life. But my wonder was not overwhelming, since for the most part
I shared the materialism of my friend. He was calmer than I as he
forced a large quantity of his fluid into a vein of the body's arm,
immediately binding the incision securely.

The waiting was gruesome, but West never faltered. Every now
and then he applied his stethoscope to the specimen, and bore the
negative results philosophically. After about three-quarters of an
hour without the least sign of life he disappointedly pronounced
the solution inadequate, but determined to make the most of his
opportunity and try one change in the formula before disposing
of his ghastly prize. We had that afternoon dug a grave in the
cellar, and would have to fill it by dawn – for although we had
fixed a lock on the house we wished to shun even the remotest
risk of a ghoulish discovery. Besides, the body would not be even
approximately fresh the next night. So taking the solitary acetylene
lamp into the adjacent laboratory, we left our silent guest on the
slab in the dark, and bent every energy to the mixing of a new
solution; the weighing and measuring supervised by West with an
almost fanatical care.

The awful event was very sudden, and wholly unexpected. I was
pouring something from one test-tube to another, and West was busy
over the alcohol blast-lamp which had to answer for a Bunsen burner
in this gasless edifice, when from the pitch-black room we had left

there burst the most appalling and demoniac succession of cries that either of us had ever heard. Not more unutterable could have been the chaos of hellish sound if the pit itself had opened to release the agony of the damned, for in one inconceivable cacophony was centered all the supernal terror and unnatural despair of animate nature. Human it could not have been – it is not in man to make such sounds – and without a thought of our late employment or its possible discovery both West and I leaped to the nearest window like stricken animals; overturning tubes, lamp, and retorts, and vaulting madly into the starred abyss of the rural night. I think we screamed ourselves as we stumbled frantically toward the town, though as we reached the outskirts we put on a semblance of restraint – just enough to seem like belated revellers staggering home from a debauch.

We did not separate, but managed to get to West's room, where we whispered with the gas up until dawn. By then we had calmed ourselves a little with rational theories and plans for investigation, so that we could sleep through the day – classes being disregarded. But that evening two items in the paper, wholly unrelated, made it again impossible for us to sleep. The old deserted Chapman house had inexplicably burned to an amorphous heap of ashes; that we could understand because of the upset lamp. Also, an attempt had been made to disturb a new grave in the potter's field, as if by futile and spadeless clawing at the earth. That we could not understand, for we had patted down the mould very carefully.

And for seventeen years after that West would look frequently over his shoulder, and complain of fancied footsteps behind him. Now he has disappeared.

II   THE PLAGUE-DEMON

I shall never forget that hideous summer sixteen years ago, when like a noxious afrite from the halls of Eblis typhoid stalked leeringly through Arkham. It is by that satanic scourge that most recall the year, for truly terror brooded with bat-wings over the piles of coffins in the tombs of Christ Church Cemetery; yet for me there is a greater horror in that time – a horror known to me alone now that Herbert West has disappeared.

West and I were doing post-graduate work in summer classes at the medical school of Miskatonic University, and my friend had attained a wide notoriety because of his experiments leading toward the revivification of the dead. After the scientific slaughter of uncounted small animals the freakish work had ostensibly stopped by order of our sceptical dean, Dr Allan Halsey; though West had continued to perform certain secret tests in his dingy boarding-house room, and had on one terrible and unforgettable occasion taken a human body from its grave in the potter's field to a deserted farmhouse beyond Meadow Hill.

I was with him on that odious occasion, and saw him inject into the still veins the elixir which he thought would to some extent restore life's chemical and physical processes. It had ended horribly – in a delirium of fear which we gradually came to attribute to our own over-wrought nerves – and West had never afterward been able to shake off a maddening sensation of being haunted and hunted. The body had not been quite fresh enough; it is obvious that to restore normal mental attributes a body must be very fresh indeed; and the burning of the old house had prevented us from burying the thing. It would have been better if we could have known it was underground.

After that experience West had dropped his researches for some time; but as the zeal of the born scientist slowly returned, he again became importunate with the college faculty, pleading for the use of the dissecting-room and of fresh human specimens for the work he regarded as so overwhelmingly important. His pleas, however, were wholly in vain; for the decision of Dr Halsey was inflexible, and the other professors all endorsed the verdict of their leader. In the radical theory of reanimation they saw nothing but the immature vagaries of a youthful enthusiast whose slight form, yellow hair, spectacled blue eyes, and soft voice gave no hint of the super-normal – almost diabolical – power of the cold brain within. I can see him now as he was then – and I shiver. He grew sterner of face, but never elderly. And now Sefton has had the mishap and West has vanished.

West clashed disagreeably with Dr Halsey near the end of our last undergraduate term in a wordy dispute that did less credit to him than to the kindly dean in point of courtesy. He felt that he was needlessly and irrationally retarded in a supremely great work; a work which he could of course conduct to suit himself in later years, but which he wished to begin while still possessed of the exceptional facilities of the university. That the tradition-bound elders should ignore his singular results on animals, and persist in their denial of the possibility of reanimation, was inexpressibly disgusting and almost incomprehensible to a youth of West's logical temperament. Only greater maturity could help him understand the chronic mental limitations of the "professor-doctor" type – the product of generations of pathetic Puritanism, kindly, conscientious, and sometimes gentle and amiable, yet always narrow, intolerant, custom-ridden, and lacking in perspective. Age has more charity for these incomplete yet high-souled characters, whose worst real vice is timidity, and who are ultimately punished by general ridicule for their intellectual sins – sins like Ptolemaism, Calvinism, anti-Darwinism, anti-Nietzscheism, and every sort of Sabbatarianism and sumptuary legislation. West, young despite his marvelous scientific acquirements, had scant patience with good Dr Halsey and his erudite colleagues; and nursed an increasing resentment, coupled with a desire to prove his theories to these obtuse worthies in some striking and dramatic fashion. Like most youths, he indulged in elaborate day-dreams of revenge, triumph, and final magnanimous forgiveness.

And then had come the scourge, grinning and lethal, from the nightmare caverns of Tartarus. West and I had graduated about the time of its beginning, but had remained for additional work at the summer school, so that we were in Arkham when it broke with full demoniac fury upon the town. Though not as yet licensed physicians, we now had our degrees, and were pressed frantically into public service as the numbers of the stricken grew. The situation was almost past management, and deaths ensued too frequently for the local undertakers fully to handle. Burials without embalming were made in rapid succession, and even the Christ Church Cemetery receiving tomb was crammed with coffins of the unembalmed dead. This circumstance was not without effect on West, who thought often of the irony of the situation – so many fresh specimens, yet none for his persecuted researches! We were frightfully overworked, and the terrific mental and nervous strain made my friend brood morbidly.

But West's gentle enemies were no less harassed with prostrating duties. College had all but closed, and every doctor of the medical faculty was helping to fight the typhoid plague. Dr Halsey in particular had distinguished himself in sacrificing service, applying his extreme skill with whole-hearted energy to cases which many others shunned because of danger or apparent hopelessness. Before a month was over the fearless dean had become a popular hero, though he seemed unconscious of his fame as he struggled to keep from collapsing with physical fatigue and nervous exhaustion. West could not withhold admiration for the fortitude of his foe, but because of this was even more determined to prove to him the truth of his amazing doctrines. Taking advantage of the disorganization of both college work and municipal health regulations, he managed to get a recently deceased body smuggled into the university dissecting-room one night, and in my presence injected a new modification of his solution. The thing actually opened its eyes, but only stared at the ceiling with a look of soul-petrifying horror before collapsing into an inertness from which nothing could rouse it. West said it was not fresh enough – the hot summer air does not favour corpses. That time we were almost caught before we incinerated the thing, and West doubted the advisability of repeating his daring misuse of the college laboratory.

The peak of the epidemic was reached in August. West and I were almost dead, and Dr Halsey did die on the fourteenth. The students all attended the hasty funeral on the fifteenth, and bought an impressive wreath, though the latter was quite overshadowed by the tributes sent by wealthy Arkham citizens and by the municipality itself. It was almost a public affair, for the dean had surely been a public benefactor. After the entombment we were all somewhat depressed, and spent the afternoon at the bar of the Commercial House; where West, though shaken by the death of his chief opponent, chilled the rest of us with references to his notorious theories. Most of the students went home, or to various duties, as the evening advanced; but West persuaded me to aid him in "making a night of it." West's landlady saw us arrive at his room about two in the morning, with a third man between us; and told her husband that we had all evidently dined and wined rather well.

Apparently this acidulous matron was right; for about three a.m. the whole house was aroused by cries coming from West's room, where when they broke down the door they found the two of us unconscious on the blood-stained carpet, beaten, scratched, and mauled, and with the broken remnants of West's bottles and instruments around us. Only an open window told what had become of our assailant, and many wondered how he himself had fared after the terrific leap from the second story to the lawn which he must have made. There were some strange garments in the room, but West upon regaining consciousness said they did not belong to the stranger, but were specimens collected for bacteriological analysis in the course of investigations on the transmission of germ diseases. He ordered them burnt as soon as possible in the capacious fireplace. To the police we both declared ignorance of our late companion's identity. He was, West nervously said, a congenial stranger whom we had met at some downtown bar of uncertain location. We had all been rather jovial, and West and I did not wish to have our pugnacious companion hunted down.

That same night saw the beginning of the second Arkham horror – the horror that to me eclipsed the plague itself. Christ Church Cemetery was the scene of a terrible killing; a watchman having been clawed to death in a manner not only too hideous for description, but raising a doubt as to the human agency of the deed. The victim had been seen alive considerably after midnight – the dawn revealed the unutterable thing. The manager of a circus at the neighbouring town of Bolton was questioned, but he swore that no beast had at any time escaped from its cage. Those who found the body noted a trail of blood leading to the receiving tomb, where a small pool of red lay on the concrete just outside the gate. A fainter trail led away toward the woods, but it soon gave out.

The next night devils danced on the roofs of Arkham, and unnatural madness howled in the wind. Through the fevered town had crept a curse which some said was greater than the plague, and which some whispered was the embodied demon-soul of the plague itself. Eight houses were entered by a nameless thing which strewed red death in its wake – in all, seventeen maimed and shapeless remnants of bodies were left behind by the voiceless, sadistic monster that crept abroad. A few persons had half seen it in the dark, and said it was white and like a malformed ape or anthropomorphic fiend. It had not left behind quite all that it had attacked, for sometimes it had been hungry. The number it had killed was fourteen; three of the bodies had been in stricken homes and had not been alive.

On the third night frantic bands of searchers, led by the police, captured it in a house on Crane Street near the Miskatonic campus. They had organized the quest with care, keeping in touch by means of volunteer telephone stations, and when someone in the college district had reported hearing a scratching at a shuttered window, the net was quickly spread. On account of the general alarm and precautions, there were only two more victims, and the capture was effected without major casualties. The thing was finally stopped by a bullet, though not a fatal one, and was rushed to the local hospital amidst universal excitement and loathing.

For it had been a man. This much was clear despite the nauseous eyes, the voiceless simianism, and the demoniac savagery. They dressed the wound and carted it to the asylum at Sefton, where it beat its head against the walls of a padded cell for sixteen years – until the recent mishap, when it escaped under circumstances that few like to mention. What had most disgusted the searchers of Arkham was the thing they noticed when the monster's face was cleaned – the mocking, unbelievable resemblance to a learned and self-sacrificing martyr who had been entombed but three days before – the late Dr Allan Halsey, public benefactor and dean of the medical school of Miskatonic University.

To the vanished Herbert West and to me the disgust and horror were supreme. I shudder tonight as I think of it, shudder even more than I did that morning when West muttered through his bandages,

"Damn it, it wasn't *quite* fresh enough!"

III   SIX SHOTS BY MOONLIGHT

It is uncommon to fire all six shots of a revolver with great suddenness when one would probably be sufficient, but many things in the life of Herbert West were uncommon. It is, for instance, not often that a young physician leaving college is obliged to conceal the principles which guide his selection of a home and office, yet that was the case with Herbert West. When he and I obtained our degrees at the medical school of Miskatonic University, and sought to relieve our poverty by setting up as general practitioners, we took great care not to say that we chose our house because it was fairly well isolated, and as near as possible to the potter's field.

Reticence such as this is seldom without a cause, nor indeed was ours; for our requirements were those resulting from a life-work distinctly unpopular. Outwardly we were doctors only, but beneath the surface were aims of far greater and more terrible moment – for the essence of Herbert West's existence was a quest amid black and forbidden realms of the unknown, in which he hoped to uncover the secret of life and restore to perpetual animation the graveyard's cold clay. Such a quest demands strange materials, among them fresh human bodies; and in order to keep supplied with these indispensable things one must live quietly and not far from a place of informal interment.

West and I had met in college, and I had been the only one to sympathize with his hideous experiments. Gradually I had come to be his inseparable assistant, and now that we were out of college we had to keep together. It was not easy to find a good opening for two doctors in company, but finally the influence of the university secured us a practice in Bolton – a factory town near Arkham, the seat of the college. The Bolton Worsted Mills are the largest in the Miskatonic Valley, and their polyglot employees are never popular as patients with the local physicians. We chose our house with the greatest care, seizing at last on a rather run-down cottage near the end of Pond Street; five numbers from the closest neighbour, and separated from the local potter's field by only a stretch of meadow land, bisected by a narrow neck of the rather dense forest which lies to the north. The distance was greater than we wished, but we could get no nearer house without going on the other side of the field, wholly out of the factory district. We were not much displeased, however, since there were no people between us and our sinister source of supplies. The walk was a trifle long, but we could haul our silent specimens undisturbed.

Our practice was surprisingly large from the very first – large enough to please most young doctors, and large enough to prove a bore and a burden to students whose real interest lay elsewhere. The mill-hands were of somewhat turbulent inclinations; and besides their many natural needs, their frequent clashes and stabbing affrays gave us plenty to do. But what actually absorbed our minds was the secret laboratory we had fitted up in the cellar – the laboratory with the long table under the electric lights, where in the small hours of the morning we often injected West's various solutions into the veins of the things we dragged from the potter's field. West was experimenting madly to find something which would start man's vital motions anew after they had been stopped by the thing we call death, but had encountered the most ghastly obstacles. The solution had to be differently compounded for different types – what would serve for guinea-pigs would not serve for human beings, and different specimens required large modifications.

The bodies had to be exceedingly fresh, or the slight decomposition of brain tissue would render perfect reanimation impossible. Indeed, the greatest problem was to get them fresh enough – West had had horrible experiences during his secret college researchs with corpses of doubtful vintage. The results of partial or imperfect animation were much more hideous than were the total failures, and we both held fearsome recollections of such things. Ever since our first demoniac session in the deserted farm-house on Meadow Hill in Arkham, we had felt a brooding menace; and West, though a calm, blond, blue-eyed scientific automaton in most respects, often confessed to a shuddering sensation of stealthy pursuit. He half felt that he was followed – psychological delusion of shaken nerves, enhanced by the undeniably disturbing fact that at least one of our reanimated specimens was still alive – a frightful carnivorous thing in a padded cell at Sefton. Then there was another – our first – whose exact fate we had never learned.

We had fair luck with specimens in Bolton – much better than in Arkham. We had not been settled a week before we got an accident victim on the very night of burial, and made it open its eyes with an amazingly rational expression before the solution failed. It had lost an arm – if it had been a perfect body we might have succeeded better. Between then and the next January we secured three more, one total failure, one case of marked muscular motion, and one rather shivery thing – it rose of itself and uttered a sound. Then came a period when luck was poor; interments fell off, and those that did occur were of specimens either too diseased or too maimed for us. We kept track of all the deaths and their circumstances with systematic care.

One March night, however, we unexpectedly obtained a specimen which did not come from the potter's field. In Bolton the prevailing spirit of Puritanism had outlawed the sport of boxing – with the usual result. Surreptitious and ill-conducted bouts among the mill-workers were common, and occasionally professional talent of low grade was imported. This late winter night there had been such a match; evidently with disastrous results, since two timorous Poles had come to us with incoherently whispered entreaties to attend to a very secret and desperate case. We followed them to an abandoned barn, where the remnants of a crowd of frightened foreigners were watching a silent black form on the floor.

The match had been between Kid O'Brien – a lubberly and now quaking youth with a most un-Hibernian hooked nose – and Buck Robinson, "The Harlem Smoke." The negro had been knocked out, and a moment's examination showed us that he would permanently remain so. He was a loathsome, gorilla-like thing, with abnormally long arms which I could not help calling fore-legs, and a face that conjured up thoughts of unspeakable Congo secrets and tom-tom poundings under an eery moon. The body must have looked even worse in life – but the world holds many ugly things. Fear was upon the whole pitiful crowd, for they did not know what the law would exact of them if the affair were not hushed up; and they were grateful when West, in spite of my involuntary shudders, offered to get rid of the thing quietly – for a purpose I knew too well.

There was bright moonlight over the snowless landscape, but we dressed the thing and carried it home between us through the deserted streets and meadows, as we had carried a similar thing one horrible night in Arkham. We approached the house from the field in the rear, took the specimen in the back door and down the cellar stairs, and prepared it for the usual experiment. Our fear of the police was absurdly great, though we had timed our trip to avoid the solitary patrolman of that section.

The result was wearily anti-climactic. Ghastly as our prize appeared, it was wholly unresponsive to every solution we injected in its black arm, solutions prepared from experience with white specimens only. So as the hour grew dangerously near to dawn, we did as we had done with the others – dragged the thing across the meadows to the neck of woods near the potter's field, and buried it there in the best sort of grave the frozen ground would furnish. The grave was not very deep, but fully as good as that of the previous specimen – the thing which had risen of itself and uttered a sound. In the light of our dark lanterns we carefully covered it with leaves and dead vines, fairly certain that the police would never find it in a forest so dim and dense.

The next day I was increasingly apprehensive about the police, for a patient brought rumours of a suspected fight and death. West had still another source of worry, for he had been called in the afternoon to a case which ended very threateningly. An Italian woman had become hysterical over her missing child, a lad of five who had strayed off early in the morning and failed to appear for dinner – and had developed symptoms highly alarming in view of an always weak heart. It was a very foolish hysteria, for the boy had often run away before; but Italian peasants are exceedingly superstitious, and this woman seemed as much harassed by omens as by facts. About seven o'clock in the evening she had died, and her frantic husband had made a frightful scene in his efforts to kill West, whom he wildly blamed for not saving her life. Friends had held him when he drew a stiletto, but West departed amidst his inhuman shrieks, curses, and oaths of vengeance. In his latest affliction the fellow seemed to have forgotten his child, who was still missing as the night advanced. There was some talk of searching the woods, but most of the family's friends were busy with the dead woman and the screaming man. Altogether, the nervous strain upon West must have been tremendous. Thoughts of the police and of the mad Italian both weighed heavily.

We retired about eleven, but I did not sleep well. Bolton had a surprisingly good police force for so small a town, and I could not help fearing the mess which would ensue if the affair of the night before were ever tracked down. It might mean the end of all our local work – and perhaps prison for both West and me. I did not like those rumours of a fight which were floating about. After the clock had struck three the moon shone in my eyes, but I turned over without rising to pull down the shade. Then came the steady rattling at the back door.

I lay still and somewhat dazed, but before long heard West's rap on my door. He was clad in dressing-gown and slippers, and had in his hands a revolver and an electric flashlight. From the revolver I knew that he was thinking more of the crazed Italian than of the police.

"We'd better both go," he whispered. "It wouldn't do not to

answer it anyway, and it may be a patient – it would be like one of those fools to try the back door."

So we both went down the stairs on tiptoe, with a fear partly justified and partly that which comes only from the soul of the weird small hours. The rattling continued, growing somewhat louder. When we reached the door I cautiously unbolted it and threw it open, and as the moon streamed revealingly down on the form silhouetted there, West did a peculiar thing. Despite the obvious danger of attracting notice and bringing down on our heads the dreaded police investigation – a thing which after all was mercifully averted by the relative isolation of our cottage – my friend suddenly, excitedly, and unnecessarily emptied all six chambers of his revolver into the nocturnal visitor.

For that visitor was neither Italian nor policeman. Looming hideously against the spectral moon was a gigantic misshapen thing not to be imagined save in nightmares – a glassy-eyed, ink-black apparition nearly on all fours, covered with bits of mould, leaves, and vines, foul with caked blood, and having between its glistening teeth a snow-white, terrible, cylindrical object terminating in a tiny hand.

IV   THE SCREAM OF THE DEAD

The scream of a dead man gave to me that acute and added horror of Dr Herbert West which harassed the latter years of our companionship. It is natural that such a thing as a dead man's scream should give horror, for it is obviously not a pleasing or ordinary occurrence; but I was used to similar experiences, hence suffered on this occasion only because of a particular circumstance. And, as I have implied, it was not of the dead man himself that I became afraid.

Herbert West, whose associate and assistant I was, possessed scientific interests far beyond the usual routine of a village physician. That was why, when establishing his practice in Bolton, he had chosen an isolated house near the potter's field. Briefly and brutally stated, West's sole absorbing interest was a secret study of the phenomena of life and its cessation, leading toward the reanimation of the dead through injections of an excitant solution. For this ghastly experimenting it was necessary to have a constant supply of very fresh human bodies; very fresh because even the least decay hopelessly damaged the brain structure, and human because we found that the solution had to be compounded differently for different types of organisms. Scores of rabbits and guinea-pigs had been killed and treated, but their trail was a blind one. West had never fully succeeded because he had never been able to secure a corpse sufficiently fresh. What he wanted were bodies from which vitality had only just departed; bodies with every cell intact and capable of receiving again the impulse toward that mode of motion called life. There was hope that this second and artificial life might be made perpetual by repetitions of the injection, but we had learned that an ordinary natural life would not respond to the action. To establish the artificial motion, noctural life must be extinct − the specimens must be very fresh, but genuinely dead.

The awesome quest had begun when West and I were students at the Miskatonic University medical school in Arkham, vividly conscious for the first time of the thoroughly mechanical nature of life. That was seven years before, but West looked scarcely a day older now − he was small, blond, clean-shaven, soft-voiced, and spectacled, with only an occasional flash of a cold blue eye to tell of the hardening and growing fanaticism of his character under the pressure of his terrible investigations. Our experiences had often been hideous in the extreme; the results of defective reanimation, when lumps of graveyard clay had been galvanized into morbid, unnatural, and brainless motion by various modifications of the vital solution.

One thing had uttered a nerve-shattering scream; another had risen violently, beaten us both to unconsciousness, and run amuck in a shocking way before it could be placed behind asylum bars; still another, a loathsome African monstrosity, had clawed out of its shallow grave and done a deed − West had had to shoot that object. We could not get bodies fresh enough to show any trace of reason when reanimated, so had perforce created nameless horrors. It was disturbing to think that one, perhaps two, of our monsters still lived − that thought haunted us shadowingly, till finally West disappeared under frightful circumstances. But at the time of the scream in the cellar laboratory of the isolated Bolton cottage, our fears were subordinate to our anxiety for extremely fresh specimens. West was more avid than I, so that it almost seemed to me that he looked half-covetously at any very healthy living physique.

It was in July, 1910, that the bad luck regarding specimens began to turn. I had been on a long visit to my parents in Illinois, and upon my return found West in a state of singular elation. He had, he told me excitedly, in all likelihood solved the problem of freshness through an approach from an entirely new angle − that of artificial preservation. I had known that he was working on a new and highly unusual embalming compound, and was not surprised that it had turned out well; but until he explained the details I was rather puzzled as to how such a compound could help in our work, since the objectionable staleness of the specimens was largely due to delay occurring before we secured them. This, I now saw, West had clearly recognized; creating his embalming compound for future rather than immediate use, and trusting to fate to supply again some very recent and unburied corpse, as it had years before when we obtained the Negro killed in the Bolton prize-fight. At last fate had been kind, so that on this occasion there lay in the secret cellar laboratory a corpse whose decay could not by any possibility have begun. What would happen on reanimation, and whether we could hope for a revival of mind and reason, West did not venture to predict. The experiment would be a landmark in our studies, and he had saved the new body for my return, so that both might share the spectacle in accustomed fashion.

West told me how he had obtained the specimen. It had been a vigorous man; a well-dressed stranger just off the train on his way to transact some business with the Bolton Worsted Mills. The walk through the town had been long, and by the time the traveller paused at our cottage to ask the way to the factories his heart had become greatly overtaxed. He had refused a stimulant, and had suddenly dropped dead only a moment later. The body, as might be expected, seemed to West a heaven-sent gift. In his brief conversation the stranger had made it clear that he was unknown in Bolton, and a search of his pockets subsequently revealed him to be one Robert Leavitt of St Louis, apparently without a family to make inquiries about his disappearance. If this man could not be restored to life, no one would know of our experiment. We buried our materials in a dense strip of woods between the house and the potter's field. If, on the other hand, he could be restored, our fame would be brilliantly and perpetually established. So without delay West had injected into the body's wrist the compound which would hold it fresh for use after my arrival. The matter of the presumably weak heart, which to my mind imperilled the success of our experiment, did not appear to trouble West extensively. He hoped at last to obtain what he had never obtained before – a rekindled spark of reason and perhaps a normal, living creature.

So on the night of July 18, 1910, Herbert West and I stood in the cellar laboratory and gazed at a white, silent figure beneath the dazzling arc-light. The embalming compound had worked uncannily well, for as I stared fascinatedly at the sturdy frame which had lain two weeks without stiffening I was moved to seek West's assurance that the thing was really dead. This assurance he gave readily enough; reminding me that the reanimating solution was never used without careful tests as to life; since it could have no effect if any of the original vitality were present. As West proceeded to take preliminary steps, I was impressed by the vast intricacy of the new experiment; an intricacy so vast that he could trust no hand less delicate than his own. Forbidding me to touch the body, he first injected a drug in the wrist just beside the place his needle had punctured when injecting the embalming compound. This, he said, was to neutralize the compound and release the system to a normal relaxation so that the reanimating solution might freely work when injected. Slightly later, when a change and a gentle tremor seemed to affect the dead limbs, West stuffed a pillow-like object violently over the twitching face, not withdrawing it until the corpse appeared quiet and ready for our attempt at reanimation. The pale enthusiast now applied some last perfunctory tests for absolute lifelessness, withdrew satisfied, and finally injected into the left arm an accurately measured amount of the vital elixir, prepared during the afternoon with a greater care than we had used since college days, when our feats were new and groping. I cannot express the wild, breathless suspense with which we waited for results on this first really fresh specimen – the first we could reasonably expect to open its lips in rational speech, perhaps to tell of what it had seen beyond the unfathomable abyss.

West was a materialist, believing in no soul and attributing all the working of consciousness to bodily phenomena; consequently he looked for no revelation of hideous secrets from gulfs and caverns beyond death's barrier. I did not wholly disagree with him theoretically, yet held vague instinctive remnants of the primitive faith of my forefathers; so that I could not help eyeing the corpse with a certain amount of awe and terrible expectation. Besides – I could not extract from my memory that hideous, inhuman shriek we heard on the night we tried our first experiment in the deserted farmhouse at Arkham.

Very little time had elapsed before I saw the attempt was not to be a total failure. A touch of colour came to cheeks hitherto chalk-white, and spread out under the curiously ample stubble of sandy beard. West, who had his hand on the pulse of the left wrist, suddenly nodded significantly; and almost simultaneously a mist appeared on the mirror inclined above the body's mouth. There followed a few spasmodic muscular motions, and then an audible breathing and visible motion of the chest. I looked at the closed eyelids, and thought I detected a quivering. Then the lids opened, showing eyes which were grey, calm, and alive, but still unintelligent and not even curious.

In a moment of fantastic whim I whispered questions to the reddening ears; questions of other worlds of which the memory might still be present. Subsequent terror drove them from my mind, but I think the last one, which I repeated, was: "Where have you been?" I do not yet know whether I was answered or not, for no sound came from the well-shaped mouth; but I do know that at that moment I firmly thought the thin lips moved silently, forming syllables which I would have vocalized as "only now" if that phrase had possessed any sense or relevancy. At that moment, as I say, I was elated with the conviction that the one great goal had been attained; and that for the first time a reanimated corpse had uttered distinct words impelled by actual reason. In the next moment there was no doubt about the triumph; no doubt that the solution had truly accomplished, at least temporarily, its full mission of restoring rational and articulate life to the dead. But in that triumph there came to me the greatest of all horrors – not horror of the thing that spoke, but of the deed that I had witnessed and of the man with whom my professional fortunes were joined.

For that very fresh body, at last writhing into full and terrifying consciousness with eyes dilated at the memory of its last scene on earth, threw out its frantic hands in a life and death struggle with the air; and suddenly collapsing into a second and final dissolution from which there could be no return, screamed out the cry that will ring eternally in my aching brain:

"Help! Keep off, you cursed little tow-head fiend – keep that damned needle away from me!"

V THE HORROR FROM THE SHADOWS

Many men have related hideous things, not mentioned in print, which happened on the battlefields of the Great War. Some of these things have made me faint, others have convulsed me with devastating nausea, while still others have made me tremble and look behind me in the dark; yet despite the worst of them I believe I can relate the most hideous thing of all – the shocking, the unnatural, the unbelievable horror from the shadows.

In 1915 I was a physician with the rank of First Lieutenant in a Canadian regiment in Flanders, one of many Americans to precede the government itself into the gigantic struggle. I had not entered the army on my initiative, but rather as a natural result of the enlistment of the man whose indispensable assistant I was – the celebrated Boston surgical specialist, Dr Herbert West. Dr West had been avid for a chance to serve as surgeon in a great war, and when the chance had come he carried me with him almost against my will. There were reasons why I would have been glad to let the war separate us; reasons why I found the practice of medicine and the companionship of West more and more irritating; but when he had gone to Ottawa and through a colleague's influence secured a medical commission as Major, I could not resist the imperious persuasion of one determined that I should accompany him in my usual capacity.

When I say that Dr West was avid to serve in battle, I do not mean to imply that he was either naturally warlike or anxious for the safety of civilization. Always an ice-cold intellectual machine: slight, blond, blue-eyed, and spectacled: I think he secretly sneered at my occasional martial enthusiasms and censures of supine neutrality. There was, however, something he wanted in embattled Flanders; and in order to secure it he had to assume a military exterior. What he wanted was not a thing which many persons want, but something connected with the peculiar branch of medical science which he had chosen quite clandestinely to follow, and in which he had achieved amazing and occasionally hideous results. It was, in fact, nothing more or less than an abundant supply of freshly killed men in every stage of dismemberment.

Herbert West needed fresh bodies because his life-work was the reanimation of the dead. This work was not known to the fashionable clientele who had so swiftly built up his fame after his arrival in Boston; but was only too well known to me, who had been his closest friend and sole assistant since the old days in Miskatonic University medical school at Arkham. It was in those college days that he had begun his terrible experiments, first on small animals and then on human bodies shockingly obtained. There was a solution which he injected into the veins of dead things, and if they were fresh enough they responded in strange ways. He had had much trouble in discovering the proper formula, for each type of organism was found to need a stimulus especially adapted to it. Terror stalked him when he reflected on his partial failures; nameless things resulting from imperfect solutions or from bodies insufficiently fresh. A certain number of these failures had remained alive – one was in an asylum while others had vanished – and as he thought of conceivable yet virtually impossible eventualities he often shivered beneath his usual stolidity.

West had soon learned that absolute freshness was the prime

requisite for useful specimens, and had accordingly resorted to frightful and unnatural expedients in body-snatching. In college, and during our early practice together in the factory town of Bolton, my attitude toward him had been largely one of fascinated admiration; but as his boldness in methods grew, I began to develop a gnawing fear. I did not like the way he looked at healthy living bodies; and then there came a nightmarish session in the cellar laboratory when I learned that a certain specimen had been a living body when he secured it. That was the first time he had ever been able to revive the quality of rational thought in a corpse; and his success, obtained at such a loathsome cost, had completely hardened him.

Of his methods in the intervening five years I dare not speak. I was held to him by sheer force of fear, and witnessed sights that no human tongue could repeat. Gradually I came to find Herbert West himself more horrible than anything he did — that was when it dawned on me that his once normal scientific zeal for prolonging life had subtly degenerated into a mere morbid and ghoulish curiosity and secret sense of charnel picturesqueness. His interest became a hellish and perverse addiction to the repellently and fiendishly abnormal; he gloated calmly over artificial monstrosities which would make most healthy men drop dead from fright and disgust; he became, behind his pallid intellectuality, a fastidious Baudelaire of physical experiment — a languid Elagabalus of the tombs.

Dangers he met unflinchingly; crimes he committed unmoved. I think the climax came when he had proved his point that rational life can be restored, and had sought new worlds to conquer by experimenting on the reanimation of detached parts of bodies. He had wild and original ideas on the independent vital properties of organic cells and nerve tissue separated from natural physiological systems; and achieved some hideous preliminary results in the form of never-dying, artificially nourished tissue obtained from the nearly-hatched eggs of an indescribable tropical reptile. Two biological points he was exceedingly anxious to settle — first, whether any amount of consciousness and rational action might be possible without the brain, proceeding from the spinal cord and various nerve-centres; and second, whether any kind of ethereal, intangible relation distinct from the material cells may exist to link the surgically separated parts of what has previously been a single living organism. All this research work required a prodigious supply of freshly slaughtered human flesh — and that was why Herbert West had entered the Great War.

The phantasmal, unmentionable thing occurred one midnight late in March, 1915, in a field hospital behind the lines at St Eloi. I

wonder even now if it could have been other than a demoniac
dream of delirium. West had a private laboratory in an east room
of the barn-like temporary edifice, assigned him on his plea that he
was devising new and radical methods for the treatment of hitherto
hopeless cases of maiming. There he worked like a butcher in the
midst of his gory wares – I could never get used to the levity
with which he handled and classified certain things. At times he
actually did perform marvels of surgery for the soldiers; but his chief
delights were of a less public and philanthropic kind, requiring many
explanations of sounds which seemed peculiar even amidst that babel
of the damned. Among these sounds were frequent revolver-shots –
surely not uncommon on a battlefield, but distinctly uncommon in a
hospital. Dr West's reanimated specimens were not meant for long
existence or a large audience. Besides human tissue, West employed
much of the reptile embryo tissue which he had cultivated with such
singular results. It was better than human material for maintaining
life in organless fragments, and that was now my friend's chief
activity. In a dark corner of the laboratory, over a queer incubating
burner, he kept a large covered vat full of this reptilian cell-matter;
which multiplied and grew puffily and hideously.

On the night of which I speak we had a splendid new specimen
– a man at once physically powerful and of such high mentality that
a sensitive nervous system was assured. It was rather ironic, for he
was the officer who had helped West to his commission, and who was
now to have been our associate. Moreover, he had in the past secretly
studied the theory of reanimation to some extent under West. Major
Sir Eric Moreland Clapham-Lee, DSO, was the greatest surgeon in
our division, and had been hastily assigned to the St Eloi sector when
news of the heavy fighting reached headquarters. He had come in
an aeroplane piloted by the intrepid Lieutenant Ronald Hill, only
to be shot down when directly over his destination. The fall had
been spectacular and awful; Hill was unrecognizable afterward, but
the wreck yielded up the great surgeon in a nearly decapitated but
otherwise intact condition. West had greedily seized the lifeless thing
which had once been his friend and fellow-scholar; and I shuddered
when he finished severing the head, placed it in his hellish vat
of pulpy reptile-tissue to preserve it for future experiments, and
proceeded to treat the decapitated body on the operating table. He
injected new blood, joined certain veins, arteries, and nerves at the
headless neck, and closed the ghastly aperture with engrafted skin
from an unidentified specimen which had borne an officer's uniform.
I knew what he wanted – to see if this highly organized body could
exhibit, without its head, any of the signs of mental life which had

distinguished Sir Eric Moreland Clapham-Lee. Once a student of reanimation, this silent trunk was now gruesomely called upon to exemplify it.

I can still see Herbert West under the sinister electric light as he injected his reanimating solution into the arm of the headless body. The scene I cannot describe – I should faint if I tried it, for there is madness in a room full of classified charnel things, with blood and lesser human debris almost ankle-deep on the slimy floor, and with hideous reptilian abnormalities sprouting, bubbling, and baking over a winking bluish-green spectre of dim flame in a far corner of black shadows.

The specimen, as West repeatedly observed, had a splendid nervous system. Much was expected of it; and as a few twitching motions began to appear, I could see the feverish interest on West's face. He was ready, I think, to see proof of his increasingly strong opinion that consciousness, reason, and personality can exist independently of the brain – that man has no central connective spirit, but is merely a machine of nervous matter, each section more or less complete in itself. In one triumphant demonstration West was about to relegate the mystery of life to the category of myth. The body now twitched more vigorously, and beneath our avid eyes commenced to heave in a frightful way. The arms stirred disquietingly, the legs drew up, and various muscles contracted in a repulsive kind of writhing. Then the headless thing threw out its arms in a gesture which was unmistakably one of desperation – an intelligent desperation apparently sufficient to prove every theory of Herbert West. Certainly, the nerves were recalling the man's last act in life; the struggle to get free of the falling aeroplane.

What followed, I shall never positively know. It may have been wholly an hallucination from the shock caused at that instant by the sudden and complete destruction of the building in a cataclysm of German shell-fire – who can gainsay it, since West and I were the only proved survivors? West liked to think that before his recent disappearance, but there were times when he could not; for it was queer that we both had the same hallucination. The hideous occurrence itself was very simple, notable only for what it implied.

The body on the table had risen with a blind and terrible groping, and we had heard a sound. I should not call that sound a voice, for it was too awful. And yet its timbre was not the most awful thing about it. Neither was its message – it had merely screamed, "Jump, Ronald, for God's sake, jump!" The awful thing was its source.

For it had come from the large covered vat in that ghoulish corner of crawling black shadows.

VI   THE TOMB-LEGIONS

When Dr Herbert West disappeared a year ago, the Boston police questioned me closely. They suspected that I was holding something back, and perhaps suspected even graver things; but I could not tell them the truth because they would not have believed it. They knew, indeed, that West had been connected with activities beyond the credence of ordinary men; for his hideous experiments in the reanimation of dead bodies had long been too extensive to admit of perfect secrecy; but the final soul-shattering catastrophe held elements of demoniac phantasy which make even me doubt the reality of what I saw.

I was West's closest friend and only confidential assistant. We had met years before, in medical school, and from the first I had shared his terrible researches. He had slowly tried to perfect a solution which, injected into the veins of the newly deceased, would restore life; a labour demanding an abundance of fresh corpses and therefore involving the most unnatural actions. Still more shocking were the products of some of the experiments – grisly masses of flesh that had been dead, but that West waked to a blind, brainless, nauseous animation. These were the usual results, for in order to reawaken the mind it was necessary to have specimens so absolutely fresh that no decay could possibly affect the delicate brain cells.

This need for very fresh corpses had been West's moral undoing. They were hard to get, and one awful day he had secured his specimen while it was still alive and vigorous. A struggle, a needle, and a powerful alkaloid had transformed it to a very fresh corpse, and the experiment had succeeded for a brief and memorable moment; but West had emerged with a soul calloused and seared, and a hardened eye which sometimes glanced with a kind of hideous and calculating appraisal at men of especially sensitive brain and especially vigorous physique. Toward the last I became acutely afraid of West, for he began to look at me that way. People did not seem to notice his glances, but they noticed my fear; and after his disappearance used that as a basis for some absurd suspicions.

West, in reality, was more afraid than I; for his abominable pursuits entailed a life of furtiveness and dread of every shadow. Partly it was the police he feared; but sometimes his nervousness was deeper and more nebulous, touching on certain indescribable things into which he had injected a morbid life, and from which he had not seen that life depart. He usually finished his experiments with a revolver, but a few times he had not been quick enough. There was that first specimen on whose rifled grave marks of clawing were later seen. There was also that Arkham professor's body which had done cannibal things before it had been captured and thrust unidentified into a madhouse cell at Sefton, where it beat the walls for sixteen years. Most of the other possibly surviving results were things less easy to speak of – for in later years West's scientific zeal had degenerated to an unhealthy and fantastic mania, and he had spent his chief skill in vitalizing not entire human bodies but isolated parts of bodies, or parts joined to organic matter other than human. It had become fiendishly disgusting by the time he disappeared; many of the experiments could not even be hinted at in print. The Great War, through which both of us served as surgeons, had intensified this side of West.

In saying that West's fear of his specimens was nebulous, I have in mind particularly its complex nature. Part of it came merely from knowing of the existence of such nameless monsters, while another part arose from apprehension of the bodily harm they might under certain circumstances do him. Their disappearance added horror to the situation – of them all West knew the whereabouts of only one, the pitiful asylum thing. Then there was a more subtle fear – a very fantastic sensation resulting from a curious experiment in the Canadian army in 1915. West, in the midst of a severe battle, had reanimated Major Sir Eric Moreland Clapham-Lee, D.S.O., a fellow-physician who knew about his experiments and could have duplicated them. The head had been removed, so that the possibilities of quasi-intelligent life in the trunk might be investigated. Just as the building was wiped out by a German shell, there had been a success. The trunk had moved intelligently; and, unbelievable to relate, we were both sickeningly sure that articulate sounds had come from the detached head as it lay in a shadowy corner of the laboratory. The shell had been merciful, in a way – but West could never feel as certain as he wished, that we two were the only survivors. He used to make shuddering conjectures about the possible actions of a headless physician with the power of reanimating the dead.

West's last quarters were in a venerable house of much elegance, overlooking one of the oldest burying grounds in Boston. He had chosen the place for purely symbolic and fantastically aesthetic reasons, since most of the interments were of the Colonial period and therefore of little use to a scientist seeking very fresh bodies. The laboratory was in a sub-cellar secretly constructed by imported workmen, and contained a huge incinerator for the quiet and complete disposal of such bodies, or fragments and synthetic mockeries of bodies, as might remain from the morbid experiments and unhallowed amusements of the owner. During the excavation of this cellar the workmen had struck some exceedingly ancient masonry; undoubtedly connected with the old burying ground, yet far too deep to correspond with any known sepulchre therein. After a number of calculations West decided that it represented some secret chamber beneath the tomb of the Averills, where the last interment had been made in 1768. I was with him when he studied the nitrous, dripping walls laid bare by the spades and mattocks of the men, and was prepared for the gruesome thrill which would attend the uncovering of centuried grave-secrets; but for the first time West's new timidity conquered his natural curiosity, and he betrayed his degenerating fibre by ordering the masonry left intact and plastered over. Thus it remained till that final hellish night, part of the walls of the secret laboratory. I speak of West's decadence, but must add that it was a purely mental and intangible thing. Outwardly he was the same to the last – calm, cold, slight, and yellow-haired, with spectacled blue eyes and a general aspect of youth which years and fears seemed never to change. He seemed calm even when he thought of that clawed grave and looked over his shoulder; even when he thought of the carnivorous thing that gnawed and pawed at Sefton bars.

The end of Herbert West began one evening in our joint study when he was dividing his curious glance between the newspaper and me. A strange headline item had struck at him from the crumpled pages, and a nameless titan claw had seemed to reach down through sixteen years. Something fearsome and incredible had happened at Sefton Asylum fifty miles away, stunning the neighborhood and baffling the police. In the small hours of the morning a body of silent men had entered the grounds and their leader had aroused the attendants. He was a menacing military figure who talked without moving his lips and whose voice seemed almost ventriloquially connected with an immense black case he carried. His expressionless face was handsome to the point of radiant beauty, but had shocked the superintendent when the hall light fell on it – for it was a wax face with eyes of painted glass. Some nameless accident had befallen this man. A larger man guided his steps; a repellent hulk whose bluish face seemed half eaten away by some unknown malady. The speaker had asked for the custody of the cannibal monster committed from Arkham sixteen years before; and upon being refused, gave a signal which precipitated a shocking riot. The fiends had beaten, trampled, and bitten every attendant who did not flee; killing four and finally succeeding in the liberation of the monster. These victims who could recall the event without hysteria swore that the creatures had acted less like men than like unthinkable automata guided by the wax-faced leader. By the time help could be summoned, every trace of the men and of their mad charge had vanished.

From the hour of reading this item until midnight, West sat almost paralyzed. At midnight the doorbell rang, startling him fearfully. All the servants were asleep in the attic, so I answered the bell. As I have told the police, there was no wagon in the street; but only a group of strange-looking figures bearing a large square box which they deposited in the hallway after one of them had grunted in a highly unnatural voice, "Express – prepaid." They filed out of the house with a jerky tread, and as I watched them go I had an odd idea that they were turning toward the ancient cemetery on which the back of the house abutted. When I slammed the door after them West came downstairs and looked at the box. It was about two feet square, and bore West's correct name and present address. It also bore the inscription, "From Eric Moreland Clapham-Lee, St Eloi, Flanders." Six years before, in Flanders, a shelled hospital had fallen upon the headless reanimated trunk of Dr Clapham-Lee, and upon the detached head which – perhaps – had uttered articulate sounds.

West was not even excited now. His condition was more ghastly. Quickly he said, "It's the finish – but let's incinerate – this." We carried the thing down to the laboratory – listening. I do not remember many particulars – you can imagine my state of mind – but it is a vicious lie to say it was Herbert West's body which I put into the incinerator. We both inserted the whole unopened box, closed the door, and started the electricity. Nor did any sound come from the box, after all.

It was West who first noticed the falling plaster on that part of the wall where the ancient tomb masonry had been covered up. I was going to run, but he stopped me. Then I saw a small black aperture, felt a ghoulish wind of ice, and smelled the charnel bowels of a putrescent earth. There was no sound, but just then the electric lights went out and I saw outlined against some phosphorescence of the nether world a horde of silent toiling things which only insanity – or worse – could create. Their outlines were human, semi-human, fractionally human, and not human at all – the horde was grotesquely heterogeneous. They were removing the stones quietly, one by one, from the centuried wall. And then, as the breach became large enough, they came out into the laboratory in a single file; led by a stalking thing with a beautiful head made of wax. A sort of mad-eyed monstrosity behind the leader seized on Herbert West. West did not resist or utter a sound. Then they all sprang at him and tore him to pieces before my eyes, bearing the fragments away into that subterranean vault of fabulous abominations. West's head was carried off by the wax-headed leader, who wore a Canadian officer's uniform. As it disappeared I saw that the blue eyes behind the spectacles were hideously blazing with their first touch of frantic, visible emotion.

Servants found me unconscious in the morning. West was gone. The incinerator contained only unidentifiable ashes. Detectives have questioned me, but what can I say? The Sefton tragedy they will not connect with West; not that, nor the men with the box, whose existence they deny. I told them of the vault, and they pointed to the unbroken plaster wall and laughed. So I told them no more. They imply that I am either a madman or a murderer – probably I am mad. But I might not be mad if those accursed tomb-legions had not been so silent.

Lisa Tuttle

Treading the Maze

And there was Lisa Tuttle thinking she'd never written a zombie story . . . According to the author, "'Treading the Maze' grew out of warm memories of a holiday romance, blissful days driving around the West Country in a little black Mini, nights spent in Bed & Breakfast establishments like the one described in the story. There was no turf maze in the adjoining field, at least not one visible to me."

"In fact," she continues, "I have never seen an actual turf maze, although I have done a lot of reading about them and am fascinated by the subject. To my mind, no one has ever satisfactorily explained what they were for, *so my story offers one suggestion."*

Lisa's most recent novel is Lost Futures *(short-listed for the 1992 Arthur C. Clarke Award), following* Familiar Spirit, Gabriel *and an award-winning collaboration with George R. R. Martin,* Windhaven. *Her short fiction has been collected in* Memories of the Body, A Spaceship Built of Stone *and* A Nest of Nightmares, *and she edited the acclaimed horror anthology by women,* Skin of the Soul.

WE HAD SEEN the bed and breakfast sign from the road, and although it was still daylight and there was no hurry to settle, we had liked the look of the large, well-kept house amid the farmlands, and the name on the sign: The Old Vicarage.

Phil parked the Mini on the curving gravel drive. "No need for you to get out," he said. "I'll just pop in and ask."

I got out anyway, just to stretch my legs and feel the warmth of the late, slanting sunrays on my bare arms. It was a beautiful afternoon. There was a smell of manure on the air, but it wasn't unpleasant, mingling with the other country smells. I walked towards the hedge which divided the garden from the fields beyond. There was a low stone wall along the drive, and I climbed onto it to look over the hedge and into the field.

There was a man standing there, all alone in the middle of the field. He was too far away for me to make out his features, but something about the sight of that still figure gave me a chill. I was suddenly afraid he would turn his head and see me watching him, and I clambered down hastily.

"Amy?" Phil was striding towards me, his long face alight. "It's a lovely room – come and see."

The room was upstairs, with a huge soft bed, an immense wooden wardrobe, and a big, deep-set window, which I cranked open. I stood looking out over the fields.

There was no sign of the man I had just seen, and I couldn't imagine where he had vanished to so quickly.

"Shall we plan to have dinner in Glastonbury?" Phil asked, combing his hair before the mirror inside the wardrobe door. "There should still be enough of the day left to see the Abbey."

I looked at the position of the sun in the sky. "And we can climb the tor tomorrow."

"*You* can climb the tor tomorrow morning. I've had about enough of all this climbing of ancient hills and monuments – Tintagel, St Michael's Mount, Cadbury Castle, Silbury Hill – "

"We didn't climb Silbury Hill. Silbury Hill had a fence around it."

"And a good thing, too, or you'd have made me climb it." He came up behind me and hugged me fiercely.

I relaxed against him, feeling as if my bones were melting. Keeping my voice brisk, mock-scolding, I said, "I didn't complain about showing you all the wonders of America last year. So the least you can do now is return the favour with ancient wonders of Britain. I know you grew up with all this stuff, but I didn't. We don't have anything like Silbury Hill or Glastonbury Tor where I come from."

"If you did, if there was a Glastonbury Tor in America, they'd have a lift up the side of it," he said.

"Or at least a drive-through window."

We both began laughing helplessly.

I think of us standing there in that room, by the open window, holding each other and laughing – I think of us standing there like that forever.

Dinner was a mixed grill in a Glastonbury café. Our stroll through the Abbey grounds took longer than we'd thought, and we were late, arriving at the café just as the proprietress was about to close up. Phil teased and charmed her into staying open and cooking for two last customers. Grey-haired, fat and nearly toothless, she lingered by our table throughout our meal to continue her flirtation with Phil. He obliged, grinning and joking and flattering, but every time her back was turned, he winked at me or grabbed my leg beneath the table, making coherent conversation impossible on my part.

When we got back to the Old Vicarage, we were roped into having tea with the couple who ran the place and the other guests. That late in the summer there were only two others, an elderly couple from Belgium.

The electric fire was on and the lounge was much too warm. The heat made it seem even smaller than it was. I drank my sweet milky tea, stroked the old white dog who lay near my feet, and gazed admiringly at Phil, who kept up one end of a conversation about the weather, the countryside, and World War II.

Finally the last of the tea was consumed, the biscuit tin had made the rounds three times, and we could escape to the cool, empty sanctuary of our room. There we stripped off our clothes, climbed into the big soft bed, talked quietly of private things, and made love.

I hadn't been asleep long before I came awake, aware that I was alone in the bed. We hadn't bothered to draw the curtains, and the moonlight was enough to show me Phil was sitting on the wide window-ledge smoking a cigarette.

I sat up. "Can't you sleep?"

"Just my filthy habit." He waved the lit cigarette; I didn't see, but could imagine, the sheepish expression on his face. "I didn't want to disturb you."

He took one last, long drag and stubbed the cigarette out in an ashtray. He rose, and I saw that he was wearing his woollen pullover, which hung to his hips, just long enough for modesty, but leaving his long, skinny legs bare.

I giggled.

"What's that?"

"You without your trousers."

"That's right, make fun. Do I laugh at you when you wear a dress?"

He turned away towards the window, leaning forward to open it a little more. "It's a beautiful night . . . cor!" He straightened up in surprise.

"What?"

"Out there – people. I don't know what they're doing. They seem to be dancing, out in the field."

Half-suspecting a joke, despite the apparently genuine note of surprise in his voice, I got up and joined him at the window, wrapping my arms around myself against the cold. Looking out where he was gazing, I saw them. They were indisputably human figures – five, or perhaps six or seven, of them, all moving about in a shifting spiral, like some sort of children's game or country dance.

And then I saw it. It was like suddenly comprehending an optical illusion. One moment, bewilderment; but, the next, the pattern was clear.

"It's a maze," I said. "Look at it, it's marked out in the grass."

"A turf-maze," Phil said, wondering.

Among the people walking that ancient, ritual path, one suddenly paused and looked up, seemingly directly at us. In the pale moonlight and at that distance I couldn't tell if it was a man or a woman. It was just a dark figure with a pale face turned up towards us.

I remembered then that I had seen someone standing in that very field, perhaps in that same spot, earlier in the day, and I shivered. Phil put his arm around me and drew me close.

"What are they doing?" I asked.

"There are remnants of traditions about dancing or running through mazes all over the country," Phil said. "Most of the old turf-mazes have vanished – people stopped keeping them up before this century. They're called troy-towns, or mizmazes . . . no one knows when or why they began, or if treading the maze was game or ritual, or what the purpose was."

Another figure now paused beside the one who stood still, and laid hold of that one's arm, and seemed to say something. And then the two figures fell back into the slow circular dance.

"I'm cold," I said. I was shivering uncontrollably, although it was not with any physical chill. I gave up the comfort of Phil's arm and ran for the bed.

"They might be witches," Phil said. "Hippies from Glastonbury, trying to revive an old custom. Glastonbury does attract some odd types."

I had burrowed under the bedclothes, only the top part of my face left uncovered, and was waiting for my teeth to stop chattering and for the warmth to penetrate my muscles.

"I could go out and ask them who they are," Phil said. His voice sounded odd. "I'd like to know who they are. I feel as if I *should* know."

I stared at his back, alarmed. "Phil, you're not going out there!"

"Why not? This isn't New York City. I'd be perfectly safe."

I sat up, letting the covers fall. "Phil, don't."

He turned away from the window to face me. "What's the matter?"

I couldn't speak.

"Amy . . . you're not crying?" His voice was puzzled and gentle. He came to the bed and held me.

"Don't leave me," I whispered against the rough weave of his sweater.

"Course I won't," he said, stroking my hair and kissing me. "Course I won't."

But of course he did, less than two months later, in a way neither of us could have guessed then. But even then, watching the dancers in the maze, even then he was dying.

In the morning, as we were settling our bill, Phil mentioned the people we had seen dancing in the field during the night. The landlord was flatly disbelieving.

"Sure you weren't dreaming?"

"Quite sure," said Phil. "I wondered if it was some local custom . . ."

He snorted. "Some custom! Dancing around a field in the dead of night!"

"There's a turf-maze out there," Phil began.

But the man was shaking his head. "No, not in that field. Not a maze!"

Phil was patient. "I don't mean one with hedges, like in Hampton Court. Just a turf-maze, a pattern made in the soil years ago. It's hardly noticeable now, although it can't have been too many years since it was allowed to grow back. I've seen them other places and read about them, and in the past there were local customs of running the maze, or dancing through it, or playing games. I thought some such custom might have been revived locally."

The man shrugged. "I wouldn't know about that," he said. We had learned the night before that the man and his wife were "foreigners", having only settled here, from the north of England, some twenty years before. Obviously, he wasn't going to be much help with information on local traditions.

After we had loaded our bags into the car, Phil hesitated, looking towards the hedge. "I'd quite like to have a look at that maze close-to," he said.

My heart sank, but I could think of no rational reason to stop him. Feebly I tried, "We shouldn't trespass on somebody else's property . . ."

"Walking across a field isn't trespassing!" He began to walk along the hedge, towards the road. Because I didn't want him to go alone, I hurried after. There was a gate a few yards along the road by which we entered the field. But once there, I wondered how we would find the maze. Without an overview such as our window had provided, the high grass looked all the same, and from this level, in ordinary daylight, slight alterations in ground level wouldn't be obvious to the eye.

Phil looked back at the house, getting in alignment with the window, then turned and looked across the field, his eyes narrowed as he tried to calculate distance. Then he began walking slowly, looking down often at the ground. I hung back, following him at a distance and not myself looking for the maze. I didn't want to find it. Although I couldn't have explained my reaction, the maze frightened me, and I wanted to be away, back on the road again, alone together in the little car, eating apples, gazing at the passing scenery, talking.

"Ah!"

I stopped still at Phil's triumphant cry and watched as he hopped from one foot to the other. One foot was clearly on higher ground. He began to walk in a curious, up-down fashion. "I think this is it," he called. "I think I've found it. If the land continues to dip . . . yes, yes, this is it!" He stopped walking and looked back at me, beaming.

"Great," I said.

"The grass has grown back where once it was kept cleared, but you can still feel the place where the swathe was cut," he said, rocking back and forth to demonstrate the confines of the shallow ditch. "Come and see."

"I'll take your word for it," I said.

He cocked his head. "I thought you'd be interested. I thought something like this would be right up your alley. The funny folkways of the ancient Brits."

I shrugged, unable to explain my unease.

"We've plenty of time, love," he said. "I promise we'll climb Glastonbury Tor before we push on. But we're here now, and I'd like to get the feel of this." He stretched his hand towards me. "Come tread the maze with me."

It would have been so easy to take his hand and do just that. But overriding my desire to be with him, to take this as just another lark, was the fearful, wordless conviction that there was danger here. And if I refused to join him. perhaps he would give up the idea and come away with me. He might sulk in the car, but he would get over it, and at least we would be away.

"Let's go now," I said, my arms stiff at my sides.

Displeasure clouded his face, and he turned away from me with a shrug. "Give me just a minute, then," he said. And as I watched, he began to tread the maze.

He didn't attempt that curious, skipping dance we had seen the others do the night before; he simply walked, and none too quickly, with a careful, measured step. He didn't look at me as he walked, although the pattern of the maze brought him circling around again and again to face in my direction – he kept his gaze on the ground. I felt, as I watched, that he was being drawn further away from me with every step. I wrapped my arms around myself and told myself not to be a fool. I could feel the little hairs standing up all along my arms and back, and I had to fight the urge to break and run like hell. I felt, too, as if someone watched us, but when I looked around, the field was as empty as ever.

Phil had stopped, and I assumed he had reached the centre. He stood very still and gazed off into the distance, his profile towards me. I remembered the man I had seen standing in the field – perhaps in that very spot, the centre of the maze – when we had first arrived at the Old Vicarage.

Then, breaking the spell, Phil came bounding towards me, cutting across the path of the maze, and caught me in a bear hug. "Not mad?"

I relaxed a little. It was over, and all was well. I managed a small laugh. "No, of course not."

"Good. Let's go, then. Phil's had his little treat."

We walked arm in arm back towards the road. We didn't mention it again.

In the months to come those golden days, the two weeks we had spent wandering around southwest England, often came to mind. Those thoughts were an antidote to more recent memories: to those last days in the hospital, with Phil in pain, and then Phil dead.

I moved back to the States – it was home, after all, where my family and most of my friends lived. I had lived in England for less than two years, and without Phil there was little reason to stay. I found an apartment in the neighbourhood where I had lived just after college, and got a job teaching, and, although painfully and rustily, began to go through the motions of making a new life for myself. I didn't stop missing Phil, and the pain grew no less with the passage of time, but I adjusted to it. I was coping.

In the spring of my second year alone I began to think of going back to England. In June I went for a vacation, planning to spend a week in London, a few days in Cambridge with Phil's sister, and a few days visiting friends in St Ives. When I left London in a rented car and headed for St Ives. I did not plan to retrace the well-remembered route of that last vacation, but that is what I found myself doing, with each town and village a bittersweet experience, recalling pleasant memories and prodding the deep sadness in me wider awake.

I lingered in Glastonbury, wandering the peaceful Abbey ruins and remembering Phil's funny, disrespectful remarks about the sacred throne and King Arthur's bones. I looked for, but could not find, the café where we'd had dinner, and settled for fish and chips. Driving out of Glastonbury with the sun setting, I came upon the Old Vicarage and pulled into that familiar drive. There were more cars there, and the house was almost full up this time. There was a room available, but not the one I had hoped for. Although a part of me, steeped in sadness, was beginning to regret this obsessional pilgrimage, another part of me longed for the same room, the same bed, the same view from the window, in order to conjure Phil's ghost. Instead, I was given a much smaller room on the other side of the house.

I retired early, skipping tea with the other guests, but sleep would not come. When I closed my eyes I could see Phil, sitting on the window ledge with a cigarette in one hand, narrowing his eyes to look at me through the smoke. But when I opened my eyes it was the wrong room, with a window too small to sit in, a room Phil had never seen. The narrowness of the bed made it impossible to imagine that he slept beside me still. I wished I had gone straight to St Ives instead of dawdling and stopping along the way – this was pure torture. I couldn't recapture the past – every moment that I spent here reminded me of how utterly Phil was gone.

Finally I got up and pulled on a sweater and a pair of jeans. The moon was full, lighting the night, but my watch had stopped and I had no idea what time it was. The big old house was silent. I left by the front door, hoping that no one would come along after me to relock the door. A walk in the fresh air might tire me enough to let me sleep, I thought.

I walked along the gravel drive, past all the parked cars, towards the road, and entered the next field by the same gate that Phil and I had used in daylight in another lifetime. I scarcely thought of where I was going, or why, as I made my way to the turf-maze which had fascinated Phil and frightened me. More than once I had regretted not taking Phil's hand and treading the maze with him when he had asked. Not that it would have made any difference in the long run, but all the less-than-perfect moments of our time together had returned to haunt me and given rise to regrets since Phil's death – all the opportunities missed, now gone forever; all the things I should have said or done or done differently.

There was someone standing in the field. I stopped short, staring, my heart pounding. Someone standing there, where the centre of the maze must be. He was turned away, and I could not tell who he was, but something about the way he stood made me certain that I had seen him before, that I knew him.

I ran forward and – I must have blinked – suddenly the figure was gone again, if he had ever existed. The moonlight was deceptive, and the tall grass swaying in the wind, and the swiftly moving clouds overhead cast strange shadows.

"Come tread the maze with me."

Had I heard those words, or merely remembered them?

I looked down at my feet and then around, confused. Was I standing in the maze already? I took a tentative step forward and back, and it did seem that I was standing in a shallow depression. The memory flooded back: Phil standing in the sunlit field, rocking back and forth and saying, "I think this is it." The open, intense look on his face.

"Phil," I whispered, my eyes filling with tears.

Through the tears I saw some motion, but when I blinked them away, again there was nothing. I looked around the dark, empty field, and began to walk the path laid out long before. I did not walk as slowly as Phil had done, but more quickly, almost skipping, hitting the sides of the maze path with my feet to be certain of keeping to it, since I could not see it.

And as I walked, it seemed to me that I was not alone, that people were moving ahead of me, somehow just out of my sight (beyond another turn in the winding path I might catch them up), or behind. I could hear their footsteps. The thought that others were behind me, following me, unnerved me, and I stopped and turned around to look. I saw no one, but I was now facing in the direction of the Old Vicarage, and my gaze went on to the house. I could see the upper window, the very window where Phil and I had stood together looking out, the point from which we had seen the dancers in the maze.

The curtains were not drawn across that dark square of glass this night, either. And as I watched, a figure appeared at the window. A tall shape, a pale face looking out. And after a moment, as I still stared, confused, a second figure joined the first. Someone smaller – a woman. The man put his arm around her. I could see – perhaps I shouldn't have been able to see this at such a distance, with no light on in the room – but I could see that the man was wearing a sweater, and the woman was naked. And I could see the man's face. It was Phil. And the woman was me.

There we were. Still together, still safe from what time would bring. I could almost feel the chill that had shaken me then, and the comfort of Phil's protecting arm. And yet I was not there. Not now. Now I was out in the field, alone, a premonition to my earlier self.

I felt someone come up beside me. Something as thin and light and hard as a bird's claw took hold of my arm. Slowly I turned away from the window and turned to see who held me. A young man was standing beside me, smiling at me. I thought I recognized him.

"He's waiting for you at the centre," he said. "You mustn't stop now."

Into my mind came a vivid picture of Phil in daylight, standing still in the centre of the maze, caught there by something, standing there forever. Time was not the same in the maze, and Phil could still be standing where he had once stood. I could be with him again, for a moment or forever.

I resumed the weaving, skipping steps of the dance with my new companion. I was eager now, impatient to reach the centre. Ahead of me I could see other figures, dim and shifting as the moonlight, winking in and out of view as they trod the maze on other nights, in other centuries.

The view from the corner of my eyes was more disturbing. I caught fleeting glimpses of my partner in this dance, and he did not look the same as when I had seen him face to face. He had looked so young, and yet the light, hard grasp on my arm did not seem that of a young man's hand.

A hand like a bird's claw . . .

My eyes glanced down my side to my arm. The hand lying lightly on my solid flesh was nothing but bones, the flesh all rotted and dropped away years before. Those peripheral, sideways glimpses I'd had of my dancing partner were the truth – sights of something long dead and yet still animate.

I stopped short and pulled my arm away from that horror. I closed my eyes, afraid to turn to face it. I heard the rustle and clatter of dry bones. I felt a cold wind against my face and smelled something rotten. A voice – it might have been Phil's – whispered my name in sorrow and fear.

What waited for me at the centre? And what would I become, and for how long would I be trapped in this monotonous dance if ever I reached the end?

I turned around blindly, seeking the way out. I opened my eyes and began to move, then checked myself – some strong, instinctual aversion kept me from cutting across the maze paths and leaping them as if they were only so many shallow, meaningless furrows. Instead, I turned around (I glimpsed pale figures watching me, flickering in my peripheral vision) and began to run back the way I had come, following the course of the maze backwards, away from the centre, back out into the world alone.

David Riley

Out of Corruption

David Riley's short fiction has been published in a wide variety of books and magazines including The Year's Best Horror Stories, The Mammoth Book of Terror, New Writings in Horror & the Supernatural, The Pan Book of Horror Stories, First World Fantasy Awards, World of Horror, Whispers, Fantasy Tales *and* Fear. *He has recently completed his third novel,* Goblin Mire.

The novella which follows is published here for the first time, and it should have you looking nervously over your shoulder the next time you have to go down into the basement . . .

The following text was discovered in the house of Raymond Gregory following his disappearance some time during October, 1934. Although no trace was ever found of its writer's body, nor any sightings reported of him alive following that date, police investigators called in at the time were unable to place any greater significance upon its contents other than an indicator of Mr Gregory's probable state of mind.

So THIS, I thought on that fine September day less than one year ago, as I drove my car round a bend in the lane and drew up before a pair of wrought-iron gates, is where he lives. Despite the brilliance of the sunshine I could not help feeling somewhat disappointed. For the drab grey building visible beyond seemed to personify for me all that had struck me as wrong about the town I had left only two miles away, before passing through the tree-lined meadows and farms along the lane. The uncurtained windows of the house, however, the leaf-strewn pathway rank with mould and long, bare streaks of clay, all these gave off such an air of desolation that I felt instantly depressed. It was certainly not a place which I would have chosen to visit at any time of the day of my own free will, and certainly not at dusk, when the shadows lengthening all about the estate seemed to intensify its ugliness. Why Poole had decided to buy such a place I could not imagine, and I roundly cursed myself for having so readily agreed to come down here to visit him over the week-end. I only hoped, as I stepped out of my car, that the inside of the house would prove to be of a more hospitable appearance than its facade.

Its blank, almost senile-looking windows stared down at me as I neared the door and rapped upon it. Soon, though, I found myself ushered deep inside the old house in Poole's redecorated study – a book-lined room full of polished wood, paintings and leather armchairs, with a coal fire roaring in an elaborately carved hearth full of ebony cupids and flowers. Poole – tall, thin, with the concealed strength of a mountaineer – was in the best of spirits. My own, in contrast, though relieved to a degree by the signs of redecoration, were overcome by a newer and less easily explainable feeling of abhorrence. There was a certain, indefinable quality about the house which I strongly disliked, and I knew then, without a shadow of a doubt, that, however much Poole might enthuse about it, this initial feeling of mine would not be changed. The more I saw of the house, in fact, as Poole showed me around it, the stronger this abhorrence grew.

Upstairs it was almost derelict, with large, grey, vacuous rooms that echoed their emptiness through fibrous veils of cobwebs and dust. Looking at them I could well imagine this place as:

> *A house without a living room*
> *For dead it was, and called a tomb!*

"I don't intend using them much," Poole explained, interrupting my thoughts, "except, perhaps, as store rooms, though I might have two or three done up for guests."

Presently we returned downstairs to the hallway where, at Poole's insistence, we turned off into an arched alcove, within which stood a sturdy wooden door that led to the cellar steps. Lighting a paraffin lamp from a shelf beside it, he unlocked the door and led me down the damp-slicked steps beyond into a tactile darkness that took us into its frigid depths like the waters of a Stygian well.

"Once, before neglect did its worst," Poole said, as he raised the lamp up above his head so that its light could filter across the cellar floor a few moments later, "this was used for storing wine in." The decaying ribs of sundered barrels, furred with mould, could still be seen across the wet flagstones, amidst the remnants of broken bottles and racks. "Some good vintages there were here too," he remarked, stooping to pick up one of the bottles. Its label slid from it like pulp. A curled spider rolled across the floor, spilled from the bottle like a withered grape.

Faint in the distance between heavy pillars I could make out extensions, like passageways. When I asked him about them Poole replied that most had been bricked up long ago. "Or were filled in with rubble when their ceilings gave way."

"Have you been down here often?" I asked, amused at his interest in the dismal place.

Surprising as an affirmative answer would have been – even from Poole, who I had long known had a somewhat morbid temperament – the way he said, "No," came in an unexpected tone of voice. Shaking his head in consternation, he went on: "Before I decided that it was a pointless task, I had some workmen in clearing it out. What they found should have been enough to keep me returning here again and again. But I rarely do."

Turning, he led me across the cellar floor, saying: "I'll show you so that you can judge it for yourself."

As we walked, the air seemed to congeal about us into diseased vapours, smothering us with the sealed-in stench of decay. Our footsteps echoed from the dim expanses of the cellar as we passed beneath the stone-built archway into one of the extensions. Though I had only expected it to be a glorified alcove, it went on for nearly thirty yards before ending in a square-shaped chamber of ancient, crumbling bricks from which the burnt-out stumps of old torches poked like bony fingers blackened with age. Hanging the lamp from one of them, Poole pointed at the floor. There, deeply cut into the unworn slabs of stone, was the intricate design of a five-pointed star, set within two circles, around and in which various signs and arabesques had been carved.

"Devil worship?" I asked, as I felt at the grooves. They were about two inches deep, almost the whole of which was filled with a foul slime.

Poole shrugged. "Probably, but I don't know for certain. I don't even know how old the thing is, nor who must have made it."

"It's old," I confirmed, standing up to look down at the design as a whole. "And authentic, I think. I recognize a few of those signs."

"So do I," Poole said sombrely. "That's the reason, I suppose, why I don't come down here often. It's the one place in this house where I actually feel afraid. Perhaps it's something to do with vibrations from the past, lingering here – I don't know. What I do know is that whatever went on here when this chamber was originally made and used could hardly have been of the more innocent nature such as our modern "fire-side" witches get up to. Why else but to conceal the reverberations of a scream should it have been placed so far underground? Maybe blood smeared this devilish creation. Maybe that slime inside those grooves is made of blood itself."

Feeling a certain revulsion at Poole's unsavoury fascination in the thing, I diverted my attention to the walls. At various points about them there were iron bolt heads riddled with rust. Though there was little of interest in them, one caught my eyes more than the others. The bricks around it appeared to be loose. Inspecting them, as Poole stepped over to join me, we began to pull one of them away to see if there was anything interesting hidden behind it. Within a few minutes five of the bricks were laid on the floor and a sizeable hole uncovered in the wall. Though at first sight it had looked as though we had only come upon a narrow crevice, further dislodgement of the bricks showed that an earth-lined burrow or tunnel large enough for a man to crawl along extended outwards at about chest height for several yards before inclining upwards out of sight. The lamplight illuminated the straggling roots hanging like lengths of matted grey hair inside it.

While Poole stared in rapt and muttering fascination along the burrow, I turned away from it to inspect the bricks we had piled on the floor. Looking one over in my hand, I noticed that it had been heavily scratched on one side as if by claws. Evidently, losing interest in the thing, some rats had tried to force a way through the wall over the years – and failed, I supposed, though their efforts had weakened the mortar enough for us to finish their work with ease.

Noticing that Poole was still staring into the tunnel, I began to feel annoyed.

Taking him by one arm, I said: "Come on. It's about time we were leaving this dismal hole. It's damp and raw down here, and though you might not mind risking rheumatics, I do . . ."

Stones and lumps of dislodged earth began to tumble down the hole, to scatter like mice across the floor at our feet. And with them, like the gases of decay, a noxious stench far worse than any we had encountered thus far emerged to blanch Poole's face in an instant – and no doubt my own as well. Barely able to restrain our nausea, we fell back from the hole.

"The sewers?" I asked. My words sounded sick in the echoing emptiness of the chamber, and slightly unreal. The air was rapidly becoming discoloured, whilst the lamp grew dim, guttering long black tails of soot. In some incomprehensible way sensing danger, I reached for the lamp, grabbing Poole's arm once again.

"Let's get out of here," I muttered coarsely, ignorant of all other impulses but to flee.

The scraping of grit tumbling down the hole filled me with alarm. A moment later we were hurrying self-consciously across the cellar towards the steps. Climbing them in an instant, we paused only at the door into the hallway. Turning, I peered back into the impenetrable dark of the cellar once more, with its mouldering barrels and decay. There was nothing to see or hear save the distant dripping of water somewhere, yet it seemed to me that some one or some thing stood, concealed in the all-encompassing darkness, glowering into my eyes. My scalp prickled and I felt a sick bout of fear overwhelm me. The next moment I was out of that hideous chamber, with the reassuringly solid weight of the door slamming shut beneath my hands.

We spoke no more of the phenomenon that night. Perhaps it was fear or nervousness that sealed our lips, but I think it was more likely shame. After all, it had been no more than a few sods of earth and a smell that sent us scurrying in the headlong flight for safety in the hallway above.

It was, however, close on midnight before we decided to retire.

Strangely – perhaps even perversely – enough, when I reached my room and prepared myself for bed my tiredness left me and insomnia set in. For what seemed like hours I lay tossing in bed, trying to compose my mind for sleep. It was as if now that I was alone, the atmosphere of the house, which I had already found distasteful, had intensified its effect upon me. At the time, depressed by the boredom that my insomnia inflicted upon me, I blamed the unsettling fright we had childishly brought upon ourselves in the cellar. Whatever it was, it was already late when I decided that I had had enough and, though I usually scorned their effectiveness and the sense of my doctor in once having prescribed them for me, I climbed out of bed to go to my suitcase to get a bottle of sleeping pills. There was nothing else for it, I knew, unless I was willing to risk the inevitable tiredness that would beggar me the next day if I did not somehow get to sleep.

As I stepped across the room to my suitcase I chanced to glance out of my window into the moonlit grounds. I can't say that the garden there was a particularly pretty sight in the stark moonlight. The gnarled trees and bushes, not to mention the reed-like grass, were as if a nightmarishly deformed jungle had quite suddenly taken root about the house. The scene was peculiarly depressing, and I was about to turn from it when I saw something move in the shrubberies. I paused and turned back to the window, pressing my face to the panes. I held my breath so that it wouldn't mist the cold glass. I could make out a man, half hidden in the interweaving shadows. It seemed that he was dressed in a dark overcoat that hung flapping in the wind about his heels. His hair, a dry-looking tangle of strands, was scattered about his shoulders as he picked his way through the trees. Despite the strong moonlight it was too dark to make out his face properly, though I could tell that it was distinctively white.

Slowly he continued on his way till he passed beyond the edge of the house and I lost sight of him, whereupon I decided that he must, undoubtedly, have been a passing vagrant – he was certainly too poorly dressed to have been a thief – and I finished off what I had set out to do, a few minutes later settling back into bed where I dry-swallowed two pills and waited for the inevitable sleep that within ten minutes overwhelmed me.

I rose late the next day, finding Poole already breakfasted when I came upon him.

"What will you have?" he asked.

"I'll just make do with some black coffee," I replied, as I settled myself down at the table.

"You look at if you slept badly last night," Poole remarked. "Did you find the air in your room too close? Or was it the bed?"

"I sometimes suffer a little from insomnia," I told him with a shrug. "It's not the room – or, at least, I don't think so. Though there was something that disturbed me." Poole glanced at me sharply – perhaps a shade too sharply, I thought. "There was a man wandering through the garden. I saw him from my window some time after one. Do you often get tramps this way?"

"A tramp?"

Was that a look of relief on Poole's face? "I supposed so at the time," I said. "Though I didn't get a very clear view of him in the gloom. Those damned elms blotted out much of the moonlight down there."

"Yes, I was thinking of having some of them cut down," Poole said, staring down at his cup.

"Have you seen prowlers here before?" I asked, suspicions sharpening the edge of my senses.

"You're more perceptive this morning than I thought you to be. But you're right, of course, I have seen someone once or twice before, though I took him to be a local poacher taking a short cut. There are some well stocked forests just a little way further on from the lane past a narrow stream." He laughed quietly. "I dare say he fancied himself less likely to be seen going through the garden than continuing any further down the lane, especially if he had had a good night and was laden with game."

When I had finished my coffee I stepped outside for a breath of fresh air. The grounds looked more healthy in the strong sunlight of a fine September day than at night, and I even found them faintly attractive, though much in need of the attention of a capable gardener. A few minutes later Poole joined me.

"Have you had a look at the house from the outside yet?" he asked, with more than a touch of pride in his voice.

Looking up at the ungainly edifice I wondered what it was about the place that appealed so strongly to Poole. "It seems to have gone through quite a few transformations in its time," I remarked tactfully, noting its early Tudor origins in the barely discernible beams about the lower floors before extensions and alterations obliterated much of them with Georgian, Queen Anne and Victorian elaborations, with a touch of the Regency Oriental in a cupola on one part of its roof – evidently an elaboration which either lack of further money or a premature death prevented from reaching fulfilment. In fact, as I began to think about this, the various changes gave off in general a half finished impression, as if succeeding owners had never possessed it long enough to complete their differing intentions. Mentioning this to Poole, he laughed indulgently and said that it was in more than one way a remarkable house.

He led me to one of the doors. "As you know," he said, "I had to have a lot of work done on the house before I could move in. The man in charge of the renovation, Mortimer (of Sletheridge, Gilbraith and Mortimer, no less) was exceptionally interested in the place, aside from the purely professional angle, which I must say I found gratifying, to say the least. Did you notice, by any chance, if any of the door or window frames were lop-sided? I'm sure I didn't when I first looked at it. He did. And he even knows why every single one of them is so, and it's not because of faulty craftsmanship, for he says that it is one of the finest houses for its age that he has seen, despite its disrepair. The main part, you see, was built during the early years of James I. Then, far more than now, the influence of superstitions on everyday life was particularly strong, far beyond any bounds we can imagine today. So much so, in fact, that they even took precautions against the supernatural in the building of their homes. And one of these was based upon the odd idea that no evil spirit could enter a house through a misshapen entranceway. Therefore the window frames, the doors, even the chimney shafts themselves, are lopsided – not too much so, but enough to reassure our ancestors that they would not be awakened in the night from their righteous sleep to find a leering succubus astride their beds."

"And did this Mortimer have any other insights into the house?" I asked. "About the cellars, perhaps?"

"He looked in once from the doorway. His only reaction was to shudder and say – rather brusquely, I felt – that it would be best to have it filled in. But I'm not too sure. It seems a waste somehow."

Feeling that "filling it in" was probably the best suggestion he could have made, I said: "You might be able to deceive yourself that what occurred last night in the cellar never happened, but I can't. Have you forgotten about it?"

Reluctantly Poole shook his head. "I went to have a look down there again a short while ago – perhaps to convince myself that we had let ourselves get carried away by our own imaginations, but . . ."

"Yes?" I prompted, impatiently.

"But, somehow – I can't explain why – I just couldn't raise the guts to take that one first step down into it. It was as if the darkness – or something I felt within it – held me back, repelled me, and I couldn't go on."

Sensing that it would do no good to press too hard on the matter, I let it drop. I said that I would like to have a look in the nearby village. "You said in one of your letters that it was a picturesque place. As long as it's better than that town I had to pass through on my way here, I'm not bothered."

"Chalk and cheese," Poole said, brightening. "I don't think you'll be disappointed. But there are several things that need doing around here this morning, so I'm afraid I won't be able to come with you. But you've got your car, and it is only a ten minute drive. It's straight down the lane; you can't miss it. There's a rather fine twelfth-century church near the green."

When, eventually, I left a short while later it was with no small feeling of relief. Few buildings, I thought as I drove down the lane beneath the overhanging branches of the trees, had such an oppressive atmosphere about them. My nerves, for some reason, seemed perpetually on edge all the time I was indoors, and were only eased a little in the grounds. Now, though, I felt relaxed once more, and at ease, and I completely looked forward to having a look around Fenley.

What our conversations had taught me, however, and over which I ruminated much on my drive into the village, was that the house was having an unhealthy effect upon my friend. He altogether lacked the spirit that had so characterized him in the long years of our friendship, and corresponded only to the dark months immediately following the death of his wife five years before, when he had nearly suffered a breakdown. But that was over and done with now. And I was certain that whatever was affecting him now had nothing to do with this. Besides, I thought, this was an altogether different type of disturbance.

It was all to do with the house, I was sure. If only for Poole's good, therefore, I decided to see if I could find out anything more about the place. Spotting the local library near the village green, I had a look inside. A small, pinched man with empty cheeks and hornrimmed glasses sat in a corner behind the desk at the entrance, while a young girl stood stamping romantic novels for a gossipy group of old ladies. The man seemed oblivious of their chatter as he read through a catalogue. I waited till the girl had finished and turned to me.

I asked her if she had any reference books on local history.

"Is there anything in particular you're interested in?" she asked. I noticed that the elderly gentleman – who I took to be the librarian – was looking across at me curiously above his glasses.

"I'm staying with a friend who recently bought an old house near here. I was interested in finding out if there is any history attached to it. It's a hobby of mine," I lied as she thought for a moment, scanning the packed bookshelves.

"Would that be Mr Poole you are staying with?" the librarian asked suddenly, rising from his chair and approaching the desk. He laid the catalogue carefully to one side.

I said that it was. "You know him?" I asked.

"In passing. He doesn't spend much time in the village, I'm afraid. Something of a recluse, I believe."

"There's a lot of work to be done on the house," I explained. "From what I can gather, it was in a pretty bad state when he took it over. I don't suppose he's had much time to spare for socializing so far." I wondered just how much of this was true. The librarian, however, whether out of politeness or agreement, accepted my explanation with a motion of his hands. "One would not have thought the house worth all the time, trouble and expense.

But there you are. But you were asking just now about books, I believe, on local history."

"About the house really," I replied. "It just strikes me that there must be something about it of interest. Its past owners must have been people of influence locally at one time or another. Is there anything you can let me have a look at that might help me in this matter?"

He smiled thinly. "There are several books I could recommend: Pitts' *The Fenley Wanderer*, or Albert Dudley's *The Barchester Landscape*, parts of which concern this area, but they are rather dry and somewhat pedantic. Not the kind of thing to spend a day like this reading through. Besides, they are neither of them very informative about certain darker aspects of the house your friend has bought."

"Then there is something?" I prompted.

The librarian nodded his greying head. "Something," he echoed. "Though exactly what I have never been able to decide."

"Was it anything to do with witchcraft or Devil worship?" I asked, remembering the pentagram in the cellar.

The librarian looked at me in surprise. "So you have heard something then," he said, "after all."

"I've heard nothing," I told him. "All I know is what I've seen." I described the strange carving we found last night, though I left out any reference to what happened afterwards. When I had finished he glanced at his pocket watch. "Look here," he said, "it's about lunchtime. If you haven't eaten yet and have some time to spare, we could go down the street to the tea shop on the corner. I think there are one or two things I can tell you which you might very well find of interest."

Agreeing to his suggestion, I waited while he told the girl he would be back in an hour, then collected his hat from a rack in the office and stepped out from behind the desk to lead me down the street.

When we reached the tea shop, a quaint, rather old world place with fox hunting scenes on its walls, the librarian introduced himself as Desmond Foster. Although he had only lived in Fenley for the last ten years, a keen interest in local history had helped give him a knowledge of the district which he was sure few locals could match. My friend's house, Elm Tree House as it was known in the area, had long fascinated him. "It has had a very long and disquieting history," he said. "Disquieting enough, in fact, to dissuade most people, even in our enlightened times, from purchasing it. Its age, of course, is apparent from its appearance alone – its peculiarly miscegenous appearance."

I said that I had noticed this about it. "It's almost as if succeeding owners had not possessed it long enough to complete their differing intentions," I re-echoed from my earlier conversation with Poole.

"Quite so. Though of the house itself, not even one stone in its entire structure, from the ground floor upwards, is a remnant from the building which originally stood on that spot. Long before Sir Robert Tolbridge, a great nephew of the third Marquis of Barchester, decided in 1608 to erect a house near Elm Tree Wood, there were the ruins of an ancient and almost forgotten abbey there, whose lichened stones were rooted in the ground. It was, as I understand it, during the thirteenth century that monks came to Fenley to build an abbey. From the start they were made welcome, and received ample help with the building of their abbey. Relations, it would seem, could hardly have been more propitious than they were. But, unfortunately, things were not destined to remain at so harmonious a level for long. It has been chronicled that the monks fell into a bad humour, growing lax in their devotions and more insatiable in their demands upon the local yeomanry. It has been chronicled that men returning home late at night from the fields saw sights at the abbey which struck fear in their hearts and heard sounds which made them think of tortured beasts howling in pain."

"Self-flagellation?" I asked.

"Perhaps," Foster replied without enthusiasm, no doubt, I thought, having opinions of his own. "However, the details are too vague for precise conjecture, except to say that to those who perceived these things there was only one explanation satisfactory to their minds. And this was that the monks had been corrupted into the worship of the Horned One, the Devil. Revealing themselves as heartless, cruel and cynical men, who took a genuine pleasure in exacting every last ounce of servitude from those they could gather in the spreading net of their power and influence, the monks became the focal point of hatred for every man, woman and child in the district, culminating after months of harsh treatment in the complete and utter destruction of the abbey building itself and the murder of every monk. The Abbot himself, however, was secured for a crueler fate. In the village green, the very one we can see from this window," he added, pointing significantly through the panes to where several boys were playing with a ball, "he was executed. It would appear, particularly from a set of woodcuts in Adrian Weeke's *Chronicles of Rural Life*, published in London in the late eighteenth century, that with a sadistic butchery, incited no doubt by the degradation he had brought upon them, the Abbot was hung by the neck from the gallows rope till almost dead. He was then cut down in time to save his life, only for the executioner to rip out his bowels and burn them before his eyes. Whereupon, as he at last expired, he was sawn into quarters, his remains being locked in an iron gibbet for the rain, decay or the summer's heat to destroy."

"Harsh justice," I remarked, "even for a man like that."

Foster raised his eyebrows in speculation. "Perhaps," he said, "though one wonders. Indeed, reaffirming whatever arguments might be put forward in favouring the justice of his fate, is the very fortitude with which he is reported to have faced it, saying as the rope was being placed about his neck – and with a sneer in his voice – a phrase of damning implications: "*Exurgent mortui et ad me veniunt!*" Or: "The dead rise and come to me!" Foster paused, watching me with inquisitive eyes above his spectacles. "It is a phrase which I happen to have come across before reading the account of his death, and which made me wonder then if the people of Fenley had not been more than justified in their dire suspicions about the abbey, culled as it is from an old book of magic, often attributed to Pope Honorius, called the *Red Dragon*."

"The phrase, said in a certain way, I suppose, could be made to sound like a threat," I suggested.

"Indeed it could. A thought which must have stirred itself in many a mind in Fenley when, on the day following his execution, it was discovered that the Abbot's remains were no longer confined in the gibbet, but had gone, utterly and without the slightest, least tangible trace. Perhaps falling back on the superstitions of the Church in hope, some said, that the Devil had come during the night to claim his own and carry him off to Hell. Personally, and not unreasonably, I think, I feel that one or more of the monks must have escaped the holocaust that took the other brothers, returning after the Abbot's death to claim his corpse, no doubt to bury it with the rites, such as they were, of their own corrupted faith. But we shall never know for certain, and the more colourful idea of a horned devil plucking out the Abbot's bones through the bars of the gibbet with his clawed fingers, as one woodcut in Weeke's book depicts, will still be the one to attract more attention from collectors of such tales."

"The pentagram would date back to the time of the abbey, I take it," I said.

"I would suppose so. The cellars were no doubt incorporated into the building erected on its site."

"With all of this I must admit to being surprised that anyone would have chosen to build a house on this spot."

"Sir Robert Tolbridge was a man, even then, I think, who would have built his house on the threshold of Hell itself if that was where he wanted it built. He didn't care a damn what others were frightened of. In fact, I really believe that this may have been one of the reasons why he built it here."

"And was he contented with it?"

"Unfortunately he did not live to enjoy the house for long. Shortly after moving in he was murdered in the grounds one night."

"Which must have brought to light the fear of ghostly revenge on every local's tongue."

"In this case, no. Two men were hanged not long afterwards for his death. It was claimed that they killed him for money. But the house has not had a happy history. Violence has seemed to hang around it. It is said to be a place of ill luck."

"What, no tales of wandering revenants?" I asked. "No screaming skulls or bloodstains on the floor?"

Perhaps taking my remarks as derisive, Foster said, stiffly, that it was not the inside of the house that was considered unlucky.

"The only deaths in there have been from natural causes," he said. "But the grounds . . ." He paused emphatically. "The grounds are a different matter altogether. Superstitious foolery, some people might say, but it is said that it is an incautious man who will wander at night through the grounds of Elm Tree House."

"Well, there's at least one local man who thinks nothing of the sort," I remarked.

"A local man, you say?" Foster asked, genuinely interested. "You surprise me. There are few men in Fenley – though fewer still who would admit it – who would willingly venture into that ill chosen ground at night. Do you know who it was, by any chance?"

I'm afraid not. It was late last night and the darkness was too dense for me to make out his face. I took him for a tramp, though Poole, who's seen him before, has the opinion that he must be a local poacher taking a short cut to the woods."

"This surprises me indeed," Foster said, "though it just goes to show how poorly one can really know a place even after nearly ten years. It is generally supposed that the only poacher in recent times to venture there was Young Teb back in the late 90s, whose torn body presented the local constabulary with an embarrassing problem for months afterwards. His murderer was never apprehended, and the example the poor fellow presented is said to have dissuaded others from going there ever since. But this was nearly thirty years ago and I suppose the younger men might think nothing of going there now."

Glancing significantly at his watch, Foster said that he really had to return to the library now. "It has been a pleasure talking to you," he said in parting, "but there is much to be seen to at the library before we close tonight. However, I hope you will call in to see me some time whenever you are here again. And if ever you want to know anything about Fenley you know where to ask."

Although I had learned a great deal during my stay in Fenley, I decided as I drove back along the lane that it was of little use to me in quelling Poole's rapture for the house. It was, in fact, just the kind of thing to allay his unease about the cellars and awaken in its place an interest in its history. I realized then that my initial idea had not been as promising as I had originally thought, and it was therefore with a feeling of frustration that I eventually pulled up before the house.

When I stepped inside the hallway I was surprised to find that Poole had gone out. Having told me before I left for Fenley that he would not be going out this afternoon, his present absence was inexplicable. It was totally unlike Poole to say one thing and do another. With more urgency, therefore, than the superficial reasons for it might explain, I began to search for him. Perhaps he had had an accident, I thought, remembering the patches of decay in several of the uncarpeted floors upstairs. As the minutes passed, room after room revealing itself empty of the least sign of him, my intangible fears began to intensify into alarm.

"Poole! Where are you?" I shouted as I strode through the hallway, looking up into the grey-brown gloom of the stairs. But my cries were re-echoed without reply through the cacophonous depths of the house.

A cold, insidious feeling of solitude began to oppress me. Enmixed with this was a feeling of foreboding, a strange premonition of doom. I knew that if Poole was in the house he would have answered me by now. I scorned myself without conviction as a panicking fool who would laugh at himself with derision when Poole, unaware of my childish alarm, returned home. But I could not suppress the feeling that something was drastically wrong. What it was, I did not know. It was too enigmatic for explanation in words. And yet, subjective though it may be, and, like hindsight, made stronger in my memory now by what happened afterwards, it was as if the very atmosphere of the house, changed or transmuted in some subtle way, confirmed for me then that something had happened while I was away. Something so awful that its presence, like the last reverberations of a scream, had not completely disappeared. Earnestly though I searched through the house, from the ground floor upwards, even to the attics themselves, there was still one place which I had ignored – perhaps, I thought guiltily, on purpose – and it was, even when all else had proved fruitless, with a feeling of reluctance that I eventually approached the cellar door. One glance, however, at the shelf alongside showed how futile my reluctance had been, for one of the two paraffin lamps stored there had gone.

Grasping the remaining lamp, I ignited it with a match and stepped to the cellar door. It came open at the merest touch. Glancing down, I saw that it was unbolted and must have swung shut – or so I surmised – after Poole had stepped inside. But why had he decided to come here? Pausing nervously at the head of the stairs I stared down into the cloying darkness, whose depths were but tenuously touched by the feeble light from my lamp. The amount of resolution that Poole must have needed to go down into that seemingly sentient darkness alone impressed itself upon me. I was afraid, and I could not deny it. After a momentary hesitation, I called out for Poole. There was one sharp, empty echo to my cry. Then, feeling even more lonely than before, I slowly began to descend the steps. I held the lamp high so that its light would spread over as wide an area as possible. Faint grey speckles of spiders, fleeing across the floor into the darkness, were the only signs of life as I crossed it; the deep shadows of the pillars gliding like massive bars, merging and mingling together as I passed between them. There was only one part of the cellar I was interested in, for although the very thought appalled me, I knew that Poole must have gone to the chamber we had investigated the day before.

Before I reached the extension leading to it, however, I saw what I at first took to be a large pile of rags lying on the ground a short distance ahead of me. As I approached it, though, I realized suddenly that it was Poole. A thin trickle of blood formed an aimless line along the flagstone beside his head. Kneeling, I felt at his face; it was as cold as the stone it had struck, cold and limp and white. I did not need to hear the harsh gasps of breath that were rasping through his lips to realize that he had been seriously hurt. It was obvious – perhaps too obvious – to me then what had happened. Firm though his resolve must have been when he started out on his way through the cellar, the darkness must have eventually unnerved him, that and the arcane evil that struck one about the chamber and its festering burrow. Panicking, he ran back along the passageway, tripped over an uneven paving stone and struck his head against the floor when he fell.

"John, John," I whispered, "why did you have to come here? Why did you have to try to prove to yourself – or to me – that there was nothing to fear in this place?" As my words were murmurously echoed I suddenly realized that I was not alone with Poole. Though nothing moved, nor any sound could be heard to disturb the profound silence around us, I knew that I was being watched. My mouth dried as I looked up from my friend and glanced along the tunnel to where the light dimmed into darkness. There, submerged in a shadowy hinterland between the two, half seen like something in a fog, I saw a motionless figure regarding me. I raised the lamp; its light spread faintly upwards, seemingly dispersing what I saw into oblivion.

When I stood up I realized that there had been nothing there, only the inhospitable void of the mouldering passageway. And yet, even now, even as I saw that I had been mistaken, I could not shrug from myself the feeling of being watched. Moment by moment the feeling grew in intensity till I felt that I could bear it no longer. Why Poole had panicked no more bewildered me. There was something about the cellar, and especially here in the extension to the chamber we had been in the night before, that could not be ignored. It had the dull persistence and mounting intensity of an aching tooth.

More hurriedly than I had intended, I pulled Poole to his feet and lowered him onto one of my shoulders, before retracing my steps towards the staircase, mounting it in an instant to make my way into the hallway. As I laid Poole out on a couch in his study he began to groan, as if he was starting to wake up. A few moments later I realized that I was mistaken. In between outbursts of unintelligible mutterings, I caught odd words and phrases that disturbed me as I tried to calm him in his delirium.

". . . scratches . . . I hear you! Scratching at the earth . . . mole, all thin . . . bleached bones . . . No! *Go away*! Bones! . . . wgah'nagl . . . I can see its head . . . No! . . . sh'sh'sh' ftharg . . . gibbering, must stop, got to leave, get away, white skinny hands all claws crawling across flesh peeling left over floor all damp and stinking eyes lit, burning. *No*! Got to leave . . . Help! God help me! Help! . . . I mustn't, can't say those words . . . mustn't, can't make me . . . No, no, no! . . . evil! . . .sh'sh'sh' . . . gibbering, must stop . . . stop . . ."

At last, after several minutes of such torment, he settled into a more easy sleep, his breathing becoming relaxed and even. But, whatever he had been through or deluded himself into believing he had been through in the cellar, must have been awful, I knew, for it to have affected him as severely as this. For a moment I thought about calling in a doctor, but I decided that Poole seemed to have recovered from the wound, such as it was, and I knew, somehow, that it was not the blow to his head that was troubling.

On an impulse I telephoned the library in Fenley and asked for Foster.

"What is the matter?" he asked a few moments later after I had introduced myself. "You sound disturbed."

I explained to him what had happened since my return to the house. "What his mutterings mean, I don't know," I said finally, "though they must be connected in some way with what happened in the cellar."

"Neurotic hallucinations?"

"No, I don't think so. Not Poole. Though he hasn't been himself this week-end, I must admit. Something happened, I think, something in the cellar. Though what, who knows?"

"But you want to find out. Is that why you phoned me?"

I admitted that it was. "You have a knowledge of the house which I lack."

"A historical knowledge? Then you believe that it is something from the building's past that has affected your friend?"

"I do. There's something about this place, something so strong, so *suffocatingly* strong that it's hardly even possible to think objectively in this place."

"So that even a man who is a complete, materialistic sceptic could begin to doubt his views and wonder if . . .?"

The ease with which Foster was assimilating what I was telling him, made me wonder for a moment if all this came as a surprise to him at all. Or did he know more than what he hinted at? Relieved that I had at least found someone with whom I could confide my fears about the place and who, moreover, had a real knowledge of it, I asked him if he would come to the house after the library had closed. "I would appreciate it immensely if you could help me. I'm sure, as well, that you'll find more than enough to interest you."

Foster laughed, admitting that he would have been disappointed if I had not asked him. "I have always wanted to investigate that house," he replied. "I am sure that in many ways it could prove as interesting as any in the country. Psychical research has always been an interest of mine, though one which I have so seldom had a chance of investigating before."

"You believe that is the explanation for all this?" I asked.

"Did you not suspect that already?" Foster responded, his voice indicating that he knew I had. And, despite the scorn I instinctively felt I should express at the idea, I could not deny it. Such things seemed far from fantastic inside Elm Tree House. I admitted that the thought had not been far from my mind.

Evidently amused at my reticence, Foster laughed, saying that in that case all doubt had been cast from his mind and he was certain in his conviction that there was definitely something "abnormal" about the house. Before hanging up, he asked if I could pick him up from his house, since he didn't own a car himself and it was a long walk from where he lived to Elm Tree House. Agreeing to this, I told him I would collect him at seven.

When this had all been settled I returned to Poole to see how he was. The peace that had settled on him after the delirium seemed to have hardly changed. I decided that it would be better to leave him as he was, making do by covering him with a blanket before writing out a note to explain where I had gone in case he woke up before I returned here with Foster. Satisfied that I had done everything I could for the time being, I went out to my car. The sun had only just started to sink lower in the sky, enriching the warm air of the late afternoon with its glow. There were three hours to go before I was due to meet Foster, three hours in which to escape from the depressing atmosphere of the house. I knew that I needed the sight of the invigoratingly healthy countryside with its trees and ferns and hedgerows to lift up my spirits. Driving off down the lane, I headed aimlessly between the rounded hills and valleys that characterize the countryside around Fenley, with its somnolent rivers, forests and glades, the small farmhouses of local stone and the tall church steeples that rise up out of the blue haze of the distance. It is a countryside notable for its subdued beauty and tranquillity. It was, in all, a diversion I had need of and which I savoured to the full. I did not, however, allow myself to forget what had happened, and I thought about it in detail as I drove. It was the sense of freedom, of release from the morbid atmosphere of the house I needed now, not forgetfulness.

At seven I drew up before Foster's house on the outskirts of Fenley, a bay-windowed building set back between rustling rhododendron. Answering the door himself, Foster showed me into his study. As my eyes adjusted to the rich brown twilight inside, I looked about the room; most of it was filled with a pair of armchairs on either side of an elderly gas fire, a rosewood table by one wall, while before the window, a bust of Goethe set on it, stood a round-topped writing desk which I judged, from the carvings about its darkened wood, to have been inherited from an ancestor who saw colonial service in India. My eyes wandered from this monumental relic to the other items in the room as a way of assessing the character of my new associate. In glass-fronted cabinets along the walls were china ornaments, statuettes, busts and various pieces of bric-a-brac. As we shook hands I turned to the neatly lined shelves of books on one wall, glancing with a nod of my head. "I see you're well read on the supernatural," I remarked, noting such volumes as

The Survival of Man by Sir Oliver Lodge, Madame Blavatsky's *The Secret Doctrine* and *Crompton's Guide to Demonology*, edited by Nicholai Caffré amongst many other books of this ilk. For a moment I had a feeling of misgiving. Though on the one hand they spoke of an erudite knowledge of the occult, on the other they spoke of a crank. The seriousness on his ascetically intelligent face helped to ease my suspicions, though.

"I didn't expect to see you again quite so soon," Foster said, smiling at my interest in his books. "Nor with anything quite so intriguing." He ushered me to one of the chairs.

"You mentioned something about glimpsing a figure in the cellar," he opened, lighting a pipe. "Can you tell me what you thought it looked like?"

"Hardly," I confessed. "If there really was anything there and I didn't just imagine it, there was hardly more than an instant in which I saw it. Barely enough time to register having seen something at all, except that it was about medium height and pale. And thin. Very thin."

Foster nodded. Looking up, he said: "Though I doubt if you have ever heard of it, there is a local legend about a 'twig-shinned' phantom which is supposed to haunt the woods about Elm Tree House. This and the thing you glimpsed could be one and the same. As the schoolboyish name implies, it is reputedly thin and pale, a wasted creature that creeps with distended fingers through the trees. I believe that Elliott O'Donnell has written about it in one of his books, though I cannot just remember which one."

"And is it known what caused this thing to be there?" I asked.

"I have always thought it must relate back to the abbey and to the Abbot whose remains disappeared so mysteriously all those years ago. '*Exurgent mortui et ad me veniunt!*' – 'The dead rise and come to me,' he said. It's possible that he believed that he would return. Perhaps he did. Somehow, through some unholy alchemy of their blasphemous malpractices, perhaps he and his acolytes were able to bring the semblance of life to his body. This is all very fanciful, I know, but there are references to stitches about the creature's body."

Feeling that we were wasting time over matters which would, in all probability have nothing whatever to do with what we were up against, I glanced out of the window at the dimming brightness of the sky. "Whatever it is that lies at the bottom of all this," I interrupted, "cannot be worse than what your suggestions conjure up. However useful they might be in preparing our minds for whatever we discover, I think we would be better spending our time now at the house with Poole. I don't like to leave him there alone, not after dusk. In his state there's no saying what he'll do if he wakes up alone."

Foster agreed. Collecting his hat from the hallway on the way out, he said: "I had forgotten about your friend in the excitement of the chase, so to speak."

The last strong rays of the sun were gilding the upper branches of the trees as we set off. These rays had passed by the time we arrived back at Poole's house, a dull grey gloom having settled about its dispiriting grounds. The house itself stood dark and lifeless against the purple haze of the sky.

"I've rarely seen a grimmer place," was Foster's only comment as we stepped out of the car and approached the house, shivering at the chill. A wind had risen with the dusk, swaying the trees as it circled the house.

Although Foster's company did something to alleviate the unease that came upon me as I opened the front door and entered the silent twilight inside, it did not disperse it altogether. Perhaps to attempt at hiding this from myself I called out for Poole, though I knew somehow that he would not have as yet recovered. I felt Foster's hand on my arm; perhaps he sensed the atmosphere as plainly as I did and understood the fear filling me now. In a subdued voice Foster said: "Grotesque rites were practised in the abbey they built here all those centuries ago. The effects of this slaughter did not die with those whose bodies were tortured on this spot. They echo through the air even now, marring the peace that should fill this place."

Switching on the light, I entered Poole's study. Thankfully he was still asleep. "I think it would be better to leave him as he is for the time being," I said. "If anything happens in the next few hours it would be better if he was oblivious of it."

Foster agreed. "He has been tried to the brink already. It is our turn next, not his. I only hope," he added, with a baleful smile that revealed just how nervous he was, "that we fare better."

"As long as we remain inside the house we'll be safe," I said. "The doors and window frames will ensure that."

"I certainly hope so," Foster replied as he shrugged his shoulders dismissively, seating himself in one of the armchairs near the hearth. The embers within it were slowly crumbling into themselves and growing dark. On an impulse I crossed the room and began piling some coal onto them. "We'll need a good fire if we're to stay up all night," I explained. "I take it you intend watching for whatever it is that prowls about the grounds."

"The poacher? Yes. Though I cannot but feel that the root cause of the whole matter lies inside the cellar. However, I don't suppose either of us would relish the prospect of going there tonight. At least the 'poacher' should cast some light on the mystery of what haunts the woods."

Eventually, as the minutes passed, we relapsed into silence, Foster patiently reading through a book he had brought in his pocket, while I spent my time alternately checking on Poole and watching the grounds through the window as dusk passed into night. The only sounds were those of a clock slowly ticking on the hearth, the soft moaning of the wind and the rustling of paper as Foster turned the pages of his book. After a while the moon rose in the sky, a grey radiance silvering the leaves of the elms. Yet nothing appeared as the long hours passed. I yawned and began to doze, the tedium tiring me even more than the events of the day.

It was in such a state, as I drifted between wakefulness and sleep and yearned for nothing more than to be able to slip between the comfortable sheets of my bed, when Foster suddenly spoke. Not catching what it was that he said, I turned from the window and looked towards him. He was staring at Poole, one hand raised into the air for silence.

There was, I realized, the sound of someone murmuring. Vague, at first, it was not for a moment that I realized it was Poole. There was an almost imperceptible twitching of his lips, as his head rolled softly from side to side. Suddenly he called out. His high-pitched, scream-like cry split the air as he leapt to his feet, shuddering. In an instant Foster was beside him. Once, twice the flat of his hand cracked hard against Poole's face, then he grabbed him by the arms and pressed him back to his seat.

"What was all that about?" I asked, bewildered.

Foster smiled thinly. There was an incipient trembling in his body which told of the tension coiled inside him. "I wish that I knew," he replied unsteadily. "All that I noticed at first were the words coming from his lips."

"What words were they?"

"Old ones – words which few civilized people speak anymore." A fit of trembling, more fierce than any which had passed through him before, shook his body. "Someone must have walked on my grave," he joked weakly. There was a deep gust of wind, and smoke billowed out of the fire. The ashes inside it were almost dead. In an effort to allay the unease that was stealing over me, I made a fuss of restoring life to the fire. A chill, which seemed to me then to be only partially relieved by the brightening glow from the fire as I poked its grudgingly igniting coals, filled the room. I made no more enquiry of Foster concerning what Poole had said. Somehow I did not want to know.

A further gust of wind suddenly rattled the window panes. Not realizing the cause for their vibration at first, I leapt to my feet in alarm, before an ensuing annoyance at my nervousness overcame it and I made to turn back to the fire. As I did so, however, I heard Poole speak in a low, uncharacteristically sibilant voice. I glanced at Foster, and was surprised to see an expression of terror writhe across his face. Before I could do anything to stop him he grasped a statuette from a cabinet by the wall and shattered it against Poole's head.

"Why the Hell – " I cried out, catching a hold of Poole as he slumped to the floor, blood flowing from an ugly gash across his forehead. "Are you mad? He's been injured once today already . . . and now, for no reason at all, you . . ."

But I could see that Foster was taking no notice of what I was saying. In silence, he stepped to the window, where he stared into the grounds outside. "Switch off the light!" he whispered authoratively a moment later. So insistent was his voice that, despite the anger I felt towards him for his attack upon Poole, there was nothing I could do but obey his command, placing my friend on the couch once more before crossing to the switch. As the light went off, the room was plunged into a pale twilight lit only by the greyish rays of the moon. Foster crouched at the window, as if to hide himself from view. Nervously I crept towards him.

"What have you seen?" I asked, but he hushed me to silence. Following his gaze I looked out into the grounds. For a moment or two, until my eyes became adjusted to the gloom, everything seemed as it should have been. The trees were swaying back and forth in the wind, portentous of a coming gale, their actions mimicked nearer the ground by the bushes and shrubs and unkempt tussocks of grass. The woods surrounding the house seemed deep and black and almost impenetrable in the darkness. But then, as the less prominent features became perceptible to me, I realized that something was crawling through the grass. "The poacher?" I whispered for wont of anything more likely to suggest.

"Poacher?" Foster laughed quietly. "And why should a poacher be prowling so secretively on his belly through the grounds? What wildfowl or game are there here for him to take?" Wiping the mist his breath had left on the window away, he pointed further to our left, adding: "Besides . . ."

Looking, I saw another shape in the grass. There was a pale blur of what I took to be flesh. Was it someone's face, looking this way? Shunning the speculations which its abnormal pallor should have given rise to, I noticed that there was another blur, this time partially concealed behind some bushes. Was I mistaken? Were my eyes deceiving me?

"They must be some children," I said uncertainly a few moments later as I made out still more figures.

"At this time of night?" Foster asked.

"Then what?" I grasped Foster's arm. "In God's name what?"

Foster pulled himself free. He pointed at Poole with a look of contempt. "Ask him."

At this I remembered the way in which Foster had attacked my friend only a few minutes before, and with it the anger I had begun to feel before my attention was diverted to whatever lay hidden outside re-emerged. No doubt discerning the altercations going on inside me as I tried to reconcile Foster's actions with reason, he said: "Can you doubt but that dabblings on *his* part must be the cause for whatever we can see outside now?"

"A few prowlers," I said dismissively.

"Prowlers! You talk as if the word brought order and normality to this house at the mere mention. Can you still not conceive what those things really are?"

There was a noise at the window as of someone scratching at the glass, and I caught sight of a thin, white hand passing down out of sight. Involuntarily I screamed. I had no choice, for it was a hand from which most of the withered flesh still adhering to it seemed to have been eaten by decay. Overcome by nausea and horror at the hideous sight, I turned away from the window. Badly shaken though he must have been as well, despite his knowledge of what we were up against, Foster had the strength of mind even now to fight against his instincts and speak rationally. "It cannot get inside the house. None of them can. The misshapen door and window frames will ensure that."

"Them?" I muttered, aghast at the thought. "What are they? What foul, unearthly abominations are those things out there?"

When he spoke it was with a voice as dry and clinical and matter-of-fact as any man could muster in the situation, dispelling at last what doubts I might have had about him. "The monks who were slaughtered at this spot all those centuries ago," he replied, "servants, even in death, of the man who founded the abysmal abbey they worshipped in, and who was hung, drawn and quartered in the village. It is them or their remnants that prowl about the house."

There was a sound outside as of twigs being snapped, and a stone came crashing through the window, scattering splinters of glass across the room. A gust of wind fluttered the curtains as it wheezed and howled about us.

"Get back!" Foster cried. "Get back as far from the window as you can." Even as he spoke a further stone hurtled through the shards of glass still surrounding the hole, and bounced off the writing desk to strike the wall at the far side of the room with a resounding crash.

"We must get Poole out of here," I insisted. "One of those stones hitting him could be fatal."

Foster nodded his agreement. "We'll carry him to an upstairs room. He'll be safer there."

Hoisting him onto our shoulders, we hurriedly vacated the study. Two more stones, crashing through what remained of the window almost simultaneously, told us just how timely our exit was. As we climbed the stairs the bangs and crashes continued without respite till it seemed, as they increased in number and ferocity, as if a monstrous hailstorm of rocks was bombarding the house.

"They are only trying to scare us into making an untimely attempt to escape," Foster said, as we peered down at the grounds after leaving Poole stretched out in the safety of the passageway. The figures, concealed by the deep shadows under the trees, were in a sense unreal. Their features were unnaturally blurred, and my eyes seemed unable to focus properly upon them. What glimpses I got of them as I strained my eyes against the gloom were of badly misshapen and gaunt bodies wrapped in dull rags, which may at one time have been the habits of monks.

There was a thud against the wall. "They're trying to reach us up here now," Foster said as we stepped out of the room. There was a piercing crash of breaking glass as the windows were shattered behind us.

"Why go to these extremes?" I asked, grasping the stair rail as we started downstairs.

"Perhaps because they are afraid of us."

"Of us?" I could hardly hide my incredulity.

Shaking his head, Foster replied: "Don't be deceived into believing them indestructible just because they appear to have conquered death. It is all a sham, a facade. They have not stopped the gnawing of the worm nor brought breath into their parchment lungs. They cannot even step through the windows they have so easily broken to reach us. Maybe, therefore," he went on, growing more confident with each word, "it is possible that we may be able to sever what thin, frail thread still binds them to the semblance of life."

"And do you have any idea how we can do this?" I asked.

"Perhaps," Foster said. "But we would have to go down to their source." At the quizzical look I cast him, he said: "To the cellar."

I shook my head. "Never! What I've already experienced down there is enough for me. Nothing, nothing on this earth could persuade me to go there again."

"If that is the case," Foster said, "so be it. I can't force you to accompany me."

"You're still seriously thinking of going down there?" I asked.

"I am. I might look like an old fool – a crank – and, God knows, in some ways I may be, at that – but I know where my duty lies. What your friend in his foolhardy residence here has unleashed, I shall do my utmost to put right."

"There was something in this place long before Poole ever ventured here," I insisted. "You admitted so yourself."

"And so there was," Foster replied, unshaken. "There was something here, alone and speechless, unable to summon up anything else. It wasn't till the thing gained access to the cellar and gained control of Poole's voice that it could speak the words needed to bring its hellish brethren back to the similitude of life." Irritably he shook his head. "We are wasting time. If you will not enter the cellar with me, will you at least do me the favour of accompanying me to the cellar door? I may need your help."

"Of course I'll go there with you," I said, "if you still insist on entering the place."

Upon reaching the cellar door, Foster paused, looking along the shelves beside it. At one end there was an untidy heap of tools: hammers, nails, a rusty pair of pliers, a saw and what looked like part of a very old brace and bit. Reaching for one of the heaviest hammers, Foster said: "This should do in case I meet with any trouble." He chuckled drily as he took down the paraffin lamp and lit it. Shaking it lightly he listened to the reassuringly loud lapping of its nearly full tank.

Tucking the hammer in his belt, he reached for the door bolt, drawing it quietly from its socket. As he pulled the door open there was a sudden smell of fetid air, a vile corruption that struck nausea in us both with one, half-gasped breath. Crying out in pure and absolute terror, Foster fell back from the doorway. There was a movement in the gloom, and I was sensible of an odd shuffling sound. With one spasmodic but determined movement, Foster raised the lamp high into the air. Its light spread into the gloom, revealing the stooped and ragged figure glaring at us with its withered and leprous abomination of a face. Its back bent double beneath the remnants of a monk's habit, it shook as if straining to keep itself erect on the topmost step.

There is no way in which I can describe the loathing horror that the creature inspired within me, with its suppurating, claw-like hands, the eye-like slits of the wrinkles in its decaying flesh, or the grotesque stains of dissolution that, in nauseatingly contrasting hues, were spread about its ravaged body. Even as I looked upon the irregular and stained stitches about its body and face, where the severed quarters of what I knew to be the Abbot's remains had been rejoined, I could not force the scream that I felt stifled within me from my lips.

In a cracked whisper I urged Foster to draw back from the doorway in case the crouched abomination should reach out for him with its talons. Perhaps numbed beyond feelings of horror, Foster merely shook his head, saying: "It can no more move its hands through the doorway than mine could penetrate stone." He laughed humourlessly, adding: "Which gives me an advantage I cannot but use to the full." With that he suddenly tugged the hammer from his belt and raised it in the air. The swaying lamp made the sharp shadows about the creature's face exaggerate its hideous decay, as if unseen maggots were writhing in torment beneath its flesh. Then, using the whole of his weight, Foster brought the hammer down onto the creature's head. The thing had barely time in which to look up as the hammer crashed into its skull. There was a dull splintering of bones, old and brittle ones, a black putrescence oozing from the obscene wound. The Abbot stiffened, its hands feebly moving as if to touch Foster, who in the instant backed away, drawing his arm out of reach. The hammer fell, forgotten, to the floor as the lich swayed in the doorway. From the wound in its skull, along with the foul fluids, other substances were being ejected in the pulsating flow: wriggling heaps of pallid worms that gathered on the stained floor. "For it is of old rumour," Foster recited to himself in awful fascination, "that the soul of the devil-bought hastes not from his charnal clay, but fats and instructs the very worm that gnaws, till out of corruption horrid life springs, and the dull scavengers of earth wax crafty to vex it and swell monstrous to plague it . . . and things have learnt to walk that ought to crawl!"

Unable to look upon the thing a moment more as it stubbornly fell to its knees in a doomed attempt to fight against the weakness plainly sweeping through its body, I stared at the floor. Horrible though it had been in "life", in its "dying" the creature had achieved new dimensions of revulsion and awfulness. Nor could I bear to see the burning penetration of its sunken eyes as it stared at us and through us into the house. There was something in that look which made panic stir itself within me.

Suddenly there was the sound of someone bounding down the stairs behind us. Surprised as I was at the unexpected sound, I was momentarily unable to react. When I did at last manage to turn round, it was to glimpse Poole as he dashed on past me. I called out to him in warning, but he shouldered me aside as he launched himself in a furious attack against Foster. The small librarian was on the point of turning round when Poole's fist struck him on the jaw. Without even so much as a groan Foster fell back against the cellar door, trying to steady himself against it. But Poole gave him no chance to regain his balance before he hit him again, pounding him in the stomach. As Foster doubled up, Poole grabbed him by one arm and propelled him towards the open doorway. Before I could do anything to stop him, Foster stumbled into the darkness at the top of the cellar steps. As if given new strength at the opportunity to wreak its vengeance upon him, the lich grasped Foster in its arms. Almost without knowing what he was doing, Foster swung the paraffin lamp, still gripped in his fingers, furiously against the creature's body. The putrescence from its skull splattered it, blotting out its light for an instant, before the lamp crashed to the ground at their feet. There was a gust as flames rippled upwards, catching on the creature's flowing robes and spreading through the pools of paraffin that were scattered at its feet. As if fed on something far more volatile than the pint or two of paraffin inside the lamp, the flames roared upwards, consuming both figures in a roaring ferocity of fire.

I cried out in despair as the sudden heat blasted out at me and I had to cover my eyes against it with my hands. I took a step forwards, but the heat was too strong and I had to step back. I looked round at Poole, and I felt a cold, unreasoning anger towards him. An anger which almost made me pound Poole into submission and force him into the growing inferno on the cellar steps. But it was an anger which died as I saw the horror and disbelief on Poole's face. The hatred that had seared his features only moments before had gone. "I . . . I couldn't stop myself," Poole muttered in his bewilderment. "I couldn't." He looked at me for support, beseechingly. "I couldn't."

I said that I understood, though there was so much that I knew I would never understand about what had happened.

I looked back at the blaze, in which the frenzied writhings of the two clasped figures had ceased. It was as if the destructive forces of those untold centuries had been unleashed upon the Abbot at last, taking their vengeful toll not only on the cleric himself but on Foster as well, till there remained, as the last few flames died down, only charred and unrecognizable fragments of bone and ashes on the floor.

As Poole collapsed, sobbing, I stepped into the study to see if there were any of the monks still lurking in the grounds. My relief could not have been more intense when I saw the faint flush of dawn penetrating the sky above the trees, now plainly etched against it. Of the creatures, not even one could be seen when I stepped to the shattered remains of the window and looked out.

I met Poole's eyes as he stepped towards me. Had my nerves been less taut, I might have felt some pity for his miserable plight, but the rigours of the night had been too much. I could tell that Poole remembered what he had done, though not why he had done it. That he had been possessed he undoubtedly realized, but not that it had been by something other than his own deranged subconscious. "How could I?" he repeated to himself. I wondered if he had seen the thing in the cellar. Or had his eyes been blinded to everything except Foster? "How could I?"

Irritation and fear building up inside me, I told him to stop being a fool. "Can't you see what it was that controlled you?" I asked.

He looked at me in alarm, that served only to intensify my annoyance, so that I grasped him by one arm and dragged him to the cellar door, where I showed him the charred fragments of bone which were all that remained as the fire died down of the Abbot. "*He* made you do it," I said callously. "Look at *him*!"

Poole shuddered as memories seemed to awaken inside him at the sight of the thing. He stepped away from it and knelt on the floor, clasping his hands to his face. "What can we do?" he asked.

What could we do? As I looked out at the stubborn darkness of the woods or into the dull twilight of the house, I felt trapped, claustrophobically and eternally trapped, as if caught within a nightmare from which there could be no escape into wakefulness and sanity. Sanity! Even the word itself seemed to verge on the ludicrous now. Sanity! What was it when even reality itself gave way to madness, when the curtains of our existence are rent apart and the grinning mask of chaos is thrust towards our eyes? What words could I utter in comfort when I felt my own mind sliding towards an oblivion of madness?

"We must get out of here," I said at last, my voice grating. "We must never return. Only death and madness lie in this place for us if we remain."

Looking up from his despair, Poole asked: "What of Foster? What can we do about him?"

"Nothing now," I replied. "He is dead and, I hope, at peace. There's nothing we can do for him now."

"But his death?" Poole asked, his voice almost shrill. "*I* caused his death."

"Not willingly," I reminded him as I looked about the hallway. "When it's light we must bury him and what's left of the Abbot beneath the flagstones in the cellar. I doubt if anyone will ever find them there. We'll do that as soon as we can, then leave . . . and hope that in the months to come we can forget what happened here last night."

Poole agreed immediately to my plan. He had no choice. He knew as well as I did that, if we were to attempt to explain any of this to the police, we would be damned straight away as liars. There was no satisfactory way in which we could explain Foster's death, even if we had possessed enough strength of will to face an enquiry, which we didn't.

On leaving the house several hours later I drove us away from Fenley to Pire, and from there we went on to Tavestock, where I live. For the next few months Poole took up residence in an hotel in town. I saw him now and again. I did not shun him particularly; it was instead as if we mutually found that each other's company brought back memories we would both of us prefer to forget. Though it seemed, to my relief, that what had happened in Fenley remained our secret, and that what fuss there was about Foster's inexplicable disappearance died down to be more or less forgotten, Poole seemed unable to recover properly from our ordeal. I doubted then that he ever really forgot, even for a moment, what had happened, and I could tell from his red-rimmed eyes and haggard face that his nights were tormented and sleepless.

He complained sometimes about feeling as if he was being watched, insisting that at night he caught glimpses of someone peering into his room from the darkened streets. I told him that it was his overwrought imagination, that it was his fear of someone finding the two charred bodies we had buried in his house and of the police watching him. "And there's no chance of any of this happening so long as you still own that house and no one is allowed inside it," I insisted. "Don't worry," I would end. "We're safe. Forget that it ever happened. It's in the past."

Over the months that followed I only hoped that the mental breakdown that kept threatening to occur would not happen and that Poole would somehow find the strength of will to fight back against his insubstantial fears. In the end he left Tavestock. Probably I reminded him too much of what happened. I was not sad to see him go. In a way it came as a welcomed relief. We still occasionally exchanged letters. These, at least, I could cast to one side if their contents disturbed me, for he continually complained even now about someone monitoring his house. I knew that he was slowly losing control. The whole thing had become an obsession with him, so intense that he would not even set foot out of doors after dark. "They are watching me," he once wrote from the new house he had bought in Pire, "waiting for the first chance they get if I slip up."

It was not till last night, when I read about his death in the *Barchester Observer & Times*, that I realized for the first time in what awful terror he must have been living for the past ten months, for his dismembered, mutilated body had been found in an alley not far from his house. No one was specifically suspected. The only clues as to who might have carried out his foul murder were the traces of mould on his scattered remains and the splintered fragments of human nails found embedded in his flesh. But the latter, as I was to learn on enquiry today, were of a puzzling nature – at least to the police investigating his death. – For they were far too old to have been broken from the fingers of living men and were supposed, by the police inspector I spoke to about it, to have been stolen by someone with a perverted sense of humour from a rifled grave and purposely implanted in Poole's dead body.

Only I know the truth of what must have happened, for I have already seen them watching my house from the darkened streets at night. That is why I no longer set foot beyond my door after dusk and have fixed a crucifix at every possible entrance to my home.

They are only waiting for me to make that one small slip such as Poole must have eventually made in order to wreak their vengeance upon me as well. You will know, by the very fact that this narrative is in your hands, that this slip must have already been made. *God have mercy on my soul when this occurs!*

Graham Masterton

The Taking of Mr Bill

Trust Graham Masterton to come up with something new and offbeat for a Mammoth *collection. Without giving too much away, "The Taking of Mr Bill" is an audacious blend of ancient myth and a certain childhood fantasy that still somehow manages to meet the criteria of this anthology.*

Some of Masterton's recent short story appearances are in Dark Voices 3 *and* 4, The Mammoth Book of Vampires, Hottest Blood *and his collection* Fortnight of Fear, *while his more than twenty horror novels include* The Hymn, Black Angel, Death Trance, Prey *and* Night of the Manitou — *the latter the second sequel to his first full-length work,* The Manitou.

IT WAS ONLY a few minutes past four in the afternoon, but the day suddenly grew dark, thunderously dark, and freezing-cold rain began to lash down. For a few minutes, the pathways of Kensington Gardens were criss-crossed with bobbing umbrellas and au-pairs running helter-skelter with baby-buggies and screaming children.

Then, the gardens were abruptly deserted, left to the rain and the Canada geese and the gusts of wind that ruffled back the leaves. Marjorie found herself alone, hurriedly pushing William in his small navy-blue Mothercare pram. She was wearing only her red tweed jacket and her long black pleated skirt, and she was already soaked. The afternoon had been brilliantly sunny when she left the house, with a sky as blue as dinner-plates. She hadn't brought an umbrella. She hadn't even brought a plastic rain-hat.

She hadn't expected to stay with her Uncle Michael until so late, but Uncle Michael was so old now that he could barely keep himself clean. She had made him tea and tidied his bed, and done some hoovering while William lay kicking and gurgling on the sofa, and Uncle Michael watched him, rheumy-eyed, his hands resting on his lap like crumpled yellow tissue-paper, his mind fading and brightening, fading and brightening, in the same way that the afternoon sunlight faded and brightened.

She had kissed Uncle Michael before she left, and he had clasped her hand between both of his. "Take good care of that boy, won't you?" he had whispered. "You never know who's watching. You never know who might want him."

"Oh, Uncle, you know that I never let him out of my sight. Besides, if anybody wants him, they're welcome to him. Perhaps I'll get some sleep at night."

"Don't say that, Marjorie. Never say that. Think of all the mothers who have said that, only as a joke, and then have wished that they had cut out their tongues."

"Uncle . . . don't be so morbid. I'll give you a ring when I get home, just to make sure you're all right. But I must go. I'm cooking chicken chasseur tonight."

Uncle Michael had nodded. "Chicken chasseur . . .," he had said, vaguely. Then, "Don't forget the pan."

"Of course not, Uncle. I'm not going to burn it. Now, make sure you put the chain on the door."

Now she was walking past the Round Pond. She slowed down, wheeling the pram through the muddy grass. She was so wet that it scarcely made any difference. She thought of the old Chinese saying, "Why walk fast in the rain? It's raining just as hard up ahead."

Before the arrival of the Canada geese, the Round Pond had been neat and tidy and peaceful, with fluttering ducks and children sailing little yachts. Now, it was fouled and murky, and peculiarly threatening, like anything precious that has been taken away from you and vandalized by strangers. Marjorie's Peugeot had been stolen last spring, and crashed, and urinated in, and she had never been able to think of driving it again, or even another car like it.

She emerged from the trees and a sudden explosion of cold rain caught her on the side of the cheek. William was awake, and waving his arms, but she knew that he would be hungry by now, and that she would have to feed him as soon as she got home.

She took a short cut, walking diagonally through another stand of trees. She could hear the muffled roar of London's traffic on both sides of the garden, and the rumbling, scratching noise of an airliner passing overhead, but the gardens themselves remained oddly empty, and silent, as if a spell had been cast over them. Underneath the trees, the light was the colour of moss-weathered slate.

She leaned forward over the pram handle and cooed, "Soon be home, Mr Bill! Soon be home!"

But when she looked up she saw a man standing silhouetted beside the oak tree just in front of her, not more than thirty feet away. A thin, tall man wearing a black cap, and a black coat with the collar turned up. His eyes were shaded, but she could see that his face was deathly white. And he was obviously waiting for her.

She hesitated, stopped, and looked around. Her heart began to thump furiously. There was nobody else in sight, nobody to whom she could shout for help. The rain rattled on the trees above her head, and William let out one fitful yelp. She swallowed, and found herself swallowing a thick mixture of fruit-cake and bile. She simply didn't know what to do.

She thought: there's no use running. I'll just have to walk past him. I'll just have to show him that I'm not afraid. After all, I'm pushing a pram. I've got a baby. Surely he won't be so cruel that he'll —

You never know who's watching. You never know who might want him.

Sick with fear, she continued to walk forward. The man remained where he was, not moving, not speaking. She would have to pass within two feet of him, but so far he had shown no sign that he had noticed her, although he must have done; and no sign at all that he wanted her to stop.

She walked closer and closer, stiff-legged, and mewling softly to herself in terror. She passed him by, so close that she could see the glittering raindrops on his coat, so close that she could *smell* him, strong tobacco and some dry, unfamiliar smell, like hay.

She thought: thank God. He's let me pass.

But then his right arm whipped out and snatched her elbow, twisted her around, and flung her with such force against the trunk of the oak that she heard her shoulder-blade crack and one of her shoes flew off.

She screamed, and screamed again. But he slapped her face with the back of his hand, and then slapped her again.

"What do you want?" she shrieked. "What do you want?"

He seized the lapels of her jacket and dragged her upright against the harsh-ribbed bark of the tree. His eyes were so deep-set that all she could see was their glitter. His lips were blue-grey, and they were stretched back across his teeth in a terrifying parody of a grin.

"What do you want?" she begged him. Her shoulder felt as if it were on fire, and her left knee was throbbing. "I have to look after my baby. Please don't hurt me. I have to look after my baby."

She felt her skirt being torn away from her thighs. Oh God, she thought, not that. Please not that. She started to collapse out of fear and out of terrible resignation, but the man dragged her upright again, and knocked her head so hard against the tree that she almost blacked out.

She didn't remember very much after that. She felt her underwear wrenched off. She felt him forcing his way into her. It was dry and agonizing and he felt so *cold*. Even when he had pushed his way deep inside her, he still felt cold. She felt the rain on her face. She heard his breathing, a steady, harsh *hah*! *hah*! *hah*! Then she heard him swear, an extraordinary curse like no curse that she had ever heard before.

She was just about to say "My baby," when he hit her again. She was found twenty minutes later standing at a bus-stop in the Bayswater Road, by an American couple who wanted to know where to find Trader Vic's.

The pram was found where she had been forced to leave it, and it was empty.

John said, "We should go away for a while."

Marjorie was sitting in the window-seat, nursing a cup of lemon tea. She was staring across the Bayswater Road as she always stared, day and night. She had cut her hair into a severe bob, and her face was as pale as wax. She wore black, as she always wore black.

The clock on the mantelpiece chimed three. John said, "Nesta will keep in touch – you know, if there's any development."

Marjorie turned and smiled at him weakly. The dullness of her eyes still shocked him, even now. "Development?" she said, gently mocking his euphemism. It was six weeks since William had disappeared. Whoever had taken him had either killed him or intended to keep him for ever.

John shrugged. He was a thick-set, pleasant-looking, but unassertive man. He had never thought that he would marry; but when he had met Marjorie at his younger brother's 21st, he had been captivated at once by her mixture of shyness and wilfulness, and her eccentric imagination. She had said things to him that no girl had ever said to him before – opened his eyes to the simple magic of everyday life.

But now that Marjorie had closed in on herself, and communicated nothing but grief, he found that he was increasingly handicapped; as if the gifts of light and colour and perception were being taken away from him. A spring day was incomprehensible unless he had Marjorie beside him, to tell him why it was all so inspiring.

She was like a woman who was dying; and he was like a man who was gradually going blind.

The phone rang in the library. Marjorie turned back to the window. Through the pale afternoon fog the buses and the taxis poured ceaselessly to and fro. But beyond the railings, in Kensington Gardens, the trees were motionless and dark, and they held a secret for which Marjorie would have given anything. Her sight, her soul, her very life.

Somewhere in Kensington Gardens, William was still alive. She was convinced of it, in the way that only a mother could be convinced. She spent hours straining her ears, trying to hear him crying over the bellowing of the traffic. She felt like standing in the middle of Bayswater Road and holding up her hands and screaming "Stop! Stop, for just one minute! Please, stop! I think I can hear my baby crying!"

John came back from the library, digging his fingers into his thick chestnut hair. "That was Chief Inspector Crosland. They've had the forensic report on the weapon that was used to cut your clothes. Some kind of gardening-implement, apparently – a pair of clippers or a pruning-hook. They're going to start asking questions at nurseries and garden centres. You never know.

He paused, and then he said, "There's something else. They had a DNA report."

Marjorie gave a quiet, cold shudder. She didn't want to start thinking about the rape. Not yet, anyway. She could deal with that later, when William was found.

When William was found, she could go away on holiday and try to recuperate. When William was found, her heart could start beating again. She longed so much to hold him in her arms that she felt she was becoming completely demented. Just to feel his tiny fingers closing around hers.

John cleared his throat. "Crosland said that there was something pretty strange about the DNA report. That's why it's taken them so long."

Marjorie didn't answer. She thought she had seen a movement in the gardens. She thought she had seen something small and white in

the long grass underneath the trees, and a small arm waving. But –
as she drew the net curtain back further – the small, white object
trotted out from beneath the trees and it was a Sealyham, and the
small waving arm was its tail.

"According to the DNA report, the man wasn't actually alive."

Marjorie slowly turned around. "What?" she said. "What do you
mean, he wasn't actually alive?"

John looked embarrassed. "I don't know. It doesn't seem to make
any sense, does it? But that's what Crosland said. In fact, what he
actually said was, the man was dead."

"*Dead*? How could he have been dead?"

"Well, there was obviously some kind of aberration in the test
results. I mean, the man couldn't have been *really* dead. Not
clinically. It was just that – "

"Dead," Marjorie repeated, in a whisper, as if everything had
suddenly become clear. "The man was *dead*."

John was awakened by the telephone at five to six that Friday
morning. He could hear the rain sprinkling against the bedroom
window, and the grinding bellow of a garbage truck in the mews
at the back of the house.

"It's Chief Inspector Crosland, sir. I'm afraid I have some rather
bad news. We've found William in the Fountains."

John swallowed. "I see," he said. Irrationally, he wanted to ask
if William were still alive, but of course he couldn't have been, and
in any case he found that he simply couldn't speak.

"I'm sending two officers over," said the chief inspector. "One
of them's a woman. If you could be ready in – say – five or ten
minutes?"

John quietly cradled the phone. He sat up in bed for a while, hug-
ging his knees, his eyes brimming. Then he swallowed, and smeared
his tears with his hands, and gently shook Marjorie awake.

She opened her eyes and stared up at him as if she had just
arrived from another country. "What is it?" she asked, throati-
ly.

He tried to speak, but he couldn't.

"It's William, isn't it?" she said. "They've found William."

They stood huddled together under John's umbrella, next to the grey,
rain-circled fountains. An ambulance was parked close by, its rear
doors open, its blue light flashing. Chief Inspector Crosland came
across – a solid, beef-complexioned man with a dripping mustache.
He raised his hat, and said, "We're all very sorry about this. We

always hold out hope, you know, even when it's pretty obvious that it's hopeless."

"Where was he found?" asked John.

"Caught in the sluice that leads to the Long Water. There were a lot of leaves down there, too, so he was difficult to see. One of the maintenance men found him when he was clearing the grating."

"Can I see him?" asked Marjorie.

John looked at the chief inspector with an unspoken question: how badly is he decomposed? But the chief inspector nodded, and took hold of Marjorie's elbow, and said, "Come with me."

Marjorie followed him obediently. She felt so small and cold. He guided her to the back of the ambulance, and helped her to climb inside. There, wrapped in a bright red blanket, was her baby, her baby William, his eyes closed, his hair stuck in a curl to his forehead. He was white as marble, white as a statue.

"May I kiss him?" she asked. Chief Inspector Crosland nodded.

She kissed her baby and his kiss was soft and utterly chilled.

Outside the ambulance, John said, "I would have thought – well, how long has he been down there?"

"No more than a day, sir, in my opinion. He was still wearing the same Babygro that he was wearing when he was taken, but he was clean and he looked reasonably well nourished. There were no signs of abuse or injury."

John looked away. "I can't understand it," he said.

The chief inspector laid a hand on his shoulder. "If it's any comfort to you, sir, neither can I."

All the next day, through showers and sunshine, Marjorie walked alone around Kensington Gardens. She walked down Lancaster Walk, and then Budge's Walk, and stood by the Round Pond. Then she walked back beside the Long Water, to the statue of Peter Pan.

It had started drizzling again, and rainwater dripped from the end of Peter's pipes, and trickled down his cheeks like tears.

The boy who never grew up, she thought. Just like William.

She was about to turn away when the tiniest fragment of memory scintillated in her mind. What was it that Uncle Michael had said, as she left his flat on the day that William had been taken?

She had said, "I'm cooking chicken chasseur tonight."

And *he* had said, "Chicken chasseur . . ." and then paused for a very long time, and added, "Don't forget the pan."

She had assumed then that he meant saucepan. But why would he have said "don't forget the pan?" After all, he hadn't been talking about cooking before. He had been warning her that somebody in Kensington Gardens might be watching her. He had been warning her that somebody in Kensington Gardens might want to take William.

Don't forget the Pan.

He was sitting on the sofa, bundled up in maroon woollen blankets, when she let herself in. The flat smelled of gas and stale milk. A thin sunlight the colour of cold tea was straining through the net curtains; and it made his face look more sallow and withered than ever.

"I was wondering when you'd come," he said, in a whisper.

"You expected me?"

He gave her a sloping smile. "You're a mother. Mothers understand everything."

She sat on the chair close beside him. "That day when William was taken . . . you said 'don't forget the Pan.' Did you mean what I think you meant?"

He took hold of her hand and held it in a gesture of infinite sympathy and infinite pain. "The Pan is every mother's nightmare. Always has been, always will be."

"Are you trying to tell me that it's not a story?"

"Oh . . . the way that Sir James Barrie told it – all fairies and pirates and Indians – *that* was a story. But it was founded on fact."

"How do you know that?" asked Marjorie. "I've never heard anyone mention that before."

Uncle Michael turned his withered neck toward the window. "I know it because it happened to my brother and my sister and it nearly happened to me. My mother met Sir James at a dinner in Belgravia, about a year afterwards, and tried to explain what had happened. This was in 1901 or 1902, thereabouts. She thought that he might write an article about it, to warn other parents, and that because of his authority, people might listen to him, and believe him. But the old fool was such a sentimentalist, such a fantasist . . . he didn't believe her, either, and he turned my mother's agony into a children's play.

"Of course, it was such a successful children's play that nobody ever took my mother's warnings seriously, ever again. She died in Earlswood Mental Hospital in Surrey in 1914. The death certificate said 'dementia', whatever that means."

"Tell me what happened," said Marjorie. "Uncle Michael, I've just lost my baby . . . you have to tell me what happened."

Uncle Michael gave her a bony shrug. "It's difficult to separate fact from fiction. But in the late 1880s, there was a rash of kidnappings in Kensington Gardens . . . all boy babies, some of them taken from prams, some of them snatched directly from their nannies' arms. All of the babies were later found dead . . . most in Kensington Gardens, some in Hyde Park and Paddington . . . but none of them very far away. Sometimes the nannies were assaulted, too, and three of them were raped.

"In 1892, a man was eventually caught in the act of trying to steal a baby. He was identified by several nannies as the man who had raped them and abducted their charges. He was tried at the Old Bailey on three specimen charges of murder, and sentenced to death on June 13, 1893. He was hanged on the last day of October.

"He was apparently a Polish merchant seaman, who had jumped ship at London Docks after a trip to the Caribbean. His shipmates had known him only as Piotr. He had been cheerful and happy, as far as they knew – at least until they docked at Port-au-Prince, in Haiti. Piotr had spent three nights away from the ship, and after his return, the first mate remarked on his 'moody and unpleasant mien.' He flew into frequent rages, so they weren't at all surprised when he left the ship at London and never came back.

"The ship's doctor thought that Piotr might have contracted malaria, because his face was ashy white, and his eyes looked bloodshot. He shivered, too, and started to mutter to himself."

"But if he was hanged – " put in Marjorie.

"Oh, he was hanged, all right," said Michael. "Hanged by the neck until he was dead, and buried in the precincts of Wormwood Scrubs prison. But only a year later, more boy-babies began to disappear from Kensington Gardens, and more nannies were assaulted, and each of them bore the same kind of scratches and cuts that Piotr had inflicted on his victims.

"He used to tear their dresses, you see, with a baling-hook."

"A baling-hook?" said Marjorie, faintly.

Uncle Michael held up his hand, with one finger curled. "Where do you think that Sir James got the notion for Captain Hook?"

"But I was scratched like that, too."

"Yes," nodded Uncle Michael. "And that's what I've been trying to tell you. The man who attacked you – the man who took William – it was Piotr."

"What? That was over a hundred years ago! How could it have been?"

"In the same way that Piotr tried to snatch me, too, in 1901, when I was still in my pram. My nannie tried to fight him off, but he hooked her throat and severed her jugular vein. My brother and my sister tried to fight him off, too, but he dragged them both away with him. They were only little, they didn't stand a chance. A few weeks later, a swimmer found their bodies in the Serpentine.

Uncle Michael pressed his hand against his mouth, and was silent for almost a whole minute. "My mother was almost mad with grief. But somehow, she *knew* who had killed her children. She spent every afternoon in Kensington Gardens, following almost every man she saw. And – at last – she came across him. He was standing amongst the trees, watching two nannies sitting on a bench. She approached him, and she challenged him. She told him to his face that she knew who he was; and that she knew he had murdered her children.

"Do you know what he said? I shall never forget my mother telling me this, and it still sends shivers down my spine. He said, 'I never had a mother, I never had a father. I was never allowed to be a boy. But the old woman on Haiti said that I could stay young for ever and ever, so long as I always sent back to her the souls of young children, flying on the wind. So that is what I did. I kissed them, and sucked out their souls, and sent them flying back to Haiti on the wind.'

"But do you know what he said to my mother? He said 'Your children's souls may have flown to a distant island, but they can still live, if you wish them to. You can go to their graves, and you can call them, and they'll come to you. It only takes a mother's word.'

"My mother said, 'Who are you? *What* are you? And he said 'Pan', which is nothing more nor less than Polish for 'Man'. That's why my mother called him 'Piotr Pan.' And that's where Sir James Barrie got the name from."

"And here, of course, is the terrible irony – Captain Hook and Peter Pan weren't enemies at all, not in real life. They were one and the same person."

Marjorie stared at her Uncle Michael in horror. "What did my great-auntie do? She didn't *call* your brother and sister, did she?"

Uncle Michael shook his head. "She insisted that their graves should be covered in heavy slabs of granite. Then – as you know – she did whatever she could to warn other mothers of the danger of Piotr Pan."

"So she really believed that she could call her children back to life?"

"I think so. But – as she always said to me – what can life amount to, without a soul?"

Marjorie sat with her Uncle Michael until it grew dark, and his head dropped to one side, and he began to snore.

*   *   *

She stood in the chapel of rest, her face bleached white by the single ray of sunlight that fell from the clerestory window. Her dress was black, her hat was black. She held a black handbag in front of her.

William's white coffin was open, and William himself lay on a white silk pillow, his eyes closed, his tiny eyelashes curled over his deathly-white cheek, his lips slightly parted, as if he were still breathing.

On either side of the coffin, candles burned; and there were two tall vases of white gladioli. Apart from the murmuring of traffic, and the occasional rumbling of a Central Line tube train deep beneath the building's foundations, the chapel was silent.

Marjorie could feel her heart beating, steady and slow.

My baby, she thought. My poor sweet baby.

She stepped closer to the coffin. Hesitantly, she reached out and brushed his fine baby curls. So soft, it crucified her to touch it.

"William," she breathed.

He remained cold and still. Not moving, not breathing.

"William," she repeated. "William, my darling, come back to me. Come back to me, Mr Bill."

Still he didn't stir. Still he didn't breathe.

She waited a moment longer. She was almost ashamed of herself for having believed Uncle Michael's stories. Piotr Pan indeed! The old man was senile.

Softly, she tiptoed to the door. She took one last look at William, and then she closed the door behind her.

She had barely let go of the handle, however, when the silence was broken by the most terrible high-pitched scream she had ever heard in her life.

In Kensington Gardens, beneath the trees, a thin dark man raised his head and listened, and listened, as if he could hear a child crying in the wind. He listened, and he smiled, although he never took his eyes away from the young woman who was walking towards him, pushing a baby-buggy.

He thought, *God bless mothers everywhere.*

J. Sheridan Le Fanu

Schalken the Painter

Joseph Sheridan Le Fanu (1814–73) was a prolific and popular novelist. Born in Dublin and educated at Trinity College, he edited a number of newspapers, as well as the Dublin University Magazine, *in which he published most of his short stories (many of them anonymously).*

Following the sudden death of his wife in 1858, he became a recluse, and began writing the majority of his weird fiction. His books include Ghost Stories and Tales of Mystery, The House By the Churchyard, Uncle Silas: A Tale of Bertram-Haugh, Wylder's Hand, Guy Deverell *and the landmark collection of short supernatural stories,* In a Glass Darkly. *During the early part of this century, most of Le Fanu's stories were rescued from obscurity by M. R. James, who published them as* Madame Crowl's Ghost and Other Tales of Mystery. *Among the best of these are "Green Tea", the classic vampire novella "Carmilla", and the story which follows.*

"Schalken the Painter" was successfully filmed by BBC-TV in 1979 as part of the "Omnibus" series. Veteran actor John Justin portrayed the corpse-like suitor Vanderhausen in writer/director Leslie Megahey's atmospheric adaptation.

"For he is not a man as I am that we should come together; neither is there any that might lay his hand upon us both. Let him, therefore, take his rod away from me, and let not his fear terrify me."

THERE EXISTS, AT this moment, in good preservation a remarkable work of Schalken's. The curious management of its lights constitutes, as usual in his pieces, the chief apparent merit of the picture. I say *apparent*, for in its subject, and not in its handling, however exquisite, consists its real value. The picture represents the interior of what might be a chamber in some antique religious building; and its foreground is occupied by a female figure, in a species of white robe, part of which is arranged so as to form a veil. The dress, however, is not that of any religious order. In her hand the figure bears a lamp, by which alone her figure and face are illuminated; and her features wear such an arch smile, as well becomes a pretty woman when practising some prankish roguery; in the background, and, excepting where the dim red light of an expiring fire serves to define the form, in total shadow, stands the figure of a man dressed in the old Flemish fashion, in an attitude of alarm, his hand being placed upon the hilt of his sword, which he appears to be in the act of drawing.

There are some pictures, which impress one, I know not how, with a conviction that they represent not the mere ideal shapes and combinations which have floated through the imagination of the artist, but scenes, faces, and situations which have actually existed. There is in that strange picture, something that stamps it as the representation of a reality.

And such in truth it is, for it faithfully records a remarkable and mysterious occurrence, and perpetuates, in the face of the female figure, which occupies the most prominent place in the design, an accurate portrait of Rose Velderkaust, the niece of Gerard Douw, the first, and I believe, the only love of Godfrey Schalken. My great grandfather knew the painter well; and from Schalken himself he learned the fearful story of the painting, and from him too he ultimately received the picture itself as a bequest. The story and the picture have become heirlooms in my family, and having described the latter, I shall, if you please, attempt to relate the tradition which has descended with the canvas.

There are few forms on which the mantle of romance hangs more ungracefully than upon that of the uncouth Schalken – the boorish but most cunning worker in oils, whose pieces delight the critics of our day almost as much as his manners disgusted the refined of his own; and yet this man, so rude, so dogged, so slovenly, in the midst of his celebrity, had in his obscure, but happier days, played the hero in a wild romance of mystery and passion.

When Schalken studied under the immortal Gerard Douw, he was a very young man; and in spite of his phlegmatic temperament, he at once fell over head and ears in love with the beautiful niece of his wealthy master. Rose Velderkaust was still younger than he, having not yet attained her seventeenth year, and, if tradition speaks truth, possessed all the soft and dimpling charms of the fair, light-haired Flemish maidens. The young painter loved honestly and fervently. His frank adoration was rewarded. He declared his love, and extracted a faltering confession in return. He was the happiest and proudest painter in all Christendom. But there was somewhat to dash his elation; he was poor and undistinguished. He dared not ask old Gerard for the hand of his sweet ward. He must first win a reputation and a competence.

There were, therefore, many dread uncertainties and cold days before him; he had to fight his way against sore odds. But he had won the heart of dear Rose Velderkaust, and that was half the battle. It is needless to say his exertions were redoubled, and his lasting celebrity proves that his industry was not unrewarded by success.

These ardent labours, and worse still, the hopes that elevated and beguiled them, were however, destined to experience a sudden interruption – of a character so strange and mysterious as to baffle all inquiry and to throw over the events themselves a shadow of preternatural horror.

Schalken had one evening outstayed all his fellow-pupils, and still pursued his work in the deserted room. As the daylight was fast falling, he laid aside his colours, and applied himself to the completion of a sketch on which he had expressed extraordinary pains. It was a religious composition, and represented the temptations of a pot-bellied Saint Anthony. The young artist, however destitute of elevation, had, nevertheless, discernment enough to be dissatisfied with his own work, and many were the patient erasures and improvements which saint and devil underwent, yet all in vain. The large, old-fashioned room was silent, and, with the exception of himself, quite emptied of its usual inmates. An hour had thus passed away, nearly two, without any improved result. Daylight had already declined, and twilight was deepening into the darkness of night. The patience of the young painter was exhausted, and he stood before his unfinished production, angry and mortified, one hand buried in the folds of his long hair, and the other holding the piece of charcoal which had so ill-performed its office, and which he now rubbed, without much regard to the sable streaks it produced, with irritable pressure upon his ample Flemish inexpressibles. "Curse the subject!" said the young man aloud; "curse the picture, the devils, the saint – "

At this moment a short, sudden sniff uttered close behind him made the artist turn sharply round, and he now, for the first time, became aware that his labours had been overlooked by a stranger. Within about a yard and half, and rather behind him, there stood the figure of an elderly man in a cloak and broad-brimmed, conical hat; in his hand, which was protected with a heavy gauntlet-shaped glove, he carried a long ebony walking-stick, surmounted with what appeared, as it glittered dimly in the twilight, to be a massive head of gold, and upon his breast, through the folds of the cloak, there shone the links of a rich chain of the same metal. The room was so obscure that nothing further of the appearance of the figure could be ascertained, and his hat threw his features into profound shadow. It would not have been easy to conjecture the age of the intruder; but a quantity of dark hair escaping from beneath his sombre hat, as well as his firm and upright carriage served to indicate that his years could not yet exceed threescore, or thereabouts. There was an air of gravity and importance about the garb of the person, and something indescribably odd, I might say awful, in the perfect, stone-like stillness of the figure, that effectually checked the testy comment which had at once risen to the lips of the irritated artist. He, therefore, as soon as he had sufficiently recovered his surprise, asked the stranger, civilly, to be seated, and desired to know if he had any message to leave for his master.

"Tell Gerard Douw," said the unknown, without altering his attitude in the smallest degree, "that Minheer Vanderhausen, of Rotterdam, desires to speak with him on tomorrow evening at this hour, and if he please, in this room, upon matters of weight; that is all."

The stranger, having finished this message, turned abruptly, and, with a quick, but silent step quitted the room, before Schalken had time to say a word in reply. The young man felt a curiosity to see in what direction the burgher of Rotterdam would turn, on quitting the *studio*, and for that purpose he went directly to the window which commanded the door. A lobby of considerable extent intervened between the inner door of the painter's room and the street entrance, so that Schalken occupied the post of observation before the old man could possibly have reached the street. He watched in vain, however. There was no other mode of exit. Had the queer old man vanished, or was he lurking about the recesses of the lobby for some sinister purpose? This last suggestion filled the mind of Schalken with a vague uneasiness, which was so unaccountably intense as to make him alike afraid to remain in the room alone, and reluctant to pass through the lobby. However, with an effort which appeared very disproportioned to the occasion, he summoned resolution to leave the room, and, having locked the door and thrust the key in his pocket, without looking to the right or left, he traversed the passage which had so recently, perhaps still, contained the person of his mysterious visitant, scarcely venturing to breathe till he had arrived in the open street.

"Minheer Vanderhausen!" said Gerard Douw within himself, as the appointed hour approached, "Minheer Vanderhausen, of Rotterdam! I never heard of the man till yesterday. What can he want of me? A portrait, perhaps, to be painted; or a poor relation to be apprenticed; or a collection to be valued; or – pshaw! there's no one in Rotterdam to leave me a legacy. Well, whatever the business may be, we shall soon know it all."

It was now the close of day, and again every easel, except that of Schalken, was deserted. Gerard Douw was pacing the apartment with the restless step of impatient expectation, sometimes pausing to glance over the work of one of his absent pupils, but more frequently placing himself at the window, from whence he might observe the passengers who threaded the obscure by-street in which his studio was placed.

"Said you not, Godfrey," exclaimed Douw, after a long and fruitful gaze from his post of observation, and turning to Schalken, "that the hour he appointed was about seven by the clock of the Stadhouse?"

"It had just told seven when I first saw him, sir," answered the student.

"The hour is close at hand, then," said the master, consulting a horologe as large and as round as an orange. "Minheer Vanderhausen from Rotterdam – is it not so?

"Such was the name."

"And an elderly man, richly clad?" pursued Douw, musingly.

"As well as I might see," replied his pupil; "he could not be young, nor yet very old, neither; and his dress was rich and grave, as might become a citizen of wealth and consideration."

At this moment the sonorous boom of the Stadhouse clock told, stroke after stroke, the hour of seven; the eyes of both master and student were directed to the door; and it was not until the last peal of the bell had ceased to vibrate, that Douw exclaimed –

"So, so; we shall have his worship presently, that is, if he means to keep his hour; if not, you may wait for him, Godfrey, if you court his acquaintance. But what, after all, if it should prove but a mummery got up by Vankarp, or some such wag? I wish you had run all risks, and cudgelled the old burgomaster soundly. I'd wager a dozen of Rhenish, his worship would have unmasked, and pleaded old acquaintance in a trice."

"Here he comes, sir," said Schalken, in a low monitory tone; and instantly, upon turning towards the door, Gerard Douw observed the same figure which had, on the day before, so unexpectedly greeted his pupil Schalken.

There was something in the air of the figure which at once satisfied the painter that there was no masquerading in the case, and that he really stood in the presence of a man of worship; and so, without hesitation, he doffed his cap, and courteously saluting the stranger, requested him to be seated. The visitor waved his hand slightly, as if in acknowledgment of the courtesy, but remained standing.

"I have the honour to see Minheer Vanderhausen of Rotterdam?" said Gerard Douw.

"The same," was the laconic reply of his visitor.

"I understand your worship desires to speak with me," continued Douw, "and I am here by appointment to wait your commands."

"Is that a man of trust?" said Vanderhausen, turning towards Schalken, who stood at a little distance behind his master.

"Certainly," replied Gerard.

"Then let him take this box, and get the nearest jeweller or goldsmith to value its contents, and let him return hither with a certificate of the valuation."

At the same time, he placed a small case about nine inches square in the hands of Gerard Douw, who was as much amazed at its weight as at the strange abruptness with which it was handed to him. In accordance with the wishes of the stranger, he delivered it into the hands of Schalken, and repeating his direction, despatched him upon the mission.

Schalken disposed his precious charge securely beneath the folds of his cloak, and rapidly traversing two or three narrow streets, he stopped at a corner house, the lower part of which was then occupied by the shop of a Jewish goldsmith. He entered the shop, and calling the little Hebrew into the obscurity of its back recesses, he proceeded to lay before him Vanderhausen's casket. On being examined by the light of a lamp, it appeared entirely cased with lead, the outer surface of which was much scraped and soiled, and nearly white with age. This having been partially removed, there appeared beneath a box of some hard wood; which also they forced open and after the removal of two or three folds of linen, they discovered its contents to be a mass of golden ingots, closely packed, and, as the Jew declared, of the most perfect quality. Every ingot underwent the scrutiny of the little Jew, who seemed to feel an epicurean delight in touching and testing these morsels of the glorious metal; and each one of them was replaced in its berth with the exclamation: "*Mein Gott*, how very perfect! Not one grain of alloy – beautiful, beautiful!" The task was at length finished, and the Jew certified under his hand the value of the ingots submitted to his examination to amount to many thousand rix-dollars. With the desired document in his pocket, and the rich box of gold carefully pressed under his arm, and concealed by his cloak, he retraced his way, and entering the studio, found his master and the stranger in close conference. Schalken had no sooner left the room, in order to execute the commission he had taken in charge, than Vanderhausen addressed Gerard Douw in the following terms:–

"I cannot tarry with you tonight more than a few minutes, and so I shall shortly tell you the matter upon which I come. You visited the town of Rotterdam some four months ago, and then I saw in the church of St Lawrence your niece, Rose Velderkaust. I desire to marry her; and if I satisfy you that I am wealthier than any husband you can dream of for her, I expect that you will forward my suit with your authority. If you approve my proposal, you must close with it here and now, for I cannot wait for calculations and delays."

Gerard Douw was hugely astonished by the nature of Minheer Vanderhausen's communication, but he did not venture to express surprise; for besides the motives supplied by prudence and politeness, the painter experienced a kind of chill and oppression like that which is said to intervene when one is placed in unconscious proximity with the object of a natural antipathy – an undefined but overpowering sensation, while standing in the presence of the eccentric stranger, which made him very unwilling to say anything which might reasonably offend him.

"I have no doubt," said Gerard, after two or three prefatory hems, "that the alliance which you propose would prove alike advantageous and honourable to my niece; but you must be aware that she has a will of her own, and may not acquiesce in what *we* may design for her advantage."

"Do not seek to deceive me, sir painter," said Vanderhausen; "you are her guardian – she is your ward – she is mine if *you* like to make her so."

The man of Rotterdam moved forward a little as he spoke, and Gerard Douw, he scarce knew why, inwardly prayed for the speedy return of Schalken.

"I desire," said the mysterious gentleman, "to place in your hands at once an evidence of my wealth, and a security for my liberal dealing with your niece. The lad will return in a minute or two with a sum in value five times the fortune which she has a right to expect from her husband. This shall lie in your hands, together with her dowry, and you may apply the united sum as suits her interest best; it shall be all exclusively hers while she lives: is that liberal?"

Douw assented, and inwardly acknowledged that fortune had been extraordinarily kind to his niece; the stranger, he thought, must be both wealthy and generous, and such an offer was not to be despised, though made by a humourist, and one of no very prepossessing presence. Rose had no very high pretensions for she had but a modest dowry, which she owed entirely to the generosity of her uncle; neither had she any right to raise exceptions on the score of birth, for her own origin was far from splendid, and as to the other objections, Gerard resolved, and indeed, by the usages of the time, was warranted in resolving, not to listen to them for a moment.

"Sir," said he, addressing the stranger, "your offer is liberal, and whatever hesitation I may feel in closing with it immediately, arises solely from my not having the honour of knowing anything of your family or station. Upon these points you can, of course, satisfy me without difficulty?"

"As to my respectability," said the stranger, drily, "you must take that for granted at present; pester me with no inquiries; you can discover nothing more about me than I choose to make known. You shall have sufficient security for my respectability – my word, if you are honourable: if you are sordid, my gold."

"A testy old gentleman," thought Douw, "he must have his own way; but, all things considered, I am not justified to declining his offer. I will not pledge myself unnecessarily, however."

"You will not pledge yourself unnecessarily," said Vanderhausen, strangely uttering the very words which had just floated through the mind of his companion; "but you will do so if it *is* necessary, I presume; and I will show you that I consider it indispensable. If the gold I mean to leave in your hands satisfy you, and if you don't wish my proposal to be at once withdrawn, you must, before I leave this room, write your name to this engagement."

Having thus spoken, he placed a paper in the hands of the master, the contents of which expressed an engagement entered into by Gerard Douw, to give to Wilken Vanderhausen of Rotterdam, in marriage, Rose Velderkaust, and so forth, within one week of the date thereof. While the painter was employed in reading this covenant, by the light of a twinkling oil lamp in the far wall of the room, Schalken, as we have stated, entered the studio, and having delivered the box and the valuation of the Jew, into the hands of the stranger, he was about to retire, when Vanderhausen called to him to wait; and, presenting the case and the certificate to Gerard Douw, he paused in silence until he had satisfied himself, by an inspection of both, respecting the value of the pledge left in his hands. At length he said –

"Are you content?"

The painter said he would fain have another day to consider.

"Not an hour," said the suitor, apathetically.

"Well then," said Douw, with a sore effort, "I *am* content, it is a bargain."

"Then sign at once," said Vanderhausen, "for I am weary."

At the same time he produced a small case of writing materials, and Gerard signed the important document.

"Let this youth witness the covenant," said the old man; and Godfrey Schalken unconsciously attested the instrument which for ever bereft him of his dear Rose Velderkaust.

The compact being thus completed, the strange visitor folded up the paper, and stowed it safely in an inner pocket.

"I will visit you tomorrow night at nine o'clock, at your own house, Gerard Douw, and will see the object of our contract;" and so saying Wilken Vanderhausen moved stiffly, but rapidly, out of the room.

Schalken, eager to resolve his doubts, had placed himself by the window, in order to watch the street entrance; but the experiment served only to support his suspicions, for the old man did not issue from the door. This was *very* strange, odd, nay fearful. He and his master returned together, and talked but little on the way, for each had his own subjects of reflection, of anxiety, and of hope. Schalken, however, did not know the ruin which menaced his dearest projects.

Gerard Douw knew nothing of the attachment which had sprung up between his pupil and his niece; and even if he had, it is doubtful whether he would have regarded its existence as any serious obstruction to the wishes of Minheer Vanderhausen. Marriages were then and there matters of traffic and calculation; and it would have appeared as absurd in the eyes of the guardian to make a mutual attachment an essential element in a contract of the sort, as it would have been to draw up his bonds and receipts in the language of romance.

The painter, however, did not communicate to his niece the important step which he had taken in her behalf, a forebearance caused not by any anticipated opposition on her part, but solely by a ludicrous consciousness that if she were to ask him for a description of her destined bridegroom, he would be forced to confess that he had not once seen his face, and if called upon, would find it absolutely impossible to identify him. Upon the next day, Gerard Douw, after dinner, called his niece to him and having scanned her person with an air of satisfaction, he took her hand, and looking upon her pretty innocent face with a smile of kindness, he said –

"Rose, my girl, that face of yours will make your fortune." Rose blushed and smiled. "Such faces and such tempers seldom go together, and when they do, the compound is a love charm, few heads or hearts can resist; trust me, you will soon be a bride, girl. But this is trifling, and I am pressed for time, so make ready the large room by eight o'clock tonight, and give directions for supper at nine. I expect a friend; and observe me, child, do you trick yourself out handsomely. I will not have him think us poor or sluttish."

With these words he left her, and took his way to the room in which his pupils worked.

When the evening closed in, Gerard called Schalken, who was about to take his departure to his own obscure and comfortless lodgings, and asked him to come home and sup with Rose and Vanderhausen. The invitation was, of course, accepted and Gerard Douw and his pupil soon found themselves in the handsome and, even then, antique chamber, which had been prepared for the reception of the stranger. A cheerful wood fire blazed in the hearth, a little at one side of which an old-fashioned table, which shone in the fire-light like burnished gold, was awaiting the supper, for which preparations were going forward; and ranged with exact regularity, stood the tall-backed chairs, whose ungracefulness was more than compensated by their comfort. The little party, consisting of Rose, her uncle, and the artist, awaited the arrival of the expected visitor with considerable impatience. Nine o'clock at length came, and with it a summons at the street door, which being speedily answered, was followed by a slow and emphatic tread upon the staircase; the steps moved heavily across the lobby, the door of the room in which the party we have described were assembled slowly opened, and there entered a figure which startled, almost appalled, the phlegmatic Dutchmen, and nearly made Rose scream with terror. It was the form, and arrayed in the garb of Minheer Vanderhausen; the air, the gait, the height were the same, but the features had never been seen by any of the party before. The stranger stopped at the door of the room, and displayed his form and face completely. He wore a dark-coloured cloth cloak, which was short and full, not falling quite to his knees; his legs were cased in dark purple silk stockings, and his shoes were adorned with roses of the same colour. The opening of the cloak in front showed the under-suit to consist of some very dark, perhaps

sable material, and his hands were enclosed in a pair of heavy leather
gloves, which ran up considerably above the wrist, in the manner of a
gauntlet. In one hand he carried his walking-stick and his hat, which
he had removed, and the other hung heavily by his side. A quantity
of grizzled hair descended in long tresses from his head, and rested
upon the plaits of a stiff ruff, which effectually concealed his neck. So
far all was well; but the face! – all the flesh of the face was coloured
with the bluish leaden hue, which is sometimes produced by metallic
medicines, administered in excessive quantities; the eyes showed an
undue proportion of muddy white, and had a certain indefinable
character of insanity; the hue of the lips bearing the usual relation
to that of the face, was, consequently, nearly black; and the entire
character of the face was sensual, malignant, and even satanic. It was
remarkable that the worshipful stranger suffered as little as possible of
his flesh to appear, and that during his visit he did not once remove his
gloves. Having stood for some moments at the door, Gerard Douw at
length found breath and collectedness to bid him welcome, and with
a mute inclination of the head, the stranger stepped forward into
the room. There was something indescribably odd, even horrible,
about all his motions, something undefinable, that was unnatural,
unhuman; it was as if the limbs were guided and directed by a spirit
unused to the management of bodily machinery. The stranger spoke
hardly at all during his visit, which did not exceed half an hour; and
the host himself could scarcely muster courage enough to utter the
few necessary salutations and courtesies; and, indeed, such was the
nervous terror which the presence of Vanderhausen inspired, that
very little would have made all his entertainers fly in downright
panic from the room. They had not so far lost all self-possession,
however, as to fail to observe two strange peculiarities of their visitor.
During his stay his eyelids did not once close, or, indeed, move in
the slightest degree; and farther, there was a deathlike stillness in
his whole person, owing to the absence of the heaving motion of the
chest, caused by the process of respiration. These two peculiarities,
though when told they may appear trifling, produced a very striking
and unpleasant effect when seen and observed. Vanderhausen at
length relieved the painter of Leyden of his inauspicious presence;
and with no trifling sense of relief the little party heard the street
door close after him.

"Dear uncle," said Rose, "what a frightful man! I would not see
him again for the wealth of the States."

"Tush, foolish girl," said Douw, whose sensations were anything
but comfortable. "A man may be as ugly as the devil, and yet, if his
heart and actions are good, he is worth all the pretty-faced perfumed

puppies that walk the Mall. Rose, my girl, it is very true he has not
thy pretty face, but I know him to be wealthy and liberal; and were
he ten times more ugly, these two virtues would be enough to counter
balance all his deformity, and if not sufficient actually to alter the
shape and hue of his features, at least enough to prevent one thinking
them so much amiss."

"Do you know, uncle," said Rose, "when I saw him standing at
the door, I could not get it out of my head that I saw the old painted
wooden figure that used to frighten me so much in the Church of St
Laurence at Rotterdam."

Gerard laughed, though he could not help inwardly acknowledging
the justness of the comparison. He was resolved, however, as far as
he could, to check his niece's disposition to dilate upon the ugliness
of her intended bridegroom, although he was not a little pleased, as
well as puzzled, to observe that she appeared totally exempt from
that mysterious dread of the stranger which, he could not disguise
it from himself, considerably affected him, as also his pupil Godfrey
Schalken.

Early on the next day there arrived, from various quarters of the
town, rich presents of silks, velvets, jewellery, and so forth, for Rose;
and also a packet directed to Gerard Douw, which on being opened,
was found to contain a contract of marriage, formally drawn up,
between Wilken Vanderhausen of the *Boom-quay*, in Rotterdam, and
Rose Velderkaust of Leyden, niece to Gerard Douw, master in the
art of painting, also of the same city; and containing engagements
on the part of Vanderhausen to make settlements upon his bride, far
more splendid than he had before led her guardian to believe likely,
and which were to be secured to her use in the most unexceptionable
manner possible – the money being placed in the hand of Gerard
Douw himself.

I have no sentimental scenes to describe, no cruelty of guardians,
no magnanimity of wards, no agonies, or transport of lovers. The
record I have to make is one of sordidness, levity, and heartlessness.
In less than a week after the first interview which we have just
described, the contract of marriage was fulfilled, and Schalken saw
the prize which he would have risked existence to secure, carried
off in solemn pomp by his repulsive rival. For two or three days
he absented himself from the school; he then returned and worked,
if with less cheerfulness, with far more dogged resolution than before;
the stimulus of love had given place to that of ambition. Months
passed away, and, contrary to his expectation, and, indeed, to the
direct promise of the parties, Gerard Douw heard nothing of his
niece or her worshipful spouse. The interest of the money, which

was to have been demanded in quarterly sums, lay unclaimed in his hands.

He began to grow extremely uneasy. Minheer Vanderhausen's direction in Rotterdam he was fully possessed of; after some irresolution he finally determined to journey thither – a trifling undertaking, and easily accomplished – and thus to satisfy himself of the safety and comfort of his ward, for whom he entertained an honest and strong affection. His search was in vain, however, no one in Rotterdam had ever heard of Minheer Vanderhausen. Gerard Douw left not a house in the Boom-quay untried, but all in vain. No one could give him any information whatever touching the object of his inquiry, and he was obliged to return to Leyden nothing wiser and far more anxious, than when he had left it.

On his arrival he hastened to the establishment from which Vanderhausen had hired the lumbering, though, considering the times, most luxurious vehicle, which the bridal party had employed to convey them to Rotterdam. From the driver of this machine he learned, that having proceeded by slow stages, they had late in the evening approached Rotterdam; but that before they entered the city, and while yet nearly a mile from it, a small party of men, soberly clad, and after the old fashion, with peaked beards and moustaches, standing in the centre of the road, obstructed the further progress of the carriage. The driver reined in his horses, much fearing, from the obscurity of the hour, and the loneliness, of the road, that some mischief was intended. His fears were, however, somewhat allayed by his observing that these strange men carried a large litter, of an antique shape, and which they immediately set down upon the pavement, whereupon the bridegroom, having opened the coach-door from within, descended, and having assisted his bride to do likewise, led her, weeping bitterly, and wringing her hands, to the litter, which they both entered. It was then raised by the men who surrounded it, and speedily carried towards the city, and before it had proceeded very far, the darkness concealed it from the view of the Dutch coachman. In the inside of the vehicle he found a purse, whose contents more than thrice paid the hire of the carriage and man. He saw and could tell nothing more of Minheer Vanderhausen and his beautiful lady.

This mystery was a source of profound anxiety and even grief to Gerard Douw. There was evidently fraud in the dealing of Vanderhausen with him, though for what purpose committed he could not imagine. He greatly doubted how far it was possible for a man possessing such a countenance to be anything but a villain, and every day that passed without his hearing from or of his niece, instead of inducing him to forget his fears, on the contrary tended more and more to aggravate them. The loss of her cheerful society tended also to depress his spirits; and in order to dispel the gloom, which often crept upon his mind after his daily occupations were over, he was wont frequently to ask Schalken to accompany him home, and share his otherwise solitary supper.

One evening, the painter and his pupil were sitting by the fire, having accomplished a comfortable meal, and had yielded to the silent and delicious melancholy of digestion, when their ruminations were disturbed by a loud sound at the street door, as if occasioned by some person rushing and scrambling vehemently against it. A domestic had run without delay to ascertain the cause of the disturbance, and they heard him twice or thrice interrogate the applicant for admission, but without eliciting any other answer but a sustained reiteration of sounds. They heard him then open the hall-door, and immediately there followed a light and rapid tread on the staircase. Schalken advanced towards the door. It opened before he reached it, and Rose rushed into the room. She looked wild, fierce and haggard with terror and exhaustion, but her dress surprised them as much as even her unexpected appearance. It consisted of a kind of white woollen wrapper, made close about the neck, and descending to the very ground. It was much deranged and travel-soiled. The poor creature had hardly entered the chamber when she fell senseless on the floor. With some difficulty they succeeded in reviving her, and on recovering her senses, she instantly exclaimed, in a tone of terror rather than mere impatience:–

"Wine! wine! Quickly, or I'm lost!"

Astonished and almost scared at the strange agitation in which the call was made, they at once administered to her wishes, and she drank some wine with a haste and eagerness which surprised them. She had hardly swallowed it, when she exclaimed, with the same urgency:

"Food, for God's sake, food, at once, or I perish."

A considerable fragment of a roast joint was upon the table, and Schalken immediately began to cut some, but he was anticipated, for no sooner did she see it than she caught it, a more than mortal image of famine, and with her hands, and even with her teeth, she tore off the flesh, and swallowed it. When the paroxysm of hunger had been a little appeased, she appeared on a sudden overcome with shame, or it may have been that other more agitating thoughts overpowered and scared her, for she began to weep bitterly and to wring her hands.

"Oh, send for a minister of God," said she; "I am not safe till he comes; send for him speedily."

Gerard Douw despatched a messenger instantly, and prevailed on his niece to allow him to surrender his bed chamber to her use. He also persuaded her to retire to it at once to rest; her consent was extorted upon the condition that they would not leave her for a moment.

"Oh that the holy man were here," she said; "he can deliver me: the dead and the living can never be one: God has forbidden it."

With these mysterious words she surrendered herself to their guidance, and they proceeded to the chamber which Gerard Douw had assigned to her use.

"Do not, do not leave me for a moment," said she; "I am lost forever if you do."

Gerard Douw's chamber was approached through a spacious apartment, which they were now about to enter. He and Schalken each carried a candle, so that a sufficiency of light was cast upon all surrounding objects. They were now entering the large chamber, which as I have said, communicated with Douw's apartment, when Rose suddenly stopped, and, in a whisper which thrilled them both with horror, she said:–

"Oh, God! He is here! He is here! See, see! There he goes!"

She pointed towards the door of the inner room, and Schalken thought he saw a shadowy and ill-defined form gliding into that apartment. He drew his sword, and, raising the candle so as to throw its light with increased distinctness upon the objects in the room, he entered the chamber into which the shadow had glided. No figure was there – nothing but the furniture which belonged to the room, and yet he could not be deceived as to the fact that something had moved before them into the chamber. A sickening dread came upon him, and the cold perspiration broke out in heavy drops upon his forehead; nor was he more composed, when he heard the increased urgency and agony of entreaty, with which Rose implored them not to leave her for a moment.

"I saw him," said she; "he's here. I cannot be deceived; I know him; he's by me; he is with me; he's in the room. Then, for God's sake, as you would save me, do not stir from beside me."

They at length prevailed upon her to lie down upon the bed, where she continued to urge them to stay by her. She frequently uttered incoherent sentences, repeating, again and again, "the dead and the living cannot be one: God has forbidden it." And then again, "Rest to the wakeful – sleep to the sleep-walkers." These and such mysterious and broken sentences, she continued to utter until the clergyman arrived. Gerard Douw began to fear, naturally enough, that terror or ill-treatment, had unsettled the poor girl's intellect, and he half suspected, by the suddenness of her appearance, the unseasonableness of the hour, and above all, from the wildness and terror of her manner, that she had made her escape from some place of confinement for lunatics, and was in imminent fear of pursuit. He resolved to summon medical advice as soon as the mind of his niece had been in some measure set at rest by the offices of the clergyman whose attendance she had so earnestly desired; and until this object had been attained, he did not venture to put any questions to her, which might possibly, by reviving painful or horrible recollections, increase her agitation. The clergyman soon arrived – a man of ascetic countenance and venerable age – one whom Gerard Douw respected very much, forasmuch as he was a veteran polemic, though one perhaps more dreaded as a combatant than beloved as a Christian – of pure morality, subtle brain, and frozen heart. He entered the chamber which communicated with that in which Rose reclined and immediately on his arrival, she requested him to pray for her, as for one who lay in the hands of Satan, and who could hope for deliverance only from heaven.

That you may distinctly understand all the circumstances of the event which I am going to describe, it is necessary to state the relative position of the parties who were engaged in it. The old clergyman and Schalken were in the anteroom of which I have already spoken; Rose lay in the inner chamber, the door of which was open; and by the side of the bed, at her urgent desire, stood her guardian; a candle burned in the bedchamber, and three were lighted in the outer apartment. The old man now cleared his voice as if about to commence, but before he had time to begin, a sudden gust of air blew out the candle which served to illuminate the room in which the poor girl lay, and she, with hurried alarm, exclaimed:–

"Godfrey, bring in another candle; the darkness is unsafe."

Gerard Douw forgetting for the moment her repeated injunctions, in the immediate impulse, stepped from the bedchamber into the other, in order to supply what she desired.

"Oh God! Do not go, dear uncle," shrieked the unhappy girl – and at the same time she sprung from the bed, and darted after him, in order, by her grasp, to detain him. But the warning came too late, for scarcely had he passed the threshold, and hardly had his niece had time to utter the startling exclamation, when the door which divided the two rooms closed violently after him, as if swung by a strong blast of wind. Schalken and he both rushed to the door, but their united and desperate efforts could not avail so much as to shake it. Shriek after shriek burst from the inner chamber, with all the piercing loudness of despairing terror. Schalken and Douw applied every nerve to force open the door; but all in vain. There was no sound of struggling from within, but the screams seemed to increase in loudness, and at the same time they heard the bolts of the latticed window withdrawn, and the window itself grated upon the sill as if thrown open. One *last* shriek, so long and piercing and agonized as to be scarcely human, swelled from the room, and suddenly there followed a death-like silence. A light step was heard crossing the floor, as if from the bed to the window; and almost at the same instant the door gave way, and, yielding to the pressure of the external applicants, nearly precipitated them into the room. It was empty. The window was open, and Schalken sprung to a chair and gazed out upon the street and canal below. He saw no form, but he saw, or thought he saw, the waters of the broad canal beneath settling ring after ring in heavy circles, as if a moment before disturbed by the submission of some ponderous body.

No trace of Rose was ever after found, nor was anything certain respecting her mysterious wooer discovered or even suspected – no clue whereby to trace the intricacies of the labyrinth and to arrive at its solution, presented itself. But an incident occurred, which, though it will not be received by our rational readers in lieu of evidence, produced nevertheless a strong and a lasting impression upon the mind of Schalken. Many years after the events which we have detailed, Schalken, then residing far away received an intimation of his father's death, and of his intended burial upon a fixed day in the church of Rotterdam. It was necessary that a very considerable journey should be performed by the funeral procession, which as it will be readily believed, was not very numerously attended. Schalken with difficulty arrived in Rotterdam late in the day upon which the funeral was appointed to take place. It had not then arrived. Evening closed in, and still it did not appear.

Schalken strolled down to the church; he found it open; notice of the arrival of the funeral had been given, and the vault in which the body was to be laid had been opened. The sexton, on seeing a well-dressed gentleman, whose object was to attend the expected obsequies, pacing the aisle of the church, hospitably invited him to share with him the comforts of a blazing fire, which, as was his custom in winter time upon such occasions, he had kindled in the hearth of a chamber in which he was accustomed to await the arrival of such grisly guests and which communicated, by a flight of steps, with the vault below. In this chamber, Schalken and his entertainer seated themselves; and the sexton, after some fruitless attempts to engage his guest in conversation, was obliged to apply himself to his tobacco-pipe and can, to solace his solitude. In spite of his grief and cares, the fatigues of a rapid journey of nearly forty hours gradually overcame the mind and body of Godfrey Schalken,

and he sank into a deep sleep, from which he awakened by someone's
shaking him gently by the shoulder. He first thought that the old
sexton had called him, but *he* was no longer in the room. He roused
himself, and as soon as he could clearly see what was around him,
he perceived a female form, clothed in a kind of light robe of white,
part of which was so disposed as to form a veil, and in her hand
she carried a lamp. She was moving rather away from him, in the
direction of the flight of steps which conducted towards the vaults.
Schalken felt a vague alarm at the sight of this figure and at the
same time an irresistible impulse to follow its guidance. He followed
it towards the vaults, but when it reached the head of the stairs, he
paused; the figure paused also, and, turning gently round, displayed,
by the light of the lamp it carried, the face and features of his first
love, Rose Velderkaust. There was nothing horrible, or even sad, in
the countenance. On the contrary, it wore the same arch smile which
used to enchant the artist long before in his happy days. A feeling of
awe and interest, too intense to be resisted, prompted him to follow
the spectre, if spectre it were. She descended the stairs – he followed
– and turning to the left, through a narrow passage, she led him,
to his infinite surprise, into what appeared to be an old-fashioned
Dutch apartment, such as the pictures of Gerard Douw have served
to immortalize. Abundance of costly antique furniture was disposed
about the room, and in one corner stood a four-post bed, with heavy
black cloth curtains around it; the figure frequently turned towards
him with the same arch smile; and when she came to the side of the
bed, she drew the curtains, and, by the light of the lamp, which
she held towards its contents, she disclosed to the horror-stricken
painter, sitting bolt upright in the bed, the livid and demoniac form of
Vanderhausen. Schalken had hardly seen him, when he fell senseless
upon the floor, where he lay until discovered, on the next morning, by
persons employed in closing the passages into the vaults. He was lying
in a cell of considerable size, which had not been disturbed for a long
time, and he had fallen beside a large coffin, which was supported
upon small pillars, a security against the attacks of vermin.

To his dying day Schalken was satisfied of the reality of the vision
which he had witnessed, and he has left behind him a curious
evidence of the impression which it wrought upon his fancy, in a
painting executed shortly after the event I have narrated, and which
is valuable as exhibiting not only the peculiarities which have made
Schalken's pictures sought after, but even more so as presenting a
portrait of his early love, Rose Velderkaust, whose mysterious fate
must always remain matter of speculation.

David Sutton

Clinically Dead

David Sutton is the winner of the World Fantasy Award and eight British Fantasy Awards. His short fiction has been published in such books and magazines as Best New Horror 2, The Giant Book of Best New Horror, Final Shadows, Cold Fear, Taste of Fear *and* Skeleton Crew, *amongst many others.*

He is the editor of the anthologies New Writings in Horror and the Supernatural 1 and 2, *and* The Satyr's Head and Other Tales of Terror, *and co-compiler of* The Best Horror from Fantasy Tales *and the* Dark Voices *and* Fantasy Tales *series. He has written two horror novels,* Earthchild *and* Feng Shui.

"Clinically Dead" grew out of the author's own experiences of visiting his mother during a lengthy hospital stay. That touch of realism adds an extra poignancy to the story's (entirely fictional) climactic horrors . . .

RUSSELL'S MOTHER WAS seriously ill in intensive care.

The sneaking suspicion was that he should never have been away on holiday when she went in for her operation. At the back of his mind he'd known he was tempting fate, but who ever believed in that? Nevertheless, his one nagging thought, as he lay on hot, gritty beaches, dozing, was that something would inevitably go wrong if he took his vacation rather than cancelling. Because his mother's aneurysm operation was to be performed a mere twelve hours before the 757 deposited him back at the airport, it hardly seemed logical to miss out on two weeks in the sun. But guilt struck any form of rationality stone dead.

He rushed to the hospital dazed, in shock, wondering if the situation could have been avoided by treating himself to a bit of healthy selflessness. To keep lady luck sweet.

Before Russell was allowed in to see his mother, he was spoken to by the senior anaesthetist, having been required to sit for fifteen minutes in a small office adjacent to intensive care.

"The operation went without a hitch," he said without preamble. "The procedure is well established and usually straightforward. In fact, your mother was coming out of surgery as we expected when there were complications." The face of the anaesthetist was alarmingly boyish; Russell thought he looked too young to be responsible for life and death in the operating theatre.

Unable to maintain eye contact, Russell stared at the man's shoes. Unexpectedly, they were white leather mules with thick wooden soles, the sort of shoes which are supposed, somehow, to do your feet good. The leather was spotted with dried blood.

"Is she –?" Russell could not finish what he wanted to ask. He'd never had to face precisely this situation before. His father had died ten years ago, at work. His death was a *fait accompli*. Having his mother halfway between this world and the next was proving to be altogether more difficult to handle. He wished that his mother and father had not had him so late, then he wouldn't have had to cope with aged parents whilst he was still relatively young.

"Your mother is, what age?" the anaesthetist asked, as if deliberately trying to avoid answering the question he must have known Russell was trying to ask.

"Sixty-six," Russell replied.

"She smoked?" There was an indifferent callousness in his tone of voice that Russell could not comprehend the need for. Nobody's perfect, after all.

Looking up, Russell nodded. "But not for the last few years," he qualified.

"Well, her age and the state of her arteries are against her, you must understand that. However, we're hopeful she'll recover, I can say that."

For a few seconds Russell's heart leaped. He could feel the beat in his chest stagger into another gear. Maybe taking his holiday and enjoying it had not, after all, destroyed his mother's life.

"But don't get me wrong," the anaesthetist continued, "she is *very* poorly indeed. And we expect her to be in intensive therapy for some time."

Only the next day would Russell be able to remember what else the man had told him in the little cluttered office that threatened to suffocate its visitants. All he could concern himself with now was the sight of his mother when he was finally allowed to briefly see her, his body trembling with the fear of death.

She was unconscious, her long, grey hair in disarray, her face absent of colour. The bed seemed huge, swamping her diminutive body, and it was raised up as if she was being offered to some malignant god on a steel-framed altar. The space around her was dimly illuminated. The continuous, quiet bleeping from a computer monitor was the only sound which accompanied her agonized, open-mouthed breathing, drawn in and exhaled with wheezing rapidity.

Russell watched the monitor high on the wall behind the bed. Red, yellow, blue and purple lines zig-zagged across it. Numbers tripped higher and lower, instantaneous calculations, forever updated. To the side of the bed were the drips, the syringe pumps and the intravenous pumps which were filling her arteries with painkillers and blood, and her stomach with food. A clear plastic tube taped to her nose was draining from her lungs a filthy brown liquid that kept hesitating in the U-bend, before being pushed on by more of the same.

A nurse appeared and emptied a urethral catheter bag, making a note of the quantity extracted. She smiled at Russell and the simple gesture reassured him more than had the anaesthetist. These people were dedicated. They were making sure his mother had every chance of survival, every chance for her own defences, her own will to live, to triumph. Her recovery was as much their concern as his.

At work the next day, he finally recalled what had been explained to him about his mother's condition. Russell was lifting and tipping what felt like the thousandth sack of the day, a bulk mailing of magazines, when a nylon strap holding the pack together split, and the magazines separated, slithering into the sorting trolley, their slippery, clear plastic envelopes helping them on their way. The bright red logo of the periodical repeated itself as the pile cascaded out of the sack. *Corpuscles* was dripping printed blood down the cover of the horror film magazine, Sissy Spacek's eyes glaring out as if shocked that the logo could do what it was doing to her face.

Russell looked away, towards the high ceiling. A haze of dust hung in the air of the sorting office, fluorescent lights glinting off specks in the middle distance. The faint sounds of radio muzak came from somewhere to his right, but the speaker could barely cope over the thump and rattle of conveyor belts and other machinery.

Then he remembered. His mother had been coming round from the first operation, but had lapsed back into unconsciousness unexpectedly. The circulation to her legs had ceased. She was rushed back to theatre as it was deemed that blood clots were preventing the circulation to the lower parts of her limbs. In a second lengthy, five hour operation, the surgeon had inserted arterial lines into both her legs, down from inner thighs to ankles. However, no blood clotting had been discovered. Instead the problem was . . . What was it Russell had been told? He couldn't really understand it. A condition called trashing, where fine crystals of blood block the capillaries. It was hoped the second operation would solve the problem in any event.

Time would tell.

On Thursday Russell wondered what had happened to all his time. He pressed the intercom button at the entrance to ITU. He was allowed through right away; some nights he had been forced to wait for up to twenty minutes while they did things: washing, physiotherapy, blood tests. As he approached the bed he was led aside by one of the sisters.

He could still see his mother wrapped in a sheet and trailed with twitching tubes. A mask covered her nose and mouth.

"As you know," the sister was saying, "Mary has had difficulty breathing and the infection on her chest has worsened. Mr Hastone considered it necessary to do something to alleviate what's becoming a life-threatening condition."

Russell blinked at the sister. She was rather tall and beautiful, her lips wide, her blue eyes bright with life and intelligence. Her forehead wore a frown, as if to ensure he meekly accept the diagnosis and its necessary treatment. For a moment, with dread upon him, Russell could only see her as part of the machinery, a fleshy cog in the whirr of ITU's vast array of equipment and plastic piping.

He hadn't said anything, but his expression must have been puzzled, because the sister continued without prompting.

"Consequently we've had to perform a tracheotomy. It's actually what we call a mini-tracheotomy, a very simple procedure done under a local anaesthetic. And it'll help us to draw off the congestion." The sister was being very matter-of-fact about what she knew must have been a further shock to Russell.

A few seconds later he was allowed to the bedside, his head like a balloon filled with scalding water, his legs trembling.

His mother's neck was covered in a mass of untidy sticking plaster surrounding one inch of plastic tube with a little pull-off cap attached. Just like you'd see on an inflatable beach-ball. A slimy brown film was drying on it, as if the nurses hadn't cleaned off the latest extraction of sputum properly.

Russell began to feel ill. Along with the new method, fluid was still being drawn off his mother's lungs from the nose tube, but it was now a dense black colour, as if her lungs were rotting away, turning into fecal slime.

He grasped her hand, more to take his mind off how he was feeling than to offer comfort to the unconscious patient. Under her skin he imagined he could see withered fatty tissues, the membranes connecting internal organs stretched and atrophied. Her rapid breathing was unchanged, the oxygen mask over her mouth and nose steaming up with each raspy exhalation. The flesh on her face looked as if it was sloughing off, drawn down around her chin, leaving the skin surrounding her eyes and forehead taut and skeletal.

She's dying, Russell whimpered to himself. The nursing staff must only have been telling him half-truths . . .

On Saturday, as he stared at the large, framed wall-mounting holding the photographs and names of the intensive care staff, one of the consultants came into the corridor where he was sitting.

"Ah, Mr Bray, isn't it?"

"Yes." He stood up.

"I'm Mr Hastone. I'd like to have a chat before you go through," he said, making Russell's heart plummet. He could not make eye contact, he was so frightened he would be unable to withhold his emotions if the news was bad.

"Did Mr Chambers explain to you about the operation and the after-effects?" he asked.

Russell nodded, trying to remember who Mr Chambers was. Numerous members of the staff had spoken to him over the last few days.

"Then you'll be aware that your mother's kidneys more or less 'shut down' after surgery?"

It *had* been explained to him that the shock of the operation to repair the aneurysm in her aorta, and the subsequent one following, had caused his mother's kidneys to stop functioning properly. That they'd ceased doing what they were supposed to do and it might take a few days for them to begin working again.

Now he knew something else had gone wrong.

"Mr Chambers has become very concerned that her kidneys aren't beginning to do their job sufficiently well to remove all the poisons in her system, and he decided she would need extra help. To give her kidneys time to recover without having the additional burden they have to contend with at the moment."

"Help?"

"So your mother has been put on a dialysis machine for the time being. We're not really equipped with the best here, but we do have a portable machine. We'll see how she progresses, but it may be that she'll need to be transferred to a hospital with a renal unit."

"Dialysis." Russell rubbed his forehead with the fingers of his right hand. There appeared to be an intangible ball of cotton wool surrounding his head, suffocating hearing, cutting off his vision and choking him.

The sight of the machine, with its aspirated sounds and the dark blood visibly pumping to and from it was a bad enough memory, but seeing his mother's feet was even worse. When he'd entered the ward, the blanket was loose at the bottom of the bed after being draped over a cage to keep her legs untouched. He peeped beneath and saw that the toes on both feet were a blotched and revolting grey-black.

What with everything else, he had been too terrified to ask what was happening to them.

On the way home rain was pummelling the pavements as if it wanted to indent the concrete. What it had succeeded in doing was soaking him so completely he knew it was foolish to have left home without an umbrella. After a few minutes walking, a cold wetness crept around his feet as if his shoes were filling up with chilled blood.

A month must have passed because, as he sorted mail, amongst the business envelopes was the plastic wrapped cover of another issue of *Corpuscles*. "Where are the living dead?" a banner headline shouted across its cover. Behind the red lettering lurked a mummified face from a film he did not recognize.

"In this place, Russ!"

Russell turned around, confused. Derek, one of his friends, with whom he'd spent his holiday, was looking over his shoulder. Russell realized he had been staring at the magazine and Derek had responded to the rhetorical question on its cover. His idea of a joke.

"Most of this lot," he nodded in general at his colleagues, "are more dead than alive."

"Right." Russell was in no mood for laughs.

"How's your mum?" Derek asked, changing tack and snatching the magazine from Russell's fingers and tossing it into a distant skip.

"She's holding her own," he replied. In fact he was unaware of whether she was nearer this life or the one beyond. What was almost unbearable was that, each time he visited the hospital, the news always got worse. So he never knew whether to believe and trust the doctors or not. And he found he couldn't talk about it to anyone.

"Bum deal," Derek said. "Watch out, here's the gaffer." He began to lift a sack and tip out piles of little boxes, groaning. "Why the fuck do they pack things up so small you can't even get a fucking label small enough to fit on 'em!"

He began tossing them without looking, accurately dispensing boxes, magazines and other envelopes into their appropriate containers.

Russell slid an elastic band off a pack of envelopes from the electricity board. The rubber smelled sickeningly familiar, the envelopes too, a sort of antiseptic tang.

"Why don't you take some time off?" Derek said, returning to Russell's obvious depression. "You'd get special leave," he added.

Russell knew he looked pretty washed out. He was existing merely to attend the hospital every evening, where he would remain for up to two hours mutely watching his mother fight for breath and for life.

"I'm better off coming in," he said. "I'd brood at home."

"Looks like you're doing that here," Derek stated. "Watch out, here's the gaffer."

Russell smiled at Derek's oft-repeated epigram.

At the end of his shift, the tips of Russell's fingers were numb from handling plastic envelopes that had begun to feel like living tissue. His fingers felt as dead as he knew his mother's feet to be.

Outside, the city centre looked changed. The rain had decided to let up, but the surface of the street was wet and gutters had become little rivers. It was the rush hour and the pedestrian zones were choked with shop and office workers heading for the bus stops. Russell felt sure they were mobile only because something else drove them, not their own desires. They were fulfilling a role, playing, unconsciously, the parts destined for them. This was a conclusion that had been forced upon him by the events of the last few weeks.

Hospital patients are like that too, Russell decided. They're unwitting actors, or movie stars, taking the stage for a day or two, swelling larger than life in the limelight of their disease, before vanishing into obscurity. And he knew them all in detail by now: the baby who'd swallowed a plastic top and nearly asphyxiated; the coronary patient on a ventilator; the car accident victim swathed in bandages; the vegetative sleeper for whom life may as well have already departed; and his mother, with a rolling panoply of complications, as if she played several parts in the drama.

He was waiting at the bus stop for home when he realized he should have been going to the hospital. He moved off, made uneasy by his forgetfulness. A hot dog man was serving through a cloud of steam. His customer squeezed a bloody, watery line of red along his onion-covered meat.

Russell turned away in disgust, heading for the bus he needed. His stomach growled for food, but he knew he couldn't eat yet. Not if he wanted it to stay down long enough to digest. His whole body felt raw, abused. As if he was starving himself.

He couldn't recall the details of his life over the past month. Memories faded in and out. He was dreaming his life, it being better than facing the truth, he could hear his mind telling him as if from far away.

At eleven-thirty he was trying to forget that the consultant was worried that his mother's circulation remained a serious predicament, slowing her recovery. She was in a lot of pain, despite the cocktail of analgesics she was being administered, and the pain was further disabling her recuperation.

Nevertheless, that evening his mother had briefly surfaced into consciousness.

Nifedipine, hydrocortisone, atropine. The words he'd sneaked a look at on his mother's chart became a litany, until he realized she was gripping his hand.

"Tell them to let me go," she hissed as he replaced the clipboard. Russell's heart swelled with hope, forcing tears into his eyes. He blinked them away as he stared at his mother. She was awake but, in spite of what she had said, did not appear to be aware of her surroundings or whose hand it was she held. At least the consciousness must mean she was beginning make progress.

He could not face telling her that her feet might have to be amputated. Yet her words hinted that she already knew. When she closed her eyes again he was saved from the necessity.

In his darkened living room, the picture on the blank television screen a reflection of his own vacant face, Russell convinced himself they were experimenting on his mother. The whole medical thing, from start to finish, was a sham. His mother was a guinea-pig. The intensive care unit was a laboratory. The doctors were testing drugs. The surgeons were performing vivisection for the gratification of their immoral souls. The machines that were keeping his mother alive were doing so only that more of the same grisly work might be accomplished.

The long road to the hospital entrance was a patchwork of autumn leaves, flattened by rain, patterning the paving slabs with brown and black blotches like rampant melanomas. The streetlamps highlighted other pedestrians skidding on the slimy mucus each leaf hid beneath itself; runny sores under scabs.

"Oh, hi! Russell Bray, isn't it?" The nearest skidder was a nurse Russell recognized as one of the ITU staff.

He nodded, unable to speak for fear of showing his emotions, knowing *she* was part of the conspiracy he'd finally uncovered the previous night.

"You might have to wait a bit this evening," she said, halting him with a hand on his arm.

"Oh?" His questioning voice was betraying his fear, but he hoped she wouldn't notice. If they knew he was on to them things could become awkward.

"There's a bit of a panic on in IT. Couple of emergencies came in. They're very busy," she added.

So why wasn't *she* there, helping them, Russell speculated. "Thanks for telling me," he replied evenly, trying to avoid her spectacled eyes.

"Watch the leaves!" the nurse stated as she stalked off, planting her flat-soled shoes firmly with each step. There was a sort of robotic motion to her walk, but it must have been the nurse's fear of falling over, and not some other vaguely mechanical workings of her body parts, that controlled her gait.

Russell ventured down the long corridor, past the coffee shop, past the chapel, past various wards announcing their function with bright red and white signs, until he turned familiarly, but uncomfortably, into the ITU reception area and waiting room. There was always an atmosphere of calm here, but it never relaxed Russell and never would now he was aware what was going on.

He lifted the phone and jabbed the button. In the earpiece he heard the echo of the distant buzzer. Seconds passed. The phone wasn't answered. He tried again, staring at the notice pinned to one of the double doors: "Absolutely No Admittance – Use Telephone". He looked from that to the photographic portraits of the staff. Some of the pictures had been removed, he saw, their names and occupations printed below blank rectangles, as if they'd suddenly been snuffed out of existence. Others continued to smile amiably, subtly concealing their real motives.

Replacing the receiver, he moved into the waiting room and sat down, intending to give himself five or ten minutes before trying the intercom again. Whenever he'd had to wait before, he always imagined the worst, but all that was happening was that his mother was undergoing physiotherapy, or some other treatment which they thought it better not to allow him to witness.

The magazines lying on top of an empty bookcase were so out of date they were thumbed to tatters, as if their covers were desiccated skin. Plastic flowers in vases looked as waxy as his mother's face. The notice board on the wall held the same information as always, advising visitors to wash their hands.

Yet, something had changed. Russell was unsure yet what it was. The two framed prints on opposing walls, one of two cute puppies, the other a pair of cute kittens, were both still askew. An oval red stain on the carpet, that must have been ink rather than blood because it had never faded, lured Russell's eyes. Every time he'd had to wait he stared at the stain, trying to see a pattern, as if it were a Rorschach test. Somewhere deep within its colour and the green of the carpet was encoded the real reason why his mother was being kept alive.

Above all he must remain controlled. He should act as subtly as the medical staff who were fooling him.

Then he knew. He walked out of the room and looked at the intercom phone on the wall. Its normally green light was red. It had never been red before. There might simply be a fault, of course.

Pressing the button again, he heard the familiar, distant buzzer hiss at the nurses' station. It sounded all right.

Yet the call remained unanswered.

Well damn the sign forbidding his entry. He looked the the blinking display on his watch and realized, dismayed, that he'd waited half an hour. That was plenty long enough.

He barged through the double doors, rehearsing his script for ignoring the mandate of the notice.

The corridor beyond was empty of life. The door to the office where he'd been informed about procedures was open. Russell peered in, ready with his explanation, but there was no one there.

He leaned his head around the entrance to the storeroom/kitchen next and saw that it was dishevelled. A tap was running into a sink unchecked and packages of dressings were strewn about the floor. An instrument tray had toppled off a table, its gleaming contents scattered amongst the dressings in a distribution reminiscent of hieroglyphics.

The emergency must be bigger than even the nurse had suggested, if the staff had found it necessary to treat the tools of their trade so carelessly.

Returning to the corridor, Russell finally came to the darkened ward. The lights were always kept turned low, but nevertheless he could not help feeling suddenly anxious at the ballooning shadows that lurked beyond curtains. There was an absence of the usual sounds. Not the bleep of a monitor, nor the swish of a nurse's starched uniform interrupted the silence.

At first this was all disorienting and unexpected. Additionally there appeared to have been some changes in the layout of the unit, particularly with regard to the whereabouts of his mother's bed. He was about to ask a member of the staff where they'd moved her to, when he realized there were no nurses, doctors, anaesthetists. ITU had become a medical *Marie Celeste*.

Russell frowned, aware that he was hanging onto the door as if in doubt about entering. His thoughts raced through a litany of words that he knew he must somehow suppress: inflammation, allergies, shock, coronary vasodilator, hypertension, sputum, gangrene.

Sweeping aside a curtain surrounding the nearest bed was both a reaction and an attempt to stem the tide of his thoughts, which he knew were turning themselves into an incantation. He knew what incantations were capable of, and how they led to unconscious acts, to a shackling of the will.

On the bed in front of him, a tube, ripped from some anonymous limb, squirted colourless liquid onto the sheets from the syringe pump to which it was attached. The bed's occupant must have been removed in a great hurry, perhaps for emergency surgery, and the nurse had failed to switch off the equipment.

A more sensible part of Russell told him they never worked like that. This place was so ordered. He was trying to work out what was happening, when a rustle of paper returned his attention to the vacant nurses' station.

He could see no one standing behind the high-fronted desk dealing with the paperwork. Perhaps a nurse had dropped a patient's notes and was bending down to pick them up? He walked back towards the desk, blinking, moisture swelling behind his eyelids, desperately wanting to know what had become of his mother and hating not having someone to comfort him.

A hand appeared, slapping against the telephone, bouncing the receiver off its cradle. The fingers looked odd and displaced and curiously transluscent before Russell realized why. The pudgy hand which appeared to be waving at him was that of a baby. Its partner rose into view, grasping the wooden ledge of the desk on its inner side. Russell was unable to see what was happening behind, in the rhombus of one of the ward's shadows.

He ceased walking towards the desk, fright halting him. There was a wheezy intake of breath, not unlike his mother's hideous gurgle, and the child's face was hauled into view by the pale hands. Its features were familiar; it was baby William, who'd come into hospital after swallowing a bottle-top, nearly choking on it. His rotund face still displayed a blue tinge from his near asphyxia. For the first time Russell took notice of the infant's eyes, which were unblinking, staring, but unseeing.

Shivering, Russell realized the baby was too young to have crawled, let alone walked, yet as this impossibility dawned, the child began to move along the desk, scattering papers and pens with its crab-like shuffle. In a moment it crashed noisily to the floor, but the fall did not appear to halt its forward momentum.

Further sounds behind him made Russell spin around, gasping. A curtain was being drawn aside from another bed, the hand that grasped it straining the hooks to breaking point.

The naked man who stepped into view trailed plastic tubing, held in place by plasters on his chest and arms. They dangled limply as if they were atrophied appendages sutured into his flesh by the vivisectionists who worked here. Blood ran sluggishly down the patient's belly, staining his pubic hair red. The face above the body tried to smile, but failed. But the expression was familiar. Russell had smiled and nodded to the man each day as he passed his bed on his way to his mother's, a gesture of support. He was the desperate coronary case who should, this very second, have been on a life-support unit.

Russell slipped suddenly, landing on his behind. His palm slid in something wet and sticky on the floor tiles which he was too scared to look at. From this new angle he could see that the man had left someone behind him, lying on the floor by his bed. It took only a second to realize it was the senior anaesthetist, his torso twitching from some severe shock or unseen wound.

Backing away, Russell dared himself to turn, wondering whether baby William had crawled near to him. He might trip over the child as he stood up, but he was no longer worried about hurting it.

He moved rapidly to his left, realizing now that his mother's bed was tucked away in the corner. He was thinking that maybe they hadn't reached her yet, the experimenters had perhaps overlooked her. Hadn't they had enough with the baby and the man?

Russell now knew for certain that it was the drugs that were causing the patients to rise up. There was too much unsupervised testing, too much willingness to inject and cut and excise. The painkillers and the narcotics were inside his mother, diluting her consciousness. No one would believe him, but he knew that, as with all the others, they had been slowly drawing off all her body fluids, in order to replace them with the secret substances which would animate her flesh once she was dead.

His mother's bed was raised high, and he felt like a small boy as he approached the mattress. There was a high-pitched whine in his head. The monitor on its adjustable arm was stretched over the bed and displayed itself towards him. On its surface, there were now six steady lines with no oscillation to impair their symmetry or the message they conveyed without words. The squeal that he imagined was emitted from the monitor should have been loud enough to summon a nurse, except that it was coming from his own throat.

The thin hollow of the bed sheet was empty, as if the occupant had been sucked from between it and the mattress. At the bottom the protective cage still hunched beneath the cover, inviting examination.

Russell drove the knuckles of his hands into his temples, a roar starting low in his throat, deep down, so deep it hurt; so deep that it wouldn't come out, his larynx strangling him.

He heard more shuffling sounds and turned. The baby and the man were moving towards him, along with other patients who had also fared for the worse. They moved with a slow synchronous grace that was none the less menacing for its lack of speed. Quickly, he looked back at the space where his mother should have been.

The gap under the leg-cage loomed as he lifted the sheet from it. Two shrivelled, black fleshy objects lay side by side as if desperately in need of further medical treatment.

Moving to one side, he dodged around the advancing figures, wrenching curtains as he went in a furious bid to find what remained of his mother. Behind one screen he discovered the bulk of the medical staff, some with hypodermics unremoved from the limbs and torsos where they had been implanted. It was plain that the experiments had taken their revenge.

"*I wanted them to let me go*," a voice spoke in Russell's head as he found her at last. The accusation was as barbed and venomous as the stainless instruments and the pharmacopoeia that had been used upon her.

Russell's mother was trying to stand up and it seemed likely she'd been mutely attempting the same procedure for some time. Her hospital nightgown was hanging off her withered shoulders, and purple blood smeared the floor next to the stumps of her ankles.

"Come on, mother," Russell said tenderly. "It's time to go home." He knew that he'd allowed her to remain in hospital far too long, but perhaps there was still time to help. He lifted her surprisingly light body in his arms and shouldered angrily past the RTA victim in his stained bandages, too fast to be cornered now.

Outside, in the corridor, he recalled what he'd almost forgotten in his haste. He must retrieve those other parts of his mother, before they began to move by themselves. Before they started to shuffle with involuntarily life to the subcutaneous beat of the drugs.

Les Daniels

They're Coming for You

Les Daniels is not exactly what you'd call prolific. However, recent short fiction appearances include Best New Horror 4, Dark Voices 4 *and* 5, The Mammoth Book of Vampires *and* After the Darkness. *A long-time devotee of comic books, he is the author of the recent bestseller* Marvel: Five Fabulous Decades of the World's Greatest Comics *and is currently working on a similar history of DC Comics. Also forthcoming is* White Demon, *the sixth novel in his series about vampire hero Don Sebastian de Villanueva.*

Daniels admits that every short story he writes somehow turns out to be a comedy. Therefore expect equal doses of humour and horror in this darkly comic tale of sundered lovers . . .

MR BLISS CAME home from work early one Monday afternoon. It was a big mistake.

He'd had a headache, and his secretary, after offering him various patent medicines, complete with their manufacturer's slogans, had said "Why don't you take the rest of the day off, Mr Bliss?"

Everyone called him Mr Bliss. The others in the office were Dave or Dan or Charlie, but he was Mr Bliss. He liked it that way. Sometimes he thought that even his wife should call him Mr Bliss.

Instead, she was calling on God.

Her voice came from on high. From upstairs. In the bedroom. She didn't seem to be in pain, but Mr Bliss could remedy that.

She wasn't alone; someone was grunting in harmony with her cries to the creator. Mr Bliss was bitter about this.

Without even waiting to hang up his overcoat, he tiptoed into the kitchen, and plucked from its magnetic rack one of the Japanese knives his wife had ordered after watching a television commercial. They were designed for cutting things into small pieces, and they were guaranteed for life, however long that happened to be. Mr Bliss would see to it that his wife had no cause for complaint. He turned away from the rack, paused for a sigh, then went back and selected another knife. The first was for the one who wanted to meet God, and the second for the one who was making those animal noises.

After a moment's reflection, he decided to use the back stairs. They were more secretive, somehow, and Mr Bliss intended to have a big secret just as soon as he could get organized.

He had an erection for the first time in weeks, and his headache was gone.

He moved as quickly and carefully as he could, sliding across the checkerboard linoleum and taking the back stairs two at a time in slow, painful, thigh-straining stretches. He knew there was a step which creaked, couldn't recall which one it was, and knew he would step on it anyway.

That hardly mattered. The groans and wails were reaching a crescendo, and Mr Bliss suspected that not even a brass band behind him could have distracted the people above him from their business. They were about to achieve something, and he wanted very much to be there before they did.

The bedroom took up the entire top floor of the house. It had been a whim of his to flatter his young bride with as spacious a spawning ground as his salary would allow; the tastefully carpeted stairs led up to it in front as inexorably as the shabby wooden stairs crept up the back.

Mr Bliss creaked at the appointed spot, cursed quietly and opened the door.

His wife's eyes, rolled back in her head, were like wet marble. Her lips fluttered as she blew damp hair from her face. The beautiful breasts that had persuaded him to marry her were covered with sweat, and not all of it was hers.

Mr Bliss didn't even recognize the man; he was nobody. The milkman? A census taker? He was plump, and he needed a haircut.

It was all very discouraging. Cuckolding by an Adonis would at least have been understandable, but this was a personal affront.

Mr Bliss dropped one knife to the floor, grasped the other in both hands, and slammed its point into the pudgy interloper at the spot where spine meets skull.

It worked at once. The man gave one more grunt and toppled over backwards, blade grinding against bone as head and handle hit the floor.

Mrs Bliss was there, baffled and bedraggled, spreadeagled naked against sopping sheets.

Mr Bliss picked up the other knife.

He pulled her up by the hair and stabbed her in the face. She blubbered blood. Madly but methodically, he shoved the sharp steel into every place where he thought she'd like it least.

Most of his experiments were successful.

She died unhappily.

The last expression she was able to muster was a mixture of pain, reproach, and resignation that thrilled him more than anything she'd shown him since their wedding night.

He wasn't done with her yet. She had never been so submissive.

It was late that night before he put down the knife and put on his clothes.

Mr Bliss had made a terrible mess. Cleaning up was always a chore, as she had so frequently reminded him, but he was equal to the task. The worst part was that he had stabbed the water bed, but at least the flood had diluted some of the blood.

He buried them in separate sections of the flower garden and showed up late for work. This was an unprecedented event. The quizzical eyebrows of his colleagues got on his nerves.

For some reason he didn't feel like going home that night. He went to a motel instead. He watched television. He saw a movie about someone killing several other people, but it didn't amuse him as much as he'd hoped. He felt that it was in bad taste.

He left the "Do Not Disturb" sign on the doorknob of his room each day; he did not wish to be disturbed. Still, the unmade bed to which he returned each night began to bother him. It reminded him of home.

After a few days, Mr Bliss was ashamed to go to the office. He was still wearing the same clothes he'd left home in, and he was convinced that his colleagues could smell him. No one had ever longed for the weekend as passionately as he did.

Then he had two days of peace in his motel room, huddling under the covers in the dark and watching people kill each other in a phosphorescent glow, but on Sunday night he looked at his socks and knew he would have to go back to the house.

He wasn't happy about this.

When he opened the front door, it reminded him of his last entrance. He felt that the stage was set. Still, all he had to do was go upstairs and get some clothes. He could be gone in a matter of minutes. He knew where everything was.

He used the front stairs. The carpeting made them quieter, and somehow he felt the need for stealth. Anyway, he didn't like the ones in the back anymore.

Halfway up the stairs, he noticed two paintings of roses that his wife had put there. He took them down. This was his house now, and the pictures had always vaguely annoyed him. Unfortunately, the blank spaces he left on the wall bothered him too.

He didn't know what to do with the paintings, so he carried them up into the bedroom. There seemed to be no way to get rid of them. He was afraid this might be an omen, and for a second considered the idea of burying them in the garden. This made him laugh, but he didn't like the sound of it. He decided not to do it again.

Mr Bliss stood in the middle of the bedroom and looked around it critically. He'd made quite a neat job of it. He was just opening a dresser drawer when he heard a thump from below. He stared at his underwear.

A scrape followed the thump, and then the sound of something bumping up the back stairs.

He didn't wonder what it was, not even for an instant. He closed his underwear drawer and turned around. His left eyelid twitched; he could feel it. He was walking without thinking toward the front stairs when he heard the door below them open. Just a little sound, a bolt slipping a latch. Suddenly, the inside of his head felt as big as the bedroom.

He knew they were coming for him, one from each side. What could he do? He ran around the room, slamming into each wall and finding it solid. Then he took up a post beside the bed and put a hand over his mouth. A giggle spilled between his fingers, and it made him angry, for this was a proud moment.

They were coming for him.

Whatever became of him (no more job, no more television), he had inspired a miracle. The dead had come back to life to punish him. How many men could say as much? Come clump, come thump, come slithering sounds! This was a triumph.

He stepped back against the wall to get a better view. As both doors opened his eyes flicked back and forth. His tongue followed, licking his lips. He experienced an ecstasy of terror.

The stranger, of course, had used the back stairs.

He had tried to forget what a mess he had made of them, especially his wife. And now they were even worse.

And yet, as she dragged herself across the floor, there was something in her pale flesh, spotted with purple where the blood had settled, and striped with rust where the blood had spilled, that called to him as it rarely had before. Her skin was clumped with rich brown earth. She needs a bath, he thought, and he began to snort with laughter that would soon be uncontrollable.

Her lover, approaching from the other side, was hardly marked. There had been no wish to punish him, only to make him stop. Still, the single blow of the TV knife had severed his spine, and his head lurched unpleasantly. The odd disappointment Mr Bliss had felt in the man's flabbiness intensified. After six days in the ground, what crawled toward him was positively puffy.

Mr Bliss tried to choke back his chuckles till his eyes watered and snot shot from his nose. Even as his end approached, he saw their impossible lust for vengeance as his ultimate vindication.

Yet his feet were not as willing to die as he was; they backed over the carpet toward the closet door.

His wife looked up at him, as well as she could. The eyes in her sockets seemed shrivelled, like inquisitive prunes. A part of her where he had cut too deeply and too often dropped quietly to the floor.

Her lover shuffled forward on hands and knees, leaving some sort of a trail behind him.

Mr Bliss pulled the gleaming brass bed around to make a barricade. He stepped back into the closet. The smell of her perfume and of her sex enveloped him. He was enveloped in her gowns.

His wife reached the bed first, and grasped the fresh linen with the few fingers she had left. She hauled herself up. Stains smeared the sheets. This was certainly the time to slam the closet door, but he wanted to watch. He was positively fascinated.

She squirmed on the pillows, arms flailing, then collapsed on her back. There were gurgles. Could she be really dead at last?

No.

It didn't really matter. Her lover crawled over the counterpane. Mr Bliss wanted to go to the bathroom, but the way was blocked.

He cringed when his wife's lover (who was this creeping corpse, anyway?) stretched out fat fingers, but instead of clawing for revenge they fell on what had been the breasts of the body beneath him. They began to move gently.

Mr Bliss blushed as the ritual began. He heard sounds that had embarrassed him even when the meat was live: liquid lurchings, ghastly groans, and supernatural screams.

He shut himself in the closet. What was at work on the bed did not even deign to notice him. He was buried in silk and polyester.

It was worse than he had feared. It was unbearable.

They hadn't come for him at all.

They had come for each other.

Hugh B. Cave

Mission to Margal

It would be almost inconceivable to publish an anthology about zombies and not include something by Hugh B. Cave. Born in 1910 in Chester, England, the author emigrated to America with his family when he was five. While editing trade journals, he sold his first pulp magazine story, "Island Ordeal", to Brief Stories *in 1929.*

During the 1930s and 40s Cave established himself as an inventive and prolific writer, and he became a regular contributor to Strange Tales, Weird Tales, Ghost Stories, Black Book Detective, Thrilling Mysteries, Spicy Mystery Stories, *and the so-called "shudder pulps",* Horror Stories *and* Terror Tales, *amongst many other titles.*

He then left the field for almost three decades, moving to Haiti and later Jamaica, where he established a coffee plantation and wrote two highly-praised travel books, along with a number of mainstream novels. During this period he also contributed fiction regularly to The Saturday Evening Post *and other "slick-paper" magazines.*

In 1977 Karl Edward Wagner's Carcosa imprint published a hefty volume of Cave's best horror tales, Murgunstrumm and Others, *which won a World Fantasy Award. A long-proposed follow-up volume,* Death Stalks the Night, *will now be published by Fedogan & Bremer. Cave returned to the genre with new stories in* Whispers *and* Fantasy Tales, *followed by a string of modern horror novels (most of them involving voodoo or the walking dead).*

A new collection of shorter works, The Corpse Maker, *edited by Sheldon Jaffery, was recently issued by Starmont House, who also published a biography by Audrey Parente,* Pulp Man's Odyssey: The Hugh B. Cave Story. *In 1991 the Horror Writers of America presented Cave with their highest honour, the Lifetime Achievement Award.*

When Cave finished "Mission to Margal" in rough draft in 1980, he decided to expand it to book-length and it finally became The Evil, *one of the most successful of his horror novels. He revised the novella for this volume, and it is published here for the first time.*

I

"OH-OH." KAY GILBERT jabbed her foot at the jeep's brake pedal. "Now what have we got, *ti-fi*?" She spoke in Creole, the language of the Haitian peasant.

In the middle of the road stood a man with his arms outthrust to stop them. Beyond him, at the road's edge, was one of the big, gaudy buses the Haitians called *camions*. Crudely painted orange and red and resembling an outsized roller-coaster car, it was pointed north in the direction they were going. Disembarked passengers stood watching two men at work under it.

The man who had stopped them strode forward as the jeep came to a halt. He was huge. "*Bon soir*, madame," he said with a slight bow. "May I ask if you going to Cap Haïtien?"

"Well . . ." The hesitation was caused by his ugliness. And, being responsible for the child, she must be extra careful.

"I beg you a lift," the fellow said, one heavy hand gripping the edge of the windshield as though by sheer force he would prevent her from driving on without him. "I absolutely must get to Le Cap today!"

She was afraid to say no. "Well . . . all right. Get in."

Stepping to the rear, he climbed in over the tailgate and turned to the metal bench-seat on her side of the vehicle. "May I move this, madame?" He held up a brown leather shoulder-bag that she had put there.

"Give it to me!" Turning quickly, Kay snatched it from his hand and placed it on the floor in front, at little Tina's feet.

"*Merci*, madame." The man sat down.

When the jeep had finished descending through hairpin turns to the Plaisance River valley, Kay was able to relax a little. Presently she heard their passenger saying, "And what is your name, little girl?"

Evidently the child did not find him intimidating. Without hesitation she replied brightly, "My name is Tina, m'sieu."

"Tina what, if I may ask?"

"Anglade."

A stretch of rough road demanded Kay's full attention again. When that ended, the child at her side was saying, "So you see, I have been at the hospital a long time because I couldn't remember anything. Not my name or where I lived or *anything*. But I'm all right now, so Miss Kay is taking me home."

"I am glad for you, *ti-fi*."

"Now tell me *your* name and where *you* live."

"Well, little one, my name is Emile Polinard and I live in Cap Haïtien, where I have a shop and make furniture. I was on my way back from Port-au-Prince when the *camion* broke down. And I'm certainly grateful to *le Bon Dieu* for causing you to come along when you did."

Darkness had fallen. Kay cut her speed again so as not to be booby-trapped by potholes. Lamps began to glow in scattered peasant *cailles*. Now and then they passed a pedestrian holding a lantern or a bottle-torch to light his way. As the jeep entered the north coast city of Cap Haïtien, rain began to fall.

In the wet darkness, Kay was unsure of herself. "I have to go to the Catholic church," she said to their passenger. "Can you direct me?"

He did so, remarking that he lived near there, himself. She stopped under a street lamp near the church entrance, the rain a silvery curtain now in the glare of the jeep's headlights. "For us, this is the end of the road, M'sieu Polinard. Tina and I will be staying here tonight with the sisters."

Their passenger thanked her and got out. To the child Kay said, frowning, "Where do the sisters live, Tina?"

"I don't know."

"But you stayed here almost a month before you came to the hospital!"

"I didn't know what was happening then."

Kay gazed helplessly at the church, a massive dark pile in the rain, then saw that Emile Polinard had stopped and was looking back at them. He returned to the jeep.

"Something is wrong, madame?"

"Well, I – I thought Tina would know where to find the sisters, but she doesn't seem to."

"Let me help. Is there a particular sister you wish to see?"

She felt guilty, keeping him standing there in the downpour. But if she did not accept his help, what would she do? "It was a Sister Simone who brought Tina to the hospital. But if she isn't there, someone else will do, I suppose."

"I know her. She should be here."

He was back in five minutes holding aloft a large black umbrella under which moved a black-robed woman not much taller than Tina. Saying cheerfully, "Hello, you two! Tina, move over!" she climbed into the Jeep. Polinard handed her the umbrella and she thanked him. "Just drive on," she instructed Kay. "I'll show you where to go."

Kay, too, thanked "ugly man" Polinard, who bowed in reply. Driving on, she turned a corner at the sister's direction, turned again between the back of the church and another stone building.

"Come," the sister commanded, and they hurried into the building. But once inside, the sister was less brisk. Giving the umbrella a shake, she closed it and placed it in a stand near the door, then hunkered down in front of Tina and put out her arms. "And how *are* you, little one?" She was Haitian, Kay noticed for the first time. And remarkably pretty.

"It's a good thing I phoned you yesterday," Kay said. Actually, she had phoned only to say that she and Tina would be passing through Le Cap on their way to the town of Trou and would stop for a few minutes. "I'm afraid I'll have to ask you to put us up for the night. Can you?"

"Of course, Miss Gilbert. What happened? Did you have car trouble?"

"We got off to a late start. Tina had one of her headaches."

"Ah, those headaches." The sister reached for Tina's hand. "Come upstairs, both of you. First your room, then we'll see about something to eat."

She put them both in the same room, one overlooking the yard where the jeep was, then disappeared. "We'll need our gear," Kay told the child. "I'll go for it while you wash up." The brown leather shoulder-bag she had brought with her, and before leaving the room she carefully slid it out of sight under a bed. Then on the stairs she met Sister Simone and a second nun coming up, each with a backpack from the jeep.

They supped on soup and fish in a small dining room: Kay and Tina, Sister Simone, Sister Anne who had helped with the backpacks, and Sister Ginette who at sixty or so was the oldest. What little conversation there was concerned only the journey. "That road is not easy, is it? . . . It so badly needs repairing . . . And the Limbé bridge is closed, so you had to come through the river . . ."

Why don't they ask about Tina – what we've been doing with her all this time at the hospital, and how she's coming along? They did talk to the youngster, but asked no personal questions. It almost seemed a conspiracy of silence.

But when the meal ended and Kay took Tina by the hand to walk her back upstairs, little Sister Simone said quietly, "Do come down again when she is in bed, Miss Gilbert. We'll be in the front room."

She found the three of them waiting there on uncomfortable-looking wooden chairs. It occurred to her that perhaps Polinard had built them. An empty chair was in place for her. On a small table in the centre of the circle lay a wooden tray on which were mugs, spoons, a pitcher of milk, a bowl of sugar. A battered coffee pot that might have been silver was being kept warm over an alcohol flame.

The nuns rose and waited for Kay to sit, managing somehow – all but Simone – to sit again precisely when she did. "Coffee, Miss Gilbert?" Simone asked.

"Please."

"Milk and sugar?"

"Black, please." It was a crime to tamper with Haiti's marvellous coffee.

Simone served the others as well – perhaps this was an aftersupper ritual – then seated herself. "Now, Miss Gilbert, please tell us how Tina regained her memory. If it won't tire you too much."

She told them how Dr Robek had hit on the idea of reading map names to Tina and how, on hearing the name Bois Sauvage, the child had snapped out of her long lethargy. "Like Snow White waking up when the prince kissed her."

They smiled.

"Then she remembered her own name. If, of course, Tina Louise Christine Anglade really is her name. We can't be sure until I get her to Bois Sauvage, can we? Or even if that's really where she came from."

The oldest sister, frowning deeply, said, "Bois Sauvage. Isn't that up in the mountains near the Dominican border?"

"According to the map, yes."

"How in the world will you get there?"

"I've been promised a guide at Trou."

"But you can't *drive* to such a place! There aren't any roads."

"I suppose we'll walk, or ride mules. I really won't know until tomorrow." Kay waited for them to sip their coffee. "Now will you tell *me* something, please? How did Tina come into your care in the first place? All we've ever heard is that she was brought to you by a priest."

"By Father Turnier," Simone said, nodding. "Father Louis Turnier. He was stationed at Vallière then and had a number of chapels even farther back in the mountains. We have a picture of him." She put her coffee mug down and went briskly, with robe swishing, to a glass-doored bookcase. Returning with a large photo album that smelled of mildew, she turned its pages, then reversed the book and held it out to Kay. "That's Father on the right, in front of the Vallière chapel. Those big cracks in the chapel were caused by an earthquake just a few days before this picture was taken. Can you imagine?"

Kay saw a husky-looking white man with a cigarette dangling from his lips. French, she guessed. Most of the white priests in the remote areas were French. He wore no clerical garment; in fact, his shirt was neither buttoned nor tucked into his pants. The way he grinned at the camera made her instantly fond of him.

"He was coming back from some far-off chapel one day," Simone said, "and stopped at this isolated native *caille* beside a little stream. He had never passed that way before, he said, but a landslide had carried away part of the usual trail and forced him to detour. He was on a mule, of course. And the animal was weary, so he thought he would just stop and talk with these people a while."

Kay gazed at the photo while she listened.

"Well, there was the child lying on a mat inside the *caille*, and the people asked Father to talk to her. She had wandered into their clearing a few days before and couldn't remember who she was or where she had come from."

"I see."

"That photo shows you the kind of man Father Turnier is. He ended up staying the night there and deciding the child must have been through some really traumatic experience and ought to have help. In any case, she couldn't remain there with those people. They didn't want her. So at daybreak he lifted her up on his mule and carried her out to Vallière, still not knowing her name or where she came from."

"Then what happened?"

"Well, he kept her there for about three weeks — he and young Father Duval who was stationed there with him — but she didn't respond as they hoped, so he brought her here to us." Sister Simone paused to finish her coffee, then leaned toward Kay with a frown puckering her pretty face. "You haven't found any *reason* for her lapse of memory?"

"None."

"On hearing the name of her village she just suddenly snapped out of it?"

"That's what happened. We've always thought there was nothing much wrong with her physically. Of course, when you brought her to us she was underweight and malnourished – not your fault; you didn't have her long enough to change that," Kay hurriedly added. "But she seemed all right otherwise."

"How strange."

"I wonder if her people in Bois Sauvage have been looking for her all this time," Ginette said. "It's been how long? Father Turnier had her for three weeks. We had her a month. You've had her for nearly six months."

Simone said, "It could be longer. We don't know that she went straight from her village to that *caille* where Father found her. Maybe *that* journey covered a long time." Life was full of puzzles, her shake of the head said. "Miss Gilbert, we can only bless you for taking her home. None of us here would be able to do it, I'm sure. But have you thought of leaving her here and having us send for the father in that district to come for her?"

"Father Turnier, you mean?"

"Well, no, it wouldn't be Father Turnier now. He's no longer there."

"It would be someone Tina doesn't know, then?"

"I'm afraid so. Yes."

Kay shook her head. "I'd better take her myself."

All the sisters nodded and looked at her expectantly. It was close to their bedtime, Kay guessed. She rose.

"I'd better make sure Tina is all right, don't you think? She has nightmares sometimes."

"And the headaches, poor thing," Simone said.

"Like this morning. Well then – until tomorrow?"

"Tomorrow," they responded in chorus, and little Simone added, "Sleep well, both of you."

Kay climbed the stairs. As she went along the corridor to their room, she heard a drumming sound overhead that told her the rain was still falling. *Please, God, let it stop soon or those mountain trails will be hell.* The room itself was a steam bath. Tina slept with her face to the wall and her arms loosely clasping an extra pillow.

In no time at all, Kay was asleep beside her.

Wearing a much-patched carpenter's apron this morning, Emile Polinard stepped back to look at a table he was working on. It was a large one of Haitian mahogany, crafted to order for a wealthy Cap Haitian merchant. The time, Emile noted, was twenty past eight. The rain had stopped just before daybreak and now the sun shone brightly on the street outside the open door of his shop.

His helper, 17-year-old Armand Cator, came from the back room and said, "I've finished the staining, M'sieu Polinard. Should I start on Madame Jourdan's chairs now?" Armand was a good boy, always respectful.

"Do that, please."

Glancing out the door at the welcome sunshine, Polinard saw a familiar vehicle coming down the street and voiced a small "Ha!" of satisfaction. He had been expecting it. To get from the church to the main north-coast highway, it would have to pass his shop. Hurrying out onto the cracked sidewalk, he waited.

Just before the jeep reached him, he waved both arms vigorously and called out, "*Bonjour,* good friends! Be safe on your journey!"

"Why, that must be Mr Polinard," said little Tina Anglade to Kay Gilbert. "That must be the furniture shop he told us about." She returned Polinard's wave.

Kay waved, too, but did not stop. They had got off to a late start again. She had overslept, and then the sisters had insisted on giving them a big breakfast.

The jeep sped on. Polinard stood on the sidewalk, hands on hips, smiling after it.

"You know those people, sir?" Armand asked from the doorway.

"Indeed, I do. They gave me a lift yesterday when the *camion* broke down. She's a charming woman. And the little girl . . . well, Armand, there's a curious story. You know what it means to lose your memory?"

"Huh?"

The jeep had disappeared from sight. Polinard re-entered the shop. "The little girl you just saw has been at that hospital in the Artibonite for a long time – months – because she could not remember her name or where she came from. She is such a bright child, too. But she has at last remembered and is going home."

"That's good."

"Yes. Provided, of course, that what she told them is not just her mind playing tricks again. By the way, don't you have a pal who came from a place called Bois Sauvage not long ago?"

"Yes, sir, I do. Luc Etienne."

"You see him often?"

"Two or three times a week."

"Ask him, then – because I am curious – if he knows of a girl about eight or nine years old who used to live there until, say, six or seven months ago. Her name is Tina Anglade."

"I'd better write it down." Armand stepped to a bench and reached for paper and a carpenter's pencil. "I may see Luc tomorrow at the cockfights."

"You spend your Saturdays at the fights, risking your hard-earned wages on chickens?"

"Only a few cobs now and then. But Luc – now there's a fellow who bets big and almost never loses. Everybody wonders how he does it."

"I don't approve of cockfights and wagering," Polinard said sternly. "But ask him about the little girl, please."

The cockfights Armand attended were held near the coastal village of Petite Anse, just east of the city. A fight was in progress as Armand approached. A white bird and a black-and-red one made the grey sand of the enclosure fly like rain as they tried to kill each other. Spectators leaned over the wall of knee-high bamboo stakes, yelling encouragement.

The white was getting the worst of it. Even as Armand located his friend across the pit, the battle suddenly ended in a spurt of blood. There was a rush to collect bets.

Armand worked his way around to his friend and was not surprised to find Luc Etienne clutching a fistful of gourde notes. Luc must have a sixth sense, he so seldom lost a wager! "Hi," said Armand, grinning. "You've done it again, hey?"

Chuckling, the tall young man stuffed the notes into a pocket of his expensive, multicoloured shirt. He offered Armand a cigarette – another expensive item these days – and the two stayed together through the remainder of the morning. With his friend's help, Armand tripled the money he had brought.

When at last they boarded a tap-tap to the city, Armand remembered to inquire about the little girl and consulted the paper on which he had written her name. "Did you know her when you lived in Bois Sauvage?" he asked.

The little bus clattered along the highway through shimmering waves of heat that rose from the blacktop. Luc gazed at Armand with an expression of incredulity.

Puzzled, Armand said, "What's the matter? All I asked was if you knew – "

"I didn't know her! No!"

"Well, don't get sore with me. What's wrong with you, anyway? I only asked because my boss told me to."

The look of incredulity faded. What took its place was the shrewd one that appeared on Luc's face when he was about to make a wager at the cockfights. "You say this girl is on her way to Bois Sauvage *now*?"

"That's right. With a nurse from the hospital where her memory came back. That is, if it really did come back. You say you never knew her, so I guess it didn't."

"When do they expect to get there?"

"How would I know? They left here yesterday morning. All I want to know for M'sieu Polinard is, was there really a Tina Anglade in your village or is she going there for nothing?"

"She is going there for nothing," Luc said, and then was silent.

Luc was the first to get off. For a moment he stood frowning after the bus as it went on down the street. Then he turned and walked slowly up a cobbled lane to a small house he shared with his latest girlfriend. The girl was not at home. Going into their bedroom, Luc climbed onto the bed and assumed a sitting position there with his back against the headboard and his arms looped about his knees. Then he closed his eyes and fixed his thoughts on a face.

Only twice before had he attempted this, and on both occasions he had only partially succeeded. The second time had been better than the first, though, so maybe he was learning, as Margal had predicted. Aware that he was sweating, he peeled off his expensive shirt and tossed it to the foot of the bed, then resumed the position and closed his eyes again. After a while the sweat ran down his chest in rivers.

The face was beginning to come, though, and there was a difference.

Before, the image had appeared only inside his head, in his mind. But not this time. This time the face of the *bocor* was floating over the lower part of the bed, out of reach.

"Margal, you've come!" Luc whispered.

The eyes stared back at him. No one but Margal had eyes as terribly piercing as those.

"I am not asking for your help at the fights," Luc said then. "This time I have something important to tell you."

The head slowly moved up and down.

"You remember that little girl, Tina Louise Anglade?"

The reply – "Of course!" – seemed to come from a great distance.

"Well, she is on her way back to Bois Sauvage right now. After she disappeared from Dijo Qualon's house she could not remember her name or where she came from, but now she has remembered. A nurse from the Schweitzer hospital is bringing her home!"

The eyes returned his stare with such force that he felt they would stop his breathing. He heard a question and replied, "Yes, I am sure." Then another question and he said, wagging his head, "No, there is nothing I can do. It's too late. They left here yesterday morning."

The floating image slowly faded and was gone. After a while Luc sank down on the bed and lay there shivering in his own sweat until he fell asleep.

II

Standing alone in a clearing, the house was a small one of wattle and clay, roofed with banana-leaf thatch. Only moments before, Kay Gilbert had wondered if her guide, Joseph, really had a stopping place in mind or was merely hoping to chance on one. Glad to have reached any kind of destination after so many hours of sitting on a mule, she gratefully swung an aching leg over the saddle and dropped to the ground.

And stumbled. And sat down hard on her bottom. And then just sat there with her arms looped about her knees, embarrassed at having made herself look foolish in the eyes of the man and woman who had just emerged from the house.

Joseph leaned from his mule to lower Tina to the ground, then leaped down himself and ran to help.

Joseph. Thank God for Joseph. She had encountered enough Haitian young men at the hospital to know the good ones. Clean, intelligent, mild of speech and manner, he was exactly the sort of guide she had hoped for. The corporal at the police post in Trou had produced him.

She had hoped to sleep in Vallière tonight. There was a church, and the priest would put them up. The late start from Cap Haïtien had put that village out of reach, though. And the trail. The trail had been a roller-coaster that made every mile a misery.

Steady climbing was not so bad; you got used to leaning forward and more or less wrapping your arms around your mule's neck. Descending was all right, too, after you accustomed yourself to leaning back, clinging for dear life to the pommel, and hoping to heaven the leather stirrups would not snap under the strain. But the constant shift from one to the other was pure hell, scaring the wits out of you while subjecting your poor tired body to torment. More than once she had envied little Tina, so confidently perched there in the crescent of Joseph's sturdy arms without a care in the world.

As she sat on the ground now, gazing up at the man and woman from the house, Joseph reached her and began helping her to her feet. "M'selle, I know these people," he said. "They will put us up for the night."

He introduced the couple as Edita and Antoine, no last names. She shook their hands. They were in their late sixties, she guessed.

Both were barefoot and nearly toothless; both wore slight facial disfigurements indicating long-ago bouts with yaws.

That curse was pretty well wiped out in Haiti now, thank God.

"Please go into the house," Antoine said. "I will attend to your animals."

"Wait." No stranger must handle the brown leather bag! Lifting it from a saddle-bag, she slung it over her shoulder.

There were two small rooms. The front one contained four homemade chairs and a table; the other, a homemade bed. No connecting door. No kitchen. Cooking was done under a thatch-roofed shelter outside.

"You and the child will use the bed," Edita said in a manner that forbade any protest. "My man and I will sleep here in the front room, as will Joseph. Joseph is my sister's son."

"Thank you." It would not be the first time she had slept in a peasant *caille*. Nurses at the Schweitzer often did things their sisters in more advanced countries might think extraordinary. The bed could harbour bedbugs, of course. More likely, the swept-earth floor was a breeding ground for the little beasties called *chigres*, which got under your toenails and laid eggs there.

"Tina should rest before supper," she said. "I'll help you with the cooking, Edita."

The woman seemed pleased. The child fell asleep as soon as she climbed onto the bed.

Supper was to be a chicken stew, Kay saw when she joined the woman in the kitchen. First, kill the chicken. Edita attended to that with a machete, then cleaned the severed head and put it into the pot along with the rest of the bird. Kay prepared malangas, leeks, and carrots. While working, they talked.

"Where are you going, M'selle, if I may ask?"

"Bois Sauvage. Tina lives there."

"Oh?"

Kay explained, stressing the child's loss of memory.

"Stranger things than that happen around Bois Sauvage," Edita said with a shake of her head. "Do you know the place?"

"No. I don't know these mountains at all. What do you mean by 'stranger things'?"

"Well . . . unnatural things."

"Voodoo?" Any time a country person talked this way, the underlying theme was likely to be voodoo. Or associated mysteries.

"I think not voodoo, M'selle. Rather, sorcery or witchcraft. Do you know about a man named Margal in that district?" More than yaws were responsible for the depth of Edita's frown.

"Margal? No. Who is he?"

"A *bocor*. You know what a *bocor* is?"

"A witch doctor?" Admit you know something and you may learn more.

Edita nodded. "Margal is a powerful one, it is said. Perhaps the most powerful one in all Haiti. Much to be feared."

"And he lives in Bois Sauvage?" Kay was not happy at the prospect of taking Tina to a village dominated by such a man.

"In Legrun, a few miles from there." The frown persisted. "Perhaps you will not encounter him. I hope not."

"I hope not, too."

Night fell while the stew was cooking. The woman used a bottle lamp in the outdoor kitchen but called on her man to bring a lantern when the food was ready to be carried to the house. Kay woke Tina and the five of them sat at the table in the front room where, with the door shut, there was a strong smell of kerosene from the lantern now hanging from a soot-blackened wall peg.

After a few moments of eating in silence, Edita looked across the table at her man and said, "These people are going near to where the crippled *bocor* is, Antoine." The frown was back on her pocked face.

"So Joseph has been telling me."

The nurse in Kay was curious. "Crippled, you say?"

They nodded. "He cannot walk," Antoine supplied. "Different tales are told about the cause of it. One is that he was hurt when a *camion* he was riding in overturned and crushed him. Another is that he became involved in politics and had his legs broken by enemies from the capital. Still another tale is that his mule fell from the cliff at Saut Diable."

"You will be seeing Saut Diable tomorrow," Edita interjected, "and can judge for yourself whether one could survive a fall from there. At any rate, Margal cannot walk but is very much alive."

"And very much to be feared," Antoine said.

Sleep followed the supper. In these remote mountain districts no one stayed up much after nightfall. For one thing, kerosene for illumination had to be transported long distances and was expensive.

But falling asleep on that peasant bed was not going to be easy, Kay discovered. At least, not with all her aches. The mattress was stuffed with some kind of coarse grass that had packed itself into humps and hollows. Each time she sought a more comfortable position, the stuff crackled as though on fire. Tina slept, thank heaven, but in the end Kay could only lie there.

The *caille* was far from quiet, too. One of the three sleepers in the front room snored loudly. In the thatch overhead, geckos croaked and clicked and made rustling sounds. Outside, other lizards sounded like people with sore throats trying to cough, and tree frogs whistled like toy trains. But the outside noises were muffled; the room had no windows. At this altitude, the problem at night was to keep warm, not cool.

A roachlike fire beetle, the kind the peasants called a *coucouyé*, came winging in from the front room, pulsing with green light as it flew. Landing on the wall, it climbed to the thatch and pulsed there like an advertising sign that kept winking on and off.

· In spite of it, Kay felt herself dozing off.

Suddenly Tina, beside her, began to tremble.

Was the child dreaming? If so, it must be another of her bad ones. She had been sleeping with her hands pressed palm to palm under one cheek, and now turned convulsively on her back and began moaning.

Damn! I don't want to wake her but I'll have to if she doesn't stop. Propping herself on one elbow, Kay peered at the twitching face, glad now for the pulsing light of the beetle above them.

Something dropped with a dull plop from the thatch onto the foot of the bed. A gecko, of course, but she glanced down to make sure. The gecko lizards were small and harmless. Kind of cute, in fact.

The nightmare was causing Tina to thrash about in a frenzy that made the whole bed shake. Kay reached for her to wake her. There was a second plop at the foot of the bed. Kay turned her head again.

The fire beetle had fallen from the thatch. Still glowing, it struggled on its back with its legs frantically beating the air, six inches from the gecko.

The lizard's head swivelled in the bug's direction and its beady eyes contemplated the struggle. Its front feet, looking like tiny hands, gripped the blanket. Its slender brown body moved up and down as though doing pushups.

Mouth agape, it suddenly lunged.

Crunch!

With the light gone, the room was suddenly dark as a pit. The child at Kay's side sat bolt upright and began screaming in a voice to shake the mountains.

The rest of what happened was so terrifying that Kay felt a massive urge to scream along with the child.

At the foot of the bed the beetle-devouring gecko had become larger. Was now, in fact, a great black shape half as big as the bed itself. Its feet spread out to grip the blanket, and its huge reptilian head turned toward Kay and the screaming child. Its enormous dragon body began to do pushups again.

It was about to leap, to open its awful jaws and crunch again!

Scarcely aware of what she was doing, Kay grabbed the child and rolled with her off the bed, onto the swept-earth floor near the doorless doorway. Not a second too soon. As she scrabbled for the doorway, pulling the shrieking youngster along with her, she heard the creature's awful jaws snap together. Then, still on hands and knees, still pulling the child after her, she reached the front room.

The screaming had aroused the sleepers there. Antoine was lighting the lantern. His woman caught hold of Tina and hugged her, telling her to stop screaming, she would be all right. Joseph, helping Kay to her feet, peered strangely at her, then turned to look into the back room as Antoine stepped to the doorway and held the lantern high to put some light in there.

Tina stopped screaming.

Kay stepped to the doorway to look into the room she had just frantically crawled out of.

Nothing.

But I saw it! It was there! It was huge and leaped at us!

After a while Antoine said, "M'selle, what frightened you?"

"I don't know."

There was nothing on the bed. Not even the small lizard that had eaten the fire beetle.

You imagined it, Gilbert. But Tina had become frightened first. Tina, not she, had done the screaming.

She looked at her watch. In an hour or so, daylight would replace the frightening dark. Backing away from the bed, she returned to the front room where Edita was now seated on a chair with Tina on her lap.

"Are you all right, M'selle?"

"I guess so. But I know I can't sleep anymore. Just let me sit here and wait for morning."

The woman nodded.

Kay sat. She had gone to bed in her clothes, expecting the night to be cold. She looked at Tina, then up at the woman's disfigured face. "Is she asleep?"

"I believe so, yes."

The silence returned.

Joseph and Antoine came back into the room. Both glanced at the child first, then focused on Kay, no doubt awaiting an explanation.

Don't, she warned herself. *If you even try, Joseph might decide to go back.*

But they were not willing just to stand there staring at her. "M'selle, what happened, please?" Joseph said.

He had to be answered somehow. "Well . . . I'm ashamed, but I believe I just had a bad dream and woke Tina up, poor thing, and she began screaming."

"That is all?"

"I'm afraid so."

By the way they looked at her, she knew they had not bought it.

III

In the village of Vallière the expedition was stalled for a time while Joseph talked with people he knew. But not for long. Beyond, the trail continued its slow, twisting climb and the stillness returned.

The mountain stillness. No bird cry or leaf rustle could have much effect on a silence so profound, nor could the muffled thumping of the mules' hoofs over the layers of leaf mold. She felt as though she were riding through another world.

Now at last the trail was levelling off and she saw Joseph ten yards ahead, looking back and waiting for her. As usual, Tina sat snugly in front of him, fenced in by his arms. Kay pulled up alongside.

"For a little while it will be hard now, M'selle," Joseph said. "Should we stop a while?"

"I'm not tired."

"Well, all right. Perhaps we should get this place behind us, anyway."

Remembering something the woman had said last night, Kay frowned. "Is this the place they call Saut Diable?" It meant, she knew, Devil's Leap.

He nodded.

She strained to see ahead. The track, mottled with tree shadows, sloped down into a kind of trench where seasonal rains had scored it to a depth of eight or ten feet. Riding through such a place, you had to remove your feet from the stirrups and lift them high. Otherwise, if the mule lurched sideways, you could end up with a crushed leg.

"You must make your animal descend very slowly, M'selle," Joseph solemnly warned.

She nodded, feeling apprehensive.

"But don't even start to go down," he said, "until I call to you from below."

"Until you call to me?"

"At the bottom, the trail turns sharply to the right, like this."

Dramatically he drew a right angle in the air. "I will be waiting there to help you."

She was not sure she understood, but watched him ride on and noticed how carefully he put his mule to the trench. Waiting at the top, she saw him disappear around a curve. It seemed a long time before she heard him calling her, from below.

Scared, she urged her own mule forward.

It was the worst stretch they had encountered, not only steep but slippery. The red-earth walls were barely far enough apart to permit passage. Her mule took short, mincing steps, stumbling at times. At one twist of the trail he went to his knees, all but pitching her over his head, then was barely able to struggle up again. With her feet out of the stirrups, she marvelled that she was able to stay on the animal's back.

Luckily, the walls were a little farther apart at the bottom of the trench, and her feet were back in place. Joseph waited for her with feet apart and hands upraised, clutching a dead stick as long as his arm. Behind him was only empty blue sky.

"Come slowly and hang on!" he shouted at her.

As she reached him, he swung the stick. *Whap!* It caught her mule across the left side of the neck and caused the animal to wheel abruptly to the right. As she clung to the pommel to keep from falling, she got the full picture and promptly wet herself.

Joseph had been standing on the edge of a sheer drop, to make sure her mule didn't take one step too many before turning. Had the animal done so, both she and it – and Joseph, too, no doubt – would have gone hurtling down into a valley hundreds of feet below!

Her mule stopped. A little distance ahead, Joseph's animal was waiting, with Tina aboard and looking back. The trail was a ribbon of rock no more than six feet wide, winding along a cliff face for a hundred yards or more with awesome heights above and those terrifying depths below. Joseph, still clutching his stick, caught up with her and gave her mule a pat on the shoulder, as if to apologize for clubbing it.

"You are all right, M'selle?"

"I'll never be all right again."

He chuckled. "Actually, I was not worried. This grey beast of yours has been here before and is not stupid. I only wanted to be sure he would remember that place. Just give him his head now and let him follow my animal along here. Okay?"

"Okay," she said, hoping he would not notice her wet pants.

He walked on ahead and swung himself into the saddle, saying something to Tina that made the child look at him with adoring eyes. His mule started forward, and Kay's clop-clopped along behind it.

Then the trail began to go dark.

Kay looked up to see what had happened to the sun. It was there but fading, and the sky began to look like a thick sheet of overexposed photographic film, becoming blacker every second.

She looked down. A dark mist rose from the valley which only a moment ago had been green. But *was* it a mist? Distinctly, she smelled smoke and saw flames. Then, like an exhalation from the earth itself, the darkness swirled up to engulf her.

Suddenly she could see nothing in front of her, nothing above or below, nothing behind. All creation was black and boiling.

Her mule stopped. Why? Because in her sudden terror she had jerked the reins, or because he, too, was now blind? What was happening was unreal. It was no more real than the harmless gecko that had become a ravenous dragon last night.

Margal, she thought. *The bocor who can't walk. We're getting closer and he doesn't want us to.*

The sky, the valley, the trail snaking along the cliffside – all had disappeared now. The darkness had engulfed them and was furiously alive, shot through with flames and reeking of smoke. The smoke made her cough and she had to cling to the saddle as she struggled to breathe.

And now the thunder. Peal upon peal of thunder, filling the fiery darkness in the valley and bouncing off the cliff in front of and behind her. Only it wasn't thunder she was hearing, was it? It was a booming of drums, ever so many drums. The sound assaulted her head and she wanted to scream but knew she must not. A scream might frighten the grey mule.

The animal wasn't easily frightened. More than once he had proved that. But he was still standing motionless, waiting for her to urge him forward again.

Should she do that? Had his world, too, gone mad? Or did he still see the trail in front of him, Joseph and Tina on the mule ahead, and the green valley below?

I can't stay here. Can't risk it. But there is no way to turn and go back.

Should she try to dismount and walk back? No, no! The world was so dark, she might as well be blind. If she tried to slide from the saddle on the cliff side, the mule might step away to make room for her. Might take a step too many and go plunging over the edge. And if she tried to dismount on *that* side without knowing where the edge was, she might drop straight into space.

She clucked to the grey as Joseph had taught her. Touched him, oh so gently, with her heels. "Go on, fella. But slow, go slow."

He gave his head a shake and moved forward through the smoke and drum-thunder, while she prayed he could see the trail and would not walk off the edge or grind her into the wall.

If he does grind me into the wall, I'll know he can't see any better than I. Then I can pull him up and at least wait. But if he goes wrong on the outside, God help me.

The mule plodded on through the unreal darkness. The drums thundered. Tongues of scarlet leaped high from the valley – high enough to curl in over the trail and stab at her feet, as if to force her to lift them from the stirrups and lose her balance. Fighting back the panic, she clutched the saddle with both hands and ground her knees into the mule's sides for an added grip.

What – oh God! – was happening to Joseph and Tina? She could not even see them now.

Saut Diable. The Devil's Leap. *Had* the man named Margal been crippled in a fall from here? She didn't believe it. No one could survive such a fall.

Dear God, how much longer?

But the grey could see! She was convinced of it now. He trudged along as though this journey through the nightmare were all in the day's work. Not once did he brush her leg against the cliff, so she had to assume that not once did he venture too close to the drop on the other side. Was the darkness only in her mind, then? Was Margal responsible for it?

Never mind that now, Gilbert. Just hang on. Pray.

It almost seemed that the one creating the illusion knew his grisly scheme was not working. Knew she had not panicked and spooked the mule into plunging over the edge with her. The thunder of the drums grew louder. She thought her skull would crack under the pounding. The darkness became a gigantic whirlpool that seemed certain to suck her into its vortex. She tried shutting her eyes. It didn't help.

I'm not seeing these things. I'm thinking them.

The big grey walked on.

The whirlpool slowed and paled. The flames diminished to flickerings. The sky lightened and let the sun blur through again. Slowly the image of the other mule took shape ahead, with Joseph and Tina on its back.

She looked down and saw darkness leaving the valley, the smoke drifting away in wisps, the green returning. It was like the end of a storm.

Ahead, Joseph had stopped where the cliff passage ended and the trail entered a forest again. Dismounting, he swung Tina down beside him. The child clung to his legs. On reaching them, Kay slid from the saddle, too.

She and Joseph gazed at each other, the Haitian's handsome face the hue of wood ash, drained of all sparkle, all life. Trembling against him, the child, too, stared at Kay, with eyes that revealed the same kind of terror.

The nightmare wasn't just for me. They rode through it, too.

Kay felt she had to say something calming. "Well . . . we're here, aren't we? Saut Diable is behind us." *Brilliant*, she thought. *Just what we didn't need.*

"M'selle . . . what happened?"

"What do *you* think happened?" *Get him talking. Get that ghastly look off his face. Off Tina's, too.*

"Everything went dark, M'selle. The valley was on fire. The flames reached all the way up to the trail and the smoke made me cough."

She only looked at him.

"Drumming," he continued hoarsely. "I heard all three drums — the manman, the seconde, the bula. And I think even a fourth. Even the giant assotor."

"It was all in our minds," Kay said. "It wasn't real."

"M'selle, it *happened*." He turned his ashen face to look at Tina. "Didn't it, *ti-fi*?"

Still too frightened to speak, the child could only nod.

"No." Kay shook her head. "The drumming was only thunder, and there was no real fire. Walk back and look."

He refused to budge. When she took him by the hand to lead him back, he froze.

"Just to the cliff," she said. "So we can see."

"No, M'selle!"

"It didn't happen, Joseph. I'm telling you, it *did not* happen. We only imagined it. Now come."

His head jerked again from side to side, and she could not budge him.

At the hospital she was known to have a temper when one was called for. "Damn it, Joseph, don't be so stubborn! Come and see!" Her yank on his wrist all but pulled him off his feet.

He allowed himself to be hauled far enough back along the trail so that he could peer into the valley. It was frighteningly far down but in no way marked by fire.

"You see? If there had really been a fire raging down there, you would still see and smell smoke. Now will you believe me?"

"I know what I *saw*!"

"You know what you think you saw, that's all." Oh God, if only there were words in Creole for this kind of discussion, but there were not. It was a bare-bones language, scarcely adequate even for dealing with basics. So few words to *think* with.

Well, then, stick to basics. Stop trying to explain things.

"All right, Joseph. There was a fire, but it's out now. Let's go, hey?"

He shook his head. "No, M'selle. Not me. I am turning back."

"*What*?"

"These things that have happened are a warning. Worse will happen if we go on."

Guessing her face was telltale white, she confronted him with her hands on her hips. "You can't do this to me, Joseph. You agreed to guide me to Bois Sauvage. I've already paid you half the money!"

"I will give it back. Every cob."

"Joseph, stop this. Stop it right now! I have to take Tina home, and you have to help me. These crazy things that have happened don't concern us. They were meant for someone else. Who would want to stop Tina from returning home?"

"I am going back, M'selle. I am afraid."

"You can't be such a coward!"

He only shrugged.

She worked on him. For twenty minutes she pleaded, cajoled, begged him to consider Tina, threatened him with the wrath of the police who had hired him out to her. Long before she desisted, she knew it was hopeless. He liked her, he was fond of the child, but he was terrified.

"All right. If you won't go any farther, you can at least tell me how to get there. Because I'm going on without you."

"M'selle, you must not!"

"Does this trail lead to Bois Sauvage, or can I get lost?"

In a pathetic whisper, with his gaze downcast, he said, "It is the only road. You will not get lost."

"Please rearrange our gear then, so Tina and I will have what we need." Extracting the brown leather shoulder-bag from her mule's saddle-bag, she stepped aside with it.

He obeyed in silence, while she and Tina watched him. The child's eyes were enormous.

"Now lift Tina onto my mule, please. I know I'll have to do it myself from now on because of your cowardice, but you can do it one more time."

He picked the child up. Before placing her on the grey mule, he brushed his lips against her cheek. His own cheeks were wet.

Kay carefully swung herself into the saddle, then turned and looked down at him. "You won't change your mind?"

"M'selle, I will wait for you at my aunt's house, where we stayed last night."

"Don't bother," she retorted bitterly. "A lizard might eat you."

Tight-lipped and full of anger, she rode on.

After the first hour, her fear began to subside. It had been real enough earlier, despite the bravado she had feigned for Joseph's benefit. But the trail was not so formidable now. At least, they had not encountered any more Devil's Leaps.

Mile after mile produced only bird-song and leaf-rustle. She and the child talked to push back the stillness.

"Will you be glad to see your mother and father, baby?"

"Oh, yes!"

"What are they like? Tell me about them."

"Maman's pretty, like you."

"Bless you. And your father?"

"He works all the time."

"Doing what?"

"Growing things. Yams, mostly. We have goats and chickens, too."

"What's his name?"

"Metellus Anglade."

"And your mother's?"

"Fifine Bonhomme."

Not married, of course. Few peasants married. But many living in *plaçage* were more faithful than "civilized" people in other countries who *were* married.

"Will you be glad to see your sister and two brothers too?"

"Yes, Miss Kay."

"Are they older than you?"

"Only Rosemarie. The twins are younger."

"Your brothers are twins? I didn't know that. It must make your family very special." In voodoo, twins played important roles. There were even special services for the spirits of *marassas*.

"Would you like to know about my village, Miss Kay?" Tina asked.

"I certainly would. Tell me about it."

"Well, it's not as big as the one we rode through this morning. Vallière, I mean. But it has a nice marketplace, and a spring for water . . ."

Just talk, to pass the time. Then, as the afternoon neared its end, the trail ascended to a high plateau, levelled off, and began to widen. Wattle and mud *cailles* appeared on either side, and people stood behind bamboo fences gazing curiously at the strangers. Had they ever seen a white woman before?

But she was not the main object of their attention, Kay presently realized. They were staring mostly at the child who sat in front of her.

Tina stared back at them. This was her village.

The road divided, and Kay reined the grey mule to a halt. "Which way, Tina?"

"That way!" The child's voice was shrill with excitement.

Kay reined the mule to the left, looked back, and saw the trailing crowd of villagers turn with her.

What did they want? And if they recognized the child, why in heaven's name weren't they calling her name and waving to her? Could the hunch that had prompted her to bring along the brown shoulder-bag be valid, after all?

The trail they followed now was only a downhill path through a lush but unkempt jungle of broad-leafed plantains and wild mangoes. More *cailles* lined its sides. More people stared from yards and doorways, then trooped out to join the silent and somehow sinister procession.

Oh God, don't tell me things are going to go wrong now that I've finally got here! What's the matter with these people?

"There it is!" Bouncing up and down on the mule, Tina raised a trembling right arm to point.

Standing by itself near a curve of the path, behind a respectable fence of hand-hewn pickets, the *caille* was a little larger than most of the others, with a roof of bright new zinc. "We're home! That's my house!" the child shrilled, all but out of her mind with excitement.

End of the line, Kay thought with relief. We made it. Be proud, gal.

She turned to look at the crowd behind them and was not proud. Only apprehensive. Worse than apprehensive. Downright scared.

At the gate in the fence she reined in the mule, slid wearily from the saddle, and reached up for Tina. Out of the house came a slender, good-looking woman of thirty or so, wearing a dress made of feed bags. Staring at Kay, she walked to the gate. Then her gaze shifted from Kay to Tina, and she stopped as though she had walked into a stone wall. And began screaming.

The sound tore the stillness to shreds and brought a man from the house, stumbling as he ran. He reached the woman in time to catch her under the arms as she sank to her knees. Standing there holding her, he too looked at the strangers and began to make noises. Nothing as loud as the woman's screaming but a guttural "huh huh huh huh" that seemed to burble, not from his mouth alone, but from his whole convulsed face.

From the crowd came a response like a storm roar, with words flashing in and out like jabs of lightning. "*Mort! Mort! Li Mort!*"

Clasping the youngster's hand, Kay pushed the gate open and walked to the kneeling woman. There was nothing she could do to stop the nightmare sounds. *Don't listen to it, Gilbert. Just do what you have to.*

"Is this your mother, Tina?"

For answer, the child threw her arms around the kneeling woman's neck and began sobbing, "Maman! Maman!"

The woman wrenched herself free and staggered erect. She looked at her daughter in horror, then turned and ran like a blinded, wild animal across the bare-earth yard, past a cluster of graves at its edge, into a field where tall stalks of *piti mi* swallowed her from sight.

The man continued to stand there, gazing at Tina as though his eyes would explode.

The child looked up at him imploringly. "Papa . . ."

"Huh huh huh . . ."

"It's me, papa. Tina!"

He lurched backward, throwing up his arms. "You're dead!"

"No, Papa!"

"Yes you are! You're dead!"

"Papa, please . . ." Reaching for him, the child began to cry. And Kay's reliable temper surged up to take over.

She strode to the man and confronted him, hands on hips and eyes blazing. "This is nonsense, M'sieu Anglade! Because the child has been missing for a while doesn't mean she's dead. You can see she isn't!"

As he stared back at her, his heavy-lipped mouth kept working, though soundlessly now. His contorted face oozed sweat.

"Do you hear what I'm saying, M'sieu? Your daughter is all right! I'm a nurse, and I know."

"You – don't – understand."

"What don't I understand?"

As though his feet were deep in the red-brown earth and he could move them only with great difficulty, he turned in the direction the child's mother had fled. Lifting his right arm as though it weighed a ton, he pointed.

"What do you mean?" Kay demanded, then looked down at the weeping child and said, "Don't cry, baby. I'll get to the bottom of this."

Metellus Anglade reached out and touched her on the arm. "Come."
He began walking slowly across the yard, his bare feet scraping the
earth. Beyond the cluster of graves toward which he walked was the
field of kaffir corn. What could there be in such a field that would
make him afraid of his own daughter?

Kay followed him, but looked back. Tina gazed after them with her
hands at her face, obviously all but destroyed by what had happened.
The crowd in the road was silent again. The whole length of the fence
was lined with starers, the road packed solid, but no one had come into
the yard even though the gate hung open. She had neglected to tie the
grey mule, she realized. Should she go back and do so, to make sure
the crowd wouldn't spook him? No. It could wait.

Metellus Anglade reached the edge of the yard and trudged on
through the gravestones – not stones, really, but crudely crafted
concrete forms resembling small houses resting on coffin-shaped
slabs of the same material. Nothing special. You saw such grave
markers all over Haiti. Kay looked beyond to the corn field.

Where was the woman?

Suddenly the leaden feet of her guide stopped and, preoccupied as
she was, Kay bumped into him. He caught her by the arm to steady
her. With his other hand he pointed to the last of the graves, one that
was either new or had been newly whitewashed.

"Look."

The name was not properly carved. Like those on the other
markers, it had merely been scratched in with a sharpened stick
before the concrete hardened. It was big and bold, though. Kay had
no difficulty reading it.

TINA LOUISE CHRISTINE ANGLADE. 1984–1992.

Kay's temper boiled to the surface again as she turned on him.
"You shouln't have done this! Graves are for people you've buried,
not for someone you only think might be dead!"

He looked at her now without flinching, and she saw how much he
resembled Tina. About thirty, he was taller than most mountain peasants and had good, clean features. "M'selle, you don't understand.
My daughter *is* buried here."

"What?"

"She died. I myself made the coffin. Her own mother prepared her
for burial. I put her into the coffin and nailed it shut, and when we
put it into this grave and shovelled the earth over her, this yard was
full of witnesses. All those people you see standing in the road were
here. The whole village."

Kay got a grip on herself. *Watch it, Gilbert. Don't, for God's sake, say the wrong thing now.* "M'sieu, I can only say you must have made a mistake."

With dignity he moved his head slowly from side to side. "There was no mistake, M'selle. From the time she was placed in the coffin until the earth covered her, the coffin was never for one moment unguarded. Either my wife or I was with her every moment."

We can't stand here talking, Kay thought desperately. Not with that mob in the road watching us. "M'sieu, can we go into the house?"

He nodded.

"And Tina? She is not dead, I assure you. All that happened was that she lost her memory for a time and could not recall who she was."

He hesitated, but nodded again.

They walked back across the yard to Tina, and Kay put a hand on the child's shoulder. "Come, baby. It's going to be all right." Metellus Anglade led the way to the house. Kay followed with Tina. The villagers by the fence still stared.

If they actually think they buried this child, I don't blame them. I'd probably do the same.

The house seemed larger than the one Tina and she had slept in the night before. But before attempting an appraisal or even sitting down, she said, "M'sieu Anglade, will you please see about my mule? He should be unsaddled and given some water, and tied were he can eat something."

He did not seem eager to comply.

"You'll have to put me up for the night or find someone nearby who will," she went on firmly. "So please bring in the saddle-bags, too." Especially the one with my shoulder-bag in it, she added mentally.

He frowned at her. "You wish to spend the night *here*?"

Kay made a production of peering at her watch, though she knew the time well enough. "I can't be expected to start back to Trou at this hour, can I? That's where my jeep is. I've brought your daughter all the way from the Schweitzer Hospital, M'sieu Anglade. Do you know how far that is?"

"All that way?" He peered at her with new respect, then looked again at Tina. What was he thinking? That if the child had been at the Schweitzer, she must not be a ghost, after all?

"The mule, please," Kay repeated. "Tina and I will just sit here until you return. Believe me, we're tired." As he turned to the door, she spoke again. "And try to find her mother, will you? I must talk to you both."

While he was gone, she asked Tina to show her around. In addition to the big front room, which was crowded with crude but heavily varnished homemade furniture, there were three bedrooms. But despite the zinc roof, which indicated a measure of wealth in such a village, the floors were of earth, hard-packed and shiny from years of being rubbed by bare feet. At least there would be no lizards dropping from the thatch.

As they waited for Metellus to return, Tina began to cry again. "Come here, baby," Kay said quietly.

The child stepped into the waiting circle of her arm.

"Listen to me, love. We don't know what's going on here, but we're not going to be afraid of it. You hear?"

"I hear, Miss Kay."

"You just concentrate on being brave and let me do the talking. For a while, at least. Can you do that?"

Tina nodded.

Kay patted her on the bottom. "Good girl. Now go sit down and try to relax. The big thing is, you're home."

It took Metellus Anglade a long time to attend to the mule. Or perhaps he spent much of that time trying to locate his woman. Daylight was about finished when at last he came through the door, lugging the saddlebags and followed by Tina's mother.

Having already decided how to handle the situation, Kay promptly rose and offered her hand. "Hello, Fifine Bonhomme, how are you? I'm Nurse Gilbert from the Schweitzer Hospital."

Tina had said her mother was pretty, hadn't she? Well, she was, or might be if she could get over being terrified. A certain firmness was called for at this point, Kay decided.

"Sit down, Fifine. I must talk to you."

The woman looked fearfully at her daughter. She had not spoken to the girl, and obviously had no intention of embracing her. But then, she actually thought she was staring at a child who was buried in that grave outside, didn't she?

Suddenly the door burst open and three children stormed into the room: a girl who resembled Tina but was a little older, and two peas-in-a-pod boys a year or so younger. Rosemarie and the twins, Kay thought. All three were out of breath but remarkably clean for country kids. Barefoot, of course, but decently dressed. And handsome.

At sight of Tina, they stopped as though they had been clubbed. Their eyes grew bigger and bigger. The girl backed up a step. The twins, as if they were one person, took two steps forward and whispered Tina's name in unison.

Tina lurched from her chair and stumbled to her knees in front of them. Wrapping her arms around their legs, she cried so hard she must have been blinded by her own tears.

Reassured, Rosemarie dared to advance again. Dared to sink to *her* knees and press her face against her sister's.

"Let the children go into another room," Kay said to their mother. "I would like to talk to you and Metellus alone."

Fifine Bonhomme only gazed at her brood in a silence of apprehension. It was their father who told them what to do.

"Now listen, both of you," Kay said. "I'm going to tell you what I know about your daughter, how she was found by Father Turnier and – " She paused. "Do you know Father Turnier?"

"The priest who used to be in Vallière?" Metellus said. "We know of him."

"All right. I'm going to tell you how he found her and what happened afterward. Then *you* are going to tell *me* why her name is on that grave out there. You understand?"

They nodded.

"After that," Kay said, "We'll decide what's to be done here."

She took her time telling it. Had to, because her Creole was not that good. She even included a brief lecture on amnesia, because it was so terribly important for them to understand that the youngster was perfectly normal.

In telling of her journey with Tina from the hospital to Bois Sauvage, though, she was very, very careful not to mention the dragon lizard or the strange occurrence at Devil's Leap.

"Now then," she said firmly in conclusion, "*you* do the talking, please. Explain that grave to me."

"Tina became ill and died," said Metellus.

"What made her ill?"

"We don't know. We asked her if she had eaten anything the rest of us had not. Only a mango, she said. A boy named Luc Etienne gave her two of them when she was passing his yard on her way home from a friend's house. One was for her, one for the twins. But nobody was at home when she got here, so she ate hers and when we returned an hour or so later, she was not well."

"How do you mean, not well?"

"Her stomach hurt and she had *la fièv*. A really high fever. I went at once for the *houngan*. He is a good man. He came and did things. Brewed a tea for her and used his hands on her – things like that. He stayed the whole night trying to make her well. But in the morning she died."

"Who said she was dead? This *houngan*?"

"All of us." Metellus returned her gaze without flinching. "It is not in dispute that she was dead when we buried her. When someone dies, the people we call in may not be as learned as your doctors at the hospital, but they know how to determine if life has ended. Tina was dead."

"And you think this mango that was given her by — by whom? — "

"Luc Etienne."

"— might have caused her death? Poisoned her, you mean?"

"*Something* made her ill. She had not been sick before."

"There were two mangoes, you said."

"Yes."

"Did anyone eat the other?"

He shook his head.

"What became of it?"

"After the funeral we opened it up, I and some others, to see if it had been tampered with. It seemed to be all right, but, of course, you can't always be sure. Some people are wickedly clever with poisons. Anyway, we buried it."

"Did you talk to this Luc Etienne?"

"Yes, M'selle."

"What did he say?"

"Only that the mangoes were from a tree in his yard, perfectly innocent, and he gave them to Tina for herself and the twins because he was fond of children. Especially of them."

Speaking for the first time, Tina's mother said, "Our children liked him. He was a nice young man."

"What do you mean, *was*?"

"He is not here now."

"Oh? When did he leave?"

"Soon after the funeral, didn't he, Metellus?"

Metellus nodded.

"Where did he go?" Kay asked.

Metellus shrugged. "We heard to Cap Haïtien, where he makes a lot of money betting on cockfights."

Feeling she had sat long enough, Kay rose stiffly and walked to the door. It was open, but would soon have to be closed because the yard was turning dark. There were still people at the fence. Turning back into the room, she frowned at Tina's father. "And there is no doubt in your mind that Tina was in the coffin when you buried it?"

"None at all. No."

"Are you saying, then, that the child I've brought back to you is not your daughter but someone else?"

He looked at his woman and she at him. Turning to meet Kay's demanding gaze again, he shrugged. "M'selle, what can we say?"

With her fists against her hips for perhaps the fourth time that day, Kay faced them in a resurgence of anger. "You can admit there's been a mistake, that's what you can say! Because, look. When the name Bois Sauvage was read to this child by a doctor reading a map, she clapped her hands and cried out, "That's where I live!" And then she remembered her name – her full name, just as you've got it inscribed on that grave out there. Tina Louise Christine Anglade. And she remembered *your* names and her sister's and the twins'. So if she isn't your Tina, who in the world do you think she is?"

The woman whispered something.

"What?" Kay said.

"She is a zombie."

"What did you say?"

"*Li sé zombie*," the woman stubbornly repeated, then rose and turned away, muttering that she had to begin preparing supper.

Only because Kay insisted did the woman allow her "zombie" daughter to sit at the supper table with her other children. After the meal, Kay stubbornly tried again to break down her resistance, and again failed.

She probably could have convinced Metellus had the child's mother been less afraid, she told herself. The father was strong and intelligent but unwilling, obviously, to make trouble for himself by challenging this woman he slept with. It was a tragic situation, with no solution in sight.

Go to bed, Gilbert. Maybe during the night Metellus will find himself some guts.

She lay with her right arm around Tina, the child's head on her breast. A lamp burned low on a chest of drawers made mostly of woven sisal.

"Miss Kay?" Tina whispered.

"What, baby?"

"They think I'm dead. Did I die, Miss Kay?"

"Of course not."

"Why do they say I did, then? Even Rosemarie and the twins."

"Because they . . ." *Oh, Christ, baby, I don't know why! I'm way out of my depth here and don't know what to do about it.*

She was so tired, so very tired. All day long on a mule, most of the time scared because Joseph had left her alone with the child in an unknown wilderness. Her knees ached, her thighs burned, her arches must be permanently warped from the stupid stirrups, even her fingers were cramped from holding the reins. And now this impasse with the child's mother.

She listened to Tina's breathing and it calmed her a little. After a while she dozed off.

There was a tapping sound at the room's only window. The window had no glass in it, and she had decided not to close the shutters lest the smell of the kerosene lamp give her more of a headache than she already had. The tapping was on one of the open shutters, and she sat up in bed and turned her head in that direction, still half asleep. The voice of Metellus Anglade whispered to her from the opening.

"M'selle . . . M'selle . . . I have to show you something!"

She looked at the watch on her wrist. Why, on this crazy pilgrimage, was she always trying to find out the time in the middle of the night?

Three-ten. Well, at least she'd been asleep for a while and would be rested tomorrow for whatever might happen.

"What do you want?"

"Come out here, please. Be careful not to wake anyone!"

"All right. Just give me a minute."

She had worn pyjamas to bed and was damned if she would get dressed at this idiot hour just to go into the yard to see what the man wanted. Pulling on her sneaks, she left the bedroom, walked silently across the dim front room with its clutter of chairs, stepped outside, and found him waiting.

"Come!" he whispered, taking her by the arm.

He led her across the yard, through moonlight bright enough to paint the ground with dark shadows of house, fence, trees, and graves. He walked her to the graves. Next to the one with Tina's name on it was a hole now, with a spade thrust upright in the excavated dirt piled at its edge.

"Look, M'selle!"

Peering into the hole, she saw what he had done. Unable to move the concrete slab that covered the grave, he had dug down beside it, then tunnelled under. Far enough under, at least, to find out what he wanted to know.

"You see? The coffin is gone!"

She nodded. There was nothing to argue about. He hadn't dug enough dirt out to risk having the slab sag into the excavation, but had certainly proved there was no wooden box under it. She stood there hearing all the usual night sounds in the silence.

"How could anyone have stolen it without moving the slab?" she asked, but knew the answer before finishing the question. Let him say it anyway.

"M'selle, we don't do the tombing right away. Not until the earth has settled. In this case, more than six weeks passed before I could go to Trou for the cement."

Which you brought back on a mule, she thought, walking the whole way back yourself so the mule could carry it. And then you built this elaborate concrete thing over the grave to show your love for a daughter whose body had already been stolen.

"Metellus, I don't understand." Let him explain the whole thing, though she guessed how he would do that, too.

"There can be only one answer, M'selle. I know I put my daughter into a coffin and buried her here. The coffin is not here now. So . . . she was stolen and made into a zombie."

"Meaning she was not really dead."

"Well, there are two kinds of zombies, as perhaps you know. Those who truly die and are restored to life by sorcery; that is one kind. Others are poisoned in various ways so they only seem to die, then are taken from their graves and restored."

"You think Tina was poisoned?"

"Now I do. Yes."

"With the mango you told me about?"

He reached for the spade and, holding it in both hands, turned to frown at her. "Luc Etienne gave her two mangoes, one for herself and one for the twins to share. Do you know what I think? I think that on the way home she got them mixed up, and when she found no one at home and ate her mango, the one she ate was the one she had been told to give to the twins."

"I don't know what you mean." This time she really did not.

"Twins are different from ordinary people," Metellus said. "He wanted them for some special purpose."

"Who? This fellow Etienne?"

"No, not Etienne." With a glance toward the house, he began quietly putting the earth back into the hole. "At least, not for himself. Luc was friendly with a much more important person at that time. With a *bocor* named Margal, who lives in Legrun. There are people here who say Luc Etienne was Margal's pupil."

"The one who can't walk," Kay said.

He stopped the spade in mid stroke. "You know of him?"

"I think he tried to stop me from coming here."

"Very likely. Because do you know what I believe happened after he stole the coffin from this grave? I think he brought Tina back to life the way they do – with leaves or herbs or whatever – and then sold her to someone in some distant place where she would not be known. He had hoped for the twins, but even Tina was worth something as a servant."

"And she wandered away from whoever bought her."

"Yes. And the priest found her."

"How could Margal have known I was bringing her back here?"

"Who can say, M'selle? But he probably knows we are standing here this very minute, discussing him." Metellus plied the spade faster now, obviously anxious to get the job finished. But again he stopped and faced her. "M'selle, Tina must not stay here. Margal will surely kill her!"

"You think so?"

"Yes, yes! To protect himself. To save his reputation!"

She thought about it, and nodded.

The hole refilled at last, he turned to her. "M'selle, I love my daughter. You must know that by now."

"I'm sure you do."

"Fifine, too, loves her. But things can never be the same here now."

Kay gazed at him in silence.

Thoughtfully he said, "I have a brother in Port-au-Prince, M'selle, who is two years younger than I and has only one child. He would give Tina a good home, even send her to school there. She must not stay here. Everyone here in Bois Sauvage knows she died and was buried in this yard and must now be a zombie. Even if Margal did not destroy her, she would forever be shunned."

"You want me to take her to your brother? Is that what you're saying?"

"Will you? I will ride out with you to where your jeep is."

Kay thought about it while he stood before her, desperately awaiting her reply. A white owl flew across the yard from the road to the field of kaffir corn. Time passed.

"I will do it on one condition," Kay said at last.

On the verge of tears, he seemed to hold his breath. "And – that is?

"That before we leave here you take me to Legrun, to visit this *bocor* who can't walk, this Margal. Will you do that?"

Trembling, he stared at her with bulging eyes. But at last he nodded.

V

The grey mule carried no saddle-bags this time, but Kay had slung the brown leather bag over her shoulder before leaving the Anglade house in Bois Sauvage. As her animal plodded along after the one ridden by Tina's father, she realized she would have had a difficult time attempting the trip by herself.

It was only four miles to Legrun, Metellus had said, but the road was difficult. That had been his word: difficult. Just beyond the Bois Sauvage marketplace, which was deserted because today was not the weekly market day, a path to the right had been marked by a cross to Baron Samedi. When asked why he had stopped and dismounted there for a moment, her guide had replied with a shrug, "It is sometimes well to ask the baron for protection, M'selle."

"You think this Margal is into voodoo, then?"

"No, no, M'selle. He is an *evil* man, a *bocor*!"

Not the same thing at all, of course. Voodoo was a religion. A *bocor* was a sorcerer, a witch-doctor, a loner. And the one they were about to confront was also a monster.

For an eternity the mules toiled up a ladder of boulders, with the high-mountain forest walling them in on both sides. At times even the sky was hidden by massed tree limbs. Then the path straggled over a rocky plateau painted gold by the sun, and plunged down through a trench.

The trench gradually widened into a grassy clearing dotted with thatch-roofed huts. Kay counted five of them. From a vertical cliff on the right tumbled a forty-foot waterfall that filled the vale with sound. Beyond the peasant huts stood a substantial, metal-roofed house painted bright red.

Margal's, she supposed. And she was looking at the first painted house she had seen since leaving Vallière. Margal the Sorcerer apparently believed in being different, and was wealthy enough to indulge his whims.

Red houses were not common in Haiti. This one brought to mind a poem, or part of a poem, she had read in a volume of verse by a Haitian writer known to be deeply interested in the occult.

> *High in a mountain clearing*
> *In a red, red house*
> *In the wilds of Haiti,*
> *Black candles burn*
> *In a room of many colors.*

Had the poet visited this place? If so, he must be a brave man to have dared write about it. But the book was in French, and Margal, being a peasant, could probably not read French. Or even any of the versions of written Creole.

In front of her, Metellus had reined his mule to a halt. As she caught up to him, he lifted an arm to point. "Margal lives there in the red house, M'selle," he said without looking at her. "I will take the mules and wait for you by the waterfall."

She drew in a breath to slow the beating of her heart. "You mean you're not going to confront him with me?"

"M'selle, no." He shook his head. "I do not have your courage."

"Very well." Disappointed but not angry, she dismounted and walked her mule the few steps to where Metellus could lean from the saddle and grasp its reins. Then, with her head high, she strode the last hundred yards alone.

On reaching the door, she lifted a hand to the brown leather bag to make sure it was still in place. Throughout the journey it had been a nuisance; now it was a comfort. She knocked. In a moment the door swung open. A boy about twelve years old, wearing only ragged khaki pants, stood gazing up at her.

She went through the usual peasant formalities. "*Honneur, ti-moun.*"

"*Respect, M'selle.*"

"I would like to speak with M'sieu Margal, if you please. I have come a long way to see him."

Motioning her to enter, the boy silently stepped back from the doorway.

The room in which she found herself surprised her, and not only for its large size. Its floor was of tavernon, the close-grained cabinet wood that was now even rarer and more expensive than Haitian mahogany. Tables and chairs, one of the latter strangely shaped, were of the same wood. Did it grow here? Probably, but Margal must have paid a small fortune to have the trees felled and cut up. The walls of the room were of clay, but each was a different colour – aquamarine, rose, black, green – and intricately decorated. The effect was startling.

"Please be seated," the boy said. "I will ask my master if he wishes to see you. Not there!" he added quickly when Kay, out of curiosity, moved toward the oddly shaped chair. "That is my master's!"

"Sorry." She veered away, but not before noticing what a really remarkable chair it was. Its back was vertical, its extra-wide seat littered with varicolored cushions. It had wide, flat, slotted arms. Fit a board across those arms, using the slots to anchor it, and the chair could be a desk, a work table, even a dining table.

She remained standing. The boy disappeared into a connecting room, leaving the door open.

In a moment the youth reappeared pushing a kind of wheeled platform on which was seated a man. Wearing a bright red nightshirt – if that was the word for it – the man weighed perhaps a hundred and fifty pounds, and would have been about five foot six had he been able to stand erect.

Apparently he could not do that. His legs, crossed in front of him, looked to Kay as though they had been broken and allowed to heal without benefit of medical attention.

The boy pushed the wheeled platform to the odd-shaped chair. Reaching behind him, the man placed both hands on the chair's arms, hoisted himself up, and worked his crippled body backward into position. After squirming to make himself as comfortable as possible, he lifted his head. It was awrithe with a thick, stringy mass that resembled the dreadlocks of Jamaican Rastafarians.

His stare was totally innocent. "I bid you welcome, M'selle. My name is Margal. Please tell me who you are and why you have come here."

It was the moment of truth. Kay took in a breath to steady herself.

"M'sieu Margal, my name is Kay Gilbert, and I am a nurse. A hospital nurse. I came here – as I think you already know – to return a lost child to her home in Bois Sauvage. A child whom you, M'sieu, turned into a zombie but whom we at the hospital were able to restore to health. And I have a proposition for you."

The man who could not walk only stared at her with unblinking eyes, saying nothing.

"I know what you are," Kay continued, using words she had silently rehearsed on the way to this place. "I also know you cannot walk. So I have come to make you an offer."

Those eyes! She could not even decide what colour they were, they were so frightening. And they were doing things to her mind. She was losing her power of concentration.

"As I say – M'sieu Margal – I am from the hospital. That hospital – in the Artibonite – which everyone in Haiti, including you, I am sure – knows about and respects. And I promise you this – that if you – if you will stop doing to people what you – what you did to Tina Anglade – if you will give me your word of honor never to – never to do such a thing again – we at the hospital will do our best to – to repair your legs so that you will be able to – to walk again."

She paused, struggling desperately to maintain control. Dear God, those eyes were making it so hard for her to think straight! Then when he did not answer her, except for a downward, ugly twist of his mouth, she added weakly, "I – I am not fluent in your – your language, M'sieu. Do you understand what – what – I – just – said?"

Something like a laugh issued from that ugly mouth, and the stare intensified. Suddenly Kay was back in the *caille* where the harmless gecko had become a giant dragon intent on devouring her and the child. And then she was sitting on a grey mule, clutching its saddle, while an unreal darkness full of smoke and flames swirled up from a far-below valley to engulf her. And she knew what Margal was doing.

Her offer of help meant nothing to him. He was bent on controlling her, perhaps destroying her. Perhaps the prospect of creating a white female zombie intrigued him. With only one move left to her, she grabbed at the brown leather bag dangling from her shoulder.

Tearing it open, she thrust her hand in and snatched out the one thing it contained – the shiny black automatic her boyfriend, a doctor at the hospital, had insisted she keep with her for safety's sake on this mad mission to the realm of Margal.

But before she could even level the weapon, that room with its multicoloured walls became something else. No longer was she standing there in a house, struggling to point a deadly weapon at another human being. All at once she was in an outdoor place of idyllic beauty where any thought of killing seemed a kind of blasphemy.

There were no weirdly painted walls here. No man with twisted legs sat on a chair in front of her, gazing at her with hypnotic eyes that merely mirrored the awful powers of his incredible mind.

What she saw was a broad valley shimmering in sunlight – a lovely, dreamlike valley carpeted with green grass and colorful wild flowers. And where Margal's chair had been was a young tulip tree with a soft, wide-eyed dove perched on one of its branches, gazing at her with pretty head atilt.

But this isn't Eden and that isn't a dove, Gilbert! You know it isn't! For God's sake, don't let him do this to you!

She still had the gun in her hand. With every ounce of will power she possessed, she forced the hand to lift it, made her eyes and mind take aim, and commanded her finger to squeeze the trigger.

In that idyllic setting there was but one living thing to aim at. The dove.

The sound of the shot shattered the illusion and jolted her out of the hypnotic spell the man on the chair had not quite finished weaving about her. She came out of it just in time to see the bullet pierce his forehead and slam his head against the back of the chair. Still in a partial daze, she pushed herself erect and stumbled forward to look at him.

He was dead. Not even Margal the Sorcerer could still be alive with such a hole in his head and most of his brains splattered over the back of the chair. Never again would be do what he had done to little Tina Anglade – and probably more than a few others.

Probably it had been a foolish notion, anyway, to think he might change his ways if given the ability to walk again.

Her trembling had subsided. In full control of herself again, she looked for the boy, who perhaps, like Luc Etienne, had hoped by serving the master to absorb some of Margal's evil knowledge. When she called to him, there was no answer. Apparently he had fled.

With a last glance at the dead man on the chair, she put the gun back into the brown leather bag and walked out of the house. At the waterfall, the father of little Tina Anglade was waiting for her, as promised. He stepped forward, frowning.

"I heard a noise like a gunshot," he said, his frown asking the unspoken question.

She shrugged. "That man made a noise to frighten me, the way he made the thunder at Saut Diable that I told you about." With his help, she climbed onto the grey mule. "I'm finished," she added. "I've done what I was sent here for. Now we can go home."

Michael Marshall Smith

Later

Michael Marshall Smith is fast becoming a talent to be recognized in horror fiction. In 1991 he won the British Fantasy Award for his debut story "The Man Who Drew Cats" (published in Dark Voices 2*) and the Icarus Award for Best Newcomer. The following year he received the short fiction award again for "The Dark Land" (from* Darklands*).*

Born in Knutsford, Cheshire, Smith grew up in the United States, South Africa and Australia before returning with his family to Britain in 1975. His short fiction has appeared in Best New Horror 2 *and* 3, The Giant Book of Best New Horror, Darklands *and* Darklands 2, *and* Dark Voices 2, 4 *and* 5. *His first novel,* Only Forward, *is published by HarperCollins in 1994.*

"Later" is a clever and moving twist on the zombie theme. When you've finished reading it, I suspect you'll agree that Michael Marshall Smith is one of the most exciting new talents the horror field has seen for a long time.

I REMEMBER STANDING in the bedroom before we went out, fiddling with my tie and fretting mildly about the time. As yet we had plenty, but that was nothing to be complacent about. The minutes had a way of disappearing when Rachel was getting ready, early starts culminating in a breathless search for a taxi.

It was a party we were going to, so it didn't really matter what time we left, but I tend to be a little dull about time. I used to, anyway.

When I had the tie as close to a tidy knot as I was going to be able to get it, I turned away from the mirror, and opened my mouth to call out to Rachel. But then I caught sight of what was on the bed, and closed it again. For a moment I just stood and looked, and then walked over towards the bed.

It wasn't anything very spectacular, just a dress made of sheeny white material. A few years ago, when we started going out together, Rachel used to make a lot of her clothes. She didn't do it because she had to, but because she enjoyed it. She used to trail me endlessly round dress-making shops, browsing patterns and asking my opinion on a million different fabrics, while I half-heartedly protested and moaned.

On impulse I leant down and felt the material, and found I could remember touching it for the first time in the shop on Mill Road, could remember surfacing up through contented boredom to say that yes, I liked this one. On that recommendation she'd bought it, and made this dress, and as a reward for traipsing around after her she'd bought me dinner too. We were poorer then, so the meal was cheap, but there was lots and it was good.

The strange thing was, I didn't even really mind the dress shops. You know how sometimes, when you're just walking around, living your life, you'll see someone on the street and fall hopelessly in love with them? How something in the way they look, the way they are, makes you stop dead in your tracks and stare? How for that instant you're convinced that if you could just meet them, you'd be able to love them for ever?

Wild schemes and unlikely meetings pass through your head, and yet as they stand on the other side of the street or the room, talking to someone else, they haven't the faintest idea of what's going through your mind. Something has clicked, but only inside your head. You know you'll never speak to them, that they'll never know what you're feeling, and that they'll never want to. But something about them forces you to keep looking, until you wish they'd leave so you could be free.

The first time I saw Rachel was like that, and now she was in my bath. I didn't call out to hurry her along. I decided it didn't really matter.

A few minutes later a protracted squawking noise announced the letting out of the bath water, and Rachel wafted into the bedroom swaddled in thick towels and glowing high spirits. Suddenly I lost all interest in going to the party, punctually or otherwise. She marched up to me, set her head at a silly angle to kiss me on the lips and jerked my tie vigorously in about three different directions. When I looked in the mirror I saw that somehow, as always, she'd turned it into a perfect knot.

Half an hour later we left the flat, still in plenty of time. If anything, I'd held her up.

"Later," she said, smiling in the way that showed she meant it, "Later, and for a long time, my man."

I remember turning from locking the door to see her standing on the pavement outside the house, looking perfect in her white dress, looking happy and looking at me. As I walked smiling down the steps towards her she skipped backwards into the road, laughing for no reason, laughing because she was with me.

"Come on," she said, holding out her hand like a dancer, and a yellow van came round the corner and smashed into her. She spun backwards as if tugged on a rope, rebounded off a parked car and toppled into the road. As I stood cold on the bottom step she half sat up and looked at me, an expression of wordless surprise on her face, and then she fell back again.

When I reached her blood was already pulsing up into the white of her dress and welling out of her mouth. It ran out over her makeup and I saw she'd been right: she hadn't quite blended the colours above her eyes. I'd told her it didn't matter, that she still looked beautiful. She had.

She tried to move her head again and there was a sticky sound as it almost left the tarmac and then slumped back. Her hair fell back from around her face, but not as it usually did. There was a faint flicker in her eyelids, and then she died.

I knelt there in the road beside her, holding her hand as the blood dried a little. It was as if everything had come to a halt, and hadn't started up again. I heard every word the small crowd muttered, but I didn't know what they were muttering about. All I could think was that there wasn't going to be a later, not to kiss her some more, not for anything. Later was gone.

When I got back from the hospital I phoned her mother. I did it as soon as I got back, though I didn't want to. I didn't want to tell anyone, didn't want to make it official. It was a bad phone call, very, very bad. Then I sat in the flat, looking at the drawers she'd left open, at the towels on the floor, at the party invitation on the dressing table, feeling my stomach crawl. I was back at the flat, as if we'd come back home from the party. I should have been making coffee while Rachel had yet another bath, coffee we'd drink on the sofa in front of the fire. But the fire was off and the bath was empty. So what was I supposed to do?

I sat for an hour, feeling as if somehow I'd slipped too far forward in time and left Rachel behind, as if I could turn and see her desperately running to try to catch me up. When it felt as if my throat was going to burst I called my parents and they came and took me home. My mother gently made me change my clothes, but she didn't wash them. Not until I was asleep, anyway. When I came down and saw them clean I hated her, but I knew she was right and the hate went away. There wouldn't have been much point in just keeping them in a drawer.

The funeral was short. I guess they all are, really, but there's no point in them being any longer. Nothing more would be said. I was a little better by then, and not crying so much, though I did before we went to the church because I couldn't get my tie to sit right.

Rachel was buried near her grandparents, which she would have liked. Her parents gave me her dress afterwards, because I'd asked for it. It had been thoroughly cleaned and large patches had lost their sheen and died, looking as much unlike Rachel's dress as the cloth had on the roll. I'd almost have preferred the bloodstains still to have been there: at least that way I could had believed that the cloth still sparkled beneath them. But they were right in their way, as my mother was. Some people seem to have pragmatic, accepting souls, an ability to deal with death. I don't, I'm afraid. I don't understand it at all.

Afterwards I stood at the graveside for a while, but not for long because I knew that my parents were waiting at the car. As I stood by the mound of earth that lay on top of her I tried to concentrate, to send some final thought to her, some final love, but the world kept pressing in on me through the sound of cars on the road and some bird that was cawing in a tree. I couldn't shut it out. I couldn't believe that I was noticing how cold it was, that somewhere lives were being led and televisions being watched, that the inside of my parents' car would smell the same as it always had. I wanted to feel something, wanted to sense her presence, but I couldn't. All I could feel was the world round me, the same old world. But it wasn't a world that had been there a week ago, and I couldn't understand how it could look so much the same.

It was the same because nothing had changed, and I turned and walked to the car. The wake was worse than the funeral, much worse, and I stood with a sandwich feeling something very cold building up inside. Rachel's oldest friend Lisa held court with her old school friends, swiftly running the range of emotions from stoic resilience to trembling incoherence.

"I've just realized," she sobbed to me, "Rachel's not going to be at my wedding."

"Yes, well she's not going to be at mine either," I said numbly, and immediately hated myself for it. I went and stood by the window, out of harm's way. I couldn't react properly. I knew why everyone was standing here, that in some ways it was like a wedding. Instead of gathering together to bear witness to a bond, they were here to prove she was dead. In the weeks to come they'd know they'd stood together in a room, and would be able to accept she was gone. I couldn't.

I said goodbye to Rachel's parents before I left. We looked at each other oddly, and shook hands, as if we were just strangers again. Then I went back to the flat and changed into some old clothes. My "Someday" clothes, Rachel used to call them, as in "some day you must throw them away". Then I made a cup of tea and stared out of the window for a while. I knew damn well what I was going to do, and it was a relief to give in to it.

That night I went back to the cemetery and I dug her up. What can I say? It was hard work, and it took a lot longer than I expected, but in another way it was surprisingly easy. I mean yes, it was creepy, and yes, I felt like a lunatic, but after the shovel had gone in once the second time seemed less strange. It was like waking up in the mornings after the accident. The first time I clutched at myself and couldn't understand, but after that I knew what to expect. There were no cracks of thunder, there was no web of lightening and I actually felt very calm. There was just me and, beneath the earth, my friend. I just wanted to find her.

When I did I laid her down by the side of the grave and then filled it back up again, being careful to make it look undisturbed. Then I carried her to the car in my arms and brought her home.

The flat seemed very quiet as I sat her on the sofa, and the cushion rustled and creaked as it took her weight again. When she was settled I knelt and looked up at her face. It looked much the same as it always had, though the colour of the skin was different, didn't have the glow she always had. That's where life is, you know, not in the heart but in the little things, like the way hair falls around a face. Her nose looked the same and her forehead was smooth. It was the same face, exactly the same.

I knew the dress she was wearing was hiding a lot of things I would rather not see, but I took it off anyway. It was her going away dress, bought by her family specially for the occasion, and it didn't mean anything to me or to her. I knew what the damage would be and what it meant. As it turned out the patchers and menders had done a good job, not glossing because it wouldn't be seen. It wasn't so bad.

When she was sitting up again in her white dress I walked over and turned the light down, and I cried a little then, because she looked so much the same. She could have fallen asleep, warmed by the fire and dozy with wine, as if we'd just come back from the party.

I went and had a bath then. We both used to when we came back in from an evening, to feel clean and fresh for when we slipped between the sheets. It wouldn't be like that this evening, of course, but I had dirt all over me, and I wanted to feel normal. For one night at least I just wanted things to be as they had.

I sat in the bath for a while, knowing she was in the living room, and slowly washed myself clean. I really wasn't thinking much. It felt nice to know that I wouldn't be alone when I walked back in there. That was better than nothing, was part of what had made her alive. I dropped my Someday clothes in the bin and put on the ones from the evening of the accident. They didn't mean as much as her dress, but at least they were from before.

When I returned to the living room her head had lolled slightly, but it would have done if she'd been asleep. I made us both a cup of coffee. The only time she ever took sugar was in this cup, so I put one in. Then I sat down next to her on the sofa and I was glad that the cushions had her dent in them, that as always they drew me slightly towards her, didn't leave me perched there by myself.

The first time I saw Rachel was at a party. I saw her across the room and simply stared at her, but we didn't speak. We didn't meet properly for a month or two, and first kissed a few weeks after that. As I sat there on the sofa next to her body I reached out tentatively and took her hand, as I had done on that night. It was cooler than it should have been, but not too bad because of the fire, and I held it, feeling the lines on her palm, lines I knew better than my own.

I let myself feel calm and I held her hand in the half light, not looking at her, as also on that first night, when I'd been too happy to push my luck. She's letting you hold her hand, I'd thought, don't expect to be able to look at her too. Holding her hand is more than enough: don't look, you'll break the spell. My face creased then, not knowing whether to smile or cry, but it felt alright. It really did.

I sat there for a long time, watching the flames, still not thinking, just holding her hand and letting the minutes run. The longer I sat the more normal it felt, and finally I turned slowly to look at her. She looked tired and asleep, so deeply asleep, but still there with me and still mine.

When her eyelid first moved I thought it was a trick of the light, a flicker cast by the fire. But then it stirred again, and for the smallest of moments I thought I was going to die. The other eyelid moved and the feeling just disappeared, and that made the difference, I think. She had a long way to come, and if I'd felt frightened, or rejected her, I think that would have finished it then. I didn't question it. A few minutes later both her eyes were open, and it wasn't long before she was able to slowly turn her head.

I still go to work, and put in the occasional appearance at social events, but my tie never looks quite as it did. She can't move her fingers precisely enough to help me with that any more. She can't come with me, and nobody can come here, but that doesn't matter. We always spent a lot of time by ourselves. We wanted to.

I have to do a lot of things for her, but I can live with that. Lots of people have accidents, bad ones: if Rachel had survived she could have been disabled or brain-damaged so that her movements were as they are now, so slow and clumsy. I wish she could talk, but there's no air in her lungs, so I'm learning to read her lips. Her mouth moves slowly, but I know she's trying to speak, and I want to hear what she's saying.

But she gets round the flat, and she holds my hand, and she smiles as best she can. If she'd just been injured I would have loved her still. It's not so very different.

Peter Tremayne

Marbh Bheo

Peter Tremayne is the pseudonym of historian and Celtic scholar Peter Berresford Ellis. Under the Tremayne alias he has published more than twenty-five books in the horror and fantasy field, most recently the Signet/Penguin omnibus volume Dracula Lives! *and* Aisling and Other Irish Tales of Terror, *his second collection of short stories, published by Brandon Books. Severn House are producing hardcover reprints of his novels, including* Swamp!, Nicor, Angelus! *and* Snowbeast.

"'Marbh Bheo' is in the tradition of the stories collected in Aisling," *explains the writer, "– a reinterpretation of Irish folk tales and legends in a way to freeze the blood. One critic, doubtless going over the top, has called me: 'A worthy successor to Sheridan Le Fanu and Bram Stoker.' So where are the royalty cheques?"*

IT WAS DARK when I reached the old cottage. The journey had been far from easy. I suppose a city-bred person such as myself would find most rural journeys difficult. I had certainly assumed too much. As the crow flies, I had been told that the cottage was only some twenty-one miles from the centre of Cork City. But in Ireland the miles are deceptive. I know there is a standard joke about "the Irish mile" but there is a grain of truth in it. For the Boggeragh Mountains,

in whose shadows the cottage lay, are a brooding, windswept area
where nothing grows but bleak heather, a dirty stubble which clings
tenaciously to the grey granite thrusts of the hills, where the wind
whistles and sings over a moonscape of rocks pricking upwards to
the heavens. To walk a mile in such terrain, among the heights and
terrible grandeur of the wild, rocky slopes and gorse you have to allow
two hours. A mile on a well-kept road is not like a mile on a forgotten
track amidst these sullen peaks.

What was I doing in such an inhospitable area in the first place?
That is the question which you will undoubtedly ask.

Well, it was not through any desire on my part. But one must
live and my livelihood depended on my job with RTÉ. I am a
researcher with Telefís Éireann, the Irish state television. Initially
it was the idea of some bright producer that we make a programme
on Irish folk customs. So that was the initial impetus which found me
searching among dusty tomes in an old occult bookstore, in a little
alley off Sheares Street on the nameless island in the River Lee which
constitutes the centre of the city of Cork. The area is often mentioned
in the literature of Cork as the place where once the fashionable world
came to see and be seen. That era of glory has departed and now small
artisans' houses and shops crowd upon it claustrophobically.

I had been told to research the superstitions connected with the
dead and I was browsing through some volumes when I became
aware of an old woman standing next to me. She was peering at the
book that I was examining with more than a degree of interest.

"So you are interested in the Irish customs and superstitions
relating to the dead, young man?" she observed in an imperious
tone, her voice slightly shrill and sharp.

I looked at her. She was of small stature, the shoulders bent, but
she wore a long black dress, with matching large hat and veil, almost
like a figure out of a Victorian drama. From such a guise it was hard
to see her features but she gave the air of a world long gone, of a time
almost forgotten.

"I am," I replied courteously.

"An interesting subject. There are many stories of the dead who
come to life again in West Cork. If you travel round the rural
communities you will hear some quite incredible stories."

"Really?" I inquired politely. "You mean zombies?"

She sniffed disparagingly.

"Zombies! That is a voodoo superstition originating in Africa. You
are in Ireland, young man. No, I mean the *marbh bheo*."

She pronounced this as "ma'rof vo".

"What's that?" I demanded.

"A corpse that lives," she replied. "You will find many a tale about the *marbh bheo* in rural Ireland."

She sniffed again. It seemed a habit.

"Yes, really, young man. There are many stories that will make your hair curl. Stories that are fantastic and terrible. Tales of being buried alive. The tale of Tadhg Ó Catháin who, in punishment for his wicked life, was condemned to be ridden every night by a hideous living corpse, a *marbh bheo*, who demanded burial and drove him from churchyard to churchyard as the dead rose up in each one to refuse the corpse burial. There are the corpses who wait in haunted lakes to devour the drowned ones, and the unholy undead creatures who haunt the raths. Oh yes, young man, there are many fantastic tales to be heard and some not a mile or so from this very spot."

An idea crossed my mind as she spoke.

"Do you know any local people who are experts in such tales?" I inquired. "You see, I am working on a television programme and want to speak to someone . . ."

She sniffed yet again.

"You wish to speak to someone who has knowledge about the *marbh bheo*?"

I smiled. She made it sound so natural as if I were merely asking to speak to someone who could advise me on bee-keeping. I nodded eagerly.

"Go to Musheramore Mountain and ask for 'Teach Droch-Chlú'. At 'Teach Droch-Chlú' you will find Father Nessan Doheny. He will speak with you."

I put down the book that I had been examining, turned to reach for my attaché case and took out my notebook. I turned back to the old lady but much to my amazement she had gone. I looked round the bookstore. The owner was upstairs and I asked him if he had seen or knew her but he had not. With a shrug, I jotted down the names that she had given me. After all, in an occult bookstore you are apt to meet the weirdest people. But I was pleased with the meeting. Here was a more interesting lead than spending days browsing through books. A good television programme relies on personalities, raconteurs, and not the recitation of dry and dusty facts by a narrator.

Musheramore is the largest peak in the Boggeragh Mountains, not far from Cork. I checked the phone book and found no listing for Father Nessan Doheny nor for "Teach Droch-Chlú". But the place was so near, and city dweller that I am, I thought I would be able to ride the twenty-one miles to Musheramore and back in one evening. I should explain that I am the proud possessor of a vintage Triumph motorcycle. Motorbikes are a hobby of mine. I thought that I could have a chat with the priest and then be back in Cork long before midnight.

I rode out of Cork on the Macroom road, which is a good straight and wide highway, and then turned north on a small track towards the village of Ballynagree with Musheramore a black dominating peak in the distance. That was easy. I stopped at a local garage, just north of Ballynagree, filled up with petrol and asked the way to "Teach Droch-Chlú". The garage man, whose name-badge on his overalls pronounced him to be "Manus", gave me an old fashioned glance, as though I had said something which secretly amused him. His face assumed a sort of knowing grin as he gave me some directions.

That was when the real journey began.

It took me an hour to negotiate the directions and reach the place. Though it shames me to say it, my Irish is not particularly good. In a country which is reputedly bilingual, but where English is more widely spoken than Irish, one can get by with little use of the language. Therefore, while I knew that "Teach" meant a house, I had no idea of the full meaning of the name. And the cottage, for such it proved to be, was harder to find than I would ever have thought.

It lay in a scooped out hollow of the mountain, surrounded by dark trees and shrubs which formed a hedgerow. It looked old, dank and depressing. And when I eventually found the place, darkness had spread its enveloping cloak all around.

I parked my motorbike and walked along a winding path, with the sharp barbs of pyracantha bushes scratching my hands and snagging my jacket. I finally reached the low lintelled door.

When I knocked on its paint peeling panels, a reedy voice bade me enter.

Father Nessan Doheny, or so I presumed the gaunt figure to be, sat in a high-backed chair by a smouldering turf fire; his hair was white, the eyes colourless and pale, seeming without animation, and his skin was like yellow parchment. His thin, claw-like hands were folded on his lap. I would have placed his age more towards ninety than younger. He was clad in a dark, shining suit with only his white Roman collar to throw it into relief. There was a chilly atmosphere in the room in spite of the smouldering fire.

"The dead?" he piped shrilly, after I had explained my purpose. His thin bloodless lips cracked upwards. It might have been a smile. "Have the living so little to interest them that they need to know of the dead?"

"It's for a television programme on folklore, Father," I humoured him.

"Folklore, is it?" he cackled. "Now the dead are reduced to folklore."

He fell silent for such a long while that I thought maybe the ancient priest had grown senile in his ageing and had fallen asleep, but he eventually raised his face to mine and shook his head.

"I could tell you many tales about the dead. They are as real as the living. Why, not far from here is a farmstead. It is the custom in these parts that when throwing away water at night, for you will find many a house that has still to draw its water from wells, that the person casting out the water should cry: "*Tóg ort as uisce*! Meaning – away with yourself from the water."

I knew this to be a rural expression better rendered into English as "look out for the water".

"Why would they say this, Father?"

"Because the belief is that water falling on a corpse burns it, for water is purity. Well, there came a night when a woman of a farm not far from here, threw out a jug of water and forgot the warning cry. Instantly, she heard a shriek of a person in pain. No one was seen in the darkness. Around midnight, the door came open and a black lamb entered the house, having its back scalded. It lay down moaning by the hearth and died before the farmer and his wife knew what to do.

"The farmer buried the lamb the next morning. At midnight that night the door came open again and the lamb entered. Its back was scalded as before. It lay down and died. The farmer buried it again. When this happened a third time, the farmer sent for me. I was then a young priest but I knew what had happened immediately and laid the dead spirit to rest by the solemnity of exorcism. The black lamb appeared no more."

I was hastily scribbling notes. I had to put down one of my notebooks on a side table as I bent to my task.

"Absolutely great, Father. That will make a nice tale. First class."

He gazed at me sourly.

"It is no game we are talking about. The dead have equal powers to the living and you should be warned not to mock them, young man."

I smiled indulgently.

"Don't worry, Father. I'll not mock them. I just want to get this programme together . . ."

Father Doheny winced as if in pain but I prattled on obliviously.

"Are there such things as zombies in Ireland?"

He sniffed. It suddenly reminded me of the old woman and the answer she had given me.

"You mean a corpse reanimated by sorcery?"

"Yes. Don't we have any stories about the walking dead in Ireland? I mean, what do you call it, a *marbh bheo*?"

His pale eyes seemed to gaze right through me.

"Of course the dead walk. There is only the faintest veil between this land of the living and the land of the dead. At the right time and with the right stimulus the dead can enter into our world with the same ease as we can enter into their world."

I could not help smirking.

"That's hardly the official Church line from Rome."

His thin lips compressed in annoyance.

"The ancients knew these things long before the coming of Christianity. It would be better not to take them lightly."

Father Nessan Doheny was a delight. I was scribbling away as fast as I could, imagining a whole series of programmes devoted to the ageing priest sitting recounting his bizarre tales.

"Go on, Father," I prompted. "How easy is it to cross through this veil, you speak of, into the land of the dead?"

"Easy enough, boy. Over at Caherbarnagh, when I was a young priest, there was living a woman. One day she was returning to her cottage when she stopped to drink by a small stream. As she rose to her feet she suddenly heard the sound of low music. A group of people were coming down the path, singing a strange, soothing song. It puzzled her and she felt a shiver of apprehension. Then she realised that close by her a tall, young man was standing watching her, his face strange and pale, the eyes wide and blank.

"She demanded to know who he was. He shook his head and warned her that she was in great danger and unless she fled with him, evil would befall her. She began to trot off with him and the people, coming down the path with their music, cried out: 'Come back!' Yet fear lent her wings and she ran and ran with the young man until they reached the edge of a small wood. The young man halted and pronounced them safe. Then he asked her to look upon his face.

"When she did so, she recognized him as her elder brother who had been drowned the year before. He was drowned while swimming in the dark waters of Loch Dalua and his body had never been recovered. What was she to do? She felt evil near and ran home to send for me, the local priest, confessing all. There was fear and trembling on her when she told me her tale and after she had made that final confession, she died."

"That's a terrific tale," I said, entering it enthusiastically in my notebook.

"There are tales of the dead in every corner of the land," nodded the old priest.

I became aware of an old clock chiming in the corner. I could not believe it. It was ten o'clock already. I sighed. Well, I was getting so much good material that it was a shame to break off now to make sure I was back in Cork at a reasonable hour.

"But what about this *marbh bheo*, Father," I asked. "These stories you have told me are more of ghosts than the walking dead. Are there stories of reanimated corpses?"

The priest's expression did not change.

"Ghosts, walking dead, the dead are dead in whatever form they come."

"But reanimated corpses?" I pressed. "What of them?"

"If I must speak, then I must," the old priest said almost half to himself, half as if speaking to some third party. "Must I speak?"

Naturally, I thought the question was addressed to me and answered in the affirmative.

"I will speak then. I will tell you a tale; a tale of a great English lord who used to own these mountains in the days before Ireland won her independence from England."

I glanced at the clock and said: "Is it a tale about the walking dead, the *marbh bheo*?"

The priest ignored me.

"The lord was called the Earl of Musheramore, Baron of Lyre and Lisnaraha. He had a great castle and estate which covered most of the Boggeragh Mountains. He and his family before him since the days of the English conquests and the flight of our noble families to Europe. The estate was a prosperous one and the Earl of Musheramore was rich and powerful."

His voice assumed a droning tone, hypnotic and soporific.

The real point of his story had taken place in the days of the "Great Hunger". During the mid nineteenth-century, the potato crops failed. Because the peasants of Ireland had been so reduced in poverty by the absentee English landlords, the potato had become the staple diet, mixed with a little poaching on the estate, game from the land and fish from the rivers and lochs. The lords of the land severely punished any people caught taking the game or the fish. One young man who had dared to poach a couple of rabbits from Lord Musheramore, to help feed his large family, was transported to Van Diemen's Land in Australia for seven years. That was the type of fate that awaited any peasant who poached on their lord's land. The law was vigorously imposed by landlord's agents, usually impoverished former officers of the British army, who were employed to run things in the absence of the owners.

So, of course, when the potato crop failed, the people began to starve. In a space of three years the population of the country had been reduced by two-and-a-half million. Yet the landlords and their agents still demanded the rent on the tiny peasant hovels, evicted people into the winter snows and frosts; men, women, children and babes in arms, if they could not pay, were evicted, their cabins torn down to prevent reoccupation. Under such straits they perished from exposure, malnutrition and other attendant diseases. Cholera struck everywhere.

Yet the landlords prospered. Great shiploads of the landlords' produce – grain, wheat, flax, cattle, sheep, poultry – were being loaded aboard the ships in Irish harbours and sent to England for sale. For every charity relief ship, raised by the Irish communities abroad, sailing into an Irish port, six ships loaded with grain and livestock were sailing out of the ports to England.

A great bitterness spread over the land. An attempt to rise up against the rulers was severely crushed by the military.

On the estate of Lord Musheramore, the peasants gathered in a body, kneeling on the well-kept green lawns outside Musheramore Castle, holding up their hands in supplication to his lordship, pleading for his help to keep them alive for the forthcoming winter, a winter that many were already doomed not to see, so wracked by malnutrition had they become.

Lord Musheramore was a vain young man. He was about thirty years old, with a dark, aquiline face and sneering mouth. Since his inheritance he had only visited his estate once. He preferred to live in a house in London where he could visit the playhouses, taverns, and the gaming houses where he loved to win or lose moderate fortunes on the throw of the dice or the fall of cards. But he had come to visit during that summer to ensure that the produce of his estate was not being squandered on any "famine relief".

He was somewhat alarmed at the concourse of people that gathered on the castle lawns. There were hundreds of people from the cottages and the villages which his estate encompassed. He sent his overseer straightaway to the military at Mallow and three companies of English hussars soon arrived and surrounded the castle to protect it from attack. The captain in charge, acting on Lord Musheramore's orders, told the people to disperse. When they hesitated, he charged his troops into them. The hussars went berserk, swinging their sabres and shouting like banshees. The result was that many died, including the local priest who had come to add his authority to the pleas of the peasants.

Now among the people gathered that day was an old woman named Bríd Cappeen. She had been shunned by the people in better days for she had the reputation of being something of a witch. She was, indeed, a wise woman. She had escaped the soldiers with no more than a sabre's cut across her thin, angular face. But the scar on her heart was deeper than that. Old Bríd Cappeen knew the ways of the ancients, the old ways that were practised from time immemorial, whose origins were forgotten even by the time of the coming of Christianity. She could search the entrails of a dead chicken and find the answer to the future in its bloodied remains.

Bríd Cappeen had fled to the gorse covered mountainside when the soldiers attacked and had hidden all day there. That night she crept down the mountain to the lawn where the corpses of the peasants had been laid out ready for disposal. She searched the pile of corpses, wild and demented, until she found the one she wanted. The body of a man whose wounds had not caused any limbs to be severed. Then with the strength derived from God alone knows where, or maybe from the Devil, Bríd Cappeen hauled that corpse away into the night. She hauled it up to her lonely cave in the mountain.

There, in the cave, she practised the old rituals, conjuring words that no scholar of the ancient Gaelic tongue would recognize. She sought and found herbs and threw them into a steam kettle on a small fire and bathed the body of the man and, finally, as the moon reached the point in the night sky which signified the hour of midnight, the limbs of the man began to tremble, to pulsate and the eyes came open.

Old Bríd Cappeen let out a growl of satisfaction.

She had created the *marbh bheo*; she had conjured the "living corpse" to her bidding.

In the ancient times it was told that vengeance could be visited on a wrongdoer by a druid or druidess who could reanimate the body of a person wrongly slain. Old Bríd Cappeen began to enact that vengeance.

She sent out the reanimated body of the corpse on its dreadful quest. Lord Musheramore, Baron of Lyre and Lisnaraha, was about to board the ship for England in Cork harbour one evening when he was attacked and literally torn apart by a man whom no one could identify. The police and soldiers swore that they opened fire and hit the attacker several times. The local magistrate took this with cynical humour, for the attacker escaped clean away and there was no blood on the cobbles of the quay except the aristocratic blood of Lord Musheramore.

The captain of the hussars was attacked next in his own quarters, safe in the barracks at Mallow. He, too, was torn apart. The attacker was evidently a man of amazing strength and iron purpose for he had broken through the stone and iron walls of the barracks to get into the captain's quarters. When they found what was left of the captain, many soldiers, veterans who had served in campaigns in India and Africa, were sick and broke down in terror.

Then, Major Farran, the overseer of Lord Musheramore's estate, was set on one evening while out with his two great hounds. Farran was a stocky man, afraid of nothing in this world nor the next, or so he boasted. He carried two hand pistols and the hounds that bounded at his side were not just for company. They had been known to tear a person to pieces at his command. Major Farran was hated amongst Musheramore's peasants. He knew it and, curious man that he was, thrived on it. He liked the aura of fear that he was able to spread around him. But he was wise enough to take precautions against any attack those who hated him might make.

But pistols and hounds did not protect him that evening.

It was three full days before all his remains were found along the bloodstrewn pathway. And the doctor confessed that he had no way of knowing the flesh of Major Farran from the flesh of the mutilated hounds.

And all the while Bríd Cappeen crooned away in her cave on the slopes of the mountain.

She was not satisfied with immediate vengeance on those who had wronged the people of Musheramore's estate. She became determined to make all who were connected with the Musheramore family pay for the deaths of her relatives and fellow villagers. Vengeance became her creed, her passion, her overwhelming desire. And the *marbh bheo* was the instrument of her vengeance.

For years, thereafter, there were reports of the demented Bríd Cappeen scouring the night shrouded country of the Boggeragh Mountains in search of vengeance with her living corpse at her side.

Father Doheny stopped talking abruptly, leaving me forward, open mouthed, on the edge of the seat.

"That's a fantastic tale, Father," I stammered at last, realising that he had come to an end of it. "Was there really such a person as Lord Musheramore?"

He made no reply, sitting gazing down at the smouldering turf.

I shivered slightly for the turf was not sending out any warmth into the tiny cottage room.

"Would you be prepared to come to our studios in Cork and talk on the programme about the *marbh bheo*? We could pay you something, of course."

I suddenly felt a draught on the back of my neck.

I turned and saw the cottage door had opened. To my surprise, because of the lateness of the hour, I saw the old woman I had met in the occult bookstore. Her black shrouded figure was framed in the gloom of its opening. Her Victorian dress seemed to be flapping around her in the wind that had risen across the mountains; flapping like the wings of a dark raven.

"Your business here is finished," she said imperiously, in a voice that cracked with age.

"I am here to see Father Doheny." I smarted at her lack of manners and turned to the old priest seeking support. "At your suggestion, too," I added, perhaps defensively.

The old man seemed to have nodded off in his high-backed wooden chair, for his jaw was lowered to his chest and his eyes were closed.

"Well, you have seen him. He has spoken to you. Begone now!"

I stared incredulously at the effrontery of the old woman.

"I rather think that it is none of your business to instruct me in another's house, madam," I said sternly.

Behind the blackness of her veil, she opened her mouth and an hysterical cackle caused the hairs on the nape of my neck to prickle with apprehension.

"I am in charge here," she wheezed, once she had recovered from her mirth, if that horrific sound was mirth.

"You mean, you are Father Doheny's housekeeper?" I could hardly keep the astonishment from my voice for the old woman looked incapable of carrying a teapot from the hearth to the table, let alone performing any of the chores expected of a housekeeper.

She cackled again.

"It is late, boy," she finally replied. "I would be about your business. There is an evil across this mountain at night. I would have a care of it."

She threw out a gnarled claw in a dismissive gesture.

I glanced again at Father Doheny but he showed no sign of stirring and so I gathered my notes, rose and put on my coat with all the dignity I could muster.

She ignored me as I bade her a "goodnight" but simply stood aside from the door.

Outside the cottage the moon was up in a sky across which fretful clouds moved hurriedly as the wind blew and wailed over the crevices of rocks. A frost lay forming its white veins over the ground. The temperature must have dropped considerably since I had arrived. In the distance I could hear the howling of dogs. The sound seemed ethereal and unreal in the night air.

I went to my motorcycle and, trusting that I was not disturbing the old priest's slumber, I kicked the starter. It took a while to get the Triumph's engine warmed and ready enough for me to begin to wind my way down the mountain track.

I had not gone more than a mile when I realised that I had left one of my notebooks on the small table in Father Doheny's cottage. With a sigh I halted and turned the Triumph gently on the muddy track and pushed back towards "Teach Droch-Chlú".

I halted my bike and made my way along the track to the dark outline of the cottage.

Something caused me not to knock but to halt outside.

A shrill chanting came to my ears.

It was the voice of the old woman. It was some time before I could actually make out the sound of the words and then they meant little to me for they were in an ancient form of Irish.

Something prompted me to peer in through the small panes of the window.

I could make out the old priest, now standing still in the middle of the room. The old woman was before him, huddled with bent shoulders, crooning away. I was surprised to see that in her hands she held one of those old fashioned cavalry sabres, with a curved blade. There was something peculiarly disturbing about the way she was carrying on, chanting and crooning in that shrill voice.

Abruptly she stopped.

"Remember, Doheny," she commanded.

The old priest stood stiff and upright, his colourless eyes staring straight above her.

"You must remember. This is what they did."

Before I could cry out a warning, the old woman had raised the sabre and, with the full force of her seemingly frail frame, she thrust the point of the weapon through the old priest just about the level of his heart. I saw the end of the blade emerge through the back of his jacket. Yet he had not even staggered under the impact of the blow.

My jaw hung open. There are no words to express the shock and terror that scene gave me.

Worse was to come.

The old woman let go of the sabre and stepped away from him.

"Remember, Doheny!"

The old priest's claw-like hands came to the handle of the sabre and then, with a mighty tug, he pulled the great blade out of his body with a slow, deliberate motion. It was bright and shining and without a speck of blood upon its blade.

I stood at the small window transfixed with terror.

I could not believe what I had seen. It was impossible. She had thrust a sharp sword through a frail old priest and the priest had not batted an eye. He had merely withdrawn it. And it had made no wound!

"Remember, Doheny!"

I suppressed a cry of fear, turned and ran back to my bike. Panic seemed to impede my every move. I tried to start the motor but everything I did seemed wrong. I heard a cry from the old woman, became aware of a shadow on the path. I could feel fetid breath on my neck. Then the bike started with a roar and I was speeding away.

The track was twisting, the mud on the road slowed the machine. I felt as if I was in some cross-country bike race, swerving, twisting, leaping down the mountain pathway in the direction of the nearest village which was Ballynagree. I had never ridden so hard in all my life, ridden as if a thousand devils from hell were at my heels.

Just as I was beginning to relax, I saw a small hump-back bridge over a winding mountain torrent. I knew it to be an old granite stone bridge which was scarcely the width of three people walking. I eased back the throttle on my machine to negotiate it in safety and then . . .

Then, by the light of my front lamp, I saw the pale figure of the priest standing in the centre of the bridge; standing waiting for me.

In fright, I tugged at the handlebars of my machine, wrenching them, as I made a silly and futile attempt to ride through the gushing stream rather than run over the bridge.

My front wheel hit a stone and the next thing I knew was that I was cartwheeling over and over in the air before smashing down on a soft muddy surface of the bank. The impact still drove the breath out of my body and I lost consciousness.

It was only a momentary loss. I remember coming to with a swimming, nauseous sensation. I blinked.

A foot away from my face was the pale, parchment features of the priest. The colourless eyes seemed to be staring through me. His breath was stale, fetid and there was a terrible stench of death on him. I felt his hands at my throat. Large, powerful claws, squeezing.

"Stop, Doheny!"

It was the old woman's shrill tones. Beyond the priest's shoulder I caught a glimpse of her, the veil thrown back, while the skull-like face was staring in triumph with a livid weal of a scar showing diagonally from forehead to cheek.

The pressure eased a little.

"He is not one of them, Doheny. Leave him be. He is to be witness to what we have done. Leave him be. What we have done will live in him and he will pass it on so that it will be known. Leave him be."

The old priest, with incredible strength, shook me as if I were no more than a rag doll.

"Leave him be," commanded the old woman again.

And then I must have fainted.

When I came to, there was no one about. I pressed my hand against my throbbing temples and rose unsteadily to my feet. For a moment or two I could not remember how I had wound up in the mud of the mountain stream. Then I did remember. I gave a startled glance about me but could see no sign of the old priest and woman. The mountainside was in darkness. The only movement was that of the trees whispering, swaying and rustling in the winds that moaned softly over the mountain.

I stood a moment or two attempting to get my bearings. Then I saw the black heap of my Triumph motorbike lying in the shallows of the stream. I tried to move it out of the water but saw immediately, by the buckled wheel and splintered spokes, that even if I could start the machine it would be useless. Nevertheless, I attempted to start it. The starter gave a weak "phutt" and remained lifeless. It was obviously waterlogged.

I manoeuvred it to the bank of the stream and then waded up to the humpback bridge. There was nothing for it but to start walking down the mountain to Ballynagree. My head was throbbing and my mind was a whirl of conflicting thoughts. Was someone playing some terrible joke, a joke which was in bad taste? But no one would go to that extreme? Surely?

It took three hours of trekking down the muddy pathway before I saw the first signs of habitation.

I finally saw the dark outline of the garage where I had stopped for petrol. I stumbled towards it numb and frozen and hammered on the door. It was a while before I heard a window go up in the room above the garage front. A light shone down and a voice cried: "Who's there?"

"My motorbike has broken down and I'm stranded," I yelled. "Can I get a taxi from here or stay the rest of the night?"

"Man, do you realize that it is three o'clock in the morning?" came the stern reply.

"I was stranded on the mountain, on Musheramore Mountain," I replied.

A woman's voice came softly to my ears although I could not hear what was said.

The window came down with an abrupt bang. I waited hopefully. A light eventually shone in the downstairs window. Then the door was opened.

"Come away in," said the male voice.

I entered, feeling ice cold and drained from my experience.

As the light fell on me, the garage man recognized me.

"You're the young man who asked me the way to 'Teach Droch-Chlú' earlier this evening, aren't you?"

I nodded. It was the man whose overalls had proclaimed his name to be "Manus".

"That's right. My motorbike has broken down. I need a cab."

The man shook his head, nonplussed.

"You look all in." He turned and drew up a bottle of Jameson from a cupboard and a glass. "This will warm you up," he said pouring the whiskey and pushing the glass into my hands.

"What were you doing up at 'Teach Droch-Chlú' at this time of night? Are you a ghost hunter? Is that it?" And without waiting for a reply he continued: "I can telephone Macroom for a car to collect you, if you like. Where do you want to get to?"

"To Cork City."

"And where did your bike break down?"

"Up the mountain track somewhere, near a river crossing. By a humpbacked bridge."

"Ah, the spot is known to me. I'll go and pick your bike up tomorrow. Give me a number where I can contact you and I'll let you know what repairs need to be done."

I nodded, frowning at him as I sipped my whiskey.

"Why did you ask if I was a ghost-hunter?"

"You asked for 'Teach Droch-Chlú'. That's what the locals call it hereabouts, the house of evil reputation. We call it that on account that it has a reputation of being haunted. You know, it is one of the old 'famine' cottages which have survived in these parts."

I gave a diffident shake of the head and pressed the whiskey to my lips, enjoying its fiery warmth through my chill body.

"I was looking for Father Nessan Doheny," I explained.

The burly man stared at me a moment as if in surprise and then gave a low chuckle.

"So I *was* right then? Well now, I hope that you didn't find him."

I stopped rubbing my hands together and gazed at him in astonishment.

"Why do you say that?"

"Because Father Nessan Doheny has been dead these last one hundred and sixty years."

A chill, like ice, shot down my spine.

"Dead one hundred and sixty years?"

"Surely. Didn't you know the story? He led his flock to Musheramore

Castle during the time of the 'Great Hunger' to plead with Lord Musheramore to help the surviving peasants and stop the evictions. The soldiers were called in from Mallow and given orders to charge the people who were kneeling on the lawn of the castle in prayer. Father Nessan Doheny was sabred to death with many of his flock."

I swallowed hard.

"And . . . and what happened to Bríd Cappeen?"

He roared with laughter.

"Then you *do* know the old legend! Of course you did. It is local knowledge that 'Teach Droch-Chlú' was her old cabin. All part of the old legend. Well frankly, I think it is simply that. No more than a legend. Poor Father Doheny and the demented Bríd Cappeen are long since dead. To think on it, the idea of an old woman reanimating the corpse of a priest to enact vengeance on Lord Musheramore and his ilk! God save us!" He genuflected piously. "It is a legend and nothing else."

Dennis Etchison

The Blood Kiss

Dennis Etchison has written one of the classic stories of the zombie genre, "The Late Shift", which I have already included in The Mammoth Book of Terror. *Therefore his contribution to this volume is a more oblique interpretation of the anthology's theme, but is nonetheless as powerful a piece of writing as you would expect from one of the finest practitioners currently working in the horror field.*

As to the genesis of this particular story, Etchison explains that it grew out of his experiences as a staff writer for a certain television anthology series: "The script outline presented here is a shortened/simplified version of an outline we developed that never got the go-ahead from the network."

A winner of both the World Fantasy Award and the British Fantasy Award, Etchison's never-prolific writing career received a recent shot in the arm with the publication of his acclaimed new novel, Shadowman, *and his editorship of the anthology* MetaHorror. *On the horizon is another full-length work,* California Gothic, *the first American hardcover of his novel* Darkside, *a new collection of stories titled* Nightland, *a stage production of "The Dark Country," and various film and television projects, including developing a series for the international television market with Dario Argento, and the feature script* American Zombie.

SHE HAD TOLD herself that it might never get this far, all the while hoping against hope that it would. Now she could no longer be sure which was the delusion and which the reality. It was out of her control.

"*Chris*? You still here?" It was Rip, the messenger boy who had hung around long enough to become Executive in Charge of Special Projects. Whatever, exactly, that denoted. He caught the door as he passed her office, pivoting on one foot and swinging the other up to cross his knee with his ankle, the graceful pose of a dancer at rest or the arch maneuver of a runner pretending that he was so far ahead he no longer had to hurry. She couldn't decide. She studied him abstractedly and feigned amusement as he asked, "Aren't you going to the party tonight?"

"Do you care whether I go to the party tonight?"

"Sure." He grinned boyishly, as though forgetting for the moment that he was thirty-five years old. "The network's going to be there, you know." He glanced up and down the hall, ducked inside and lowered his voice to make a joke of his naked ambition. "You hear what we're getting for Milo?"

"Let me guess," she said. "A belly dancer? No, that was for his birthday. A go-go boy from Chippendale's?"

Rip imploded a laugh. "You've got to be kidding. He can't come out of the closet till the third season."

"You never know." You wish, she thought. Closet, my ass. I could tell you some things about Milo, if you really want to know. But you probably wouldn't believe me; it wouldn't fit your game plan, would it? Milo the Trouser Pilot. Dream on. "I give up," she said, "what?"

Rip closed the door behind him. "We hired this bimbo from Central Casting. She's going to come in – rush in at five minutes of twelve, all crying that she just totaled Milo's car out front. You know, the white 450 SL? She's so sorry, she's going to pay for everything, *if her insurance hasn't expired*. Milo's freaking, right? So she gets him up to the bedroom where the phone is, she's looking for the number, she starts to break down, she whips off her dress and offers herself – when all of a sudden, surprise! It's a strip-o-gram! Happy Valentine's Day! We're all coming. You got a camera, Chrissie?"

"I'll bring my 3-D."

"What?"

"See you there, R. Right now I've got to retype my outline." What time's it getting to be? she wondered.

"You mean 'Zombies'? I thought it was all set."

"It is. But Milo had some last-minute suggestions. Nothing major. He wants it on his desk tomorrow morning."

"Great," said Rip, no longer listening. "Well, don't work too hard."

If I don't, she thought, who will?

"And Chrissie?"

"Yeah?"

"Have yourself a fabulous evening, stag or drag. Remember, *Don't Open the Door's* headed straight for Number One – we've got it made! Uh, thanks to your episode, of course. 'Queen of the Zombies' is going to put us over the top!"

"Thanks for telling me that, R."

And don't call me Chrissie, she thought, as he let himself out.

I have it made, you have it made, they have it made, we have it made . . . I'd like to see them, Milo or anybody else in this production company, do the real work for once: interviewing writers, extracting stories, rewriting all night so there's something more than high concept to give the network . . . I should have stayed a secretary. At least I'd sleep better.

But then where would they be? And where would *I* be? Back in Fresno, she thought. At my parents'. Instead of here, scuttling around behind the scenes to hold this surrogate family together. If I had a dollar for every time I've saved Milo's tight little ass the night before a pitch . . .

With stories like this one, she thought, shuffling papers.

I finally found the right one. Oh, didn't I. This time, miraculously, it was all there when it came in over the transom; the only real work I had to do was to punch it up a bit and hand it to M for the presentation. The perfect episode to launch the second season. That's what they called it. I wanted them to think it was mine, let's be honest. And it worked. Am I really supposed to give back this office for the sake of an abstraction? Who is Roger Ryman? With the specifics changed it will be all but unrecognizable by the time it shoots – I'll see to that; they'll let me do the script. Who else? And with it will come a full credit at last, Guild membership . . . Who will be the wiser? Ryman is probably earning an honest living somewhere, and better off in the long run. He'll never see it. I'll bet he doesn't even have cable.

But what if one of his friends sees it?

Forget it, Chrissie. *Chris.* You're psyching yourself out.

You wanted in this way, admit it. You did.

She removed the last sheet of her latest revision from the typewriter, the one incorporating the changes from today's meeting with Milo, and began proofreading from page one:

QUEEN OF THE ZOMBIES
by
Christine Cross

1. 24-HOUR SUPERMARKET – NIGHT

Three o'clock in the morning. The market is under siege – by the walking dead.

Zombie shoppers converge on the **produce department**, where the NIGHT MANAGER and a CHECKER, his girlfriend, are hiding behind the lettuce. He's got to get her out of there before they spot her. They want something more than fruit and vegetables.

He makes it to the p.a. system, grabs the microphone, announces a special on liver as a diversion. The zombies shamble off to the **meat department**.

He sends the CHECKER crawling to the front door – but now zombie reinforcements are pouring in from outside. She changes course, sidles between the aisles, is pressed back to the **meat department**, where the zombies are busy feasting on liver.

One lone zombie arrives at the end of the cold case. All the meat is gone. Rings the bell with thick, jerky movements. No answer. So he climbs up over the counter, grabs the BUTCHER hiding there, lifts him, sticks a hand into the BUTCHER'S abdomen and takes his liver.

As the feeding frenzy continues, the CHECKER is splattered with blood and guts. She screams.

"CUT!"

We see that a movie is being shot in the market. But the GIRL, who plays the CHECKER won't stop screaming. As the zombies take off their masks she runs from the set, hysterical.

"Great!" the DIRECTOR says to his FX MAN. "Only next time more blood, okay, Marty?"

He goes off to find the GIRL.

* * *

2. OUTSIDE

In the parking lot, the DIRECTOR comforts her. She wants to please, knows she's not giving him what he needs, but it's too much for her. She's cracking. She's about ready to get on the bus back to Indiana.

The DIRECTOR needs her. She's going to be the Queen of the Zombies. He sends her back to the Holiday Inn. A hot bath, rest — what else can he do for her? He'll even rehearse her later, in private, if that's what it takes.

She put down the pages. Perfect, and so was the rest of it. Now it really moved. Screw the outline, she thought; I could go to script right now, while I've got the momentum, if Milo didn't need to send this version to the network for approval first. A formality. I could keep working — I didn't want to go to that god-awful party, anyway. I can have it done ahead of schedule . . . They'll finally realize how important I am to this operation. It might even occur to Milo that he needs an Associate Producer. Why not?

Was he still in his office? She could pay her respects now, beg off for the evening, explain that she's going home to work. That would impress the hell out of him. Wouldn't it?

She clipped her pages together and reached for her purse.

The hallway smelled faintly of disinfectant, and in the distance she heard already the bump and rattle of waste baskets as the cleaning woman moved from room to room in the building, wiping up other people's messes for them and making things right again. As Chris passed the reception area she saw the cart of brooms and cleansers behind a half-closed door, and beyond, through the window in Rip's office, the skyline darkening under a band of air made filthy by another day in the city. It was later than she had thought.

"Good night," she called out.

The cleaning woman straightened and wiped her heavy hands on her uniform, then let her arms hang limp with palms open, as if afraid to be accused of stealing. Her face was flat and expressionless.

"Have a nice — nice holiday," Chris added. Well, it wasn't really a holiday. Did the woman even understand English?

Before she went on they exchanged a last glance. The other's gaze was steady and all-accepting, beyond hope and yet strangely at peace. There was a hint of disapproval in the deadpan face; it left Chris vaguely uneasy, as if she were a teenager spotted sneaking in or out of her bedroom. In fact the look was almost pitying. Why? She lowered her eyes and moved away.

She rapped on Milo's door, then entered without waiting for permission.

The room was empty. Of course he hadn't bothered to say good night. Why should he? He never had before. That would change, of course. She had had her office for three days, but it would take awhile for that to sink in for all of them. Things would be different around here soon enough.

She saw the usual signs of a hasty departure. A row of empty Coke cans, a drawer still pulled out for Milo's feet, a flurry of message slips like unfilled prescriptions curling next to the phone, a rat's nest of papers teetering at the edge of the desk.

In spite of herself she found the sight more touching than appalling. He needed someone to bring order to his life, to tidy up after hours each night. He couldn't do it alone. It wasn't his fault, she reasoned; it was his nature . . . She felt like the sister who corrected his homework for him while he slept, the girlfriend who slipped him answers to the big test, the mother who saw to it that his hair was combed before he left for school. She was none of these things, she knew, but soon he would recognize her worth. The days of being taken for granted were over.

She smiled as she crossed the office and set her corrected outline triumphantly on the glass desktop, where it would be waiting for him in the morning. He couldn't miss it.

She stacked the message slips, centering her pages between the overflowing ashtray and the rings left by his coffee cup. She positioned his paperweight to hold the pages in place, aligned a pencil on either side to frame them, and started to leave.

The cart was clattering out of Rip's office, heading this way.

What if the cleaning woman rearranged things further, slid the pages to the bottom of the wrong pile?

Chris would have to tell her not to touch the desk.

But what if she could not make the woman understand?

She sighed and emptied the ashtray herself, dumped the cans into the waste basket, wiped the glass top and lined up the rest of his artifacts so that nothing on the desk would have to be touched. As she pushed his notepad under the phone and made ready to leave before being caught in the act, the bell within the phone mechanism tolled once, disturbed by the impact. She blinked.

And saw what was written on the top page of the pad.

She blinked again, reread it, her mind racing to understand.

It was in Milo's familiar scrawl, his last memo of the day. She had no trouble making it out. It read:

BILL S. TO WRITE QUEEN OF THE Z'S. WHO'S HIS AGENT?

She stared at it.

She put her hands on her hips, shifted her weight to one foot, then the other, looked out the window and saw nothing but blackness, and read it one more time before her eyes began to sting. The meaning was unmistakable.

Milo had already assigned someone else to do the full script.

She was not even in the running.

She never had been.

She would be lucky to receive a split credit. No, probably not even that much.

Suddenly the scales lifted from her eyes.

She could already envision another writer's name on the screen. Perhaps Milo's alone. It had happened before.

It follows, she thought. God, does it ever.

And I didn't even see it coming.

Of course she wouldn't be able to file a protest, because that could lead to an arbitration that might reveal the true author whose work she herself had appropriated.

I have, she thought, been had. Again.

But this time I'm not going to settle for the bone they've tossed me. Not now.

This time it stops here.

She picked up the ashtray and hurled it across the room. It smashed into the framed LeRoy Nieman print hanging on the wall. Then she took back the pages and walked out of the office, bits of broken glass sticking to the soles of her shoes and grinding underfoot.

Startled, the cleaning woman stepped aside.

"Not this time," Chris told her through tears of rage. "*Comprende?* I – I'm sorry. Excuse me . . ."

I've made a mistake. A terrible, terrible mistake.

Or someone has.

In her office, she riffled through the file until she found the original draft synopsis, submitted without an agent by an unknown whom she had never met, Roger R. Ryman. He had included both his home and work phone numbers on the title page.

She throttled the receiver, breaking a fingernail as she dialed.

At first he didn't recognize her name. But when she said the magic words, *Don't Open the Door*, he remembered the series and his submission and almost squeezed through the phone to lick her face.

Yes, he would meet her anywhere, anytime.

She gave him Milo's address.

He didn't think it at all odd that she asked him to meet her at a Valentine's party.

3. AT THE HOLIDAY INN

She calls home tearfully. She's getting ready for that bath, when the DIRECTOR walks in.

Everything's going to be all right. You can do it, he tells her. He'll work with her personally. He takes the part of a zombie during their run-through, touches her, grabs her, enfolding her. She responds desperately, forgetting the script. She needs him. And she thinks he needs her.

4. LATER

She calls home again — but with a different story this time. Yes, she's doing okay. She's going to make it out here, after all.

"And Mama? I met a man. Not just any man. He's wonderful, so kind. He really cares what happens to me . . ."

Great, she thought. Now the only question is, Which one is he?

Bodies of all sizes and shapes streamed past her, arrayed in costumes of one sort or another — heart-shaped hats, dresses with arrows, shoes with cuddly designs, kitschy T-shirts, enameled pins, patterned headbands, pastel jogging suits from the Beverly Center, ersatz camp from Melrose Avenue. Teddy bears lurked in corners with *billets-doux* pinned to their bibs; mylar balloons drubbed at the ceiling like air bubbles at the surface of an aquarium. She gasped for breath as unidentifiable people bobbed around her, all luminous collars and teeth under the ultraviolet lights, and searched for an opening before the pressure of the music closed in on her again. As she swam against the flow for the nearest door, something like a pincer tried to grasp her thigh, while in the shadows the bears with their shiny black sharks' eyes seemed to move their heads, following her progress.

Another record began to pound, "Waiting Out the Eighties" by the Coupe de Villes, as long-necked men with trimmed moustaches collected around a garish buffet in the kitchen. She had almost passed through when she noticed a huge dyed paté, its top cleaved to resemble the wings of a gull in flight. The center collapsed to reveal a dull, livery interior as the men dipped *hors d'oeuvres* into the mold and made jokes, a thin film of workout sweat glazing their receding hairlines. She recognized the most animated of the conversationalists.

"Rip . . ."

He grasped her shoulder and drew her to arm's length, holding her until he finished his joke, as though she had intruded on an audition. When he finished he threw his head back and laughed too loudly, his Adam's apple bouncing up and down in a vigorous swallowing motion. Finally he turned to her.

"Chrissie, love!" He pulled her closer. "Mark, I'd like you to meet our new Story Editor."

"Rip, have you seen . . .?"

"No, I don't know where Milo's scampered off to. But I'll bet he's up to no good." He hooked a thumb at the ceiling. "Try topside."

"Rip, if anyone asks for me . . ."

"If I were you, love – " Rip winked. "I wouldn't disturb him just yet."

I'm on my own, she thought. I always have been. The rest was an illusion.

"Never mind." She hoisted a fresh champagne glass, emptied it. "See you at midnight," she said, slipping through to the stairs.

There were a lot of voices up there. Perhaps that was where she would find what she was looking for. It was getting late, and she had to have everything in place before the fireworks started.

5. MAKEUP AREA – THE NEXT DAY

She's in the chair, getting the coddling she needs from her new family. The MAKEUP MAN is kind, sensitive. She may have left her real family back home, but at last she feels that she belongs somewhere.

When she leaves the chair, the MAKEUP MAN and CREW change their tune. The poor kid's getting to be a pain. She's too nervous, high-strung, dangerously unstable. But it's too late to replace her. Time is running out.

6. ON THE SET

She breaks down again. The DIRECTOR tries to coach her but it's still not enough. She's too insecure. After take twelve, she pleads with him for the chance to do it again.

"Tell me the way you told me last night. I only want it to be good."

"That's all I want, too," he tells her.

The dim stairway was tricky. A blur of zippy, ironic faces as she ascended: young men without sideburns and casually elegant young women dragged along like camp followers, their made-up smiles fixed and grimly determined. Her wrist brushed something cold and slick. It was a heart-shaped satin pillow, carried as an offering by someone of indeterminate gender. She drew away and hugged the wall as she stepped over sodden paper plates; she made out an imprint of two lovebirds billing and cooing beneath half-eaten potato salad and drooping chicken wings.

"Excuse me," she said.

"Excuse *me*," said the person with the pillow. "Are you the one?"

"I hope so," she said, averting her eyes and hurrying on. Then the words and the masculine timbre of the voice registered. She stopped, looking back.

"I beg your pardon," she said, "but . . ."

Below, a nostalgic sixties strobe light flickered over dancing heads, rendering them all as anonymous as a second-unit crew.

She felt as if she were still trapped in a pattern that had been set decades ago. It would never change unless she did something about it. This was no time to falter. She remembered something her father had said to her before he went away. *When you sit, sit. When you stand, stand. But don't wobble.* The last few hours had brought his words home to her; now she understood.

Where was he? Time was running out.

She scanned the tops of the heads below, but the man with the heart was gone.

She started back down the stairs, panicking. He must not get away.

From the other side of the stairwell, something shiny thrust out to touch her.

"You are," said the man with the satin pillow. "I can tell."

"Thank God."

She pressed him up the stairs to the second landing. A dimmer hallway stretched ahead, cut across by shafts of subdued light from the several bedrooms. She did not remember which was Milo's but knew she must find it before the appointed hour. From below she heard a rush of excitement. Was the girl Rip had hired here already?

"Come with me," she said. "We have to talk."

7. HOTEL DINING ROOM

The DIRECTOR is having dinner with his PRODUCER. The pressure is on to finish in time. But the DIRECTOR can do it. He's done it before. The last scene is going to be a killer.

In the scene the GIRL'S boyfriend, the NIGHT MANAGER from the supermarket, will lead soldiers to a graveyard to rescue her. There will be lots of pyrotechnics.

Now the GIRL appears in the dining room. She sits down without being invited, expecting to be warmly received. She assumes that she is part of the DIRECTOR'S life now. She waits for his greeting. But he only looks at her. He takes her aside and tells her impatiently to grow up. This is real life.

8. FX TRAILER

The DIRECTOR goes to his FX MAN for help. The GIRL is hanging everybody up. He can't let it go on this way. Nothing is more important than the picture.

What scenes does she have left? They go over the storyboards: only the Burning of the Zombies. The NIGHT MANAGER will lead the attack on the graveyard, shotgunning dummies of zombies behind the gravestones. Then the National Guard lobs grenades in – the boyfriend will have to run a careful path around the explosive charges. Once the dummies are blown, he'll torch them with a flamethrower.

All they need from the GIRL is a close-up of her as she receives a blood squib from the shotgun, her shocked expression as she comes to her senses and recognizes her lover at the instant he kills her. Then cut to an exploding dummy.

Is there a way to shoot around her? Long shots, a better dummy, more bloody and effects to cover? The other zombies will be blown away using dummy substitutes, but they need her for the reaction shots – she's the Queen of the Zombies.

MARTY is always one step ahead. He's saved the DIRECTOR'S ass time and again. This time he's already made an alginate cast of the GIRL. He's got a full latex body mold of her ready as a back-up. It is lifelike to the tiniest detail. It's more than a dummy – it can be worn by a double, if necessary. Now they can finish with or without the GIRL.

You're a genius, the DIRECTOR tells him. This is going to be a bloody masterpiece regardless of actors. They're nothing but trouble, anyway.

She led him on down the hall. There was a lilting peal of laughter from the first bedroom; from the second she heard boisterous chatter, and through the unlatched door glimpsed a pale hand with razor blade describing furiously in the air above a horizontal mirror. The third was closed, with a crude sign attached to the doorknob: PRIVATE — OFF LIMITS. That, she guessed, was Rip's doing.

She pulled the man with the heart into the adjoining bathroom. The connecting door was ajar; in the bedroom, the soft, filtered glow of a small lamp. It was enough. "Here, we can be alone . . ."

He stood uncertainly in the middle of the bathroom floor. "I've been waiting for you," he said.

"I know. I've been waiting for you, too," she told him, and heard giggles and footsteps approaching in the hall.

"Busted," he said.

"No." She backed up to secure the door. "Not us."

Leaning against it, she allowed her eyes to flutter shut. She waited for the room to stop spinning so that she could make the speech she had rehearsed. When she opened her eyes, he had moved closer.

He stood before her and tilted his head quizzically.

"But you don't know what I've got planned, do you?" she said. "I should explain."

"You don't have to," he said. "I think I understand."

"How could you?"

"I told you. I've been waiting a long time."

"Forgive me. I'm being rude. I don't mean to be. It's just that it's all happened so fast . . ."

"Take it easy," he said. He withdrew to give her breathing space and sat on the edge of the tub. "I don't mind waiting a little longer." A reflection from the tiles glinted playfully in his eyes.

Good, she thought. He's game.

"As long as it's not too long," he said.

In the hall, the footsteps and the giggling drew nearer.

9. ON THE SET

The GIRL arrives with notes in hand, more eager than ever to please her director.

But he's not in his chair. Somebody else is — a woman.

The DIRECTOR'S WIFE. The crew is gathered around, laughing and reminiscing. The WIFE is now the center of attention. The GIRL is displaced.

She finds the DIRECTOR and tells him off. He uses people. He doesn't care about anything but blood, blood and more blood. Why did he lead her on? She'll tell the world, starting with his WIFE.

He tells her the facts of life. "She already knows." He doesn't need the GIRL anymore. The relationship is a wrap.

As she runs from the set, the WIFE observes. How sweet and innocent the GIRL looks. "I hope she doesn't take it too seriously. I used to — but now we lead separate lives. I learned a long time ago that this is his only real world — making movies. It's all he lives for. Real flesh and blood can't compete. The only thing he's truly married to is his capacity for illusion . . ."

10. GRAVEYARD – THE LAST NIGHT

The crew is working feverishly to rig everything for the climax.

The DIRECTOR lingers after the rest of the crew have gone home. At 4 a.m. he finishes checking every detail. The zombie dummies are propped up on armatures behind the tombstones, the oil-smoke pots are ready, the crosses are tilted just so. Nothing left but to call "action" at dawn. For now, he'll catch an hour's shuteye in his trailer.

"It won't be long," she said when the footsteps passed.

He shook his head sadly. "It's been such a long, long time," he said at last. "I'd almost given up hope. But you are the one, aren't you? Yes. You are."

"I'm the one," she said. "Now listen . . ."

He waved the stuffed heart. "I've been carrying this around, trying to find the right person to give it to." He made a sound that was halfway between a laugh and a shudder. "But no one would take it."

"You didn't need to do that," she said. Something to recognize him by? She could not remember any mention of it on the phone. It was a good idea, of course; it would have made him easier to spot. Or was it a gift? "What is it?"

He stood and came closer, holding it out. "What does it look like? I wanted to give it away, but there were never any takers. I wonder why that is? But now you're – "

"Yes, of course. There isn't much time. I don't know where to begin. You must be wondering why I brought you here."

"It doesn't matter."

"It does! That's what I'm trying to tell you. I see a lot of people . . ."

"So do I," he said. "Or I did. That's all over now."

Somehow he had gotten across the floor and was now only inches from her. She couldn't see his face; in the shadows he could have been anyone. She recalled a brief flash on the stairs: kind features, pained eyes, a hangdog expression. That only made her feel worse. She forced herself to go on. She could make things right. It was not too late.

Before she could speak, he braced his hands on either side of her head and leaned in to kiss her.

At first she was too dumbfounded to resist. Then she thought, Oh Christ, not at a time like this. Then she thought, What did he imagine when I called him, led him here . . .?

My God.

"Wait," she said, breaking and turning aside.

But he pressed her and enfolded her mouth again.

At that moment someone pushed on the other side of the door at her back, trying to gain entry. Her front teeth struck his with a grinding like fingernails on a blackboard.

"Sorry," mumbled a voice from the hall.

She spread her hands against his chest. "No," she said, "please, you don't understand. That's not what this is about."

"What *is* this about, then?"

"Will you hurry up in there?" said the voice from the hall.

She was shaken, confused. But there was no time for that. The clock was ticking.

Now there was a pounding on the door.

"This way," she said, and dragged him through the connecting door to the bedroom.

"I wish you'd make up your mind."

"Listen," she said, "my name's – "

"I don't care."

"You sent me a story, right? I showed it to my producer. He liked it. So much that he wants it for next season. *But not to buy it.* Oh, I'm sorry, I'm not making myself clear. It's my fault, too. I'll tell you about that later. But you'd better get down to WGA Manuscript Registry first thing in the morning. File whatever you've got – preliminary drafts, notes, anything."

"Why should I do that?"

"I'm trying to help you! They're going to steal your story. When Milo comes up here, I want you to tell him who you are."

She took the pages of the original version from her purse.

"I had to warn you. Whatever he says, don't back down. We're in this together. Now any minute all hell's going to break loose. Regardless of anything, know that I'll stand up for you. I want to make it up somehow. Maybe you'll end up hating me, I don't know. But I've got to try. I'm truly sorry. Believe that."

She inhaled, exhaled, wishing her heart would slow down. In the bathroom a few feet away, someone locked the doors.

The bedroom was quiet, the lighting cool. On the nightstand the contents of a lava lamp flowed together, heated up and broke apart again into separate bodies, endlessly. Her mouth hurt; it was warm and wet. There was a sound of water running.

"What, may I ask," the man said, "are you talking about?"

"I'm trying to tell you that I'm all for you," she said, "no matter what."

Impatience flared in his eyes.

"Make up your mind," he said.

11. AT HIS TRAILER

The graveyard is spooky – he almost feels that he's being followed. He's about to enter the trailer when a ghoul appears. It's the GIRL, in full ghastly makeup.

He tries to get rid of her, knowing she's not really needed. But this time she's coming on differently. Not whining and needful, but happy as a puppy dog and all set to please. See? She's ready, and she's going to be perfect. She's even worked out a little something extra for her moment of death. It's her own idea and she's sure he's going to like it. If she can just try it out on him first.

She seems to have accepted reality. She really wants more than anything else for the picture to be good, after all. The same thing he wants. It's all that matters. She realizes that now.

"You've taught me a lot. More than you know. Now let me give you something back – what you really want. I want it now, too."

* * *

12. IN THE TRAILER

She runs through her expressions as he stands in for her lover.
She screams on cue. Almost perfect. She needs to try it with
the shotgun. She's brought it with her, already loaded with
wax blood bullets. She's thought of everything.

"You want it to be real, don't you?" She presses him to take
the prop gun. "We have to do it right. I want you to see how
much I'm willing to give you. Let's do it all the way. And this
time you're going to get everything you want. I promise."

He's reluctant, but he plays it out. When she starts screaming,
he fires the shotgun. The look in her eyes is one of peace at last,
as blood explodes and she sinks down the wall to the floor.

"Jesus, that was great! What a take! If we'd had a camera . . ."
He leans down, shakes her. "Cut. That's it. You've finally got
it. Hey, what's the . . .?"

He touches the wound. **It's real**. When she handed him the
gun, it had a live round in the chamber. She had planned it
that way.

He cleans up frantically to get rid of the evidence – no one will
believe what really happened.

What about the body?

A desperate plan. He'll replace her dummy on the set with
the real thing, propping her up behind the tombstone like
all the other dummies. The evidence will be blown to hell,
then burned to a cinder. When the flamethrower hits her,
the rubber makeup will burn like napalm. There won't be
anything left.

He'll put her into position himself. No one will notice.

"I'm doing you a favor," she told him. "At least that's what I'm trying
to do. If you'll let me."
   "Are you the one?" he repeated more forcefully.
   "Yes. I mean no." She evaded his grasp once again. "I mean . . ."
   "But you said you're the one." He waved the heart-shaped pillow.
   "Not like that," she said. "This is about something more important.
Don't you see?"
   "I should have known. You're not who I thought you were."

"Yes!"

"Which is it?" he said, angry now.

"Just – not the way you mean it!"

He was about to leave.

"This is very important to me," she said.

"To you," he said. "It always gets down to that."

"And to you! What's the matter with you? Haven't you heard a word I've been saying? Can't you . . .?"

He glared down at her. He tapped the pillow into her chest. "It never changes. You're just like all the rest." He tapped her again more aggressively. "It's always me, isn't it? *Isn't it.*"

"What do you mean?"

"What do *you* mean?" he said fiercely, directly into her face.

Her scalp began to crawl. Who is this man? she thought. I've made another mistake, the biggest one of all.

"Wh-who are you?" she said.

"Who are *you*," he said, "to ask that? Who the fuck do you think you are?"

She tried to dodge him as he lunged for her, a lifetime of disappointment igniting his rage. He grabbed her and flung her against the hall door before she could get it open, pushed himself in front of her. The pillow thrust up under her chin, forcing her head back. It wasn't soft, after all. It had something dangerously hard inside it. In fact it wasn't a pillow. It was an elaborate, padded Valentine gift box.

He raised it high. She saw the red heart poised to strike her, the satin covering worn, tattered, stained but still a deep crimson, like his face and the roadmap of years there, like the blood that ran from his cut lip. She didn't know who he was. He could have been anyone.

He was a madman.

Suddenly the door rattled. It rammed into her spine as someone tried to open it. She was driven into his arms.

"Huh? Oh. Sorry." Milo's voice through the crack, and behind him the sound of hysterical, theatrical weeping. "Come on. There's another phone down the hall."

"Wait!"

"Have fun . . ."

The man in front of her hesitated. In that moment she made her move and sprang for the doorknob. But he was on her. She twisted around and snatched the heart, heavier than she had imagined, and hit him with it. When he would not let go of her she swung it at his face again and again. She heard a dull breaking sound as she struck bone. The box broke and lumps of candy went flying, shriveled and hard as rocks. He dropped to his knees, a mystified look in his eyes, and toppled forward.

Then other people were in the room, Rip leading the way. Cheerful whispers turned to gasps.

"*What have you done?*" someone said.

"I didn't do anything! He – he was – "

"He was what? What did he do?" A tall woman moved to comfort her. She smoothed Chris's hair, saw the bruised lips, the torn buttons, the wild look. "It's all right now. He tried to assault you, didn't he? I've seen his kind before. The bastard."

"Who is that guy?" someone else said. "Who invited him?"

"I'll call a doctor."

"It was self-defense," said the woman, holding Chris too tightly. "Don't say a word to anybody. Do you understand? You had no choice. Who knows what he would have done to you if he'd had the chance? Something much worse. You know that, don't you?"

Chris had never seen her before. Now she could not remember any of the other faces, either.

She tore free and rushed to the stairs.

Below, in the empty living room, the music had stopped. One solitary young man remained. He stood up self-consciously.

"Excuse me," he said, "but do you know a Christine Cross?"

She stared at him dumbly. She could not think of an answer.

"Well, if you see her, would you mind telling her that I've been looking for her? My name's Roger. I'm supposed to meet her here. Hey, is something wrong? Is that blood on your . . .?"

Without breaking stride she ran outside, the taste of blood, her own or someone else's, drying to salt on her lips.

13. DAWN

All is ready: backlight through fog, tilted crosses. Zombies propped up like shooting gallery targets.

The DIRECTOR tells MARTY to use extra-strength charges. He doesn't want to see anything left when the smoke clears, not even the animal blood and guts inside the dummies.

"ACTION!"

The boyfriend, the NIGHT MANAGER, runs like a soldier through a mine field. Dummies are shotgunned one by one, then blown up, then torched. All except the GIRL. She will be the last shot. Where is she for her close-up?

We don't need her, says the DIRECTOR, winking at MARTY.

She's not on the set? Who knows where she is — probably on the bus back to Indiana. Who cares? This is my picture and I say we don't need her. We've got a perfect dummy. Just blow it up — now.

"ACTION!"

The NIGHT MANAGER advances on her, shotgun ready. But before he can fire, her head lolls to one side.

"Wait," calls the SCRIPT GIRL. "Her head's out of position — it won't match."

"I'll fix it," says MARTY.

"No!" The DIRECTOR can't let anyone handle her — they'll discover it's a real body. He'll have to do it himself.

"Watch your step!" yells MARTY.

The DIRECTOR threads a careful path to her tombstone. Tries not to look at her face as he adjusts the head. There. He stands back.

Ready?

"Hold it," says MARTY. Now there's blood running out of her mouth. The shot still won't match.

"Just get it, will you?" says the DIRECTOR. He grabs the shotgun and prepares to fire the blood pellet into her himself. But before he can pull the trigger, her head lolls again as she starts to come to. She's not dead!

He pumps a shot into her, another. But the bullets aren't real this time. Her eyes open and look at him, seeing him there in her moment of triumph. She smiles.

"Die," he mutters, "die . . .!"

She raises her arms, zombie-like, as if to embrace him.

He lunges at her, his hands going for her throat to make it right for the last time. Her arms go around him, pressing him to her in a final paroxysm — and the wires attached to her body make contact, setting off the charge. They are blown up together, married in blood for all eternity.

It's the last shot, the best effect of the film.

END

Christopher Fowler

Night After Night of the Living Dead

Christopher Fowler lives and works in London, where he runs The Creative Partnership, a Soho film promotion company that, uniquely in Britain, specializes in selling movies to the public. His first short story collection, City Jitters, *featured interlinked "Tales of Urban Malevolence". He has since had three further volumes of short stories published,* City Jitters Two, The Bureau of Lost Souls *and* Sharper Knives. *His story "The Master Builder" was recently aired as a CBS-TV movie starring Tippi Hedren, while another, "Left Hand Drive", has been filmed for British television.*

His first four novels, Roofworld, Rune, Red Bride *and* Darkest Day *loosely make up a "London Quartet", and other projects include another novel,* Spanky; Menz Insana, *a series of adult graphic tales about an insane doctor illustrated by John Bolton, and* High Tension, *an original screenplay.*

In case you couldn't guess by the title, Fowler says he wrote the following story after watching the George A. Romero movie trilogy one Sunday afternoon and asking himself why everyone so readily accepted the concept of the living dead.

"Romero addressed the question of what happened in the days following the awakenings," explains the author, "but nobody concerned themselves with matters

of logic. First and foremost, why did the dead awake? How did reanimated corpses manage to force themselves out of the ground? And how the hell would eating living people help them?

"The answer, I imagined, was that adults didn't ask themselves questions like these. That's what children are provided for. So it made sense to look at the problem through the eyes of a child."

Fowler also admits to once burying a dead tortoise as a child, and digging it up weeks later to see if the shell was empty. "We were horrified to find the thing moving about by itself in its box," he reveals. "It had been reanimated thanks to some heavy maggot activity, so we took this to be proof not of reanimation but reincarnation, and therefore the permanence of the soul."

All of which hopefully gives you some idea of what to expect during the "Night After Night of the Living Dead" . . .

THE BEST THING about the dead is you can't get pregnant from sitting on a chair they've just been sitting on, like you can with live people. When live people warm up the seat (especially the toilet seat – that's where AIDS comes from) and you sit on it after them and it's still warm, the heat activates the hormones in your body and fertilizes the eggs, and nine months later you have a baby. But the dead don't leave warm seats because their body temperature is about the same as winter tap water.

The worst thing about the dead is they don't sleep, so if you go downstairs for a glass of water in the middle of the night you're liable to find my grandpa sitting at the kitchen table staring off into the dark, and this frankly gives me the creeps. We have the Night Of The Living Dead to thank for all of this. The most interesting thing about that occasion (apart from the fact that it happened in the middle of the afternoon) is that such a cataclysmic event didn't seem to bother many people at the time. Personally speaking I find that weird because I was only eleven when it happened and it fucked me up considerably, I can tell you.

You probably know all about it – I mean you'd have to have been living in a monastery on the Orkney Islands for the last three years to avoid knowing – but I'll tell you anyway, because (a) it will give like a personal perspective on the whole thing and (b) I'm doing this as my mid-term English essay.

For a start, it was nothing like the movie.

If you saw that particular classic, you'll remember how the dead came out of the ground and stumped about in waist-high mist with their arms stretched out like sleepwalkers. This was not exactly accurate. Think about it; when they bury someone the coffin is sealed and put in a hole that's packed with earth and tamped down, so we're talking about several hundred pounds of wet dirt to push up, assuming that you can get the lid of the box open in the first place – which you wouldn't be able to do because there's not enough depth in most coffins to give your arms the necessary leverage. The simple fact is, nobody came out of the ground. When the dead came back to life it was only the ones in the morgues and hospitals that reawoke, and if any others were lying around above ground for any reason, they would have risen too.

They didn't walk with their arms raised either; their hands hung limply at their sides and they didn't really move about much, although they did fall over a lot. But the main difference with the film is that they didn't kill people and try to eat their brains. If you think it through logically, how could they? They were dead, and that means brain-dead, and wanting to eat someone else's brains suggests conscious thought, which they don't have. Eating a brain isn't going to restore your own. That's like saying if you eat part of a cow you'll grow four stomachs. Also, if you wanted to eat someone's brains you'd have to get their head open, which I shouldn't think is as easy as it looks on the screen. It's like the vampire thing in movies. You know, the biting part, when Dracula makes two holes in someone's neck and sucks the blood out. Excuse me, but did someone just cancel the laws of physics or something? When you open a tin of condensed milk you have to make a hole on either side of the can to allow the milk to escape. So a vampire would have to make sure that his mouth only went over one of the holes, otherwise he wouldn't be able to suck any blood out – unless he could really suck, in which case the person he was sucking would sort of dent inwards like a punctured football.

So. No coming out of the ground, no eating brains. That's the trouble with the living dead, they're nothing like their movie counterparts. In fact, they're really boring. These days some of them can do rudimentary root-memory things like read *The Sun* or hum songs from *Cats*, but you can't train them any more than you can train really stupid insects or our biology teacher's dog. You can point up in the air and they'll follow your finger but then they'll stay like that for hours, like chickens expecting rain. And it's because they're dead, end of story. I mean, dead is it, finito, after you're dead you don't understand the punchlines to jokes or remember to set the video, it's all over, baby. I don't specifically remember much about the night it happened except that it was a Wednesday, it was raining hard and I was late home from school. I'd been caught unravelling the elastic inside a golf ball during Social Studies and had been made to stay behind for Detention. I remember walking home and seeing one of the dead shuffling ahead, a man of about fifty. My first sighting. It was a weird experience, as though I'd been waiting all of my admittedly short life to see something like this, and now that I had it made sense of everything else.

The figure before me was drifting more than walking, his feet barely rising from the ground. As far as I could see in the fading light he was dressed in normal street clothes, although they were dirty, as though he'd been in a fight. His head was lowered a little but he was staring forward and seemed to know where he was going. As I drew abreast of him I caught an overpowering stench of chemicals, formaldehyde I suppose, as though he had just heaved himself up from the mortuary slab. His face was grey and speckled, the texture of my Dad's IBM slipcase, but his eyes were the real giveaway. They had this fixed dry look, like doll's eyes, I guess because there was no fluid to lubricate them and they were stuck in one position. I kept pace with him as I passed, and it was then that I realized I wasn't really scared.

When someone is dangerous they give off warning signals, and if you're receptive to the signals you back away. But this guy was just dead and there weren't any signals, good or bad, and I instinctively knew that the worst thing that could happen was he could fall over and land on top of me. The street was pretty empty, and the few people who passed us didn't seem to see anything wrong. I guess in the rain-hazed dimness there was nothing unusual to see beyond the fact that the old man didn't have a raincoat on and was getting pretty soaked. Finally I arrived at my turning, and the dead guy just shuffled onwards into the gloom. I watched him go for a while, then headed home.

I missed the early evening TV news but asked my mother if there had been anything about the dead coming back to life and she made a face and said no. I remembered noticing that her eyes were puffy and red, as if she'd been crying about something and was trying not to let me see. Later, on the portable in my room, the footage appeared. There right in front of me, live on cable, the anchorwoman was awkwardly reading a report that several cadavers in a hospital morgue in Leeds had been found walking along the corridors of the building. She said similar phenomena were being reported all over the world, although I don't think she believed a word of it. Then some ecosystems guy who looked like he'd just got out of bed kept patting down his hair and saying it was all to do with the ozone layer, and I thought As If. I mean, you don't have to be a rocket scientist to figure out that there's no link between the depletion of the ozone layer and the reanimation of dead tissue. That's like saying Nintendo games give you rabies or something, get a grip.

I tuned the TV to CNN because they repeat the same stories over and over, and there it was, actual footage of ZOMBIES lumbering along roads and bumping into walls and generally looking thick. I rang my friend Joey "Boner" Mahoney to tell him to turn on the TV but his dog stepmother answered and told me it was too late to talk to him.

The next day I attempted to discuss what was happening with my friends at school, but no one was that interested except Simon Waters. Unfortunately Simon believes that crop circles are made by Venusians, not by a couple of sad guys with a piece of rope and a plank, and is desperate to believe in any scenario that's more interesting than his own miserable existence, which consists of getting lousy marks at school and going home to a father who is having an affair with a foot specialist. That was when I began my Deadwatch, which is a notebook marked out so that I can record each dead sighting as it happens.

With each passing day there were more and more sightings as the walking dead took to the streets. Soon I was recording as many as ten or fifteen on a single Saturday morning (the women are particularly fond of milling around the Trolley Collection Point outside Sainsbury's), and I stopped bothering with the book because there were too many to keep up with. To begin with, most of these ambulatory cadavers were in pretty good condition. I mean their jaws and ears weren't hanging off or anything, but once in a while you'd see one in a really bad state. There was a guy on the bus in a hospital gown, and the stitches down the front of his chest had burst open so that his intestines were hanging out and rolling from side to side as the bus turned corners. That was pretty gross. But in the early days most of the corpses seemed to stay in one piece.

You see, it wasn't just a Night Of The Living Dead, as we had thought at first. It was a Night After Night. The effects of whatever had revived them were sticking around, so the authorities had to come up with some kind of legislation to cope with the problem. They simply arranged for bodies to be buried at a new standard depth and for mortuary doors to be kept locked. Still, an awful lot of Deadies seemed to be walking around, more every day, so either someone was letting them out (which I'd seen a Right-To-Life group doing on the news) or they were finding ways to escape prior to burial.

The government couldn't settle on a reason for what was happening, and still haven't come up with a satisfactory cause to this day. They set up an independent enquiry to investigate what was going on — i.e. cut open some corpses and have a poke around — but found nothing conclusive. The corpses were just inert organisms that wouldn't lay still. They had no heartbeats and coagulated blood and hardened veins and leathery skin and dry staring eyes. At first the scientists thought it was radiation in the atmosphere, then Rogue Viral DNA, but I knew they really didn't have a clue when everyone started to blame the French. Anyway, none of this really touched my family or our lives. We continued to see the dead sitting in bus-shelters looking neither happy nor sad (looking like they were waiting for a bus really). We saw them in gents outfitters staring vaguely at the shelves, we saw them standing shellshocked outside cinemas and pizza parlours (they weren't allowed near food but they seemed to enjoy being in queues) and we saw them sunbathing in park deckchairs with newspapers over their faces, and the only way you could tell they were dead was because it was raining.

I guess this was about a month after the actual NOTLD, and now that everyone could see the dead weren't going to hurt anybody, all kinds of trouble started. For one thing, no matter how harmless they were, the dead tended to creep people out. It was only natural; the way they looked and smelled was depressing to say the least. The police wanted special powers to round them up because they were always falling onto railway lines and wandering into busy traffic, but all kinds of groups began protesting, arguing that because they were still walking around the dead had souls and therefore had human rights.

Then doctors began worrying that the bodies would decompose and put everyone at risk from germs, but the corpses didn't really rot. Because the newly dead leaked so much they slowly got drier and more leathery, and this was helped by the fact that it was winter and a lot of them had taken to sitting in libraries where the central heating caused an arid atmosphere.

They got damaged and tatty-looking from constantly bumping into things, and some of them lost fingers and clumps of hair, which made them even creepier looking. (Oddly enough, they managed to keep a natural sense of propriety. If one of them tore his trousers he would tug the hole around so that people wouldn't have to sit on the tube facing his willy.) While television shows and newspaper articles preached respect for the dead, teenage gangs began going out and tampering with the bodies, cutting bits off or dressing them in inappropriate clothes to make them look silly. My friend Joey once saw an old man in the high street wearing a glitter wig and a ballet tutu. Also, some unscrupulous entrepreneurs hung advertising on them, but most people disapproved of this.

The dead weren't supposed to travel on the tubes because they never bought tickets, but one or two always managed to get through the barriers, only to spend the entire day trying to open the drawers on the platform's chocolate machines. They never made much noise, I think their vocal chords sort of dried out over time, but God, the older ones started to look awful. The problem was, even if they fell into the river and floated about for a few days being run over by motorboats, they would eventually drift to the shore, to climb out and begin aimlessly walking around again. Hospital crews collected the most disgusting ones and took them away somewhere.

Around this time I remember seeing an old woman fall off a Routemaster bus and get dragged around the block on her face. I followed her just to see what would happen if her coat-strap managed to disentangle itself from the pole. When the poor old love finally hauled herself to her feet (nobody was willing to help her – the dead are kind of ignored now, like the homeless) the remaining part of her face fell off like torched wallpaper, leaving her with tarmac-scraped bone and a surprised expression. It was not a pleasant sight.

A few weeks after this, one wet Saturday afternoon, my grandpa died. He had lived in the house with us for years even though my mother had never liked him, and at first nobody realized that he had died. He just stayed in his armchair all day staring at the television, but I knew something was wrong because he would normally start shouting at the screen when the wrestling came on and today he didn't. He did make himself a cup of tea, but he left the teabag in the mug, drank it scalding and immediately peed it back out. My father wouldn't let my mother call the hospital and they had a huge row, after which it was decided that grandpa could stay for a while so long as he didn't get in anyone's way. My mother refused to change his clothes, but Dad argued that they wouldn't need changing very often as he no longer had operative sweat glands. Still, it was difficult to break the old geezer of his teamaking habit. I guess when you've been making 10 cups of Brooke Bond a day for 60 years you don't need motor-neurons.

Grandpa wasn't allowed out by himself because he had a tendency not to come back and we would have to go looking for him. Once I was allowed to go on a grandpa-hunt with my Dad, and we had to search the park just as it was starting to get dark. There were dozens of them – Deadies – sitting motionless beneath the rustling elm trees. They were seated in deckchairs around the bandstand with their hands in their laps, quietly waiting for the music to start. It was a strange sight. I stopped going to the park after that.

A few days later I took grandpa to the cinema. I guess it was an odd thing to do, but I was supposed to be looking after him and there was a film I really wanted to see, one of those slasher films with music that creeps up on you, and I managed to pass grandpa off as alive, although the usherette looked suspiciously at us. Halfway through the film, just when the heroine had gone to the cellar to look for her cat even though she knew there was a homicidal maniac loose, I turned to find the old man staring at me with wide, flat eyes. He wasn't breathing of course, and his mouth hung open to reveal a thick dry tongue that looked as if it had been carved out of Spam. What bothered me most was the way he repeated one of his living mannerisms, tilting his head slightly to look at me, so that for a moment I couldn't tell if he was really dead. It was just the illusion of life, of course, but an unsettling one.

A few weeks later, grandpa took it upon himself to revive another root-memory and peel some potatoes. He remembered the peeler but unfortunately forgot to use it in conjunction with a vegetable, and succeeded in removing most of the skin from his fingers before I came home from school and found him staring at a set of bony protrusions that looked like badly sharpened pencils. The very next day he sat down on the stove while the burners were lit and seared himself badly. My mother threatened to leave us if my father didn't arrange for him to be put somewhere, so the following morning found me standing on the doorstep waving goodbye to grandpa as he stared sightlessly back and stumbled off across the flowerbeds, led by a disinterested hospital porter smoking a joint.

I rarely leave my bedroom now. I don't go to school anymore. There are just too many dead people about, and it bothers me. They blunder into the garden at night and follow you to the shops and fall down the steps of public lavatories and float past you on the ferry, and it's undignified. My mother seems to understand how I feel, and lets me have most of my meals in my room. She's become overfriendly with the cocktail cabinet these days, anyway. The extraordinary thing is, the living dead don't seem to count anymore. It doesn't matter that the stench of corruption is all around us. We've grown used to the smell. The government continues to chair pointless debates and issue toothless white papers. The general public has ceased to care or even notice. The fabric of society is gently rotting through, even if the dead aren't. So I'm formulating a plan, because someone has to do something. Somebody has to care. Somebody has to take affirmatve action before it's too late.

Kevin Grady, Upper 4B

"It makes you wonder what he thinks about," whispered Mrs Grady, pulling the tablecloth in by the corners and removing it. "He'll sit like that for hours on end, just staring down into the street, watching the people come and go."

"You should be thankful," said her neighbour, helping her clear away the cups and saucers. "My Joey's a holy terror these days, out every night mixing with heaven knows what kind of riff-raff."

She looked across at the chalk-faced child seated before the window, and a cloud of doubt momentarily formed in her mind. It was unnatural for a teenaged boy to sit so still. When you spoke to him he stared back in accusing silence. And the terrible way he looked at you, with murder in those deep-set eyes. "Joey tells me he's doing his homework," she continued, "but I know damned well he's running with that gang of his. I have no control over him, and his father's absolutely no help at all. But your Kevin . . ." She furrowed her brow and uneasily turned aside as the boy glanced at her in suspicion. No wonder his mother was bashing the Bristol Cream these days, with her son wandering about the house dressed in black, narrowing his eyes at every passing adult. He'd probably grow up to be a serial killer.

"Kevin's a good boy," said his mother firmly. "He's terribly bright. And sensitive. He and his granddad were very close. He's been a lot quieter since the old man died. Wouldn't even come with us to the funeral. I hope it doesn't have any lasting effect on him."

"I shouldn't think so," the neighbour whispered back. "Children are resilient. He's very quiet, though. He should go outside more and get some fresh air. Mix with the others. Swim. Play football." She threw the torpid child a look of desperation. "Anything."

Mrs Grady unfolded her arms from her ample chest and looked about for the sherry bottle. "I wish he would, but he prefers to stay in his room watching horror films all the time." She poured overgenerous measures into a pair of amber glasses. "It gives him such an overactive imagination. I think Kevin sees the world differently to most children. He has some very odd ideas. I'm sure it's just a phase, but right now, well . . ." She turned to her friend and brought her face closer, confiding.

"It's . . . the way he looks at us sometimes. Almost as if he wishes we were dead."

Robert Bloch

The Dead Don't Die!

Robert Bloch is probably getting tired with me keep referring to him as the author of Psycho, *so I'll just mention such recent projects as his new collection,* Tales from Arkham, *and the anthology* Monsters in Our Midst. *He has also written the first volume of his autobiography,* Once Around the Bloch, *which promises to make fascinating reading.*

In the meantime, here's what he had to say about the following novella when it was originally published as the cover story in the July 1951 edition of the pulp magazine Fantastic Adventures:

"As to the present yarn – 'The Dead Don't Die!' – perhaps a couple of words may be in order. The first thing I want to explain is that I didn't choose the title. Your editor chose the title and sent it to me, together with a letter suggesting that I write a story around said title and have it in his hands within four weeks – or else. Or else what, he didn't say. I wired him 'Yes' and went to work.

"But at the time he wrote me and at the time I wired him, I wasn't aware that I'd suddenly be left with an office full of work as a sort of souvenir of my associate's trip to Florida. Yet, that's what happened. No sooner did I consent to write than my associate (he's really my boss, but I don't tell anybody that) left town for the Everglades. And I began to sweat it out. The more I sweated, the more I realized what a lousy title I had to use – 'The Dead Don't Die!'

"It just wasn't true. I was dead, dead on my feet and dead on whatever I used for support while writing. And I was not only dead, but constantly dying.

Nobody in the world could possibly have felt worse than I did – except your editor, if I'd managed to get my hands on him.

"But he's in New York, I'm in Milwaukee, and the story is in Fantastic Adventures *for you. All I can say is, I hope he's happy in New York, I hope I'm happy in Milwaukee, and I hope you'll be happy with the story."*

Although "The Dead Don't Die!" has not been widely reprinted, in 1974 it was turned into a fun television movie (sans the exclamation mark) by director Curtis Harrington from Bloch's own script. The impressive B-movie cast included George Hamilton, Linda Cristal, Joan Blondell, Ralph Meeker, James McEachin, Reggie Nalder, Milton Parsons, Yvette Vickers, and Ray Milland as the mysterious zombie master.

THIS IS A story that never ends.

This is a story that never ends, but I know when it started. Thursday, May 24th, was the date. That night was the beginning of everything for me.

For Cono Colluri it was the end.

Cono and I were sitting there, playing two-handed stud poker. It was quiet in his cell, and we played slowly, meditatively. Everything would have been all right except for one thing. We had a kibitzer.

No matter how calmly we played, no matter how unemotional we appeared to be, we both were aware of another presence. The other, the kibitzer, stayed with us all night long.

His name was Death.

He grinned over Cono's shoulder, tapped him on the arm with a bony finger, selected the cards for every shuffle. He tugged at my hands, poked me in the back when I dealt.

We couldn't see him, of course. But we knew he was there, all right. Watching, watching and waiting; those big blind holes in the skull sneaking a look at the clock and counting the minutes, those skeleton fingers tapping away the seconds until dawn.

Because in the morning, no matter what cards turned up and no matter how much money changed hands, Death would win the game. The game, and Cono Colluri.

It's funny, looking back on it now, to figure out how the three of us happened to get together that particular evening – Cono, myself, and Death.

My story's straight enough. About six months beforehand I'd taken a Civil Service exam and ended up for a probationary period as a guard at State Pen. I wasn't too excited about the job when I got it, but I felt it might give me routine, a small but steady income, and a chance to turn out a book on the side. By the time a few months had passed, I knew I was wrong. The idea of turning out a novel in a background of security sounded fine when I started. but there was no security in a guard's life. I found I couldn't write. The bars and the concrete penned me in just as much as any of my charges. And I began to develop my own sense of guilt.

I guess my trouble was too much empathy. That's a big word – meaning the ability to put yourself in the other fellow's place. "There but for the grace of God go I" – you know that feeling. I had it, but double. Instead of writing at night, I tossed around on my bunk and suffered the torments of the thousand men under my charge.

That's how I got friendly with Cono, I guess – through empathy.

Cono came to the death cell in an awful hurry. His had been a short trial and a merry one – the kind of thing the newspapers like to play up as an example of "quick justice". He'd been a professional strong man with a carnival – the James T. Armstrong Shows. The story was that he got too jealous of his wife and one of the other performers. At any rate, one morning they found Cono lying dead drunk in his trailer. His wife was with him, but she wasn't drunk – merely dead. Somebody had pressed two thumbs against the base of her neck, and something had snapped.

It was an ideal setup for "quick justice" and that's just what Cono Colluri got. Within three weeks he was on his way to the death-house, and for the past two weeks he'd been a guest of the state. A temporary guest. And he was moving out tomorrow morning – for good.

That, of course, explains why Death showed up at our little card party. He belonged there.

Oh, perhaps not for the entire night. He undoubtedly had rattled down the short – oh so terribly short! – corridor to the little room with the big chair. He'd probably peered and eaves-dropped on the electricians who tested the switches. He'd certainly have stopped in at the warden's office to make sure that the mythical pardon from the Governor wasn't on its way.

Yes, Death must have checked all those things to make certain that this was really a farewell card party. And now the uninvited guest was kibitzing as Cono and I dealt our hands.

I knew he was there, and Cono knew it too, but I have to hand it to the big man. He was cool. He'd always been cool; on the stand, swearing his innocence, he'd never lost his temper. Here in the cell, talking to the warden, to the other guards, to me, he'd never broken down. Just told his story over and over again. Somebody had slipped a Mickey in his drink and when he woke up, Flo was dead. He'd never harmed her.

Of course, nobody believed him at the trial. Nobody believed him in the prison, either; the warden, the guards, even the other convicts knew that he was guilty and ready to fry.

That's why I had the honor of spending the last night with him – he'd made a special request for my presence. Because, believe it or not, I believed him.

Blame it on empathy again, or on the very fact that I noticed he never lost his temper. The way he talked about the case, the way he talked about his wife, the way he talked about the execution – everything was out of character for a "crime of passion" murderer. Oh, he was a big brute, and a rough-looking one, but he never acted on impulse.

I guess he took to me right away. We used to talk, nights, after I drew guard assignment on his bloc. He was the only prisoner awaiting execution, and it was natural that we'd get to talking.

"You know I didn't do it, Bob," he'd tell me – over and over again, but there was nothing else to talk about, for him – "It must have been Louie. He lied at the trial, you know. He had been drinking with me, no matter what he says, and he offered me a slug out of the bottle behind the cookhouse, after the last show. That's the last thing I remember. So I figure he must have done it. He was always hanging around Flo anyway, the little crumb. The Great Ahmed warned me, said he saw it in the crystal. But of course, he came into court with this alibi and – oh what's the use?"

There was no use at all, and he knew it. But he told me over and over again. And I believed him.

Now, this last night, he wasn't talking. Maybe it was because Death was there, listening to every word. Maybe it was because they'd shaved his head and slit his trouser legs and left him to wait out these last few hours.

Cono wasn't talking, but he could still grin. He could and he did – smiling at me and looking like a great big overgrown college boy with a crew haircut. Come to think of it, he wasn't much more than just that; only Cono had never gone to college. He went with his first carney at fifteen; married Flo when he was twenty-three, and now he was going to the chair two days before his twenty-fifth birthday. But he smiled. Smiled, and played poker.

"My king is high," he said. "Bet a quarter."

"See you," I answered. "Let's have another card."

"King still high. Check. Funny thing, aces aren't coming up much tonight."

I didn't answer him. I didn't have the heart to tell him that I was cheating. I'd taken the Ace of Spades out of the pack and put it in my pocket before the game started. I didn't want him to get that particular card on the table tonight of all nights.

"Fifty cents on the king," said Cono.

"See you," I said. "I've got a pair of nines."

"Pair of kings." He turned up his cards. "I win."

"You're just naturally lucky," I told him – and wished I hadn't.

But he smiled. I couldn't face that smile, so I looked at my watch. That was another mistake, and I realized it as soon as I made the gesture.

His smile didn't alter. "Not much time left, is there?" he said. "Seems to be getting light."

"Another hand?" I suggested.

"No." Cono stood up. Shaved head, slit trousers and all, he was still an impressive sight. Six feet four, two hundred and ten pounds, in the prime of life. And in just an hour or so they would strap him into the chair, turn on the juice, twist that smile into a grimace of agony. I couldn't look at him, thinking those thoughts. But I could feel Death looking; gazing and gloating.

"Bob, I want to talk to you."

"Shall we order breakfast? You know what the warden said – anything you want, the works."

"No breakfast." Cono put his hand on my shoulder. The fingers that were supposed to have broken a woman's neck barely pressed my skin. "Let's fool 'em all and skip the meal. That'll give the nosey reporters something to talk about."

"What's up?"

"Nothing much. But I got things to tell you."

"Why me in particular?"

"Who else is there left? I got no friends. Got no family I know of. And Flo's gone . . ."

For the first time I saw a look of anger flicker across the big man's face. I knew then that whoever had killed Flo was lucky when Cono got the chair.

"So it has to be you. Besides, you believe me."

"Go on," I said.

"It's about the dough, see? Flo and me, we were saving for a house. Got better'n eight grand stashed away. Somebody's gonna, get it, so why not you? I wrote this here letter, and I want you to have it."

He pulled the envelope out from under his bunk. It was sealed, and scrawled across its face in the sprawling handwriting of a schoolboy was the name, "The Great Ahmed".

"Who's he?"

"I told you, he's the mitt reader with the carney. A nice guy, Bob. You'll like him. He stuck up for me at the trial, remember? Told about Louie hanging around Flo. Didn't do any good because he couldn't prove nothing, but he was – what did the lawyer say? – a character witness. Yeah. Anyhow, he banks for all us carneys with the show.

"Take the letter. It says to give you the money. He'll do it, too. All you got to do is look him up."

I hesitated. "Wait a minute, Cono. You'd better think this over. Eight thousand dollars is a lot of money to pass out to a virtual stranger – "

"Take it, pal." Again he smiled. "There's a string tied to the bundle, of course."

"What do you want?"

"I want you to use some of that dough to try and clear me. Oh, I know you haven't got much of a chance, and nothing to work on. But maybe, with the dough, you'll get an angle, turn something up. You're leaving this joint anyway."

I jerked my head at that. "How did you know?" I asked. "Why, I only told the warden yesterday afternoon – "

"Word goes around." Cono smiled. "They give me the office that you're springing yourself out of here this Saturday. That you aren't satisfied to be a screw the rest of your life. So I says to myself, why not give him the eight grand as a kind of going-away present? Seeing as how we're both going away."

I balanced the envelope on my palm. "The Great Ahmed, eh? And you say he's with the show?"

"Sure. You'll find their route in *Billboard*." Cono smiled. "They must be somewhere around Louisville right now. Heading north as it gets warmer. I'd sort of like to see the old outfit again, but . . ."

The smile faded. "One more favor, Bob."

"Name it."

"Scram out of here."

"But – "

"You heard me. Scram. I expect visitors pretty soon, and I don't want you to stick around."

I nodded, nodded gratefully. Cono was sparing me that final ordeal – the warden, the priest, the mumbling farewell, the shuffling down the corridor.

"Goodbye, Bob. Remember, I'm depending on you."

"I'll do what I can. Goodbye, Cono."

The big hand enveloped mine. "I'll be seeing you around," he said.

"Sure."

"I mean it, Bob. You don't believe this is the end, do you?"

"Maybe you're right. I hope so." I had no intention of getting into a discussion about the after-life with Cono, in his situation. Personally, I had a pretty good idea that once the juice was turned on, Cono would be turned off – forever. But I couldn't tell him that. So I just shook hands, put the letter in my pocket, unlocked the cell, and walked out.

At the end of the corridor I turned around and looked back. Cono stood against the bars, his body outlined against the yellow light but blending into the shadows that come with dawn. There was another shadow behind him – a big, black shadow outlining a ghost of a figure.

I recognized the shadow. Old Man Death.

That was the last I saw – just the two of them, waiting together. Cono and Old Man Death.

I went downstairs, then, to my bunk. The night shift came off and the day shift went on. They were all talking about the execution. They tried to pump me, but I didn't say anything. I sat there on the edge of the bunk, looking at my watch and waiting.

Upstairs they must have gone through the whole routine, just the way you always see it in the B movies. Opening the door. Handcuffing him to a guard on either side. Marching down the corridor. Yes, just about now it would be happening. The night shift went outside to get the news, leaving me alone on my bunk. I looked at my watch again. Now was the time.

They'd be strapping him down now, putting that damned black cloth over his eyes. I could see him sitting there; a big, gentle hulk of a man with a tired smile on his face.

Maybe he was guilty, maybe he was innocent – I didn't know. But the whole stupid business of execution, of "justice" and "punishment" and "the full penalty of the law" hit me in the pit of the stomach. It was cruel, it was senseless, it was wrong.

The seconds ticked away. I watched the little hand crawl around the face of the watch and tried to figure it out. One minute Cono would be alive. A jolt of electric current and he'd be dead. Trite idea. But it's the eternal mystery all of us live with. And die with.

What was the answer? I didn't know. Nobody knew. Nobody except the kibitzer. Old Man Death knew the answer. I wondered if he had a watch. No, why should he? What's Time to Death?

Thirty seconds.

Sure, I'd quit my job. I'd try to clear Cono. But what good would it do him? He'd never know. He'd be dead.

Twenty seconds.

The hand crawled around, and the thoughts crawled around. What's it like to be dead? Is it a sleep? Is it a sleep with dreams? Is it just dreams but no rest, no peace?

Ten seconds.

One moment you're alive, you can feel and hear and smell and see and move. And the next – nothing. Or – something. What's the change like? Like suddenly turning out the lights?

Now.

The lights went out.

First they dimmed, then they flickered, then they went out. Only for a second, mind you. But that was long enough.

Long enough for Cono to die.

Long enough for me to shudder.

Long enough for Death to reach out, grinning, and claim his prey in the dark . . .

I was still in a daze when I hit the railroad station on Saturday morning. So much had happened in the last two days I still couldn't figure it out.

First of all, there was that business about Cono's body. I'd gone to the warden, of course, with the story about the money, and I more or less expected to handle funeral expenses from Cono's funds when I got them.

"His cousin will bury him," the warden told me. "Got a call this morning."

"But I thought he had no relatives."

"Turns out he has, all right. Fellow named Varek. Oh, it's legitimate, we always check. The Doc insists – makes him mad every time somebody shows up and cheats him out of an autopsy."

The warden had chuckled, but I didn't laugh.

And the warden hadn't chuckled long. Because the next day, Louie had confessed.

Louie the contortionist, that is – the man Cono claimed had given him the knockout drops in his drink. The warden got a wire, of course, but the whole story hit the papers that afternoon. It seems he'd just walked into the station-house in Louisville and confessed. Came out with the entire statement without a sign of emotion. Said he just wanted to clear his conscience once he knew Cono was dead. He'd hated Cono, wanted Flo, and when she repulsed him he rigged up the murder to get revenge on both of them.

The story was lurid enough, but it had gaps in it. The report I read claimed Louie was a hophead. He was too calm, too unemotional. "Glassy-eyed" was the way they put it. They were going to give him a psychiatric test.

Well, I wished them luck, the whole lot of them – psychiatrists and district attorneys and smart coppers and penologists. All I knew was that Cono was innocent. And he was dead.

By this time I'd already checked on the Armstrong Shows through *Billboard*. They were playing Louisville this week, all right. I sent through my wire Friday afternoon. Saturday morning I got a telegram signed by the advance agent in Paducah.

GREAT AHMED LEFT SHOW THREE WEEKS AGO STOP OPENING OWN MITT CAMP IN CHICAGO STOP WILL CHECK FORWARDING ADDRESS AND NOTIFY LATER

So I was on my way to Chicago and eight thousand dollars. I'd hole up in some hotel and wait for news on the Great Ahmed. And after that – well, with the money, my writing problems would be solved.

Actually, I should have been happy enough at the way it had all turned out. Cono's name was cleared, I was out of the whole sordid grind forever, and I had eight grand coming, in cash.

But something bothered me. It wasn't just the irony of Cono Colluri's innocence. It was the inexplicable feeling that things weren't settled, that they were only beginning. That I had somehow been caught up in something that would sweep me along to –

"Chicago!" bawled the conductor.

And there I was, in the Windy City at 5 p.m. on Saturday, May 25th. It wasn't windy today. As I lugged my grip out of the LaSalle Street Station I walked straight into a pouring rain.

There's something about a storm in Chicago. It seems to melt all the taxicabs away. I stood there, contemplating the downpour, watching the cars inch along under the El tracks. The sky was dark and dirty. The water dribbled inkstains along the sides of the buildings. I couldn't stand watching it in my present mood.

So I walked. I turned corners several times. Pretty soon there was a hotel. It wasn't a good hotel. It was located too far south to be even a decent hotel. But that didn't matter. I needed a place to stay in for a couple of days until the money was located. And right now, I had to get out of the rain. My suit was soaked, and the cardboard in the luggage had taken a beating.

I went in, registered. A bellboy took me up to my room on the third floor. Apparently he hadn't expected me. At least, he didn't know about my coming in time to shave. But he opened my door, deposited my luggage and asked if there'd be anything else now. Then he held out his hand. It would have taken me all day to give him a decent manicure, so I put a quarter in his palm instead. He was just as happy with that.

Then he left, I opened my grip, changed clothes, and went out to eat. The rain had moderated to a drizzle. I stopped in the lobby long enough to get eyed by the night clerk, the house dick, and a woman with improbable red hair.

During the pause I managed to send off a telegram to the advance man of the carney, giving him my new address and requesting action on locating the Great Ahmed. That concluded my business for the day.

At least, I thought it did at the time.

Nothing happened to change my mind during supper. I ate at a fish joint and contemplated the delightful prospect of returning to my crummy room and holing up for the weekend.

I don't know if you've ever spent a Sunday alone in downtown Chicago, but if you haven't, I offer you one word of advice.

Don't.

There's something about the deserted canyons on a Sunday that tears the heart out of a man. Something about the grey sunlight reflected from grimy roofs. Something about the crumpled bits of soiled paper flopping listlessly along empty streets. Something about the mournful rattle of the half-empty elevated trains. Something about the barred shop-windows and chained doors. It gets to you, does things to your insides. You start wondering whether or not, in the midst of all this death and decay, you're really alive.

The prospect didn't please me at all. I finished my meal, put another quarter in another palm, and wandered out down the street.

After all, it was still Saturday night. And Saturday night was different. The rain had definitely stopped now, and the street was black and gleaming. Neon light reflections wriggled like crimson and gold serpents across my path.

You know what serpents do, of course. They tempt you. These particular neon serpents were saying, "Come in. Have a drink. You've got nothing to do tonight anyway, and nobody to do it with. Sit down. Place your order. Relax. You're due for a little relaxation after six months in prison. It's a long sentence. You know what a con does after he's sprung. You're entitled to a little fun."

There were serpents all around me. Serpents spelling out the names of taverns, night-clubs, come-on joints, clips, dives. All I had to do was take my choice.

Instead, I walked back to the hotel, went in the lobby, and checked with the night clerk to make sure my telegram was really on the way to the carney. Then I went up to my room and rid myself of all money except for a ten-dollar bill. I wasn't taking any chances on getting rolled.

The night was still young. I'd probably feel young myself with a few drinks in me. I went back down to the lobby and toyed with the notion of the hotel bar.

The improbable redhead had disappeared, and so had the house dick. The place was almost deserted now. Almost, but not quite. There was a blonde sitting in a chair near the elevator. I'd looked at her once when I'd come downstairs and now I looked at her again.

She was worth a second look.

Genuine. That's the only word to describe her. Genuine. To begin with, she was a real blonde. No peroxide glint, no unnatural accent in makeup. The fur she wore was real, and so were the diamonds.

Those diamonds really stopped me. The ring was too big to be phoney. Even if the stone were flawed, it must have set her (or somebody) back a pretty penny. And the same went for the big choker that clung to her neck in a glittering caress.

Her smile seemed genuine, too.

And that was the phoney part.

Why should she smile at me? Me, with my forty-dollar suit and my ten-dollar bill tucked away in its watch pocket?

I didn't get it. And I didn't want it. I walked towards the lobby entrance to the hotel bar. She stood up and followed.

I walked into the dimly-lit bar, around it, and out the front door to the street. I'd do my drinking somewhere else, thank you.

There was a little place across the street down the block. I ran into it, crossing in mid-traffic. Before I opened the door I glanced back to make sure that she wasn't following. Then I went in.

The joint was small – an oval bar and five or six booths grouped on either side of a juke-box. The bartender on duty was lonesome.

"What'll it be, Mac?"

"Rye. Top shelf."

He poured. I drank. Just like that. Fast. The stuff was bonded, like a bank messenger.

"Refill, please."

He poured. I watched his black bowtie. It was beginning to wobble in anticipation of the conversation forming in his larynx. Abruptly it stopped wobbling.

Because the door opened and she came in. Big as life, and even blonder. The neon on the juke-box did things to her diamond choker.

There was no place to hide. No real reason for me to hide, for that matter. She came right over, sat down, motioned to the bartender. "The same," she said. Nice, rich, husky voice.

She watched the man pour, then transferred her gaze to me. Her eyes matched the diamonds she was wearing.

"Let's sit in a booth," she suggested.

"Why?"

"We can talk there."

"What's wrong with right here?"

"If you prefer."

"What's the proposition?"

"I want you to come with me, to meet somebody."

"You'll have to talk plainer than that, lady."

"I said we should take a booth."

"Nothing wrong with mentioning names right here in the open."

"No." She shook her head. Those diamonds shed enough light to blind a pedestrian walking across the street. "I am not permitted to mention names yet. But it will be to your advantage to come with me."

"Sorry, lady. I'd have to know more about it." I looked down at my glass. "For example, who sent you to me. How you found me. Little details like that. Maybe they're nothing to you. Me, I find them fascinating."

"This is no time to make jokes."

"I'm serious. And I say I'm not playing unless you tell me the name of the team."

"All right, Bob. But – "

That did it. The name. Of course, she could have picked it up off the hotel register easily enough. But it jarred me more than anything else up to that point. It jarred me right on down to my feet.

"Good-night," I said.

She didn't answer. As I walked out, she was still staring at me. Blue diamond eyes winked me out of the tavern.

I walked out. I didn't go back to my room and I didn't go to another tavern. I headed north, crossed under the El tracks into the Loop. There was a burlesque show. I bought a ticket and sat through a dreary performance of which I remember nothing except the old blackout skit about the photographer in the park who complained that the squirrels were nibbling his equipment.

I spent my time trying to fit the pieces together. Who was this girl? A friend of Cono's? A friend of Flo's? A friend of the Great Ahmed's? A friend of the carney advance man? Or just a friend?

Cono was dead and Flo was dead. They couldn't tell her where to find me. Ahmed didn't know I existed, let alone where I was. The carney advance man wouldn't know my address until the telegram arrived.

Could it be that she had a line into the prison and had learned I was about to receive eight thousand dollars?

Was she simply working the hotel, picking my name from the register at random?

But if so, what was this story about a proposition, and meeting somebody?

It didn't make sense. I sat there a while and tried to figure the deal out, then I left.

Eleven o'clock. I headed back to the hotel. This time I peeked into the lobby before entering. She wasn't around. I slid unobtrusively past the entrance so the night clerk wouldn't pay attention. He was reading a science-fiction magazine and didn't look up.

The elevator operator took me to the fifth floor without removing his eyes from the Racing Form. Quite a bunch of students in this hotel. Probably working their way through mortician's school.

I walked down to the door of my room very quietly. I listened at the keyhole before I unlocked the door. Then I opened it fast and switched on the light.

No blonde.

I examined the closet, the washroom. Still no blonde. Then and only then I went to the phone, called room service, and ordered a pint of rye and some ice.

It was still Saturday night and I was still entitled to a drink, without strange blondes butting in.

But when the drinks came, I found the blonde was still with me. Prancing around inside my skull, making propositions, winking her diamonds at me.

It didn't take me long to finish the bottle and it didn't take the bottle long to finish me.

Somewhere along the line I managed to undress, don pyjamas, and slump across the bed. Somewhere along the line I drifted off to sleep.

And that's when it started.

I was back in the burlesque house, sitting in the crummy seat, watching the stage. This time the performance was more interesting. There was a new comic in the cast – a tall fellow with a shaved head. He looked something like Cono. In fact, he was Cono. Big as life. A chorus line danced out behind him; eight, count 'em, eight nifty little numbers. They danced, kicked, whirled. Cono noticed them. He did a little shuffling dance of his own, gyrating to the end of the line. Then he reached out – in the old familiar gesture used by the late Ted Healy in chastising his stooges – and flicked them across the neck. One by one. As his fingers touched each girl in turn, she changed.

Heads dangled limply from broken necks. The eight dancing girls became eight dancing cadavers. Eight, count 'em, eight. The dancing dead. The dancing dead, with skulls for heads. Skulls with diamond eyes.

Dead arms reached out and scrabbled in dead skull-sockets. They picked out the diamonds and threw them at me. I twisted and turned, sweated and squirmed, but I couldn't dodge. The diamonds hit me, seared me with icy fire.

Cono laughed. The girls danced off stage and he was all alone. All alone except for the chair. It stood there in the center of the stage and the lights went down. As the spotlight narrowed, Cono moved towards its center, closer to the chair. He had to stay within the circle of light or die.

Then the circle narrowed still further and he was sitting in the chair. As if by magic, squirrels danced out on the stage. They each carried a tiny thong, and each bound the thong around Cono's arm or leg or neck until he sat there crisscrossed with thongs that lashed him to the chair.

I don't have to tell you what kind of a chair it was. What else would it be?

And I don't have to tell you what was going to happen next. Even in my dream I knew it, and I struggled frantically to wake up.

But I couldn't. I couldn't even leave my seat in the theatre. Because while I had been watching Cono getting bound into the chair, somebody had bound me!

Now I was sitting in an electric chair, hands tied, feet tied, electrodes clamped and ready. I tugged and tore, but I couldn't move. They had me, all right. It had all been a trick, a dirty trick to get my attention away from myself.

I knew that now. Because suddenly Cono burst his bonds with a flick of his fingers, the same fingers that had killed the dancing girls. He stood up and laughed because it was a joke. A joke on me.

He wasn't going to die. I was. He'd live. He'd get the eight thousand dollars and the blonde, and I'd fry. Just as soon as they turned on the juice. The bonded juice. The neon lights were winking now and the bartender was ready to pull the switch as soon as the conductor called out "Chicago!" and now they were getting ready to give the signal. While waiting, Cono stood on the stage and amused me with card tricks. He pulled the Ace of Spades out of his mouth and held it up for me to see.

Then it was time. Somebody came onstage and handed him a telegram from the carney and that was the signal for them to yell "Chicago!"

The switch was ready. I felt the cold sweat running down my spine, felt the electrodes bite into the side of my leg, the side of my head. And then, they pulled the switch –

I woke up.

I woke up, sat up in bed and stared out the window.

Through the windowpane, the blonde stared back at me.

I could only see her face, and that was funny, because it was a full window. Then I realized it was because she wasn't vertical, but horizontal. And only her face was pointed towards me.

Shall I make it plainer?

I mean she was floating in empty air outside my window.

Floating in empty air and smiling at me with her icy eyes aglitter.

Then I really woke up.

The second dream, or the second part of the dream, was so real I had to stagger over to the window and convince myself that there was no one outside. It took me a minute before my trembling legs would support me and carry me that distance, so if she really had been at the window there'd have been enough time for her to get back down the fire-escape and disappear.

Of course she wasn't there.

And she couldn't have been, because there was no fire-escape. I gazed down at a sheer drop of five floors to the closed and empty courtyard below. It was black down there, black as the Ace of Spades.

I don't know what I should have done under the circumstances; all I know is what I did do.

I shoved my head under the cold water faucet, towelled my face dry, dressed, and rushed out of my room in search of a drink.

And that's when the next nightmare started.

There was this little joint three blocks south of the hotel. I ran all the way, couldn't stop running until I'd covered that much distance. The street was deserted and it was dark, and only this little joint had a rose light burning in the window. It was the light that drew me, because I was afraid of the dark.

I opened the door and a blast of smoke and sound hit me in the face but I ploughed through it blindly to the bar.

"Shot of whiskey!" I said, and meant it.

The bartender was a tall, thin man and he had a glass eye that almost fell out as he bent his head while pouring my drink. I didn't pay very much attention to it at the time; I was too busy getting the drink down.

Then it fascinated me. I didn't want to stare at it, so I looked away – looked down the bar, into the seething center of smoke and sound.

That was a mistake.

Sitting on the stool next to me was a little man who was sipping a glass of beer. He had to sip, because he had no arms. He lapped at the glass the way a cat laps at a saucer of cream. Watching him was a blind man. Don't ask me how I knew he could see, but I got the impression of watching from the tilt of the head, the focus of the dark glasses.

I whirled around and nearly collided with the man on crutches. He was standing there arguing with the man on the floor – the one without legs. Down the bar a way; somebody was banging with a steel hook affixed to his elbow. I could scarcely hear the thumping because the juke box was playing so loudly. Sure enough, there were dancers present; the inevitable two women, both of them engrossed in their movements. They had to watch carefully, because both of them were on crutches.

There were others present, too – others in the booths. The man with the bandaged head. The man with the hole where his nose should be. The man with the great purple growth bulging over his collar. The lame, the halt, the blind.

They didn't pay any attention to me. They were having fun. And in a moment I realized what I'd stumbled into. It was a street beggar's tavern. I saw the tin cup set alongside the shotglass, the placard resting against the beer bottle. What was the name of the dump in Victor Hugo's *Notre Dame de Paris*? "The Court of Miracles" he called it. And this was it.

They were happy enough, drinking. They forgot their physical ills. Maybe liquor would cure me of my mental ills. It was worth a try. So I had another drink.

Along about the third drink somebody must have slipped out. Along about the fourth drink somebody must have come back. And in a minute or two, she walked in.

I didn't see her, at first. The reason I sensed her presence was because the noise cut down. The juke box stopped and didn't start again. The conversation dropped to a hush.

That's when I looked around and noticed her. She was sitting in a booth, all alone, just watching me.

She made a little gesture of invitation and I shook my head. That was all. Then she raised her glass and offered me a silent toast.

I turned, noted my re-filled glass, and toasted her. Then I downed my drink. The bartender with the glass eye had another waiting for me.

"On the lady," he said.

"No thanks, chum."

He looked at me. "Whatsa matter? She's a nice lady."

"Sure she is. Nobody's questioning that."

"So whyn'cha drink it?"

"I've had enough, that's why." I had, enough and to spare, I suddenly realized. The room was beginning to spin a little.

"Come on, drink up. We're all friends here."

The bartender didn't look friendly. Neither did anyone else. For the first time I grew aware of the fact that everyone was looking at me. Not at her – at me. The legless, the armless, the blind. In fact, the blind man took off his dark glasses in order to see me better, and one of the crowd slapped his crutch on the bar and walked a little closer.

The Court of Miracles! Where the blind see and the lame walk! Of course it was; and half of these beggars were fakes. They were as sound as I was – sounder, perhaps.

And there was a whole roomful of them, all looking at me. None of them seemed happy any longer. They were quiet; so quiet I could hear the click of the key in the lock as the armless man locked the door.

Oh, he had arms now; they'd emerged from beneath a bulky vest. But I wasn't interested in that. I was interested in the fact that the door was locked. And I was here, inside.

She stared and they stared.

The bartender said, "How about it, chum?"

"Not today." I stood up. That is, I tried to stand up. My legs were wobbly. Something was wrong with them. Something was wrong with my eyes, too.

"What's the trouble?" drawled the bartender. "Afraid of being slipped a Mickey?"

"No!" It was hard to talk. Only gasps came out. "You already slipped me one the drink before this. When she came in, and gave you the signal."

"Wise guy, huh?"

"Yes!" I managed to spin around, fast. Fast enough to grab the whiskey-bottle off the bar and hold it cocked. My other hand supported me.

"Now – open that door or I'll let you have it," I panted. "Come on, move fast."

The bartender shrugged. There was neither fear nor malice in his glass eye.

My own eyes were turning to glass. I tried to focus them on the bartender, tried not to look at the creeping, crawling cripples that slithered closer all around me, brandishing canes and crutches and uttering little grunts and whimpers and moans.

"Open that door!" I wheezed, while they crept closer and closer, stretching out their arms and tensing to spring.

"All right, chum!"

That was the signal for them to rush me. Somebody swung a crutch, somebody clawed at my legs. I began to spin and go down.

I swung the bottle, clearing an arc, and they fell back, but only for a moment. The bartender aimed a punch, so I swung the bottle again.

Then they came back. It was like fighting underwater, like fighting in a dream. And this was a dream, a nightmare of crawlers, of slithering shapes tearing at me, dragging me down.

The bartender hit me again, so I raised the bottle and brought it down. It landed on his head with a dull crunch.

For a moment he stood there, and the glass eye popped out of its socket and rolled along the bar. It stared up at him and watched as he sagged slowly and fell.

Then it stared at me as the man with the artificial arm hit me across the neck with the hook.

I felt the blow land and melt my spine.

The glass eye watched as I collapsed into roaring darkness and when I went down, it winked.

When I woke up, she was stroking my forehead.

Not bad. Lots of men would have traded places with me at the moment – lying there in the cool dusk, on a comfortable bed, with a beautiful blonde stroking my forehead.

Too bad some other guy didn't show up, because I would have traded him in a flash.

I'd have thrown in a splitting headache, free of charge, and a taste in the mouth like the bottom of the Chicago Drainage Canal.

But nobody showed up to take my place, so I just stayed there. When she said, "Drink this," I drank. When she said, "Close your eyes and wait for the pain to go away," I closed my eyes and waited.

Miraculously, the pain went away.

The headache and the taste vanished. I opened my eyes again, wiggled my fingers and toes.

I was lying on this bed in a darkened room. The shades were drawn, but enough light filtered through to bring life to the diamond choker and the diamond ring and the diamond eyes. The diamond eyes regarded me candidly.

"Feel better now?"

"Yes."

"That's good. Then there's nothing to worry about."

How right she was. Nothing to worry about except where I was, and why. I suppose a little of my bitterness crept over into my reply.

"Thanks," I said. "Thanks for everything you've done for me. Including getting me knocked out."

"That's no way to look at it," answered the blonde. "After all, I saved your life."

"You mean those beggars would have killed me?"

"No. But the police might."

"Police?"

"Yes." She drew a long breath. "After all, you did murder that bartender."

"What?"

"You hit him with the bottle. He's dead."

I sat up, faster than I would have believed possible. "Come on, let me out of here," I snapped.

"They'll be on the lookout for you," she told me. "It's not safe for you to go just now. You're among friends here."

"Friends!"

"Don't misunderstand. If you'd only listened to me in the first place and come along sensibly, all this would never have happened."

I had no answer for that one. All I knew was that if she spoke the truth, I was a murderer. And I knew what they did to murderers. They sat them down in a chair and turned on the juice and fried them. A faint odor of singed flesh tainted my nostrils.

"How do I know you're not lying?" I asked.

"I can furnish proof if you like, later. Right now, I want you to meet a friend." She put her hand on my shoulder and even through the shirt I could feel the icy coldness of her flesh. She was cold and hard, like a diamond.

"As long as I'm meeting friends, we might as well establish a few facts," I suggested. "You know my name. Now, what's yours? And where am I?"

She smiled and stood up. "My name is Vera. Vera LaValle. We are in a home on the South Side. And, although you didn't think to ask me, it's Monday evening. You've been unconscious for almost forty-eight hours."

I stood up, then. It wasn't a spectacular performance. I glanced down at myself in the dim light and what I saw wasn't pretty.

"Why don't you go in and bathe, clean up a bit?" Vera suggested. "I'll go out and bring back some food. You can eat it before our meeting."

Without waiting for my reply, she went out. Went out and locked the door.

It was getting to be a habit. Everybody that I met locked me in. Of course, that's what you do with murderers. Dangerous people to have around. Always killing bartenders, for instance. And if I was a murderer . . .

I doubted it. The whole thing was phoney from start to finish. Things like that just didn't happen to me. I was the original timid soul. Couldn't lick my weight in wild flowers.

Then, again . . .

There was blood on my suit. Blood on my shirt. Blood on the back of my neck, crusted blood from where the steel hook had landed.

I went into the bathroom, filled the tub, undressed, bathed. There was a nice array of soap and towels, all laid out and waiting for me.

I even found an electric shaver to plug in. I felt a lot better once I was cleaned up.

When I dressed, I was surprised to discover a fresh white shirt conveniently placed on top of a clothes hamper. My genial host or hostess thought of everything.

By the time I stepped out of the bathroom she had returned. She had four sandwiches wrapped in cellophane, a double cardboard cup of coffee, and a wedge of pie. She didn't say anything while I ate. It only took me about six minutes to dispose of the meal and latch onto a cigarette from my pocket. I offered her one.

"No, thanks. I do not smoke."

"Funny. I thought all women did nowadays."

"I tried it once. Many years ago. Of course, it wasn't a cigarette."

This didn't seem to be getting me anywhere. "About that friend I was going to meet. Where is he?"

"Waiting outside the door," she said. "Shall I ask him in?"

"By all means. Don't keep the gentleman waiting." My tone was facetious, but I didn't feel very gay. I don't know what I really expected. Years of reading – and writing – horror fiction had conditioned me to almost everything. A Mad Doctor, perhaps, coming to recommend a certain brand of cigarettes. A Mad Scientist with a beaker-full of monkey glands. A Mad Professor with a driver's license for a flying saucer.

The last person I expected to see when the door opened was a friend. But it was a friend who walked in. It was Cono.

Cono Colluri. The man who died in the electric chair.

He stood there in the twilight and looked at me. He wore a battered trench-coat with the collar turned up, and he had a hat pulled down over his eyes like a movie gangster, but I recognized him. It wasn't a double, or a stooge, or somebody made up to resemble him. It was Cono. Cono in the flesh. The dead flesh – reanimate and alive!

Changed? Of course he had changed. There was a dreadful facial tic, where the muscles had been pulled and torn by the convulsive spasm of the shock. And he was pale. Pale as death. But he lived. He walked. He talked . . .

"Hello, Bob. I've been waiting for you."

"She – she told me."

"Too bad you wouldn't come at once. I should have used more sense, let her tell you who wanted to see you. But I figgered you wouldn't of believed her."

"Yes. I guess that's right." I fumbled for words while he stood there, stood there looking at me. "How – how are you?"

That was a fine thing to ask. But he didn't seem to mind.

In fact, he smiled. The smile creased the side of his face and got tangled up in the tic, but he made it. "Oh, I'll live," he said. "I'll live forever."

"What?"

"That's the pitch, Bob. That's why I had to see you. I'm going to live forever. Varek fixed that."

Varek? Where had I heard that name before?

"He's the one who claimed my body. You remember."

Yes, I remembered. The mysterious cousin. "But how did he know you weren't dead, and how did he revive you?"

"I was dead, Bob. Deader'n a doornail. And he fixed me up. He can fix anybody up, Bob. Bring them back. Make it so's they never die. And that's where you come in."

"Me?"

"I been telling him about you. About how smart you are, all that stuff you write. He needs somebody like you for the outside – to front. Somebody with brains. Young. And alive."

Alive. I was alive, all right, but I wondered if I was awake and sane. Talking to a dead man . . .

"Come here, Bob. I can see you don't believe me."

I moved closer to Cono.

"Feel my skin. Go ahead."

I put my hand on his wrist. It was cold. Cold, but solid. Up close I could see the waxen pallor of Cono's face. Cono's death-mask. The tic rippled across it and he smiled again.

"Don't be scared. I'm real. It's real. He can do it. He can bring back the dead. Don't you see what it means? What a big thing it is, if it's handled right?"

"I see. But I still can't understand where I fit in."

"Varek will tell you all about it. Come on, I want you to talk to him."

I followed Cono Colluri out of the room. Vera smiled and nodded as we left, but she didn't accompany us as we walked down the long corridor to a stairway. Descending the stairs into the soft, subdued light of the parlors below, I became conscious of a peculiar odor. It smelled like stale air, steam heat and the scent of mingled flowers.

"Say, just where are we, anyway?" I asked.

"Funeral home," Cono answered. "Didn't you know?"

I hadn't known. But I might have guessed. Living quarters

upstairs and down here the parlors. The parlors, the soft lights and the scent of flowers.

We walked across a carpeted hallway, and I glanced around me. It was the way Cono had said; this was a funeral home, and a rather shabby one. Perhaps that's why there were no bodies lying in state, no mourners. Varek had set this up for a front, and I rather suspected that if I made a dash for it and tried the front door I would find it locked.

But I didn't make a dash for it. I followed Cono into the darkened parlor to the left, to meet Mr Varek.

I walked in and Cono lumbered over to the corner. He walked stiffly, awkwardly. The muscles in his body were taut with shock. But he did pretty well for a dead man.

He was turning on a lamp in the corner, he was closing the door behind us. I paid no attention. I was staring down at the coffin on the trestle. Staring down at the body in the coffin. The body of the man with the glass eye.

It was the bartender I'd killed.

He lay there on the cheap satin, dressed in a worn black suit. Somebody had put the glass eye back in place and it stared up at me sardonically. The other eye was closed, and the general effect was that of a wink.

There we were – me and the man I'd killed. I looked at him, and he looked at me.

He looked at me!

Yes. It happened. The eyelid rolled back. The eye opened. It focussed on me. And the mouth, the bound mouth, relaxed its smirk. The lips parted.

And from the corpse came the voice: "Hello, Bob. I'm Nicolo Varek."

"You – "

"Oh, I'm not the bartender you killed. He's dead enough, as you can see for yourself. His body isn't breathing."

It wasn't, either. The corpse was still a corpse, but something was alive, something lived inside it. Lived and looked and talked.

"I'm just taking temporary residence. So that I can talk to you, without having to travel a great distance. You can appreciate the convenience."

I couldn't, at that moment. I could only stand and gape and feel the sweat trickling down under my armpits.

"You've been a long time coming, Bob. But it was inevitable that we should meet. Cono has told me all about you, and of course I have other ways of gaining information. Many ways."

"I'm sure." It came out before I could stop it, but the corpse chuckled. The sound was a death-rattle.

"How typical of you to say that. How characteristic! Ah, yes, I've studied your background, your work. You interest me greatly. That is why I have gone to all this trouble to arrange our meeting."

I nodded, but said nothing. I was waiting.

"I'm inclined to give Cono credit for finding you. It's quite true, I can use you."

"Dead or alive?" That remark came out before I could stop it, too.

"Alive, of course. But don't think I'm not appreciative of the distinction. You're a man of keen wit, sir. And I admire you for it. One seldom finds acerbity in these decadent days."

"Look," I said, beginning to recover a little composure. "I'm not used to indulging in character analysis with a corpse. Just what do you want of me?"

"Your services, sir. Your professional services. For which, needless to say, you will be generously rewarded. In perpetuity, I might add."

"Cut the double-talk. I've had enough from Vera, and from poor Cono – "

"*Poor* Cono? I would hardly endorse the adjective. Were it not for me, my dear sir, Cono would be languishing in an unmarked grave. Whereas, thanks to my efforts, he is among the quick rather than the dead. And if you wish plain talk, sir, you shall have it.

"I am Nicolo Varek, man of science. I have perfected a means, a methodology, a therapy if you like, which defeats what men call death. Defeats death? It goes beyond that, far beyond. For those whom I revive also possess the boon of eternal life. Eternal life!"

Crazy talk. But it was coming from the mouth of a corpse, and I believed it. There was no hint of fakery or collusion – no ventriloquist could open that cadaver's eye, manipulate his dead lips. I saw, and I heard. And I believed.

"Yes, I can give life to the dead. As to the how and the why of it, well, that's my secret. My priceless, precious, perfect secret.

"And what do you think the use of that secret is worth, Sir? What is the proper fee for the boon of eternal life? A million dollars, perhaps?

"There are many men with a million dollars in this world, my friend. Do you think any of them would hesitate to part with that sum if I could assure them of continued existence?

"But there's the rub. They must be assured. And at the same time the secret must remain a secret. For this reason I must continue to operate anonymously. There is nothing men would stop at in order to extract my secret from me – if I were known to them as its possessor. How often I've faced torture and death myself at the hands of those who suspected I might save them!

"You say I have helpers aplenty? That I can summon up an army of the dead, if need be, to assist me in my aims? That is true – but only within certain limits. The dead must be controlled. And I cannot carry out my plans completely without the aid of living humanity. I need a man of prescience, a man of integrity. Such as yourself, sir."

"I don't see what you're driving at."

"A business arrangement. You might even go so far as to call it a partnership. With myself as the silent partner. You as the go-between. Our product: Eternal life. Our goal: Unlimited wealth, unlimited power."

"Sounds a bit too easy."

"Do not mistake it, my friend. There are innumerable obstacles to overcome, many problems to face and to solve. I can provide for them all, however. This has been a cherished dream of mine for centuries. Yes, centuries."

"Who are you, anyway?"

The corpse chuckled. "So many men have asked that question of me, so many times! Yet I find it best not to answer. My handiwork is proof that I speak truth, and that is all you need. Trust me, and we shall rule.

"Yes, rule! Surely you can see what power lies in my secret. The hold it will give us both over the great ones of this world, now and forever! We'll seek our fortunes first, and the rest shall come.

"I have the plans well laid. You will be able to go forth and proclaim the gift of eternal life to the world. Nor shall you lack for assistance. I can summon a host to your command, to do your bidding and mine. We shall broadcast the tidings: There is no more death, for those who can pay the price! Eternal life, and more; special powers, new powers.

"But you'll learn all this and more in time to come. You'll learn the methods I've devised for bringing the news to the world. Of course, it would never do to make a really public announcement or statement; it must all be cloaked in mysticism and the proper formulae. We'll start a cult, attract the wealthy, and reveal the truth only to the select few.

"Now, sir, how does my proposal strike you? Eternal life, eternal riches, eternal power?"

I didn't say anything for a long moment. I stared at the corpse that told me men could live forever.

"Silence means consent," said the voice.

"Not necessarily. I was just wondering – what if I refuse?"

"I'm sorry you even mention the possibility. For it forces me to remind you that you really have no choice in the matter."

"You mean you'll kill me if I don't? Kill me and animate my corpse, I suppose?"

"Come now, surely you give me credit for more subtlety than that? I've already gone to a great deal of trouble and risk to bring you here, as you know. I cannot jeopardize my plans to any further extent. And you would be of no use to me as a corpse. Besides, there is no need for me to kill you. If you walk out of here, you're as good as dead anyway."

"Meaning?"

"Meaning that you are wanted for murder. For killing this poor one-eyed citizen of a free republic. The bartender."

"But he's alive, you've revived him – "

"Not like the others. It's purely temporary, you understand. I can keep him animated as long as I choose, and I will do so if you consent. I'll even put him back to work in the bar." Again the chuckle. "It won't be the first time a dead man has walked abroad with none the wiser. If only you knew or even suspected how many of the dead presently mingle with the living, thanks to the Varek method!"

I shuddered. The single eye of the corpse was omniscient. The voice purred on: "If you refuse, he becomes a corpse again. With a dozen witnesses to swear you killed him. I'll not wreak vengeance – the full majesty of the law will attend to that. And your story of mysterious women and corpses that talk and a walking dead man will not help you or save you. I believe you realize that.

"But you won't refuse. Because you can see what I'm offering you. Wealth and power. The goals, the dreams of every man. A chance for eternal life yourself, such as I enjoy. Think it over, sir, think well upon it. Life or death?"

I thought. I thought well upon it. And everything within me clamored for assent. Oh, it's easy enough to be a hero when there's no temptation. But the cynic who said every man has his price knew human nature. There aren't many who wouldn't settle for eternal life, eternal wealth and eternal power even at the price of their souls – and the souls of everyone else, for that matter.

The souls of everyone else . . .

I looked at Cono. My friend, Cono Colluri. The late Cono Colluri who went to his death looking like an overgrown college boy. Cono, who left me eight thousand bucks and a promise to clear his name.

Where was Cono now?

He wasn't here in this room. His body was here, and it moved and it talked, but the soul . . .

There was a tic, there was torment, there was twisting torture. Not real life. This was a stranger, a bulking walking corpse. No emotions, no warmth, no humanity.

Sure, I could sell myself out. But I couldn't sell out the world.

So I stared down at the corpse and I said, "No. I'm sorry, Varek. I've got to refuse, and take my chances."

"The decision is final?"

"Final."

"Very well. You've had your chance."

The mouth shut. The eye closed. The dead bartender was truly dead again. I saw the light fade away from the countenance, then I moved back. Back, into Cono Colluri's arms.

I might have known Varek would lie. That he'd never let me out of that room alive. If I hadn't realized it before, I knew it now. Because the cold arms wrapped around me. And the great thumbs rose up to my neck, ready to press and squeeze.

"Cono!" I gasped. "It's me – your friend – don't – "

You can't argue with a corpse.

You can only fight. Fight and pant, and try to keep the strangling hands away from your throat. I hit him with everything I had. Nothing happened. Nothing happened, except that he bent me back, back . . .

I sagged then. Sagged so suddenly that he went down with me. As I fell, I twisted. His grip broke. I rolled under the trestle. He groped after me. I dumped coffin and all on his head. He went down. Blind corpse-eyes sought me. I ran. I made it down the hall with no one to stop me. He lumbered to his feet, came groping after me.

I knew the front door would be locked. But there was a glass panel, and next to it in the hall somebody had placed a large urn.

I grabbed it up, smashed the glass, and stepped through.

Then I was out on the street, running. It was night. The air was cool.

It was good to be free.

Free, and wanted for murder.

Have you ever wondered what it feels like to be a murderer?

I can tell you.

It feels like rabbits who bear the baying of a hunting dog. It feels like lying in bed with the covers pulled over your head and Pa coming up the stairs to give you a spanking. It feels like waiting for the Doctor to sterilize the instruments.

You don't walk down the street when you're a murderer. You skulk through the alleys. You don't take the streetcar and you don't pass any cops. And when you finally get down-town to your hotel, you walk a long time before you go inside the lobby. You look around very carefully to make sure it's deserted.

And when you do go in, you don't ask for the key to your room. The police might be waiting up there. Or somebody else. Somebody that's dead, but alive. Waiting to grab you and −

I had the feeling, but I kept it out of my face and voice long enough to ask the clerk and the desk whether or not there had been any message for me.

You see, I had to play one hunch; that the hotel hadn't been tipped off. Varek wouldn't, as long as he thought I was coming in with him. And now, there was still that chance. If I could only get the message . . .

It was waiting for me, the precious little yellow envelope stuck in the pigeonhole. The telegram from the carney. I ripped it open and read:

GREAT AHMED AT FORTY THREE EAST BRENT STREET UNDER NAME RICHARDS.

That was all, and it was enough. Brent was a street on the near North side. Walking distance, I could take an El and bypass the Loop, if I was willing to risk it.

I was. Ahmed, or Richards, had the money.

I had to. Ahmed, or Richards, could save me.

I did. Ahmed, or Richards, was the answer.

Brent Street was about a mile across the bridge after I left the El. It was a long, hard mile, I kept to the shadows, kept my face averted from passersby. But nothing happened. I stopped in front of the dingy old brownstone frost that was graced with the numerals 43, lit my last cigarette, and went up the steps to preas the buzzer.

Then I waited.

It was a good two minutes before the door opened. During

that time I speculated quite a bit about the man I was going to meet.

Would it be the Great Ahmed in a turban? A swarthy man with a pointed beard, deepset burning eyes and a singsong voice?

Would it be the suave, cultivated, cosmopolitan Mr Richards, a con man from the carney, dressed a little too garishly, with a voice too soft and smooth?

It was important for me to know. Because I'd have to throw myself on the man's mercy.

The door opened to answer my question.

"The Great Ahmed?" I asked.

"Yes. Please come in."

I came in. Into the light of the hall-way, where I could see my host.

He wasn't Ahmed and he wasn't Richards, either.

He was nobody.

A small man of about fifty, with thin, greying hair. Wrinkled face, watery blue eyes, almost grey. Come to think about it, his skin was grey, too. And he wore a grey suit. Quiet and inconspicuous. About as far away from a carney type as I could have possibly imagined.

How to describe him? In Hollywood, he'd be what they'd call a Barry Fitzgerald type without the smile and the brogue. Somebody's uncle. The kindly bachelor uncle.

I hoped he'd be mine.

"You are the Great Ahmed?" I asked, still not sure, still not sold.

"Yes. You want a reading?"

"Uh . . . yes."

I might as well stall for a while until I was sure. The way things had been happening, I wouldn't have trusted my own brother.

It was a big house, an old house, one of those places built for people to live in at a time when most families had eight or nine children instead of a television set.

The Great Ahmed led me down a long hallway, past two or three doors leading, inevitably, to a sunporch, a parlor, a library. The room he ushered me into was a sort of secondary parlor, towards the rear of the house. It had plenty of solid mahogany in it; old pieces, but durable. There was a massive center table and the inevitable grouping of chairs as if for a seance. But there was nothing of the medium's workshop or the clairvoyant's clip-joint about this place.

I took advantage of the light in the room to study my host a little more closely, but I can't say I learned much. He was just a tired, middle-aged man, and I wondered how he managed the grift with a tough carney outfit. He didn't look the part of an Oriental mystic at all.

Even when he told me to sit down and produced a crystal ball from a cupboard, I wasn't impressed. The ball itself was small, and a trifle dusty. As a matter of fact, he brushed it off with his sleeve, smiling sheepishly as he did so.

Then he sat down, stared into the ball, and smiled again.

"The reading is three dollars," he said. "An offering, you understand, not a fee. Fee's against the law here."

"Shoot the three bucks," I said.

"Very well." His eyes left my face. They focussed on the ball. Grey eyes, a trifle bloodshot.

I sat very quietly while he stared. He cleared his throat. He fidgeted. Then he spoke.

He told me my name.

He told me where I'd been working.

"You are a friend of the late Cono Colluri," he said, his eyes downcast. "And you are here to collect his money. A sum amounting to eight thousand, two hundred and thirty-one dollars."

He paused. I felt the perspiration running along the collar of my nice white shirt – the one from the funeral parlor, probably stolen off a stiff.

He paused, and I stared at him. Nice little man in grey, but he knew too much. I'd never believed in "occult powers", and yet here he was, telling me these things.

After what I'd gone through in the past three days, I felt that I couldn't take much more. My whole concept of the universe was shattering, and along with it, my sanity. Dead men walking, me a murderer, and now a man who actually reads minds. It was too much . . .

"Take it easy, friend." The Great Ahmed stood up, slowly. "I didn't mean to upset you so. It was a cheap trick, I guess."

His hands moved upwards from under the table. They held an envelope and a sheet of paper.

With a start, I recognized Cono's letter.

"Picked it out of your pocket when I brushed against you in the hall," smiled the little man. "Then held it under the table and read it while you thought I was reading the crystal. Old bit of business, but effective."

I nodded, and tried to smile in a way that conveyed my relief.

"So you're Cono's friend," said the Great Ahmed. "He wrote me about you, you know. A couple of weeks ago. Didn't mention the money, though. It was a tragedy, wasn't it?"

"Then you know about the confession?"

"Yes. Louie was a rat." The smile left his face. "Too bad, a messy business. I'm glad I left the show."

He walked around to the cabinet, stooped, and opened the lower drawer with a small key. He took out a big black tin box. Another key opened it. He began to pile bills on the table – big bills, hundreds and thousands.

"Here's your money," he said, sorting a pile and pushing it across to me.

"But . . . don't you want some kind of paper, some kind of identification or signature?"

"You're Cono's friend. I trust you."

He smiled shyly, and his hands made a gesture of dismissal.

"You trust me, eh?"

"Why not?"

I took a deep breath and came out with it. I had to come out with it to somebody, or go crazy. "Because I'm wanted for murder, that's why!"

The Great Ahmed sat down again, still smiling. "And you want to tell me all about it, is that it? Well, go ahead. I'm listening."

I went ahead, and he listened. It took up a long time, but I told him the whole story – from the time I hit town until the time Cono hit me.

He sat there, a little grey idol, quietly gazing off into the gloom.

"And so now you want to clear your name, eh? And rescue Cono, I suppose? And put the finger on this man Varek, whoever he may be?"

I nodded.

"That's a big order. A mighty big order, friend. You know, of course, that your whole story sounds a bit implausible?"

"It sounds screwier than blazes," I told him. "But it's true. Every word of it."

"Granted. So the problem arises, where do we go from here?"

I glanced at the eight grand plus, lying before me on the table. Suddenly I shoved it back across to him.

"Will this help you to figure things out for me?" I asked. "Because if it will, take it. Part of it or all of it. Whatever it may cost to clear me, to save Cono. To pin a rap on that rat, Varek."

"You trust me to come in with you?" he asked.

"I've trusted you with my story. With my life. The money isn't important. If you're Cono's friend, you'll help."

"Good enough." The Great Ahmed sorted the bills and stacked them up next to the tin box. "From now on, I'm your man. Full time. Now to our problem." He pushed the crystal ball aside. "This won't help us any, I'm afraid. We have to face facts."

"Fact number one," I said, "is that the heat is on me."

"Which means you'll have to lay low. That makes me the outside man," he said.

"Correct. So it's your move."

"My move is to the hotel," Ahmed answered. "To your room. Sooner or later somebody is going to show up there, looking for you. The law will be around. But so will your blonde charmer, and some of the rest of Varek's friends. Perhaps even Cono himself. At any rate, chances are I'll find someone to tail; someone who will lead me to the funeral home or wherever else Varek hides out. He probably has a dozen or more places to hang his hat. If he wears a hat."

"I keep wondering," I mused. "What kind of a creature is this man? And his secret of eternal life – "

"He may have it," Ahmed retorted, "but you don't. And from the looks of you, a little sleep is in order. I'll take you upstairs to a bedroom. You might as well get a good night's rest while I go to work."

I didn't argue with him. The weariness pulled at my knees as I followed him up the stairs.

"You'll have to trust to me and to luck," said the little grey man. "Right now all I can tell you is I'm playing a hunch. That I can go back to the hotel, pick up the trail, and somehow have it lead me to Cono. He's the weak spot in the whole setup, for us. If I can handle him, he'll tell me what we have to know about Varek. Then we'll figure out how to deal with him."

"Sounds logical," I said, as we entered a small bedroom at the end of the corridor.

"Sounds mighty weak and flimsy, to tell the truth," replied my host. "But it's all we have to work on right now. I hope that by the time I return there'll be a little more to work on. Now – here we are. You don't fit into my pyjamas, but I think you'll find the bed is comfortable enough. I'll be on my way. Go to sleep, and pleasant dreams to you."

He waved and went out. I sank back on the bed, scarcely mindful of the click of the key in the lock. Then I sat up. "Here we go again!" I muttered.

My voice must have carried, because he called from beyond the door. "Locking you in. Got a cleaning woman who gets here in about an hour, and I don't want to take any chances. If your description has been broadcast, that is."

"Good enough," I answered. "But you'd better come back."

"I'll be back: And with good news. Don't you worry about a thing. When the Great Ahmed takes over, he takes over."

I lay back, kicked off my shoes, loosened my tie and belt, and then crawled under the covers. His footsteps receded into silence.

Here I was, in a strange house, in a strange bed, my future dependent on the integrity and the ability of a man I hadn't known a half hour.

Somehow, though, I trusted him. I had to trust him, of course, because there was nobody else. I wondered about the Great Ahmed, or Richards — if that was his real name. What he'd been doing hanging around a carney. Why he'd set up a three-dollar-a-throw crystal reading parlor here. Little colorless middle-aged nobody, without even a good line of patter to hand out. But the son-of-a-gun knew how to pick pockets!

That reassured me. He wasn't the schmoe he appeared to be. But was he good enough to handle a man who raised the dead?

I couldn't answer that one now. There was nothing to do but wait. Wait and rest. Rest and sleep.

The room was dark. The night came in at me through the window. I got up and pulled the shade. I didn't want the night. It contained too much that could hurt me. Police, detectives, Varek and the walking dead. Better the special darkness of the room, the special darkness behind my closed eyes. The darkness of sleep.

The darkness of dreams . . .

Funny, the people you run into when you're asleep. Like this negro, for instance. He was just a common citizen, like hundreds of thousands of others on Chicago's South Side. He was riding on the El and I was riding on the El, hanging on the strap next to him.

I wouldn't have even given him a second glance, except for one little thing.

He was dead.

Yes, he was dead. When the El lurched, and he toppled against me, and I saw the rolling whites of his empty eyes, felt the cold, the ebon coldness of his black skin, I knew he was dead. A black corpse, hanging to a strap in the El.

I knew he was dead, and he knew I knew it. Because he smiled. And the deep bass voice rumbled up from the depths — from the depths of his empty grave, his plundered and cheated grave – and he said, "Don't look at me. 'Cause I ain't the only one. They's a lot of 'em dead around heah. A lot of 'em. Look!"

I looked. I gazed down the aisle of the lurching El and I saw them, recognized them. Some of the passengers were alive, of course, and I could tell that at a glance. But there were others. Many others. The quiet ones. The ones with the fixed, cold stares. The ones who didn't talk. Who sat alone. Who carefully avoided touching other bodies. They were pale, they were stiff, they were dead.

Most of the men wore their good suits, because that's the way they were dressed in the undertaking parlors. Most of the women wore too much powder and rouge, because the morticians fixed them that way. Oh, I recognized them. And the Negro nudged me with his icy finger and grinned a grin that held neither mirth nor malice nor any human emotion.

"Zombies," he said. "Tha's what they calls us. Zombies. Walkin' dead. Walkin', talkin' dead. Walkin' and talkin' because the Man say so. The Man. The Big Voodoo Man."

"Varek!" I said.

The El lurched again. The lights went out. Something was happening to the power. Maybe because I'd spoken the name.

The black corpse thought so. In the darkness all I saw was eye-white and tooth-white, flashing at me. "You went and done it," the voice rumbled. "Sayin' the name!"

And all the corpses in all the cars groaned and murmured, "He said the name!"

Suddenly the car gave a sickening lurch and I knew we were going off the track, going over. The corpses rolled against me in waves, and we were twisting and turning, falling, falling . . .

I landed. You're supposed to wake up before you land, but I didn't. Because I went too deep. The car crashed down into the sewers. I wasn't hurt. I was flung free. And I crawled along in the darkness, without eye-white and tooth-white flashing. Just red, this time. Little red lights.

"Rats," I told myself. "Rat eyes."

"We take the form of rats, yes. And of bats. And of other things. But we are not animals. We are not men either." The voice at my ear was soft but imperative. "They call us – vampires!"

I couldn't see him, or the others, but I heard the chittering laughter rise all around me, rise and turn to metallic mockery as it boomed off the sewer walls.

"Vampires. He raised us from the dead, he made us. In the big church up on Division Street, Father Stanislaus makes the Holy Sign against us. But we do not care. He is fat and old, that priest, and he will die. We can never die. We walk the night, we feast, and we own the world below."

Another voice droned in: "It's like this under the whole city, did you know that? And under every city. There's always places to hide, if you're clever. You can tunnel from place to place, come and go as you please, and nobody knows. Nobody sees. Nobody hears. And you can lift the manhole covers, drag down what you want, and dispose of what's left without leaving any evidence. Oh, it's clever and no mistake, and we can thank the Master for it all."

I nodded. "You mean Varek," I said.

They howled at that, and the sound nearly tore my head in two as the echo hammered from the metal walls. They howled, and then they scrabbled towards me in the darkness, but I ran. I ran and waded and crawled and swam through muck and filth, seeking an opening, seeking a light, seeking an escape from the world of death and darkness here below.

I found it, found it at last. The round metal lid above my head which led to safety. Safety and the cool darkness of a cellar. A chink of light guided me to a stairway and the door above. I came out into a kitchen, moved past to the bedroom, and peered through the door.

Edgar Allan Poe sat by the bedside and made strange motions with his slim white hands. Two doctors were in attendance, and all focussed their gaze on the apparition lying on the bed; the gaunt, skeletal countenance peered up from the pillows with glazed and glassy eyes.

The patient had white whiskers and incongruously black hair; outside of the animation in his eyes he might have passed for dead, and none would be the wiser.

But Poe's hands moved, commanding the sleeper to awake, and as I watched, he awakened.

Ejaculations of "Dead! dead!" absolutely burst from the tongue and not the lips of the sufferer, and his whole frame at once – within the space of a single minute or even less, shrunk – crumbled – absolutely rotted away. Upon the bed, before that whole company, there lay a nearly liquid mass of loathsome, of detestable putridity.

Then I fled, screaming, from the house of M. Valdemar.

But wherever I went, there were the dead.

Poe couldn't raise Valdemar. But Varek could. And he had. In my dream, I saw the proof. I tramped the streets of Chicago and recognized the faces. That stiff-lipped, unsmiling doorman in front of the ritzy Gold Coast hotel – he was dead. The black-haired girl on the end of the switch-board at the Merchandise Mart, the one who said, "Number please?" in such a mechanical fashion – she was Varek's puppet, too. There was an elevator operator at Field's and three men who worked the night shift at a big steel plant out near Gary. An old precinct sergeant over in Garfield Park was a walking corpse and even his wife didn't suspect. But what the precinct sergeant didn't know was that his captain was also a cadaver, and neither of them knew the secret of one of the Cook County judges.

The dead – there were hundreds of them. Maybe thousands. Because Chicago isn't the only city in the world, and Varek had been everywhere.

I walked along, and then I ran. Because I couldn't stand it any longer, couldn't stand to see the faces, the empty eyes. I couldn't stand being jostled by a corpse in the crowded Loop. I ran and I ran until I came to the Great Ahmed's house and I came up to the bedroom, battered down the locked door, and crawled in bed here with myself again, knowing that I was safe at last, I was here, I could wake up into a world of reality – *where dead men still walked*!

"And they have other powers, too."

Who had told me that? Varek himself, in the bartender's body. *Other powers*. Powers like levitation – like floating through space, through windows high off the ground . . .

It had happened once before in a dream, and now it was happening again.

I could see her face at the bedroom window. Vera's face. The pale blonde hair. The diamond choker. Floating outside the window, bumping against it. Her hands groped out. She was opening the window from outside.

Funny that I should see it that way, because I'd pulled the shade down, and it was up now. So was the window. She was coming into the room, floating in gently, softly, ever so quietly. And now she landed, without a bump or a thump or a shudder, on the tips of her delicate toes. She was dead, too, of course. I knew it now. Her stare was glassy. She moved by automatic compulsion only. It was like a hypnotic trance, with every motion directed by an outside, an alien force.

Glassy-eyed, like a drugged Assassin. And like an Assassin, she drew the dagger from her waist. It was a long, slim, feminine-looking weapon, but it was deadly. The steel was diamond-bright. Why did she remind me of diamonds? Because of the choker. I gazed at the choker now as she tiptoed over to the bed. I wanted to watch it.

Better than watching the dagger. Because the dagger was a menace. It was coming up over my throat. In a moment it would come down, the point would bury itself in my neck, over the jugular.

All I had to do was watch the diamonds in her choker. And in a minute it would be all over. The knife was coming down, the knife that would end my life, the knife that would make me one with Varek's army – the army of the dead.

It came down, fast.

The glitter of that frantically falling blade broke the spell. Instantaneously, I realized that I was seeing it. There was a knife, and it was coming down at my throat.

I jerked my head to one side on the pillow and slammed my body forward, upward. My hands closed around solid flesh. Cold flesh.

Vera LaValle twisted wildly in my arms.

I sat up, hands moving to her wrist. I pressed it back until the knife dropped to the carpet. She fought me silently, her face a Medusa's mask, blonde curls tumbling like serpents over her cold, bare shoulders.

Suddenly her head dropped. I caught a glimpse of strong white teeth grimacing towards my neck. Vampire teeth, seeking my jugular.

I tore at her throat. My hands ripped the choker, dug beneath it. It came free, and fell. My hands closed around her neck, then came away.

I could not touch the thin red line, the scar that encircled her neck completely.

My hands came away, and I slapped her, hard.

Abruptly, she sank to the bed. The glassiness left her eyes and something like recognition flooded her face.

"Where am I?" whispered Vera LaValle.

"In a bedroom on Brent Street," I answered. "The Great Ahmed's place. You floated through the window and tried to kill me."

"He put me under," she murmured. "Then he sent me here and levitated me. I didn't know."

I nodded, but said nothing.

"You believe me, don't you?" she implored. "I didn't know. He promised me that he'd never make me do that again. But he did. He always does. Even now, I can't trust him. He can do anything he likes with me, because I'm – "

She stopped abruptly, and I filled it in for her.

"Because you're dead," I told her. "I know."

Her eyes widened. "How did you find out?"

For answer, I pointed at her throat. She noticed then that the choker had been torn away. Her hands covered the red scar on her neck and she stared at me for a long moment. Then, with a sigh, she swept her hair back into place.

"Tell me about it," I said. "Maybe I can help."

"Nobody can help. Nobody."

"I can try. And the more you tell me, the more I have to work with. That is, if it's safe to talk."

She thought that one over for a moment. "Yes, it will be, for at least a half hour now. He goes into a sort of coma when he levitates one of us; it requires terrific concentration. But if he comes out of it and discovers I've failed, anything can happen."

The fear was coming back into her eyes, and I sought to capture her attention again, quickly.

"Half an hour," I said. "That's time enough. Tell me about it from the beginning. What happened to you?"

Vera LaValle sighed. Her hands stroked the scar, softly. "All right," she said.

I lighted a cigarette and sat up, offering her the pack. She shook her head and I said. "Oh, that's right, I remember now. You don't smoke, do you?"

"I can't," said Vera LaValle. "I haven't been able to smoke, or drink, or eat. Not since I was beheaded – in 1794."

In 1794, the Terror ruled France. You could run into almost anything under the Terror. You might encounter a Citizen Robespierre or a man called – ironically enough – St Just.

If you did so, the chances were that they would introduce you to still another man with a more apt name – Samson, the executioner.

And Samson, in turn, would direct you to La Guillotine.

Everybody in France knew La Guillotine. Despite the feminine appellation, La Guillotine was not a giddy female – although she turned a lot of heads.

La Guillotine was the Terror incarnate. The head-chopping Terror. The beheading blade that waited until you were ripe for it, then chopped and filled the basket beneath it with rich and rotting fruit.

In 1794, the Terror ruled France, and you might run into almost anything. If you were Vera LaValle, age 20, daughter of Lucien LaValle the wealthy merchant, you walked in constant danger of your life.

Wealthy merchants were not popular these days. Wealthy merchants had to twist and turn, fawn and cringe, resort to almost any stratagem in order to try and escape from Paris before the order came – the fatal summons to the Tribunal. Better to ride out of the city in a dung-cart than to the Place de la Concorde in a tumbril.

No wonder Lucien LaValle betook himself to desperate measures and consorted with strange people in an effort to procure a means of deliverance before it was too late. Paris was aswarm with rogues and adventurers, thieves and sharpers who fattened on the misery of the remaining members of the nobility or the well-to-do. Some of them, for a price, could procure passports or arrange an unauthorized passage across the border or the English Channel.

Lucien LaValle, wealthy widower with a handsome, marriageable daughter, thought that he had found a solution.

Somewhere, somehow, in heaven knows what den or dive or stew, he encountered Nicolo Varek. Varek, the friend of the illustrious Comte St Germain. Varek, the *confidant* of the mighty Cagliostro. Varek, the alchemist, the mystic, the seeker of the Philosopher's Stone. Varek who boasted of powers greater than those of the two great charlatans he claimed to have known – and taught. Varek, the unsmiling, the cold, the ageless. But – and this was the crux of the matter – Varek the foreigner. Varek, the holder of the priceless possession, the Russian visa. The passport to freedom for himself and family.

Varek had no family, now. But Vera LaValle was young, she was *chic*, she was eminently well dowered. If she were a wife, and Lucien LaValle an official member of Varek's family – then what would there be to stop the *ménage* from leaving France?

It was a reasonable proposition, and Lucien LaValle presented it to Varek on many occasions.

He shrugged. There was work to be done here in Paris, he said. Great things were afoot. He had never been presented to Mademoiselle LaValle, and no doubt she was all her fond father proclaimed her to be but still . . . A man in Varek's position is above matrimony and the calls of the flesh. And as to money (and here Varek shrugged again), he fortunately was in a position to command a fortune whenever he wished. No, it would not be advisable to leave the country now. As a matter of fact, everything depended upon remaining.

Lucien LaValle was eloquent. When eloquence fell upon deaf ears, he was insistent. When insistence failed, he resorted to tears. He sank to his knees. He wept and implored. And in the end, Nicolo Varek consented to meet the merchant's daughter, to talk to her.

That was enough for LaValle. He returned home elated, and put his case to Vera.

"Consider now how much depends upon your conduct," he told her. "Be charming – sprightly – gay. This Varek, he has a long face. He needs cheering. He needs your youth."

Vera LaValle nodded dutifully. No need to instruct her in coquetry. Long before he revealed his hopes and plans, she was miles ahead of her father. He had found a man who could save them – at a price. What the price was did not matter. Her father would pay his share and she would gladly pay hers.

She bathed, dressed, perfumed and painted for the interview. The meeting took place in the parlor and it was unchaperoned. A carriage drove up in the dusk, and Vera LaValle met Nicolo Varek under candlelight.

And it was thus that Varek, the friend of the nobility, the mentor of magicians, the peer of alchemists – Varek, the man who was above matrimony or the commonplace emotional reactions of ordinary men – fell in love.

Candlelight and coquetry definitely won the day, and the night. The suave, cold middle-aged man became a stammering, intense importuner. As to the matter of age, Varek was quite explicit on that point.

"Do not think of me as old, my dear," he reassured her. "For I am truly ageless. There are secrets I possess, secrets you shall share with me. Oh, we will share a great deal, you and I!"

He began to boast then, like any love-sick youth, and to confide.

Varek was Russian by birth, but the date of that birth and the details of his parentage would (he smirked) astound her. Suffice for him to say that he came of noble blood. He had been educated at the leading universities of Europe, but the bulk of his learning came from extended sojourns in Mongolia and Hindustan where he had studied occultism and the forbidden mysteries. Upon his return to Europe, he had visited Italy and imparted some of his wisdom to Cagliostro – wisdom which Cagliostro misused in his unscrupulous career. Varek, still seeking disciples, later gave instruction to the Comte de St Germain, whose mastery of mass illusion and the principles of levitation enabled him to win fame and fortune.

But he, Varek, was not interested in such trivia. True, as an alchemist he had sought to transmute baser metals to gold. But he soon realized that cultivation of other powers was more important.

Once he had developed them, fame and fortune would be his for the asking.

There were two secrets, and two only, which were worth possessing. One of them was the secret of eternal youth, and the other, the secret of eternal life.

To the discovery of these secrets, Varek had dedicated himself for scores of years.

It was a costly study, an expensive search. In order to finance himself he had, at times, resorted to base means. As an alchemist he was acquainted with the group that centered around La Voisin, and he admitted assisting that notorious female in her preparation of poisons. He had also been familiar with the clique surrounding the infamous de Montespan.

"But that was ages ago!" cried Vera, when she heard him. "Over a hundred years!"

Nicolo Varek, the unsmiling one, smiled. "Exactly," he said. "You see, I succeeded in at least part of my quest. I did discover the secret of eternal youth. Discovered it and possessed myself of it."

"You are over a hundred?" Vera murmured.

Varek inclined his head. "I assure you, time is a relative concept. You will not find me less ardent a lover due to my age, no less honorable a man because of my past associations. As you realize, we who seek the mysteries have always been on the fringes of society. We skulk in darkness, we consort with the underworld, we compound with the charlatans simply because we have never been accepted by the scholars and the savants. They are jealous of our achievements, these so-called "men of science" – although virtually all they know or hope to know has come from our work.

"Yes, it is we alchemists who have given them their chemistry, we sorcerers who have preserved what little is known of medicine and physiology and biology, we mystics who have the only knowledge which can develop into a science of the mind."

"I don't understand," Vera said. "What are you trying to tell me?"

"I'm telling you not to be afraid of me." he answered. "It has been said that I am a cheat, a liar, a fraud, a scoundrel, a magician, a murderer. Very well – I am all these things, but to a purpose. That purpose is power, power greater than you can dream!

"I've played my part behind the scenes these years past, my dear – and you've seen the result! I've had my interview with Mademoiselle Charlotte Corday, and Marat died. I've talked to Citizen Robespierre's brother, and Danton is no more. I've ways and means to pull the strings and make the puppets dance. And the end will be power. Great power. Once France is properly disrupted, there are other lands ripe for revolution.

"Revolution, my dear, always ends in dictatorship. Dictatorship, my dear, always ends in megalomania on the part of those who rule. And what would a megalomaniac do for the secret of eternal youth or the secret of eternal life – or both?

"Ah, yes, it will end only one way: My way. I shall rule the rulers! Think of that, my dear. Within a few years, Nicolo Varek will be the unseen ruler of the world. And you, his empress, his queen."

Varek came closer, and Vera could see the paper thinness of his bloodless lips. He might have been forty, he might have been four hundred. "The secret of eternal youth. How does that please you, my little one? To be always young, always as you are today? To live, to rule, to enjoy the senses to the full forever? I have that gift for you, that dowry.

"And soon – sooner than I dare tell you – I shall have the other, too. The Great Secret. Eternal life! I've a laboratory here – you must see it – where I experiment. In times like these, there is no shortage of subjects. Samson sells me the unclaimed ones every day." The bloodless lips formed a bloody smile. "I'm getting closer and closer to the solution," Varek told her. "And once it's gained, the world is mine. Ours!"

It was mawkish melodrama, but it was also naked nightmare. For the little lisping, whispering, sniggering creature came closer and closer, and then he was no longer braggart or stammerer but merely a lustful automaton. He pawed at Vera LaValle and she endured his carrion breath upon her neck for a moment. But only for a moment. Then she wrenched free, and Varek, losing his balance, tumbled grotesquely to the floor.

Vera LaValle laughed.

She didn't refuse his offer of marriage. She didn't call him an old man, a liar, a murderer, a repulsive fool. She didn't do anything but laugh.

Her laugh said all those things.

Nicolo Varek rose, tugged at his ruffled clothing, and bowed coldly. "*Adieu*," he said. And left.

Vera LaValle waited. She waited for Lucien to scamper in, rubbing his hands briskly in anticipation. She waited for the effect of her story upon him; his crestfallen stare, his agitation, his frantic reiteration of, "Why, why, why? He was our only hope, out only chance! Why?"

She waited, then, for the summons. It came soon enough.

Somebody had denounced Citizen LaValle and his daughter. As usurers, as enemies of the People.

She waited for the trial, and it was short. Lucien sobbed when he heard the verdict, but she shrugged.

She waited, then, for the tumbril.

Waited, those last few days, alone. For Lucien LaValle hung himself one gloomy Sunday morning and she was left alone.

She was alone, and waiting, that last night when Varek came.

Citizens were not allowed to visit with prisoners in their cells on the eve of execution. But Varek was not a citizen. He was not a man at all in the ordinary concept of the word. He was a mocking shadow that glided silently to her cell.

One moment nothing, and the next, Varek was there. Whispering in the darkness.

"Vera, Vera LaValle, listen to me! I have news for you. Great news!"

Silence, as he waited for a reply. But she said nothing. After a moment, he continued: "Remember what I told you? About the laboratory, the experiments, the secret of eternal life? I have it at last, Vera – I have it at last! Oh, it's not exactly all I'd hoped, and much remains to be done in refining the method. But it's the goal of sorcery through the ages, the dream of science. And I have it. For you. For us!"

Silence once more. Vera LaValle did not move. He spoke again: "Eternal life, Vera! I swear it's the truth; I can give you eternal life. All you need do is say the word and you're free. I can get you out as easily as I got you in. And now you can be young forever, alive forever! You must believe me, you must!"

Vera turned and faced him through the bars of the cell. She could not see his face in the darkness of the corridor, but he could see her countenance – and the lineaments of loathing.

"I do believe you," she said. "And I tell you that I prefer to die tomorrow morning rather than spend eternity – or a single living moment – with you."

Varek's laugh grated through the gloom. "A plain answer, Mademoiselle LaValle. But I wonder if you have rightly considered what's in store for you. When the tumbril rolls and the sun is gleaming, gleaming on the bright blade of the guillotine? Have you see the heads in the basket, Mademoiselle? Have you seen Samson lift them by the hair and exhibit them to the crowd?"

"You can't frighten me," she whispered.

"Do you know what it's like to be dead? Dead forever and ever?

They'll put you in the ground, Mademoiselle, in the cold wet ground.
You'll lie there in eternal darkness, lie there and rot and decay into
slime and dust. And the lips that you withhold from me will feed
kisses to the worms.

"Aren't you afraid of death, Mademoiselle LaValle?"

She shook her head and smiled into the blackness beyond the bars.
"Not as much as I fear life with you," she said. "Now, go and leave
me in peace."

He broke down, then. The creature cried and begged. "I don't
understand, it's never happened before — that a woman, a girl, a
mere child should do this to me! I thought I was immune to folly, but
since the moment I laid eyes on you I cannot endure the thought of
not possessing you. You are a burning in my blood, you must know
that and you cannot refuse — you cannot! But you must be mine of
your own free will, not by force. I want you willingly, and I must
have you." Varek sobbed, and it was the dry and dusty sobbing of
a reanimated mummy, rustling in the darkness.

Once again, Vera LaValle shook her head. "No," she said.

Varek's sob held not grief but rage. "Good enough," he cried. "If
I'm not fit for you, I commend you to a new lover. To Death! Death
shall embrace you, twine his bony fingers in your curls, take your
head as a souvenir of his conquest. *Adieu* — I leave you to hold tryst
with your beloved. He'll not be long now!"

And he left her.

Then and only then did Vera break down. For she had lied.
She did fear death. The thought of dying terrified her past all
comprehension, and now in the darkness she could almost see the
grinning presence of Death incarnate; the skeleton in the black coat,
the grinning skull covered with a cowl.

He was still with her the next morning, when the guards came.
He walked with her to the tumbril, and as she and five other
weeping and bedraggled women took their places, Death climbed
in beside them.

Death grinned at Vera LaValle as she rode through the streets of
Paris to the site of execution. Death pointed his finger at the roaring
crowd, the prancing Citizen Samson and his grimacing assistants.
Death showed her the shrieking silhouette of the knife against the
dawn-drenched sky.

Death was with her as she walked to the platform. Death helped
her up the stairs, and it seemed to Vera in the delirium of the last
few moments that not Samson but Death himself was the executioner
— removing her cloak, binding her arms forcing her to kneel and gaze

down at the bottom of the basket when all the time she wanted to gaze up; gaze up at the knife, the bright blade of the knife which was the only real thing left in the world.

Then, as the roar of the crowd came up, the blade of the guillotine came down.

Death took Vera LaValle in his arms.

And – released her!

"You want to know what it's like, of course," she told me, sitting there on the bed, thousands of miles and lifetimes later. "But I don't remember. There was no pain, no sensation, and yet I *felt*, I was conscious in a new way. There was no sense of duration, either.

"Then the pain came back, and I was alive.

"I had this pain in the throat, and in the head.

"I opened my eyes. I saw the bandage on my neck. I saw the silver tube coiling to the top of my spine. And I saw Varek.

"You know what happened, of course. Samson had sold me to Varek after the execution. He took me to his laboratory and brought me back to life.

"I realized it, naturally, at once. But I can never convey to you the horror of that moment – when I discovered that he had sewed my head back on my body!

"It was grotesque, it was ludicrous, and it was somehow blasphemous. But despite it all, in the weeks to come, I learned to respect the power, the wisdom, the genius of Nicolo Varek.

"My convalescence, if you can call it that, was slow. It was not easy, with the crude techniques he had painfully evolved, for Varek to keep me alive and nurse me back to a semblance of health and sanity. But he did it. Since that time I've learned a great deal about what he does to reanimate the dead, and still I haven't grasped the true secret."

She paused, and I cut in: "You say he sewed your head back on? But that's . . . incredible."

Vera pointed at the scar and smiled wanly. "Would you find it equally incredible if I told you that there's a metal plate covering half of my skull – that there is metal, some sort of machinery, extending down the neck and into the upper spine? That Varek, in 1794, was using electrical voltage and a sort of miniature dynamo for metabolic regulation? That the control he exercised and still exercises is a combination of hypnotism and an extension of brain-waves transformed into electric current? Yet it's true, all of it. I am an automaton – operating on the power generated from within plus the current fed me by Varek at a distance. I'm alive yet not alive. I do not age or change, I do not eat or sleep. But there's something worse than sleep. Something much worse." She shuddered. "That's when he *turns me off*."

Either she was crazy or I was. Or both of us. This I knew. But I believed her. I believed the cold-eyed, cold-skinned creature with the livid scar who talked to me across the centuries.

"He's done it to me, many times, temporarily and to suit his convenience or his needs. But I've seen him do it to others – permanently. It's horrible. They die, then; die a second death. A hideous death, forever.

"That's the hold he has over me, over all of us. The ability to turn us off. Because there's something inside that wants to live, fights to live. Oh, how can I tell you the story of what took a hundred and sixty years to live?" Vera glanced around the room, and for a moment her agitation seemed completely human. "There's not time; he'll come out of it now, hear us."

I pressed her. I had to know the rest. "Quickly, then," I urged. "What happened after you recovered?"

"He was still experimenting. I was his first complete success. There were other . . . corpses . . . that he revived temporarily. But they were damaged, warped. Completely insane. At the time, he hadn't perfected his methodology of control. Several escaped. There was an ugly scandal. And Robespierre's dictatorship fell. He went to the guillotine himself. Varek no longer had protection in Paris. So we fled.

"The Embargo was on, and the only ship we could find was bound for the colonies. We ended up in Haiti, just the two of us.

"It was a strange relationship. He no longer desired me, of course – and I think he almost regretted his monstrous act of revival. Gradually he set about to make me his servant. And of course, he succeeded. I was alone, helpless, literally dependent on him for my existence.

"I offer no apologies for serving Varek. I had no choice. And he was master.

"It didn't take long for him to establish himself in Haiti and in San Domingo. He had brought money and jewels. We took a mansion; he posed as a planter. And immediately set about fomenting an insurrection. You know what happened to Haiti a few years later, when Toussaint L'Ouverture, Dessalines and Christophe revolted against the French. Varek played his part. Blood flowed, and there were bodies for Varek's new laboratories. Black bodies to experiment upon. Black bodies to toil on the plantations.

"It was at this time that a new superstition arose. The one about zombies. The walking dead. Can you understand now just why and how this belief was born?"

I nodded, thinking of my dreams. There was a horrid logic and conviction behind her words. Varek had created the concept of the zombie. His creatures walking the world.

"The blacks were primitive, simple. Varek bungled often. He was still groping, evolving methods and techniques. The botched jobs were the zombies.

"And the vampires – that was Hungary, of course."

I raised an eyebrow. "But Varek isn't responsible for the belief in vampires. That's an ancient superstition."

"Correct," answered Vera. "But we went to Hungary from Haiti because of the belief. Because, there, tales of the walking dead would be ascribed to superstition and no one would investigate too closely if some of Varek's experiments moved freely over the countryside. Also, Varek wished to follow the latest developments in European scientific research. Even before the Revolution, he had worked briefly with Anton Mesmer in the development of hypnotism. Now he was interested in the new psychology.

"You see, attaining the power he dreams of is a long and a complicated process. It involves much more than merely the ability to control the reanimated bodies of the dead. At first, Varek could not keep a corpse alive except by constant hypnotic control. He had to focus his own energies every moment. Then he reached a stage were he could fix a behavior pattern for hours, or days, and turn to other matters. But that is not enough.

"Each reanimated corpse must be provided for – given a new identity, a new life, a new *role* to play. Varek moulds the puppets, breathes life into them, and then he must manipulate the strings. Dozens, scores of puppets, on dozens of separate stages; all play their part in one involved drama.

"He had to enter into scientific fields, enter into politics. How much of the intrigue behind the Third Empire in France was due to his work, I'll never know. For in 1847 I rebelled; I tried to get away. And as punishment he *turned me off for seventy years!*"

Vera's white death-mask contorted in remembered agony. "For seventy years I followed Varek across the world as baggage – in an ice-packed coffin. And meanwhile he meddled with science, he pulled strings, and he waited. What's time to Varek?

"I awoke in Russia, during the Revolution. By this time he'd come to realize that he needed living allies; men to work in front of the public. Dupes and spies. He'd made some connection with a monk,

Rasputin. There was a plan to kill the young Tsarevitch and then bring him back to life again; the Czar and Czarina would be at his mercy, from that point on. But somebody murdered Rasputin, and we fled Russia for a spell. That's when I was reanimated again.

"Varek believes in Revolution, you know. A time of turmoil and disruption is what he needs; it gives him an opportunity to profit by confusion. New and untried leaders arise, and he comes to them with hints of what he can do. He presents plans and attempts to gain control of those who form governments.

"We returned to Russia, and I aided him. I had no choice. It was that or lying in darkness – refrigerated darkness, now, thanks to modern conveniences." She smiled wryly. "You can guess what he's been up to since then. You can guess who was behind the scenes in some of Pavlov's experiments. Varek reached members of that group. You can guess that sooner or later the Comintern got wind of it. But what you do not know – and what history does not show – is just how perilously close Russia came to developing a truly mechanized army in the 1930's. An army of the dead!"

I lit a cigarette and tried not to look at the clock on the bureau; the clock that was ticking the minutes away.

"We were in Germany, then, and Varek attempted to sell his notion to the New Order. But his spokesmen fell out of power, and in 1939 we fled again. We were in Canada for a few years, in Manitoba and further north. Varek waited out the war. But he has infinite patience, infinite cunning.

"He can afford to wait – wait for centuries, if necessary. He's a strange man, Varek. He has possessed vast wealth, and lost it time and time again fleeing from country to country. He has a chameleon-like ability to alter his personality his appearance. He is – But what's the use of telling you? You're doomed."

I crushed out the cigarette.

"Now let's get down to cases," I suggested. "He sent you to kill me. Why?"

"Because you know about Cono. His offer was genuine, at first. He is still looking for a man, for many men, who will serve him as living allies. But you refused, and because you understand his power, you must die."

"Yet, Cono is such an insignificant cog in his machine," I persisted. "A dumb strong-man from a carnival. I can't see why a man with Varek's gigantic plans would bother with such a trivial matter."

"Then you don't know Varek. He has plans within plans. He's

not lived quietly for the past few years for nothing. He's been waiting – waiting for the next war. The big one. The one his plans have indirectly fomented.

"There's a great laboratory set up already, somewhere in Sorora. It is capable of . . . processing . . . the dead almost on a factory assembly line. Its services will be offered to the highest bidder when the time comes. Whichever side runs out of manpower and needs a new army of workers, a new army of fighters. Don't you understand? That's where it all leads to, Varek's dream; to create a world run by slaves – by the dead!"

"He'll never get away with it."

"I'm not so sure. The past few years have brought the scientific developments he needs. There are new methods of controlling bodies *en masse*. Radio, electronics, blood plasma all play a part in his schemes.

"For years now he's been in the background, waiting for the right time. When war comes he will have emissaries ready to approach the new leaders. He knows how to get to the wealthy, the powerful, and intrigue them. That has been my job in the past. He intended to have your help, too – and probably the help of a hundred men like you."

"That's the one point that isn't clear to me yet," I told her. "Just exactly how does he manage to insinuate himself into the confidence of the men on top?"

Vera smiled. The ghost of a smile, the smile of a ghost. "Simple. Have you ever heard of the Fox sisters? Or D. D. Home or Angel Annie or Madame Blavatsky?"

I nodded. "Spiritualist mediums or mystics, weren't they?"

"Yes. During my . . . sleep . . . Varek was able to hit on that gambit. The same one used earlier by St Germain and Cagliostro. Through the ages the wealthy, the powerful have always had one weakness. A belief in superstition. A longing to pierce the veil of the Mysteries. They've always followed the seers, flocked to the occultists, confided in them. No need to explain the phenomenon. It exists."

"True enough." I said. "So Varek allies himself with the mediums. They act as his front men. They attract the rich. And Varek watches, waits, chooses those he wants or can use, and then steps into the picture and reveals his plans."

"Exactly." Vera sighed. "It was that way with Rasputin, if you remember. He was the key to the Czar's influence. And he's ready to start again."

"But the mediums aren't trustworthy, many are frauds," I argued.

"And many are not. Take D. D. Home, for example. No less a scientist than Crookes verified the fact that Home levitated himself out of a third storey window and floated back in through another. It actually happened, time and time again. But what Crookes didn't know is that little, tubercular, wan Mr Home had been dead for a year – and Varek animated him, hypnotized him, and then levitated him by concentration. Just as he levitated me tonight and sent me to kill you."

Vera paused. I stared at her white face in the gloom. And as I stared, something happened. A spasm contorted her countenance, the same dreadful tic that had afflicted Cono. I watched her as her mouth opened and a voice came out. But it was not Vera LaValle's voice. It was the voice of the dead bartender, the voice of Varek.

"Yes," it told her, as much as it told me. "I sent you to kill him. And you failed. Failed and then talked. I cannot afford to have you talk any more, Vera. I'm going to turn you off. *Forever*."

The voice shut off abruptly. It had to shut off, for there was no longer a means of utterance. The spasm in Vera's face swept down over her body in a single hideous horripilation. For a moment she swayed there, shuddering convulsively. Then – she *melted*.

There was a change, and it wasn't a collapse. It was a running together, as though flesh were falling in on splintering bone. She shrank, dwindled before my eyes – and then she crumbled.

Somebody had taken the wax doll that was Vera LaValle, and held it over a roaring flame. In an instant she ran together, fused.

I stared at the floor, stared at the heap of fine white ash surrounding a charred and twisted cluster of wires linked to a metal plate.

Vera LaValle was gone.

Vera was gone and I was alone in the bedroom. Or was I?

If I'd had any doubts about Varek's power, they were gone now. They'd vanished with Vera, and taken a part of my sanity with them.

Let's face it; I was panicked. Varek knew where I was, and that meant I would no longer be safe here. Not safe from him, not safe from the police. I wondered what had happened to Ahmed. For all I knew, Varek had attended to him, too. And I couldn't stick around and wait.

I went over to the door. It was locked, of course, and I'd have to force it. I gave it the old college try. You see them do it every day in the movies and on television. Brawny, broad-chested hero puts his shoulder to the locked door. The door gives way. Simple.

Try it sometime. Desperate as I was, all I managed to gain was a bruised shoulder. Then I picked up a chair. That was a better deal. The panel splintered. I broke the lock.

Then I was running down the hall in darkness, groping at the head of the stairs, clumping down them, racing through the hall to the front door. If a cleaning-woman had showed up, she didn't show.

I made the door, opened it. The night air hit me. So did a hand.

"What's the rush, friend?"

I gasped with panic, then with relief.

Ahmed bustled in, rubbing his hands. "Hold it," he said. "I've got news for you."

I shook my head. "I've got news for you, too," I said.

"What do you mean?"

I decided to risk it. He had to be shown. I took him by the arm and steered him back up the stairs. If you think it wasn't hard for me to force myself into that room again, you've got another guess. But it had to be done that way.

"Take a look," I said.

His little gray eyes examined the charred ashes on the floor. He stooped and picked up the metal plate, contemplated the dangling wires protruding from it.

"What's this?"

"All that remains of Vera LaValle. She visited me with a knife. I got her to talk and then she was . . . shut off."

"I don't follow you."

"Sit down," I sighed. "I'll have to explain, but I want to make it fast."

I did. The Great Ahmed nodded. He wasn't upset, he wasn't alarmed, he wasn't horrified. Somehow, his very calmness managed to reassure me.

"It ties together," he said, as I concluded. "It fits. Every bit of it."

"How do you know?"

"Because I've seen Cono. You were right about the hotel, friend. He came back. And when he found me hiding in the closet he tried to kill me." Ahmed smiled and help up a skeleton key. "I needn't tell you how I got in the room," he grinned. "But to make a long story short, the same thing happened as must have happened to you and Vera here. I managed to calm him down – he recognized me, of course. To be brutally frank, I resorted to an old Varek trick; a little hypnosis of my own. Varek must have been directing his own energies elsewhere, possibly to levitate Vera LaValle.

"At any rate, Cono talked, Of course, he's newly reborn, as it were, and he doesn't have too many details. Also, he's not the best example of a scientific mind." Ahmed smiled, briefly. "Still, he told more than he thought he was telling.

"Did you know that Varek has hideouts established in almost every principal city in the world? And that each of them contains anywhere from a dozen to several hundred bodies under refrigeration, ready for reanimation at any time? A sort of dead storage.

"Also, there are the walkers. More of them than you'd suspect. Although it's really quite easy to detect them because they all have one thing in common – the red scar on the neck."

I started at that. "You mean, he cuts off their heads before he revives them?"

Ahmed shrugged. "Not completely, now. But an operation is performed. A deep incision is made at the base of the brain. The metal plate is grafted into place and the wires" – here he picked up the charred mass from the floor and waved it – "are put into place. Meanwhile, the hypnotic control is being established."

"It's a form of hypnotism, then? But I don't get it."

The Great Ahmed shook his head. "It isn't easy. But then, what do any of us understand about the life process? We don't know what governs our physiological continuity; makes our hearts beat and our lungs take in and expel air without conscious control. You might say we operate our own bodies through autohypnosis and that keeps us alive.

"And what's death? Various organs 'die' at different times after the heart stops. We can understand the process of decay, but we can't define or truly measure death. Why, I defy anyone to tell me exactly what sleep is, let alone death!

"Sleep – that's a form of hypnosis, too.

"And, somehow, Varek has harnessed that portion of the mind which functions automatically in life, in sleep; kept it going in the state we describe as death. The common denominator is electrical energy; brain-waves, which can be measured electrically, you know. Varek has managed to apply hypnotic principles to the electric current of the body; magnetism controlling magnetism. That's why he performs the operation, inserts the metal plates in the brain and the spine. To alter the 'hookup', you might say."

The little man spoke earnestly, as though he were lecturing a backward pupil. I listened with equal earnestness now as he waved his finger at me.

"Let me put it simply. You might compare the human body to a radio set, and Varek to a radio station. His operation consists of putting in the proper tubes and condensers to make the set forever receptive to his hypnotic wave-length. It's all electrical. Once control is established, he can broadcast impulses forever. That's a vast oversimplification, but you get the idea."

"Not completely," I said. "What about the bartender?"

"Oh, there are exceptions. The bartender was one. There Varek resorted to a temporary hookup. Probably gave his entire concentration to animating him temporarily, just to talk to you. As he concentrated entireiy to levitate Vera. Those special things require special efforts. But with the vast army of dead, Varek — to return to our little analogy of a radio station — merely sends out a host of previously prepared 'transcriptions' in the shape of hypnotic suggestions. The dead then 'play' the hypnotic suggestions through for hours. And Varek need pay no more attention to them than an engineer who puts on long-playing records for broadcasting. They operate automatically.

"And that, of course, is the weakness. Sometimes Varek doesn't pay attention; or he watches the wrong body. Then it's possible for someone else with a stronger hypnotic wavelength to 'jam' reception in a corpse — capture its attention, divert its purpose. As I did with Cono tonight at the hotel. And as you did with Vera."

"Lucky for both of us we did," I said. "But what else happened? What else did you find out? Why is Varek operating in Chicago now? And — this is the jackpot question — what's the secret of his own eternal life?"

The Great Ahmed smiled. "You want a lot for a few hours' work, friend," he answered gently. "Some of those questions you'll have to find out about for yourself. All I can do is give you that opportunity."

"Meaning?"

"Meaning I made a deal with Cono. And I think he can be trusted — as long as Varek doesn't get to him. Cono has promised to lead you direct to Varek himself tonight."

"Now?" I was genuinely startled.

Ahmed glanced at his wristwatch. "In about three quarters of an hour. You're to meet him in the lobby of the Wrigley Building at eleven-thirty. Alone."

I didn't like that at all, and he could see it even before I spoke. "What's the big idea?" I asked. "Why aren't you coming along?"

The little man returned my gaze with unmoved composure. "For a very obvious reason; it might be a trap. Then Varek'd have both of us. As it is, you'll have to take your chances. And if anything does go wrong, I'll still be able to carry on, to follow through. After all, that's why you hired me. And I aim to finish the job."

He was silent for a moment. "Think it over," he said. "You don't have to go, you know. And I don't mind telling you I'd hesitate before taking such a risk."

I nodded. "Somebody's got to do it," I said. "So if you'll call a cab for me . . ."

Ahmed smiled and held out his hand. "Good boy," he said. He turned and led the way downstairs. He phoned for a cab in the hall.

"I don't know where you're going or what you'll get into," he mused. "And of course, under the circumstances, you can't have the cops tagging along. You'll just have to use your head. Try and keep in touch with me, tip me off what's going on and what to do."

"Why don't you follow me in another cab?" I suggested. "Then, no matter where Cono takes me, you'll at least have the address."

"Good idea." Ahmed stepped to the phone and put in another call. Then he nudged me. "And here's a little idea of my own," he said.

He held out his hand next to my pocket and dumped something cold and hard. I reached for it and came up with a .38 fully loaded.

"Just in case," he told me. "I'll feel better if you have something along for company."

I grinned my gratitude as we walked out of the door of 43 East Brent and waited for the cabs to arrive. Mine rolled up first, but his turned the corner a moment later.

"Let's go," he said. "Be careful now."

"Same to you," I answered. Then, "Wrigley Building," I told the driver. And we were off.

It was a nice, warm, moonless night. I leaned back in the cab as we jolted downtown and tried to relax. I'll give you three guesses how well I succeeded.

We kept stopping at corners, corners with cops on them. I hid my face and thanked my lucky stars there was no moon.

When we hit Chicago Avenue and a red light, I took a long chance. I leaned out of the cab, yelled at a newsboy, and bought a paper. Just idle curiosity. I wanted to see if they had my picture in today. With some of the latest gossip. Such as the offering of a reward, dead or alive.

I riffled through the pages rapidly, but no success greeted my efforts. Maybe they didn't care. Maybe they were used to killing bartenders in Chicago.

Killing –

The little squib caught my eye. With the Louisville dateline. James T. Armstrong Shows . . . Louis Preusser, 43 . . . Confessed murderer of . . . Psychiatrists declared under influence of hypnosis and drugs . . .

It was the follow-up on the story of Louie's confession. He'd walked in, glassy-eyed, and confessed. I wondered what the whole deal was. The Great Ahmed would know. Maybe I'd better ask him before I went on.

I glanced behind to see if his cab was trailing mine. Nothing was in sight. Maybe his driver had taken Clark Street instead. He'd catch up to me. Nobody seemed to have any trouble at all catching up to me whenever they wanted to.

Take Vera LaValle, for instance. She'd found me at the Great Ahmed's after I'd been there for less than an hour. That was one question I needed an answer for. How did she – and Varek – know I was there?

I'd remember to ask Ahmed that.

But – *would he tell me?*

Maybe you're a scientist, a great scientist. Maybe you're a sorcerer too, a wizard. You can raise the dead, and you stay alive yourself. But it's still quite a trick to pick one person out of four million and send a killer right to his door. Unless somebody tips you off.

The tip off. That was it.

Ahmed goes out. Ahmed sells out. Of course! He went to the hotel, just as he said he would, with the eight grand in his pocket. Maybe he saw Cono there, maybe he saw somebody else. Maybe he even saw Varek himself. And he made a deal. He told Varek where I was. Varek sent Vera to kill me.

When enough time had passed, Ahmed came back to see if the job was accomplished. It must have surprised him to find me alive.

So he came up with the story about meeting Cono. Why? It hadn't, come to think of it, sounded too good at the time. This business about winning Cono over with hypnosis. And Cono leading me to Varek.

But seeing me alive, he'd told me the story for a purpose. Ahmed was a great guy for purposes, all right. He must even have given me the gun for a purpose.

I tried to figure it out as we roared down Michigan. I could see the gleaming lighted spire that chewing gum built, right ahead. I'd be there in a minute now.

What had Varek said? Something about not bothering to kill me because the law would do it.

And here I came riding up to the Wrigley building, with a gun in my pocket. An armed murderer.

I knew what to look for now. It wouldn't be Ahmed's cab; he wouldn't show up at all, I was sure. I was looking for a black prowl car.

I wouldn't see Cono standing in the lobby with a white carnation in his buttonhole, ready to guide me on a conducted tour of Varek's snug harbor. I was more likely to see a couple of downtown boys with their hands in their topcoat pockets. The reception committee from the downtown station.

We started to edge towards the curb, and I added up my score. Exactly 100 per cent right. There was the squad car, there were the boys. They stood patiently, just waiting for somebody to show up. If I knew Ahmed, I felt sure he'd furnish them with a very good description.

We nosed in, slowing down. "Here we are — " the driver began.

"No, we're not," I cut in. "Back to 43 East Brent. And fast. I have another appointment."

We kept going, over the bridge. Nobody looked up. Nobody followed. I kept my hand on the butt of the .38 all the way back. I didn't want to lose it, you see.

It was the Great Ahmed's, and I intended to make sure that I gave it to him.

The house was dark, but then it was always dark. I had the cab park around the corner because I didn't mind walking. In fact, I preferred it. Preferred it so much I went around to the back of the house – the long way around, mind you. Didn't bother me a bit. Nor did it bother me to climb in through a rear bedroom window on the first floor.

I was quiet. Very quiet. Sort of a slow, seething quiet. Little thoughts kept bubbling up in me about what I'd do to Ahmed when I got my hands on him.

So he wasn't the type for a carney grifter, eh? Well, he'd taken me in soon enough. And sold me out even sooner.

I landed on the bedroom floor and padded out, down the hall. No cleaning-woman was around and I knew now that there never had been. Ahmed had locked me in to keep me on ice for Vera LaValle or whoever Varek might send.

Ahmed and Varek – a good team. Maybe Ahmed was the guy Varek needed for a front man!

Of course, he wouldn't look quite so presentable after I got through with him . . .

I tiptoed down the hall, peeked into the library. It was dark. The whole house was dark. I stopped, listened. After a long moment, I became convinced of the truth. I was alone. Ahmed had gone out in his cab but he hadn't returned.

I reached a stairway going up – that led to the bedroom and the other rooms on the second floor. But behind it was another set of stairs, going down. I decided to have myself a look. Curiosity killed a cat of course – but *this* cat carried a .38.

The basement was big and dusty. Old fashioned furnace, the usual stationary washtubs, a coal-bin, a fruit-cellar. I pushed open the door and stared at the usual assortment of dusty, empty jars in the light thrown by a naked bulb dangling from the center of the small room.

Nothing in the cellar to interest me. My hunch was cold.

I was cold!

Standing in the deserted fruit-cellar a little past midnight of a warm May evening, I was cold. Cold as ice! I felt the cold air all around me. But where was it coming from?

A draft blew against my trouser cuffs. I looked down.

There was a round metal lid set in the floor of the fruit-cellar. I stooped, touched it. The iron was icy. I groped for the ring, lifted the lid. I gazed down into darkness.

Then I walked away, making a circuit of the cellar until I found what I needed and expected to find – the inevitable handy flashlight.

I returned to the fruit-cellar and pointed the beam down. It focussed on the iron rungs of a ladder. I took the flashlight in one hand, the gun in the other, and left enough fingers free on both for me to cling to the rungs as I descended.

I lowered myself into icy cold – the coldness of a vast black refrigerator. I went down, down, rung after rung. Finally my feet hit slimy, damp stone. I joggled the flashlight until it bisected a wall with its beams. Eventually I located a light switch.

I flicked it. The light went on, and I saw everything.

I was standing in the center of Varek's laboratory.

Varek – Ahmed. Ahmed – Varek.

It all added up now.

More lights went on.

They went on in the little room with the big filing cabinets. I pried open a lot of drawers that night; the drawers containing the certificates, the visas, the affidavits, the fake credentials, the diplomas, the letters of identity (hadn't Varek convinced the warden he was Cono's cousin?) and all of the mingled memorabilia of hundreds of years of impersonations, imposture, and disguise. Floods, tons of paper. The dust fairly flew.

And more light was shed. I found the long closet with the wardrobe; the Ahmed wardrobe, the sportsman's garments, the shabby workman's garb complete even to the battered tin initialled lunchbox and the union button. The accoutrements of Varek the wealthy man of the world were there, too – and a box containing diamonds and other gems that reminded me of poor Vera LaValle.

Then there was another room, with more files. Letters and newspaper clippings. Ads from the *Personal* columns of ten thousand papers, in a score of languages. *Help Wanted* notices. Lonely Hearts messages. And letters, letters, letters – messages from the millions who later turned up missing. Those who answered Varek's appeal for a wife, a husband, an employee. I got a picture of him sitting there, year after year, sending out his letters, interviewing prospects, recruits for his army of the dead. Recruits who would not be missed, searched for.

There were more lights in other rooms. The big surgery, with the gigantic autoclave; completely modern, completely equipped. I wondered how he'd managed to assemble it here, and then I thought of the dead; the tireless dead who steal, who strain, who slave day and night.

Beyond the modern surgery was medieval horror.

The round, dungeon-like room, dominated by the huge table on which rested the alembics and retorts of an ancient alchemist. The beaker filled with the brownish-red, crusting liquid. The herbs and powders on the shelves; the dried roots in bottles, and the great jars filled with monkeys floating in a nauseous liquid, and other things that looked like monkeys but weren't. The stock of chalk and powders. The great circle drawn upon the floor with the zodiacal signs inscribed in blue before it. The jar of combustible powder – that was used to make the circle of fire inside a pentagon, according to the thaumaturgists. And on the iron table rested the iron book; the *Grimoire* of the sorcerer.

* * *

Sorcery and science! Surgery and Satanism! That was the link, the combination! Sorcery had led to science, as Varek said. His original alchemic experiments had brought him to actual research and enabled him to perfect his method of reanimating the dead.

But that didn't explain his own continued life, his boasts of eternal youth. That was sorcery. That was selling your soul, after lighting the fires and invoking the Author of All Evil.

The rooms, the lighted rooms, seemed to present a panorama of Varek's entire existence across the centuries. Everything was here – and I wondered, now, if he'd told me the truth. If in every great city, unsuspected, beneath a house or a factory or a tenement there existed a duplicate of this place. What had he said? A sort of "dead storage", that was it.

"Dead storage." But where were the dead?

There was another room, beyond the alchemic chamber. I entered it, and the coldness engulfed me. This was *it*. The refrigerator storage space. Where you keep the cold meat.

The cold meat . . .

They lay on slabs, but they weren't sheeted. I could see them all, see their staring faces. Men, women, children, young, old, rich, poor – lavish your categories upon them, they were all here. A host, a hundred or more. Silent but not sleeping, inert but not immovable, rigid without *rigor*. They lay there, waiting, like toys that would soon be wound up by cunning hands and set about to walk in make-belief of life.

It was cold in that room, but cold alone did not make me shiver. I walked through rows of dead, staring into the faces that stared into mine. I don't know what I expected to see. None of them looked familiar – except, perhaps one little blonde who reminded me of someone I'd run into before somewhere.

Then, all at once, I knew what I must do. There was fire outside, and it would serve more purposes than that of conjuring up demons. It could also be used to put them to rest.

I walked back into the other room and picked up the powder box which, when its contents were kindled, traced a pattern of flame on the floor. A circle of fire protected you from demons, it was said, after you evoked them.

I ripped the lid off the box and began to sprinkle the powder about. I worked quickly, but not quickly enough.

Because when I looked up, somebody was standing in the room. He only stood there for a moment, and then he started for me.

It was Cono.

*　　*　　*

He didn't say anything and I didn't say anything. He came on and I backed away. The cold arms reached out; I'd felt them before. The tic-like grimace leered, and I knew it would keep on leering no matter how many bullets I might waste.

Because the dead don't die.

Because this was the end.

Because he was coming at me like a demon.

But demons can be warded off with fire.

I pulled out the .38 and pressed the trigger. I didn't aim at Cono; I aimed at the powder on the floor.

A circle of flame shot up, almost in Cono's face. He stopped. Dead or alive, fire destroys flesh. And he couldn't get through. Not as long as the fire flared.

I wondered how long that would be. When would the powder's potency be exhausted? Ten minutes, five, two? Whatever the time, I had that long to live and no longer – unless I could convince him.

I talked then. Told him what I thought he'd understand. About Varek being the Great Ahmed, hiding out with the carney for a while and perfecting plans. About seeing Cono and deciding to make him a recruit, then rigging up the murder charge by hypnotizing Louie, getting him to drug Cono and kill Flo.

I told him something about what Varek was, what he planned, what he'd do to Cono, to me, to the whole world if he wasn't stopped and stopped soon. I told him about the sorcery and the science and the bodies that walked everywhere in every city.

The fire began to flicker, to fade, to die down. I talked louder, faster.

And it didn't do any good.

It was like talking to a stone wall.

It was like talking to a dead man.

With a sickening feeling, I realized I'd been in this spot once before. I'd tried then, tried to tell Cono I was his friend, tried to reach his heart, his soul. But dead men have no hearts. Varek was his heart. And I knew of nothing that could touch his soul. Nothing he cared for, nothing he loved. Except Flo!

Then I remembered, remembered the next room and the blonde on the slab. The little blonde with the familiar face – Flo!

"Cono," I said. "Listen to me. You've got to listen. She's in there, too. You didn't know that, did you? He didn't tell you. But he's greedy, he wants them all. He not only took your body, he took Flo's too. She's in the next room. Cono. He cut off her head, put in his damned wires and plates, and now she'll walk for him forever!"

He was blind. Blind and deaf. The flames died, he moved towards me, he caught me up in his arms. I waited for the squeezing strength of his fingers to wrench my life away. But he merely held me, held me and lumbered across the ashes into the next room.

"Show me where," he said, and the tic rippled horribly across his face.

I pointed. Pointed at the face I remembered from a photograph he'd shown me.

Cono saw her. He released me, and his hands went to his head. He kept staring at her, staring and staring, even after Varek came into the room.

That's how it happened. One second we were alone and the next moment he was there – little grey shadow, silent and suave.

No emotion, no surprise, no tension.

Just his soft, quiet voice saying, "Kill him, Cono."

He might have been asking the big man for a match.

But as I stared at Varek – stared at the quiet little middle-aged man with the paper-thin lips – I saw many things.

I saw a vulgar charlatan in a carnival who was in turn a gypsy in Spain who was in turn a Polish count who was in turn a Haitian planter who was a London barrister who was a Polynesian trader who was a Tulsa wildcatter who was a physician in Cairo who was a trapper with Jim Bridger who was a diplomat of Austria who was – it went on and on that way, a hundred incarnations and a hundred lives and all of them were evil.

He faced us with all of that evil, the evil of a hundred and a thousand men, concentrated but quietly so, and he said to Cono again in the voice that could not be denied because it was the voice of mastery, the voice of life over death – "Kill him, Cono."

Cono set me down and I felt his arms close about my body, his hands grasp my throat. He was a robot, an automaton, he could not refuse; he was a zombie, vampire, all the evil legends, all the fear of the dead that return, the dead that never die.

Cono bent me back. And Varek, with a look in his eyes that was a grey ecstasy, came closer and waited for Cono to finish.

That's what Cono wanted, too.

For when Varek came close, Cono moved. One instant he held me – the next, I was free and those huge arms had reached out to engulf Varek.

The little grey man rose, shrieking, in the air. Cono squeezed – there was a sound like somebody stepping on a thin board – and the body of Varek writhed and twisted on the floor like a snake with a broken back.

Cono helped me with the powder, then. There were chemicals, too; enough to start a good-sized blaze.

"Come on," I said. "Time to get out of here."

"I'm staying," he said. "I belong here."

I had no answer to that one. I turned away.

"You got to go now," Cono told me. "Leave me the gun to start the fire. I give you five minutes to get out."

The thing on the floor was mewing. Neither of us looked at it.

"One thing," Cono said. "I want you should know it so you'll maybe feel better. About that bartender. You didn't knock him off. You hit him with a bottle, but that didn't kill him. Varek killed him, later, when they dragged him in back to see how bad he was hurt. But he was going to pin the rap on you. I found out at the funeral home."

"Thanks," I said.

"Now go away," said Cono.

And I went. I walked through the rooms and didn't look back. I climbed the ladder back to the basement. When I reached the top I heard the muffled sound of a shot from below me, far away.

Long before the flames spread, I was out of the house and on my way to the Loop.

Next morning I read about the place burning to the ground, and that was the end.

But this is a story that never ends.

I keep thinking of those "dead storage" places in other cities. I keep wondering if Varek had turned everybody off that night – or if others walked in other places. The way he and Cono and Vera had all told me. "If you only knew how many . . ."

That's what frightens me.

That's why, wherever I go now, I'm afraid of women wearing high collars and chokers. Men in turtleneck sweaters or even a clergyman's collar. I think of the red scar under the scarf. And I wonder.

I wonder when someone or something will float through my window again. I wonder what walks abroad at night and waits to drag me down.

I wonder how I, or you, or anyone can tell, as we go about our daily rounds, which are the living and which are the dead. For all we know, they may be all around us. Because:

The dead don't die!

Kim Newman

Patricia's Profession

I always expect Kim Newman to come up with something different, so here's an offbeat science fiction *zombie story from the author of such novels as* The Night Mayor, Bad Dreams, Jago, Anno Dracula *and* The Quoram. *Newman is also co-editor (with Paul J. McAuley) of the anthology* In Dreams, *and has written various non-fiction volumes, the short story collection* The Original Dr Shade and Other Stories, *and what he describes as several "young adult sex and violence novels" under the name Jack Yeovil.*

The idea for "Patricia's Profession" occurred to him one evening while listening to a woman wonder what to call her kissogram company. He wrote a draft version in two hours and then took seven months to think of a title.

"Originally, it was called something that gave too much away," he explains, "then I nearly called it Working Girl, *which later turned up on a hit movie. For a five-page story it has been oddly attractive to film-makers. Director Laurens C. Postma (perhaps best known for the David Cronenberg documentary* Long Live the New Flesh) *actually turned it into a four-minute movie, titled* Happy Birthday, *for a Channel 4 TV series. Though it was never aired, for "political reasons", a brief glimpse of Patricia can be seen in the Film on 4,* Midnight Breaks.

"This happened because Laurens was in a coffee bar in Soho's Old Compton Street, having learned that he couldn't get the rights to the Philip K. Dick story he wanted to do, even though he had the crew and shooting time ready. He happened

to overhear me and Lisa Tuttle talking and, gathering that we were writers, asked
if we had any ideas, whereupon Lisa suggested this then recently-published story.
Subsequently, after running into someone at the Troy Club in London, I sold film
rights to a British producer and haven't heard from him since.

"A sequel, 'Pamela's Pursuit', appeared in Arrows of Eros, *and I reserve*
the right to do 'Pandora's Predilection' in the future."

WHEN THE CALL came, Patricia was going FF through the latest
snuffs. She was a subscriber to the *120 Days in the City of Sodom*
part-work, but, since Disney had run out of de Sade and been
forced to fall back on their own limited psychopathology, the series
had deteriorated. After a few minutes of real-time PLAY, she had
twigged that the 104th day was just one of the fifties with a sexual
role reversal, Mouldy chiz. Colin broke into the vid-out.

"Patti," he said. "Goto PRINT."

Colin had blanked before she could work out whether he was live
or a message simulacrum. The printer retched a laconic strip.

JAY DEARBORN, DEARBORN ESTATE, TWENTY ONE
O'CLOCK HIT, 2-NITE.

The mark was on screen. The Firm had a four-second snip from
regular call, Dearbone was a sleek, expensive, youngish man. He
had on a collarless, fine-stripe shirt. Silently, he repeated a phrase.
Something about cheekbones, Patricia's lip-reading was off.

She switched to greenscreen and speed-read Dearborn's write-up.
Executive with Skintone, Inc., the second-largest fleshwear house.
Married, Euro-citizen. Not cleared for parenthood. No adult criminal
record. Alive. Solvent.

Colin came back, real-time. "Our client is Philip Wragge. More
middle management at Skintone. He likes us. He's used us before."

"Why does he want Dearborn hit?"

"Getting curious, Patti?" Colin smiled. "That's not in your usual
profile. I think it's the mark's birthday."

Patricia's birthday was in August. When she was little, her parents
had always taken her to their cottage in Portugal for the school
holidays. She had escaped until she was twelve. That year, Dad's
job became obsolete, and the cottage had to be marketed. At tea-time
on her birthday, the other children had come round to Patricia's house
and killed her.

Colin faded, and the scheduled program popped up on the slab.
Patricia rarely watched real-time. A Luton house-husband guessed
that Seattle, Washington was the capital of the US. The Torture Master grinned, and his glamorous assistant thrust his/her bolt-cutters

into the hot coals. "Wrong," sang the man in the dayglo tux, "I'm afraid it's Portland, Oregon. That puts you in a tricky spot, Goodman. You have only three questions and two toes left, so take your time with this next one. Who, at the time of this recording, is the Vice-President of the Confederate States of America . . .'

Patricia off-switched. It was twenty to nineteen. Chord would be here soon. She put her uniform on. Black spiderweb tights, black lace singlet, black armlength talon glove, black butterfly tie. She shrugged into the white shoulder holster, and pulled a comfortable heavy white Burberry over her shoulders. She perched a black beret on her Veronica Lake bob. She white-fixed her face, and blacked her lips and eyelids. Neat.

She palmed her desk-top, and the safety cabinet unsealed. She took out the roscoe and disassembled it. There had been some question about the foresight, but it seemed okay to her eye. She replaced the lubricant cartridge and snapped the machine back together. She shoved a new clip of slugs into the grip, and holstered the roscoe.

It could manage up to one hundred and seventy rounds per second. At that rate, the slugs left the eleven-inch barrel as molten chips. At Sixth Form College, the Firm's instructor had given a demonstration. She had turned a cow carcass into a piece of abstract expressionism, a study in red and intestine. Patricia didn't like to use her roscoe as a hosepipe, and usually kept the rate adjusted to a comfortable twenty-five r.p.s.

Outside, the car called to her. Patricia sealed her flat, negotiated the checkpoint in the foyer, and stepped onto the steaming pavement. If she stood still for a few minutes, the yellow ground mist would eat holes in her unprotected shins. Harry Chord, at ease in his reinforced chauffeur's puttees and Lone Ranger mask, held the Old's door open for her. She slid onto the sofa-sized back seat. The Olds purred. Chord took the console.

The sturdy, box-like, black car had only recently been converted. Chord had done the job himself, and was quietly pleased with it. When they stopped at the Gordon's station to tank up, he pointed out the minute scars on the hood and running boards. Otherwise, it was impossible to tell from the exterior that the cash-wasting petrol engine had been replaced with the latest model booze-burner.

Patricia was tense, impatient. As always before a hit. She had been to the lavatory twice since Colin's call, but there was still a tingle in her lower abdomen. Some of the other girls pill-popped, but she needed, and wanted, the cold-rush of unfiltered sensations.

Of course, there had been less popping since Rachel. The girl had taken too many zippers, waltzed into her mark's office singing

'Paper Moon', and shot the man through the brain. By the time the termination officers arrived, she had switched to 'Stardust'. The firm had lost its 100 percent efficiency rating.

Patricia had heard Chord, and several of the other back-up personnel, refer to Rachel's humpty dumpty hit, ". . . all the king's horses, and all the king's men . . ." The flippancy irritated her. Killing people might seem like a fun job, but you had to take it seriously. If nothing else, Rachel had proved that.

The Dearborn Estate was out in the Green Belt. They were well ahead of schedule, so she had Chord program a route that would avoid the disemployment centre. Shit City, the claimants called it. Nissen huts covered in ghastly, mock-cheerful murals. The dope dole. The Ghetto Blaster gangs. There had recently been a rash of documentaries, but, having spent six years in Shit City, Patricia couldn't get off on poverty porn.

Evidently, Dearborn's wife was in on the hit. At the estate entrance, a cobra terminal snaked into the Olds and hovered over Patricia's lap. HELLO! IDENTIFICATION? She palm-printed the slab, and keyed in the Firm's trademark. PURPOSE OF VISIT? She had typed MURDER before noticing that the need for a reply had been countered on the print of Gillian Dearborn. HAVE A PLEASANT VISIT.

The crackling electrodes in the gravel drive went briefly dead as the Olds rolled over them. There were other cars, low and streamlined, ranked in front of the house. Over the roof landing floated a small dirigible, shifting gently on its mooring. The house, Victorian but remodelled in early Carolian, was lit by banks of old-mode disco lamps.

Dearborn was having a birthday party, with live music. Patricia recognised the popular song "Throw Yourself Off a Bridge". The ballad was being performed by a small swing combo; an unfamiliar, somehow inapt, arrangement. A girl sinatra was trying to croon to the up-tempo,

> *When I get too depressed,*
> *Crawling along in a ditch,*
> *I get right up,*
> *Walk on down,*
> *And throw myself off a bridge . . .*

Patricia left Chord with the Olds, and walked unconcerned across the lawn. A few stray guests, in designer rags, noticed her. She hated Depression Chic. The bulk of the party was behind the house between the L of its two wings and the skimming pool. She tried to move easily among the rich.

A man with a plumed mohawk, an epitome of the New Conservatism, reached inside her Burberry. She sliced his forehead with a soporific talon. He fell onto a trestle table, between the swan cutlets and the cocaine blancmange. He would be able to tell the other Young Rotarians he had won second prize in a duel.

> *I could put myself through a mangle,*
> *I could drink the water in Spain,*
> *From a home-made noose I could dangle,*
> *It's the end to all my pain . . .*

Dearborn was an easy mark. He was holding a helium balloon with **BIRTHDAY BOY** on it, he was squiffed, but standing. A plump, dapper man, and an elegant woman with fashionable facial mutilations were propping Dearborn up. Wragge and Gillian? They saw her coming and confirmed their identities by rapidly moving out of her line.

Abandoned, the mark lurched forward into a personal spotlight. No hole-in-the-head innocent bystanders in the way. Terrific.

> *If I feel like cracking up*
> *And locking myself in the fridge,*
> *I get on out*
> *And take a high jump,*
> *To throw myself off a bridge . . .*

Patricia reached with her bare hand for the roscoe. The Burberry slid from her shoulders. There were a few werewolf whistles. She shimmied across the lawn, getting in close to compensate for the possibly dodgy foresight. She did a few elementary gold-digger steps, and adopted the Eastwood position; legs apart, weight evenly distributed, left hand on right wrist, elbows slightly bent to absorb the kickback.

The bandleader, surprised but adaptable, had his instruments segue into "Happy Birthday to You". The sinatra picked it up immediately, and led the less out-of-it guests in the chorus.

The mark was looking around, gasping. ". . . Phil? You . . ." The balloon went up.

She took out his left kneecap. He staggered sideways, tripping into an abandoned urn but not falling. She upped the r.p.s. and sprayed Dearborn's flailing right arm. His hand came off at the wrist. Most of the guests had to laugh. She closed in, and fired a final, free-ranging burst into his torso. She had a glimpse of churning innards. He did an awkward piroutte and, with a satisfying splash, fell into the pool. The purple scum rippled. There were cheers. Patricia took a bow.

By the time she had retrieved her coat, the resurrection men were there. The kildare was passing a vivicorder over the corpse. A nurse Patricia knew ticked off the necessary repairs. Most of the vat-bred organs and ossiplex bones would be in the Firm's ambulance. The front man was assuring Gillian Dearborn that her husband would be on his feet by morning, and preparing the legal and medical waivers for her palm.

"Good job, lassie," Wragge hugged and kissed her. Even for a regular customer, he was overdoing it. "When Jay sees himself on the playback, he'll die all over again."

He stuffed a thousand note down her cleavage. Not a bad gratuity. He also gave her a hundred in Sainsbury's Redeemable for Chord. She was invited to the resurrection party, but cried off.

Tired, she gave Chord authority to get·back to town by the quickest route. As she drove through Shit City, she cleaned the roscoe. She remembered her own deaths, and wondered whether the DHSS still had a budgetary allocation for resurrecting the underemployed.

She hadn't had the kind of luxury treatment Dearborn was getting. There had been problems with her anglepoise vertebrae throughout her middle teens. She had not had the funds for a proper rebuild until she started working for Killergrams.

That first time, the other children had dragged her out of the house and hanged her from a swan-neck lamp-post. Her party dress was torn, and her legs were badly bitten by midges. Dangling in the late afternoon, the last thing that had crossed her mind was that this was supposed to be funny.

Joe R. Lansdale

On the Far Side of the Cadillac Desert with Dead Folks

I've left the most outrageous until last. Joe R. Lansdale is well known for his often bizarre stories, and they don't come much weirder than "On the Far Side of the Cadillac Desert with Dead Folks", which in 1990 won both the Bram Stoker Award and the British Fantasy Award.

Some of the author's best stories have been collected in By Bizarre Hands, Bestsellers Guaranteed *and* Stories By Mamma Lansdale's Youngest Boy, *and his novels include* The Nightrunners, The Drive-In (A B Movie with Blood and Popcorn, Made in Texas) *and the inevitable* The Drive-In 2 (Not Just One of Them Sequels).

More recently, he has written a Batman novel for adults, Captured By the Engines, *and another for children,* Terror on the High Skies, *and Cemetery Dance has published a limited edition of Lansdale's first novel,* Act of Love *(1981), with a new afterword by the author.*

Perhaps this is how the world ends; not with a bang, but with zombie nuns . . .

I

AFTER A MONTH'S chase, Wayne caught up with Calhoun one night at a little honky-tonk called Rosalita's. It wasn't that Calhoun had finally gotten careless, it was just that he wasn't worried. He'd killed four bounty hunters so far, and Wayne knew a fifth didn't concern him.

The last bounty hunter had been the famous Pink Lady McGuire – one mean mama – three hundred pounds of rolling, ugly meat that carried a twelve-gauge Remington pump and a bad attitude. Story was, Calhoun jumped her from behind, cut her throat, and as a joke, fucked her before she bled to death. This not only proved to Wayne that Calhoun was a dangerous sonofabitch, it also proved he had bad taste.

Wayne stepped out of his '57 Chevy reproduction, pushed his hat back on his forehead, opened the trunk, and got the sawed-off double barrel and some shells out of there. He already had a .38 revolver in the holster at his side and a bowie knife in each boot, but when you went into a place like Rosalita's it was best to have plenty of backup.

Wayne put a handful of shotgun shells in his shirt pocket, snapped the flap over them, looked up at the red-and-blue neon sign that flashed ROSALITA'S: COLD BEER AND DEAD DANCING, found his center, as they say in Zen, and went on in.

He held the shotgun against his leg, and as it was dark in there and folks were busy with talk or drinks or dancing, no one noticed him or his artillery right off.

He spotted Calhoun's stocky, black-hatted self immediately. He was inside the dance cage with a dead buck-naked Mexican girl of about twelve. He was holding her tight around the waist with one hand and massaging her rubbery ass with the other like it was a pillow he was trying to shape. The dead girl's handless arms flailed on either side of Calhoun, and her little tits pressed to his thick chest. Her wire-muzzled face knocked repeatedly at his shoulder and drool whipped out of her mouth in thick spermy ropes, stuck to his shirt, faded and left a patch of wetness.

For all Wayne knew, the girl was Calhoun's sister or daughter. It was that kind of place. The kind that had sprung up immediately after that stuff had gotten out of a lab upstate and filled the air with bacterium that brought dead humans back to life, made their basic motor functions work and made them hungry for human flesh; made it so if a man's wife, daughter, sister, or mother went belly up and he wanted to turn a few bucks, he might think: "Damn, that's tough about ole Betty Sue, but she's dead as hoot-owl shit and ain't gonna be needing nothing from here on out, and with them germs working around in her, she's just gonna pull herself out of the ground and cause me a problem. And the ground out back of the house is harder to dig than a calculus problem is to work, so I'll just toss her cold ass in the back of the pickup next to the chain saw and the barbed-wire roll, haul her across the border and sell her to the Meat Boys to sell to the tonks for dancing.

"It's a sad thing to sell one of your own, but shit, them's the breaks. I'll just stay out of the tonks until all the meat rots off her bones and they have to throw her away. That way I won't go in some place for a drink and see her up there shaking her dead tits and end up going sentimental and dewy-eyed in front of one of my buddies or some ole two-dollar gal."

This kind of thinking supplied the dancers. In other parts of the country, the dancers might be men or children, but here it was mostly women. Men were used for hunting and target practice.

The Meat Boys took the bodies, cut off the hands so they couldn't grab, ran screws through their jaws to fasten on wire muzzles so they couldn't bite, sold them to the honky-tonks about the time the germ started stirring.

Tonk owners put them inside wire enclosures up front of their joints, started music, and men paid five dollars to get in there and grab them and make like they were dancing when all the women wanted to do was grab and bite, which, muzzled and handless they could not do.

If a man liked his partner enough, he could pay more money and have her tied to a cot in the bag and he could get on her and do some business. Didn't have to hear no arguments or buy presents to make promises or make them come. Just fuck and hike.

As long as the establishment sprayed the dead for maggots and kept them perfumed and didn't keep them so long hunks of meat came off on a fellow dick, the customers were happy as flies on shit.

Wayne looked to see who might give him trouble, and figured everyone was a potential customer. The six foot two, two-hundred fifty pound bouncer being the most immediate concern.

But, there wasn't anything to do but to get on with things and handle problems when they came up. He went into the cage where Calhoun was dancing, shouldered through the other dancers and went for him.

Calhoun had his back to Wayne, and as the music was loud, Wayne didn't worry about going quietly. But Calhoun sensed him and turned with his hand full of a little .38.

Wayne clubbed Calhoun's arm with the barrel of the shotgun. The little gun flew out of Calhoun's hand and went skidding across the floor and clanked against the metal cage.

Calhoun wasn't outdone. He spun the dead girl in front of him and pulled a big pigsticker out of his boot and held it under the girl's armpit in a threatening manner, which with a knife that big was no feat.

Wayne shot the dead girl's left kneecap out from under her and she went down. Her armpit trapped Calhoun's knife. The other men deserted their partners and went over the wire netting like squirrels.

Before Calhoun could shake the girl loose, Wayne stepped in and hit him over the head with the barrel of the shotgun. Calhoun crumpled and the girl began to crawl about on the floor as if looking for lost contacts.

The bouncer came in behind Wayne, grabbed him under the arms and tried to slip a full nelson on him.

Wayne kicked back on the bouncer's shin and raked his boot down the man's instep and stomped his foot. The bouncer let go. Wayne turned and kicked him in the balls and hit him across the face with the shotgun.

The bouncer went down and didn't even look like he wanted up.

Wayne couldn't help but note he liked the music that was playing. When he turned he had someone to dance with.

Calhoun.

Calhoun charged him, hit Wayne in the belly with his head, knocked him over the bouncer. They tumbled to the floor and the shotgun went out of Wayne's hands and scraped across the floor and hit the crawling girl in the head. She didn't even notice, just kept snaking in circles, dragging her blasted leg behind her like a skin she was trying to shed.

The other women, partnerless, wandered about the cage. The music changed. Wayne didn't like this tune as well. Too slow. He bit Calhoun's earlobe off.

Calhoun screamed and they grappled around on the floor. Calhoun got his arm around Wayne's throat and tried to choke him to death.

Wayne coughed out the earlobe, lifted his leg and took the knife out of his boot. He brought it around and back and hit Calhoun in the temple with the hilt.

Calhoun let go of Wayne and rocked on his knees, then collapsed on top of him.

Wayne got out from under him and got up and kicked him in the head a few times. When he was finished, he put the bowie in its place, got Calhoun's .38 and the shotgun. To hell with the pigsticker.

A dead woman tried to grab him, and he shoved her away with a thrust of his palm. He got Calhoun by the collar, started pulling him toward the gate.

Faces were pressed against the wire, watching. It had been quite a show. A friendly cowboy type opened the gate for Wayne and the crowd parted as he pulled Calhoun by. One man felt helpful and chased after them and said, "Here's his hat, Mister," and dropped it on Calhoun's face and it stayed there.

Outside, a professional drunk was standing between two cars taking a leak on the ground. As Wayne pulled Calhoun past, the drunk said, "Your buddy don't look so good."

"Look worse than that when I get him to Law Town," Wayne said.

Wayne stopped by the '57, emptied Calhoun's pistol and tossed it as far as he could, then took a few minutes to kick Calhoun in the ribs and ass. Calhoun grunted and farted, but didn't come to.

When Wayne's leg got tired, he put Calhoun in the passenger seat and handcuffed him to the door.

He went over to Calhoun's '62 Impala replica with the plastic bull horns mounted on the hood – which was how he had located him in the first place, by his well known car – and kicked the glass out of the window on the driver's side and used the shotgun to shoot the bull horns off. He took out his pistol and shot all the tires flat, pissed on the driver's door, and kicked a dent in it.

By then he was too tired to shit in the back seat, so he took some deep breaths and went back to the '57 and climbed in behind the wheel.

Reaching across Calhoun, he opened the glove box and got out one of his thin, black cigars and put it in his mouth. He pushed the lighter in, and while he waited for it to heat up, he took the shotgun out of his lap and reloaded it.

A couple of men poked their heads outside of the tonk's door, and Wayne stuck the shotgun out the window and fired above their heads. They disappeared inside so fast they might have been an optical illusion.

Wayne put the lighter to his cigar, picked up the wanted poster he had on the seat, and set fire to it. He thought about putting it in Calhoun's lap as a joke, but didn't. He tossed the flaming poster out the window.

He drove over close to the tonk and used the remaining shotgun load to shoot at the neon ROSALITA'S sign. Glass tinkled onto the tonk's roof and onto the gravel drive.

Now if he only had a dog to kick.

He drove away from there, bound for the Cadillac Desert, and finally Law Town on the other side.

II

The Cadillacs stretched for miles, providing the only shade in the desert. They were buried nose down at a slant, almost to the windshields, and Wayne could see skeletons of some of the drivers in the cars, either lodged behind the steering wheels or lying on the dashboards against the glass. The roof and hood guns had long since been removed and all the windows on the cars were rolled up, except for those that had been knocked out and vandalized by travelers, or dead folks looking for goodies.

The thought of being in one of those cars with the windows rolled up in all this heat made Wayne feel even more uncomfortable than he already was. Hot as it was, he was certain even the skeletons were sweating.

He finished pissing on the tire of the Chevy, saw the piss had almost dried. He shook the drops off, watched them fall and evaporate against the burning sand. Zipping up, he thought about Calhoun, and how when he'd pulled over earlier to let the sonofabitch take a leak, he'd seen there was a little metal ring through the head of his dick and a Texas emblem dangling from that. He could understand the Texas emblem, being from there himself, but he couldn't for the life of him imagine why a fella would do that to his general. Any idiot who would put a ring through the head of his pecker deserved to die, innocent or not.

Wayne took off his cowboy hat and rubbed the back of his neck and ran his hand over the top of his head and back again. The sweat on his fingers was thick as lube oil, and the thinning part of his hairline was tender; the heat was cooking the hell out of his scalp, even through the brown felt of his hat.

Before he put his hat on, the sweat on his fingers was dry. He broke open the shotgun, put the shells in his pocket, opened the Chevy's back door and tossed the shotgun on the floorboard.

He got in the front behind the wheel and the seat was hot as a griddle on his back and ass. The sun shone through the slightly tinted windows like a polished chrome hubcap; it forced him to squint.

Glancing over at Calhoun, he studied him. The fucker was asleep with his head thrown back and his black wilted hat hung precariously on his head – it looked jaunty almost. Sweat oozed down Calhoun's red face, flowed over his eyelids and around his neck, running in rivulets down the white seat covers, drying quickly. He had his left hand between his legs, clutching his balls, and his right was on the arm rest, which was the only place it could be since he was handcuffed to the door.

Wayne thought he ought to blow the bastard's brains out and tell God he died. The shithead certainly needing shooting, but Wayne didn't want to lose a thousand dollars off his reward. He needed every penny if he was going to get that wrecking yard he wanted. The yard was the dream that went before him like a carrot before a donkey, and he didn't want any more delays. If he never made another trip across this goddamn desert, that would suit him fine.

Pop would let him buy the place with the money he had now, and he could pay the rest out later. But that wasn't what he wanted to do. The bounty business had finally gone sour, and he wanted to do different. It wasn't any goddamn fun anymore. Just met the dick cheese of the earth. And when you ran the sonofabitches to ground and put the cuffs on them, you had to watch your ass 'til you got them turned in. Had to sleep with one eye open and a hand on your gun. It wasn't any way to live.

And he wanted a chance to do right by Pop. Pop had been like a father to him. When he was a kid and his mama was screwing the Mexicans across the border for the rent money, Pop would let him hang out in the yard and climb on the rusted cars and watch him fix the better ones, tune those babies so fine they purred like dick-whipped women.

When he was older, Pop would haul him to Galveston for the whores and out to the beach to take potshots at all the ugly, fucked-up critters swimming around in the Gulf. Sometimes he'd take him to Oklahoma for the Dead Roundup. It sure seemed to do the old fart good to whack those dead fuckers with a tire iron, smash their diseased brains so they'd lay down for good. And it was a challenge. 'Cause if one of those dead buddies bit you, you could put your head between your legs and kiss your rosy ass goodbye.

Wayne pulled out of his thoughts of Pop and the wrecking yard and turned on the stereo system. One of his favorite country-and-western tunes whispered at him. It was Billy Conteegas singing, and Wayne hummed along with the music as he drove into the welcome, if mostly ineffectual, shadows provided by the Cadillacs.

> *My baby left me,*
> *She left me for a cow,*
> *But I don't give a flying fuck,*
> *She's gone radioactive now,*
> *Yeah, my baby left me,*
> *Left me for a six-tittied cow.*

Just when Conteegas was getting to the good part, doing the trilling sound in his throat he was famous for, Calhoun opened his eyes and spoke up.

"Ain't it bad enough I got to put up with the fucking heat and your fucking humming without having to listen to that shit? Ain't you got no Hank Williams stuff, or maybe some of that nigger music they used to make? You know, where the coons harmonize and one of 'em sings like his nuts are cut off."

"You just don't know good music when you hear it, Calhoun."

Calhoun moved his free hand to his hatband, found one of his few remaining cigarettes and a match there. He struck the match on his knee, lit the smoke and coughed a few rounds. Wayne couldn't imagine how Calhoun could smoke in all this heat.

"Well, I may not know good music when I hear it, capon, but I damn sure know bad music when I hear it. And that's some bad music."

"You ain't got any kind of culture, Calhoun. You been too busy raping kids."

"Reckon a man has to have a hobby," Calhoun said, blowing smoke at Wayne. "Young pussy is mine. Besides, she wasn't in diapers. Couldn't find one that young. She was thirteen. You know what they say. If they're old enough to bleed, they're old enough to breed."

"How old they have to be for you to kill them?"

"She got loud."

"Change channels, Calhoun."

"Just passing the time of day, capon. Better watch yourself, bounty hunter, when you least expect it, I'll bash your head."

"You're gonna run your mouth one time too many, Calhoun, and when you do, you're gonna finish this ride in the trunk with ants crawling on you. You ain't so priceless I won't blow you away."

"You lucked out at the tonk, boy. But there's always tomorrow, and every day can't be like at Rosalita's."

Wayne smiled. "Trouble is, Calhoun, you're running out of tomorrows."

III

As they drove between the Cadillacs, the sky fading like a bad bulb, Wayne looked at the cars and tried to imagine what the Chevy-Cadillac Wars had been like, and why they had been fought in this miserable desert. He had heard it was a hell of a fight, and close, but the outcome had been Chevys and now they were the only cars Detroit made. And as far as he was concerned, that was the only thing about Detroit that was worth a damn. Cars.

He felt that way about all cities. He'd just as soon lie down and let a diseased dog shit in his face than drive through one, let alone live in one.

Law Town being an exception. He'd go there. Not to live, but to give Calhoun to the authorities and pick up his reward. People in Law Town were always glad to see a criminal brought in. The public executions were popular and varied and supplied a steady income.

Last time he'd been to Law Town he'd bought a front-row ticket to one of the executions and watched a chronic shoplifter, a red-headed rat of a man, get pulled apart by being chained between two souped-up tractors. The execution itself was pretty brief, but there had been plenty of buildup with clowns and balloons and a big-tittied stripper who could swing her tits in either direction to boom-boom music.

Wayne had been put off by the whole thing. It wasn't organized enough and the drinks and food were expensive and the front-row seats were too close to the tractors. He had gotten to see that the red-head's insides were brighter than his hair, but some of the insides got sprinkled on his new shirt, and cold water or not, the spots hadn't come out. He had suggested to one of the management that they put up a big plastic shield so the front row wouldn't get splattered, but he doubted anything had come of it.

They drove until it was solid dark. Wayne stopped and fed Calhoun a stick of jerky and some water from his canteen. Then he handcuffed him to the front bumper of the Chevy.

"See any snakes, Gila monsters, scorpions, stuff like that," Wayne said, "yell out. Maybe I can get around here in time."

"I'd let the fuckers run up my asshole before I'd call you," Calhoun said.

Leaving Calhoun with his head resting on the bumper, Wayne climbed in the back seat of the Chevy and slept with one ear cocked and one eye open.

Before dawn Wayne got Calhoun loaded in the '57 and they started out. After a few minutes of sluicing through the early morning greyness, a wind started up. One of those weird desert winds that come out of nowhere. It carried grit through the air at the speed of bullets, hit the '57 with a sound like rabid cats scratching.

The sand tires crunched on through, and Wayne turned on the windshield blower, the sand wipers, and the headbeams, and kept on keeping on.

When it was time for the sun to come up, they couldn't see it. Too much sand. It was blowing harder than ever and the blowers and wipers couldn't handle it. It was piling up. Wayne couldn't even make out the Cadillacs anymore.

He was about to stop when a shadowy, whalelike shape crossed in front of him and he slammed on the brakes, giving the sand tires a workout. But it wasn't enough.

The '57 spun around and rammed the shape on Calhoun's side. Wayne heard Calhoun yell, then felt himself thrown against the door and his head smacked metal and the outside darkness was nothing compared to the darkness into which he descended.

IV

Wayne rose out of it as quickly as he had gone down. Blood was trickling into his eyes from a sligh forehead wound. He used his sleeve to wipe it away

His first clear sight was of a face at the window on his side; a sallow, moon-terrain face with bulging eyes and an expression like an idiot contemplating Sanskrit. On the man's head was a strange, black hat with big round ears, and in the center of the hat like a silver tumor, was the head of a large screw. Sand lashed at the face, imbedded in it, struck the unblinking eyes and made the round-eared hat flap. The man paid no attention. Though still dazed, Wayne knew why. The man was one of the dead folks.

Wayne looked in Calhoun's direction. Calhoun's door had been mashed in and the bending metal had pinched the handcuff attached to the arm rest in two. The blow had knocked Calhoun to the center of the seat. He was holding his hand in front of him, looking at the dangling cuff and chain as if it were a silver bracelet and a line of pearls.

Leaning over the hood, cleaning the sand away from the windshield with his hands, was another of the dead folks. He too was wearing one of the round-eared hats. He pressed a wrecked face to the clean spot and looked in at Calhoun. A string of snotgreen saliva ran out of his mouth and onto the glass.

More sand was wiped away by others. Soon all the car's glass showed the pallid and rotting faces of the dead folks. They stared at Wayne and Calhoun as if they were two rare fish in an aquarium.

Wayne cocked back the hammer of the .38.

"What about me," Calhoun said. "What am I supposed to use?"

"Your charm," Wayne said, and at that moment, as if by signal, the dead folk faded away from the glass, leaving one man standing on the hood holding a baseball bat. He hit the glass and it went into a thousand little stars. The bat came again and the heavens fell and the stars rained down and the sand storm screamed in on Wayne and Calhoun.

The dead folks reappeared in full force. The one with the bat started through the hole in the windshield, heedless of the jags of glass that ripped his ragged clothes and tore his flesh like damp cardboard.

Wayne shot the batter through the head, and the man, finished, fell through, pinning Wayne's arm with his body.

Before Wayne could pull his gun free, a woman's hand reached through the hole and got hold of Wayne's collar. Other dead folks took to the glass and hammered it out with their feet and fist. Hands were all over Wayne; they felt dry and cool like leather seat covers. They pulled him over the steering wheel and dash and outside. The sand worked at his flesh like a cheese grater. He could hear Calhoun yelling, "Eat me, motherfuckers, eat me and choke."

They tossed Wayne on the hood of the '57. Faces leaned over him. Yellow teeth and toothless gums were very near. A road kill odor washed through his nostrils. He thought: now the feeding frenzy begins. His only consolation was that there were so many dead folks there wouldn't be enough of him left to come back from the dead. They'd probably have his brain for dessert.

But no. They picked him up and carried him off. Next thing he knew was a clearer view of the whaleshape the '57 had hit, and its color. It was a yellow school bus.

The door to the bus hissed open. The dead folks dumped Wayne inside on his belly and tossed his hat after him. They stepped back and the door closed, just missing Wayne's foot.

Wayne looked up and saw a man in the driver's seat smiling at him. It wasn't a dead man. Just fat and ugly. He was probably five feet tall and bald except for a fringe of hair around his shiny bald head the color of a shit ring in a toilet bowl. He had a nose so long and dark and malignant looking it appeared as if it might fall off his face at any moment, like an overripe banana. He was wearing what Wayne first thought was a bathrobe, but proved to be a robe like that of a monk. It was old and tattered and moth-eaten and Wayne could see pale flesh through the holes. An odor wafted from the fat man that was somewhere between the smell of stale sweat, cheesy balls and an unwiped asshole.

"Good to see you," the fat man said.

"Charmed," Wayne said.

From the back of the bus came a strange, unidentifiable sound. Wayne poked his head around the seats for a look.

In the middle of the aisle, about halfway back, was a nun. Or sort of a nun. Her back was to him and she wore a black-and-white nun's habit. The part that covered her head was traditional, but from there down was quite a departure from the standard attire. The outfit was cut to the middle of her thighs and she wore black fishnet stockings and thick high heels. She was slim with good legs and a high little ass that even under the circumstances, Wayne couldn't help but appreciate. She was moving one hand above her head as if sewing the air.

Sitting on the seats on either side of the aisle were dead folks. They all wore the round-eared hats, and they were responsible for the sound.

They were trying to sing.

He had never known dead folks to make any noise outside of grunts and groans, but here they were singing. A toneless sort of singing to be sure, some of the words garbled and some of the dead folks just opening and closing their mouths soundlessly, but, by golly, he recognized the tune. It was "Jesus Loves Me."

Wayne looked back at the fat man, let his hand ease down to the bowie in his right boot. The fat man produced a little .32 automatic from inside his robe and pointed it at Wayne.

"It's small caliber," the fat man said, "but I'm a real fine shot, and it makes a nice little hole."

Wayne quit reaching in his boot.

"Oh, that's all right," said the fat man. "Take the knife out and put it on the floor in front of you and slide it to me. And while you're at it, I think I see the hilt of one in your other boot."

Wayne looked back. The way he had been thrown inside the bus had caused his pants legs to hike up over his boots, and the hilts of both his bowies were revealed. They might as well have had blinking lights on them.

It was shaping up to be a shitty day.

He slid the bowies to the fat man, who scooped them up nimbly and dumped them on the other side of his seat.

The bus door opened and Calhoun was tossed in on top of Wayne. Calhoun's hat followed after.

Wayne shrugged Calhoun off, recovered his hat, and put it on. Calhoun found his hat and did the same. They were still on their knees.

"Would you gentleman mind moving to the center of the bus?"

Wayne led the way. Calhoun took note of the nun now, said, "Man, look at that ass."

The fat man called back to them. "Right there will do fine."

Wayne slid into the seat the fat man was indicating with a wave of the .32, and Calhoun slid in beside him. The dead folks entered now, filled the seats up front, leaving only a few stray seats in the middle empty.

Calhoun said, "What are those fuckers back there making that noise for?"

"They're singing," Wayne said. "Ain't you got no churchin'?"

"Say they are?" Calhoun turned to the nun and the dead folks and yelled, "Y'all know any Hank Williams?"

The nun did not turn and the dead folks did not quit their toneless singing.

"Guess not," Calhoun said. "Seems like all the good music's been forgotten."

The noise in the back of the bus ceased and the nun came over to look at Wayne and Calhoun. She was nice in front too. The outfit was cut from throat to crotch, laced with a ribbon, and it showed a lot of tit and some tight, thin, black panties that couldn't quite hold in her escaping pubic hair, which grew as thick and wild as kudzu. When Wayne managed to work his eyes up from that and look at her face, he saw she was dark-complected with eyes the color of coffee and lips made to chew on.

Calhoun never made it to the face. He didn't care about faces. He sniffed, said into her crotch, "Nice snatch."

The nun's left hand came around and smacked Calhoun on the side of the head.

He grabbed her wrist, said, "Nice arm, too."

The nun did a magic act with her right hand; it went behind her back and hiked up her outfit and came back with a double-barreled derringer. She pressed it against Calhoun's head.

Wayne bent forward, hoping she wouldn't shoot. At that range the bullet might go through Calhoun's head and hit him too.

"Can't miss," the nun said.

Calhoun smiled. "No you can't," he said, and let go of her arm.

She sat down across from them, smiled, and crossed her legs high. Wayne felt his Levis snake swell and crawl against the inside of his thigh.

"Honey," Calhoun said, "you're almost worth taking a bullet for."

The nun didn't quit smiling. The bus cranked up. The sand blowers and wipers went to work, and the windshield turned blue, and a white dot moved on it between a series of smaller white dots.

Radar. Wayne had seen that sort of thing on desert vehicles. If he lived through this and got his car back, maybe he'd rig up something like that. And maybe not, he was sick of the desert.

Whatever, at the moment, future plans seemed a little out of place.

Then something else occurred to him. Radar. That meant these bastards had known they were coming and had pulled out in front of them on purpose.

He leaned over the seat and checked where he figured the '57 hit the bus. He didn't see a single dent. Armored, most likely. Most school buses were these days, and that's what this had been. It probably had bullet-proof-glass and puncture-proof sand tires too. School buses had gone that way on account of the race riots and the sending of mutated calves to school just like they were humans. And because of the Codgers – old farts who believed kids ought to be fair game to adults for sexual purposes, or for knocking around when they wanted to let off some tension.

"How about unlocking this cuff?" Calhoun said. "It ain't for shit now anyway."

Wayne looked at the nun. "I'm going for the cuff key in my pants. Don't shoot."

Wayne fished it out, unlocked the cuff, and Calhoun let it slide to the floor. Wayne saw the nun was curious and he said, "I'm a bounty hunter. Help me get this man to Law Town and I could see you earn a little something for your troubles."

The woman shook her head.

"That's the spirit," Calhoun said. "I like a nun that minds her own business . . . You a real nun?"

She nodded.

"Always talk so much?"

Another nod.

Wayne said, "I've never seen a nun like you. Not dressed like that and with a gun."

"We are a small and special order," she said.

"You some kind of Sunday school teacher for these dead folks?"

"Sort of."

"But with them dead, ain't it kind of pointless? They ain't got no souls now, do they?"

"No, but their work adds to the glory of God."

"Their work?" Wayne looked at the dead folks sitting stiffly in their seats. He noted that one of them was about to lose a rotten ear. He sniffed. "They may be adding to the glory of God, but they don't do much for the air."

The nun reached into a pocket on her habit and took out two round objects. She tossed one to Calhoun, and one to Wayne. "Menthol lozenges. They help you stand the smell."

Wayne unwrapped the lozenge and sucked on it. It did help overpower the smell, but the menthol wasn't all that great either. It reminded him of being sick.

"What order are you?" Wayne asked.

"Jesus Loved Mary," the nun said.

"His mama?"

"Mary Magdalene. We think he fucked her. They were lovers. There's evidence in the scriptures. She was a harlot and we have modeled ourselves on her. She gave up that life and became a harlot for Jesus."

"Hate to break it to you, sister," Calhoun said, "but that do-gooder Jesus is as dead as a post. If you're waiting for him to slap the meat to you, that sweet thing of yours is going to dry up and blow away."

"Thanks for the news," the nun said. "But we don't fuck him in person. We fuck him in spirit. We let the spirit enter into men so they may take us in the fashion Jesus took Mary."

"No shit?"

"No shit."

"You know, I think I feel the old boy moving around inside me now. Why don't you shuck them drawers, honey, throw back in that seat there and let ole Calhoun give you a big load of Jesus."

Calhoun shifted in the nun's direction.

She pointed the derringer at him, said, "Stay where you are. If it were so, if you were full of Jesus, I would let you have me in a moment. But you're full of the Devil, not Jesus."

"Shit, sister, give ole Devil a break. He's a fun kind of guy. Let's you and me mount up . . . Well, be like that. But if you change your mind, I can get religion at a moment's notice. I dearly love to fuck. I've fucked everything I could get my hands on but a parakeet, and I'd have fucked that little bitch if I could have found the hole."

"I've never known any dead folks to be trained," Wayne said, trying to get the nun talking in a direction that might help, a direction that would let him know what was going on and what sort of trouble he had fallen into.

"As I said, we are a very special order. Brother Lazarus," she waved a hand at the bus driver, and without looking he lifted a hand in acknowledgement, "is the founder. I don't think he'll mind if I tell his story, explain about us, what we do and why. It's important that we spread the word to the heathens."

"Don't call me no fucking heathen," Calhoun said. "This is heathen, riding around in a fucking bus with a bunch of stinking dead folks with funny hats on. Hell, they can't even carry a tune."

The nun ignored him. "Brother Lazarus was once known by another name, but that name no longer matters. He was a research scientist, and he was one of those who worked in the laboratory where the germs escaped into the air and made it so the dead could not truly die as long as they had an undamaged brain in their heads.

"Brother Lazarus was carrying a dish of the experiment, the germs, and as a joke, one of the lab assistants pretended to trip him, and he, not knowing it was a joke, dodged the assistant's leg and dropped the dish. In a moment, the air conditioning system had blown the germs throughout the research center. Someone opened a door, and the germs were loose on the world.

"Brother Lazarus was consumed by guilt. Not only because he dropped the dish, but because he helped create it in the first place. He quit his job at the laboratory, took to wandering the country. He came out here with nothing more than basic food, water and books. Among these books was the Bible, and the lost books of the Bible: the Apocrypha and the many cast-out chapters of the New Testament. As he studied, it occurred to him that these cast-out books actually belonged. He was able to interpret their higher meaning, and an angel came to him in a dream and told him of another book, and Brother Lazarus took up his pen and recorded the angel's words, direct from God, and in this book, all the mysteries were explained."

"Like screwing Jesus," Calhoun said.

"Like screwing Jesus, and not being afraid of words that mean sex. Not being afraid of seeing Jesus as both God and man. Seeing that sex, if meant for Christ and the opening of the mind, can be a thrilling and religious experience, not just the rutting of two savage animals.

"Brother Lazarus roamed the desert, the mountains, thinking of the things the Lord had revealed to him, and lo and behold, the Lord revealed yet another thing to him. Brother Lazarus found a great amusement park."

"Didn't know Jesus went in for rides and such." Calhoun said.

"It was long deserted. It had once been part of a place called Disneyland. Brother Lazarus knew of it. There had been several of these Disneylands built about the country, and this one had been in the midst of the Chevy-Cadillac Wars, and had been destroyed and sand had covered most of it."

The nun held out her arms. "And in this rubble, he saw a new beginning."

"Cool off, baby," Calhoun said, "before you have a stroke."

"He gathered to him men and women of a like mind and taught the gospel to them. The Old Testament. The New Testament. The Lost Books. And his own Book of Lazarus, for he had begun to call himself Lazarus. A symbolic name signifying a new beginning, a rising from the dead and coming to life and seeing things as they really are."

The nun moved her hands rapidly, expressively as she talked. Sweat beaded on her forehead and upper lip.

"So he returned to his skills as a scientist, but applied them to a higher purpose – God's purpose. And as Brother Lazarus, he realized the use of the dead. They could be taught to work and build a great monument to the glory of God. And this monument, this coed institution of monks and nuns would be called Jesus Land."

At the word "Jesus," the nun gave her voice an extra trill, and the dead folks, cued, said together, "Eees num be prased."

"How the hell did you train them dead folks?" Calhoun said. "Dog treats?"

"Science put to the use of our Lord Jesus Christ, that's how. Brother Lazarus made a special device he could insert directly into the brains of dead folks, through the tops of their heads, and the device controls certain cravings. Makes them passive and responsive – at least to simple commands. With the regulator, as Brother Lazarus calls the device, we have been able to do much positive work with the dead."

"Where do you find these dead folks?" Wayne asked.

"We buy them from the Meat Boys. We save them from amoral purposes."

"They ought to be shot through the head and put in the goddamn ground," Wayne said.

"If our use of the regulator and the dead folks was merely to better ourselves, I would agree. But it is not. We do the Lord's work."

"Do the monks fuck the sisters?" Calhoun asked.

"When possessed by the Spirit of Christ. Yes."

"And I bet they get possessed a lot. Not a bad setup. Dead folks to do the work on the amusement park – "

"It isn't an amusement park now."

"– and plenty of free pussy. Sounds cozy. I like it. Old shithead up there's smarter than he looks."

"There is nothing selfish about our motives or those of Brother Lazarus. In fact, as penance for loosing the germ on the world in the first place, Brother Lazarus injected a virus into his nose. It is rotting slowly."

"Thought that was quite a snorkel he had on him," Wayne said.

"I take it back," Calhoun said. "He *is* as dumb as he looks."

"Why do the dead folks wear those silly hats?" Wayne asked.

"Brother Lazarus found a storeroom of them at the site of the old amusement park. They are mouse ears. They represent some cartoon animal that was popular once and part of Disneyland. Mickey Mouse, he was called. This way we know which dead folks are ours, and which ones are not controlled by our regulators. From time to time, stray dead folks wander into our area. Murder victims. Children abandoned in the desert. People crossing the desert who died of heat or illness. We've had some of the sisters and brothers attacked. The hats are a precaution."

"And what's the deal with us?" Wayne asked.

The nun smiled sweetly. "You, my children, are to add to the glory of God."

"Children?" Calhoun said. "You call an alligator a lizard, bitch?"

The nun slid back in the seat and rested the derringer in her lap. She pulled her legs into a cocked position, causing her panties to crease in the valley of her vagina; it looked like a nice place to visit, that valley.

Wayne turned from the beauty of it and put his head back and closed his eyes, pulled his hat down over them. There was nothing he could do at the moment, and since the nun was watching Calhoun for him, he'd sleep, store up and figure what to do next. If anything.

He drifted off to sleep wondering what the nun meant by, "You, my children, are to add to the glory of God."

He had a feeling that when he found out, he wasn't going to like it.

V

He awoke off and on and saw that the sunlight filtering through the storm had given everything a greenish color. Calhoun seeing he was awake, said, "Ain't that a pretty color? I had a shirt that color once and liked it lots, but I got in a fight with this Mexican whore with a wooden leg over some money and she tore it. I punched that little bean bandit good."

"Thanks for sharing that," Wayne said, and went back to sleep.

Each time he awoke it was brighter, and finally he awoke to the sun going down and the storm having died out. But he didn't stay awake. He forced himself to close his eyes and store up more energy. To help him nod off he listened to the hum of the motor and thought about the wrecking yard and Pop and all the fun they could have, just drinking beer and playing cars and fucking the border women, and maybe some of those mutated cows they had over there for sale.

Nah. Nix the cows, or any of those genetically altered critters. A man had to draw the line somewhere, and he drew it at fucking critters, even if they had been bred so that they had human traits. You had to have some standards.

'Course, those standards had a way of eroding. He remembered when he said he'd only fuck the pretty ones. His last whore had been downright scary looking. If he didn't watch himself he'd be as bad as Calhoun, trying to find the hole in a parakeet.

He awoke to Calhoun's elbow in his ribs and the nun was standing beside their seat with the derringer. Wayne knew she hadn't slept, but she looked bright-eyed and bushy-tailed. She nodded toward their window, said, "Jesus Land."

She had put that special touch in her voice again, and the dead folks responded with, "Eees num be prased."

It was good and dark now, a crisp night with a big moon the color of hammered brass. The bus sailed across the white sand like a mystical schooner with a full wind in its sails. It went up an impossible hill toward what looked like an aurora borealis, then dove into an atomic rainbow of colors that filled the bus with fairy lights.

When Wayne's eyes became accustomed to the lights, and the bus took a right turn along a precarious curve, he glanced down into the valley. An aerial view couldn't have been any better than the view from his window.

Down there was a universe of polished metal and twisted neon. In the center of the valley was a great statue of Jesus crucified that must have been twenty-five stories high. Most of the body was made of bright metals and multicolored neon, and much of the light was coming from that. There was a crown of barbed wire wound several times around a chromium plate of a forehead and some rust-colored strands of neon hair. The savior's eyes were huge, green strobes that swung left and right with the precision of an oscillating fan. There was an ear to ear smile on the savior's face and the teeth were slats of sparkling metal with wide cavity-black gaps between them. The statue was equipped with a massive dick of polished, interwoven cables and coils of neon, the dick was thicker and more solid looking than the arthritic steel-tube legs on either side of it; the head of it was made of an enormous spotlight that pulsed the color of irritation.

The bus went around and around the valley, descending like a dead roach going down a slow drain, and finally the road rolled out straight and took them into Jesus Land.

They passed through the legs of Jesus, under the throbbing head of his cock, toward what looked like a small castle of polished gold bricks with an upright drawbridge interlayed with jewels.

The castle was only one of several tall structures that appeared to be made of rare metals and precious stones: gold, silver, emeralds, rubies and sapphires. But the closer they got to the buildings, the less fine they looked and the more they looked like what they were: stucco, cardboard, phosphorescent paint, colored spotlights, and bands of neon.

Off to the left Wayne could see a long, open shed full of vehicles, most of them old school buses. And there were unlighted hovels made of tin and tar paper; homes for the dead, perhaps. Behind the shacks and the bus barn rose skeletal shapes that stretched tall and bleak against the sky and the candy-gem lights; shapes that looked like the bony remains of beached whales.

On the right, Wayne glimpsed a building with an open front that served as a stage. In front of the stage were chairs filled with monks and nuns. On the stage, six monks – one behind a drum set, one with a saxophone, the others with guitars – were blasting out a loud, rocking rhythm that made the bus shake. A nun with the front of her habit thrown open, her headpiece discarded, sang into a microphone with a voice like a suffering angel. The voice screeched out of the amplifiers and came in through the windows of the bus, crushing the sound of the engine. The nun crowed "Jesus" so long and hard it sounded like a plea from hell. Then she leapt up and came down doing the splits, the impact driving her back to her feet as if her ass had been loaded with springs.

"Bet that bitch can pick up a quarter with that thing," Calhoun said.

Brother Lazarus touched a button, the pseudo-jeweled drawbridge lowered over a narrow moat and he drove them inside.

It wasn't as well lighted in there. The walls were bleak and grey. Brother Lazarus stopped the bus and got off, and another monk came on board. He was tall and thin and had crooked buck teeth that dented his bottom lip. He also had a twelve-gauge pump shotgun.

"This is Brother Fred," the nun said. "He'll be your tour guide."

Brother Fred forced Wayne and Calhoun off the bus, away from the dead folks in their mouse-ear hats and the nun in her tight black panties jabbed them along a dark corridor up a swirl of stairs and down a longer corridor with open doors on either side and rooms filled with dark and light and spoiled meat and guts on hooks and skulls and bones lying about like discarded walnut shells and broken sticks; rooms full of dead folks (truly dead) stacked neat as firewood, and rooms full of stone shelves stuffed with beakers of fiery-red and sewer-green and sky-blue and piss-yellow liquids, as well as glass coils through which other colored fluids fled as if chased, smoked as if nervous, and ran into big flasks as if relieved; rooms with platforms and tables and boxes and stools and chairs covered with instruments or dead folks or dead-folk pieces or the asses of monks and nuns as they sat and held charts or tubes or body parts and frowned at them with concentration, lips pursed as if about to explode with some earth-shattering pronouncement; and finally they came to a little room with a tall, glassless window that looked out upon the bright, shiny mess that was Jesus Land.

The room was simple. Table, two chairs, two beds – one on either side of the room. The walls were stone and unadorned. To the right was a little bathroom without a door.

Wayne walked to the window and looked out at Jesus Land pulsing and thumping like a desperate heart. He listened to the music a moment, leaned over and stuck his head outside.

They were high up and there was nothing but a straight drop. If you jumped, you'd wind up with the heels of your boots under your tonsils.

Wayne let out a whistle in appreciation of the drop. Brother Fred thought it was a compliment for Jesus Land. He said, "It's a miracle, isn't it?"

"Miracle?" Calhoun said. "This goony light show? This ain't no miracle. This is for shit. Get that nun on the bus back there to bend over and shit a perfectly round turd through a hoop at twenty paces, and I'll call that a miracle, Mr Fucked-up Teeth. But this Jesus Land crap is the dumbest, fucking idea since dog sweaters.

"And look at this place. You could use some knick-knacks or something in here. A picture of some old naked gal doing a donkey, couple of pigs fucking. Anything. And a door on the shitter would be nice. I hate to be straining out a big one and know someone can look in on me. It ain't decent. A man ought to have his fucking grunts in private. This place reminds me of a motel I stayed at in Waco one night, and I made the goddamn manager give me my money back. The roaches in that shit hole were big enough to use the shower."

Brother Fred listened to all this without blinking an eye, as if seeing Calhoun talk was as amazing as seeing a frog sing. He said. "Sleep tight, don't let the bed bugs bite. Tomorrow you start to work."

"I don't want no fucking job," Calhoun said.

"Goodnight, children," Brother Fred said, and with that he closed the door and they heard it lock, loud and final as the clicking of the drop board on a gallows.

VI

At dawn, Wayne got up and took a leak, went to the window to look out. The stage where the monks had played and the nun had jumped was empty. The skeletal shapes he had seen last night were tracks and frames from rides long abandoned. He had a sudden vision of Jesus and his disciples riding a roller coaster, their long hair and robes flapping in the wind.

The large crucified Jesus looked unimpressive without its lights and night's mystery, like a whore in harsh sun-light with makeup gone and wig askew.

"Got any ideas how we're gonna get out of here?" Calhoun asked.

Wayne looked at Calhoun. He was sitting on the bed, pulling on his boots.

Wayne shook his head.

"I could use a smoke. You know, I think we ought to work together. Then we can try to kill each other."

Unconsciously, Calhoun touched his ear where Wayne had bitten off the lobe.

"Wouldn't trust you as far as I could kick you," Wayne said.

"I hear that. But I give my word. And my word's something you can count on. I won't twist it."

Wayne studied Calhoun, thought: Well, there wasn't anything to lose. He'd just watch his ass.

"All right," Wayne said. "Give me your word you'll work with me on getting us out of this mess, and when we're good and free, and you say your word has gone far enough, we can settle up."

"Deal," Calhoun said, and offered his hand.

Wayne looked at it.

"This seals it," Calhoun said.

Wayne took Calhoun's hand and they shook.

VII

Moments later the door unlocked and a smiling monk with hair the color and texture of mold fuzz came in with Brother Fred, who still had his pump shotgun. There were two dead folks with them. A man and a woman. They wore torn clothes and the mouse-ear hats. Neither looked long dead or smelled particularly bad. Actually, the monks smelled worse.

Using the barrel of the shotgun, Brother Fred poked them down the hall to a room with metal tables and medical instruments.

Brother Lazarus was on the far side of one of the tables. He was smiling. His nose looked especially cancerous this morning. A white pustule the size of a thumb tip had taken up residence on the left side of his snout, and it looked like a pearl onion in a turd.

Nearby stood a nun. She was short with good, if skinny, legs, and she wore the same outfit as the nun on the bus. It looked more girlish on her, perhaps because she was thin and small-breasted. She had a nice face and eyes that were all pupil. Wisps of blond hair crawled out around the edges of her head gear. She looked pale and weak, as if wearied to the bone. There was a birthmark on her right cheek that looked like a distant view of a small bird in flight.

"Good morning," Brother Lazarus said. "I hope you gentlemen slept well."

"What's this about work?" Wayne said.

"Work?" Brother Lazarus said.

"I described it to them that way," Brother Fred said. "Perhaps an impulsive description."

"I'll say," Brother Lazarus said. "No work here, gentleman. You have my word on that. We do all the work. Lie on these tables and we'll take a sampling of your blood."

"Why?" Wayne said.

"Science," Brother Lazarus said. "I intend to find a cure for this germ that makes the dead come back to life, and to do that, I need living human beings to study. Sounds kind of mad scientist, doesn't it? But I assure you, you've nothing to lose but a few drops of blood. Well, maybe more than a few drops, but nothing serious."

"Use your own goddamn blood," Calhoun said.

"We do. But we're always looking for fresh specimens. Little here, little there. And if you don't do it, we'll kill you."

Calhoun spun and hit Brother Fred on the nose. It was a solid punch and Brother Fred hit the floor on his butt, but he hung onto the shotgun and pointed it up at Calhoun. "Go on," he said, his nose streaming blood. "Try that again."

Wayne flexed to help, but hesitated. He could kick Brother Fred in the head from where he was, but that might not keep him from shooting Calhoun, and there would go the extra reward money. And besides, he'd given his word to the bastard that they'd try to help each other survive until they got out of this.

The other monk clasped his hands and swung them into the side of Calhoun's head, knocking him down. Brother Fred got up, and while Calhoun was trying to rise, he hit him with the stock of the shotgun in the back of the head, hit him so hard it drove Calhoun's forehead into the floor. Calhoun rolled over on his side and lay there, his eyes fluttering like moth wings.

"Brother Fred, you must learn to turn the other cheek," Brother Lazarus said. "Now put this sack of shit on the table."

Brother Fred checked Wayne to see if he looked like trouble. Wayne put his hands in his pockets and smiled.

Brother Fred called the two dead folks over and had them put Calhoun on the table. Brother Lazarus strapped him down.

The nun brought a tray of needles, syringes, cotton and bottles over, put it down on the table next to Calhoun's head. Brother Lazarus rolled up Calhoun's sleeve and fixed up a needle and stuck it in Calhoun's arm, drew it full of blood. He stuck the needle through the rubber top of one of the bottles and shot the blood into that.

He looked at Wayne and said, "I hope you'll be less trouble."

"Do I get some orange juice and a little cracker afterwards?" Wayne said.

"You get to walk out without a knot on your head," Brother Lazarus said.

"Guess that'll have to do."

Wayne got on the table next to Calhoun and Brother Lazarus strapped him down. The nun brought the tray over and Brother Lazarus did to him what he had done to Calhoun. The nun stood over Wayne and looked down at his face. Wayne tried to read something in her features but couldn't find a clue.

When Brother Lazarus was finished he took hold of Wayne's chin and shook it. "My, but you two boys look healthy. But you can never be sure. We'll have to run the blood through some tests. Meantime, Sister Worth will run a few additional tests on you, and," he nodded at the unconscious Calhoun. "I'll see to your friend here."

"He's no friend of mine," Wayne said.

They took Wayne off the table, and Sister Worth and Brother Fred and his shotgun, directed him down the hall into another room.

The room was lined with shelves that were lined with instruments and bottles. The lighting was poor, most of it coming through a slatted window, though there was an anemic yellow bulb overhead. Dust motes swam in the air.

In the center of the room on its rim was a great, spoked wheel. It had two straps well spaced at the top, and two more at the bottom. Beneath the bottom straps were blocks of wood. The wheel was attached in back to an upright metal bar that had switches and buttons all over it.

Brother Fred made Wayne strip and get on the wheel with his back to the hub and his feet on the blocks. Sister Worth strapped his ankles down tight, then he was made to put his hands up, and she strapped his wrists to the upper part of the wheel.

"I hope this hurts a lot," Brother Fred said.

"Wipe the blood off your face," Wayne said. "It makes you look silly."

Brother Fred made a gesture with his middle finger that wasn't religious and left the room.

VIII

Sister Worth touched a switch and the wheel began to spin, slowly at first, and the bad light came through the windows and poked through the rungs and the dust swam before his eyes and the wheel and its spokes threw twisting shadows on the wall.

As he went around, Wayne closed his eyes. It kept him from feeling so dizzy, especially on the down swings.

On a turn up, he opened his eyes and caught sight of Sister Worth standing in front of the wheel staring at him. He said, "Why?" and closed his eyes as the wheel dipped.

"Because Brother Lazarus says so," came the answer after such a long time Wayne had almost forgotten the question. Actually, he hadn't expected a response. He was surprised that such a thing had come out of his mouth, and he felt a little diminished for having asked.

He opened his eyes on another swing up, and she was moving behind the wheel, out of his line of vision. He heard a snick like a switch being flipped and lightning jumped through him and he screamed in spite of himself. A little fork of electricity licked out of his mouth like a reptile tongue tasting air.

Faster spun the wheel and the jolts came more often and he screamed less loud, and finally not at all. He was too numb. He was adrift in space wearing only his cowboy hat and boots, moving away from earth very fast. Floating all around him were wrecked cars. He looked and saw that one of them was his '57, and behind the steering wheel was Pop. Sitting beside the old man was a Mexican whore. Two more were in the back seat. They looked a little drunk.

One of the whores in back pulled up her dress and cocked it high up so he could see her pussy. It looked like a taco that needed a shave.

He smiled and tried to go for it, but the '57 was moving away, swinging wide and turning its tail to him. He could see a face at the back window. Pop's face. He had crawled back there and was waving slowly and sadly. A whore pulled Pop from view.

The wrecked cars moved away too, as if caught in the vacuum of the '57's retreat. Wayne swam with his arms, kicked with his legs, trying to pursue the '57 and the wrecks. But he dangled where he was, like a moth pinned to a board. The cars moved out of sight and left him there with his arms and legs stretched out, spinning amidst an infinity of cold, uncaring stars.

". . . how the tests are run . . . marks everything about you . . . charts it . . . EKG, brain waves, liver . . . everything . . . it hurts because Brother Lazarus wants it to . . . thinks I don't know these things . . . that I'm slow . . . I'm slow, not stupid . . . smart really . . . used to be a scientist . . . before the accident . . . Brother Lazarus is not holy . . . he's mad . . . made the wheel because of the Holy Inquisition . . . knows a lot about the Inquisition . . . thinks we need it again . . . for the likes of men like you . . . the unholy, he says . . . But he just likes to hurt . . . I know."

Wayne opened his eyes. The wheel had stopped. Sister Worth was talking in her monotone, explaining the wheel. He remembered asking her "Why" about three thousand years ago.

Sister Worth was staring at him again. She went away and he expected the wheel to start up, but when she returned, she had a long, narrow mirror under her arm. She put it against the wall across from him. She got on the wheel with him, her little feet on the wooden platforms beside his. She hiked up the bottom of her habit and pulled down her black panties. She put her face close to his, as if searching for something.

"He plans to take your body . . . piece by piece . . . blood, cells, brain, your cock . . . all of it . . . He wants to live forever."

She had her panties in her hand, and she tossed them. Wayne watched them fly up and flutter to the floor like a dying bat.

She took hold of his dick and pulled on it. Her palm was cold and he didn't feel his best, but he began to get hard. She put him between her legs and rubbed his dick between her thighs. They were as cold as her hands, and dry.

"I know him now . . . know what he's doing . . . the dead germ virus . . . he was trying to make something that would make him live forever . . . it made the dead come back . . . didn't keep the living alive, free of old age . . ."

His dick was throbbing now, in spite of the coolness of her body.

"He cuts up dead folks to learn . . . experiments on them . . . but the secret of eternal life is with the living . . . that's why he wants you . . . you're an outsider . . . those who live here he can test . . . but he must keep them alive to do his bidding . . . not let them know how he really is . . . needs your insides and the other man's . . . he wants

to be a God . . . flies high above us in a little plane and looks down
. . . Likes to think he is the creator, I bet . . ."

"Plane?"

"Ultralight."

She pushed his cock inside her, and it was cold and dry in there,
like liver left overnight on a drainboard. Still, he found himself ready.
At this point, he would have gouged a hole in a turnip.

She kissed him on the ear and alongside the neck; cold little kisses,
dry as toast.

". . . thinks I don't know . . . But I know he doesn't love Jesus . . .
He loves himself, and power . . . He's sad about his nose . . ."

"I bet."

"Did it in a moment of religious fervor . . . before he lost the belief
. . . Now he wants to be what he was . . . A scientist. He wants to grow
a new nose . . . knows how . . . saw him grow a finger in a dish once
. . . grew it from the skin off a knuckle of one of the brothers . . . He
can do all kinds of things."

She was moving her hips now. He could see over her shoulder into
the mirror against the wall. Could see her white ass rolling, the black
habit hiked up above it, threatening to drop like a curtain. He began
to thrust back, slowly, firmly.

She looked over her shoulder into the mirror, watching herself fuck
him. There was a look more of study than rapture on her face.

"Want to feel alive," she said. "Feel a good, hard dick . . . Been
too long."

"I'm doing the best I can," Wayne said. "This ain't the most
romantic of spots."

"Push so I can feel it."

"Nice," Wayne said. He gave it everything he had. He was
beginning to lose his erection. He felt as if he were auditioning for
a job and not making the best of impressions. He felt like a knothole
would be dissatisfied with him.

She got off of him and climbed down.

"Don't blame you," he said.

She went behind the wheel and touched some things on the upright.
She mounted him again, hooked her ankles behind his. The wheel
began to turn. Short electrical shocks leaped through him. They
weren't as powerful as before. They were invigorating. When he
kissed her it was like touching his tongue to a battery. It felt as if
electricity was racing through his veins and flying out the head of his
dick; he felt as if he might fill her with lightning instead of come.

The wheel creaked to a stop; it must have had a timer on it.
They were upside down and Wayne could see their reflection

in the mirror; they looked like two lizards fucking on a window pane.

He couldn't tell if she had finished or not, so he went ahead and got it over with. Without the electricity he was losing his desire. It hadn't been an A-one piece of ass, but hell, as Pop always said, "Worst pussy I ever had was good."

"They'll be coming back," she said. "Soon . . . Don't want them to find us like this . . . Other tests to do yet."

"Why did you do this?"

"I want out of the order . . . Want out of this desert . . . I want to live . . . And I want you to help me."

"I'm game, but the blood is rushing to my head and I'm getting dizzy. Maybe you ought to get off me."

After an eon she said, "I have a plan."

She untwined from him and went behind the wheel and hit a switch that turned Wayne upright. She touched another switch and he began to spin slowly, and while he spun and while lightning played inside him, she told him her plan.

IX

"I think ole Brother Fred wants to fuck me," Calhoun said. "He keeps trying to get his finger up my asshole."

They were back in their room. Brother Fred had brought them back, making them carry their clothes, and now they were alone again, dressing.

"We're getting out of here," Wayne said. "The nun, Sister Worth, she's going to help."

"What's her angle?"

"She hates this place and wants my dick. Mostly, she hates this place."

"What's the plan?"

Wayne told him first what Brother Lazarus had planned. On the morrow he would have them brought to the room with the steel tables, and they would go on the tables, and if the tests had turned out good, they would be pronounced fit as fiddles and Brother Lazarus would strip the skin from their bodies, slowly, because according to Sister Worth he liked to do it that way, and he would drain their blood and percolate it into his formulas like coffee, cut their brains out and put them in vats and store their veins and organs in freezers.

All of this would be done in the name of God and Jesus Christ (Eees num be prased) under the guise of finding a cure for the dead folks germ. But it would all instead be for Brother Lazarus who wanted to have a new nose, fly his ultralight above Jesus Land and live forever.

Sister Worth's plan was this:

She would be in the dissecting room. She would have guns hidden. She would make the first move, a distraction, then it was up to them.

"This time," Wayne said, "one of us has to get on top of that shotgun."

"You had your finger up your ass in there today, or we'd have had them."

"We're going to have surprise on our side this time. Real surprise. They won't be expecting Sister Worth. We can get up there on the roof and take off in that ultralight. When it runs out of gas we can walk, maybe get back to the '57 and hope it runs."

"We'll settle our score then. Whoever wins keeps the car and the split tail. As for tomorrow, I've got a little ace."

Calhoun pulled on his boots. He twisted the heel of one of them. It swung out and a little knife dropped into his hand. "It's sharp," Calhoun said. "I cut a Chinaman from gut to gill with it. It was easy as sliding a stick through fresh shit."

"Been nice if you'd had that ready today."

"I wanted to scout things out first. And to tell the truth, I thought one pop to Brother Fred's mouth and he'd be out of the picture."

"You hit him in the nose."

"Yeah, goddamn it, but I was aiming for his mouth."

X

Dawn and the room with the metal tables looked the same. No one had brought in a vase of flowers to brighten the place.

Brother Lazarus's nose had changed however; there were two pearl onions nestled in it now.

Sister Worth, looking only a little more animated than yesterday, stood nearby. She was holding the tray with the instruments. This time the tray was full of scalpels. The light caught their edges and made them wink.

Brother Fred was standing behind Calhoun, and Brother Mold Fuzz was behind Wayne. They must have felt pretty confident today. They had dispensed with the dead folks.

Wayne looked at Sister Worth and thought maybe things were

not good. Maybe she had lied to him in her slow talking way. Only wanted a little dick and wanted to keep it quiet. To do that, she might have promised anything. She might not care what Brother Lazarus did to them.

If it looked like a double cross, Wayne was going to go for it. If he had to jump right into the mouth of Brother Fred's shotgun. That was a better way to go than having the hide peeled from your body. The idea of Brother Lazarus and his ugly nose leaning over him did not appeal at all.

"It's so nice to see you," Brother Lazarus said. "I hope we'll have none of the unpleasantness of yesterday. Now, on the tables."

Wayne looked at Sister Worth. Her expression showed nothing. The only thing about her that looked alive was the bent wings of the bird birthmark on her cheek.

All right, Wayne thought, I'll go as far as the table, then I'm going to do something. Even if it's wrong.

He took a step forward, and Sister Worth flipped the contents of the tray into Brother Lazarus's face. A scalpel went into his nose and hung there. The tray and the rest of its contents hit the floor.

Before Brother Lazarus could yelp, Calhoun dropped and wheeled. He was under Brother Fred's shotgun and he used his forearm to drive the barrel upwards. The gun went off and peppered the ceiling. Plaster sprinkled down.

Calhoun had concealed the little knife in the palm of his hand and he brought it up and into Brother Fred's groin. The blade went through the robe and buried to the hilt.

The instant Calhoun made his move, Wayne brought his forearm back and around into Brother Mold Fuzz's throat, then turned and caught his head and jerked that down and kneed him a couple of times. He floored him by driving an elbow into the back of his neck.

Calhoun had the shotgun now, and Brother Fred was on the floor trying to pull the knife out of his balls. Calhoun blew Brother Fred's head off, then did the same for Brother Mold Fuzz.

Brother Lazarus, the scalpel hanging from his nose, tried to run for it, but he stepped on the tray and that sent him flying. He landed on his stomach. Calhoun took two deep steps and kicked him in the throat. Brother Lazarus made a sound like he was gargling and tried to get up.

Wayne helped him. He grabbed Brother Lazarus by the back of his robe and pulled him up, slammed him back against a table. The scalpel still dangled from the monk's nose. Wayne grabbed it and jerked, taking away a chunk of nose as he did. Brother Lazarus screamed.

Calhoun put the shotgun in Brother Lazarus's mouth and that made him stop screaming. Calhoun pumped the shotgun. He said, "Eat it," and pulled the trigger. Brother Lazarus's brains went out the back of his head riding on a chunk of skull. The brains and skull hit the table and sailed onto the floor like a plate of scrambled eggs pushed the length of a cafe counter.

Sister Worth had not moved. Wayne figured she had used all of her concentration to hit Brother Lazarus with the tray.

"You said you'd have guns," Wayne said to her.

She turned her back to him and lifted her habit. In a belt above her panties were two .38 revolvers. Wayne pulled them out and held one in each hand. "Two-Gun Wayne," he said.

"What about the ultralight?" Calhoun said. "We've made enough noise for a prison riot. We need to move."

Sister Worth turned to the door at the back of the room, and before she could say anything or lead, Wayne and Calhoun snapped to it and grabbed her and pushed her toward it.

There were stairs on the other side of the door and they took them two at a time. They went through a trap door and onto the roof and there, tied down with bungie straps to metal hoops, was the ultralight. It was blue-and-white canvas and metal rods, and strapped to either side of it was a twelve gauge pump and a bag of food and a canteen of water.

They unsnapped the roof straps and got in the two seater and used the straps to fasten Sister Worth between them. It wasn't comfortable, but it was a ride.

They sat there. After a moment, Calhoun said, "Well?"

"Shit," Wayne said. "I can't fly this thing."

They looked at Sister Worth. She was staring at the controls.

"Say something, damn it," Wayne said.

"That's the switch," she said. "That stick . . . forward is up, back brings the nose down . . . side to side . . ."

"Got it."

"Well, shoot this bastard over the side," Calhoun said.

Wayne cranked it, gave it the throttle. The machine rolled forward, wobbled.

"Too much weight," Wayne said.

"Throw the cunt over the side," Calhoun said.

"It's all or nothing," Wayne said. The ultralight continued to swing its tail left and right, but leveled off as they went over the edge.

They sailed for a hundred yards, made a mean curve Wayne couldn't fight, and fell straight away into the statue of Jesus, striking it in the head, right in the midst of the barbed wire crown. Spot lights shattered, metal groaned, the wire tangled in the nylon wings of the craft and held it. The head of Jesus nodded forward, popped off and shot out on the electric cables inside like a jack-in-the-box. The cables pulled tight a hundred feet from the ground and worked the head and the craft like a yoyo. Then the barbed wire crown unraveled and dropped the craft the rest of the way. It hit the ground with a crunch and a rip and a cloud of dust.

The head of Jesus bobbed above the shattered ultralight like a bird preparing to peck a worm.

XI

Wayne crawled out of the wreckage and tried his legs. They worked.

Calhoun was on his feet cussing, unstrapping the shotguns and supplies.

Sister Worth lay in the midst of the wreck, the nylon and aluminum supports folded around her like butterfly wings.

Wayne started pulling the mess off of her. He saw that her leg was broken. A bone punched out of her thigh like a sharpened stick. There was no blood.

"Here comes the church social," Calhoun said.

The word was out about Brother Lazarus and the others. A horde of monks, nuns and dead folks, were rushing over the drawbridge. Some of the nuns and monks had guns. All of the dead folks had clubs. The clergy was yelling.

Wayne nodded toward the bus barn, "Let's get a bus."

Wayne picked up Sister Worth, cradled her in his arms, and made a run for it. Calhoun, carrying the guns and the supplies, passed them. He jumped through the open doorway of a bus and dropped out of sight. Wayne knew he was jerking wires loose, trying to hotwire them a ride. Wayne hoped he was good at it and fast.

When Wayne got to the bus, he laid Sister Worth down beside it and pulled the .38s and stood in front of her. If he was going down he wanted to go like Wild Bill Hickock. A blazing gun in either fist and a woman to protect.

Actually, he'd prefer the bus to start.

It did.

Calhoun jerked it in gear, backed it out and around in front of Wayne and Sister Worth. The monks and nuns had started firing and their rounds bounced off the side of the armored bus.

From inside Calhoun yelled, "Get the hell on."

Wayne stuck the guns in his belt, grabbed up Sister Worth and leapt inside. Calhoun jerked the bus forward and Wayne and Sister Worth went flying over a seat and into another.

"I thought you were leaving," Wayne said.

"I wanted to. But I gave my word."

Wayne stretched Sister Worth out on the seat and looked at her leg. After that tossing Calhoun had given them, the break was sticking out even more.

Calhoun closed the bus door and checked his wing-mirror. Nuns and monks and dead folks had piled into a couple of buses, and now the buses were pursuing them. One of them moved very fast, as if souped up.

"I probably got the granny of the bunch," Calhoun said.

They climbed over a ridge of sand, then they were on the narrow road that wound itself upwards. Behind them, one of the buses had fallen back, maybe some kind of mechanical trouble. The other was gaining.

The road widened and Calhoun yelled, "I think this is what the fucker's been waiting for."

Even as Calhoun spoke, their pursuer put on a burst of speed and swung left and came up beside them, tried to swerve over and push them off the road, down into the deepening valley. But Calhoun fought the curves and didn't budge.

The other bus swung its door open and a nun, the very one who had been on the bus that brought them to Jesus Land, stood there with her legs spread wide, showing the black-pantied mound of her crotch. She had one arm bent around a seat post and was holding in both hands the ever-popular clergy tool, the twelve-gauge pump.

As they made a curve, the nun fired a round into the window next to Calhoun. The window made a cracking noise and thin crooked lines spread in all directions, but the glass held.

She pumped a round into the chamber and fired again. Bullet proof or not, this time the front sheet of glass fell away. Another well-placed round and the rest of the glass would go and Calhoun could wave his head goodbye.

Wayne put his knees in a seat and got the window down. The nun saw him, whirled and fired. The shot was low and hit the bottom part of the window and starred it and pelleted the chassis.

Wayne stuck a .38 out the window and fired as the nun was jacking another load into position. His shot hit her in the head and her right eye went big and wet, and she swung around on the pole and lost the shotgun. It went out the door. She clung there by the bend of her elbow for a moment, then her arm straightened and she fell outside.

The bus ran over her and she popped red and juicy at both ends like a stomped jelly roll.

"Waste of good pussy," Calhoun said. He edged into the other bus, and it pushed back. But Calhoun pushed harder and made it hit the wall with a screech like a panther.

The bus came back and shoved Calhoun to the side of the cliff and honked twice for Jesus.

Calhoun down-shifted, let off the gas, allowed the other bus to soar past by half a length. Then he jerked the wheel so that he caught the rear of it and knocked it across the road. He speared it in the side with the nose of his bus and the other started to spin. It clipped the front of Calhoun's bus and peeled the bumper back. Calhoun braked and the other bus kept spinning. It spun off the road and down into the valley amidst a chorus of cries.

Thirty minutes later they reached the top of the canyon and were in the desert. The bus began to throw up smoke from the front and make a noise like a dog strangling on a chicken bone. Calhoun pulled over.

XII

"Goddamn bumper got twisted under there and it's shredded the tire some," Calhoun said. "I think if we can peel the bumper off, there's enough of that tire to run on."

Wayne and Calhoun got hold of the bumper and pulled but it wouldn't come off. Not completely. Part of it had been creased, and that part finally gave way and broke off from the rest of it.

"That ought to be enough to keep from rubbing the tire," Calhoun said.

Sister Worth called from inside the bus. Wayne went to check on her. "Take me off the bus," she said. ". . . I want to feel free air and sun."

"There doesn't feel like there's any air out there," Wayne said. "And the sun feels just like it always does. Hot."

"Please."

He picked her up and carried her outside and found a ridge of sand and laid her down so her head was propped against it.

"I . . . I need batteries," she said.

"Say what?" Wayne said.

She lay looking straight into the sun. "Brother Lazarus's greatest work . . . a dead folk that can think . . . has memory of the past . . .

Was a scientist too . . ." Her hand came up in stages, finally got hold of her head gear and pushed it off.

Gleaming from the center of her tangled blond hair was a silver knob.

"He . . . was not a good man . . . I am a good woman . . . I want to feel alive . . . like before . . . batteries going . . . brought others."

Her hand fumbled at a snap pocket on her habit. Wayne opened it for her and got out what was inside. Four batteries.

"Uses two . . . simple."

Calhoun was standing over them now. "That explains some things," he said.

"Don't look at me like that . . ." Sister Worth said, and Wayne realized he had never told her his name and she had never asked. "Unscrew . . . put the batteries in . . . Without them I'll be an eater . . . Can't wait too long."

"All right," Wayne said. He went behind her and propped her up on the sand drift and unscrewed the metal shaft from her skull. He thought about when she had fucked him on the wheel and how desperate she had been to feel something, and how she had been cold as flint and lustless. He remembered how she had looked in the mirror hoping to see something that wasn't there.

He dropped the batteries in the sand and took out one of the revolvers and put it close to the back of her head and pulled the trigger. Her body jerked slightly and fell over, her face turning toward him.

The bullet had come out where the bird had been on her cheek and had taken it completely away, leaving a bloodless hole.

"Best thing," Calhoun said. "There's enough live pussy in the world without you pulling this broken-legged dead thing around after you on a board."

"Shut up," Wayne said.

"When a man gets sentimental over women and kids, he can count himself out."

Wayne stood up.

"Well boy," Calhoun said. "I reckon it's time."

"Reckon so," Wayne said.

"How about we do this with some class? Give me one of your pistols and we'll get back-to-back and I'll count to ten, and when I get there, we'll turn and shoot."

Wayne gave Calhoun one of the pistols. Calhoun checked the chambers, said, "I've got four loads."

Wayne took two out of his pistol and tossed them on the ground. "Even Steven," he said.

They got back-to-back and held the guns by their legs.

"Guess if you kill me you'll take me in," Calhoun said. "So that means you'll put a bullet through my head if I need it. I don't want to come back as one of the dead folks. Got your word on that?"

"Yep."

"I'll do the same for you. Give my word. You know that's worth something."

"We gonna shoot or talk?"

"You know, boy, under different circumstances, I could have liked you. We might have been friends."

"Not likely."

Calhoun started counting, and they started stepping. When he got to ten, they turned.

Calhoun's pistol barked first, and Wayne felt the bullet punch him low in the right side of his chest, spinning him slightly. He lifted his revolver and took his time and shot just as Calhoun fired again.

Calhoun's second bullet whizzed by Wayne's head. Wayne's shot hit Calhoun in the stomach.

Calhoun went to his knees and had trouble drawing a breath. He tried to lift his revolver but couldn't; it was as if it had turned into an anvil.

Wayne shot him again. Hitting him in the middle of the chest this time and knocking him back so that his legs were curled beneath him.

Wayne walked over to Calhoun, dropped to one knee and took the revolver from him.

"Shit," Calhoun said. "I wouldn't have thought that for nothing. You hit?"

"Scratched."

"Shit."

Wayne put the revolver to Calhoun's forehead and Calhoun closed his eyes and Wayne pulled the trigger.

XIII

The wound wasn't a scratch. Wayne knew he should leave Sister Worth where she was and load Calhoun on the bus and haul him in for bounty. But he didn't care about the bounty anymore.

He used the ragged piece of bumper to dig them a shallow side-by-side grave. When he finished, he stuck the fender fragment up between them and used the sight of one of the revolvers to scratch into it: HERE LIES SISTER WORTH AND CALHOUN WHO KEPT HIS WORD.

You couldn't really read it good and he knew the first real wind would keel it over, but it made him feel better about something, even if he couldn't put his finger on it.

His wound had opened up and the sun was very hot now, and since he had lost his hat he could feel his brain cooking in his skull like meat boiling in a pot.

He got on the bus, started it and drove through the day and the night and it was near morning when he came to the Cadillacs and turned down between them and drove until he came to the '57.

When he stopped and tried to get off the bus, he found he could hardly move. The revolvers in his belt were stuck to his shirt and stomach because of the blood from his wound.

He pulled himself up with the steering wheel, got one of the shotguns and used it for a crutch. He got the food and water and went out to inspect the '57.

It was for shit. It had not only lost its windshield, the front end was mashed way back and one of the big sand tires was twisted at such an angle he knew the axle was shot.

He leaned against the Chevy and tried to think. The bus was okay and there was still some gas in it, and he could get the hose out of the trunk of the '57 and siphon gas out of its tanks and put it in the bus. That would give him a few miles.

Miles.

He didn't feel as if he could walk twenty feet, let alone concentrate on driving.

He let go of the shotgun, the food and water. He scooted onto the hood of the Chevy and managed himself to the roof. He lay there on his back and looked at the sky.

It was a clear night and the stars were sharp with no fuzz around them. He felt cold. In a couple of hours the stars would fade and the sun would come up and the cool would give way to heat.

He turned his head and looked at one of the Cadillacs and a skeleton face pressed to its windshield, forever looking down at the sand.

That was no way to end, looking down.

He crossed his legs and stretched out his arms and studied the sky. It didn't feel so cold now, and the pain had almost stopped. He was more numb than anything else.

He pulled one of the revolvers and cocked it and put it to his temple and continued to look at the stars. Then he closed his eyes and found that he could still see them. He was once again hanging in the void between the stars wearing only his hat and cowboy boots, and floating about him were the junk cars and the '57, undamaged.

The cars were moving toward him this time, not away. The '57 was in the lead, and as it grew closer he saw Pop behind the wheel and beside him was a Mexican puta, and in the back, two more. They were all smiling and Pop honked the horn and waved.

The '57 came alongside him and the back door opened. Sitting between the whores was Sister Worth. She had not been there a moment ago, but now she was. And he had never noticed how big the back seat of the '57 was.

Sister Worth smiled at him and the bird on her cheek lifted higher. Her hair was combed out long and straight and she looked pink-skinned and happy. On the floorboard at her feet was a chest of iced-beer. Lone Star, by God.

Pop was leaning over the front seat, holding out his hand and Sister Worth and the whores were beckoning him inside.

Wayne worked his hands and feet, found this time that he could move. He swam through the open door, touched Pop's hand, and Pop said, "It's good to see you, son," and at the moment Wayne pulled the trigger, Pop pulled him inside.